Y0-CBC-195

THE VALUATION OF MORTGAGE-BACKED SECURITIES

Good analytics make smart people better;
Better analytics don't make people smart.

THE VALUATION OF MORTGAGE-BACKED SECURITIES

William W. Bartlett
Senior Vice President
Lehman Brothers

IRWIN
Professional Publishing

Burr Ridge, Illinois
New York, New York

© RICHARD D. IRWIN, INC., 1994

Project editor: Susan Trentacosti
Production manager: Ann Cassady
Designer: Larry J. Cope
Art manager: Kim Meriwether
Compositor: Graphic Sciences Corporation
Typeface: 10.5/12 Times Roman
Printer: R. R. Donnelley & Sons Company

Library of Congress Cataloging-in-Publication Data

Bartlett, William W.
The valuation of mortgage-backed securities / William W. Bartlett.
p.   cm.
Includes index.
ISBN 1-55623-973-4
1. Mortgage-backed securities—Valuation. 2. Portfolio management. I. Title.
HG4655.B37 1994
332.63'2044—dc20   93–33172

Printed in the United States of America
1 2 3 4 5 6 7 8 9 0 DOC 0 9 8 7 6 5 4 3

To Françoise Bartlett

Without whose developmental and writing skills this book would not have been possible.

PREFACE

This book has been written for portfolio managers of fixed-income securities seeking a valuation guide to mortgage-backed securities (MBSs). Its purpose is, first, to define relative value of MBSs and to identify the kinds of questions that need to be asked in order to sort through the complex universe of MBSs—pass-throughs, CMOs, and their derivatives. Second, the book seeks to translate the complexity of the MBS market and its attendant analytics and terminology into the vernacular for portfolio managers, analysts, traders, salespeople, and students.

The MBS market, born in 1970, has grown faster in size and complexity than any other fixed-income market in the history of the financial marketplace. By June 1993, outstandings of MBSs had grown to almost $1.5 trillion. Three major eras have characterized this brief but explosive evolutionary process. The first, the 1970s, was the adolescent phase of the MBS market, the period of introducing MBSs to institutional investors totally unfamiliar with the mortgage market. Until 1977 MBSs were traded to a 12-year life assumption, with price calculated assuming no prepayments until the 12th year, whereupon the security would prepay in full. In 1977, Dexter Senft (then at The First Boston Corporation) introduced single monthly mortality (SMM) as a prepayment measure and HTG (Honest to God) yield, which evolved into what we now call cash flow yield.

The second era, the coming of age of MBS analytics, stretched from the late 1970s into the mid-1980s with the definition of the prepayment option by Stanley Diller (then at Goldman Sachs). Option-adjusted spread technology evolved shortly thereafter.

The third era, one of powerful growth, massive capital commitment to large trading positions, and the dominance of the REMIC form of the MBS, came with the emergence of Louis Ranieri, who initiated large-scale MBS trading positions at Salomon Brothers in the early 1980s, and with the introduction of the CMO by First Boston and Freddie Mac in 1983. There followed the landmark REMIC legislation in 1986 and a proliferation of CMO derivatives, which added greatly to the complexity (and opportunity as well as risk) of the MBS marketplace. The growth in MBSs following the REMIC launch was phenomenal: From $46 billion in 1984 to $226 billion in 1986, MBS outstandings grew to $1.4 trillion by 1992 year-end, of which 65 percent were issued as REMICs.

A fourth era in the growth of the MBS market may now be evolving following the upheaval of the 1991–1993 successive refinancing waves—one that looks ahead to the maturation of the MBS market, substantially reduced prepayment volatility, and changed demographics that will probably temper the pace of housing turnover and mortgage creation. MBS technicals will likely be focused less on prepayment risk and more on the shape of the yield curve and its impact on MBS cash flows and on whether to buy the MBS as a pass- through or in REMIC form. Such, at least, are the predominant themes that are presented in this book as questions that must be answered to the intuitive satisfaction of the MBS investor.

ORGANIZATION OF THIS BOOK

The book consists of fifteen chapters, with the first six chapters focusing on the characteristics of MBSs, risk/reward considerations, technical considerations, and the definition of prepayment and option-adjusted spread. Included is a unique chapter on the outlook for housing demographics (Chapter 5) by Phillip Kidd, a housing economist. Chapter 1 defines the coming new era in MBS dynamics and valuation as well as the new risk-based capital and mark-to-market regulations. Chapter 2 presents the characteristics of pass-throughs and the relative performance of the current-coupon, premium-priced, and discount-priced seasoned pool sectors of the MBS market. Chapters 3, 4, and 6 cover the analytical tools, such as the components of the OAS, and prepayment models and technical considerations, including the impact of yield curve shifts and price and prepayment volatility on MBS cash flow valuation.

Chapters 7 through 10 define CMOs, their bond forms, valuation methodologies, and the CMO deal structure. Chapters 11 through 14 provide (in sequence) an overview of whole-loan MBSs, CMO floaters and inverse floaters, ARM MBSs, and stripped MBSs. Finally, Chapter 15, provided by Raymond Beier, a partner of Coopers & Lybrand, offers accounting guidelines for the proper reporting of pass-through, CMO, and stripped MBS cash flows.

The book concludes with a comprehensive glossary of commonly used MBS terms, including definitions of the new CMO derivative forms introduced in recent years.

ACKNOWLEDGMENTS

First, to Francoise Bartlett, my partner in life and development editor of this text. If the text is found to be user-friendly and the complexities of MBSs comprehensive, it is to her credit. Second, to Lehman Brothers and Bloomberg Financial Markets for the use of their research, with special thanks due to John Tierney, Nicole Vianna, and Chuck Webster of Lehman, who provided extensive comments on various technical discussions in the text. Special appreciation is due to Ralph Rieves, executive editor of Irwin Professional Publishing, who over two years encouraged me with great patience to undertake and complete the project.

Also contributing significantly were Thomas Ho, president of Global Advanced Technology, who provided the investment properties of IOs and POs; Kenneth Scott, vice president of Clayton Brown & Associates, Chicago, who closely reviewed the text. Others who made significant contributions include Lawrence Penn of Lehman Brothers who contributed the text and graphics on CMO structuring which make up Chapter 10 and Paul Wang, formerly of Lehman Brothers and now at Merrill Lynch Mortgage Research, who provided much of the description of prepayment models. Harry Forsyth, private consultant, contributed to the OAS and strips discussion. I am grateful to Phillip Kidd for his timely chapter on demographic trends and to Raymond Beier, then a partner of Deloitte Touche and now a partner at Coopers & Lybrand, who wrote Chapter 15 on accounting for MBS investments. Others of Lehman who thoughtfully reviewed various chapters include Chris Ames, Jeff Biby, Byron Boston, Alan J. Brazil, Betty Carey, David Harris, and Kirk Hartman. Finally, many thanks to the capable staff in Lehman support services, especially Shelley Block and Mary Weston, who assisted in preparing the text for publication.

William W. Bartlett

CONTENTS

LIST OF FIGURES

MOST COMMONLY USED ACRONYMS

AD	accretion directed (bond)
AFS	Advance Factor Services
ARM	adjustable-rate mortgage
AVR	asset valuation reserve
BDA	benchmark default assumption
BEY	bond-equivalent yield
CAB	capital appreciation bond
CAGE	calculated loan age
CBOT	Chicago Board of Trade
CDR	conditional default rate
CFY	cash flow yield
CMO	collateralized mortgage obligation
CMT	constant-maturity Treasury
COFI	cost of funds index
COFI-ARM	cost of funds-indexed adjustable-rate mortgage
CPP	constant percent prepayment
CPR	constant prepayment rate
CY	current yield
DM	discount margin
EM	effective margin
FASB	Financial Accounting Standards Board
FFIEC	Federal Financial Institutions Examination Council
FHA	Federal Housing Administration
FHLB	Federal Home Loan Bank
FHLBB	Federal Home Loan Bank Board
FIRREA	Financial Institutions Reform, Recovery, and Enforcement Act of 1989
FHLMC	Federal Home Loan Mortgage Corporation
FNMA	Federal National Mortgage Association
GAAP	generally accepted accounting principles
GDP	gross domestic product
GEM	graduated equity mortgage

GIC	guaranteed investment contract
GNMA	Government National Mortgage Association
GPM	graduated payment mortgage
HELS	home equity loan (asset-backed) security
HPR	holding-period return
IMR	interest maintenance reserve
IO	interest only
IRR	internal rate of return
IRS	interest rate spread
LIBOR	London Interbank Offering Rate
LOC	letter of credit
LOCOM	lower of cost or market
LTV	loan to value
MBA	Mortgage Bankers Association
MBB	mortgage-backed bond
MBS	mortage-backed security
MEY	mortgage-equivalent yield
MFY	mutual fund yield
MIP	monthly insurance premium
MSA	Metropolitan Statistical Area
MSD	Mortgage Securities Division (of AFS)
MSVR	Mandatory Securities Valuation Reserve
NAH	National Affordable Housing Act of 1990
NAIC	National Association of Insurance Commissioners
NAR	National Association of Realtors
NPV	net present value
OAD	option-adjusted duration
OAM	option-adjusted margin
OAS	option-adjusted spread
OCC	Office of the Comptroller of the Currency
OTS	Office of Thrift Supervision
PAC	planned amortization class
P&I	principle and interest
PO	principle only
PSA	Public Securities Association
QTL	qualified thrift lender
REMIC	real estate mortgage investment conduit
RFC	Residential Funding Corporation
RTC	Resolution Trust Corporation
SDA	standard default assumption
SMART	Structured Mortgage Asset REMIC Trust (Lehman Brothers)

SMB	stated maturity bond
S&P	Standard & Poor's
TBA	to be announced
TIMS	Trusts for Investment in Mortgages
VOE	verification of employment
WAC	weighted average coupon
WAL	weighted average life
WALA	weighted average loan age
WAM	weighted average maturity

CHAPTER 1

OPPORTUNITY AND RISK IN MORTGAGE-BACKED SECURITIES

THE NEW AGE IN MORTGAGE-BACKED SECURITIES

The year 1993 marked a watershed in terms of how mortgage-backed securities (MBSs) would be evaluated—a period of transition in which the primary concern shifted from prepayment risk to extension risk. As the decade-long decline in mortgage rates wound down, it became more likely that future opportunities to refinance would be diminished. The factors underlying mortgage cash flow dynamics will likely be determined by two new developments. First, a secular shift in the demographic profile of the U.S. population will likely slow housing formations and housing turnover from the feverish pace of the 1980s. Second, refinancings are likely to be driven not so much by the traditional refinancing pattern, for example, from a 30-year mortgage to another loan for a 2 percent differential between the rate of the loan held and a lower market rate loan. Rather, refinancing is more likely to be to a 15-year loan, balloon, or adjustable-rate mortgage to pay down debts, finance education, or manage taxes.

The mechanism for determining value also shifted dramatically. As the new risk-weighted capital rules and the Federal Financial Institutions Examination Council (FFIEC) high-risk security measures took full force, with depository institutions facing the reality of market-based accounting, the performance characteristics of the variant forms of MBSs began to take precedence over high stated yield alone. At the same time, MBS bond forms were considered more for their intrinsic value than for their labels. For example, the concern shifted from "Can the PAC prepayment bands ever be broken?" (they were) to "How will a broken PAC perform?" Emphasis also shifted from intercoupon swaps (rolling up or down in coupon) in response to prepayment shifts to barbell trades to deal with yield curve risk. Finally, some skepticism emerged of black box analytics based on assumptions and methodologies known primarily to the analyst who programmed it.

This book is a guide to the new dynamics that will drive mortgage cash flows in the 1990s. The process of evaluating MBSs can start only one way—by asking the right questions, and that is the theme of this book.

WHAT IS THE QUESTION?

As the post-Renaissance philosopher-mathematician René Descartes lay dying, his disciples, gathered at his bedside, queried, "What is the answer?" Countered the sage, "What is the question?" Although probably apocryphal, the anecdote highlights the central mission of this text: to define the key questions regarding the risk/reward of MBS investing. The holistic question is, What is the convexity?[1] Central to this question is the host of concerns that make up the risk/ reward compendium. Investors, traders, analysts, and students are provided with ample answers regarding the expected behavior of MBS cash flows and investment expectations, particularly those of bond salespersons and MBS analysts. The investor who can properly construct the questions to qualify the investment advice and analysis offered is likely to be rewarded. The art of good questioning is to ask specific questions whose answers will be revealing versus general questions that often invite deceptively simple answers.

To illustrate, the most commonly asked question by investors is, Where is the best yield available in the MBS market today? What is meant by "best"? The highest stated yield? Or the strongest expected performance defined as maintenance of price and basis points yield spread to Treasuries? For example, assume the following as a reasonably conservative answer to the question of where is the best yield: Take an FHLMC 7.5 percent PC priced at 99 1/2 to yield 104 basis points over the 10-year Treasury. This could be a good answer to the question. The Freddie Mac PC carries an agency guaranty, is highly liquid, and is priced just under par, so it

---

[1]Convexity defines the degree of positive price response to change in yield. (For a discussion of convexity, see Convexity and Duration in Chapter 3.) The definition of the convexity profile of a given MBS is one of the key relative value considerations examined in this text.

offers high current yield without subjecting the investor to the potential prepayment risk of premium-priced MBSs.

But what if the question were more specific: What will be the best-*performing* MBS with a 5-year average life for maintaining positive convexity, assuming high price volatility? Now we must provide an MBS with a 5-year average life. A high-coupon, fast-prepaying MBS would have the shorter average life, but it would *NOT* provide positive convexity, so we might suggest a PAC (see Chapter 7) to give protection against prepayment risk. And to ensure positive convexity, we might suggest a discount-priced PAC (to provide performance in a bull market) with high-coupon collateral (to maintain prepayment speed in a bear market). Such a bond might be offered at a yield spread of 90 basis points to the 5-year Treasury, a much lower stated yield than the FHLMC 7.5 percent PC, but the proper bond to fit the second, more specific question.

We could phrase the question "What is the best MBS investment?" in many ways, and each would provide a very different answer.

Question: What will offer the absolute highest stated yield?

Answer: A volatile 5-year-average-life CMO support[2] bond with a stated spread of 250 basis points to the 5-year Treasury.

Risk: The average life can vary from 2 months to 15 years given a 500 PSA point swing in prepayment speed.

Reward: Support bonds are often offered at sufficient yield spread that on an option-adjusted spread (OAS) basis they offer fair value (see Chapter 3, Relative Value Analysis: The Analytic Tools).

In the last example the investor is getting the high stated yield, but there is a possibility the stated yield will not be realized. The support bonds in the CMO structure are the ones that absorb the greatest prepayment risk and generally do not offer favorable convexity characteristics. So we see there are many investment questions that must be thoughtfully constructed to ensure the answers

---

[2]Support (or companion) bonds are those that support and stabilize the PAC bonds. (See Anatomy of PAC Bonds in Chapter 7.)

to them will identify MBSs that meet investors' risk/reward expectations.

The Investor's Perspective—Yield versus Performance

The text illustrates with case histories the key risk/reward considerations for two basic categories of investors. One investor category may best be defined as total-return, or performance-oriented, investors. This category includes bond fund managers, money management advisers, and insurance company and pension fund portfolio managers. The primary risk/reward questions the text defines for these types of investors are:

- What is the convexity profile?
- What is the duration?
- What will be the bond's performance measured in total return?
- Which are the rich/cheap sectors in the MBS market?
- What is the probable pattern of the future for:
  - Prepayments.
  - MBS to Treasury yield spreads.
  - Impact of market volatility.
  - Impact of yield curve risk.
  - Supply issues.
  - Other "event risk" concerns.

The second investor category consists of depository institutions, which tend to focus on high stated yield and yield spread to a cost of funds, usually called the liability base. These investors are primarily concerned with maintaining a stable maturity match of assets to liabilities and with maximizing the yield spread between the return on the investment (the asset) and the cost of carry (the liability—CDs, borrowed funds, etc.). For this category of investors the text emphasizes questions designed to derive the following information:

- Stated yield versus probable realized yield.
- Impact of duration drift on the assets to liabilities match.
- Impact of interest rate risk and yield curve shape on the assets to liabilities yield spread.

Where Is the Risk?

With MBSs, evaluation is more complex than with other fixed-income securities. The difficulty in defining the risk considerations and the complexity of the analytical techniques applied to the discovery of relative value explains in large part why these federal agency-guaranteed, very liquid securities offer so much yield premium to Treasury securities.

MBSs differ from all other fixed-income investments because:

1. Principal is returned as a monthly annuity or cash flow stream over the life of the investment rather than at maturity, as with most fixed-income investments.
2. Interest is received monthly rather than semiannually or annually.
3. The principal and interest (P&I) cash flows are passed through with interest delays of from 14 to 54 days.
4. The *amount* and *timing* of each monthly cash flow differ depending on the prepayment speed of the MBS collateral underlying the pool.
5. The amount of monthly interest declines over time rather than being a fixed interest payment.
6. The MBS pool is priced to an *average life* rather than to a final maturity.

Of these characteristics, the most troublesome and the most analyzed and discussed is (4), the uncertainty of the amount and timing of monthly P&I cash flows. This uncertainty arises from the homeowner's right to prepay the mortgage—referred to as the prepayment option.

The relative value considerations most pertinent to valuation of MBSs are as follows:

1. Prepayment risk (see Chapter 4, Dynamics of Mortgage Prepayments)

   • Prepayment risk alters the timing of monthly cash flow.
   • Prepayment risk injects call and extension risk.

2. Volatility and yield curve risk (see Chapter 6, Technical Considerations)

- Volatility affects the valuation of the prepayment option.
- Yield curve shape affects the valuation of the front-end cash flows.

3. Performance risk (see Chapter 3, Relative Value Analysis: The Analytic Tools)

   - Widening of the MBS to Treasury spread depresses value.

4. Structure and tail risk (see Chapter 2, Characteristics of Pass-Throughs)

   - Deal structures of MBSs may reduce or increase prepayment risk.
   - The liquidity of some custom structures may be poor.
   - Tail risk is the cash flows that extend beyond the average-life point.
   - The length of the cash flow[3] window defines reinvestment risk and the asset to liabilities match of cash flows.

5. Technical considerations (see Chapter 6)

   - Supply/demand factors affect MBS yield spreads.
   - Competitive fixed-income securities affect MBS prices.

6. Credit risk (see Chapter 11, Whole-Loan Mortgage-Backed Securities)

   - Private label credit-enhancement adequacy determines credit agency rating.
   - Government-sponsored enterprise capital adequacy is sometimes a market concern.

7. Regulatory risk (see this chapter, pages 8–19)

   - Regulatory prohibition of investment in certain types of MBSs structures reduces liquidity.

Figure 1.1 illustrates the maximization of reward at minimum risk, with the greatest reward for less risk represented by the northwest quadrant (upper left quarter) and the greatest risk for less reward by the southeast quadrant (lower right quarter). It is hard to find investments that truly reside in the northwest quadrant and all too easy to be drawn to those in the southeast quadrant.

---

[3]The cash flow window is the period from the receipt of the first principal dollar of pool cash flow to the last.

FIGURE 1.1
MBS Performance (Total Return, January 1987–December 1990)

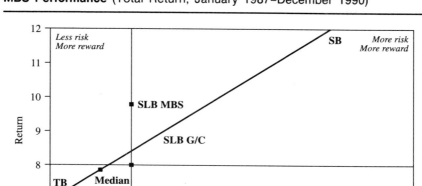

SLB MBS = Shearson Lehman Mortgage Security Index   SP = S&P Stock Index
SLB G/C = Shearson Lehman Government/Corporate Index   TB = Treasury Bills

Source: Lehman Brothers Fixed Income Research.

REGULATORY IMPACT ON PORTFOLIO MANAGEMENT

The passage of the **Financial Institutions Reform, Recovery, and Enforcement Act (FIRREA) of 1989** dramatically altered the landscape of portfolio management practices, initially for thrift institutions. Ultimately, however, it has affected how regulators of virtually all financial institutions oversee the investing practices of their constituent members. National banks came heavily under its influence in 1991, and by 1993 insurance companies were investing with new guidelines that restrict assets identified as high risk for inclusion in their portfolios.

Return on Assets versus Return on Equity

The thrust of the new investment regulation is to shift the emphasis of institutional investing from return on assets (ROA) to return on equity (ROE). In effect, the purpose of FIRREA is to cause financial institutions to shift the focus from high *stated* yield per se to greater evaluation of the risk factor—that is, that the stated yield may not be realized either as a function of credit risk or of volatility risk. (Volatility as it relates to MBSs refers primarily to prepayment risk, which in turn leads to price volatility.) Before FIRREA and its appendant regulation, a construction loan with high stated yield was often considered a better choice than a federal agency-guaranteed REMIC with a lower stated yield. FIRREA, in essence, has led to a view that the institution choosing the construction loan may do so, but within limits. The limits are imposed by assigning a higher capital requirement to be set aside to support the construction loan than to hold the agency REMIC. With depository institutions this requirement is met through risk-based capital guidelines that were imposed on thrift and banking institutions in stages through 1990 and 1991. The year 1993 brought a stratification of reserve requirements imposed by the National Association of Insurance Commissioners (NAIC) on the insurance industry. The result has been twofold: (1) a higher-base capital requirement imposed on national banking and thrift institutions (8 percent); and (2) a modification of the capital requirement regulations, permitting a lower-base capital requirement (to a minimum of 3 percent core capital) through the risk-adjusted guidelines. (For a more complete summary of the capital regulations, see the appendix to Chapter 15.) The following section is an overview of the central issues for MBS practitioners.

Regulatory Issues for Portfolio Investing

Four regulatory issues in particular that concern portfolio investing are:

1. Risk-based capital guidelines for banks.
2. FFIEC policy statement on high-risk mortgage securities.
3. Risk-based capital standards for insurance companies.
4. FASB accounting standards and proposals.

1. Risk-Based Capital Guidelines for Banks
Table 1.1 summarizes the risk-based capital (RBC) guidelines for national banks, supervised by the Office of the Comptroller of the

TABLE 1.1
Risk-Based Capital Guidelines for Banks

	OCC (%)	OTS (%)
Cash, U.S. Treasuries, Ginnie Mae MBSs	0	0
Fannie Mae, Freddie Mac MBSs	20	20
Private MBSs AAA, AA (SMMEA)[a]	50	50
Whole loan		
Qualifying	50	50
Nonqualifying	100	100
CMOs Backed by agency MBSs	20	20
Recourse sales/ subordinated interests	Same as collateral; based on full issue	
Goodwill	Deduct from assets and capital	Deduct nonsupervisory goodwill; phase out supervisory goodwill
IOs/POs	100[b]	100[b]
Residuals	100[b]	100[b]
REO, loans 90 days past due; equity risk investment	100	200
Capital/risk-adjusted assets	8	8

[a]Secondary Mortgage Market Enhancement Act of 1986.
[b]Pending introduction of guidelines for interest rate risk, which when instituted would reassign these classes to a risk weight based on that of the issuer.

Source: John Tierney, Lehman Brothers.

Currency (OCC), and for thrift institutions, supervised by the Office of Thrift Supervision (OTS). The guidelines for national credit unions are similar. The impact of the risk-based capital guidelines may be assessed in part by conducting a breakeven analysis comparing the stated return of a proposed investment to its equivalent ROE.

Breakeven Spread Analysis.[4] With the new risk-based capital framework, an analysis of the investment outlook for potential assets must include a detailed examination of the incremental cost of capital associated with each asset, as well as of differences in credit risk, interest rate risk, and administrative expenses.[5] Analyzing the cost of capital requires calculating the breakeven spread requirement associated with different credit risk categories. The basic formula is given in Table 1.2, and an example is presented in Table 1.3. Equation 1 in Table 1.2 represents the income statement of a thrift. Net income is equal to the yield on assets minus the interest cost of liabilities and administrative expenses. In Equation 2, ROE depends on the spread performance of the assets and liabilities, leverage, general administrative expenses, and taxes. This basic for-

TABLE 1.2
Marginal Cost of Capital

Formula for ROE calculation:

$$\text{After-tax ROE} = \frac{\text{Net income}}{\text{Capital}}$$

$$NI = (Ya \cdot A - Yl \cdot L - G/A) \cdot (1 - t) \qquad (1a)$$
$$NI = [Ya \cdot (L + E) - Yl \cdot L - G/A] \cdot (1 - t) \qquad (1b)$$
$$NI = (Ya \cdot L + Ya \cdot E - Yl \cdot L - G/A) \cdot (1 - t)$$
$$NI = [(Ya - Yl) \cdot L + Ya \cdot E - G/A] \cdot (1 - t)$$
$$\frac{NI}{E} = \left(\frac{(Ya - Yl) \cdot L - G/A}{E} + Ya\right) \cdot (1 - t) \qquad (2)$$

where:

NI = Net income
Ya = Asset yield
Yl = Cost of liabilities
A = Total assets
L = Total liabilities
E = Equity
G/A = Other expenses
t = Tax rate

Source: John Tierney, Lehman Brothers.

---

[4]This breakeven analysis was prepared by John Tierney, Senior Vice President, Manager, Mortgage Market Analysis, Lehman Brothers.

[5]This approach is useful for marginal asset acquisitions where the institution is not capital constrained.

mula may also be used to solve for the spread required to achieve a target return on equity.

The example in Table 1.3 applies the formula in the context of a simple balance sheet and income statement. The asset yield is assumed to be 10.4 percent, the cost of liabilities 8.5 percent, and general administrative (G/A) expenses 1.5 percent of total assets ($1,000). After-tax income is $6, providing an after-tax ROE of about 10 percent. To achieve a target after-tax ROE of 15 percent, the required yield on the asset increases to 10.85 percent. Note that the total spread required to achieve the target ROE is 2.35 percent (10.85 − 8.5). Of this, 150 basis points are required to cover administrative expenses and 85 basis points to cover the cost of capital. If the asset has potential exposure to other risks, such as credit risk or interest rate risk, as compensation the institution will require additional spread.

This analytical approach is used in Tables 1.4A and 1.4B

TABLE 1.3
Application of Formula Given in Table 1.2

	Amount ($)	Yield (%)
Assets	1,000	10.40
Liabilities	940	8.50
Equity	60	
G/A expenses		1.50
Interest income	103.994	
Interest expense	79.900	
Net interest income	24.094	
G/A expenses	15.000	
Income tax (34%)	3.092	
Net income	6.002	

$$\text{After-tax ROE}^a = \frac{\text{Net income}}{\text{Capital}} = \frac{6.00204}{60} = 10.00\%$$

$$\text{After-tax ROE} = \frac{[(Ya - Yl) \cdot L - G/A + Ya] \cdot (1 - .34)}{E}$$

$$= \frac{[(.1040 - .0850) \cdot 94 - .015 + 0.1040] \cdot .66}{.06} = 10.00\%$$

[a]For a target after-tax ROE of 15%, required asset yield = 10.85%.

Source: John Tierney, Lehman Brothers.

TABLE 1.4A
Thrift Industry Credit Category Breakeven Analysis: Credit Risk Capital
Equal to 6 Percent of Risk-Weighted Assets (Interest Rate Risk Assumed
Constant)

Credit Risk (%)	Target After-Tax ROE = 15%				
	0%	*20%*	*50%*	*100%*	*200%*
0	0 bp	17 bp	43 bp	85 bp	171 bp
20		0	26	68	154
50			0	42	128
100				0	86
200					0
	Target After-Tax ROE = 10%				
0	0	8	20	40	80
20		0	12	32	72
50			0	20	60
100				0	40
200					0

to calculate the marginal spread on assets across different credit risk categories required to meet a target after-tax return on equity of 15 percent and 10 percent. The 15 percent ROE example in Table 1.4A shows the required incremental spread associated with moving from a lower credit risk class, listed in the first column, to one of the higher classes, listed in subsequent columns. For example, if a Fannie Mae MBS asset in the 20 percent risk class were sold and the funds used to originate a consumer loan (100 percent credit risk category), the loan would have to yield 68 basis points more than the MBS asset to compensate for the cost of the additional capital and achieve the target ROE. The cost of capital spread premium critically depends on the required ROE (or marginal cost of capital). At a required ROE of 10 percent, the transaction just described would require only 32 basis points additional spread. This example assumes that the institution is not capital constrained—that is, it has capital reserves in excess of the minimum leverage ratio—and is in a position to take advantage of the marginal capital requirement. A capital-constrained institution would have to put up capital equal to at least 3 percent of the asset.

TABLE 1.4B

Thrift Industry Credit Category Breakeven Analysis: Credit Risk Capital Equal to 8 Percent of Risk-Weighted Assets (Interest Rate Risk Assumed Constant)

Credit Risk (%)	Target After-Tax ROE = 15%				
	0%	*20%*	*50%*	*100%*	*200%*
0	0 bp	23 bp	57 bp	114 bp	228 bp
20		0	34	91	295
50			0	57	171
100				0	114
200					0
	Target After-Tax ROE = 10%				
0	0	11 bp	27 bp	53 bp	107 bp
20		0	16	42	96
50			0	26	80
100				0	54
200					0

Note: The breakeven spreads indicate the additional spread required to achieve a constant after-tax ROE. They are net of any marginal costs associated with the asset (e.g., origination costs, servicing costs, and loan losses).

Assumptions: (1) Fixed G/A expenses remain constant; (2) marginal tax rate = 34 percent.

Source: John Tierney, Lehman Brothers.

   Tables 1.4A and 1.4B show the cost of capital requirements based on risk-based capital ratios of 6 percent and 8 percent, respectively. The risk-based capital ratio for thrifts is currently 8 percent, but it is expected to drop to 6 percent after the interest rate component is finalized. The spread premium required to cover the cost of capital varies with the amount of capital required to carry an asset (or, alternatively, the degree of leverage employed) and with the target ROE. Additional sensitivity analyses could be prepared using different marginal tax rates. The cost of capital spread premium associated with different asset classes varies among institutions, depending on the ROE objective, leverage, and the tax rate.

2. FFIEC Policy Statement on High-Risk Mortgage Securities[6]

In 1991 the FFIEC issued a supervisory policy statement outlining what the regulators consider to be unsuitable investments and investment practices for most depository institutions. Among its provisions are:

- Institutions must establish and document a prudent investment plan.
- Securities must be reported as held for investment, sale, or trading purposes, in accordance with the investment plan.

Certain trading activities and practices (nine "deadly sins") may not be used in connection with the investment portfolio:

1. Delegation of discretionary investment authority.
2. Covered call writing.
3. Gains trading.
4. "When-issued" securities trading.
5. "Pair-offs."
6. Corporate or extended settlements for Treasury/agency securities.
7. Repositioning repurchase agreements.
8. Short sales.
9. "Adjusted trading" or "bond swapping."

The FFIEC guidelines identify types of securities containing volatile price or other high-risk characteristics that are categorized in general as unsuitable for most depository institutions. The securities identified include zero coupon bonds (including stripped Treasury securities), stripped MBSs (IOs and POs), certain high-risk CMO tranches, and residuals. *High-risk CMO tranches are broadly defined as tranches bearing a greater than normal share of risk inherent in the collateral.* These include Z-bonds, inverse floaters, and certain support class bonds. The language proposed does not include specific quantitative criteria for defining "high-risk" tranches (e.g., average-life variability over a range of interest rates).

The so-called unsuitable securities may be held only if the in-

---

[6]The discussion of capital risk weight and FFIEC investment guidelines is based largely on research papers prepared by John Tierney.

stitution can document that they pass a stress test designed by the FFIEC or serve a specific hedging purpose so as to reduce the overall interest rate-risk position of the portfolio. Furthermore, this position must be monitored regularly to confirm that the hedge strategy is operating as expected. If it is not working, the hedge must be rebalanced or removed.

FFIEC High-Risk Securities Test. All proposed MBS investments must pass the FFIEC test in order to be eligible for inclusion in the investment portfolio. The test is most generally applicable to MBS derivative products. Figure 1.2 summarizes the test and gives the FFIEC position on the risk associated with MBS derivative products. (Examples of the application of the FFIEC test are given throughout the text. The derivative products outlined in Figure 1.2 are described in more detail in Chapter 9.)

Provisions of the FFIEC Test. If a derivative product fails *any* of the following tests, it is considered high risk:

1. The mortgage derivative product has an average weighted life greater than 10 years.
2. The expected weighted average life of the product
   a. Extends by more than four years, assuming an immediate and sustained parallel shift in the yield curve of +300 basis points.
   b. Shortens by more than six years, assuming an immediate and sustained parallel shift in the yield curve of −300 basis points.
3. The estimated change in price is more than 17 percent, due to an immediate and sustained parallel shift in the yield curve of ±300 basis points.

Standard industry calculators used in the mortgage securities marketplace are acceptable and are considered independent sources for determining whether a security is high risk. Once a derivative product has been designated as high risk, it may be redesignated as non-high risk if at the end of two consecutive quarters it does not meet the definition of a high-risk security. Non-high-risk securities continue to have to be tested on a yearly basis. The FFIEC is still considering designating a class of mortgage derivative products that, after being tested at purchase, would be exempt from further test-

FIGURE 1.2
Derivative MBS Forms

FFIEC High-Risk Security Test:	Regulators[a] of thrifts, national banks,
1. Average life not to exceed 10 years at pricing.	and credit unions have determined these MBS forms are generally
2. Average life not to extend over 4 years + 300 bp[b]. Average life not to contract over 6 years − 300 bp[b].	high-risk investments. Guidelines for investment are: • Suitable *only* if pass FFIEC test or • Serve clearly documented hedge purpose.
3. Price not to change over 17% up/down 300 bp[b]. FFIEC test determines investment suitability for depository institutions (available on Bloomberg).	

MBS Type	Comment
IO strip Interest stripped from the principal.	Only bearish investment (yield rises when rates rise). Generally unsuitable for investors who cannot have a negative return. Principal investors: money managers, insurance companies, private pension funds. PAC IOs less volatile.

Inverse floaters
  Coupon resets to opposite of index.
  Indexes—LIBOR, CMT.
	Coupon goes down when rates go up—floor zero or higher. Principal investors: money managers, public and private pension funds, insurance companies. No risk of loss of principal.

Support class bonds Protect the PAC bond class from prepayment risk.	Prepayment volatility varies greatly. Some can pass FFIEC risk test—most not. Suitable for depository institutions if pass FFIEC test.
PO strip Principal separated from coupon.	Moderate risk—no risk of loss of principal investment; used primarily for hedging prepayment risk (mortgage originators) or as a substitute for long Treasury strips.
Z-bond An accrual bond for 5–15 years; pays monthly P&I when prior coupon classes retired.	Potentially greater price volatility due to typically longer durations. Principal investors: pension funds, insurance companies. No risk of loss of principal.

[a]OTS = Office of Thrift Supervision; regulates Federal S&Ls.
OCC = Office of Controller of the Currency; regulates national banks.
NCUA = National Credit Union Administration; regulates credit unions.
NAIC = National Association of Insurance Commissioners; oversees life insurance companies.
FFIEC = Federal Financial Institutions Examinations Council.
[b]Denotes interest rate shift plus or minus 300 bp to stress average life, price sensitivity.

Source: Lehman Brothers Fixed Income Research.

ing. High-risk mortgage securities are to be reported as trading assets at market value or as held-for-sale assets at the lower of cost or market.

Floating-rate mortgage securities need meet only the price volatility test unless they have reached a cap. Once the cap is reached, they are to be stressed under the test like other derivative products. Institutions may buy caps to reinstate the exemption from the 10-year average life and average-life stress tests.

3. Risk-Based Capital Standards for Insurance Companies[7]

In 1993 insurance companies were subjected to investment standards (Table 1.5) that restrict their holdings of commercial real estate and below-investment-grade corporate bond assets. The RBC requirements have four risk components: asset-, insurance-, interest rate-, and business-risk measures.

Asset Risk.   Table 1.5 summarizes asset-risk standards.

Adjustments to Asset Risk.   Two adjustments must be applied to the asset-risk capital measure. First, there is an adjustment for the amount and diversification of corporate bond holdings. The preferred corporate bond portfolio is one consisting of more than 1,000 different issuers held in more or less equal amounts. For a corporate bond portfolio of 1,000 issuers the adjustment factor to the asset-risk measure is 1 (no adjustment). For portfolios with less than 1,000 issuers, the factor increases up to a maximum of 2.5 for portfolios consisting of less than 50 issuers. For purposes of deriving the factor, securities issued or guaranteed by a federal agency (including agency-guaranteed MBSs) are excluded. Figure 1.3 illustrates the adjustment factor for corporate bond holdings.

The adjustment in Figure 1.3 is clearly an issue primarily for small- to intermediate-size insurance companies for whom diversification into several hundred different corporate names is not feasible from the viewpoint of a credit-maintenance review. However, for conservative insurance companies not burdened with commercial real estate or below-investment-grade corporates this adjustment factor may not be an issue.

---

[7]This discussion of capital standards for insurance companies was prepared by David Harris, Senior Vice President, Manager, Portfolio Strategies, Lehman Brothers.

TABLE 1.5
Asset-Risk Standards for Insurance Companies

	Capital Required as a Percentage of Asset
Cash, U.S. Treasuries, Ginnie Mae MBSs	0
Fannie Mae, Freddie Mac MBSs	0.3
Private MBSs, AA	0.3
CMOs	
Agency collateral	0.3
Other collateral (A rating or better)	0.3
Whole loans[a]	2.0
Commercial mortgages[a]	3.0
Real estate	10.0
Corporates	
A or better	0.3
BBB	1.0
BB	4.0
B	9.0
CCC	20.0
Below CCC	30.0

[a]These percentages are then multiplied by a factor to reflect past delinquency experience compared to industry averages.

Source: David Harris, Lehman Brothers.

FIGURE 1.3
RBC Adjustment Factor for Corporate Bond Holdings

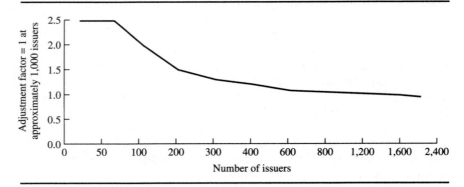

Source: NAIC and Lehman Brothers Fixed Income Research.

The second factor is a concentration factor. The concentration factor doubles the risk-based capital factor for the 10 largest assets to a maximum of 30 percent. Excluded from this calculation are common stock, policy loans, bonds with a zero asset value reserve requirement, category 1 bonds, preferred stock, and any asset with an RBC requirement of less than 1 percent.

Insurance Risk. Insurance risk covers the risk of mispricing the insurance product itself. Existing reserves are expected to cover the anticipated costs of mortality, morbidity, lapses, interest rate risk, and expenses. The interest rate RBC is designed to provide protection beyond existing reserves for risks unforeseen in the original actuarial and pricing assumptions (AIDS, for example).

Interest Rate Risk. Interest rate risk covers the mismatching of assets and liabilities, cash flow testing required under New York Regulation 126, and the actuarial opinion and memorandum regulation.

The interest rate RBC factors are derived by stressing the investment and annuity portfolio of assets to six scenarios:

1. From base interest rate to *up* 500 basis points over years 1 to 5 and back to base from years 5 to 100.
2. From base interest rate *down* 500 basis points for the same 1 to 5 and 5 to 10 years, as in (1).
3. From base interest rate to *up* 500 basis points from years 1 to 10, then held at up 500 basis points to year 15.
4. From base to *down* 500 basis points from years 1 to 10, then held to year 15.
5. Instantaneous shock from base to *up* 300 basis points and held at up 300 basis points to year 15.
6. Instantaneous shock from base to *down* 300 basis points and held to year 15.

Vectors 1, 3, and 5 are illustrated in Figure 1.4.

Business Risk. There is a risk charge for guarantee fund assessments equal to 2 percent of life and annuity premiums and 0.5 percent for accident and health premiums. Figure 1.5 illustrates the application of the four RBC standards for insurance companies.

Accounting for Gains and Losses.   The National Association of Insurance Commissioners (NAIC) changed the regulations covering

FIGURE 1.4
Interest Rate Stress Vectors

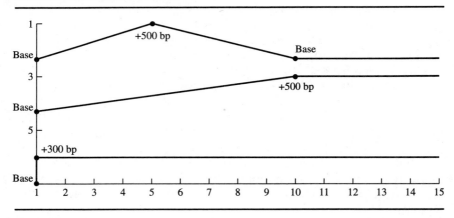

Source: Lehman Brothers Fixed Income Research.

FIGURE 1.5
Application of RBC Factors

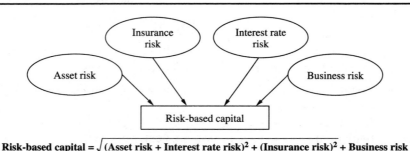

Risk-based capital = $\sqrt{\text{(Asset risk + Interest rate risk)}^2 + \text{(Insurance risk)}^2 + \text{Business risk}}$

Source: Lehman Brothers Fixed Income Research.

gains and losses accounting at life insurance companies effective December 31, 1992.

The **Mandatory Securities Valuation Reserve (MSVR)** was replaced by two new reserves: the **Asset Valuation Reserve (AVR)** and the **Interest Maintenance Reserve (IMR)**. In the past all gains and losses were taken into MSVR in the same year they were realized. Most analysts considered the MSVR part of surplus and added it to surplus when analyzing the capital position of a company. Now gains and losses are separated into interest rate related and credit related. All credit-related gains and losses are placed in the AVR, which is considered part of surplus, whereas interest rate-related gains and losses are included in the IMR, which is considered a liability. For risk-based capital purposes, the AVR is counted as part of surplus, and the IMR cannot be used to help a company meet its minimum capital requirement.

Credit-Related or Interest Rate-Related Gains and Losses. NAIC rules determine whether gains and losses are treated as credit related or interest rate related. If the beginning rating of the bond did not change by more than one NAIC class during the time it was held, the gain or loss is interest rate related; all other losses are credit related. For bonds purchased before 1991, the bond's rating as of December 31, 1990 is used as the beginning rating. Gains or losses on mortgage loans are considered interest rate related unless such a loan is in default, in which case the gain or loss is credit related. A gain or loss on a defaulted mortgage loan is considered credit related. For AVR purposes, mortgage securities such as CMOs and MBSs are treated the same as bonds. The majority of gains or losses are interest rate related because few bonds have dropped more than one NAIC class since the beginning of 1991. For example, Table 1.6 shows that an A3 bond would have to drop to Ba1 for a gain or loss to qualify as credit related.

Applications of IMR and AVR. The IMR is amortized into income based on the expected maturity of the security sold. For securities other than MBSs, the expected maturity date is simply the maturity date. For bonds and preferred stock without a maturity date, the expected maturity is 30 years. For residual mortgages and

TABLE 1.6
NAIC Bond Ratings

NAIC Rating Class	Moody's Ratings	Maximum AVR Factor (%)
1	Aaa–A3	1
2	Baa1–Baa3	2
3	Ba1–Ba3	5
4	B1–B3	10
5	Caa and below	20
6	In default	20

MBSs the maturity is one half the period of time to the final maturity. For newly issued CMOs, the expected maturity is the weighted average life at the time of issue using the prepayment-speeds assumption of the issue. If purchased after the original issue, the insurance company can recalculate the average life based on the pricing prepayment speed as long as this method is used "consistently" for all "similar" CMOs held.

A reserve against all types of credit risks, the AVR is handled in a similar manner to that used with the old MSVR. Over time it builds up a reserve against credit losses and counts as capital in the proposed risk-based capital regulations. The AVR includes two components, the default component and the equity component. The default component handles bonds, preferred stocks, and mortgage loans, whereas the equity component handles equity and real estate. All credit-related gains and losses are added to the AVR along with an annual reserve contribution.

Reserve Contribution for Each Asset.   The reserve contribution is set based on the assumption the AVR does not have to be funded to the maximum level in the year an asset is purchased but may be funded over a longer period of time. To determine the contribution, the maximum AVR is first calculated by applying a maximum reserve factor to the book value of each asset. The maximum factor for each asset varies by type of asset and within certain sectors perhaps by credit quality. The yearly contribution is based on the difference between the maximum and the accumulated reserve, with the contribution equaling 20 percent of the difference between the maximum AVR and the actual accumulated AVR.

Bonds. All securities backed by the full faith and credit of the United States are exempt from the AVR and require no contribution. These securities include Treasuries, Ginnie Maes, and CMOs backed by Ginnie Mae collateral.

The maximum reserve factors for bonds, which increase as credit quality decreases, apply to all securities with an NAIC rating that are reported in Schedule D of the annual statement. CMOs and MBSs are considered bonds and receive the same maximum AVR factor as similarly rated corporate bonds.

Preferred Stock. The maximum factors for preferred stock are shown in Table 1.7. These factors increase dramatically with decreasing credit quality.

Mortgage Loans. Mortgage loans have required a reserve con-

TABLE 1.7
Classes of NAIC Preferred Stock Ratings

NAIC Rating Class	Moody's Ratings	Maximum AVR Factor (%)
1	Aaa–A3	3
2	Baa1–Baa3	4
3	Ba1–Ba3	7
4	B1–B3	12
5	Caa	22
6	Ca, C	22

Source: David Harris, Lehman Brothers.

tribution since the beginning of 1993. For mortgage loans the factor is 3.5 percent multiplied by an adjustment factor. The adjustment factor is the insurance company's delinquency rate over the last two years before the calculation divided by the industry's delinquency rate over the equivalent two years. Historically, industry delinquency rates were 3.37 percent in 1989, 4.32 percent in 1990, and 6.32 percent in 1991, giving a two-year industry average of 5.32 percent.

$$\text{Delinquency rate} = \frac{\text{90-day overdue loans} + \text{Loans in foreclosure process} + \text{Foreclosed loans}}{\text{Mortgage book value} + \text{Foreclosed loans during period}}$$

The adjustment factor can range from 0.5 to 3.0, resulting in maximum mortgage factors of from 1.75 to 10.5 percent.

Real Estate and Equity. Real estate, with a maximum factor of 7.5 percent, required a reserve contribution for the first time in 1992. The maximum factor for unaffiliated life insurance common stock remains 33 1/3 percent. Affiliated common stock requires no AVR contribution, whereas affiliated nonlife equity has a maximum factor of 20 percent.

Phase-in of AVR Contribution. The AVR contribution was implemented over a three-year phase-in beginning January 1, 1993. The phase-in schedule calls for a 10 percent annual contribution for 1992, 15 percent for 1993, and 20 percent for 1994 (as of this writing).

4. FASB Accounting Standards and Proposals[8]

The Financial Accounting Standards Board (FASB) in June 1993 issued FAS statement 115 that effectively mandates market value accounting for marketable equity securities and all debt securities.
*This rule applies to all publicly held companies that hold securities,
including banks, thrifts, credit unions, insurance companies (but not
mutuals), and industrial corporations effective December 15, 1993.*
The proposal has been controversial, however, and it applies to assets only. From a theoretical standpoint, including liabilities would
make economic sense since changes in the market value of assets
and liabilities should tend to offset each other. However, the FASB
concluded that too many practical problems were associated with
determining the market value of most liabilities.

Three categories for classifying securities are provided for in
FAS 115. On the surface these categories appear similar to those
used under current generally accepted accounting procedures
(GAAP), but there are subtle underlying differences. The next sec-
tion reviews current GAAP and is followed by a discussion of the
FAS 115 statement on market value accounting.

Pre-115 GAAP

Under pre-FAS Statement 115 (old GAAP) securities were accounted for in one of three different ways:

Investment Portfolio. Most banks have historically held securities in the investment portfolio, where they were accounted for at
historical cost. In theory, institutions were to assign securities to the
investment portfolio only if they had the intent as well as the ability
to hold them over the long term. In practice, some institutions conducted extensive trading activity out of the investment portfolio,
sometimes selling to take gains while holding the losers—that is,
gains trading. Long a concern of regulators, this practice led to proposals by the Securities and Exchange Commission (SEC) and the
current FASB rule to require that marketable securities be marked
to market.

Held for Sale. Securities the institution anticipated selling in
the foreseeable future were supposed to be categorized as held for

---

[8]This discussion of FASB proposals was prepared by John Tierney.

sale and accounted for under lower of cost or market (LOCOM). Unrealized losses were to be run through the income statement for financial (GAAP) reporting purposes, but had tax consequences. If the position subsequently rose in price, unrealized gains could be recognized (and run through the income statement) up to the initial or amortized cost. Unrealized gains had no tax consequences. The following is a simple example of how gains and losses were treated under LOCOM accounting:

1. An investor purchases $100 face value of securities at par and places them in the investment portfolio on 1/2/92. The price subsequently rises to 103. The investor transfers them to the held-for-sale portfolio at par on 2/1/92.

2. Also on 2/1/92 the investor decides to purchase additional securities—$100 face value at 103—to be held in the held-for-sale portfolio.

3. The book value of the held-for-sale portfolio is 203:

$$
\begin{array}{lll}
\text{1/2/92 purchase} & 100 @ 1.00 = & 100 \\
\text{2/1/92 purchase} & 100 @ 1.03 = & \underline{103} \\
& & 203
\end{array}
$$

4. Now assume the market price falls to 102. How is the portfolio to be marked to market? GAAP allows at least two approaches:

   a. First, the portfolio can be marked on a security-by-security basis. The initial (1/2/92) position is unchanged, and the new position (2/1/92) is marked down to 102, resulting in a loss of $1:

$$
\begin{array}{lll}
\text{1/2/92 purchase} & 100 @ 1.00 = & 100 \\
\text{2/1/92 purchase} & 100 @ 1.02 = & \underline{102} \\
& & 202
\end{array}
$$

$$202 - 203 = -1$$

   b. Alternatively, the two positions may be treated as a portfolio, with unrealized losses netted against unrealized gains. The unrealized loss of $1 on the 2/1/92 purchase is netted against the unrealized gain of $3 on the 1/2/92 purchase; the net unrealized gain of $2 is not recognized under LOCOM accounting.

The approach in (b) is clearly the less aggressive (or more favorable) one because it effectively allows the institution to make use of unrealized gains. In the approach in (a), gains may be used to offset losses only by selling securities. In practice, depository institutions use both approaches.

Trading Portfolio. Securities held for very short time periods or to profit from a bid/ask spread could be assigned to a trading portfolio, where they were subject to full mark-to-market accounting. All unrealized gains and losses were run through the income statement; there were no tax consequences unless gains or losses were realized.

FAS Statement 115: Market Value Accounting Standards

The FAS 115 standards provide for three categories for classifying securities:

Investment Portfolio. Securities in the investment portfolio qualify for historical cost accounting, but the criteria for qualifying for investment portfolio status will be rigorous. Institutions using this category will have to demonstrate that they intend to hold the securities indefinitely under virtually all possible scenarios.

Available for Sale. Generally speaking, securities that are likely to be sold under specified conditions should be assigned to this category. This category includes securities held for managing interest rate risk, for facilitating management of assets and liabilities, for speculative purposes, and so on. As a practical matter, most securities fall into this group. Available-for-sale securities will have to be marked to market on the balance sheet, but unrealized gains and losses may be booked directly to the capital account. Unlike the held-for-sale category under old GAAP, they will not have to be run through the income statement. Table 1.8 compares the accounting treatment for the old held-for-sale category and the FAS 115 available-for-sale category (new) for a security acquired 12/31/93.

Trading Portfolio. This category is similar to current GAAP. Securities assigned to it are generally held for a very short term or with the intent of profiting from a bid/ask spread. Securities would be marked to market regularly, and unrealized gains or losses would be run through the income statement.

TABLE 1.8
Held for Sale versus Available for Sale[a]

	Market Value	Held for Sale (Old)	Available for Sale (New)	Income		Capital	
		Book Value		Old	New	Old	New
12/31/93	100	100	100	0	0	0	0
3/31/94	102	100	102	0	0	0	+2
6/30/94	98	98	98	−2	0	−2	−4

[a]Security acquired 12/31/93.

Source: John Tierney, Lehman Brothers.

INTEREST RATE-RISK-BASED CAPITAL GUIDELINES

Even if opponents successfully delay implementation of an FASB market value standard, bank and thrift regulators are moving ahead to implement an interest rate-risk-based capital framework that would have a similar if less visible impact on bank and thrift asset/liability management policies.

The framework for determining capital risk just described covers only credit risk. Interest rate risk would be measured as the change in the net market value of the institution for a parallel 100 basis points shift in interest rates and would be expressed as a percentage of total assets. This calculation would take into account all assets, liabilities, and off-balance sheet items. Institutions would be required to hold additional capital to cover any change in net market value beyond 1 percent. The regulators would use call report data and duration-based factors to estimate each institution's interest rate risk.

The OTS has also released for public comment a similar proposal. It would require institutions to subject their total asset, liability, and off-balance sheet positions to a 200 basis points interest rate shock. As with banks, described earlier, interest rate risk would be measured as the change in net market value as a percentage of total assets. A change in net market value above 2 percent would trigger an additional capital requirement equal to 50 percent of the change above the 2 percent threshold.

A fascinating aspect of the OTS proposal is that mortgage derivatives, which are now assigned to the 100 percent risk-based capital category for credit risk, would be classified based on the underlying collateral. Agency-backed IOs and residuals, for example, would be assigned to the 20 percent risk-weight category. The OTS believes the interest rate risk inherent in these securities would be effectively captured in the interest rate-risk test and that mortgage derivatives should be evaluated in a portfolio context rather than as individual securities.

Impact on Financial Institutions

Over time, interest rate-risk-based capital guidelines should force institutions to reorient their entire asset/liability management process away from a historical cost accounting and GAAP analysis framework toward a market-valuation approach. Such an approach, in turn, could lead to more creative use of liability and off-balance-sheet-based strategies to better manage interest rate risk and the duration/convexity characteristics of the overall portfolio.

FINANCIAL ACCOUNTING STANDARDS

FAS 107 is an intermediate milestone of the FASB's Financial Instruments and Off-Balance Sheet Financing Project. The broader project is also working on the market value accounting proposal for marketable securities that was put out for public comment late in 1992. The ultimate goal of the entire project is to develop market value accounting standards for all—or at least most—financial instruments, although it may take years to accomplish this objective. As an intermediate step, the FASB requires companies to provide as complete a disclosure as possible of the fair value of financial assets and obligations.

Scope of FAS 107

Under FAS 107 companies are required to disclose the fair value or market value of all financial assets and obligations, including securities, loans, debentures, and off-balance sheet agreements, with the exception of the following items:

- Pension benefits, other postretirement benefits, employee stock purchase/option plans, and other forms of deferred compensation.
- Defeased debt.
- Most insurance contracts (other than financial guarantees and investment contracts).
- Lease contracts.
- Warrant obligations and contracts.
- Certain investments, including minority interest or equity investment in consolidated subsidiaries and equity instruments issued by the entity and classified under stockholders' equity in the balance sheet.

These items are excluded from the scope of FAS 107 because either they are treated under other accounting standards or they pertain primarily to nonfinancial items (e.g., a fire insurance contract on an office building).

FAS 107 is not a market value accounting standard. It does not affect the financial assets and liabilities reported on the balance sheet, and changes in fair value are not reported in the income statement. The purpose of FAS 107 is to provide investors with additional information for making investment decisions. FAS 107 disclosures may be made either in the body of the financial statements or in footnotes. The methods and significant assumptions used to derive fair value of financial instruments must be disclosed.

Guidance for Applying FAS 107

The FASB recognizes that whereas active markets exist for some financial instruments, making it easy to ascertain their market value, other instruments are essentially illiquid. For dealing with these latter instruments the FASB has provided general rather than specific guidance. Generally speaking, the FASB believes that companies should estimate fair values for illiquid instruments to the extent "practicable," but they have the flexibility not to do so for specific instruments if the costs associated with providing these estimates are deemed excessive. However, companies must disclose why estimating fair value was not practicable for them.

FAS 107 provides the following more specific guidelines:

- The fair value of a financial instrument is the price at which reasonable quantities of the instrument could be exchanged in a transaction between willing parties, rather than the price that might be obtained in a forced sale or liquidation.
- Some loans, such as credit card receivables or mortgages, may be valued by referencing the appropriate secondary securities markets.
- The fair value of commercial and industrial loans may be estimated by discounting projected cash flows by a discount rate that reflects both current market rates and an appropriate spread for credit risk.
- Trade receivables and payables can generally be valued at face value.
- Deposit liabilities with no defined maturity (for example, transaction accounts and pass-book savings) are to be valued at the amount payable as of the reporting date. Institutions cannot take into account the value of long-term deposit relationships; deposit intangibles are viewed as nonfinancial items.
- For deposit liabilities with defined maturities (for example, CDs) fair value can be estimated by discounting projected cash flows at an appropriate market discount rate.

Potential Problems

By offering only general guidance, the FASB provides both companies and auditors with a degree of flexibility in applying the standard and at the same time generates a degree of confusion about how to comply with the requirements of FAS 107. Critics have pointed out that the combination of flexibility and confusion may lead to widely differing methods for calculating fair market valuation across companies, making it difficult for investors to make apples-to-apples comparisons. The view of the FASB is that its general guidelines give companies leeway to provide useful information without incurring excessive costs.

In any case, companies will incur fairly significant costs in complying with FAS 107. They must, for example, contend with the risk that the fair market valuations and historical cost statements may be inconsistent with each other. For example, fair value statements may show that a securities position is significantly under water, whereas at the same time there may be no provision for loss on the historical statements (since the firm expects to recoup the entire principal balance). These potential misunderstandings might well lead to greater uncertainty and lower stock prices.

CHAPTER 2

CHARACTERISTICS OF PASS-THROUGHS

KEY QUESTIONS

1. What are the characteristics of pass-throughs?
2. How do payment delays affect MBS yield?
3. How do I use CAGE and WALA?
4. What is all the fuss about?
5. What are the valuation issues?
6. What are the MBS sector considerations?
7. What are the features of other MBS forms?

1. WHAT ARE THE CHARACTERISTICS OF PASS-THROUGHS?

All MBSs have a coupon, or pass-through rate; an issue date; a final, or stated, maturity date; an average life (which shifts with prepayment cycles); and a payment delay. The cash flow of principal and interest (P&I) generated by the underlying pool of mortgage collateral is in the form of a monthly annuity. Box 2–1 gives definitions of the terms associated with MBSs.

Cash Flows of MBS Pools

The P&I payments of a standard, level-pay mortgage are scheduled as a series of equal monthly installments, but over time the proportion of interest declines, with the principal portion becoming greater in the later years. Figure 2.1 illustrates the distribution of P&I and servicing payments for a level-pay, 30-year amortizing 9.75 percent mortgage, less 75 basis points total servicing spread. The pass-through rate is 9 percent, the WAM is 360 months, and no prepayments are assumed.

BOX 2-1
MBS Terminology

- The **pass-through rate** is the net interest rate passed through to investors after deducting the average servicing spread from the average gross mortgage rate or WAC (see below).

- The **servicing spread** consists of the **service fee** paid to the servicer of the pool for collecting the monthly P&I from individual homeowners and a **management and guarantee fee** paid to the federal agency that guarantees the P&I payments due the investor.

- The **issue date** is the date of issuance of the MBS pool.

- The **stated maturity date** is calculated as the last payment date of the latest-maturing mortgage in the pool.

- The **weighted average coupon (WAC)** is calculated as the weighted average of the gross interest rates of the mortgages underlying the pool as of the pool issue date (the WAC is updated by Fannie Mae and Freddie Mac for most pools).

- The **weighted average life (WAL)** is the weighted average time to the receipt of a principal dollar. The WAL is not a half-life or midpoint of the cash flows; rather, the key is in the *weighting of the timing of the cash flows*. The WAL is prepay dependent and is not a fixed characteristic of a pool.

- The **weighted average maturity (WAM)** is calculated as of the *issue date* as the weighted average of the stated maturities of the mortgages underlying the MBS pool.

- The **weighted average remaining maturity (WARM)** is the weighted average remaining term calculated as the number of payments remaining to the contractual maturity date of the pool and is usually calculated as of a date *subsequent* to the date of issuance of the pool.

- The **weighted average loan age (WALA)** reflects the weighted average of the number of months *since* the date of mortgage origination; therefore, WALA is an excellent measure of the seasoning of the pool. Freddie Mac reports the WALA on all its pools.

- The **calculated loan age (CAGE)** is calculated by Fannie Mae and provided for all its pools. CAGE differs somewhat from WALA in that CAGE provides an *inferred* age similar to the WAM calculation. Ginnie Mae does not provide data comparable to WALA or CAGE. However, since Ginnie Mae does not permit pooling of seasoned loans into its MBS pools, such information is less important to have except to the extent that curtailments (partial prepayments) may distort the WAM calculation.
- The **weighted average original loan term (WAOLT)** is another piece of data provided by Freddie Mac on its PCs. WAOLT is helpful in differentiating between loans with some seasoning and those that were originated with a shorter than normal original term.
- The **payment delay** is the time lag in days from the first day of the month following the month of issuance of the pool to the date the pass-through P&I is actually remitted to the investor.
- The **cash flow window** is the time period from the first payment of principal to the last payment, or to the final (projected or stated) maturity.
- The **tail** is the principal cash flow that extends from the average life point to the final maturity.

Although an MBS pass-through is designed as a mirror image of the P&I payments that are "passed through" from the underlying mortgage pool, the mortgage pool cash flows are passed through to the MBS investors less a servicing spread and with a payment delay.

The Servicing Spread

The **servicing spread** is the difference in basis points between the mortgage rate (or the WAC) of the mortgage collateral underlying the pool and the pass-through rate, net of servicing and guarantee fees. Note from Figure 2.1 that the servicing spread is a percentage of the unpaid principal balance of the mortgage remaining, which declines over time. As a consequence, the total cash flows paid to the MBS investor increase slightly over time.

FIGURE 2.1

Scheduled Mortgage Cash Flow, 9.75 Percent Mortgage, 360-Month WAM, Contractual Amortization, Zero PSA

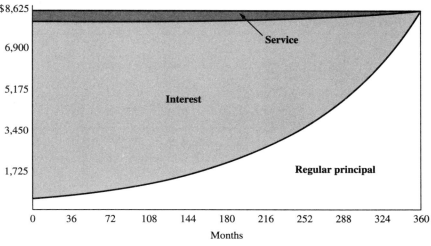

Source: Bloomberg Financial Markets.

2. HOW DO PAYMENT DELAYS AFFECT MBS YIELD?

Mortgage payments are made in arrears; that is, the homeowner owes the first payment on the first day of the month following the month in which the mortgage was originated. In effect, the **payment delay** pushes the actual pass-through of P&I payments forward in time, thereby somewhat reducing the present value of the annuity paid to the MBS investor. The length of the payment delay depends upon the securitization program employed to form the MBS, as illustrated by Figure 2.2

Figure 2.2 shows the flow of P&I payments. The figure is structured to assume the MBS pool was issued at point A in month 1. The first homeowner payments are due at point C, with the P&I passed through to the MBS holders at point D. It should be noted that the placement of point D in the time sequence differs among MBS programs. For example, the payment delay is 14 days for

FIGURE 2.2
How Payment Delays Work, Primary Market

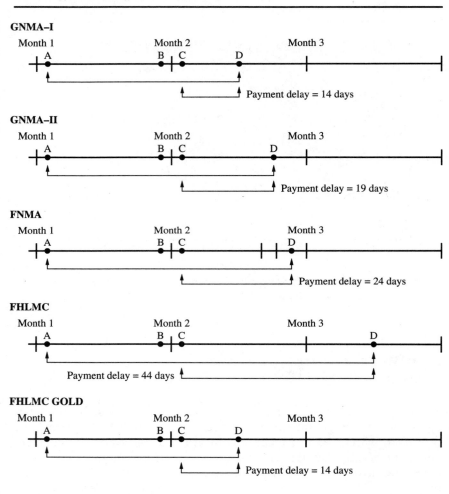

A: Investor buys security on origination date
B: First record date (of security ownership)
C: First payment due from homeowner
D: First payment actually made to pass-through investor

Source: Lehman Brothers Fixed Income Research.

GNMA-I and 19 days for GNMA-II. With Freddie Mac PCs the payment delay is 44 days for the original Freddie Mac program and 14 days for the Freddie Mac Gold program, introduced in the spring of 1990.

Payment delays are often incorrectly stated. For example, the correct payment delay for a Ginnie Mae is 14 days, but the delay is sometimes incorrectly stated as 45 days. The reason is that some analysts count from the first day of the month of origination (month 1 in Figure 2.2) to the date of the pass-through of P&I to the investor (15th day of month 2) and call the delay 45 days. However, the payment *is* received on the 15th of the month, and even by this erroneous counting the delay is only 44 days. The actual delay is from February 1 to February 15—which is 14 days. The day count for calculating accrued interest with MBSs is 30/360—that is, there is no recognition of the shorter or longer *actual* day count of specific months.

A synopsis of the flow-through of P&I for a Freddie Mac PC is given in Box 2-2. Subsequent months follow the pattern illustrated for July. Application of the pool factor method to a hypothetical Guarantor PC pool formed on or before the 15th day of a month differs from the illustration given in Box 2.2. In this instance, the second pool factor, which is published on or about the first day of the month after the month of PC pool formation (May 1 in the box), is not an estimate by Freddie Mac but reflects the actual unpaid principal balance of the mortgages as of the 15th day of the month of PC pool formation (April in the box). This report, which is prepared by the mortgage servicers, reflects principal payments and prepayments that were made between the 1st and 15th days of the month.

Bond-Equivalent Yield

The P&I of a pass-through is received monthly (versus semiannually for a traditional bond), thereby enabling the monthly compounding of the coupon. The monthly coupon is treated as though it were collected and reinvested at the yield to maturity (or cash flow yield if a prepayment assumption is applied). This assumption is not realistic, of course, because in periods of declining interest rates the coupon would probably be reinvested at a rate below the purchase yield—and vice versa if rates are rising.

BOX 2-2
Synopsis of Payment Delay, Freddie Mac PC

The following illustrates the payment of principal by application of the Pool Factor method to a hypothetical Guarantor PC Pool formed on April 22 (i.e., after the 15th day of the month):

April 1	The initial Pool Factor, which is not published, is equal to 1,000,000. This is the date of PC Pool Inception.
April 22	Settlement on the PC Pool takes place and the PC Pool is formed. The Original Unpaid Principal Balance of the PC Pool is equal to the unpaid principal balance of the Mortgages as of April 1, as reported at delivery to Freddie Mac by the seller.
By April 29	Within five business days after PC Pool formation, servicers report and remit any prepayments in full of Mortgages received from April 1 through April 22 and repurchase any Mortgages that became delinquent during such period.
On or about May 1	The May Pool Factor is published, reflecting a reduction in the unpaid principal balance of the Mortgages equal to Freddie Mac's estimate of scheduled amortization on the Mortgages from April 1 through April 15.
By May 22	Within five business days after May 15, servicers report the outstanding principal balance of the Mortgages as of May 15. This balance will be used in calculating the June Pool Factor and will reflect principal payments received by servicers and paid to Freddie Mac, including full and partial prepayments and any repurchases of

	Mortgages by servicers, from April 1 through May 15.
On or about June 1	The June Pool Factor is published, reflecting the May 15 unpaid principal balance reported by servicers, including full and partial prepayments, and any repurchases of Mortgages as of May 15.
June 15	The first payment is made to Holders. The aggregate principal payment to Holders is equal to the difference between the April and May Pool Factors multiplied by the Original Unpaid Principal Balance.
By June 22	Within five business days after June 15, servicers report the outstanding principal balance of the Mortgages as of June 15. This balance will be used in calculating the July Pool Factor and will reflect principal payments received by servicers, including full and partial prepayments, and any repurchases of Mortgages by servicers, from May 16 through June 15.
On or about July 1	The July Pool Factor is published, reflecting the June 15 unpaid principal balance reported by servicers, including full and partial prepayments, and any repurchases of Mortgages as of June 15.
July 15	The second payment is made to Holders. The aggregate principal payment to Holders is equal to the difference between the May and June Pool Factors multiplied by the Original Unpaid Principal Balance.

Source: Federal Home Loan Mortgage Corporation.

Parity Price

Because of the payment delay, a 9.5 percent GNMA priced at par does not yield 9 percent: It yields 9.45 percent. Table 2.1 illustrates the yields of various MBSs priced at par and, conversely, the price at which each MBS would yield 9 percent, the **parity price**.

The Cash Flow Window

The **cash flow window** is the period of time from receipt of the first P&I payment to receipt of the last payment. In the MBS pool illustrated in Figure 2.1 it is 30 years. As we examine the impact of prepayments on the distribution of the pool cash flows, we need to interject the concept of average life. The average life of the MBS illustrated in Figure 2.3 is 9.6 years. Compare the cash flow structure illustrated in Figure 2.3 with that in Figure 2.1.

The principal cash flows in Figure 2.1 may be said to be back-end loaded—that is, the principal is deferred to the later years of the pool cash flow cycle. Note that the interjection of prepayments, as shown in Figure 2.3, pushes the principal cash flows forward, causing the distribution of principal cash flows to be more front-end loaded.[1] Note also that the cash flow window extends for many years beyond the average life point. This extension is referred to as the **tail**. The length of the tail is an important relative value consideration in MBS investing. The nature of the cash flow window, or tail, has an important bearing on the probability distribution of the average life of the MBS. (Another important aspect of the cash flow window is examined in Wide versus Narrow Windows in Chapter 7, where MBS types with very narrow windows—one year or less—are discussed.)

Impact of WAC and WAM

The WAC may have an important bearing on the anticipated prepayment pattern of the pool. With Ginnie Maes, WAC considerations are less important because the servicing spread is always 50

---

[1]Front-end loading of principal has a dramatic impact on the WAL calculation. At zero PSA the weighting of the later cash flows causes the average life to be extended well beyond the midpoint of the cash flows. With prepayments and the rapid advancement of principal cash flows the average life is shifted forward significantly.

TABLE 2.1
MBS Parity Price (Price Where Yield = Pass-Through Rate)

MBS		Price	Yield (%)[a]	Delay (days)
GNMA	7.50	99-23	7.50	14
FNMA	7.50	99-16	7.50	24
FHLMC[b]	7.50	98-28	7.50	44
GNMA	7.50	100	7.44	14
FNMA	7.50	100	7.40	24
FHLMC[b]	7.50	100	7.21	44

[a]Monthly Yield. The bond equivalent (BEY) will be higher.
[b]Original program Freddie Mac PC pools. Gold PCs provide the same price/yield results as Ginnie Mae MBSs.

Source: Bloomberg Financial Markets.

FIGURE 2.3
Cash Flows, FHLMC 9 Percent PC, 30-Year Amortization, 150 PSA

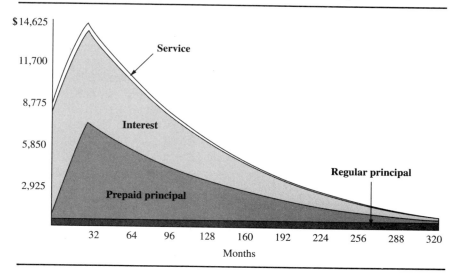

Source: Bloomberg Financial Markets.

basis points (except for special programs such as mobile homes and projects), but the WAC is generally a valuation consideration with conventional pools. Pools with a high WAC generally will prepay somewhat more consistently to a higher prepayment rate than those with a more typical WAC of about 75 basis points above the pass-through rate. (Ginnie Mae securities, which, except for some GNMA-II pools, always have a WAC of 50 basis points above the pass-through rate, are not relevant to this discussion.) The key to identifying value in WAC pools is finding a consistent pattern of paying to a higher prepayment rate. If the pool has paid to a higher prepayment rate on only a few reporting periods, the real intrinsic value is small.

3. HOW DO I USE CAGE AND WALA?[2]

Before the WALA measure became available, loan age was estimated by subtracting the updated remaining term from the original term. For example, a pool with a WARM of 345 months was assumed to have an age of 15 months (360 minus 345). The problem with this assumption is that WARM is *not* a chronological measure. Whereas WAM means weighted average maturity, it is *not* the average number of months to the loan's stated maturity dates.

If a homeowner prepays a portion of the mortgage, the "extra" amount is applied to the remaining principal balance. As the amount of principal owed is reduced, the mortgage maturity shortens but the loan age remains the same. If one were to evaluate the shortened WARM alone, the pool would appear much older.

WAM[3] is recalculated by Freddie Mac and Fannie Mae to take into account the effect of partial prepayments, or curtailments, so that *the current WAM equals the average number of scheduled payments remaining.* (See the discussions of WALA and CAGE on pages 43 and 44, respectively.) For example, assume a mortgagor's 12th payment originally called for $100 of interest and $1.00 of principal, whereas the scheduled principal for the 13th payment

---

[2]This discussion of WALA is based on Catherine Lidy and Michael McCabe, "WARMing Up to WALAs and WAOLTS," *Mortgage Finance.* Washington, DC: Freddie Mac, August 1991.

[3]This discussion of WAM was provided by Nicole Vianna, Vice President, Mortgage Strategies Group, Lehman Brothers.

is $1.10. Before the 12th payment is made, the WAM would be 349 months. If a payment of $101 is made, then the new WAM would be 348 months. If the payment is $102.10, the new WAM would be 347 months, or 2 months shorter than the original WAM.

The following two case studies illustrate the impact of curtailments.[4]

Case 1: The borrower has a 30-year, $100,000 mortgage with a 12 percent interest rate. The monthly payment is calculated to be $1,028.61. The first payment includes $1,000 of interest and $28.61 of principal. After this payment is made, the number of payments left to amortize the loan is calculated to be 359.

Case 2: The borrower prepays an additional $500 of the mortgage balance with the first monthly payment. This is an example of a curtailment. The loan balance after one month ($99,471.39) is calculated by subtracting the first month's principal amortization of $28.61 and the $500 curtailment from the original balance. Each month after the curtailment, payments are assumed to be made at the original payment amount of $1,028.61 until the loan balance is repaid. The calculations show that the remaining term drops to 343 months. Thus, even a small curtailment can sharply reduce WARM.

If loan age were not disclosed, mortgage analysts might assume that this loan is 17 months old. In fact, it is one month old. Why does loan age matter? It matters because borrowers are less likely to prepay mortgages in the early months of a loan's life than later. This tendency is represented in the Public Securities Association (PSA) prepayment curve. A mortgage pool that prepays at 100 PSA has an annualized prepayment rate which increases from zero by 0.2 percent each month for 30 months and then levels off at 6 percent. Yields on MBSs are often quoted assuming prepayments of a specific multiple of PSA chosen based on the characteristics of the underlying loans. For example, 200 PSA refers to loans prepaying twice as fast as this schedule.

WALA provides better information about where loan pools are on the PSA curve. Thus, mortgage analysts are able to apply models for predicting prepayments and pricing mortgage securities more accurately because these models specify a relationship between loan

---

[4]The case studies were provided by Joel Katz, Manager, Structured Finance Marketing, Freddie Mac. His case studies first appeared in *Secondary Mortgage Markets,* Summer 1991, Freddie Mac.

age and prepayment rates. Analysts are also better able to translate a given paydown into the correct implied multiple of PSA. The monthly release of WALA may be especially useful to investors in derivative products backed by PCs because returns on these securities can vary greatly with relatively small changes in predicted prepayment speeds.

A problem with the old WAM calculation arises if one assumes the mortgages backing a 30-year security pool all have 30-year original terms.[5] In fact, Freddie Mac, Fannie Mae, and Ginnie Mae allow mortgages with original terms greater than 180 months and less than or equal to 360 months to be included in 30-year security pools. Knowing the WALA, WARM, and WAOLT of a particular pool will keep analysts from incorrectly assuming that pools with 25-year WARMs are 30-year loans that have seasoned for five years. In this case WAOLT, which is the weighted average of the number of monthly P&I payments the homeowner will make over the life of the mortgage for all the mortgages in a security pool, would reveal whether the mortgages are new 25-year loans.

CAGE, calculated by Fannie Mae, also accounts for curtailments but may not catch the presence of a short-maturity mortgage that was included in the pool at the time of issue.[6] Under CAGE the age of the loan is calculated by subtracting the *original* WAM of a pool from the *original maturity* and then adding the number of months elapsed since the original data provided at the time of issue. For example, a 360-month pool issued July 1 with an original maturity of 359 months would have a CAGE of 4 months in October (360 − 359 + 3 months = 4 months). This method accounts for curtailments because the formula uses the original WAM of the pool, which is not distorted by curtailments. On the other hand, the WARM, calculated as of a subsequent date, is affected by curtailments.

The problem with CAGE, however, is that it does not account for loans included in the pool that have original maturities less than the stated maturities because the CAGE calculation is based on an assumption that all loans in the pool have a uniform original maturity of 360, 180, or 84 months.

The loan age determines the cash flows of the MBS or CMO if

---

[5]See Lidy and McCabe.

[6]This discussion of CAGE is from the *Mortgage-Backed Securities Letter* 6 (51), December 23, 1991. New York: Investment Dealers Digest.

the prepayment assumption is defined as a percentage of the PSA standard.[7] Loan age is irrelevant for cash flow calculations if the prepayment is defined as a percentage of CPR.

- WALA equals the weighted average number of months since loan origination and is fairly chronological.
- The WALA will change by more than 1 month only if the loans in the pool are heterogeneous.

WALA determines where on the PSA curve the amortization calculation is made. For example, assume the WAM is 350 months and the WALA is 5 months. The stream of CPRs implied by 100 PSA is dramatically different from when WALA is 10 months, as shown in Table 2.2.

Generic MBSs: Overview

Current-coupon MBSs, that is, those in current production, are perhaps the most familiar to a broad range of investors. Newly issued MBS pools carry all the attributes that cause many investors to shy away from MBS investing: monthly cash flows in amounts that may vary from month to month, prepayment risk, negative convexity—all the "buzz" words commonly applied to MBSs with equal zest by both the experts and the uninformed.

4. WHAT IS ALL THE FUSS ABOUT?

A federal agency-guaranteed MBS bears virtually no credit risk; the current coupon is highly liquid and offers a generous yield spread over intermediate-term Treasury securities. Where is the risk? Figure 2.4 illustrates the risk associated with the tail cash flows of a FHLMC 9 percent PC. It has a WAC of 9.70 percent and a WAM of 29 years, 3 months, also typical of recent newly issued current-coupon product.[8] The pool has a 9.17-year average life at 150 PSA and would be priced at a yield spread off perhaps the 9- or, more likely, the 10-year Treasury security. Note first all the "noise" that

---

[7]This discussion of loan age was provided by Nicole Vianna.

[8]A theoretical new-issue pool would have a WAM of 30 years, but in reality because of processing time and variation in mortgage origination dates most pools have WAMs of less than 30 years when they are newly issued.

TABLE 2.2
CPR Implied by 100 PSA

Month from Now	Pre-WALA Age Assumption = 10		WALA = 5	
	Age	CPR	Age	CPR
0	10	2.0	5	1.0
1	11	2.2	6	1.2
2	12	2.4	7	1.4
3	13	2.6	8	1.6
4	14	2.8	9	1.8
5	15	3.0	10	2.0
6	16	3.2	11	2.2
7	17	3.4	12	2.4
8	18	3.6	13	2.6
9	19	3.8	14	2.8
10	20	4.0	15	3.0
11	21	4.2	16	3.2
12	22	4.4	17	3.4
13	23	4.6	18	3.6
14	24	4.8	19	3.8
15	25	5.0	20	4.0
16	26	5.2	21	4.2
17	27	5.4	22	4.4
18	28	5.6	23	4.6
19	29	5.8	24	4.8
20	30	6.0	25	5.0
21	31	6.0	26	5.2
22	32	6.0	27	5.4
23	33	6.0	28	5.6
24	34	6.0	29	5.8
25	35	6.0	30	6.0
26	36	6.0	31	6.0
27	37	6.0	32	6.0
28	38	6.0	33	6.0
29	39	6.0	34	6.0
30	40	6.0	35	6.0

Source: Nicole Vianna, Lehman Brothers.

surrounds the average-life point. Investors often picture a 9-year-average-life MBS as a security that looks and feels like a 9-year bullet-maturity Treasury. It does not. In fact, Figure 2.4 clearly illustrates that most of the cash flows are at some point *other* than 9 years, and extend into a long tail that runs to 30 years.

FIGURE 2.4

Principal Cash Flow, FHLMC 9 Percent Gold PC; 30-Year Amortization; 150 PSA; WAM 29 Years, 3 Months; WAC 9.70 Percent

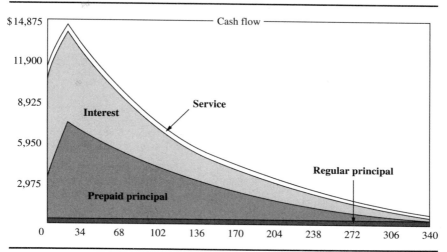

Source: Bloomberg Financial Markets.

Structural Considerations

From examining Figure 2.4 some important structural considerations emerge:

Cash flows	Monthly
Cash flow window	29 years, 3 months
Tail beyond average life	20.08 years

Table 2.3 illustrates the cash flows of this PC. Note the net cash flow, which is the sum of the interest, contractual principal, and prepaid principal cash flows. The net cash flow is in significant six-figure numbers only for the first 7 years. By the 9-year-average-life point it is below six figures, and $679,135 of cash flow—68 percent of the total—follows the average-life point. Table 2.4 illustrates the average-life drift of the FHLMC PC in Figure 2.4. Note that although the pool has an average life of 9.17 years at one specific PSA prepayment-speed assumption, the only certainty is the prepayment speed will *not* remain at 150 PSA from month to month through its pool life. Note that the average-life drift spans 11.11

TABLE 2.3
Cash Flow Table, FHLMC 9 Percent Gold PC; WAM 29 Years, 3 Months;
WAC 9.70

Year	Date	Principal Balance	Interest	Regular Principal	Prepaid Principal	Net Cash Flow
1	2/15/93	947,351.95	88,086.11	6,268.98	46,379.07	140,734.17
2	2/15/94	864,413.46	81,999.92	6,469.00	76,469.48	164,938.41
3	2/15/95	780,436.10	74,274.28	6,501.56	77,475.81	158,251.64
4	2/15/96	704,002.48	67,032.79	6,516.52	69,917.10	143,466.42
5	2/15/97	634,433.62	60,441.76	6,531.52	63,037.34	130,010.62
6	2/15/98	571,111.66	54,442.63	6,546.56	56,775.39	117,764.59
7	2/15/99	513,474.36	48,982.14	6,561.63	51,075.67	106,619.45
8	2/15/00	461,010.06	44,011.81	6,576.73	45,887.57	96,476.11
9	2/15/01	413,253.15	39,487.50	6,591.87	41,165.03	87,244.31
10	2/15/02	369,779.94	35,369.09	6,607.05	36,866.16	78,842.31
11	2/15/03	330,204.86	31,620.04	6,622.26	32,952.82	71,195.12
12	2/15/04	294,177.04	28,207.10	6,637.50	29,390.31	64,234.91
13	2/15/05	261,377.21	25,100.02	6,652.78	26,147.05	57,899.85
14	2/15/06	231,514.80	22,271.27	6,668.10	23,194.31	52,133.67
15	2/15/07	204,325.42	19,695.79	6,683.45	20,505.93	46,885.17
16	2/15/08	179,568.46	17,350.79	6,698.83	18,058.13	42,107.75
17	2/15/09	157,024.96	15,215.52	6,714.25	15,829.24	37,759.02
18	2/15/10	136,495.69	13,271.11	6,729.71	13,799.56	33,800.38
19	2/15/11	117,799.33	11,500.37	6,745.20	11,951.16	30,196.74
20	2/15/12	100,770.87	9,887.67	6,760.73	10,267.72	26,916.12
21	2/15/13	85,260.19	8,418.79	6,776.29	8,734.39	23,929.47
22	2/15/14	71,130.64	7,080.77	6,791.89	7,337.66	21,210.32
23	2/15/15	58,257.89	5,861.83	6,807.53	6,065.23	18,734.59
24	2/15/16	46,528.78	4,751.26	6,823.20	4,905.90	16,480.37
25	2/15/17	35,840.37	3,739.30	6,838.91	3,849.51	14,427.72
26	2/15/18	26,098.95	2,817.08	6,854.65	2,886.77	12,558.50
27	2/15/19	17,219.26	1,976.50	6,870.43	2,009.26	10,856.19
28	2/15/20	9,123.70	1,210.22	6,886.24	1,209.31	9,305.78
29	2/15/21	1,741.68	511.56	6,902.10	479.93	7,893.58
30	2/15/22	.00	26.06	1,728.01	13.67	1,767.74

Source: Bloomberg Financial Markets.

TABLE 2.4
Average-Life Drift, FHLMC 9 Percent PC; WAM 29 Years, 3 Months;
WAC 9.70

PSA	50	100	150	200	250	300	400
Average life	15.24	11.61	9.17	7.46	6.25	5.34	4.13

Source: Bloomberg Financial Markets.

years, from a slow PSA speed of 50 to a relatively fast PSA speed of 400. So it is essential to establish a view on the outlook for prepayment speeds over the period of your investment horizon (see Chapter 4 for a discussion of prepayment dynamics).

The complete prepayment history of all FHLMC 7.5s and 9s is illustrated in Figures 2.5A and 2.5B. Note that the pattern of prepayments indicates a low PSA of 75–100 in the early 1980s (1983–1985), a high PSA of 1,341 in March 1992 (the peak of the 1991–1992 refinancing cycle), and an overall range of about 125 to 200 PSA.

5. WHAT ARE THE VALUATION ISSUES?

The first valuation question should be, What is my convexity? Convexity measures the rate of change in price to the change in yield. The price of a security with *positive convexity* will rise at an increasing rate as market yields decline and decline at a decreasing rate as market yields increase. The price of a security with *negative convexity* does the opposite; when market yields decline the price of negatively convex securities increases at a decreasing rate. In the case of a premium-priced MBSs, for example, the price will eventually plateau when market yields decline sharply. This characteristic of premium-priced MBSs is referred to as **price compression** (see page 51 for a discussion of price compression). The option-adjusted spread (OAS) assigned to the MBS will indicate whether the MBS in question will be characterized as positively or negatively convex. OAS measures the value of the prepayment option embedded in the MBS root and adjusts the stated MBS to Treasury yield spread for the option value. Premium-priced MBSs characteristically carry a high option value, which causes them to be negatively convex. The value of the option is therefore referred to as a convexity cost. *So another question should be, What is the OAS of my proposed MBS investment?* (For a full discussion of OAS and its derivation and applications, see What Are the OAS and Prepayment Model Components? in Chapter 3.)

The OAS of the current-coupon MBS will be the most favorable when

- The yield curve is positive.
- Prepayments are stable or declining.

FIGURE 2.5A
Prepayment History, FHLMC 7.5s

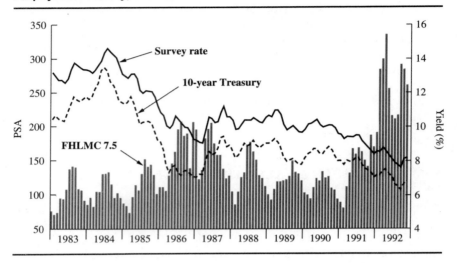

Source: Lehman Brothers Fixed Income Research.

FIGURE 2.5B
Prepayment History, FHLMC 9s

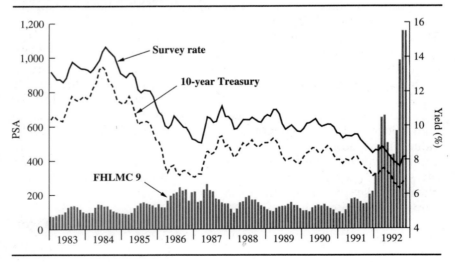

Source: Lehman Brothers Fixed Income Research.

- Volatility is relatively low.
- The MBS supply is moderate and demand is high.

A positive yield curve encourages CMO/REMIC production, assuring a good "deal bid" for the current-coupon MBS, the primary source of CMO/REMIC collateral. A positive yield curve also reduces the cost of carry—the yield spread between the financing cost and the MBS coupon—and encourages investors to seek relatively longer-duration securities.

Stable or declining prepayments reduce the convexity cost, resulting in an OAS that is relatively close to the stated yield. The current coupon, assuming it represents recently issued pools collateralized by new production mortgages, will enjoy considerable call protection for some time (see Pool Age: Seasoning in Chapter 4). *A note of caution: Not all MBSs carrying the current coupon are new issues.* (For example, if the current coupon is 8.5 percent, there were 8.5s issued every year from 1985 to the present.) *A further caution: Not all newly issued MBS pools are collateralized by new mortgage loans.* A Freddie Mac Guarantor PC, for example, may have been recently issued to securitize seasoned loans in a bank portfolio restructuring. *So watch the WAM of your current-coupon MBSs*—if the WAM or WARM is less than 350 months, the collateral is not new.

Relative price volatility is a consideration given too little attention by most MBS investors. The current coupon tends to display the most low-percentage volatility of the generic MBS forms, suffering price compression above the 101 dollar price and duration extension at prices below 99 (lower prices imply rising interest rates, slower prepayments, and average-life extension). Price compression defines in part the negative convexity that is the bane of MBS investors: Price compression in a bull market deprives the MBS of price performance, a key ingredient of total return; duration extension is what is least desired in a rising interest rate environment.

Supply/demand considerations include

- Housing economics/demographics.
- REMIC demand.
- Dollar roll demand.
- Investor demand.
- Competitive market technicals.

Supply/Demand Overview

The state of the housing market will obviously dictate the supply side of the MBS supply/demand equation. In the boom years of home price appreciation of the mid- to late 1980s mortgage origina- tions and MBS production were high. At the same time, demand was somewhat limited because until 1986 thrift institutions were the principal buyers of MBSs, and since 1982 thrifts have been net sellers of MBSs. After the 1986 Tax Reform Act, the REMIC legis- lation vastly broadened the market for MBS product. Commercial banks, which under the 1986 Tax Reform Act lost the ability to ar- bitrage tax-free municipals against tax-deductible CD interest, sub- stantially increased their holdings of MBSs from 1987 to 1992. Insurance companies soon followed as junk bond and commercial real estate holdings were reduced in favor of securitized mortgage product.

In the early 1990s the supply/demand equation reversed fur- ther as the boom faded into history and stagnating home prices re- duced housing turnover (see Chapter 5). Even as the supply side was diminishing, REMIC demand accelerated rapidly, particularly in 1991 and 1992. The result was a dramatic tightening of the MBS to Treasury yield spread, even when prepayments accelerated in the fourth quarter of 1991. As prepayment speeds continued their ac- celeration into 1992 and MBS issuance (supply) increased signifi- cantly, MBS to Treasury spreads widened only moderately. This experience was in contrast to that of 1986–1987 when MBS to Treasury spreads widened to well over 200 basis points.

The reasons for the reversal of the supply/demand equation were twofold. First, the success of the REMIC structure assured a continuing demand for MBSs as collateral, a situation that did not exist in the pre-REMIC 1986–1987 refinancing cycle. Second, the REMIC efficiently redistributes the prepayment option, enabling investors who are averse to prepayment risk to avoid the risk and still participate in the MBS market without forcing yield spreads to compensate for uncertainty. (See Chapter 6 for a further discussion of supply/demand considerations.)

Dollar Roll Demand
When REMIC demand is high the roll value of current-coupon MBSs becomes high as the scramble for collateral to fill REMIC deals leaves the MBS dealers short of collateral. In fact, in 1990 the

dollar volume of MBSs pledged as collateral for REMIC deals exceeded that year's total MBS origination. In 1991 REMICs absorbed 95 percent of total conventional MBS issuance. The result was a dollar roll market with month-to-month price drops that exceeded economics by a wide margin: The equivalent cost of carry in the dollar roll market was below the repo market cost (see Table 2.5). One valuation consideration for current-coupon MBSs, therefore, is which issue (for example, Fannie Mae versus Freddie Mac) and coupon are likely to be in greatest demand in the dollar roll market. The answer, of course, is the one with the highest REMIC deal demand and the lowest origination level.

Competitive Market Technicals

Technical considerations that influence nonmortgage-related fixed-income securities will also strongly influence MBS demand considerations. For example, in strong bull markets performance-oriented investors will frequently swap out of MBSs (particularly the current coupon, which is the most broadly traded MBS market) to buy noncallable securities, generally intermediate Treasuries. Such activity may add significantly to the supply of MBSs when demand is less. Conversely, when event risk strikes other markets, as it did corporate bonds in 1989–1990 and asset-backed securities in 1991, investors will favor MBSs. Other supply factors such as Resolution Trust Company (RTC) selling adds supply, although in 1991 that was not a detriment to MBSs.

Prepayment Activity
When prepayment activity is high, as was the case in 1986–1987 and again in 1991–1992, the volume of MBS issuance is increased by refi-

TABLE 2.5
Dollar Roll versus Repo Financing Costs, December 18, 1992

	1-Month Drop (32nds)	Equivalent Financing Cost (%)	1-Month Repo Rate (%)
GNMA 7.5	12	2.42	3.62
FNMA 7.5	15	1.22	3.67
FHLMC 7.5	10	3.34	3.67

Source: Bloomberg Financial Markets.

TABLE 2.6

Agency and Nonagency Issuance Summary ($ Billions)

Total Date	Agency[a]				Nonagency[b]				1-4-Family Mortgage Debt	
	Net Issuance	Issuance	Outstanding	Paydowns (%)	Total Issuance	Net Issuance	Outstanding	Paydowns (%)	Total	Sectorized (%)
1984	60.9	45.6	284.2	n.a.	0.2	n.a.	n.a.	n.a.	1,344.0	26.1
1985	109.3	80.5	364.6	10.2	2.0	n.a.	n.a.	n.a.	1,501.4	29.2
1986	264.6	160.3	524.7	28.6	7.0	n.a.	n.a.	n.a.	1,719.7	32.9
1987	234.9	139.7	663.6	18.1	11.1	n.a.	27.8	n.a.	1,963.0	36.6
1988	152.4	85.5	747.7	10.1	15.4	7.1	34.9	30.1	2,201.2	36.9
1989	201.0	126.1	869.8	10.0	14.2	8.5	43.3	16.6	2,429.7	39.0
1990	234.3	147.6	1,013.4	10.0	24.4	10.0	53.3	33.3	2,765.1	40.2
1991	270.9	142.6	1,156.0	12.7	49.4	30.7	84.0	35.0	2,781.1	45.4
1992	461.9	119.6	1,275.6	29.6	89.5	48.0	132.0	49.4	2,981.0	46.9

[a]Agency issuance includes only pass-throughs.

[b]Nonagency issuance includes REMICs and pass-throughs.

Sources: Federal Reserve Bulletin, *Inside Mortgage Securities*, Lehman Brothers.

nancing activity. In the spring and summer of 1992, refis, which represented 60 percent of total originations, added incrementally to the supply. Table 2.6 illustrates the annual issuance of MBSs from 1984 through 1992. The column labeled paydowns represents refinancing activity. Note the large paydown numbers for 1986 and 1992. The net-issuance column is total issuance less paydowns. Concomitantly, even as refi activity was high, primary originations remained relatively low as a function of the stagnation in home sales.

Investor Demand

Throughout the early 1990s investor demand has remained high as a result of (1) the success of the REMIC structure in attracting new investors to the MBS market; (2) the dramatically redefined regulatory and accounting environment whereby bank, thrift, and insurance company investors were discouraged from pursuing their traditional investments (see Chapter 1); and (3) the refinancing activity of 1991–1993, which returned to investors a vast amount of principal, in the form of prepayments, that had to be invested—much of it back into MBSs.

6. WHAT ARE THE MBS SECTOR CONSIDERATIONS?

The MBS pass-through market may be divided into the current-coupon portion, which includes TBA offerings; the seasoned, pool-specific market; and the premium-priced MBS sector.

Current-Coupon MBSs

The current-coupon investor should evaluate the relative cheap/rich considerations of alternative sectors, such as:

- Ginnie Maes versus conventional MBSs (Freddie Macs/ Fannie Maes).
- 30-year versus 15-year MBSs.
- Generic versus REMIC structures.

With Ginnie Maes versus conventionals, considerations are:

- Ginnie Maes have longer duration.

- Ginnie Maes have slower prepayment speeds.
- Ginnie Maes are in shorter supply.
- Ginnie Maes are in less frequent demand as REMIC collateral.
- Ginnie Maes are preferred risk-weighted capital.

With 30-year versus 15-year MBSs, the factors to consider are:

- The 30-year has greater extension risk.
- The 30-year is the most liquid market.
- The 15-year has greater prepayment risk.
- The 15-year is in greater demand as REMIC collateral.
- The 15-year is in ample supply primarily when refinancings are high—otherwise supply is short of demand.
- The 15-year has larger allocation of principal in the early years.

With generic versus REMIC structures, characteristics to evaluate are:

- The generic is more liquid.
- The generic is more easily understood by a wide spectrum of investors.
- The generic avoids criticism on the part of regulators.
- The cash flow structure of the generic is evaluated better in a flat yield curve environment.
- The generic has the benefit of an active dollar roll market.
- REMIC reallocates cash flow into better-defined maturity sectors.
- REMIC more efficiently redistributes the prepayment option to those who want it.
- REMIC's narrow cash flow windows allow the short-average-life CMO bond classes to roll down the curve efficiently.
- REMIC's narrow cash flow windows provide better performance in a steep yield curve environment.

Seasoned MBSs

Seasoned MBS pools are those that have been issued with specific pool numbers and that have been outstanding at least 30 months.[9] There is a three-tiered market for 30-year, original-dated seasoned pools, which somewhat loosely identifies seasoned pools as slightly seasoned if issued and outstanding for less than 30 months, moderately seasoned if outstanding for 2.5 to 5 years, and fully seasoned if outstanding for 10 years or more. The 5- to 10-year age group is a gray area, with some analysts considering it fully seasoned and some not. The three-tiered market is described more fully below.

Seasoned pools are regarded as having value because of their stability (reduced prepayment volatility), shorter WAM, and the characteristic that as they march down the amortization curve and age, the monthly cash flow consists of an increasing percentage of principal, which in most cases will have been purchased at a price discounted from par. Seasoned pools offer

- Generally positive convexity.
- Relatively long, stable duration.
- A relatively steady prepayment pattern in both volatile and stagnant markets.
- Reduced prepayment drift.
- Opportunity for selective, pool-specific investing.

For seasoned pools investment decisions must take into account the following factors:

- The age effect.
- Structural considerations.
- Prepayment stability and burnout.
- WAC and dispersion of loan coupons.
- WAM (WALA) and dispersion of loan maturities.
- The three-tiered seasoned pool market.
- Demographic and geographic patterns.

---

[9]The PSA, the self-governing body of securities dealers, defines seasoned Ginnie Mae pools as 30-year, single-family pools with coupons of 9 percent or less with a maturity of 2008 or earlier; coupons over 9 percent but less than 10 percent with a maturity of 2009 or earlier; and coupons of 10 percent or higher with a maturity of 2010 or earlier.

- Technical considerations such as assumability, pool size, and amount by origination year.

The Age Effect

The absolute age effect captures such long-term factors as interest rate cycles, demographic patterns, and family growth cycles.

In essence, as it ages the MBS pool follows the life cycle of a family. When new the pool is relatively insensitive to refinancing or transfer opportunities. As time passes the family grows, and new job opportunities stimulate transfers. Eventually the children move away and careers stabilize. Finally comes retirement. This family life cycle reflects the pattern of the MBS pool, where prepayments are very slow the first year or two but gradually increase to the end of the PSA ramp (30 months). As family and career activity accelerates, prepayments tend to be their most active from the 5th through 10th years, to plateau between years 12 and 20, and, finally, to escalate near the end of the cycle.

Ginnie Mae and conventional pools differ with respect to the pattern of the seasonal cycle, with the plateau coming later with Ginnie Maes (typically after year 7) and with less volatility throughout the cycle. (For a discussion of the technical aspects of the seasoning process, see Pool Age: Seasoning in Chapter 4 and Burnout in Chapter 3.)

The prepayment pattern may be summarized as follows:

1. Prepayment rates of new pools increase at first, then eventually decline.
2. Prepayment rates of seasoned discounts are most active in midcycle.
3. Prepayments on all pools gravitate to a norm over time, lending prepayment stability to seasoned pools but mitigating the long-term benefits of seeking "fast-pay" pools.
4. Over the cycle Ginnie Maes prepay at a slower speed than conventionals.

Note on relative value: To capture the maximum *yield* benefit of purchasing seasoned discounts in a bull market, buy pools that are not too new and not too old. Very seasoned pools will be more stable and will be priced to a short WAM (farther down the term structure of the Treasury curve).

Structural Considerations

The economic benefit of the seasoning effect is twofold: (1) With age the monthly cash flows become predominantly return of principal, which lends stability to the pool cash flows; and (2) with age the WAM shortens and the pool "rolls down the curve." The first point is particularly significant when the pool cash flows were purchased at a substantial discount. The yield benefit of the early return of principal is a direct function of the percentage of the monthly cash flow represented by principal. Table 2.7 illustrates the difference in return of principal for various months of age for the same pass-through coupon.

The second benefit of the seasoning effect is illustrated by Table 2.8, which shows the pricing structure of 7.5 percent MBSs. In this case the MBS to Treasury is constant, but the WAM varies, and the pricing of the pool is to shorter points on the Treasury curve term structure as the WAM declines. Although the table makes the point, in reality several points need to be considered in determining how these WAM bonds would trade in the real world:

1. The market would trade the shorter WAM bonds to a tighter spread because there is implied stability of the shorter WAM (more seasoned) bonds, and the MBS spreads to Treasuries tighten for shorter maturities.

2. If the WAM bonds under consideration were priced to a premium, the price might actually *decline* because of the shorter time to amortize the premium, as shown in Table 2.9.

Prepayment Stability and Burnout

Pools that have passed through one or more refinancing cycles tend to be less sensitive to the opportunity to refinance, lending a modicum of prepayment stability. The higher the burnout factor, the greater the stability. (See Chapters 3 and 4 for technical discussions of burnout.) This stability is illustrated by Figure 2.6, which compares the 1992 prepayment patterns of 11 percent GNMAs issued in 1980 versus 1985.

Notice the 1980-issue GNMA 11s exhibited consistently slower PSAs than the 1985-issue 11s. The 1980-issue pools had the opportunity to refinance in 1983 and again in 1986 and therefore were exhibiting some burnout. For the 1985-issue pools the 1986–1987 period was the first refi opportunity. Figure 2.7 illustrates the cycles

TABLE 2.7

$1 Million Face FNMA 8 Percent MBS, Pool Cash Flows at 150 PSA

Months since Issue	Principal ($)		Total Principal ($)	Total Pool Cash Flow	Principal (%)
	Schedule	Prepayments			
0	587	250	837	7,504	22.3
50	638	5,770	6,408	11,325	56.5
100	617	3,691	4,308[a]	7,455	57.8
150	596	2,295	2,888	4,850	59.5
200	576	1,359	1,935	3,097	62.5
300	539	317	856	1,130	75.8

[a]The absolute dollar amount of principal is highest near the peak of the PSA ramp (see Chapter 4). As a *percentage* of the pool distribution of cash flows, however, the amount increases with age.

Source: Bloomberg Financial Markets.

TABLE 2.8

FNMA 7.5 Percent MBS Priced at a 95 Basis Points Spread to the Treasury Curve at 150 PSA for Various WAMs

WAM (months)	Average Life (years)	Reference Treasury	Treasury Yield (%)	MBS to Treasury Spread	MBS Yield (%)	MBS Price
348	9.0	10 year	6.71	95	7.66	99-9
300	8.90	7 year	6.41	95	7.36	100-30
180	5.75	5 year	6.06	95	7.01	102-2

Source: Bloomberg Financial Markets.

TABLE 2.9

FNMA 9 Percent MBS Priced at 125 Basis Points Spread to the Treasury Curve at 250 PSA for Various WAMs

WAM (months)	Average Life (years)	Reference Treasury	Treasury Yield (%)	MBS to Treasury Spread	MBS Yield (%)	MBS Price
348	6.12	5 year[a]	6.06	125	7.31	107-30
300	5.5	5 year	6.06	125	7.31	106-20
180	4.5	5 year	6.06	125	7.31	105-22

[a]Note that even when the pool is priced to the 5-year Treasury for all WAMs at a constant spread the price declines.

Source: Bloomberg Financial Markets.

FIGURE 2.6
GNMA 11 Percent MBSs, 1980 and 1985 Issues; 1992 Prepayments in PSA

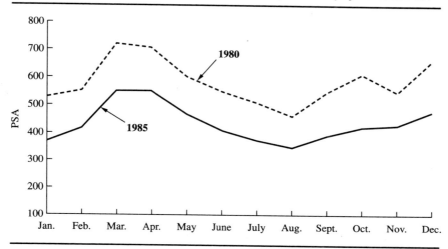

Source: Lehman Brothers Fixed Income Research.

FIGURE 2.7
Thirty-Year Fixed Mortgage Rates, 1981–1987

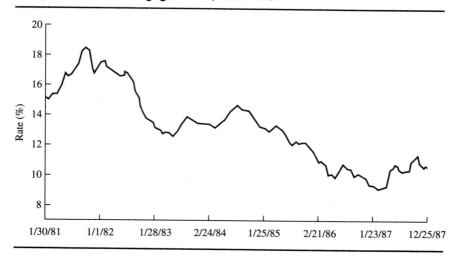

Source: Lehman Brothers Fixed Income Research.

of mortgage rates from 1981 through 1987. Notice the key refinancing opportunities from summer 1982 to May 1983 and from the first quarter of 1986 to April 1987.

Impact of Burnout

Short-term or cyclical burnout (see Cyclical Burnout in Chapter 4) can have a significant impact on the performance of premium-priced MBSs. For example, in 1992 FHLMC 10s showed signs of burnout in the second quarter of 1992.

Figure 2.8 illustrates the pattern of prepayments measured in PSA for FHLMC Gold 9, 9.5, and 10 percent coupons for 1992. Note that the PSA of the 10 percent Gold coupons declined rapidly during April and May and *remained slow into the second 1992 refinancing wave in the summer of 1992. The Gold 9.5s, in contrast, reaccelerated, peaking at over 1,000 PSA in the fourth quarter.* This example of a higher coupon (10s) prepaying at a slower PSA rate than a lower coupon is an excellent example of cyclical burnout.

FIGURE 2.8
FHLMC Gold, 9, 9.5, and 10 Percent Coupons; 1992 Prepayments in PSA

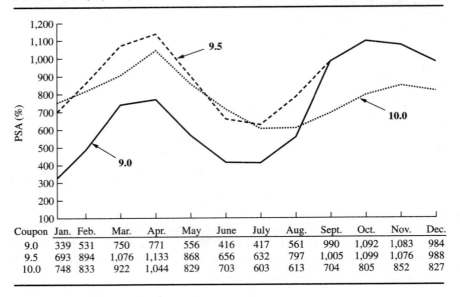

Coupon	Jan.	Feb.	Mar.	Apr.	May	June	July	Aug.	Sept.	Oct.	Nov.	Dec.
9.0	339	531	750	771	556	416	417	561	990	1,092	1,083	984
9.5	693	894	1,076	1,133	868	656	632	797	1,005	1,099	1,076	988
10.0	748	833	922	1,044	829	703	603	613	704	805	852	827

Source: Lehman Brothers Fixed Income Research.

Cyclical burnout may be interrupted or delayed by short-term shifts in interest rates and/or the yield curve. For example, if interest rates temporarily bounce upward during a market rally, the refinancing cycle is interrupted as interest rates back up; then, as interest rates resume their decline, there tends to be a rush to not miss the second chance. Such was the situation in 1992, as shown by Figure 2.9. Note that as interest rates started to back up at year-end 1991 there was a rush of applications in the hope of not missing the refi window. Then, when interest rates again declined, there was another surge in applications.

The shape of the yield curve also had an impact, causing 8.5 percent coupons to prepay at an interest rate level that the old models would not have anticipated would provide a prepayment opportunity. However, when the yield curve is steep, with the existence of alternative mortgage forms, such as 15-year, adjustable-rate, and balloon mortgages, the borrower can refinance to rates much lower than the 30-year rate, which used to be the only alternative. (For a technical discussion of the yield curve effect, see FNMA 8.5s and the Yield Curve Effect in Chapter 4.)

FIGURE 2.9
MBA Application Index, January 1991–December 1992

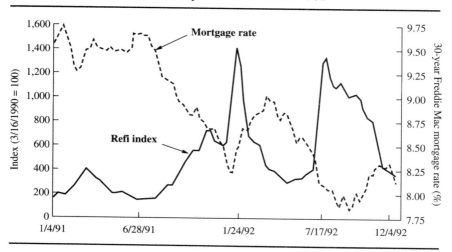

Source: Mortgage Bankers Association and Lehman Brothers.

WAC and Dispersion of Loan Coupons

There may be considerable differences among the WACs of seasoned pools. Pools with high WACs will typically prepay much faster than low-WAC pools. Investors seeking the potential prepayment benefits of a high WAC should determine the dispersion of coupons within the pool. If a high WAC is caused by a few loans with a substantially higher coupon than the bulk of the loans in the pool, the benefits sought may be short-lived. *Be aware that the WAC of the pool will likely change*—that is, drift to a lower WAC. The higher-coupon loans are highly likely to prepay sooner than the lower-coupon loans, resulting in a loss of the higher prepayment potential. An even dispersion of mortgage coupons within the pool will result in greater cash flow stability.

WAM (WALA) and Dispersion of Loan Maturities

Pools with a short WAM—200 months or less—are deemed to possess a high degree of the most favorable aspects associated with seasoning and will generally trade to a substantially tighter yield spread than generic pools of the same coupon and issuer. Reliance on WAM alone, however, can be deceptive because the growing application of partial prepayments (curtailments) by homeowners in the early 1990s has led to distortions in the WAM calculation. Investors seeking to benefit from substantial seasoning and a short WAM should obtain the WALA of the pool under consideration. Sometimes with age the WAM extends if the older loans prepay sooner than more recent originations, so be sure you have updated data.

The Three-Tiered Seasoned Pool Market

The seasoned pool market recognizes stratas of seasoning generally defined in terms of final stated maturity (before or after 2009, 2016, 2022, etc.). This pattern relates to seasoning events in the past that are identified as significant in defining the prepayment characteristics of the three groups. Figure 2.10 illustrates three tiers of seasoned GNMA 8s issued in 1977 and 1987 and slightly seasoned 8s issued in 1991.

1. 1991 Issues—Slightly Seasoned

Pools seasoned two years or less are referred to as **slightly seasoned**. Generally, pools of such recent issue are relatively insensitive to

FIGURE 2.10
GNMA 8 Percent MBSs, 1977, 1987, 1991 Issues (Prepayment History, 1984–1992; Prepayments in CPR)

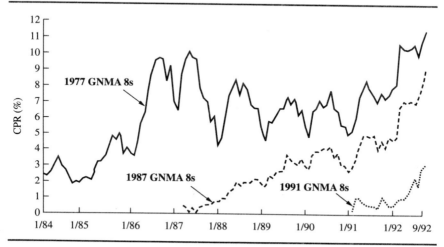

Source: Lehman Brothers Fixed Income Research.

prepayments. (See Chapter 4 for a discussion of the prepayment sensitivity of new pools.) This resistance is illustrated (Figure 2.10) by the fact that the CPR of 1991-issue 8s did not reach 6, the benchmark CPR for seasoned pools. Pools aged 18 months (third quarter 1992) should theoretically be paying at about 3.6 CPR, according to the PSA ramp (see Chapter 4), which is about what they did.

It is interesting that the 1991-issue 8s held so close to the PSA predicted prepayment ramp, with 1992 having been the year of the sharpest acceleration in prepayments experienced to date with mortgage securities. Of course, the GNMA 8s are backed by 8.5 percent mortgages, which were not provided with a strong refinancing window (30-year mortgage rates did not fall much below 7.5 percent and thus failed to provide sufficient incentive). Nevertheless, in periods of dramatic declines in mortgage rates the housing market historically has responded with a surge in home sales, generating in turn transfer-related prepayments in discount-priced coupons. Unique to the 1991–1992 decline in mortgage rates, this did not occur until the first quarter of 1993 because of the 1991–1992 recession. For these reasons, the market does not generally assign any particular value above that assigned to generic TBA pools for slightly seasoned pools, except for recognition of some temporary call protection, until the pools are farther up the PSA ramp.[10]

2. 1987 Issues

The distinguishing characteristic of 1987 issues is that they were originated *after* the 1986–1987 refinancing cycle; therefore, although by 1992 these pools were 5 years seasoned, they were not yet tempered with burnout. Some traders expected the 1987-issued pools to be slow because the 1988 stall-out of home price appreciation left these homeowners, who had bought at the peak of the housing boom, with a potential home equity shortfall, making refinancing difficult. In 1992, however, the CPRs of this group reached 9 percent. A good guess is that a number of these homeowners took advantage of the lower rates to refinance down to a 15-year mortgage (to build home equity faster) without having to take on a substantially increased monthly payment. Cash-out refis to pay down credit card debts were also probably part of the stimulus. As these pools age into the mid-1990s and beyond, they are likely to accrue value because of the burnout benefit bestowed the pool by its having passed through the mammoth 1991–1992 refinancing cycle.

3. 1977 Issues—Fully Seasoned

Pools issued in 1977 passed through their first refinancing window in 1979, another in 1983–1984, and another in 1986–1987. The strong prepayment response to the 1986–1987 decline in mortgage rates is related more to home sales than to refinancings. The decline in mortgage rates from January 1986 through the first quarter of 1987 provided many homeowners with the first opportunity to trade the house in as many years. By this point in time many families were overcrowded in houses too small for growing families, and many baby boomers had been waiting years for the opportunity to buy their first home. So prepayments associated with housing turnover were very high. The interest rate cycle for this period is illustrated in Figure 2.11. Looking back to Figure 2.10, note that the burnout effect shows up in the January 1988–January 1991 period

---

[10]Higher coupons on slightly seasoned MBSs, such as 9s and 9.5s, exhibited sufficient prepayment sensitivity to suggest the PSA ramp was shortened for CUSP coupons by the 1992 refi event. (CUSP refers to coupons with a WAC that has reached the refinancing threshold.)

FIGURE 2.11
Thirty-Year Fixed Mortgage Rates, 1984 through First Quarter 1992

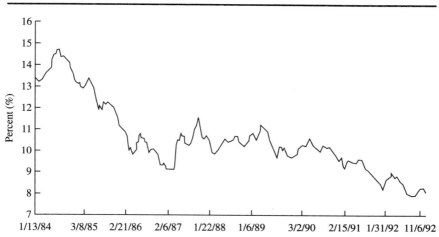

Source: Lehman Brothers Fixed Income Research.

for the 1977-issue GNMA 8s, whereas the prepayment cycles are very much seasonally cyclical (low in winter, high in summer).

Demographic and Geographic Patterns

Some investors seek specific pools with a geographic concentration. For example, California and the Rocky Mountain states were seen for many years as "fast-pay" states; New York has always been known as a "slow-pay" state.

Fannie Mae and Freddie Mac provide geographic pool information on the factor tapes they run every month. Also, with Freddie Mac Guarantor pools issued by regional banks there is a high probability that all the loans pooled by these banks are within their geographic lending area. Caution must be exercised here, however: Many banks in the mid- to late 1980s expanded aggressively into mortgage banking and as a consequence issued widely dispersed pools.

Some MBS dealer firms make a specialty of tracking the zip code distribution of specific pools and develop highly technical "speed stories" based on the demographic, migration, and employment histories of very specific areas—sometimes represented by a single statistical metropolitan area (SMA) that may make up all or a large part of a specific pool.

Technical Considerations

Assumability[11]

Assumability has historically been a consideration distinguishing Ginnie Mae pools (the FHA/VA loans backing Ginnie Maes are assumable) from conventionals. Through the mid- to late 1980s assumability was not an issue—home prices had accelerated so rapidly during those years that few loans were economically feasible to assume because the amount required to purchase the home had generally increased substantially above the paid-down balance of the loan that was to be assumed. Following the 1988 home price appreciation wall, however, a home buyer found it more possible to assume a post-1987-issued mortgage. For example, if the home price rose in tandem with the national median between January 1987 and January 1990, the current loan to value (LTV) ratio on an 8.5 percent, 30-year mortgage originated in January 1987 was approximately 82 percent, close to the 80 percent level generally required to obtain conventional financing. With mortgage rates ranging between 11.25 and 9.75 percent during the period, it was clearly advantageous for an FHA/VA-qualifying borrower to assume the 8.5 percent loan. Figure 2.12 compares the 1988–1990 prepayment patterns of 1977 GNMA 8s with those originated in 1987. Notice how much slower are the 1987-issue 8s.

Pool Size

Pool-specific investors should seek pools that were originally issued for the largest size possible. It is difficult to find old pools (1977–1982) that were issued for more than $1 million—the origination market was not yet mature enough. But the limitations of small pools are:

1. Prepayment patterns are irregular—one $50,000 loan that prepays can jump the prepayment CPR of a $1 million pool a lot (it is 20 percent of the original pool balance). In

---

[11]This discussion of assumability is based on analysis by Nicole Vianna.

FIGURE 2.12
GNMA 8 Percent MBSs, 1977 versus 1987 Issues (Prepayment History, 1988–1990)

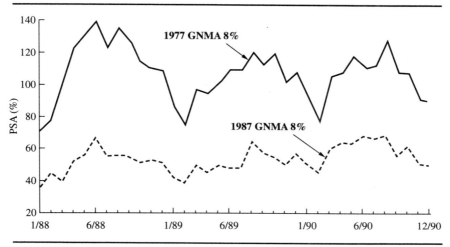

Source: Lehman Brothers Fixed Income Research

addition, with small pools there can be times when there are no prepayments within a given month.

2. A pool originated 5 to 10 years ago in a small amount will by now be paid down to such a small balance that it is hardly worth the trouble to research it—and such a pool has virtually no liquidity. Pools with a paid-down balance of less than $25,000 are not eligible for good delivery under PSA guidelines and might be bid for sale only to individual investors. That means selling them to the public through a stockbroker, who expects a commission of 2 to 4 points, which will be taken out of your bid price!

Amount by Origination Year

Avoid coupons issued in years with very low originations for the coupon in question. Liquidity is reduced, and the prepayment data are unreliable because the data are not based on a statistically significant base pool of information. Table 2.10 shows the amounts outstanding for GNMA 8s from 1974 through December 1992.

TABLE 2.10
GNMA 8 Percent MBS Issuance Data, 1974–1992

Issue Year	Amount Outstanding[a] ($ millions)
Total	52,563
1992	24,880
1991	3,443
1990	927
1989	907
1988	236
1987	12,986
1986	1,355
1978[b]	1,567
1977	3,140
1976	1,905
1975	443
1974	343

[a]Data as of December 1992.
[b]There were no 8 percent coupon GNMA MBSs issued from 1979 through 1985.

Source: Lehman Brothers Fixed Income Research.

Premium-Priced MBSs

Premium-priced MBSs are generally defined as coupons that are 1.5 percent above the current coupon or higher. Their principal characteristic is negative convexity, or the propensity of premium-priced MBSs to "cap out" in price. Figure 2.13 illustrates the negative convexity of MBSs. As yields decline and Treasury prices continue to climb, the MBS price curve flattens. This is an illustration of price compression. The figure may be read two ways. Reading from right to left we see the negative convexity as the MBS price flattens when it passes the cusp. Looking at the graph from left to right we see that when yields start to rise and Treasury prices fall, the MBS premium-priced issues hold their price. For this reason premium-priced MBSs are sometimes referred to as cushion bonds. This unique price pattern of premium-priced MBSs is related to the market's perception of the value of the prepayment option and the impact that prepayments and a change in average life have on the valuation of MBS cash flows when they are purchased at a premium.

FIGURE 2.13
Negative Convexity of MBSs

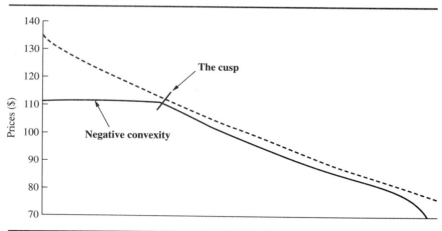

Source: Nicole Vianna, Lehman Brothers.

Prepayment Impact on Realized Value

The impact of prepayments on the realized value of an MBS is similar to that of a callable bond. For example, an investor who buys a 10 percent coupon, 10-year maturity bond that is called in 5 years has lost 5 years of anticipated coupon. If market rates are lower at the time of the call (presumably they are—if they are not, the bonds would not be called), the investor has lost for 5 years the difference between the original 10 percent coupon and the new market rate currently available. For this reason, when yields start to decline, callable bonds become priced to the call date rather than to the maturity.

With premium-priced MBSs the situation is similar. As interest rates decline the opportunity to refinance becomes greater, and the value of the implied prepayment option grows. However, since the MBS market is *anticipatory*, the price of an MBS that is priced above par will begin to compress on the *expectation* that prepayments will increase long before they actually do. Likewise, when prepayments have become high and the now premium-priced MBS is trading to a relatively high yield spread, the market will pay up for those cash flows if the market believes prepayments have peaked and are soon to decline. The analogy of the callable bond applies here. Assume an investor bought the hypothetical 10 per-

cent callable bond priced to the *call* date, only to discover yields
went back up to 10 percent and the bonds were never called. That
investor would now have a windfall. Although such a situation is
not likely with corporate bond investing because in this market
calls are exercised efficiently, in the MBS market about one third of
all MBSs whose prepayment option has gone into the money are
never called, even when they remain a premium for many years
(see Pool Age: Seasoning and Table 4.12 in Chapter 4). In summary, the risks are that:

- High anticipated coupon is called away.
- There is less time than expected to write down the premium.
- The investor is subjected to reinvestment risk as the return of
  cash flows accelerates in a low interest rate environment.

Investment Considerations
Investment considerations include price compression, the widening
of yield spreads on premium-priced MBS in a bull market, and the
impact of seasoning and burnout (see Box 2–3). In 1992 some

BOX 2–3
Synopsis of Premium Investment Considerations

When Prepayments Are Accelerating

- GNMAs may offer some call protection versus conventionals.
- GNMAs will tend to outperform conventionals.
- The yield curve extends refinancing options when it is steep.

When Prepayments Are Peaking

- The market will anticipate early burnout.
- The highest coupons will show burnout first.
- The yield curve effect can delay burnout.
- The highest prepaying MBSs perform best in prepayment
  slowdowns.
- Burnout benefit is highest with the fastest payers.

"WAM" bonds (those with WAMs of 10 years or less) became premium-priced as they rolled down the curve and were priced as a spread to 4- to 5-year Treasury securities then yielding 5 or 6 percent. Some investors were caught by surprise by this phenomenon because WAM bonds are normally thought of as discounts.

Prepayments alter the response of MBS price changes to interest rate changes. MBSs do, in fact, normally increase in price as yields decline, but when the decline in rates is sufficient to induce refinancings, the price will rise less than would be expected were there no prepayment option. For example, note in Table 2.11 the prices of selected Treasury and MBSs as reported on Telerate on December 3, 1991, the date the November Freddie Mac prepayment speeds were released. On this date the PC Gold 9.5s slid over the prepayment cusp, and their price was crushed down 7/32 in price when the Treasury 7.5 of 11/1/01 (current 10-year) was up 8/32. Note also that PC Gold 7.5s and 9.5s were also up and the higher premiums were down only a bit. Here is an illustration of the classic negative convexity of an MBS coupon when its prepayment experience first begins to accelerate. MBSs priced at par (really parity, reflecting the payment delay) will not reflect a yield impact from a change in average life. No matter when the principal is returned, the MBS will continue to yield the pass-through rate on the remaining unpaid principal balance. If the MBS is purchased at

TABLE 2.11
Selected Treasury and MBS Prices, December 3, 1991

Coupon	Bid Price	Price Change
December PC Gold Prices		
7.5	96-05	+06
9.0	104-06	+01
9.5	105-28	−07
10.0	107-10	−03
11.0	108-17	−02
11.5	110-30	−01
10-Year Treasury Bond		
7.5	101-30	+08

Source: Telerate Mortgage Data Services.

a premium, prepayments lower the realized yield because the paydown of principal reduces the anticipated coupon stream (interest lives off principal). The investor is thereby deprived of earning some portion of the now above-market coupon. Furthermore, the time to write down the premium has been reduced, requiring the unamortized premium to be written off against income. Finally, when the average life is shortened, so is the duration. When yields are declining investors generally prefer long-duration securities. The impact of accelerating prepayments on premiums is referred to as the **call risk**. The call risk results in price compression—that is, the premium MBS loses ability to gain in price. This price compression results in negative convexity (see Figure 2.13). Of course, if prepayments slow down, the realized yield of the premium-priced MBS is enhanced and the high-coupon cash flow is extended, as is the time to write down the premium. For this reason premium-priced MBSs are sometimes referred to as cushion bonds and are sought after by investors who anticipate rising interest rates.

Widened Yield Spreads of Premium MBSs[12]

During periods of declining interest rates MBS to Treasury spreads tend to widen substantially. In this discussion the yield spread and price patterns of premium-priced MBSs are reviewed comparing the 1986–1987 experience with the 1991–1993 cycle. On February 28, 1986 GNMA 9s were the current coupon, yielding 9.26 percent, or 115 basis points more than the 10-year Treasury. The January 1986 prepayments (the latest available to the market during February 1986) were mostly unchanged from December levels for issues below 11 percent. However, 11s and 12s almost doubled (11s rose from 2.8 to 5.7 CPR, and 12s increased from 4.9 to 9.2 CPR). These increases flattened the price curve for coupons between 10.5 and 11 percent and also for those above 12 percent. On the whole, however, there remained a substantial price differential between most premium issues at the end of February 1986 (see Figure 2.14). March and April brought even faster prepayments. Figure 2.15 illustrates the prepayment speeds of slightly seasoned GNMA 11, 12, and 13 percent prepayments from January 1985 through March

---

[12]This discussion of widened yield spreads of premium-priced MBSs in 1986–1987 was provided by Nicole Vianna.

FIGURE 2.14

Price Curve, Ginnie Mae Current Coupon and Premium, Selected Dates

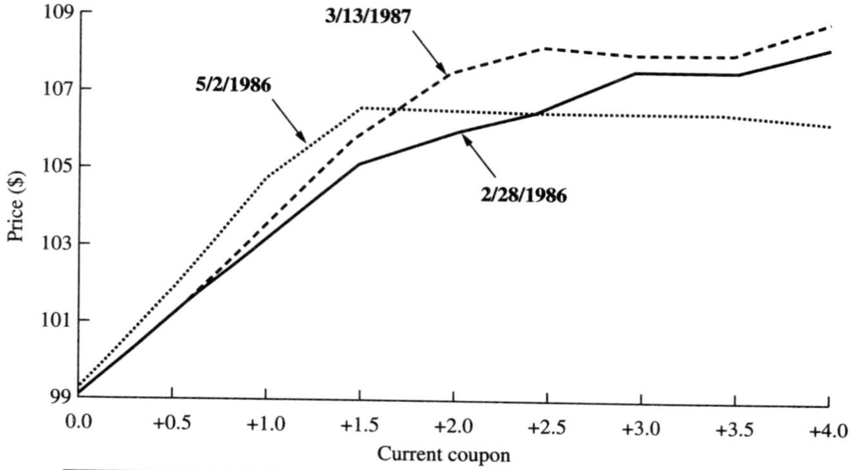

2/28/86	9	9 1/2	10	10 1/2	11	11 1/2	12	12 1/2	13
5/2/86	9	9 1/2	10	10 1/2	11	11 1/2	12	12 1/2	13
3/13/87	8	8 1/2	9	9 1/2	10	10 1/2	11	11 1/2	12

Source: Nicole Vianna, Lehman Brothers.

1988. Figure 2.16 provides the same information for FNMA 11, 12, and 13 percent coupons.

The price effect of the rapid rise was dramatic. Although the 10-year Treasury rallied by 60 basis points between February 28 and May 2, 1986, the yield on GNMA 9s improved by only 2 basis points because the yield spread to the 10-year Treasury was pushed to 173 basis points. Prepayments on high-coupon issues surged, with GNMA 11s doubling (to 11.2 CPR) from their January levels and GNMA 12s tripling (to 30.5 CPR). The price curve for GNMA 10.5s and above became slightly downward sloping, with dollar prices for all issues within 1/4 point of each other. Lower-premium issues (9.5s–10.5s) appreciated during this period, perhaps because sellers of higher premiums tried to maintain their coupon income by buying lower-premium issues in the hope that they would be safe from substantial increases in prepayments.

FIGURE 2.15
GNMA 11, 12, and 13 Percent Coupons, 1983 Issues (January
1985–March 1988; Prepayments in PSA)

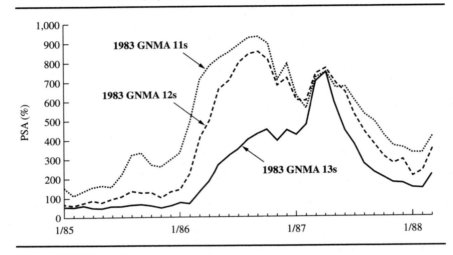

Source: Lehman Brothers Fixed Income Research.

FIGURE 2.16
FNMA 11, 12, and 13 Percent Coupons, 1983 Issues (January
1985–March 1988; Prepayments in PSA)

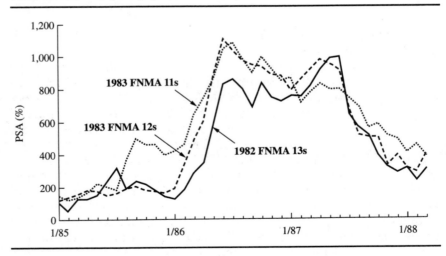

Source: Lehman Brothers Fixed Income Research.

The rally continued for another year, with Treasury and MBS yields reaching their lows in March 1987. On March 13, 1987 GNMA 8s were the current coupon, yielding 8.20 percent, or 99 basis points more than the 10-year Treasury.

The MBS market began trading premium issues to high-prepayment rate assumptions that considerably shortened their average lives. Compared to Treasuries in the 2- to 4-year-average-life sector, these issues had high yields. The result was good demand on the part of investors with short-duration targets, for whom the average lives of mortgage pass-throughs had previously been too long. The intercoupon price spreads of issues 1.5 percent and more above the current coupon, as a consequence, returned to a more normal pattern.

The 1991–1993 Experience. The performance of premium-priced MBSs was quite different in the 1991–1993 refinancing cycle for three reasons. First, interest rates did not drop as much in the 1991–1993 cycle as they did in 1986–1987, declining from about 9.75 percent in January 1991 to about 7.5 percent by March 1993 (225 basis points). In the earlier period the decline, by contrast, was about 575 basis points, from 14.74 to just over 9 percent.

Second, the prepayments increase was much higher, with 9.5 percent coupons (comparable to 11.5 and 12 percent coupons in 1986–1987) soaring to well over 900 PSA in the spring and summer of 1992 and to over 1,000 PSA in the spring of 1993.

Third, and most significant, the yield spreads of the premium-priced coupons most affected by the refinancing wave of 1991–1993 did not widen as much in 1991–1992 as they did in 1986–1987. The price compression was also less severe in the 1991–1993 experience. The 1992 high price for GNMA 7s (then the current coupon) was 99-25, reached on September 8, 1992 (see Table 2.12); for the FNMA 7s it was 99-09. The Ginnie Mae premium coupons (9 through 10.5) traded at spreads of roughly 1 point apart. The price compression for the more prepayment sensitive Fannie Mae premiums was somewhat tighter. It is interesting to note the GNMA 10.5s reached a considerably higher price (111-0) than the FNMA 10.5s (108-30), reflecting the lesser prepayment sensitivity of the Ginnie Maes (for a discussion of the relative prepayment sensitivity of Ginnie Mae versus Fannie Mae issues,

TABLE 2.12
Price Data, Selected Ginnie Mae and Fannie Mae Coupons

Issue	Coupon	Price 9/8/92	Yield (BEY)	Price 3/4/93	Yield (BEY)
GNMA	7	99-25	7.09	101-27	6.76
GNMA	9	107-17	6.97	107-30	6.87
GNMA	9.5	108-19	7.04	109-01	6.92
GNMA	10.0	109-28	6.92	110-15	6.75
GNMA	10.5	111-00	6.88	111-26	6.65
FNMA	7	99-09	7.15	101-07	6.81
FNMA	9	106-20	6.68	106-16	6.72
FNMA	9.5	107-18	6.77	107-16	6.80
FNMA	10.0	108-07	6.56	108-25	6.73
FNMA	10.5	108-30	6.87	110-06	6.42

Source: Bloomberg Financial Markets.

see Chapter 4). The 1993 price experience for the first half of 1993 was similar when the GNMA 7s hit their high price of the period on March 3 at 101-27.

The explanation for the higher prepayment speeds achieved in 1991–1992 is a result of a combination of the yield curve effect and higher consumer awareness. The yield curve effect was a function of the steep yield curve that marked the period, which provided mortgage borrowers with a wide array of alternative refinancing options, most significantly 15-year mortgages but also adjustable-rate and balloon mortgage forms. Consumer awareness was high because of intense focus by the media and promotional education by bank originators directed at mortgage holders (for a discussion of the yield curve effect and consumer awareness, see FNMA 8.5s and the Yield Curve Effect in Chapter 4).

GNMA versus Conventional Prepayment Sensitivity

The other significant performance differential is that between Ginnie Maes and conventional MBSs. Ginnie Maes have historically prepaid to significantly lower PSA speeds at the peak of the cycle than have conventionals. The reason has to do with demographic and assumability differences between the FHA and conventional home borrower (see FHA versus Conventional Collateral in Chapter 4). Look at the 9.5 percent coupon, the highest prepaying coupon of the refinancing cycle, and compare the Ginnie Mae PSAs to those of the Fannie Mae prepayment experience (see Figure 2.17). Note that the FNMA 10.5s were exhibiting burnout, declining close to the PSA level of the GNMA 10.5s. This illustrates the slower burnout of Ginnie Mae premium coupons compared to conventional premiums. See, however, the reference to research by Deepak Narula in Chapter 3 suggesting this historic relationship may be changing, with Ginnie Maes prepaying somewhat faster than in the past.

Seasoning Impact on MBS Value

The principal *negative* factor that seasoning brings to premium-priced MBSs is that as the pool ages, a greater portion of the

FIGURE 2.17
GNMA versus FNMA 7 to 12 Percent Coupons, December 1992; Prepayments in PSA

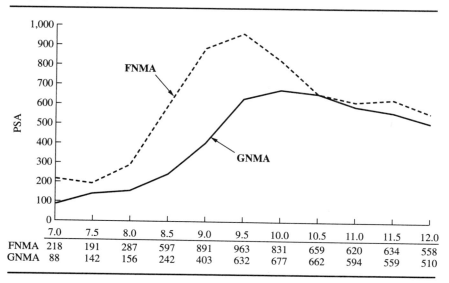

	7.0	7.5	8.0	8.5	9.0	9.5	10.0	10.5	11.0	11.5	12.0
FNMA	218	191	287	597	891	963	831	659	620	634	558
GNMA	88	142	156	242	403	632	677	662	594	559	510

Source: Lehman Brothers Fixed Income Research.

monthly cash flow consists of principal. When these cash flows are purchased at a premium price, the more rapid amortization of principal is a negative to the investor's realized yield if returned faster than expected. Also, even if prepayments are not high, the percentage of pool interest payments generated is diminished by the relatively greater amount of principal as the amortization schedule seasons. The high percentage of principal in seasoned MBS cash flows thereby reduces the value of the high coupon on the premium issues.

The principal *benefit* of seasoning is that it endows the pool with burnout, which usually significantly mutes the pool's sensitivity to prepayments. This attribute of seasoned premiums is still undervalued. In general, the yield spread of all premium-priced MBSs tends to widen rapidly when the prepayment speed accelerates, lending considerable relative value to the seasoned pools. In time the burnout value is generally recognized, so that, as with all MBS investing, it is necessary to anticipate the value before it has been broadly recognized. Recall the more extensive discussion of burnout earlier in this chapter. Also refer back to Figure 2.6 for an illustration of burnout in premium coupons (GNMA 11s).

7. WHAT ARE THE FEATURES OF OTHER MBS FORMS?

Stability of 15-Year MBSs

Because of their much shorter final maturity, 15-year MBSs are in high demand by investors when prepayment speeds are slow; they are also in high demand for CMO deal collateral because of the more rapid "fronting" of principal on the 15-year amortization schedule. MBSs backed by 15-year loans issued by Ginnie Mae are referred to as Midgets and those backed by Fannie Mae 15-year loans as Dwarfs. Freddie Mac used to call its PCs backed by 15-year loans Gnomes, but now they are called simply 15-year PCs.

While it is reasonable to expect a 15-year pass-through to trade at equivalent OAS to 30-year mortgages, investor segmentation may keep the 15-year sector tighter than the 30-year. Certain investors with final-maturity constraints prefer 15-year securities. In addition, within the CMO market short-average-life CMOs (4 years and under) trade tighter than long-average-life CMOs. The faster amortization of 15-year collateral allows for a larger percentage issuance of CMO bonds with shorter average lives. (For a further discussion of the value of 15-year MBSs as CMO Collateral, see Collateral Features of 15-year MBSs in Chapter 8.)

Supply Forecast

The 1992 refinancing experience indicated that 15-year mortgages appear to be predominantly a refinancing-related product (see New Prepayment Patterns Emerge in Chapter 4). Therefore, if prepayments remain moderate for some time, the supply of 15-year mortgages is likely to stay at around 15 percent of originations, whereas the demand for them is likely to increase as prepayment speeds slow in the mid-1990s and investors became more concerned with extension risk.

Balloon MBSs[13]

First introduced in January 1990 by Fannie Mae, the monthly origination level for balloon MBSs has risen to about $1.2 million for Fannie Mae 7-year balloon loans for a total of $11.6 million in 1992. Freddie Mac's 1992 issuance volume for its 5-year balloon Guarantor program was $19.2 million. A principal reason for the rapid growth in balloon loan origination is that the balloons appear to be gaining popularity among borrowers as an affordable fixed-rate alternative to adjustable-rate mortgages (ARMs). According to data provided by Fannie Mae, the contract rate on 7-year balloon mortgages averages 0.375 to 0.50 percent below that of traditional 30-year fully amortizing loans. The 7-year balloon contract rate is about 0.125 percent below that of a 15-year amortizing mortgage. The more recently introduced 5-year balloon loan may be expected to offer an even lower borrowing rate to the home buyer.

---

[13]This discussion of balloon mortgages is based on information provided by Nicole Vianna.

The savings are considerable. On a $100,000 mortgage, the monthly payment on a 10 percent balloon loan is $28 less than the $877 a month payment on a 10.375 percent 30-year amortizing loan and $200 a month less than on a 10.125 percent 15-year amortizing loan.

The balloon mortgage is expected to be popular with economically mobile home buyers who anticipate moving frequently and who are seeking the most house for the mortgage amount for which they can qualify. It is also becoming popular with corporations that have active employee relocation programs as a way to save on company-sponsored mortgage subsidy plans.

Mortgage Description

The **balloon mortgage** has a 30-year, fixed-rate amortization schedule and a balloon, or bullet, payment due at the end of 5, 7, 10, or 15 years. The borrower is not subject to prepayment penalties and, under most circumstances, is guaranteed to be offered new financing at the balloon maturity date. A common formula for the refinancing is to guarantee that a loan will be offered at the then 60-day commitment rate offered by Fannie Mae for 30-year mortgages purchased by it plus 0.5 percent.

Investment Characteristics of Balloons

- The principal payment is guaranteed by Fannie Mae or Freddie Mac.

- The principal payment for a 7-year balloon represents 94 percent of the original principal balance.

- Total outstandings for all balloon MBSs as of 1992 year-end were as follows:

	5-Year Balloon ($ millions)	7-Year Balloon ($ millions)
FHLMC	25,655.9	12,088.8
FNMA	–0–	18,622.0

- Prepayment speeds of balloon MBSs are typically very fast, probably because of the homeowner's preference for a 10- or 30-year fixed-rate mortgage when it becomes available at rates competitive with those offered on the balloon.

CHAPTER 3

RELATIVE VALUE ANALYSIS: THE ANALYTIC TOOLS

KEY QUESTIONS

1. How do I determine relative value?
2. What are the risk components?
3. What are the OAS and prepayment model components?
4. How do I apply relative value analysis?

1. HOW DO I DETERMINE RELATIVE VALUE?

Relative value analysis aggregates a universe of securities within a common framework of comparable risks. The objective of relative value analysis is to compare one's investment alternatives—for example, to compare MBSs (the generic pass-throughs and their variant derivative forms) to other traditional fixed-income securities. The product of the exercise is the determination of the required yield spread increase (over that of comparable Treasury securities) that is required to compensate the MBS investor for relative risk/reward investing considerations. The portfolio manager determines the correct compensation relative to the risk/reward inherent in the MBS versus an alternative security. Finally, the valuation process enables MBSs to be valued within the context of asset/liability management.

Derivation of MBS to Treasury Yield Spread

The key to deriving the appropriate basis points yield spread to the Treasury for an MBS is to define its fair value, taking into consideration the convexity and duration characteristics of the proposed investment. The greater the uncertainty that the anticipated yield will be realized, the wider must be the expected MBS to Treasury yield spread gain to provide a fair risk/reward opportunity for the investor. The estimate of the required yield (the comparable-maturity Treasury yield plus the risk-required yield spread to the Treasury) is based primarily on prepayment risk and price-volatility assumptions. Investors can compare the total return, breakeven prepayment rate, and implied breakeven basis points spread to the Treasury to determine the relative risk/reward justification for alternative investments. Ultimately, *option-based pricing methodology should offer the best results.*

Trends in MBS to Treasury Yield Spreads

There appears to be a persistent trend to tighter MBS to Treasury yield spreads, which will likely prevail into the 1990s. This trend is a function of maturation of the MBS market, changing demographics, and improved analytical and deal structuring technology.

As the MBS market has matured, the supply-demand technical factors within the MBS market have strengthened. The risk-based capital guidelines imposed on depository institutions in the early 1990s and more recently on insurance companies have driven financial intermediaries to shift away from accepting increased credit risk as a means of maximizing return. Mortgage product, as a result, has been the beneficiary of increased focus from a broader universe of institutional investors.

Meanwhile, the demographically dictated weakness in housing suggests a lessened demand for starter homes. Most new loan demand is coming in the higher-priced new home market where fewer of the related mortgages find their way into MBS pools.

Finally, and perhaps most important, homeowner refinancing activity in the 1990s is likely to take place at a less torrid pace than in the 1970s and 1980s, meaning that origination levels and prepayment volatility will be reduced. From the mid-1980s into 1993, as much as 60 percent of new MBS originations was directly attributable to refinancings. These were years in which mortgage rates declined by about 7 percent—from 14.63 percent in July 1983 to below 7.5 percent in the first quarter of 1993. Following the 1991–1993 refinancing experience, the MBS market was significantly restructured. Currently, half of all MBS coupons are below 8.5 percent. With the interest rates of most existing mortgages now at cyclical lows, refinancing opportunities may be marginal for many years, and if that is so, remaining high-coupon MBSs will have an opportunity to season to a burned-out state.[1] In addition, if home equity accumulation remains sluggish, the cash-out refi, which peaked in popularity in the late 1980s, would contribute little to refinancing-related originations. Against this scenario prepayment risk associated with refinancings would be diminished. Meanwhile, the overwhelming success of REMIC structures, which offer a wide range of prepayment volatility (from PACs to support, or companion, classes), maturities, and cash flow windows, has broadened the demand from a widening base of institutional investors. Each REMIC deal itself has provided the most aggressive bid for the generic MBS as deal collateral.

In addition, the rapidly advancing technology for structuring more predictable MBS derivative products, such as PACs and TACs (targeted amortization class—a PAC-like CMO bond form with modified prepayment-protection bands), as well as more prepayment or interest rate-sensitive derivatives, such as PAC IOs and inverse floaters with caps and floors, has extended the viability of these securities as portfolio hedges. Demand from non-U.S. investors has also expanded significantly.

With all capital markets now linked to global trends, however, market volatility and shifts in the yield curve may be expected to increase. Thus, the long-term trend for MBS to Treasury spreads may be toward moderation, but with intermittent spikes related to technical factors that can catch investors off guard.

The Valuation Process

The foundation of the valuation process is a dependable pricing methodology. The MBS pricing process projects the P&I cash flows of the MBS, and these cash flows are then discounted back to a present value. This discounted yield is then compared to other fixed-income investment opportunities. The most common alternative is simply to compare the projected yield spread of the MBS to yield spread levels of comparable securities. Making such comparisons is standard procedure with corporate, federal agency, and Treasury securities. The valuation process becomes more compli-

---

[1]Burnout refers to a pool that has experienced sufficient refinancing exposure that the pool has become relatively prepayment insensitive.

cated when the bond has option characteristics, especially in mortgages when the option cannot be precisely defined.

Several pricing methodologies and valuation techniques have evolved in just the past few years. The principal component of most of these techniques is the valuation of the prepayment option(s) embedded within the MBS collateral pools.

The MBS valuation process is complicated not only by the valuation of the prepayment options but also by the proliferation of MBS derivatives that have been created, mostly since 1983 when the CMO was introduced. Since that time the MBS product menu has added adjustable-rate and stripped MBSs, floating-rate CMOs, and a host of CMO derivatives, including PACs, TACs, and support, or companion, classes.

The complexity of the valuation process now extends well beyond the relatively simple comparison of GNMA 8s to a comparable-duration Treasury. Now the process must incorporate a comparison of adjustable-rate MBSs to high-yielding, short-term, traditional fixed-rate securities or an examination of a strip MBS as a portfolio hedge tool or even a comparison of a synthetic portfolio, such as an IO strip MBS matched with an inverse floater, to a Treasury portfolio. A holistic valuation process is necessary to perform such varied comparisons.

2. WHAT ARE THE RISK COMPONENTS?

The components of an individual MBS are represented by the combination of a long position in a noncallable coupon bond and a short position in a series of prepayment call options, one call to each homeowner represented in the pool of mortgages underlying the MBS collateral. Option-based methodology is best utilized for this aspect of the valuation process.

Price Volatility Risk

Increases in market volatility raise the value of the options embedded in the MBS, just as volatility increases the value of any option. The more frequently market prices change, the greater the probability that a market option may be exercised. Since the MBS investor is short the prepayment call options embedded in the MBS, an increase in the value of these options lowers the price of the investor's MBS. **Current-coupon**[2] MBSs and those priced at a slight premium are the most volatile.

Yield Curve Risk

The shape of the yield curve also influences the value of the MBS. An inverted yield curve tends to depress the MBS price for three key reasons:

1. The MBS cash flows positioned on the inverted portion of the Treasury curve will be discounted at the high (inverted) discount rate (for a technical discussion of yield curve risk with MBSs, see How Does the Yield Curve Affect Price Performance, page 262.
2. The ability to create CMOs is impaired, thereby reducing the demand for MBSs as deal collateral.
3. Investors shy away from longer-duration securities when short-term yields are higher than long-term yields.

Price Performance Risk

When the required basis points spread an MBS must yield over the Treasury curve widens, the MBS will underperform because the price of the MBS will have to decline to accommodate the higher required yield dictated by the spread-widening process. The factors that cause performance risk are accelerating prepayments and increasing supply, interest rate volatility, and the shape of the yield curve. Each of these risk factors is examined in the text that follows.

Convexity and Duration: The Keys to Total-Return Investing

Convexity measures the *rate of change* in the relationship between price and yield. Convexity is generally defined as the second derivative of the Treasury price/yield curve (duration is the first derivative). The term "convexity" is derived from "convex," which refers

---

[2]Current coupon refers to newly originated MBSs. Slight premium-priced MBSs of recent issue are often referred to as **CUSP** or **CUSPY** *bonds* because they are on the edge of the point at which the economic incentive to refinance first becomes apparent.

to a curved line. More specifically, while duration measures how *much* the price of a security changes in response to a yield change, convexity measures the *rate* at which the price changes. Figure 3.1 illustrates the duration tangent of a Treasury security. The tangent is the straight line that defines the mathematically defined duration of the security. It is well known that in reality the price of a Treasury security does not follow a linear path but rather a convex line, as shown in the figure. Convexity therefore explains the *difference* between the theoretical price path (as defined by the duration tangent) and actuality. The shaded area in the figure illustrates the optimization of the security's price induced by the phenomenon of convexity.

What occurs is as the price of a security is rising its duration is extending, therefore causing the price to increase at an accelerating rate as it is multiplied by a slightly larger duration number at each iteration. This occurrence, of course, causes the price curve to curl up and away from the linear duration tangent line. When the price is declining, the duration shortens slightly, thereby causing the declining price to be multiplied by a somewhat smaller duration number. The result is a deceleration in the price decline, causing

FIGURE 3.1
Duration Tangent, Current 30-Year Bond, 10 Percent

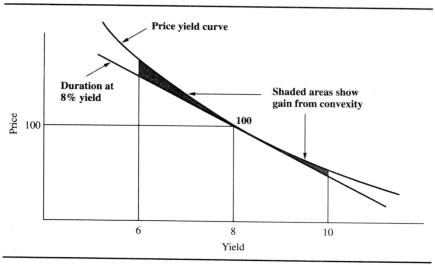

Source: Lehman Brothers Fixed Income Research.

the price curve to again curl away from the linear duration tangent.

In higher mathematics optimization theory is used to define a feasible region, shown as the shaded area in Figure 3.1, which refers here to the spread relationship of a security to points on the Treasury yield curve. The intersection of the plot points on a yield curve is a convex region, and determining the spread relationship, or feasible region, refers to identifying the saddle point of a function, which in turn is used to determine that feasible region we refer to as the change in price explained by convexity. The solution can result in either a positive or a negative number.

Duration measures the percentage change in price for a percentage change in yield. In other words, *duration measures the relative price volatility of the bond, whereas convexity describes the rate of change in duration as interest rates change.* When interest rates change, the duration of the security changes. Investors typically prefer securities that shorten slightly in duration when rates rise (or become less interest rate sensitive, meaning the price declines at a decelerating rate) and that lengthen somewhat when rates decline (the price increases at an accelerating rate). Such securities are referred to as *positively convex.*

With negatively convex securities present in the MBS product universe, *the ultimate question in the valuation process becomes, What kind of convexity is inherent to a given MBS form?* The more the *price performance* of the MBS is to be compared to that of the Treasury, the more desirable it is that the MBS be positively convex. On the other hand, if the MBS is to be used as a *hedge or to enhance portfolio yield, negative convexity may be acceptable.* The issue of convexity preference is to a large degree linked to the question, What is your investment objective? If price performance and maximum total return to a horizon are the primary goals, then positive convexity is a critical attribute for the MBS under consideration. On the other hand, if maximum yield to maturity is the key investment objective, then negatively convex, high-yielding MBSs may best achieve the goal. Figure 3.2 illustrates the positive convexity of Treasuries compared with the negative convexity of MBSs.

Two cautionary notes must be interjected here. First, the difference between stated yield and actual realized yield is likely to be dramatically different with negatively convex MBSs, especially if the securities bear a high degree of prepayment sensitivity, which is likely to be the case. In sum, the issues in a market with price volatility are, first:

FIGURE 3.2
MBS versus Treasury Price/Yield Curves

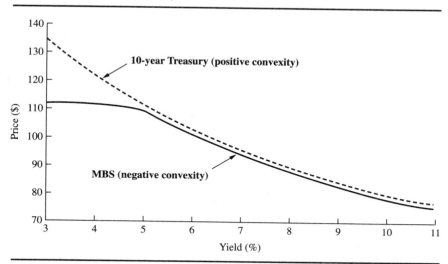

Source: Nicole Vianna, Lehman Brothers.

1. Do you want to buy or sell convexity (i.e., increase or decrease exposure to call risk)?
2. Are you paying a discount or premium price?
3. What is the value of the prepayment option?

Second, *history has proved that the yield-driven investor has generally paid too much for high stated yield and has undervalued MBSs with strong performance characteristics—that is, prepayment stability and positive convexity.* Stated another way, investors who choose to forgo (sell) convexity will be paid a higher yield to do so. Conversely, total-return-driven investors will give up yield to secure a high certainty of positive convexity. *Given this assumption, the idea is not necessarily to avoid prepayment (call) risk or uncertain convexity but rather to ensure adequate compensation for doing so.*

The value of the prepayment option causes the price of the MBS to change in the future unless volatility is, in fact, zero. The issue is not that of price change due to a change in interest rates; the issue, rather, is related to the change in the timing of the (MBS) cash flows. If one were to hold an 8 percent Treasury (i.e., a security with fixed payments) purchased at par to maturity, one *would* realize a yield of 8 percent. When the timing of the cash flows changes, the realized yield changes up or down depending on how the cash flows were purchased (premium or discount).

The overwhelming concern with negatively convex securities and MBSs priced to a premium is a product of the market environment that prevailed throughout the 1980s. A decade-long decline in interest rates and high price volatility caused MBS investors to lose money on the option component in the MBS (see Valuing the Call Option, page 94). The issue may be viewed in this way: If you sell a call on a bond, you will be paid a premium (the call price), and if prices do not change or decline, you keep the premium and let the call expire worthless. But if rates decline and the call is exercised, you lose money. The 1980s and early 1990s (into 1993) caused MBS investors to generally lose money on the MBS prepayment option (it was often called).

3. WHAT ARE THE OPTION-ADJUSTED SPREAD AND PREPAYMENT MODEL COMPONENTS?

The most widely used pricing and valuation techniques use static cash flow assumptions as the basis for calculating price and yield. The most simplistic approach to pricing fixed-income securities is **current yield (CY:** coupon divided by price). CY is not a good measure of value for any fixed-income security and is virtually useless with callable securities. It recognizes no passage of time or reinvestment opportunity (or risk). **Yield to maturity (YTM)** is a somewhat better measure because it takes into account a reinvestment assumption and the present value of money. YTM does not, however, provide for the presence of the prepayment option in MBSs.

Price to Cash Flow Yield

The **cash flow yield (CFY)** pricing process does utilize a prepayment assumption, albeit a constant, or static, prepayment assumption. This technique applies a single prepayment assumption to the projection of monthly cash flows, creating an assumed average life and a final maturity date. CFY, then, may be defined as the monthly internal rate of return of the MBS priced to a projected P&I cash flow annuity estimated by a prepayment model.

Net present value (NPV) in cash flow yield is computed by adding the series of projected monthly cash flows to the WAMs and discounting them back to present value, as follows:

$$NPV = \frac{cf_1}{(1 + r)^d} + \frac{cf_2}{(1 + r)^{d+1}} + \frac{cf_m}{(1 + r)^{m+d-1}} \qquad (3.1)$$

where

cf = Cash flow for the ith period (usually one month)

m = To maturity

r = Investor-required discount rate (IRR)

d = Interest-free delay expressed as a fraction, for example, $14/360 = .032$

Advantages and Limitations of CFY

The principal advantage of pricing to CFY is that a single prepayment assumption may be selected that best reflects the nature of the collateral (high coupon versus low coupon; FHA versus conventional) and the WAC of the underlying mortgages. The typical pricing convention is to use the actual CPR of the past three months or past experience as the prepayment speed assumption, although in times of high prepayment volatility, or with highly prepayment-sensitive MBS forms, such as CMO support class bonds or IO strips, a more conservative (faster or slower) prepayment assumption may be applied. The cash flows are then discounted to their present values, using as the discount rate the rate required by MBS investors (the IRR) as measured by the basis points spread of the MBS to the comparable-duration Treasury. The required IRR will generally be derived by one of the relative value analytical tools described in this chapter. For example, assume the MBS to be valued is a GNMA 8 percent pass-through and the appropriate prepayment assumption is 8 percent CPR, giving the MBS a 10-year average life. If the 10-year Treasury is yielding 8 percent and the IRR basis points spread to the Treasury yield is 115 basis points, then the IRR would be $8.00 + 115 = 9.15$ percent.

The chief limitation of CFY is its static nature. It does not adjust the prepayment assumption to allow for prepayment volatility. The seasonal cycle alone, for example, will increase the prepayment rate by 20 to 25 percent with the spring/summer prepayment speeds and will lower the rate by a comparable amount during the fall/winter cycle. The other and potentially more serious limitation is the duration value derived from the static nature of the CFY calculation, which assumes that the price sensitivity of the MBS arises from changes in market-driven interest rates. In technical terms the duration captures the impact of the change in discount rate, but not the change in the timing of the cash flows. This is true, of course, but since the CFY technique does not model prepayment-related changes in the timing of the pool cash flows, CFY never produces either negative duration or negative convexity. *Investors who rely totally on CFY-based calculators to derive the duration of premium-priced MBSs and other prepayment-sensitive MBS derivatives are running a substantial (and unnecessary) risk.*

Valuing the Call Option

The MBS has already been identified as a composite security consisting of a noncallable coupon bond component (the long position to the MBS investor) and a call option (the homeowner's prepayment option, or the short position to the MBS investor). This composition may be expressed as:

$$NPV(MBS) = V(NC) - V(CO) \tag{3.2}$$

where

$NPV(MBS)$ = Price, or NPV, of the MBS

$V(NC)$ = Value of the noncallable coupon bond component

$V(CO)$ = Value of the prepayment call option

The MBS investor is short the call option, so the value of the call is a minus in the component-pricing equation. Since the value of the call option is subtracted from the value of the noncallable component, an increase in the value of the call option reduces the total NPV value (price) of the MBS. When interest rates are declining, or are *expected to decline*, the MBS therefore loses ability to increase in price. This results in price compression of the premium-priced MBS coupons and induces negative convexity. Figure 3.3 illustrates the price compression and negative convexity of the MBS in a declining interest rate environment. The shaded area represents the value of the prepayment call option, which is shown to increase as interest rates decline.

FIGURE 3.3
Value of Embedded Option Induces Negative Convexity

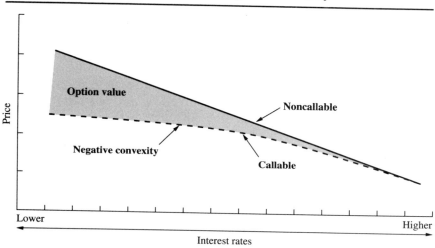

Isolating the value of the call option separately from the coupon component provides an orderly theoretical approach to the MBS valuation process. The market value of any callable bond equals the present value of the stated coupon and principal cash flows to maturity minus the implied value of the call option. The market value of the callable bond therefore equals the present value of all the cash flows following the call date less the exercise price (value) of the call. Clearly, if interest rates remain high enough that the call remains out of the money, the call will not be exercised, and the cash flows following the call date will be earned as originally priced.

Application of this approach to option-value pricing provides an intuitive approach to MBS pricing. The principal difference, of course, is that there is not a similar degree of certainty in defining the value of the MBS cash flows which succeed some theoretical call period, which with the MBS would commence at the beginning of the homeowner's opportunity to refinance.

Finally, and most vexing, *there is not one call but a bundle of calls embedded in the MBS,* and not all of them will be exercised even when they remain in the money year after year.

Static Yield Spread versus OAS

The stated, or static, MBS to Treasury yield spread is generally derived as a basis points spread differential between the MBS and a given Treasury security at a single point on the Treasury curve (for example, to the 7-year or the 10-year Treasury). The Treasury curve point that is selected is typically the Treasury note or bond with a maturity comparable to the average life of the MBS under consideration. Static yield spread is calculated using a single (static) prepayment assumption to derive a yield spread to a given point on the Treasury yield curve based on one set of cash flows.

By contrast, OAS utilizes option-based methodologies that simulate the performance of the MBS under many different interest rate (and prepayment rate) scenarios. (See Box 3.1 for a definition of OAS.) Under each scenario the MBS will have a different set of cash flows, thereby creating a different WAL. *The OAS model then solves for the yield spread differential that must be added across each point of the Treasury yield curve so that the average present value of the simulated MBS cash flows equals the current market price of the MBS.*

Because of the cost of the embedded prepayment options, the OAS will almost always be less than the static or conventional spread to Treasuries. Thus, the value, or cost, of the prepayment options reduces the realized return on the MBS. The difference between the conventionally static yield spread and the OAS is called

---

BOX 3.1
Defining OAS

1. **What is option-adjusted spread?** The **option-adjusted spread (OAS)** measures relative value. It calculates the expected yield spread of the MBS over the entire Treasury curve adjusted for the value of the prepayment call options embedded in the MBS. The value of the option is a function of the homeowner's economic incentive to refinance.

2. **What is the convexity cost?** The convexity cost calculates the change in yield if rates deviate stochastically. It can be interpreted as the time value of the option.

the **convexity cost** because it measures the reduction in expected yield that is attributable to prepayment volatility. (Many OAS models attempt to measure the impact on realized yield spread of other variables such as housing turnover and burnout.) The OAS is the difference between the zero-volatility yield (no change in interest rates) and the convexity cost of the prepayment option. *Therefore, the OAS spread represents a spread to the entire Treasury curve rather than to a particular point on the curve.* Figure 3.4 illustrates the process of subtracting the convexity cost (shaded area) from the stated spread (assuming static prepayment assumptions) to derive the OAS.

Option-Based Methodologies

The objective of option-based methodology is to define the anticipated MBS cash flow using an approach as reasonably reflective of

FIGURE 3.4
Stated and Option-Adjusted Yield Spreads

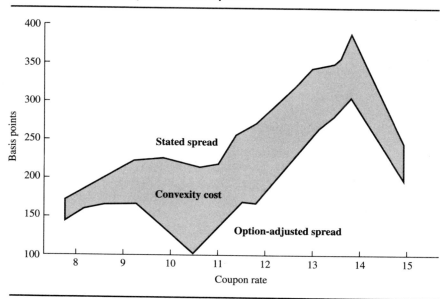

Source: Salomon Brothers Mortgage Research.

economic reality as current technology permits. In contrast to the relatively simple simulation that is used to determine the OAS for a callable Treasury or corporate bond, the greater number of variables in a mortgage security makes the calculation far more complex. The starting point is the generation of a random simulation of the future course of interest rates. These paths are then used to generate a series of interest rate-path-dependent mortgage prepayment rates. Finally, a *cash flow diagram* is established that will then be used to create a series of present values. (The cash flow diagram refers to the lattice of cash flows generated by running the OAS model over a series of interest rate paths.) One can then use an OAS model to determine the basis points differential, expressed as a spread, to the entire Treasury yield curve. The starting point can be current prices, which would be used to calculate the OAS. Alternatively, one can start with an OAS spread—for example, 50 OAS—and then determine a price based upon a specific interest rate/prepayment rate scenario. Central to the accuracy of the OAS calculation are the input variables relating to the MBS under consideration. Figure 3.5 is a cash flow diagram of five interest rate paths generated in an interest rate scenario in which there is a drop of 50 basis points.

FIGURE 3.5
Cash Flow Diagram

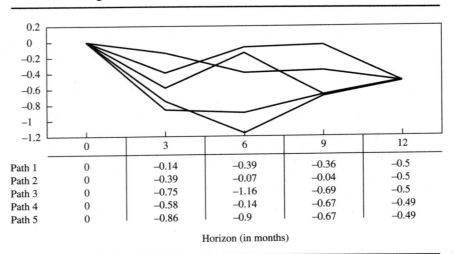

	0	3	6	9	12
Path 1	0	−0.14	−0.39	−0.36	−0.5
Path 2	0	−0.39	−0.07	−0.04	−0.5
Path 3	0	−0.75	−1.16	−0.69	−0.5
Path 4	0	−0.58	−0.14	−0.67	−0.49
Path 5	0	−0.86	−0.9	−0.67	−0.49

Horizon (in months)

Source: Lehman Brothers Fixed Income Research.

The figure illustrates the path dependency of the scenario analysts applied. The point is, all the paths end down 50 basis points at the end of the horizon, but one drops 116 basis points (1.16 percent) before rising back to end at −50 basis points. In other words, there are a lot of different ways to travel to the same future interest rate levels. Compare the implications of the down 116 basis points at midpoint to down 50 basis points at the end of the scenario horizon on an IO strip to that of a current-coupon MBS. The IO strip would lose considerable value while it passed through the down 116 basis points path; this path, therefore, produces far different results for the IO than would a linear decline to down 50 basis points. The impact on a current-coupon MBS would be far less critical.

Application of an option-based methodology generally produces better results than CFY in deriving MBS values, durations, and convexities. The option-based approach to valuing MBSs is similar in concept to that employed in valuing a traditional callable agency corporate bond. In essence, the process defines the value of a call option as the sum of the value of all the cash flows of the bond that occur after the call date.

The process of deriving the value of the MBS option is considerably more complex, however. First, the series of call options granted to the collective homeowners are not all equally subject to call. Some of the options will not be called even when in the money (the homeowner is locked in or not prepayment sensitive); some options will be called on different dates (some homeowners refinance at the first opportunity to do so, whereas others wait to see whether rates will drop further); and many homeowners exercise the option when it is out of the money—the homeowner moves and pays off the mortgage without regard to the current level of interest rates. Furthermore, changing demographics and/or falling or static home prices may alter housing turnover trends. Finally, prior interest rates determine how many of the original homeowners who remain in the pool are likely to respond to the next window of refinancing opportunity (interest rate-path dependency).

The analytical process for weighing these variables is the econometric prepayment model linked to an OAS model. The prepayment model simulates MBS cash flows, which track a series of interest rate paths projected by the OAS model, and these cash flows may be used to determine MBS value measurements. These measurements, such as modified duration and convexity, are then expressed in terms of their option-adjusted value and are used to derive a spread differential to the Treasury yield curve. The idea is to simulate MBS cash flow under different projections and then quantify the cash flow after making adjustments for its "option value."

The OAS measure may be used in a variety of ways. Most obviously, it is a more rigorous alternative to the application of conventional yield spread comparisons to other fixed-income securities. The level of OAS for a specific security can be monitored over time as an indicator of fair value. When the OAS narrows, the MBS is becoming more expensive relative to comparable MBSs that may have a wider OAS.

Limitations of OAS Methodology

OAS methodology has become increasingly adopted by total-return-oriented investors as a means of identifying risk/reward. *Note, however, that the estimate of option cost derived by the OAS model is highly dependent upon the assumptions inserted into the model by the analyst operating it—and these assumptions can be highly subjective. The same is true of the prepayment model upon which the OAS model is dependent.*

Questions Relating to OAS Modeling Variables

- *What is the coupon rate of the MBS and/or its collateral,* and what is the relationship of that coupon rate to "current" market interest rates? A comparison of collateral coupon rates to current rates determines the relative value of the implied option held by the homeowner and establishes its nearness to an at the money state. From a purely quantitative point of view, the value of the implied prepayment option in an MBS determines the rate of prepayment attributable to refinancing that will be used as the starting point for entering the calculations generated by the OAS model.

- *What is the volatility assumption to be applied?* To correctly determine the implied option value, a volatility assumption must be used in any option-pricing framework. The greater the value of the implied option, the greater the likelihood the option will be exercised—that is, that the homeowner will refinance.

- *What is the price of the MBS?* If the price of the subject security is at a substantial discount or premium to par ($100), then greater emphasis must be placed upon volatility. Generally speaking, when interest rates are declining, MBSs priced at a premium of greater than 2 points will display price compression (negative convexity and lower volatility). But discount MBSs will perform better than most other fixed-income securities (positive convexity and higher volatility). When interest rates are rising, premium-priced MBSs decompress (the option value of the prepayment declines), and discounts retain positive convexity.

- *What is the age of the MBS pool and/or collateral?* Seasoned collateral has a tendency to become more predictable, or to conform to a historic prepayment curve, as the collateral ages. *Newer MBS collateral tends to be less predictable and to possess a greater degree of prepayment rate volatility.*
- *How much weight is assigned to the demographically influenced tendency to prepay within the subject collateral pool?* In general, most prepayment models simply apply a normal statistical distribution when relating to purely demographic factors such as population shifts, death and divorce rates, and family size. As discussed in Chapter 5 on demographic patterns of the 1990s, it is important to define these factors specifically. A prepayment model, and its influence upon the OAS determination, may vary the weight assigned to demographic influences dependent upon such variables as age of the collateral, zip code distribution, and price trends in the single-family market.

OAS Yield and Spread Calculations

All yield calculations begin with a negative cash flow, cf_0, which represents the cash outlay necessary to purchase the security. When the calculation involves a traditional bond, such as a Treasury or corporate, one simply has to know the elements of the bond—that is, coupon, maturity, dated date, redemption value, and price or yield.[3] One can then use either price or yield to calculate yield or price by adding each cash flow, cf_0, cf_1, cf_2, ... $cf_{n,n+1}$, representing each interest payment, and then adding the last cash flow, cf_n,

---

[3]All bond calculations are performed in accordance with the Securities Industry Association's recommendations as contained in Lynch and Mayle, *Standard Securities Calculations Methods.* New York: Securities Industry Association, 1986.

consisting of the last interest payment and the principal payment. When the calculation begins with a yield, the yield establishes the discounting rate, or NPV; for example, the NPV figure common to all yield calculations is relatively simple when the discounting percentage rate and the cash flows are known and are not subject to change, as they are with a callable bond like an MBS.

The NPV formula is essentially the same as Equation 3.1:

$$NPV = \frac{cf_1}{(1 + i)^1} + \frac{cf_2}{(1 + i)^2} + \ldots + \frac{cf_n}{(1 + i)^n} \qquad (3.3)$$

where

NPV = NPV of discounted cash flow(s)

cf_n = Cash flow at period

The NPV calculation simply involves adding all of the cash flows and then discounting each back to the present value, taking into account the length of time to the date of receipt of the cash flows. The bond calculator knows the beginning (negative) number and the sum of the interest and principal payments (positive) numbers. Yield is expressed as the ratio, given the time value of money, of the positive cash flows over the negative cash flow.

The goal of any measurement of value relating to MBSs is basically the same as the preceding NPV calculation: When the beginning value equals x (price) and the ending value equals $x+$, what is the yield or return? The problem arises when one attempts to quantify the nature of the future cash flows. As is the case with all *price to yield* calculations, the formula involves the use of a series of guesses, expressed as a loop (Σ, the sigma or sum sign). The bond calculator undergoes a number of calculation loops until it arrives at a yield that is within 0.0001 of 1 percent of the NPV. The MBS calculation is complicated by the fact that an additional guess function must be added to the equation in the form of assumptions relating to the size and timing of the receipt of the future cash flows.

Given that a prepayment model has estimated the future cash flow diagram of an MBS, we can now solve for yield when we know the price by using Equation 3.4:

$$P = \sum_{j=1}^{n} \frac{cf_j}{(1 + y_t + s_c)^j} = \sum_{j=1}^{n} \frac{cf_j}{(1 + y)} \qquad (3.4)$$

where

> P = Price
>
> j = Time until receipt of cash flow ($to - ti$)
>
> cf_j = Cash flow at time j
>
> y = Yield of MBS under consideration (cash flow yield)
>
> y_t = Yield of reference Treasury
>
> S_c = Static spread to the benchmark Treasury

Price is arrived at by the same kind of loop process that would be used to calculate the price of any other bond. With an MBS, however, the extra step of looping through the cash flows is added, so that the payment stream can be discounted back to a present value.

When we add the following variables, we can also solve for a static spread to the Treasury yield curve and OAS:

> r_j = The implied forward rate
>
> i = An interest rate path (1, 2, etc.)
>
> k = The designated yield curve point
>
> zv = Zero volatility spread

To solve for static spread to the Treasury yield curve:

$$P = \sum_{j=1}^{n} \frac{cf_j}{\prod_{k=1}^{j} (1 + r_k + zv \ spread)} \tag{3.5}$$

To solve for the OAS:

$$P = \frac{1}{n \ paths} \sum_{i=1}^{n \ paths} \sum_{j=1}^{n} \frac{cf_{ij}}{\prod_{k=1}^{j} (1 + r_{ik} + OAS)} \tag{3.6}$$

To solve for the number of paths and then average back price:

$$P = \frac{1}{n \ paths} \sum_{i=1}^{n \ paths} \sum_{j=1}^{n} \frac{cf_{ij}}{\prod_{k=1}^{j} (1 + r_{ik} + OAS)} \tag{3.7}$$

The correct determination of the OAS is arrived at through the execution of the preceding three distinct but linked simulations executed by the interest rate model, the prepayment model, and the actual OAS model.

To develop an understanding of the determination of the yield of a given MBS, one must keep all of these steps firmly in mind. In addition, one cannot lose sight of the fact that each step is constructed on top of the step it succeeds. An interest rate model really amounts to nothing more than a fairly straightforward statistical simulation. Most models rely upon a Monte Carlo–type simulation, which is more than sufficient to estimate the future value of most noncallable bonds.

Considering the sensitivity of the MBS cash flows to prepayments, however, we find the utilization of a prepayment model is necessary. The objective of the model is to determine the future cash flow of the MBS under consideration. Using the simulation generated by the interest rate model (step 1), the prepayment model adds another analytical function—that is, a series of guesses relating to the remaining number of mortgages in a given security (step 2). These guesses are referred to as prepayment rate. The length of time within which the model uses a specified prepayment rate is determined by the interest rate simulation, as well as by any demographic factors that affect prepayment. Once the cash flow diagram has been projected, the yield and spread calculations may be done (step 3).

Determining a series of prepayment rate projections to derive an average life of an MBS pool, together with entering the correct cash flow information, provides the base data to derive a yield and the point on the yield curve against which the MBS will be compared. With these results, one can identify the OAS and determine how it may change given a projected change in prepayment rates.

In summary, OAS is a measurement of the value of a given MBS, on a relative basis, as measured against the Treasury yield curve, and of any possible changes in the shape of the yield curve. Because of the complexity of the MBS cash flow, the utilization of technical value measurements such as modified duration, convexity, and option-adjusted yield or spread enhances the process of weighting the relative value of MBS investment forms against one another as well as against traditional fixed-income investments.

Synopsis of OAS

- Derives spread over the Treasury curve.

- Plots all the yield spreads versus the Treasury curve within the OAS model.
- Gives an indication of the bond's risk/return.

Advantages

- Does not rely on workout pricing assumptions.
- Does not rely on reinvestment assumptions.
- Is extremely useful in buy versus hold decisions—for example, PAC IOs, inverse floaters, and support bonds.
- Is computationally possible given today's technology.
- Is an extremely useful diagnostic tool.

Disadvantages

- Is not really a clean indicator of total return.
- Does not capture reinvestment of cash flows.
- Cannot be used alone.
- Requires understanding of the bond.

Functional Components of the OAS Model

An OAS model is constructed upon a series of building blocks. In sequential order these are:

1. An interest rate model is used to generate a series of future interest rate paths, or yield curves. Monthly interest rates for a period of up to 30 years, or the remaining life of a pass-through MBS, are generated, creating hundreds—or often thousands—of interest rate paths.
2. A prepayment model is used to forecast the changes in pool cash flow according to the interest rate paths generated and the specific collateral characteristics selected. The prepayment projection is dependent upon projected interest rate paths and demographic influences on mortgage pool life.
3. A cash flow model is used to calculate the monthly distributions of P&I according to the projections of the prepayment model. This is a relatively straightforward process for pass-throughs, but becomes extremely complex when applied to CMOs and their related derivatives. A probability distribu-

tion of possible average lives is generated by linking the pre-payment model to the distribution of interest rate paths.

Figure 3.6 is a schematic of the functional steps related to the electronic derivation of OAS.

The Interest Rate Model (as Developed by John Tierney, Lehman Brothers)

The interest rate model begins with the current interest rate and, using a random number generator referred to as a **Monte Carlo simulation**, casts out a series of possible interest rates 1 month forward. (The term Monte Carlo refers to the random nature of the interest rate-path selection process.) The 1-month forward rates are, in turn, used to generate a set of interest rates 2 months forward, and so on, until one path consisting of 360 months of random observations is completed. This process is repeated for the requisite number of paths, each representing one possible sequence of future monthly interest rates.

Construction of the Interest Rate Model

To derive an arbitrage-free distribution of future interest rates, the current Treasury yield curve must be used to derive the spot-rate curve, sometimes referred to as the term structure of interest rates. The Treasury yield curve is constructed from the yields to maturity of the "on-the-run" Treasury securities. Individual yields to maturity that comprise the yield curve denote the average yield required to discount the cash flow of a given security to the current market

FIGURE 3.6
Simulation Analysis: OAS Model Functions

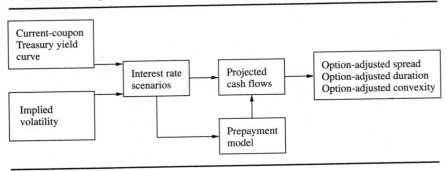

Source: Lehman Brothers Fixed Income Research.

price. However, if the yield curve is not flat (but is upward or downward sloping), the true yield or discount rate for each cash flow will be different. For example, when the yield curve is upward sloping, the market requires a lower yield for principal or interest payments to be received in 6 months or 1 year than it does for payments scheduled to be received in 12 or 15 years.

Discount rates that apply to specific periods, such as 6 months or 12 years, are called spot rates, and the profile of spot rates across the maturity spectrum is called the term structure. The term structure provides several critical pieces of information for generating an arbitrage-free distribution of interest rates. First, the spot-rate profile defines the credit risk and option-free interest rate for each maturity. Second, the term structure may easily be converted into a corresponding price (or discount) function that defines the theoretical price of zero coupon bonds at each maturity. When the term structure is used to discount cash flows, each cash flow is discounted by the spot rate that corresponds to the maturity of the cash flow. Therefore, a series of cash flows—such as monthly mortgage security cash flows—is viewed as a series of individual zero coupon bonds.

Finally, the term structure provides the link for setting prices and yields in the cash (spot) and forward markets and defines the current option-free interest rates across all maturities at any given point in time. Spot rates define the current cost of money (interest rate) for various maturities beginning today. Forward rates represent the current interest rate quote for a given maturity starting at some future time—for example, the 10-year rate a year from today.

A tight arbitrage pricing relationship normally exists between the cash and forward markets, so an investor normally cannot earn an excess return by taking hedged or risk-free positions between the cash and forward Treasury markets. Investors who want to earn the current 2-year spot rate over a 2-year horizon should be indifferent to purchasing a 2-year or a 1-year security in the cash market and a 1-year security in the forward market for delivery in 1 year. If one of these strategies provides a superior return, then arbitrage activity should realign prices so that the expected incremental return of the superior strategy returns to zero. Using spot rates to calculate the forward rate for a given maturity at any future point is straightforward. The forward rate is calculated simply as the geometric average that links two spot rates.

One particularly useful series salient to this discussion is the 1-month forward rate series across the entire term structure. This forward rate series defines the monthly risk-free rate for all months over a 30-year horizon, consistent with current pricing of the Treasury cash market. The monthly forward rates, in turn, can be rolled together to give the spot rates at each maturity. In general, let $r_n t$ denote the spot rate for maturity n at time t, where $n = 1, 2 \ldots,$ 360. Then r_n 0; $n = 1, 2, \ldots, 360$ denotes the current term structure. The implied monthly forward rates are represented by $r_{1,t}$; $t = 1, 2, \ldots, 359$). In particular, the sequences are related by Equation 3.8:

$$(1 + r_{n,0}) = [(1 + r_{1,0}) \prod_{t=1}^{n-1}(1 + r_{1,t})]^{(1/n)} \qquad (3.8)$$

for $n = 2, 3, \ldots, 360$

The interest rate projection model was designed to generate random interest rate scenarios, subject to the arbitrage pricing relationship between spot and forward Treasury rates. In particular, the model generates individual scenarios of 359 monthly Treasury bill (bond-equivalent) forward rates. Each month's rate is generated using a variant of the log-linear random walk model of the form shown by Equation 3.9:

$$Ln\bar{r}_{1,t,j} = Ln\bar{r}_{1,t-1,j} + c_t + a_{t,j} \qquad (3.9)$$

for $t = 1, 2, \ldots, 359$

where

$\bar{r}_{1,t,j}$ = The projected 1-month Treasury bill forward rate in month t for scenario j, where $j = 1, 2, \ldots, J$, and $t = 1, 2, \ldots, 359$

$\bar{r}_{1,0,j} = \bar{r}_{1,0}$ for $j = 1, 2, \ldots, J$

$a_{t,j}$ = The random shock in month t for scenario j, distributed normally and independently with zero mean and constant variance equal to the assumed level of volatility

c_t = A centering term chosen empirically to ensure that the expected forward discount function is equivalent to the discount function consistent with the current term structure.

Since the model generates a logarithmic series of interest rates, the distribution of rates at any point in time will be distributed log-normally. A log-normal distribution has the useful property that the interest rates are constrained to range from zero to infinity, with decreasing probability density assigned to very low and very high rates. Each scenario may be viewed as a series of monthly projected or hypothetical Treasury bill forward rates that can be rolled into a series of spot rates.

To ensure that the results of the model for noncallable securities are consistent with current market pricing, and to eliminate the simplest risk-free arbitrage opportunities, the interest rate projection model is constrained by a sequence of term structure adjustment terms (ct, $t = 1, 2, \ldots, 359$). In practice, this sequence is basically a centering mechanism whereby an array of 359 constants, one for each month of the projection, is added to the corresponding projected rate in each scenario. These constants are derived empirically, so that the mean of the distribution of discount functions is congruent to the discount function that is consistent with the current term structure. This constraint may be represented by Equation 3.10:

$$(1 + r_{n,0})^{-n} = J^{-1} \sum_{j=1}^{J} (1 + \bar{r}_{n,0,j})^{-n} \tag{3.10}$$

where

$$\left(1 + \bar{r}_{n,0,j}\right) = \left[\left(1 + r_{1,0}\right) \prod_{t=1}^{n-1} \left(1 + \bar{r}_{1,t,j}\right)\right]^{(1/n)}$$

for $n = 2, 3, \ldots, 360$

J = The number of simulated scenarios

While admittedly not elegant, Equation 3.10 does achieve the goal of eliminating simple arbitrage opportunities between the spot Treasury market and the projected forward Treasury scenarios. The price-centering specification in Equation 3.10 may appear at first to be a cumbersome process; however, the simpler and perhaps more intuitive approach of centering the distribution of projected yields about the term structure does not result in arbitrage-free interest rate scenarios.

Two-State Models

Many interest rate models are **two-state** in that for each month two paths are generated—a short-term rate (usually tied to Treasury short rates) and a longer-term rate tied to the 10-year Treasury rate. The short-term rate is used to discount the cash flows to present value and the long-term rate to generate the mortgage-rate assumption used to project prepayments. Figure 3.7 gives an example of a series of paths.

Most interest rate models generate a series of interest rate paths following a **log-normal distribution.** This means that the percentage interest rate change from one period to the next follows a normal bell-shaped distribution. *The principal variables in the distribution of the interest rate paths are (1) the assumption used to define the percentage of interest rate volatility and (2) the basis for the probability distribution of interest rate paths.*

Although the casting out of interest rate paths is accomplished through a random walk, the OAS model does look to the structure of forward rates to determine the distribution of these random paths. For example, in a steep yield curve environment (long rates are higher than short rates) the model will generate more high interest rate paths than low interest rate paths. When the prepayment model runs the MBS cash flows over more high-rate than low-rate paths, it will generate a distribution of average lives reflecting the greater number of high-rate paths; that is, slower prepayments.

Volatility Assumption. The greater the percentage of the volatility assumption, the greater the value attributed to the implied call option, and the higher the option cost. This outcome is intuitively logical because the greater the volatility of swings in yield, the greater the probability of the opportunity to refinance. This is something we see with *all* options—increased volatility leads to a higher option value.

Mean Reversion. Without some form of reverting the generated interest rate paths to some mean, interest rates will obtain unreasonably high and low levels. Volatility over time would theoretically approach infinity. Figure 3.8A illustrates pure diffusion-yield volatility without mean reversion. Figure 3.8B illustrates mean-reverting diffusion.

FIGURE 3.7
Interest Rate Path Simulation

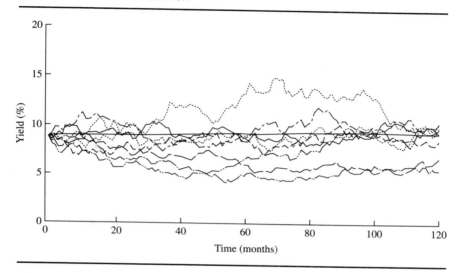

FIGURE 3.8A
Pure Diffusion

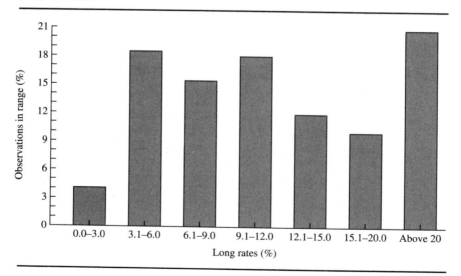

FIGURE 3.8B
Mean-Reverting Diffusion

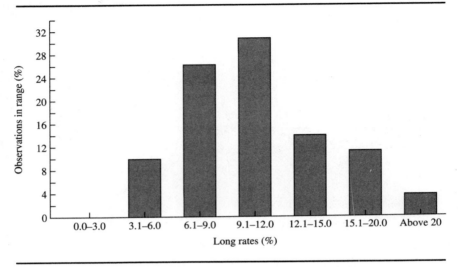

Source: Lehman Brothers Fixed Income Research.

Volatility Impact on OAS

The volatility assumption has a profound impact on the OAS because the MBS investor is short the option, and high volatility leads to high option cost. The following discussion of volatility is based on a report on OAS methodologies and the impact of volatility on the OAS model results by Terrance Belton of Freddie Mac.[4]

Table 3.1 demonstrates the extent to which volatility affects the results. The table gives calculations of OASs and durations at 12, 17, and 22 percent volatility. Although the duration estimates tend to be only mildly sensitive to the assumed volatility, the OAS may move by as much as 40 basis points if volatility increases by 10 percentage points. Using a 10.5 percent coupon as an example from the table, one sees that the OAS drops from 76 at 12 percent volatility to 34 at the higher 22 percent volatility—a drop of 42 basis points; the duration, by contrast, drops only from 4.5 to 4.1.

---

[4]"The New Breed': Option Adjusted Spreads" by Terrance M. Belton, Senior Economist, FHLMC, Washington, DC. In *Secondary Market Reports*, Freddie Mac, Winter 1988–1989.

TABLE 3.1

OASs and Duration under Alternative Volatility Estimates (Freddie Mac PCs, August 26, 1988)

		Volatility (%)[a]					
		12		17		22	
Coupon (1)	Price (2)	OAS (bp) (3)	Duration (4)	OAS (bp) (5)	Duration (6)	OAS (bp) (7)	Duration (8)
10.5	100-09	76	4.5	53	4.3	34	4.1
10.0	98-01	74	5.1	56	4.8	40	4.6
9.5	95-17	71	5.6	58	5.3	46	5.1
9.0	93-01	64	6.0	55	5.7	48	5.4

[a]Volatility of short-term rate. The volatility of the mortgage rate is set at 9, 14, and 19 percent, respectively. The correlation coefficient is equal to 0.60 in all cases.

Source: Terrance Belton, Freddie Mac.

Note also the cusp (10 percent and 10.5 percent) coupons are the ones most affected.

Different assumptions about volatility can reverse the direction of trades designed to arbitrage perceived mispricing across different sectors of mortgage coupons. An investor who assumed 22 percent volatility, for example, might buy the 9 percent FHLMC PC and sell the 10.5 percent PC to arbitrage the fairly large OAS differences in column (7) of Table 3.1. If the true volatility were 12 percent, however, the opposite trade should be made: Low volatility means the investor should buy the 10.5 percent coupon and sell the relatively rich 9 percent coupon.

Although trading strategies are dependent on volatility, accurately estimating the volatility parameter is difficult. Modelers use various approaches, such as estimating volatility based on recent interest rate movements or calculating implied volatility from observed security prices. No method provides completely satisfactory estimates of this critical variable, however. In part, this is because of the differences between implied versus historical volatility.

OASs also tend to be extremely sensitive to the degree of correlation between long- and short-term rates the model assumes. Table 3.2 illustrates that, for three estimates of the correlation coefficient between the short-term Treasury rate and the mortgage rate, the OAS declines sharply for modest changes in the assumed degree of correlation. This sensitivity stems from the fact that prepayments are based on changes in mortgage rates, whereas short-term rates are used in the model for discounting. As a result, the greater the assumed correlation coefficient between mortgage rates and short-term rates, the higher the option cost embedded in the mortgage.

Many option-based one-factor models assume for simplicity that long and short rates are perfectly correlated. Such an assumption is equivalent to saying that prepayments are perfectly correlated with changes in short-term Treasury rates. In reality, prepayments tend to follow movements in mortgage rates; and, historically, the correlation coefficient between short-term Treasury rates and mortgage rates has ranged only between 0.4 and 0.9, depending on the time period. Moreover, prepayments depend upon other factors besides interest rates, so they will not be perfectly correlated with short-term interest rates even if long and short rates are perfectly correlated.

Assuming perfect correlation between short-term Treasury rates and prepayments will overstate the option cost of the mortgage and, therefore, bias in a downward direction the estimated

TABLE 3.2

OASs[a] under Alternative Correlation Coefficients (Freddie Mac PCs, August 26, 1988)

Coupon (1)	Price (2)	Correlation Coefficient (bp)		
		0.30 (3)	0.60 (4)	1.0 (5)
10.5	100-09	84	53	16
10.0	98-01	84	56	26
9.5	95-17	84	58	35
9.0	93-01	84	55	38

[a]Based on 17 percent volatility of the short-term rate and 14 percent volatility of the mortgage rate.

Source: Terrance Belton, Freddie Mac.

OAS on the mortgage security. In addition, as Table 3.2 indicates, the bias may be larger for current-coupon mortgages than for discount mortgages. This situation may create the appearance that an arbitrage opportunity exists when, in reality, all mortgages are being fairly priced. On August 26, 1988, for example, 9 percent PCs appear to have been mispriced by 22 basis points relative to 10.5 percent PCs under an assumed correlation coefficient of 1.0. At more realistic estimates of the correlation coefficient, however, this perceived arbitrage opportunity begins to disappear.

Estimates of volatility and the degree of correlation between long and short rates may significantly affect the results of an option-based model. The parameters of the prepayment function are also important, but at least these can be estimated on the basis of historical data on mortgage prepayments. In this sense, uncertainty about the prepayment function is less worrisome than uncertainty about interest rate volatility and correlation, the parameters of the interest rate process.

While rate volatility can be based on real data, correlation is frequently based on simple assumptions, intuition, or data that may not be relevant to the current interest rate environment. The inherent complexity of mortgage cash flows makes all methods for valuing MBSs subject to error. The new option-based models do not change this fact, but they offer a substantial improvement over static measures of duration and value.

Projecting Market Interest Rates[5]
The mortgage valuation model, as noted earlier, typically depends on a simulated distribution of future interest rate scenarios. In particular, stochastic scenarios of monthly observations of short-term Treasury bill yields (bond-equivalent) are generated using a variant of the log-linear random walk model. Furthermore, the distribution of these scenarios is constrained to eliminate potential Treasury yield curve arbitrage opportunities. This condition is derived from option-pricing theory, in which a risk-free hedge or investment can earn no more than the risk-free rate.

---

[5]From *Option Valuation Analysis of Mortgage-Backed Securities* by Michael R. Grupe, Ph.D; John P. Tierney, CPA; and Catherine Willis, Ph.D. New York: Kidder Peabody Mortgage-Backed Securities Research, July 1988.

The Cash Flow Model[6]

Given the probability distribution of future interest rate paths and the related prepayment forecast, calculating the cash flows associated with these assumptions is reasonably straightforward. The projected cash flows must now be discounted back to present value using the sequence of short-term rates generated for the path selected and averaging the resulting present values over all interest paths selected as applicable. Mathematically, the discounting process is expressed in Equation 3.11:

$$ P = E\left[\frac{c_1}{(1 + r_1 + z)} + \frac{c_2}{(1 + r_1 + z)(1 + r_2 + z)} \cdots \right] \quad (3.11) $$

where

P = Price

E = The expected value operator

c_1 = The cash flow for period 1

r_1 = The one-period stochastic forward rate

z = The OAS

This method of discounting the cash flows, frequently called **path-dependent discounting,** is an important step in capturing the embedded option cost in the mortgage. To illustrate, assume that current interest rates are 10 percent and either will rise to 12 percent in the next period and remain there or fall to 8 percent and remain there. Suppose that each path has a 50 percent probability of occurring and that investors have a choice between a two-period noncallable 10 percent bond and a two-period 10 percent nonamortizing mortgage.

The noncallable bond pays a $10 coupon at the end of the first period and $110 at the end of the second period, regardless of which path interest rates take. If rates increase, the mortgage should behave just as the noncallable bond: Borrowers pay the $10 interest payment at the end of the first period and the $110 P&I payment at the end of the second period. If rates fall to 8 percent, however,

---

[6]This discussion of the cash flow model was provided by Terrance M. Belton, FHLMC.

borrowers will prepay the mortgage at the end of the first period, and the investor will receive the 10 percent interest rate for only one period.

These cash flows may now be valued by calculating their expected present value. Since the probability of each path occurring is 50 percent, the value of the noncallable bond is calculated as in Equation 3.12:

Price of bond = 0.50 [present value of cash flows in path 1]
    +0.50 [present value of cash flows in path 2]

$$= 0.50 \left[\frac{\$10}{1.1} + \frac{\$110}{(1.1 \times 1.12)} \right] \tag{3.12}$$

$$+ 0.50 \left[\frac{\$10}{1.1} + \frac{\$110}{(1.1 \times 1.08)} \right]$$

The price of the mortgage is similarly calculated (3.13):

Price of mortgage = 0.50 [present value of cash flows in path 1]
    +0.50 [present value of cash flows in path 2]

$$= 0.50 \left[\frac{\$10}{1.1} + \frac{\$110}{(1.1 \times 1.12)} \right] \tag{3.13}$$

$$= + 0.50 \left[\frac{\$110}{1.1} + \frac{\$0}{(1.1 \times 1.08)} \right]$$

$$= 0.50 \, [98.38] + 0.50 \, [\$100] = 99.19$$

Although both securities pay a 10 percent coupon, the prepayment option on the mortgage reduces the expected present value of the security by 84 cents relative to the value of the noncallable bond. This occurs because prepayments prevent the present value of the mortgage cash flows in the low interest path from rising above $100. Of course, mortgage values can exceed par once the full range of interest rate and prepayment paths is considered. Nevertheless, path-dependent discounting still accounts for the cost of the prepayment option in the same general way: Prepayments in low interest rate paths reduce the value of the mortgage security relative to the value of a noncallable bond.

Even with a completely general set of interest rate paths, the expected present value approach provides only a theoretical estimate of the value of the mortgage cash flows. In practice, applying this method to actual mortgage securities almost always results in overestimation of their value because the method assumes the MBS cash flows are equivalent to Treasuries—that is, yield spread equals zero. To calibrate the model to observed market prices, modelers add an additional parameter—the OAS.

Operationally, the OAS is a constant spread that, when added to the short-term rates the model has derived, makes the expected present value of the mortgage security equal to its observed price. It is an estimate of the spread over Treasury securities after taking into account the model-determined fair value of the option costs of the mortgage. The OAS may represent costs associated with the mortgage security that the model omits, such as credit risk, liquidity concerns, or prepayment uncertainty unrelated to interest rate movements, or it may simply represent errors in the pricing model. By construction, the OAS on a Treasury security is zero, so the OAS also provides an estimate of the net yield advantage of the mortgage over a comparable-duration Treasury security.

The Prepayment Model

A primary component in the process of determining the OAS is the prepayment model. The key ingredients of the prepayment model are:

Model Inputs

- Point on the seasonal cycles.
- Age (WAM) of mortgage collateral.
- Mortgage rate (WAC) of mortgage collateral.

Model Building Blocks

- Linkage of prepayment speeds to historic shifts in interest rates.
- Lag response reflecting time required to process refi application.
- Path-dependency characteristics of mortgage collateral.

- Application of a burnout simulation to premium-priced coupons.
- Application of the yield curve effect.

Prepayment Model Methodologies

Most prepayment models consist of two components—one to monitor housing turnover, which relates primarily to discount-priced MBSs (age and seasonal and demographic factors prevail), and one for prepayments, which relates to premiums (the refinancing incentive prevails). Econometric prepayment models store historic data relating the prepayment sensitivity of the mortgage pool to interest rate changes and seasonal cycles. The models contain, in turn, a mathematical function that links prepayment rates to pool age, seasonal cycles, changes in interest rates, changes in yield curve shape, and sometimes housing turnover. The seasoning (the age and the prior path of interest rates the pool passed through) modifies the prepayment sensitivity of the pool according to the historic profile of pools of the same coupon and agency guaranty and of similar age. Some models incorporate an assumption for housing turnover, generally through derivation of an affordability index.

Functional Components of Prepayment Models[7]

A typical prepayment model forecasts prepayments by comparing the observed prepayment activity of a pool of mortgages to certain standards established from historic performance. For example, the prepayment model has stored in memory as a benchmark the typical aging pattern and seasonal cycle of each issue and coupon (for example, FNMA 9s) of a given WAM. The future prepayment pattern of a pool may then be forecast according to scenarios relating to interest rate changes and age based on the historic performance of the benchmark. The functional components of the prepayment model are age, seasonality, the incentive to refinance, and burnout.

Establishing a Base CPR

The analyst must first establish a base case CPR assumption, which will be adjusted up or down by the factors discussed in the text that

---

[7]This discussion of functional components of prepayment models was provided by Paul C. Wang, Vice President, Merrill Lynch Mortgage Research.

follows. In establishing the base CPR, historic data are used to construct a CPR ramp that replicates the demographic and economic profile of the current coupon. This profile is then used to project a CPR ramp for the current coupon to be modeled at a given point in time. Some analysts have used seasoned pools that capture identifiable demographic and economic characteristics as a means of deriving a target CPR assumption. For example, pools issued with a concentration on the East or West Coast during a period of heavy East-West migrations would reflect the housing turnover associated with such migrations. Pools with a high WAC imply homeowners who accepted relatively high mortgage rates. Such homeowners will likely be less stable than those with sounder economic footing leading to higher turnover (faster prepay). Low WAC pools suggest the opposite. Other pools may have been issued in a year with a large share of ARM originations, reflecting the yield curve effect. In a year with heavy ARM originations, pools of fixed-rate mortgages would represent the most conservative profile of homeowners for that year (low prepay).

The CPR ramps of pools with specific years of issue may be plotted, each having a different CPR profile. For example, a mid-1993–issue pool might have a projected CPR of almost 8; a seasoned pool with a slow prepayment demographic profile might have a projected CPR of a little less than 5. Assuming 6 CPR is the norm, the first pool had a factor of more than 1 applied to project its CPR; the second, a factor of less than 1. Note that over time, a little past the year 2000, the projected CPRs of all four pools merge, indicating that with full seasoning most of the demographic and economic differences have worked out of the pool. This result demonstrates again the stability of well-seasoned pools.

Age

The age or seasoning pattern of an MBS may be plotted by tracking the profile of a series of MBS issues of the same coupon sorted by WAM (age). The theoretical prepayment pattern may then be charted and stored as a reference for the pure aging effect. When the pool is within 1 to 2 years of issue it would be assigned a seasoning factor of less than 1 (for discussion of the age effect on MBS pools, see Chapter 4). As the pool seasons into years 3 through 7, the period of maximum transfers related to economic and demographic-driven migration patterns (family growth, job transfer, etc.), it would likely be assigned a factor of greater than 1. A factor of less than 1 would cause the prepayment model to apply a reduction in the base-line prepayment assumption; as the pool seasons and the transfer effect becomes greater, the model would adjust the base prepayment assumption by a factor of greater than 1, and so on.

Seasonality

The seasonal cycle is implemented by applying a factor greater than 1 for the summer months and less than 1 for the winter months. The seasonal factors would be best derived from the seasonal prepayment cycle of pre-1980–issue pools with a pass-through rate of 8 percent or less. With the selection of pool issues that are well seasoned, and the relatively low pass-through rate, it could be ensured that the prepayment options are out of the money, leaving prepayment changes from month to month attributable primarily to seasonal factors. The average prepayment speed for the full-year cycle would have a factor of 1. The seasonal peak in prepayments is generally in August, which might be assigned a factor of about 1.3; the low, in February, a factor of about 0.8. This information would be applied in the model as a plus 30 percent or minus 20 percent increase or decrease in the base case average prepayment. In-between months would have the appropriate percentage applied—that is, minus 7 percent for April (0.93 factor) and plus 2 percent for October (1.02 factor). Note that the seasonal factor must be plugged in for each month of the cash flow series in the forecast.

The Incentive to Refinance

Application of the refinancing factor, which is really the economic incentive to refinance, has been the most important and complex function of the prepayment model. It is generally expressed as the percentage of monthly savings that can be realized by refinancing. This would be plotted as a ramp reflecting the refinancing functions for prepayment modeling as the difference increases between the currently available (market rate) mortgage rate and the mortgage rate held by the borrower. This difference is referred to as the interest rate spread (IRS).

The incentive to refinance increases as the IRS becomes greater, and as the IRS declines, the incentive to refinance is less. A negative IRS means that current mortgage rates are higher than the rate of the mortgage held, and the prepayment option is out of the money. To the extent there are prepayments when the IRS is flat or negative, these prepayments must be explained by housing turnover—that is, the decision to sell the house regardless of the relative level of interest rates. The IRS is expressed mathematically in Equation 3.14:

$$IRS = 100 \times \left[1 - \frac{CM}{CP} \right] \qquad (3.14)$$

where

IRS = Percentage of monthly saving

CM = Payment requirement refinanced to prevailing market rate

CP = Payment requirement at original mortgage rate

A simpler approach sometimes used is to use the spread between current market rates and the WAC of the MBS pool under consideration:

$$RI = Max[WAC - FHCR, 0] \qquad (3.15)$$

where

RI = Refinance incentive

WAC = Mortgage rate on subject pool

$FHCR$ = Freddie Mac mortgage contract rate[8]

Burnout

The burnout effect captures the economic and demographic factors that cause some percentage of homeowners to fail to refinance when the economic incentive to do so persists over time. Those factors include inadequate home equity to qualify for refinancing (decline in property value), a negative change in employment of one or more members of the household, and/or a negative change in the credit status of the borrower(s). Other factors could be presence of a subsidy in the mortgage rate or simply unawareness or unresponsiveness on the part of the homeowner. **Burnout,** then, may be quantified as a function of how much interest rate savings have been forgone for a given period of time. In Figure 3.9 the vertical axis represents the monthly mortgage payment, and the shaded area represents savings that could be realized by refinancing. The question then becomes, How much will the homeowner leave on the

---

[8]Paul Wang, Merrill Lynch.

FIGURE 3.9
Forgone Savings over Time

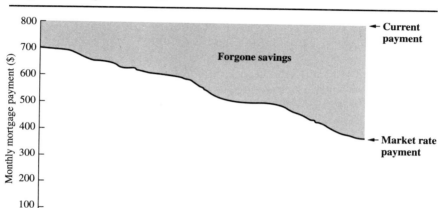

Source: Lehman Brothers Fixed Income Research.

table, and for how long? The amount of savings forgone may be modeled as a factor representing time multiplied by the dollars of opportunity, or savings, lost each month. The opportunity loss is added up month by month. At a point after 7 to 9 months of forgoing the savings, the borrower becomes dramatically less likely to ever take advantage of the opportunity. The burnout factor can be modeled by summing from time t to $t + 12$. The burnout factor is, first, a function of $t + 1$ in the sense that the more time $t + 1$ represents, the lower will be the burnout factor (application of a smaller factor reduces the prepayment assumption). Second, the greater the sum of forgone savings, the lower the factor. Figure 3.9 illustrates the forgone savings with the passage of time.

The Yield Curve Effect
When the yield curve is very positively sloped (short-term rates are significantly lower than long-term rates) homeowners have a variety of alternative mortgage forms for extending their refinancing options (ARMs, 5- and 7-year balloons, and 15-year mortgages). The yield curve effect may be carried in the computer as a factor of the

spread between the shorter end of the Treasury term structure and the 30-year fixed rate held by the homeowner, or more simply as the spread from the 2-year Treasury to the 10-year Treasury.

Figure 3.10 illustrates the derivation of the yield curve factor. For example, when the yield spread from the 2-year Treasury to the 10-year Treasury is 350 basis points, the yield curve is very positively steeply sloped (short rates are much lower than long rates). This scenario is illustrated at the top of Figure 3.10 and is represented by the top (solid) curve in the graph. A normal 2- to 10-year spread is about 150 basis points and has a factor of 1. A flat yield curve would be 50, 0, or −50 basis points. The higher the yield curve factor, the greater will be the prepayment projection, thus reflecting how a steep yield curve encourages refinancing activity.

How to Sum It Up. The prepayment function, or single monthly maturity (SMM), is a prepayment measure for 1 month (see Measuring Prepayment Speeds in Chapter 4) and is the sum of all the factors described. It may be derived as in steps 1 through 4.

Step 1:   Start with the base case CPR projection.

FIGURE 3.10
Yield Curve Factors

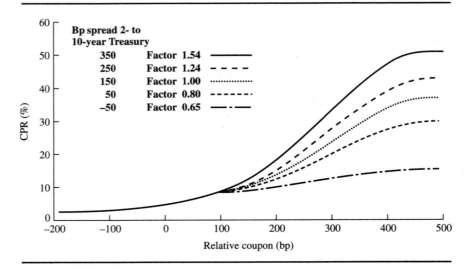

Step 2: Multiply the base CPR projection by the seasonal factor.

Step 3: Multiply the refinancing function by YC to adjust the IRS for the yield curve effect. Some analysts also multiply the base case CPR by the YC on the theory that the yield curve carries implications regarding the economic state; for example, a steep yield curve may suggest low inflation and relatively low interest rates (faster prepayments), and a flat yield curve may imply higher inflation and higher interest rates (slow prepayments).

Step 4: SMM = (Base CPR × Seasonal factor) + (Refi × YC).

Limitations of Prepayment Models

All prepayment models are basically **econometric models.** This means that their projections are predicated on the assumptions that (1) forecasted conditions will be similar to benchmark conditions in the past (1981–1982 housing recession, 1986–1987 refinancing cycle versus 1991–1992 cycle) and that those conditions are accurately contained in the model; and (2) the known "world" has not materially changed with respect to the demographic, regulatory, and structural make-up of financial intermediaries.

State of the world changes that did occur since the 1986–1987 benchmark for modeling many of the prepayment factors programmed into the prepayment models of the early 1990s include the cessation of the yearly acceleration in home prices that drove much of the home sale activity of the 1980s until 1988. Since then, home prices have been sluggish and have actually *declined* in many markets. Other factors are dissolution of the savings and loan industry, regulatory and accounting-related initiatives stemming from the 1989 FIRREA legislation, and the introduction of the yield curve effect and related mortgage forms that broadened homeowners' refinancing options.

What the Prepayment Models Missed

Other sensitive assumptions are the analysts' predictions of the business cycle, the relative degree of home affordability, and the linkage between interest rates and prepayments. In the late 1980s and early 1990s most models went astray in several respects:

1. The models carried the 1986–1987 prepayment experience

as the historic benchmark for the bull market response of prepayments to a decline in interest rates. In the 1991–1993 refinancing cycle a number of economic factors were very different from the 1986–1987 experience.

2. The underlying assumption that *any* decline in interest rates would result in an acceleration in prepayments was violated by the 1990 experience, which witnessed a temporary decoupling of the linkage between prepayments and interest rates. The linkage breakdown was largely related to the 1991–1992 recession and the cessation of the mid-1980s boom in home prices.

3. In 1988–1989, prepayment models that lacked a factor for housing turnover were forecasting prepayment speeds that were too fast because they failed to catch the decline in home sales resulting from the post-1988 cessation in home price inflation. They also neglected to identify a slower housing turnover rate related to demographic changes associated with the demise of the baby boom and a shift in the predilection of U.S. consumers from spending and borrowing to debt reduction. The prepayment models that were tracking housing turnover by 1980s standards forecast prepayments that were too fast; those that contained a housing turnover factor were better able to capture the prepayment slowdown.

4. In the 1991–1993 refinancing surge, many prepayment models were too slow in their forecasts because the burnout factor was too aggressive. The burnout factor built into most prepayment models was based on the 1986–1987 experience, when the refinancing option for most homeowners was restricted to refinancing from 30-year fixed rate to 30-year fixed rate. That experience indicated that when the IRS shrank to less than 1.5 percent there would be diminished economic incentive to refinance—that is, to refinance a 9.5 percent mortgage to 8 percent. In the 1991–1993 period, however, other mortgage forms were available and became particularly significant in the spring of 1992 when the yield curve steepened. For the holder of a 9.5 percent mortgage the effective spread ranged from 0.7 (30-year fixed to 30-year fixed) to 3.1 (30-year fixed to ARM), but the prepayment model knew only the 0.7 IRS from the 9.5 percent 30-year fixed held to the 8.8 percent 30-year fixed. The result was an extension of the refinancing option and a delay

in burnout. *Many prepayment models therefore underestimated the prepayment speeds of high premiums (9.5 percent coupon and above) in the first half of 1992.* This was later corrected with the addition of the yield curve effect to the prepayment models (see Functional Components of Prepayment Models, page 119).

5. According to research by Deepak Narula,[9] the underestimation of prepayment speeds in the spring and fall of 1992 was related to the introduction of zero-point financing. The zero-point financing lowered the cost of the refinancing transaction, thereby causing the savings required to trigger a refi to occur at a narrower differential between the mortgage rate held and that available for a refinancing.

6. Also, according to Narula's research, many prepayment models then *overestimated* the prepayment speeds of the high premiums in the first half of 1993 when mortgage rates again declined, this time to below 8 percent. The models did not account for the burnout that finally set in by 1993 for the 9.5 percent and higher coupons. That burnout was credit related, according to Narula, because by this point in the cycle the homeowners remaining on loans backing the 9.5 and above coupons consisted of those who had inadequate home equity to refinance in the face of income restrictions. By contrast, "in the 1986–1987 refinancing wave home appreciation was much stronger and credit-related burnout was not a factor."[10]

7. Many prepayment models overestimated the expected prepayment volatility of Ginnie Maes in early 1992. These securities prepaid far slower than predicted because of the impact of the newly imposed FHA insurance premium (see Impact on Low-Premium Ginnie Maes of New FHA MIP in Chapter 4). In addition, the 1991–1992 recession appeared to be especially painful for FHA borrowers, causing them to pass up refinancing opportunities for lack of the cash or job security to undertake the refinancing.

8. However, the relative sensitivity of Ginnie Mae pools versus conventionals shifted dramatically with the introduction by

---

[9]Deepak Narula, Senior Vice President, Mortgage Strategies Group, Lehman Brothers.
[10]Deepak Narula.

FHA of a streamlined refi program in October 1992, according to Narula. The streamlined refi enabled FHA borrowers to effectively achieve 100 percent financing, thereby closing the gap between FHA (i.e., Ginnie Mae) and conventional prepayment activity. Narula sees this as a *long-term trend* for Ginnie Maes.

In summary, the difficulty arises from the functional characteristic of a regression model (which is the prepayment model) that is composed of one dependent variable and one or more explanatory variables. The dependent variable is usually expressed as a rate or probability of prepayment defined as CPR or PSA. Some prepayment models restrict the explanatory variables to the basic three— interest rate sensitivity, seasonality, and pool age. In times of high interest rate volatility the interest rate-spread differential will dominate the other two variables; however, in times of modest interest rate volatility the underlying rate of housing turnover is more important—and far more difficult to input accurately (with many models it is not input at all).

It should be noted that most of the variables implicit in the prepayment model are themselves variable. The lag response, for example, is keyed as three to four months with most models. However, at the start of the refinancing cycles in 1986 and again in 1992, refinancing activity became so heavy that the actual lag time was stretched out because of the extra processing time required to accommodate an overflow of business. However, by late 1992 mortgage originators had become so efficient the lag shortened to about six weeks. The hightened efficiency of originators, and aggressive marketing programs targeted to refinancing opportunities, together with the zero-point refinancing already described, contributed to higher than expected refinancing activity in late 1992 and early 1993.

Another inconsistent factor has been the burnout syndrome. Burnout proved to be far less protective of the call risk of somewhat seasoned premium-priced coupons in the 1992 refinancing experience than was the case in 1986–1987 when the primary refinancing was from 30-year fixed rate to 30-year fixed rate. Burnout was further muted with the introduction of zero-point refinancing, which substantially reduced the cost to refi. So the core prepayment rate may be adjusting to a higher plateau.

Finally, the model primarily predicts the *availability* of the opportunity to refinance. Accurately predicting the percentage of in the money prepayment options that will actually be exercised has so far proved elusive. The changes in housing economics from the 1980s to the 1990s as they relate to regional and national patterns in home prices, demographics, consumer spending patterns, and household formations occurred at too rapid a pace to be accurately programmed on a timely basis.

Longer-range projections are often still faulty in their lack of recognition that demographic and life style changes which took place between the 1980s and 1990s will govern the underlying core demand for housing (see Chapter 5).

Telerate Advance Factor Service

In May 1991 Telerate Mortgage Market Services introduced a market data base as a means of predicting prepayment rates. Called Advance Factor Services (AFS), the service estimates prepayment trends based on data gathered from title search companies. AFS has an exclusive agreement with some 50 title search companies across the nation that notify AFS whenever a title search occurs relating to mortgages backing Ginnie Maes and Freddie Macs.

The title search normally occurs about three months before the loan closing on a home sale, thereby providing AFS with advance notice that a given mortgage is scheduled to be retired under due on sale. Refinancings also require a title search, which normally occurs two to three weeks prior to the closing.[11] AFS publishes prepayment predictions on its market information screens, which are available to Telerate subscribers. Also available from AFS are custom prepayment predictions for private subscribers providing information by year of issue and by region.

Mortgage Bankers Association Weekly Mortgage Application Survey

The Mortgage Bankers Association (MBA) issues a weekly report that tabulates data related to mortgage applications. The data are compiled from a survey of about 20 national mortgage banking companies. Data relating to loan purpose (purchase or refinance) are consolidated into indexes, one to track applications to purchase mortgages and the other to track applications to refinance. The baseline date for the indexes is March 16, 1990. Changes in application

---

[11]Some analysts have pointed out that orders for title searches may be overstated because of multiple mortgage applications.

volume are subsequently reported by purpose as a percentage of the March 16 application volume. (See Tracking the 1991–1993 Prepayment Experience in Chapter 4 for a detailed discussion of the MBA refinancing index through the 1991–1993 refinancing cycle.)

Applications of OAS

Clearly, a means to derive a proper value for the prepayment option is a significant contribution to the ability to identify the best relative values within the MBS market. Since it is the value of the prepayment option that causes the price of the MBS to deviate from that of a comparable straight-coupon bond, a properly designed OAS model incorporates all of the valuation variables in order to properly price the MBS.

The distinguishing characteristic of OAS-derived pricing is that when the MBS duration shortens, negative durations and negative convexities are derived and applied—as against Macaulay duration, which does not recognize the possibility of a negative duration. In addition, options-based methodology may be applied to the valuation of strips and CMO-related derivatives. The OAS is also applicable to ARMs, where the option analysis applies more specifically to the interest rate caps, which are valued as short puts. The most common application of the OAS model is to derive the convexity cost, zero-volatility OAS, and option-adjusted duration.

Zero-Volatility OAS. Zero-volatility OAS is the benchmark OAS—also called the zero-volatility spread. It is the spread to the *entire* Treasury curve assuming that interest rate volatility is zero—that is, that the current yield curve tells the whole story. One interest rate path is used as both the current rate *and* the forward rate curve. The zero-volatility spread is *not* comparable to the static spread because, like OAS, it is relative to the entire Treasury curve, not just a single point on the curve.

Convexity Cost. Convexity cost is the reduction in static yield spread due to the value of the prepayment option. The static spread minus the convexity cost equals the OAS (see Table 3.3).

Option-Adjusted Duration

Duration as defined by Macaulay measures the percentage change in the price of a security to a change in the market-required yield. The three principal applications of duration are:

TABLE 3.3
OAS Analysis for Sequential CMOs (November 2, 1992)

Base Treasury	Static[a] Spread	Average Life	Macaulay Duration	Zero[b] Spread	Zero A/L	Option-Adjusted Duration	Convexity Cost	OAS
2-year	140	2.4	2.2	77	3.0	3.1	4	73
3-year	158	3.4	3.0	80	4.5	4.4	6	74
4-year	142	4.3	3.7	78	5.9	5.3	6	72
5-year	140	5.6	4.6	88	7.8	6.2	5	83
7-year	135	7.5	5.7	89	10.2	7.3	4	85
10-year	130	10.5	7.0	92	13.8	8.6	3	89
30-year	70	18.5	9.2	88	22.0	9.8	1	87

[a]Static, or stated, spread to Treasuries.
[b]Zero-volatility OAS.

Source: Lehman Brothers Fixed Income Research.

1. To predict the change in the price sensitivity of one security (perhaps to be purchased) or of two (to evaluate the impact of a swap) or of a whole portfolio by comparing the durations of the securities to be bought or sold.
2. To define hedge ratios for trading positions or to desensitize a portfolio.
3. To define asset/liability matching objectives or to structure a managed arbitrage such as a coupon swap or to leverage earnings through spread arbitrage, matching an asset to a funding liability.

The difficulty with MBSs is that with the introduction of prepayments, the price no longer changes as a linear function of price to yield. Furthermore, the investor-required value of the MBS to Treasury yield spread changes as prepayment speeds accelerate (the spread widens) or slow down (the spread narrows).

The **option-adjusted duration (OAD)** is the price sensitivity of the MBS taking into account the impact of prepayments. It must be computed electronically because no closed-end formulas have been defined to deal with the many variables associated with payment uncertainty.

Negative Duration

Macaulay's duration informs us that price is inversely sensitive to yield: As yields decline, the price rises, and vice versa. This relationship holds for MBSs as long as the prepayment option holds only intrinsic value—that is, the prepayment option even when out of the money always has some value just because it always has the potential to become operative. When the option goes into the money, however, the MBS price becomes compressed and in extreme situations may even decline as interest rates decline. **Negative duration,** therefore, describes a relationship between price and yield wherein the MBS price is changing in the same direction as interest rates. The duration of the MBS is said to be negative to distinguish it from positive duration, which denotes the MBS price is changing in the opposite direction as yield. The significance of negative duration will be apparent in Chapters 8 and 14, which deal, respectively, with support class CMO bonds and strips. With MBSs in which the prepayment option is dominant the duration shortens as interest rates decline and lengthens as rates rise.

OAS-Adjusted Convexity

Convexity describes the rate at which duration changes in response to changes in interest rates. Clearly, investors prefer securities that become less price sensitive when interest rates rise (duration shortens) and enjoy maximum price sensitivity when interest rates decline (duration lengthens). Such securities are positively convex.

Negative convexity describes securities whose duration lengthens when rates rise and shortens when rates decline, for example, high-premium MBSs, IO strips, and some highly prepayment-sensitive CMO derivatives. It may be said that investors in negatively convex bonds own securities with limited price performance when interest rates decline but may enjoy hedge benefits when interest rates rise.

Limitations of OAS Methodology

OAS modeling is dazzling in its capacity to take into account a range of variables. Users of OAS technology must appreciate, however, that the results are a product of a number of assumptions intuitively derived in large part by the analyst operating the OAS model. These variables include the analyst's assumptions concerning the impact of seasonality, the link between interest rate direction and prepayment sensitivity, and the underlying rate of housing turnover; and, as noted earlier, a major variable is the volatility assumption applied by the analyst.

Furthermore, even given that the above assumptions are reasonably close to the mark, the option model by itself is still incapable of capturing all of the economic and demographic variables associated with each homeowner who makes up the series of options embedded in the pool. Consider, for example, the large number of MBSs remaining outstanding with underlying mortgage rates in excess of 12 percent in spite of years of opportunity to refinance (see Table 4.11 in Chapter 4).

Finally, the OAS model tends to bias the value of the prepayment option in accordance with the assumption that the shape of the yield curve is a predictor of the direction of interest rates. Thus, when the yield curve is positively sloped, the OAS model assigns higher probabilities to the rising interest rate paths generated by the Monte Carlo simulator, and the prepayment model, therefore, assigns a higher distribution probability to longer average-life assumptions. This bias became most evident in the spring of 1992 when OAS designations for IO strips were as high as 800 based on the model's bias that since the yield curve was steep, prepayment speeds would soon slow down dramatically. With OAS models linked to a prepayment model that incorporates the yield curve effect, there will be compensation because application of the yield curve factor accelerates prepayments when the prepayment model reads the steep yield curve.

Total-Return Analysis

A major theme of this text is that many MBS investors overpay for stated yield and undervalue good potential price performance (that is, good convexity characteristics). MBS investors have historically been dominated by yield buyers, who are logically attracted to MBSs with very high stated yield spreads to Treasuries. However, when the stated yield is high, so generally is the prepayment risk and the consequent probability that with increases in market volatility the stated yield at the time of purchase will not be realized. In other words, the bond fails to perform. Indeed, a greater risk, which many people do not realize, is the risk that MBS spreads may widen. Widening will generally occur in periods of rising market volatility, particularly if the volatility is biased to higher prices—that is, lower interest rates (increased prepayment risk).

Perhaps the most rigorous simulation of MBS performance is measuring the **total rate of return** against a predefined holding-period return (HPR), a process referred to as **scenario analysis,** or **horizon analysis.** The components of total rate of return consist of coupon income, the scheduled principal plus prepayments and other unscheduled principal (defaults), reinvestment income on all P&I cash flows, and market gains or losses recognized upon termination of a predefined holding period (horizon). A total-return analysis generally provides the best estimate of the potential performance of an MBS against other fixed-income securities. Total rate of return is expressed in Equation 3.16:

$$TR = \frac{(PVe - PVb) + PI + R}{PVb} \qquad (3.16)$$

where

TR = Total return

PVb = The price of the investment at the beginning of the holding period

PVe = The price at the end of the period

PI = The total PI payments received over the period

R = The total reinvestment income received over the holding period

The analysis is generally performed electronically, stressing the proposed investment to a series of interest rate scenarios whereby the interest rate is shifted up and down by 100 basis points increments. The prepayment rate is then shifted according to projections generated by a prepayment model. A yield, average life, and HPR are thereby generated for each of the scenarios.

A summary of the advantages and disadvantages of total-return analysis is given in Box 3.2. The distinguishing characteristic of the

---

BOX 3.2
Synopsis of Total-Return Considerations

Advantages

- Begins to show risk.
- Begins to be a useful diagnostic tool.
- Works well with simple scenarios.
- Is more rigorous than CFY.
- Is easier to comprehend than OAS technology.

Disadvantages

- Is effective only with a small number of scenarios.
- Doesn't generally incorporate yield curve dynamics.
- Requires accurate workout prices—often quite difficult to have confidence in.
- Long horizons capture reinvestment assumptions more than risk in the bond.
- Results are not succinct.

total-return valuation method is that it estimates the terminal market value of the portfolio asset. This attribute makes total return truly a *valuation method,* whereas OAS is more the ultimate (so far) *pricing model* for MBS valuation analysis.

Total return is generally applied as a horizon analysis, taking into account the impact of up and down incremental shifts in interest rates. Yield curve shifts may be shown as well, to reflect the impact of pure interest rate changes. The basic total-return analysis is generally run to parallel shifts in interest rates (the short and long ends of the Treasury yield curve are assumed to shift in tandem— for example, parallel). A further testing of total return to flat, positive, and negative yield curve vectors is sometimes applied, particularly if the investor is liability sensitive—for example, a thrift institution carrying longer-term assets with short-term, interest rate-sensitive liabilities. Table 3.4 illustrates the calculation of the HPR of a CMO, the FHLMC R128E class.

One note of caution here is a comment on the methodology applied in calculating the terminal price, which is to hold yield spreads constant. In reality, if interest rates have declined, the price of a typical fixed-income security will, of course, increase, and the price increase may be calculated by application of Macaulay's duration. With an MBS, however, declining interest rates suggest an acceleration in prepayments that would lead to price compression. Stated another way, the MBS to Treasury yield spread will widen, leading to some reduction in the total price appreciation that may be realized.

TABLE 3.4
Calculation of HPR, FHLMC R128E

Beginning price = 107-04					
Yield curve shifts	+200	+100	0	−100	−200
Ending PSA	140	150	185	335	505
Yield	7.32	7.32	7.32	7.18	6.43
Ending price	98-12	102-10	106-14	110-17	110-08
WAL	5.01	5.01	5.01	4.38	2.48
HPR	0.24	3.83	7.54	11.16	10.89

Source: Lehman Brothers Fixed Income Research.

Scenario-Specific HPR Case Study

Inherent to the total-return analysis, of course, is integration of the sensitivity of prepayments to interest rate shifts. The objective of the horizon analysis is to project the impact of shifting interest rates and changes in prepayments on the performance of the MBS.

The robustness of the total-return valuation process is illustrated in Figure 3.11, which illustrates scenario-specific HPRs for various Fannie Maes to a 1-year (12-month) holding period. The HPR of Fannie Maes is tested to six interest rate scenarios (three rising and three declining) against the base case, or current interest rate scenario.

Seasoned FNMA 8s

The seasoned FNMA 8s in Figure 3.11 display good convexity, showing a strong increase in total return in the falling interest rate scenarios and a decline in HPR in the rising interest rate scenarios. This performance is attributable entirely to the strong price appreciation that results when rates decline and the loss of price when rates increase. The overwhelming impact of price appreciation/depreciation on the total return of a positively convex security in rising and declining interest rate scenarios is amply illustrated here.

FIGURE 3.11
Scenario-Specific HPR Comparison

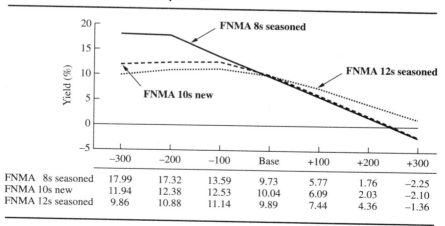

	−300	−200	−100	Base	+100	+200	+300
FNMA 8s seasoned	17.99	17.32	13.59	9.73	5.77	1.76	−2.25
FNMA 10s new	11.94	12.38	12.53	10.04	6.09	2.03	−2.10
FNMA 12s seasoned	9.86	10.88	11.14	9.89	7.44	4.36	−1.36

Source: Lehman Brothers Fixed Income Research.

The seasoned 8s enjoy such excellent price appreciation because they are priced at a discount in the base case scenario. And since they are seasoned, the acceleration in prepayments is not as rapid as with newly issued pools. (For a discussion of the prepayment sensitivity of new versus seasoned MBS pools, see Pool Age: Seasoning in Chapter 4.)

Newly Issued FNMA 10s

The newly issued FNMA 10s in Figure 3.11 offer a higher yield (10.04 percent) in the base case because these pools are less convex than the seasoned pools. Although a new pool is relatively insensitive to prepayments for two years or so, ultimately it has more potential for prepayment stress than a seasoned pool.

The HPR of the new FNMA 10s increases somewhat as interest rates decline, but not nearly as much as the discount-priced 8s. Note that in the −300 basis points scenario the HPR of the 10s actually declines; the reason is that with this much decline in interest rates the new 10s start to prepay rapidly. Here is an instance of the impact of negative convexity induced by the exercise of the homeowner's prepayment call option.

In the rising-rate scenarios the HPR of the new 10s declines pretty much in line with the seasoned 8s. Although the 10s retain some initial yield advantage over the 8s, in the +300 basis points scenario the margin is very thin.

Seasoned FNMA 12s

The FNMA 12s in Figure 3.11 are priced to a slight premium, and although they enjoy some increase in HPR, to 11.14 percent in the −100 basis points scenario, the HPR increase for the 12s is less than that for either the 10s or the 8s. And as prepayments fairly quickly overwhelm the performance of the 12s in the −200 and −300 scenarios, the HPR declines. This is so because price compression actually forces the price to decline in the severe bull market scenarios. Note, on the other hand, that in the rising-rate scenarios, although the 12s lose some HPR, they significantly outperform the 10s and the 8s. The reason is that the 12s benefit from the extension in average life as the interest rate increase shuts the refinancing window for the premiums. With the ensuing extension of collateral life, more interest is generated for a longer average life, thus generating to the MBS holder greater interest cash flow. The extension in average life, in addition, enables the investor to earn the 12 percent coupon for a longer time than had originally been anticipated, thus enhancing the HPR of this investment.

Scenario-Specific Average-Life Comparison

Figure 3.12 illustrates the extension and call risk characteristics of the three Fannie Maes just examined. Of the three, the newly issued pool has the greatest swing in average life, with an 8.18-year range from the shortest (1.94) to the longest (10.12). This wide range is due primarily to the vulnerability of the new pool to very high prepayment speeds when it passes through its first refinancing cycle. The premium-priced FNMA 12s do not shorten much—they already have a relatively short average life—but show vulnerability to significant extension in the high interest rate scenario. The seasoned FNMA 8s display the shortest swing—only 4.05 years—from the high to the low interest rate scenarios. This short swing illustrates the interest value in seasoned MBS pools—they resist prepayment stress better than the new pools, having likely already passed through at least one refinancing cycle. At the same time, because of the steady turnover of mortgages seasoned 10 years or more, seasoned pools retain some prepayment sensitivity in the rising interest rate scenarios better than new pools, which pretty much go dead in the water when rates increase early in the life of the pool.

FIGURE 3.12
Scenario-Specific Average-Life Comparison

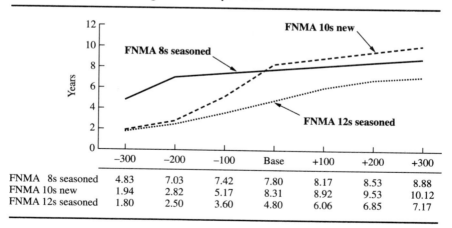

	−300	−200	−100	Base	+100	+200	+300
FNMA 8s seasoned	4.83	7.03	7.42	7.80	8.17	8.53	8.88
FNMA 10s new	1.94	2.82	5.17	8.31	8.92	9.53	10.12
FNMA 12s seasoned	1.80	2.50	3.60	4.80	6.06	6.85	7.17

Source: Lehman Brothers Fixed Income Research.

Breakeven Analysis

A good litmus test of relative value is to determine how much prepayments would have to increase, or MBS to Treasury spreads widen, for the MBS to underperform a comparable-maturity Treasury security. Investors may assess the potential value of an MBS by comparing its breakeven prepayment rate to the actual observed prepayment rate and then determining how much the MBS prepayment rate could change before the MBS would perform no better than the benchmark security. The benchmark security might be a current-coupon MBS trading close to par or a comparable-duration Treasury. Since mortgages prepay at par, an increase in prepayments would raise the yield for discount coupons but lower it for premium coupons. If the breakeven rate for a discount coupon far exceeds the most recent prepayment rate, the security may be considered rich to the benchmark because its prepayment rate has to increase substantially in order to raise the yield to that of the benchmark coupon.

Conversely, a premium coupon is considered cheap to the benchmark if its most recent prepayment rate lies far below, and seems unlikely to approach, the breakeven rate. If the premium coupon is yielding far above the benchmark, its prepayment rate would have to be raised to equate its yield with that of the benchmark. Table 3.5 illustrates a breakeven analysis of GNMAs with coupons ranging from 8.5 percent to 12 percent.

Although generally a good analytical tool, this traditional breakeven analysis is seriously limited when dealing with premium coupons: It does not recognize that rising prepayment rates shorten the duration of premium coupons. Since shorter-duration securities provide lower yields than longer-duration securities, in a positively sloped yield curve environment premium coupons need not yield the same as the benchmark. A more realistic breakeven analysis, therefore, would incorporate the term structure of interest rates and compare mortgage securities to their comparable-duration Treasuries.

Starting from the formula for HPR, we may reverse engineer a breakeven spread as follows.[12] The basic total-return formula may be simplified as Equation 3.17:

---

[12]This analysis of breakeven yield spread was provided by John Tierney, Lehman Brothers.

TABLE 3.5
Breakeven Analysis (GNMA MBS Coupons, 8.5–12 Percent)

GNMA Coupons	Duration-Comparable Treasury	Static Spread[a]	Rates Unchanged		-50		+50	
			6 Months	12 Months	6 Months	12 Months	6 Months	12 Months
8.5	7	1.34	+12	+24	+18	+30	+5	+16
9.0	7	1.44	+13	+26	+18	+30	+7	+20
9.5	7	1.6	+14	+30	+15	+30	+10	+27
10.0	7	1.71	+16	+35	+7	+25	+15	+32
10.5	5	1.74	+22	+50	+11	+40	+15	+42
11.0	5	1.72	+24	+53	-16	+10	+29	+60
11.5	4	1.41	+22	+50	-42	-25	+47	+70
12.0	4	1.09	+18	+40	-39	-25	+59	+80

[a]Amount the static yield spreads must widen (basis points spread: bps) for the HPR on the security to be equal to the HPR on the comparable-duration Treasury. For example, if interest rates remain unchanged, the static spread of GNMA 8.5s can widen 24 basis points to a 12-month horizon before the HPR of the GNMA 8.5s would only break even with the comparable-duration Treasury.

Source: Lehman Brothers Fixed Income Research.

$$TR = \frac{EP + \frac{C}{12} \times M - BP}{BP} \tag{3.17}$$

where

TR = The estimated total return to the selected horizon

EP = The ending price

C = The annual coupon

M = The holding period in months

BP = The beginning price

The total-return equation may be restated as Equation 3.18:

$$EP = BP(1 + TR) - \left[\frac{C \times 12 \times M}{12} \right] \tag{3.18}$$

Assume

BP = 100

C = 12

M = 6 months

TR = 5% (10% per year)

Inserting these assumptions into Equation 3.18:

$$EP = 100(1 + .05) - \left[\frac{12 \times 100 \times 6}{12} \right]$$

we derive Equation 3.19:

$$EP = 105 - 6 \atop EP = 99 \tag{3.19}$$

The breakeven spread could be derived by means of electronic analysis:

1. Identify the prepayment speed of the collateral at a price of 100.

2. Derive the prepayment resulting from a price decline to 99. (*Note:* The price has fallen, so implicitly yields have risen.)

3. Assume a new spread (*BP*) that would cause the price to decline to 99. For example, Equation 3.20:

$$BPS(EP) - BPS(BP) = Breakeven\ BPS \qquad (3.20)$$

where

BPS   = Basis point spread

BPS(EP) = Basis point spread at ending price

BPS(BP) = Basis point spread at beginning price

Assume

BPS(EP) = 127

BPS(BP) = 120

Then

$$127 - 120 = 7\ \text{basis points} \qquad (3.21)$$

The breakeven spread is 7 basis points.

Assumptions

- There is no reinvestment risk.
- The total return derived from the breakeven analysis process is expressed in mortgage-equivalent yield (MEY). Since the total return of a Treasury spread "bogey" would be on a bond-equivalent yield (BEY) basis, the results must be converted to a MEY basis to use the formula just given.

4. HOW DO I APPLY RELATIVE VALUE ANALYSIS?

The first step in identifying relative value within the fixed-income market as a whole—or, more likely, within a market segment of specific interest, such as the mortgage market—is to construct a matrix of relative returns available for a range of maturities and credit risks.

Defining the Risk/Reward Continuum

Figure 3.13 is an example of identifying relative stated yield spreads for a range of MBSs and asset-backed securities (ABSs; these include securitized consumer loans such as auto and credit card receivables

FIGURE 3.13

The Relative Value Matrix

Low risk   Moderate risk

	Security	Agency-Guaranteed MBSs	AAA Super Senior	AAA	AA	Subordinated A/NR	Whole Loans
		Basis Point Yield Spread to Comparable-Duration Treasury					
1-year and less	Government						
	Agencies	5					
	5-year CMO floater	60	85	95	105		
	1-year CMT ARM	75			150	100-250	200
	11th Dist. COFI ARM (monthly)	71		105	115	100-220	180
	Clean CMO	65	140	160	195	100-220	
	Auto ABS		100				
2-year	Government						
	Agencies	7					
	PAC CMO	83	120	125			
	Clean CMO	140	225	235		100-250	
	Credit cards (premium)		65			100	
	Fixed HEL (premium)		140				
	5-year balloon			110	125	150	

Maturity	Instrument					
3-year	Government					
	Agencies	16				
	PAC CMO	86	125	135	150	
	Clean CMO	155	220	230	250	100-250
	Credit cards (premium)		60			140
5-year	Government					
	Agencies	17				
	PAC CMO	93	130	140		
	Clean CMO	140	225	235		100-250
	Credit cards (premium)		65			100
	15-year FNMA PT	113				
7-year	Government					
	Agencies	22				
	PAC CMO	96	130	140		
	Clean CMO	138	200	210		100-250
10-year	Government					
	Agencies	24				
	PAC CMO	92	130	140		
	Clean CMO	127	200	210		
	30-year FNMA PT	122				250

Source: Lehman Brothers Fixed Income Research.

145

and home equity loans [HELs]) at year-end 1992. The relative value matrix illustrated here defines a range of maturities of from 1 to 10 years (vertical axis) and credits from federal agency-guaranteed MBSs through AAA, AA privately issued CMOs, and whole-loan collateralized MBSs to whole loans (horizontal axis).

The matrix may be viewed as a first castoff simply to identify rich/cheap sectors within the MBS/ABS secondary market at a point in time. For example, a 1-year constant-maturity Treasury (CMT) ARM at a spread of 75 basis points, given its ability to adjust upward in rate should the yield curve flatten, seems to be a good relative value compared to a 1-year sequential-pay CMO at a spread of 65 basis points to the curve. Likewise, AAA-rated, 1-year-average-life, whole-loan CMOs appear relatively cheap at a spread of 160 basis points. The 75 basis points offered in excess of the 1-year agency-guaranteed CMO appears generous for the difference in credit. Most of the extra yield is offered as compensation for the lesser liquidity of the privately issued CMO. Two-year HELs at a premium bear some risk of early call, but at a spread of 140 bear closer analysis as possibly cheap. Looking farther down the maturity scale, note that a 5-year sequential-pay CMO at 140 seems to offer good value against the 5-year PAC CMO at a spread of 93; the 10-year sequential-pay CMO at a spread of 127 looks attractive against the 30-year Fannie Mae pass-through at a spread of 122, and so on.

This approach, of course, is only a starting point. Relative value analysis must be applied to define the relative prepayment and credit risk of these securities. The analytical tools described in this chapter provide the means to undertake a more rigorous risk/reward analysis.

CHAPTER 4

DYNAMICS OF MORTGAGE PREPAYMENTS

KEY QUESTIONS

1. What are the principal factors that affect prepayment dynamics?
2. What are the demographic considerations?
3. How do seasonal cycles affect prepayments?
4. How do economic and demographic considerations affect home sale activity?
5. What sparks the incentive to refinance?
6. What does the term "seasoning" really mean?
7. What is the impact of prepayments?
8. How do I measure prepayments?

Prepayment dynamics in the 1990s are likely to be very different from those of the 1980s, with volatility probably lower, assuming mortgage rates remain in the range of 7.5 to 9 percent. The base level may be somewhat higher than it was in the late 1980s and early 1990s given the outlook for a revival in the rate of household formations through the mid-1990s. This chapter examines these differences and provides an in-depth review of the factors that drive prepayment activity.

For reference purposes historic mortgage and prepayment rate cycles are illustrated in Figures 4.1 and 4.2. Figure 4.3 portrays the Freddie Mac survey rate for 30-year, fixed-rate mortgages from January 7, 1984 through June 11, 1993. Every Wednesday the agency conducts a survey of mortgage commitment rates, assuming 2 points to be paid at closing.

FIGURE 4.1
Prepayments, FNMA 7.5s

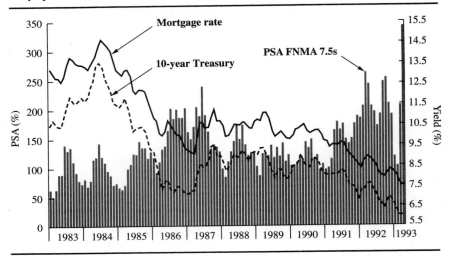

Source: Lehman Brothers Fixed Income Research.

FIGURE 4.2
Prepayments, FNMA 10s

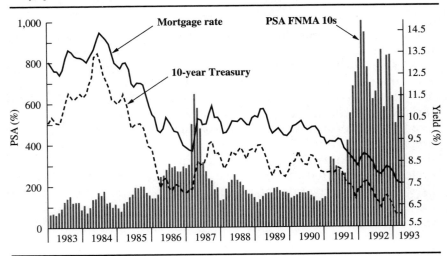

Source: Lehman Brothers Fixed Income Research.

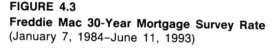

FIGURE 4.3
Freddie Mac 30-Year Mortgage Survey Rate
(January 7, 1984–June 11, 1993)

Source: Lehman Brothers Fixed Income Research.

1. WHAT ARE THE PRINCIPAL FACTORS THAT AFFECT PREPAYMENT DYNAMICS?

A prepayment on a mortgage is any payment made in addition to the scheduled payments called for under the terms of the mortgage. *The three principal sources of prepayments are housing turnover (home sales), refinancings, and involuntary prepayments related to default, divorce, death, and other factors. In general, home sales account for the bulk of prepayments for discount-priced coupons, whereas refinancing dominates prepayments for premium-priced coupons* (see Box 4.1). The prepayment is typically made for the full amount of the remaining unpaid principal balance of the mortgage, although partial prepayments, or curtailments, are sometimes made to build home equity or to accelerate the amortization schedule. Curtailments have recently become more common.

BOX 4.1
Developing a View on Prepayments

Short Term

- Seasonality: Are you now looking at winter or summer prepayment speeds?
- Recent path of interest rates: Will it drive prepayments up or down?
- Changes in housing market strength: Is housing turnover picking up or slowing? Use the past two to three months' prepayment experience as a base. Are prepayments likely to increase or decrease?
- What is the outlook for interest rate changes?
- Is there any secular MBS program change, for example, an FHA insurance premium increase?

Intermediate Term

- What are the recent and expected paths of interest rates?
- What are expectations concerning the economy and the housing market?

Longer Term

- The 1980s were mostly interest rate driven.
- The 1990s will be mostly demographically driven.

Other Aids

- Econometric prepayment models.
- Historic prepayments.
- MBA mortgage application survey: 2- to 4-month lead on prepayment patterns.
- AFS (title search data): 1- to 3-month lead on prepayment projections.
- Telerate/PSA median: Wall Street prepayment projections.

Source: This overview of prepayments was provided by Nicole Vianna.

2. WHAT ARE THE DEMOGRAPHIC CONSIDERATIONS?

The most visible demographic consideration is the distinction between FHA/VA and conventional borrowers. Regional considerations are highly significant as well—so much so that the focus of Chapter 5 is demographics and regional diversity.

The cost of the home, which is the principal determinant of the size of the mortgage, is also an important factor in terms of prepayments. Upscale homes tend to turn over more often than less expensive ones, leading to faster prepayments on large mortgages. In economic hard times, however, large homes are difficult both to sell and to obtain financing for (except at very low LTVs), so that prepayments tend to be slower for large mortgages.

FHA/VA versus Conventional Collateral

A constant is the difference between FHA-insured and VA-guaranteed collateral and conventional (not government-insured or guaranteed) collateral. Government-backed loans have consistently demonstrated less prepayment sensitivity than conventional loans to virtually all prepayment factors. One reason for the lower sensitivity of FHA/VA loans is that they are assumable by the new home buyer, a consideration which has become important since the post-1988 moderation in home price increases has made assumability more realistic. Conventional loans contain a due on sale requirement; that is, the mortgage must be paid off upon sale of the home.

One notable exception to this general rule occurs when prepayment activity is in decline following a period of high prepayment activity. The FHA/VA collateral is slower to burn out than conventional loans. Therefore Ginnie Mae premiums may tend to prepay faster for a short time than their conventional counterparts until the burnout takes effect on the government loans.

Assumability becomes less of an issue with time as the LTV ratio of the mortgage declines because of a combination of reduction of the balance of the mortgage and price appreciation of the house. At a point the down payment required to assume the outstanding mortgage becomes too great an expense for most home buyers.

There are also demographic differences between FHA/VA and conventional borrowers. On average, FHA and VA mortgagors earn lower incomes and put down smaller down payments than conventional mortgagors, making refinancing more difficult. Because of the smaller average mortgage balance carried by FHA and VA borrowers, refinancing is less advantageous because the application and appraisal costs are fixed. The less affluent FHA borrower often does not have the cash required to refinance. Furthermore, the 30-year FHA/VA borrower has fewer refinancing alternatives. There is no FHA/VA balloon program and as yet no VA ARM program. Obtaining 15-year financing would mean an increase in the monthly payment unless the reduction in the interest rate is over 300 basis points.

Impact on Low-Premium Ginnie Maes of New FHA MIP[1]

In July 1991, under the National Affordable Housing (NAH) Act of 1990, a new monthly insurance premium (MIP) structure for FHA single-family mortgages was imposed for the first time. (This supplemental MIP was withdrawn for refis in July 1991.) The annual fee, amounting to 50 basis points, was in addition to the premium paid at the closing of the loan.

The new fee reduced the sensitivity of above-market rate FHA mortgages while it was in force because it effectively raised the coupon on 1991-originated FHA mortgages by 50 basis points. The extent of the impact of the MIP on the refinancing incentive of FHA homeowners was also a function of the current LTV, which determined whether the FHA borrower could avoid the fee by refinancing into a conventional loan. Most homeowners with low LTV mortgages were able to avoid the cost of the MIP by shifting to conventional refinancing. However, those who required a loan with an LTV of 85 percent or higher found conventional financing either unavailable or uneconomic compared to FHA financing, even with the MIP. Freddie Mac and Fannie Mae will not pool loans with LTVs above 90 percent, and both require private mortgage insurance (PMI) for LTVs between 80 and 90 percent. The result was a significant muting of GNMA 9 and 9.5 percent MBSs during the first 1991–1992 refinancing experience (Table 4.1).

---

[1]This discussion of the new fee is from Nicole Vianna, "New FHA Fees Make Low Premium GNMAs Look Attractive," *MBS Outlook*. New York: Lehman Brothers, April 1991.

TABLE 4.1

GNMA versus FNMA Prepayments (PSA), May 1991 versus January 1992 (9-10 percent)

	May 1991			*January 1992*		
Coupon	*GNMA*	*FNMA*	*Difference*	*GNMA*	*FNMA*	*Difference*
9.0	120	173	53	133	325	192
9.5	141	211	70	257	596	339
10.0	201	325	124	402	748	346

Source: Lehman Brothers Fixed Income Research.

3. HOW DO SEASONAL CYCLES AFFECT PREPAYMENTS?[2]

Absent significant shifts in interest rates or boom/bust economics, the seasonal cycle is the major influence on prepayment activity. Prepayments are consistently highest in the spring (starting in April) and summer (peak in August), slower in the late fall (starting in November), and at the bottom in the winter (lowest in February). The school calendar is an important factor because most families prefer to move over the summer, between school years. In addition, new family formations tend to be highest from May through September. Interestingly, the seasonal cycle is apparent even when other factors such as interest rates are also influencing housing turnover, as shown in Figure 4.4.

Figure 4.4, prepared by Nicole Vianna, who also provided the comments related to it, profiles prepayment patterns absent refinancings (GNMA 8s have been below the refinancing threshold since the early 1970s, although they became refinanceable again in the spring of 1993) and reflects the pure seasonal effect with pools issued in 1977. The figure illustrates the steady, year-in and year-out seasonal cycle displayed by the seasonal, 1977-issue GNMA 8s. The newer-production 1987 GNMA 8s, which have very low CPRs in their year of issue but increasing CPRs as they age, nevertheless display a seasonal pattern even as they are seasoning. Notice the gradual sloping of the prepayment pattern of the 1987-issue 8s as they season (PSA smooths out this effect; the prepayment pattern

---

[2]This discussion of seasonality is based on research developed by Nicole Vianna.

FIGURE 4.4
Seasonal Prepayment Patterns in CPR, GNMA 8s, 1977 and 1987 Issues

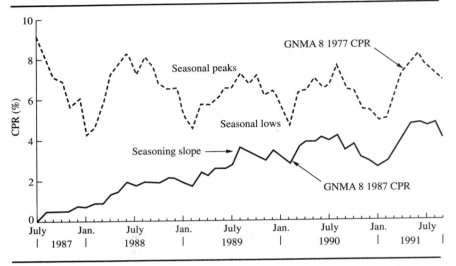

Source: Nicole Vianna, Lehman Brothers.

here is in CPR). It is also interesting to note that the very high CPRs for the 1987 peak partially reflect the strong housing market prevailing at the time—which, of course, was also near the peak period of the 1986–1987 refinancing cycle.

Figure 4.5, also prepared and commented on by Nicole Vianna, demonstrates that seasonality is very evident when prepayments are measured in PSA. Note that most of the seasoning slope in the 1987 issue of GNMA 8s has been eliminated by application of the PSA prepayment measure. Note also that the level for the 1987 originations is muted by the loss of home price appreciation from 1988 into 1993. The swing from the base prepayment speed to the seasonal peak and trough is about 25 percent, as shown in Figure 4.6.

4. HOW DO ECONOMIC AND DEMOGRAPHIC CONSIDERATIONS AFFECT HOME SALES ACTIVITY?

Prepayments made to pay off the mortgage on the sale of the home are a function of housing turnover and are most responsive to the overall demand for housing. (See Chapter 5 for a look at demo-

FIGURE 4.5
Prepayments in PSA, GNMA 8s, New versus Seasoned

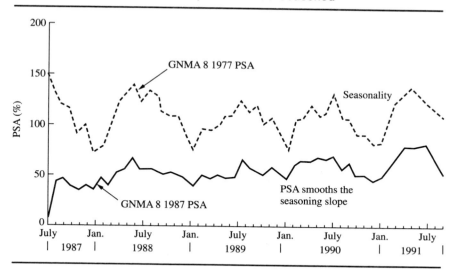

Source: Nicole Vianna, Lehman Brothers.

FIGURE 4.6
Seasonal Prepayment Factors, GNMA 8s, 1977 Issue

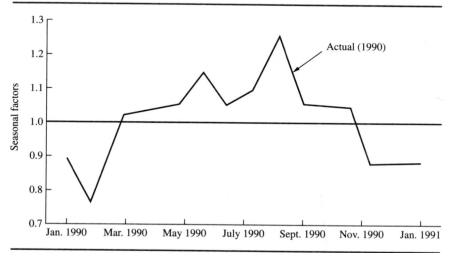

Source: Salomon Brothers Mortgage Research.

graphic trends that will have an impact on home sales activity in the 1990s.) Housing demand, in turn, is a function of the relative affordability of home financing, house prices, and demographic factors, which include family formations and growth in family size, migration patterns from region to region, and job transfers.

The general level of economic activity has a strong impact on the relocation decision, which may be positive or negative. The overall level of economic activity as well as regional migration patterns affects housing turnover. Good economic times raise consumer confidence and thereby stimulate housing activity. Regional economic hardship may lead to housing turnover as well, in the form of increased out-migration and foreclosures. The evolution of new technologies stimulates housing activity, just as economic stagnation in certain regions hurts it. An example is the defense cutback of the early 1990s, which had an impact on the already vulnerable markets of Boston, New York, and St. Louis and the states of Washington and, particularly, California. The reversal of the once thriving technology industry in Massachusetts and defense activities in California are among the most memorable reversals of the late 1980s (Massachusetts) and early 1990s (California). Of course, the earlier collapse of energy-related businesses in Texas and Oklahoma served as the first of the economic slowdowns of the mid-1980s that ultimately contributed to the demise of the housing boom in 1988 and the ensuing recession of 1991. On the other hand, it did stimulate migration.

The profile of population age has an important impact as well. The 20- to 30-year period following a baby boom produces a large number of first-time home buyers, an essential ingredient to stimulating the housing turnover cycle, as was evidenced from the mid-1960s through the mid-1980s. Without an ample supply of first-time home buyers, families seeking to trade up to a second home will lack buyers, thus locking them into their own first homes. As the population ages, migration patterns will shift to favor retirement homes to the extent that the stagnation in home prices permits it.

Home price inflation is also an important factor in home sales activity. When prices appreciate steadily, homeowners are encouraged to trade in on their equity to invest in a larger house. In times of home price stagnation the homeowner is locked in, in the worst case with an outstanding mortgage equal to or possibly greater than the market value of the house. At such times the house is looked upon less as an investment and more as simply a home. If more

FIGURE 4.7

Prepayments on 1986 FNMA 8.5s versus Home Sales

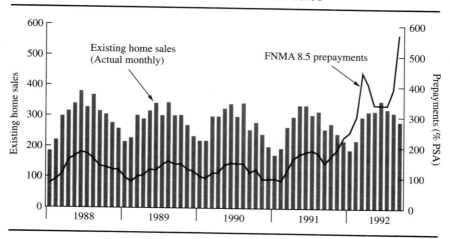

Source: Lehman Brothers Fixed Income Research.

space is required, renovations and additions to the existing home may be more economical than a house trade.

The level of interest rates also affects housing turnover. Relatively low mortgage rates (below 9.5 percent) improve home affordability and normally stimulate housing turnover (although not in 1991–1992). Very high mortgage rates (above 12.5 percent) induce a home affordability crisis that dampens home sales activity. The diversion of home sales patterns related to interest rate cycles and mortgage prepayments is illustrated in Figure 4.7. The figure shows the prepayments of seasoned FNMA 8.5s plotted against existing home sales. Note that from 1988 through 1991 there was a close correlation between rising home sales activity and an increase in FNMA 8.5 percent prepayment activity.

In 1992, prepayments of FNMA 8.5s soared even though home sales activity remained flat over the 1988 through 1990 seasonal cycles, a time when home sales activity was relatively sluggish. Mortgage rates, which fell a little below 8 percent only briefly in the fall of 1992, do not explain this surge—the drop to 8 percent is not enough to induce high levels of refis on 9 percent mortgages, which are behind the 8.5 percent pass-through rate. The explanation lies in the yield curve effect, which induced high refinancing activity into ARMs and balloons that offered rates as low as 4 to 7 percent. (The yield curve effect is examined in detail later in this chapter.)

5. WHAT SPARKS THE INCENTIVE TO REFINANCE?

Prepayments to refinance the mortgage may be made to obtain a lower mortgage rate or to take out home equity, or both. The first reason is primarily a function of a decline in interest rates and represents *the refinancing incentive;* the second reason is simply to liquidate accumulated home equity, often referred to as a cash-out refi.

If the current mortgage rate is lower than the contractual coupon rate of the existing mortgage, the homeowner can pay off the remaining principal and refinance the mortgage at a lower rate. The refinancing incentive is therefore a function of the difference between the coupon payment of the existing mortgage and the current mortgage market rate. *The incentive, therefore, truly exists as the saving in a reduced monthly mortgage payment.* It has been well documented that prepayment rates depend nonlinearly on the interest rate spread between these rates. In fact, the relationship between the prepayment rate and the interest rate is often modeled as a call option, with the strike rate being a little lower than the current market rate to reflect the cost of the refinancing transaction. In other words, the functional shape is convex, with the prepayment rates accelerating when mortgages are at a slight premium, generally 1.5 to 2 percent above market rates. Based on the 1992 refinancing experience, the required spread to induce a refinancing appears to have narrowed and is now closer to the 1.5 percent spread from the old 2 percent norm. In fact, by mid-1993, a spread of as little as 75 basis points appeared to stimulate some refinancing activity.

Another method for modeling the refinancing incentive is to define a ramp of the monthly savings to the homeowner (see Prepayment Model Functions in Chapter 3).

The Prepayment Option

The ability of the homeowner to prepay the mortgage at any time is generally viewed as a call option where the homeowner effectively has the option to call the mortgage away from the lender and the security pool at par. Since the homeowner is long that call, it follows as well that the MBS security holder is short the call.

The prepayment option inherent in the MBS pool is complicated by the fact that there is a *bundle of options embedded in the
MBS*. Each homeowner has a unique set of demographic and economic considerations. These considerations include income, market
value of the home, the amount of unencumbered equity in the
home, and the transaction cost of refinancing. Therefore, within
any given interest rate scenario the incentive and timing of a prepayment decision will differ for each homeowner. The prepayment
option held by the population of homeowners within a given pool
of mortgages, then, must be viewed as a bundle of options, each of
which is subject to somewhat different thresholds that may trigger
the exercise of that option—that is, a prepayment.

The Lock-in Effect

In the late 1990s a further consideration was added to the
homeowner's prepayment decision: If the market value of the house
has declined, the homeowner may be unable to refinance because of
negative equity (the value of the home is less than the present mortgage balance). Even if the home value is equal to the mortgage balance, refinancing will not be available because the lender will require
about 80 percent LTV. The propensity of people to borrow heavily
in the 1980s led to poor credit reports on some applicants, which
locked them out of refinancing opportunities. The dramatic upgrad-
ing of underwriting standards in the late 1980s and early 1990s pre-
cluded homeowners who had obtained a 90 or 95 percent LTV loan
in the early to mid-1980s from refinancing in the late 1980s when 80
percent LTV became the maximum. Finally, the deteriorating employment market of the early 1990s reduced the availability of cash
to many homeowners. The **lock-in effect** is therefore applicable in instances in which the homeowner (1) cannot meet the underwriting
requirements for a new loan; (2) lacks sufficient home equity to enable refinancing; or (3) does not have the cash to pay the transaction
cost of refinancing. To the extent homeowners are caught by the
lock-in effect refinancings will be muted.

Cost Considerations

Transaction costs of refinancing include not only *explicit* costs such
as discount points, legal fees, and loan origination fees but also *implicit* opportunity costs. For example, a homeowner may be in financial distress and not able to take advantage of a lower current

mortgage rate. In addition, the transaction costs burden is lower for homeowners who have built a large equity value compared with those who have a small equity value. However, transaction costs become less relevant when the stimulus to relocate is high, such as a requirement to transfer or to seek new employment elsewhere.

Whenever current mortgage interest rates drop below the rate on the existing mortgage, the homeowner faces the question of whether to refinance. To determine the attractiveness of refinancing, homeowners must weigh the prospective after-tax saving from lower interest costs against the refinancing costs of the transaction. These include mortgage fees (points), application and appraisal fees, and other costs that may be associated with obtaining a new mortgage, such as a prepayment penalty on the existing mortgage.

Impact of Points

The points charged by the originator will determine to a large degree the spread at which it is attractive to refinance.[3] For example, in instances in which the mortgage lender offers a no-point loan, the borrower may refinance for only a 1 percent spread. The other consideration is how long it will take for the homeowner to break even on the closing costs at the new loan rate.

Finally, the amount of the mortgage relative to the borrower's income will have a bearing. If the mortgage is relatively small (under $100,000) and the income is large (over $100,000), the saving from refinancing may not be sufficient to provide a refinancing incentive. On the other hand, for a homeowner on a marginal income and burdened with debt, any saving may precipitate a refinancing.

Table 4.2 illustrates how to calculate the time required to recover the transaction costs of refinancing. The vertical column at the left gives a range of transaction costs. The horizontal row at the bottom represents a range of amounts saved in the monthly mortgage payment through the refinancing. The time to recoup the transaction costs is at the point where the row and column intersect. For example, if the transaction cost is $3,000 (left column) and the monthly saving is $125 (bottom row), 24 months will be required to break even on the refinancing.

---

[3]One point is equal to 1 percent of the amount borrowed and is paid at the loan closing, or in some cases in part on loan application with the balance at closing.

TABLE 4.2
Mortgage Refinancing Calculator

Refinancing Cost	Months to Recapture								
7,000	140	94	70	56	47	40	35	32	28
6,000	120	80	60	48	40	35	30	27	24
5,000	100	67	50	40	34	29	25	23	20
4,000	80	54	40	32	27	23	20	18	16
3,000	60	40	30	24	20	18	15	14	12
2,000	40	27	20	16	14	12	10	9	8
1,000	20	14	10	8	7	6	5	5	4
Monthly P&I savings	50	75	100	125	150	175	200	225	250

Generally speaking, if a rise or a fall in rates of the same amount is viewed as equally likely, and the saving currently available from refinancing is relatively modest, the typical homeowner with a fixed-rate mortgage would probably choose to wait. The most that could be lost in the event of rising rates would be the relatively small currently available saving—a large rise in rates would have no more adverse effect than a small rise in rates. But a large drop in rates in the future would allow a large reduction in interest costs, so that the possible benefits of waiting to refinance would outweigh the possible costs. If such a rate drop is viewed as a secular bottom the response will be explosive.

Timing Considerations

One consideration is the possibility that the homeowner will sell the property before the mortgage maturity date, thus reducing the total (and present value) of saving on future interest. If the property is sold relatively soon after a refinancing, the saving in interest costs that had accumulated by that time would probably not offset the transaction costs associated with obtaining the new loan, unless the rate reduction was unusually large. This uncertainty concerning length of residence is one reason that most rules of thumb about whether to refinance incorporate the dictum that the costs of refinancing be recoverable within two years.

Uncertainty about the future course of interest rates also affects the refinancing decision. Seemingly, a homeowner should refinance whenever interest rates drop enough to generate a positive net saving on interest costs within a reasonable period of time. However, the timing of this decision is important, because if interest rates continue to fall, the homeowner would reap even larger savings by deferring the refinancing. Thus, the decision to refinance depends on the homeowner's expectations for future interest rates weighed against the amount of savings available from an immediate refinancing. This issue rests with the homeowner's willingness to forgo a known gain for the possibility of a larger future gain.

To illustrate the process, assume the homeowner is considering the refinancing of a $100,000 mortgage where the loan origination fees are 2 points ($2,000) and the other closing costs are $1,000, for a total cost of $3,000. Further, assume the mortgage will be refinanced from 11.5 to 9.5 percent. The after-tax saving will be reduced somewhat because a lower interest rate means a smaller tax deduction. For most homeowners, the actual after-tax saving works out to be approximately 70 percent of the pretax number. That represents $105 a month, or $1,260 a year, on the $100,000 refinanced in this example. With closing costs of $3,000, it will take 29 months for the reduction in the mortgage payment to recoup the transaction costs of refinancing.

The Lag Cycles

Homeowners respond with some delay, historically two to four months, to the opportunity to refinance. People need first to become aware that the refinancing opportunity exists. They then generally take some time to research the opportunity, allocate time to visit a mortgage lender, and schedule a closing. Finally, there are usually about two months between the time of commitment and the actual closing. In some cases the lag represents a deliberate delay on the part of the homeowner, who wants to see whether rates will drop even lower.

Box 4.2 is a look ahead to the probability that the issue of prepayment risk which dominated the concerns of MBS investors throughout the 1980s and into 1993, when mortgage rates dropped from the high teens to below 7.25 percent by April 1993, will be displaced by other issues such as demographics, the shape of the yield curve, and whether the issuance of REMICs is at a level sufficient to provide a strong bid for pass-throughs as collateral for the REMIC structures.

BOX 4.2
Prepayments in Transition: Less Volatility Ahead?

Prepayments may be less volatile in the 1990s than in the 1980s, when mortgage rates declined from 14 percent early in the decade to 7.5 percent and below by 1993. Should mortgage rates decline below 7 percent, the prepayment rate would accelerate, but probably not to 1992 levels.

The stratospheric mortgage rates of the early 1980s and the subsequent long decline provided multiple refinancing opportunities from the mid-1980s into 1993. Following a major drop in rates and a related massive and prolonged acceleration in prepayments starting in the fall of 1991 and continuing throughout 1992, mortgage rates bottomed at cyclical lows in the second quarter of 1993, hitting 7.38 percent the week ended April 30, 1993. Thus, the potential for large-scale refinancings appears to be sharply reduced, perhaps for years into the future. The force driving prepayments in the coming decade will be demand for housing. The baby boom was the engine that drove the housing market of the 1970s and 1980s. But in 1988, excess borrowing by both individuals and institutions brought the boom of the 1980s to an end, and from 1988 through 1991 the housing market stalled with it. Census figures released in the fourth quarter of 1992 suggest a pickup in household formations following the 1988–1991 low period in housing activity, which apparently bottomed in 1991 at the lowest level since 1946. That increase in households may support a steady base for housing turnover, but it would be at a level below the feverish resale market of the mid-1980s (see Chapter 5).

At the same time, in the early 1990s homeowners became much more sophisticated in recognizing and responding to refinancing opportunities—for example, refinancing to a 15-year mortgage to build home equity, and with the benefit of partial prepayments. It may be that homeowners who were unable to refinance during the 1991–1993 refi window because of inadequate home equity or income and credit constraints may yet do so as the economy permits a favorable change in their home equity or income status. As the level of mortgage activity moderates, mortgage originators may also be expected to become innovative in finding ways

(continued)

BOX 4.2 (*concluded*)

to justify refis. They could do so by lowering the cost to the home-owner with zero-point financing or streamlined documentation. *The pattern of the early to mid-1990s may evolve toward increased sensitivity among homeowners to refinancing opportunities, but with fewer opportunities to do so and with a reduced population of homeowners with the potential to refinance.*

New Prepayment Patterns

Significantly, prepayments in the 1980s were mostly from 30-year, fixed-rate to 30-year, fixed-rate mortgages when the rate differential between the old loan and the new mortgage available reached 2 percent or more.

Fifteen-Year Mortgages

In 1992 there was a strong shift to alternate mortgage forms, particularly 15-year mortgages but also to ARMs and balloons. Table 4.3 shows the pattern of refinancings at Fannie Mae during 1992. Almost 50 percent of Fannie Mae's 30-year, fixed-rate mortgages that were refinanced used a 15-year mortgage as the new loan. (Freddie Mac reported a similar pattern with its refinanced 30-year mortgages.) This percentage was up from a 10 to 15 percent share of total originations for 15-year mortgages when refinancings are not active. Certainly the steep yield curve was a factor favoring the 15-year mortgage, with a rate differential of 0.5 percent or more below that of the 30-year mortgage.

TABLE 4.3

Refinancing Choices for 9 Months (1992 Fannie Mae Mortgage Loan Portfolio)

	Refinanced into			
Original Loan	*30-Year (%)*	*15-Year (%)*	*ARM (%)*	*Other (%)*
30-year fixed rate	44.4	47.9	5.9	1.8
15-year fixed rate	15.0	80.2	3.7	1.2
Adjustable rate	46.3	36.7	10.2	6.9

Source: Federal National Mortgage Association.

Curtailments Become a New Factor[4]

Following a brief refinancing window in February 1991, in October of that year prepayments once again accelerated, with the pattern continuing through 1992. One surprise was the acceleration in prepayment speeds of lower MBS coupons (9s and below) at a time when seasonal patterns would suggest that prepayment-insensitive coupons should reflect a slower prepayment rate. Normally coupons below the cusp (the prepayment call option is out of the money) will respond only to seasonal factors or to an acceleration in housing turnover. The seasonal factors in October 1991 were, of course, heading into the slow-prepayment winter period—and housing turnover was stagnant at best. Table 4.4 illustrates the prepayment acceleration that occurred in October 1991 versus the September to October pattern for 1988 and 1989. The table shows that during the September to October period the prepayment rates of Ginnie Mae and Fannie Mae MBSs actually increased significantly in 1991, whereas over the same period in 1988 and 1989 prepayments declined, reflecting the start of the seasonal winter effect.

The contrary performance of the 1991 8 percent through 9 percent coupons is attributable to a dramatic reversal of the economic

TABLE 4.4

September to October Prepayment Increase (MBS Coupons 1988–1991)

	1991			*1989*			*1988*		
	Sept.	*Oct.*	*Increase (%)*	*Sept.*	*Oct.*	*Increase (%)*	*Sept.*	*Oct.*	*Increase (%)*
GNMA									
8.0	82	93	13	80	79	−1	93	81	−13
8.5	87	91	5	79	81	3	78	76	−3
9.0	100	110	10	97	97	0	93	85	−9
FNMA									
8.0	121	131	8	113	118	4	138	126	−9
8.5	138	162	17	140	135	−4	158	142	−10
9.0	146	168	15	148	143	−3	170	142	−16

Source: Lehman Brothers Fixed Income Research.

[4]This discussion of curtailments was provided by Nicole Vianna.

dynamics of 1991 versus that of the 1980s. The principal factor was a secular shift in consumer attitudes away from incurring debt toward reducing debt. The result was a shift to:

1. Consolidation of credit card and home equity debt through refinancing.
2. Acceleration in partial prepayments (curtailments) stimulated by low CD rates, which made mortgage debt reduction a more attractive form of saving than short-term money market securities.
3. Refinancing from 30-year to 15-year mortgages (to build equity faster) and to balloon mortgages or teaser-rate ARMs to minimize the mortgage cost.

FNMA 8.5s and the Yield Curve Effect[5]

FNMA 8.5 percent coupon MBSs followed a unique prepayment pattern, as shown by Figure 4.8. These securities responded only moderately to the refinancing window provided by the July 1991 to January 1992 decline in mortgage rates. A drop in the rate of long-term, fixed-rate mortgages to 8.25 to 8.5 percent did not provide the typical 1.5 to 2 percent incentive for much refinancing of the 9 to 9.5 percent mortgages (the range of mortgage rates on an 8.5 percent pass-through). Starting in the second half of 1992, however, the prepayment rates of FNMA 8.5s accelerated dramatically, as shown in Table 4.5 and Figure 4.8. Note the contrast between the prepayment patterns of the FNMA 8.5s and the 9.5s. As mortgage rates fell to 8 percent the traditional refinancing incentives do not explain the acceleration in PSA of the 8.5 versus 9.5 FNMA MBSs. The latter responded strongly to the fourth quarter 1991 decline in mortgage rates. The reason is that the 10 to 10.5 percent mortgages represented in the 9.5 percent pools were within the refinancing threshold as mortgage rates dropped below 8.75 percent in September 1991.

With the Federal Reserve Bank initiative in the spring/summer of 1992 to significantly lower short-term interest rates, short-maturity mortgage forms such as ARMs and balloons suddenly became available at considerably lower rates. This phenomenon provided the first experience in which a shift in the yield curve strongly influenced the pattern of mortgage prepayments. The

---

[5]This analysis of the yield curve effect was provided by John Tierney.

FIGURE 4.8
Prepayments, FNMA 8.5s and 9.5s, in PSA

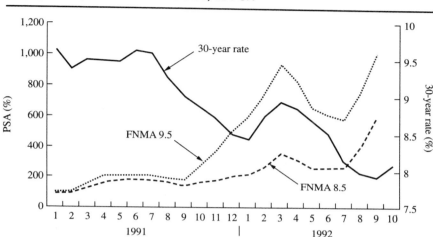

Source: Lehman Brothers Fixed Income Research.

yield curve effect as it existed by the spring of 1992 is shown in Figure 4.9.

The 1990s will differ from the 1980s for several reasons:

- The passing of the baby boom, the aging of the population, declining family formations, and changing life styles will slow home sales and housing turnover.
- The composition of MBS coupons has been redistributed so that the proportion of MBSs with pass-through rates that are likely to be cusp coupons as mortgage rates may range from 7

TABLE 4.5
FNMA 8.5 Percent Prepayment Rates

1992	PSA
June	267
July	265
August	398
September	602

Source: Lehman Brothers Fixed Income Research.

FIGURE 4.9
Contract Fate for Various Mortgage Types

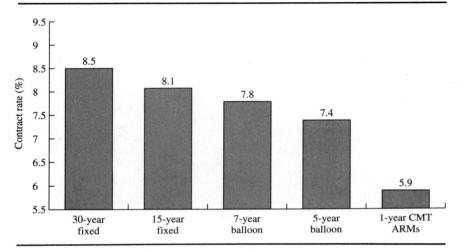

Source: Mortgage Bankers Association.

percent and up is much reduced. In 1986, 65 percent of all coupons were 10.5 percent and above; by the first quarter of 1993, 54 percent of all conventional MBS coupons were 8.5 percent and lower, and only 3 percent of all conventional MBS coupons and 8 percent of Ginnie Mae MBSs were 10.5 percent or higher. The callability of the MBS market has thereby been much reduced.

- With mortgage rates having reached a secular low of 6.97 percent the week ended August 27, 1993, prepayment volatility is not likely to be a significant concern from mid-1994 and beyond until mortgage rates once again rise above 9.5 percent to provide some future refinancing potential.

- Sluggish home prices once again make the FHA/VA assumability option meaningful; Ginnie Maes will therefore be even slower to prepay than conventionals, which are due on sale.

- Equity cash-out refis will be less frequent and for different purposes; from the mid-to-late 1980s cash-out refis were utilized to finance conspicuous consumption; in the 1990s they are more likely to be a means to manage education and tax requirements.

• For the remainder of the decade such issues as the relative level of home sales and starts, regional differences in economic and housing trends, year of issue (before or after the 1988 top-out of home prices and before or after the 1991–1992 refinancing cycle), and affordability are likely to be more important to prepayment dynamics than refinancing opportunities. (For a discussion of other aspects of the pre-1991 prepayment cycle, see Trends in MBS to Treasury Yield Spreads in Chapter 3.)

Historical Perspective: 1991–1993 versus 1986–1987[6]

The two major refinancing cycles experienced in the era of MBSs were in 1986–1987 and 1991–1993. The 1986–1987 wave was the basis for the OAS and prepayment models designed in the late 1980s and revised in 1993 to reflect new patterns provided by what proved to be the "mother" of refinancing cycles.

There were important differences between the spring periods of 1987 and 1992. In 1987, the trough mortgage rates at 9 percent were 75 basis points higher than they were in the first refi wave of 1992 and 125 basis points higher than in the second wave, which began in the summer of 1992. Significantly, the increase in rates in the spring of 1987 aborted abruptly the 1987 refi cycle. In 1992 mortgage rates remained low for a much longer period of time. In 1987 the economy was stronger, there was a bull market in real estate, and the housing sector was healthy. Arguably, there were also demographic differences—in particular, baby boomers were six years younger and were buying in large numbers either their first homes or trade-up homes in which they planned to raise families. Nevertheless, the similarities between the two periods are striking. Of particular significance was the high concentration of refinanceable premiums and the almost uncanny ability of consumers to time refinancing decisions to coincide with what proved to be mortgage rate bottoms.

The first wave of refinancing in 1992 was similar to the 1986–1987 experience, with a rush to refinance as mortgage rates backed up from the January low of 8.23 percent to 9.03 percent in late

---

[6]Portions of this comparison of the 1986–1987 and 1991–1993 experiences were provided by John Tierney.

FIGURE 4.10
MBA Application Index versus Freddie Mac Survey Rate

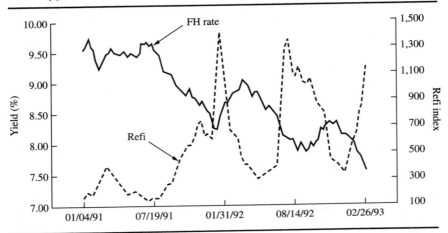

Source: Mortgage Bankers Association.

January (see Figure 4.10). This was similar to the mortgage rate increase in the spring of 1987. However, in the second 1992 refinancing wave through the third and fourth waves in the spring and fall of 1993 the refinancing cycle stretched out much longer. The major differences between the two periods may be summarized as follows:

1986–1987

- The 1986–1987 experience was principally a single cycle that started early in 1986 and ended abruptly when mortgage rates bounced off a low of 9.08 percent in March 1987 and shot up to 10.70 percent in June.
- The 1986–1987 experience came on the heels of a tremendous pent-up housing demand resulting from seven years of mortgage rates that were unaffordable for most first-time home buyers.
- Pent-up demand coupled with record home price appreciation fed a boom in home sales that swelled primary originations. This new production, when added to the refis, produced a record supply of MBSs—a supply far in excess of investor demand at the time.

- GNMA MBS to Treasury yield spreads briefly widened to 235 basis points and remained in a range of 175 to 200 in the face of the confusion and uncertainty created by the loss of premium-priced coupon income. (Spreads on conventional MBSs reached about 260 basis points.)

1991–1993

- The 1991–1993 wave consisted of four cycles. The first, rather modest and short-lived, came in January 1991 following the Gulf war and a consequent upsurge in consumer confidence coupled with a brief drop in mortgage rates to 9.25 percent in mid-February. The second wave came in the spring of 1992, the third from the summer to the end of 1992, and the fourth and fifth from the fourth quarter of 1993, finally trailing off, perhaps, in mid-1994.

- The 1991–1993 experience came in the midst of a housing slump, with demand dampened by stagnant home prices and the 1989–1991 recession. Housing demand picked up only moderately in 1993 after mortgage rates fell below 7.5 percent.

- Primary originations were therefore muted throughout 1993, although MBS issuance increased substantially because of the extraordinary acceleration in refis.

- MBS to Treasury yield spreads widened only moderately because the very steep yield curve encouraged REMIC production (except in the fourth quarter of 1992), assuring a strong demand for the collateral. Furthermore, the evolution of call-protected MBS forms enabled investors to mitigate the prepayment risk when investing in MBSs.

- In addition to the expected 30-year to 30-year refinancing, there was substantial refinancing to 15-year mortgages to build home equity, often with no reduction in the monthly mortgage payment. The incentive, in other words, was as much related to debt reduction as to a saving in the monthly mortgage payment, and much more so than in 1986–1987.

- In the 1991–1993 refinancing cycle, the window was open for over two years, from September 1991 into mid-1994. In the 1986–1987 experience, the refi window was a much shorter 15 months (January 1986 to March 1987).

The 1991–1993 refinancing cycle may be said to have started early in 1991 when the Freddie Mac survey rate for 30-year, fixed-rate mortgages fell briefly to 9.25 percent in February and then backed up, peaking at 9.67 percent in June and then going into a steady decline to below 7 percent in the fourth quarter of 1993. During this first phase of the cycle, the 9 to 10 percent MBS coupons were the most prepayment sensitive, soaring to PSA levels comparable to 11 to 13 percent coupons in 1986–1987. Interestingly, 8.5 to 9.5 percent coupons also contributed less visibly to prepayment activity during this period—but less visibly because of curtailments, according to a study by Joseph Hu.[7] Mr. Hu does not believe that curtailments were a factor in the 1986–1987 prepayment experience. The decline in short-term investment rates (for example, bank CDs) made in paying down the mortgage in 1991 through 1993 more attractive than remaining invested short term.

Tracking the 1991–1993 Prepayment Experience

Figure 4.11A shows the MBA refinance application volume index plotted against the Freddie Mac survey rate. The graph shows that mortgage rates provided an interim refinancing window in the first quarter of 1991, with mortgage rates falling to 9.25 percent the week ending February 22. This drop in rates precipitated the first shock wave of refinancing that led ultimately to the super refinancing cycle of 1991–1993. Prepayments of 9.5 to 11 percent MBS coupons showed gains in the 45 to 60 percent range and began to decline in earnest at the end of July 1991 as mortgage rates dropped from about 9.6 percent on July 19 to 8.23 percent on January 10, 1992. (Refer to Figures 4.1 through 4.3, which track historic mortgage interest rates and prepayment rates.) The refinancing index climbed steadily from 138 the week ended July 5 (its low point for 1991) to a peak of 1,428 the week ended January 17, 1992. Mortgage rates began their final descent for the cycle in mid-December 1992, dropping through 7.5 percent in March 1993 and reaching a new low of 7.38 percent on April 30. Mortgage rates remained below 7.5 percent into the summer of 1993 with the possibility of even lower rates by year-end. The refi index responded in January 1993, climbing to a peak of 1,465 the week of March 12

---

[7]"Recent Prepayments in a Historical Perspective," by Joseph Hu, Senior Vice President, Director, Mortgage Research, Nomura Securities International, New York. In *MBS Letter,* June 3, 1991.

FIGURE 4.11A
MBA Refinance Application Volume Index

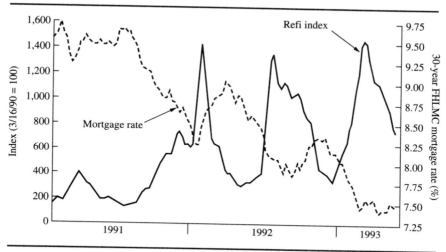

Source: Mortgage Bankers Association and Lehman Brothers.

and then falling through the 1,000 level the second week of May. Prepayment speeds rose again in late 1993 but were expected to decline by the fall of 1994.

Sluggish Housing Turnover. As refinancings soared, home sales, as shown by the purchase index,[8] remained sluggish throughout the cycle of low mortgage rates (see Figure 4.11B). This pattern held in spite of the dramatic drop in mortgage rates from the 11 percent range in 1989 to below 7 percent by the fourth quarter of 1993. The decline in home sales appears to be related to the dual and interrelated functions of the 1988–1989 home price appreciation wall and the 1991–1992 recession that followed (and that was in large part caused by the appreciation wall).

Alternative Mortgage Forms Fooled the Models
The prepayment patterns of the 1986–1987 refinancing experience formed the basis of most assumptions applied to prepayment sensi-

[8] The MBA purchase index tracks turnover as a function of home sales. September 1992 home sales were down in spite of the lowest mortgage rates in 20 years.

FIGURE 4.11B
MBA Total and Purchase Application Index

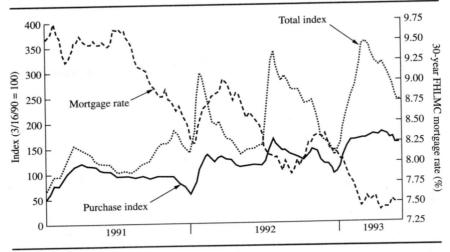

Source: Mortgage Bankers Association and Lehman Brothers.

tivity within the models as the market entered the 1991–1992 surge. In the two earlier experiences the predominant refinancing option was from 30-year fixed to 30-year fixed, and generally a positive spread of about 2 points between the gross WAC of the mortgages in the pool and the market mortgage rate available at the time of analysis was required to generate sufficient savings over the cost of refinancing to precipitate a prepayment. In the 1991–1993 experience, teaser-rate ARMs and balloon loans considerably extended the savings associated with the incentive to refinance. Consider the options available to the holder of a 9.5 percent mortgage on January 10, 1992 (Table 4.6).

In January, according to Table 4.6, the spread of a 9.5 percent, 30-year, fixed-rate mortgage to the 8.3 percent, 30-year, fixed rate was only 120 basis points. This narrow spread led the prepayment model to assume there was not sufficient incentive to stimulate substantial refinancing of the 9.5 percent mortgage, at least by 1986–1987 standards. However, the spread of the 9.5 percent, 30-year, fixed-rate mortgage to a 1-year CMT ARM is over 2¾ points, and to a 5-year balloon it is over 2 points. The incentive to refinance to 15-year mortgages was more to build equity than to save on the

TABLE 4.6
Alternative Mortgage Rates

	January 10, 1992		October 9, 1992	
	Rate (%)	Spread to 9.5%, 30-Year (bp)	Rate (%)	Spread to 9.5% 30-year (bp)
30-year fixed	8.3	120	7.9	160
1-year CMT ARM	6.8	270	4.8	470
5-year balloon	7.4	210	6.3	320
15-year fixed	7.8	170	7.4	170

Source: Federal Home Loan Mortgage Corporation.

mortgage payment. These options were missed by most analysts (and prepayment models) until early 1992.

On October 9, Table 4.6 indicates, the 30-year, fixed contract rate[9] was 7.9 percent; the 15-year fixed 7.4 percent; the 7-year balloon 6.3 percent; and the first-year ARM 4.8 percent, and in some cases lower. By October 9, the 30-year, fixed rate was below 8 percent, providing incentive for any 30-year, fixed-rate mortgages at 9.5 percent or above to refinance to the 30-year rate or to the CMT ARM, now at a spread of about 470 basis points below the 9.5 percent fixed rate. The result was that mortgages backing the 9.5 percent coupon MBS pools prepaid rapidly. In fact, the availability of initial ARM rates of 4 to 5 percent, capped for life at 9 or 10 percent, altered the historic relationship between mortgage rates and prepayment rates. Before the 1991–1993 refinancing experience only 30-year to 30-year mortgage rates were compared to derive prepayment forecasts. The 1992 experience saw the introduction of the yield curve effect into the prepayment model to take into account the availability of mortgages on the shorter-term structure of the yield curve.

The Lag Effect

The lag in prepayment activity during the spring and summer refi waves illustrates two key points: First, consumers must respond to

---

[9]Effective with points, these rates were 30-year fixed, 8.40; 15-year fixed, 8; 7-year balloon, 7.70; and ARM, 5.6.

FIGURE 4.12A
Prepayment Lag, FNMA 9.5 PSA versus 30-Year Contract Rate

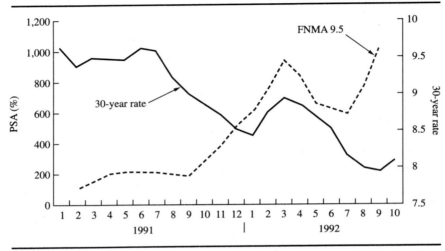

Source: Lehman Brothers Fixed Income Research.

the decline in rates, and there is a processing time to turn refi applications into closed loans that actualize the refi. Second, rates must decline sufficiently to provide sufficient savings to induce the refinancing. The first point is illustrated in Figure 4.12A. The figure illustrates the lag of FNMA 9.5 percent prepayment rates to changes in 30-year mortgage rates. Note that the Freddie Mac 30-year mortgage survey rate peaked at 9.67 percent the week ended June 28, 1991, and the prepayment rate of FNMA 9.5 percent MBSs first accelerated in September, representing a lag of two months (July and August).[10] Figure 4.12B shows that the MBA application refinancing index turned in June 1992, following by three months the decline in mortage rates in March.

The second point is also illustrated in Figure 4.12B, which shows that the lag in the refi index was much longer in the second wave, which commenced in July, four months after the 30-year survey rate dropped again, starting in April, from 9.50 percent. The

---

[10]The October prepayment report reflects Fannie Mae prepayments collected from August 16 to September 15.

FIGURE 4.12B
MBA Application Refinancing Index Leads 30-Year Contract Rate

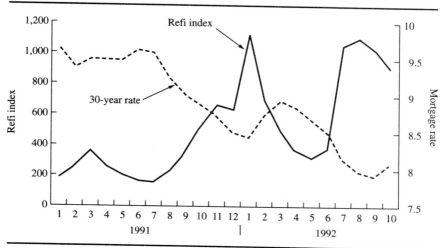

Source: John Tierney, Lehman Brothers.

reason is that 9.50 percent was not now a low enough mortgage rate to provide the incentive to refinance. It was not until the 30-year rate fell below 9 percent in September that it was to provide a refinancing in its own right. The stimulus for the second wave of refinancings was related more to the July 2 ease in short-term interest rates, which stimulated yield curve roll-down refinancings to 15-year mortgages, balloons, and ARMs. By this point the 30-year to 30-year refinancing activity already exhibited considerable burnout. Note from Figure 4.12C that the 8.5 percent coupons were only moderately responsive to the decline in mortgage rates in the second half of 1991 and into the first quarter of 1992, whereas the 9.5s responded strongly starting in September 1991.

The 8.5s finally did show accelerating refinancing activity in July 1992 in response to the steepening of the yield curve following the Federal Reserve's initiative starting July 2 to drive down short-term rates. This steepened the yield curve and led to shorter mortgage rates on alternative mortgage forms such as the ARM, balloon, and 15-year mortgages. This yield curve steepening induced the yield curve effect.

FIGURE 4.12C
Prepayment Lag in PSA, FNMA 8.5 versus 9.5 Coupons

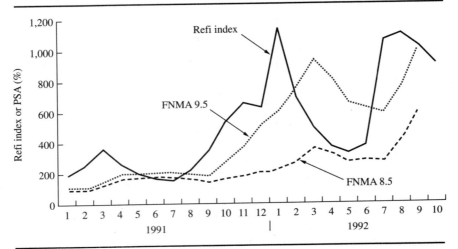

Ginnie Maes: Superior Call Protection[11]

It is interesting to note how much the difference in prepayments between the same-coupon Fannie Mae and Ginnie Mae pass-throughs increased in September 1992, which was near the peak of the 1991–1993 refinancing cycle. FNMA 9s prepaid nearly 600 PSA faster than GNMA 9s. In July, that difference stood at 225 PSA. For the 9.5 coupon, the difference had ballooned—from under 250 PSA to over 400 PSA—in two months, and for 8.5s it soared from 119 PSA to nearly 400 PSA. The steep curve during that period provided for more efficient refinancing options for conventional mortgages, with options for refinancing a 30-year loan distributed all along the yield curve—from 1- to 5-year ARMs, 5- and 7-year balloons, and 15- and 30-year fixed-rate mortgages. In contrast, the high LTV typical of FHA/VA borrowers made refinancing more difficult for them. And as previously discussed, refinancing into a 15-year mortgage requires higher monthly payments unless the difference between the old and new interest rates is 300 basis points. The higher payment required of the 15-year mortgage made it a less

---

[11]This discussion of Ginnie Mae call protection was provided by John Tierney.

attractive option for the FHA/VA borrower than for conventional borrowers.

1986–1987 Revisited[12]

Throughout the early 1980s mortgage rates were high, with the Freddie Mac weekly primary market survey rate for fixed-rate mortgages above 12 percent from November 1979 through June 1985. (The peak was 14.74 percent in July 1984.) A long-term bull market in bonds began in mid-1984, with mortgage rates, as measured by the Freddie Mac survey rate, falling steadily from 14.74 percent in July 1984 to a low of 9.07 percent in late March 1987 (Figure 4.13). The survey rate fell below 11 percent for the first time in nearly seven years at the beginning of 1986, fluctuated between 9.5 and 11 percent for most of the year, and then fell below 9.5 percent for four months, from December 1986 through March 1987.

FIGURE 4.13

Freddie Mac Monthly Commitment Rate (July 1984–December 1987)

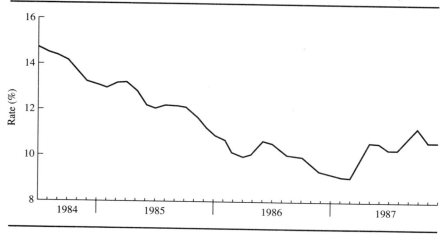

Source: Lehman Brothers Fixed Income Research.

[12]This discussion of 1986–1987 revisited was provided by John Tierney.

FIGURE 4.14
Prepayments for Slightly Seasoned Fannie Mae Premiums (January 1985–March 1988)

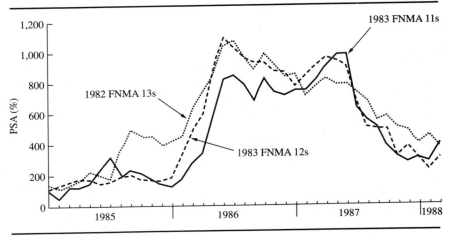

Source: Lehman Brothers Fixed Income Research.

The downward progression of rates led borrowers to refinance successively lower-coupon mortgages. Slightly seasoned, conventional 13 percent coupon MBSs prepaid at about 400 PSA in September 1985 after mortgage rates fell to the 12 percent level in the summer of 1985 and accelerated to 1,000 PSA in the summer of 1986 (Figure 4.14). Prepayments of conventional 12s rose above 400 PSA in March 1986 and reached 1,000 PSA by midsummer 1986. Conventional 11 percent coupon MBS prepayments reached 400 PSA in May 1986, but did not peak in the 850 PSA range until April–June 1987, based on the 9 percent cyclical low in mortgage rates in February and March 1987.

GNMA prepayment rates accelerated in approximately the same pattern, but peaked at lower levels. As a result, GNMA 13 prepayment rates rose to above the 400 PSA level five months after conventional 13s and peaked in the low 900 PSA range. Likewise, GNMA 12 prepayments accelerated two months later than conventional 12s, and GNMA 11s three months later than conventional 11s. GNMA 12 speeds peaked at about 850 PSA in the fall of 1986 and GNMA 11 speeds at 750 PSA in April 1987 (Figure 4.15). The principal reason is the longer processing time required with the

FIGURE 4.15

Prepayments for Slightly Seasoned Ginnie Mae Premiums (January 1985–March 1988)

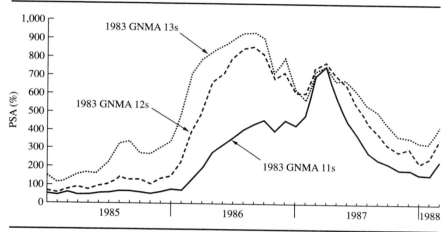

Source: Lehman Brothers Fixed Income Research.

more complex FHA loan paper work. Also, the FHA borrower is typically somewhat slower to respond to the refinance opportunity.

In April 1987, the bond bull market ended abruptly: The 10-year Treasury yield rose from 7.33 percent in late March to 8.75 percent in late May; the Freddie Mac mortgage survey rate rose even more—from 9.07 percent in late March to 10.81 percent in late May, ending the refinancing boom (Figure 4.16). After settling in the mid-10s through the summer of 1987, the Freddie Mac rate rose sharply again in September and reached a high of 11.58 percent in mid-October. The Freddie Mac rate came down again after the October 19, 1987 stock market crash, as a result of a flight-to-quality rally in the bond market, but remained at or above the 10 percent level until late 1989.

The refinancing boom ended equally abruptly. By July 1987, prepayments started plummeting as the final wave of refinancers cleared the mortgage application pipeline. By the fourth quarter of 1987, prepayments on GNMA 12s and 13s were below 400 PSA, whereas similar-coupon conventionals were below 500 CPR. Prepayments on 11s and 11.5s fell even more sharply, to about 200 PSA for Ginnie Maes and 300 PSA for conventionals.

FIGURE 4.16
Freddie Mac Monthly Commitment Rate (July through December 1987)

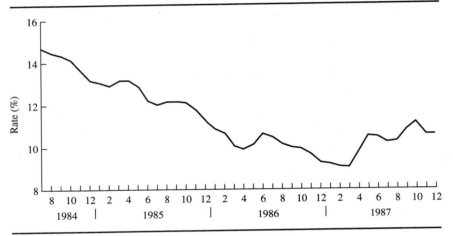

MBS Issuance, 1986–1987[13]

MBS issuance for 1986 and 1987 totaled $494 billion. About $193 billion was replacement supply, or issuance required to maintain the outstanding balance at a constant level—that is, to replace paydowns caused by refinancings and amortization. These paydowns caused problems for the MBS market because they were concentrated in a short period of time, catching many new MBS investors by surprise. The real pressure on spreads, however, came from the additional $301 billion in net new supply that caused MBSs outstanding to grow by over 80 percent during 1986 and 1987, to $668.4 billion (Table 4.7). About two thirds of this net new supply was the result of increased securitization of mortgage originations, with the rest coming from growth in outstanding residential debt. Between year-ends 1985 and 1987, residential debt grew from $1.501 trillion to $1.962 trillion, and the share that was securitized through agency MBS programs jumped nearly 10 percentage points, from 24.4 percent to 34.1 percent. If the MBS share of total residential debt had remained constant at 24.4 percent through 1987, net new agency supply during 1986–1987 would have been a more

[13]This discussion of MBS issuance, 1986–1987, is from Lehman Brothers Fixed Income Research, *MBS Outlook*, October 1991.

TABLE 4.7
MBS Issuance and Paydown Activity, 1985–1990 ($ Billions)

	Issuance	Paydowns	Net New Supply	Year-End Balance	Percentage of Outstanding Balance[a]		MBS as Percentage of Outstanding 1–4 Family Mortgage Debt
					Paydowns[a]	New Supply	
1984	—	—	—	286.2	—	—	21.3
1985	108.3	27.5	80.8	367.0	9.6	28.2	24.4
1986	258.9	96.9	162.0	529.1	26.4	44.1	30.8
1987	234.9	95.5	139.4	668.4	18.1	26.3	34.1
1988	151.3	69.8	81.5	749.9	10.4	12.2	34.1
1989	199.7	78.7	12.0	871.0	10.5	16.1	35.8
1990	234.9	88.4	146.5	1,017.5	10.1	16.8	37.6

[a]Paydowns as a percentage of the outstanding balance as of the previous year.

Source: Lehman Brothers, *Financial World Publications.*

FIGURE 4.17
FNMA 11 Prepayments (Prepayment Lag Effect)

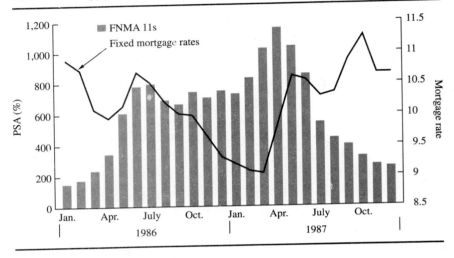

Source: Nicole Vianna, Lehman Brothers.

manageable $112 billion. If the 1986–1987 paydowns had occurred in this constant MBS market share scenario, it is unlikely that spreads would have widened as much as they did, especially considering, at that time, the need to reinvest principal paydowns and the influx of new investors.

The 1986–1987 Lag Experience[14]

Figure 4.17 illustrates the lag experience of Fannie Mae 11s in 1986 and 1987. Note that prepayments continued to accelerate even after mortgage rates began to rise in February 1987. In fact, the highest prepayment levels came as homeowners locked in the lower rates in a now-or-never rush.

In the 1991–1992 refinancing wave, the lag was even longer as homeowners watched mortgage rates decline from over 9.5 percent in the summer of 1991 to below 8.5 percent in the fall. As pointed out earlier in this chapter, however, when the mortgage rate decline paused in September, refinancing applications that had been pend-

---

[14]This discussion of the lag experience is based on research by Nicole Vianna.

ing since the summer were processed swiftly starting in the last two weeks of October.

In the brief refinancing flurry in the winter of 1991, the lag time from opportunity to refinance to execution was only about one and a half to two months. Part of the explanation is that originators were much better prepared to deal with an acceleration in loan-processing volume. A combination of better technology and improved productivity learned during the 1986–1987 refinancing bonanza also contributed to greater efficiency. Heightened consumer awareness of the benefits of refinancing from the heavy media focus on the issue also stimulated a faster response by consumers (the media were less involved in the 1986–1987 period). However, by mid-January 1992, with refinancings representing about 70 percent of originations, the originators became overwhelmed, and processing time alone could take up to three months, extending the lag to four months or so.

As refinancing activity accelerated, the pipeline backed up when mortgage rates reversed in January 1992. By late February, the processing lag was again three to four months.

The 1992 Lag Experience

In the 1992 refinancing experience the lag effect was significantly reduced in the early phase of the cycle. A major reason was the implementation of an education program by mortgage servicers designed to encourage homeowners to refinance. This experience was in contrast to that of 1986–1987 when less media attention was given to the refinancing opportunity. The difference appears to lie with a major change in the mortgage financing process from the 1980s to the 1990s. In the 1980s, a large percentage of mortgage originations were held in portfolio by S&Ls. These S&Ls had little incentive to encourage refinancings that would eliminate the higher-coupon mortgages from their portfolios. By the 1990s, as the number of S&Ls remaining that could or would originate mortgages for portfolio was largely liquidated, mortgage originations became almost entirely done for sale, with the economic incentive shifting to the creation of servicing. The shift from portfolio lending to mortgage banking caused the mortgage originator to become concerned primarily with keeping the servicing portfolio intact. The best defense then becomes to encourage refinancing so that the mortgages are kept on the books of the servicer and not refinanced elsewhere. In other words, a 7.5 percent mortgage contributing 3/8 servicing that will maintain its economic life has more future value than a 10 percent mortgage in portfolio that might be refinanced at any time.

It is interesting to note that the traditional three-month lag between a drop in mortgage rates through the threshold and an observed change in prepayments shortened considerably in the winter of 1991 when refis were the only game in town and were processed fast; primary originations (for home purchase) were very low. By the winter/spring of 1992, however, refinancing activity overwhelmed mortgage origination and loan-processing capability, and the lag had extended to up to four months. The MBA reported in January 1992 that loan-processing time was averaging 50 days, up from an average of 30 to 40 business days as the norm.

On balance it appears that homeowners have become far more astute in recognizing refinancing opportunities. Thus, the lag response will probably shorten, and participation is likely to be broader than in the past.

Refinancing versus Purchase Lag.   Data provided by the MBA indicate that the lag between a drop in mortgage rates and a home purchase is more than twice as long as the lag between a mortgage rate drop and a pickup in the refinancing rate. This pattern is intuitively logical because the process of making a home purchase decision and locating a suitable home is more complex and incurs greater commitment on the part of the consumer than the simpler decision to refinance an existing mortgage.

The Fannie Mae versus Freddie Mac Lag

The prepayment speeds reported for Freddie Mac PCs lag those of the Fannie Mae MBSs. The speeds reported for Freddie Mac PCs often appear to be lagging those of the Fannie Mae MBSs when rapid changes in prepayment speeds are taking place. This lag reflects the difference in how the two agencies report any prepayments. Fannie Mae reports prepayments from the first day of a month to the last, thereby picking up a full month's prepayment activity. Freddie Mac, by contrast, reports from mid-month to mid-month.

Figure 4.18 compares the prepayment pattern for Fannie Mae and Freddie Mac MBSs. Note that the Freddie Mac PCs are picking up only half of each subsequent faster month, whereas the Fannie Maes pick up the full month, making the Fannie Mae appear to be prepaying faster. The figure illustrates this lag. The lag is clearly reflected in the data for the 1992 prepayment acceleration, shown in Table 4.8.

FIGURE 4.18
FNMA versus FHLMC 1989-Issue 9s (Prepayment Lag)

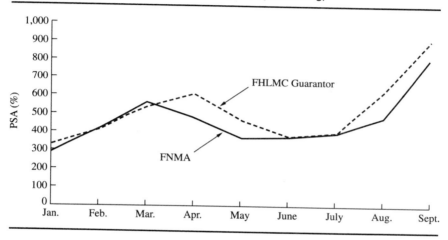

Source: Lehman Brothers Fixed Income Research.

TABLE 4.8
Fannie Mae versus Freddie Mac Prepayments, 1992

	1989 9s		1989 9.5s	
	FNMA	*FHLMC Guarantor*	*FNMA*	*FHLMC Guarantor*
Jan.	292	325	535	509
Feb.	415	409	665	615
Mar.	555	535	824	736
Apr.	475	604	726	844
May	371	459	564	650
June	375	378	566	552
July	397	395	529	540
Aug.	623	480	704	609
Sept.	910	819	948	864

Source: Lehman Brothers Fixed Income Research.

6. WHAT DOES THE TERM "SEASONING" REALLY MEAN?[15]

Seasoning refers to the time since origination, or the age of a mortgage or of the mortgages in a pool. The weighted average age of the mortgage pool is important because of the implications for average life and yield. Seasoning also affects the assumptions made with respect to prepayment rates. *Newly formed pools will have very little prepayment activity for the first two or three years.*

Homeowners who have just borne the expense of a mortgage closing will be relatively insensitive to refinancing opportunities—they are generally out of pocket for a year or two. The other factors that influence prepayments—job transfers, desire to trade up, deaths, and divorces—are unlikely events for new homeowners. A couple seeking new job opportunities or a larger house or heading for the divorce court would not have been likely to have purchased the home to begin with. This phenomenon is recognized by the PSA prepayment model; the base scenario (100 PSA) assumes that prepayments increase successively by 0.2 CPR each month until the prepayments level out at 6 CPR by month 30. Thus, the mortgage is seasoned 2.5 years after origination. This period of time is referred to as the **PSA ramp**.

What Is Weighted Average Life?

Table 4.9 shows the relationship between seasoning and average life for different pass-through rates and prepayment assumptions. The **weighted average life (WAL)** of a security is the average number of years that any dollar of principal will be outstanding. As indicated in the table, average life increases with the level of pass-through rates regardless of prepayment assumptions. The reason is that the interest component of the monthly payment is larger with higher interest rates. Thus, repayment of principal is delayed, increasing the average life. As the underlying mortgage pool ages, average life declines. The decline is accentuated when prepayments are introduced. Higher prepayment rates mean that principal is being repaid

---

[15]This discussion of seasoning is based largely on research by Nicole Vianna.

TABLE 4.9
Effect of Seasoning or Age of the Pool on Average Life

Pass-through Rate (%)	Average Life (Years)					
	No Prepayment			Prepayment of 0.50% per Month		
	New Pool	Aged 5 Years	Aged 10 Years	New Pool	Aged 5 Years	Aged 10 Years
8	20.84	16.70	12.78	11.37	10.06	8.52
9	21.38	17.11	13.06	11.57	10.24	8.67
10	21.88	17.49	13.34	11.75	10.41	8.81
11	22.35	17.86	13.60	11.92	10.57	8.95
12	22.78	18.21	13.86	12.07	10.72	9.08
13	23.18	18.54	14.10	12.21	10.86	9.21
14	23.55	18.85	14.33	12.33	10.99	9.32

at a faster rate. A reduction in the time required to repay principal translates into a shorter average life.

As the **weighted average maturity (WAM)** of a pass-through security decreases, average life declines as it would for a pool that is aging. Remaining term to maturity is simply an alternative way to express age given the initial life of the pool. The effect of seasoning is evident from Table 4.10. Specifically, for the discount security shown, as the remaining term to maturity is reduced from 30 years to 20 years (i.e., the mortgage pool is aging from new to 10 years) the average life of the security falls, which causes the cash flow yield to increase. Additionally, over time the difference between average life and remaining term narrows.

Burnout

The burnout phenomenon is the tendency for mortgage pools with prolonged exposure to attractive refinancing opportunities to prepay more slowly after the mortgagors most able to refinance and most attentive to interest rates have exited the pool. It first became apparent in early 1987 as MBS coupons of 12 percent and above prepaid at slower speeds than they did in 1986, even though rates had dropped further. The initial impact of burnout was modest, however. Conventional 12s, 12.5s, and 13s continued to prepay

TABLE 4.10
Effect of Seasoning on Cash Flow Yield

	Age of Pass-through		
	New	5 Years	10 Years
Remaining term	30	25	20
Average life	12.07	10.72	9.08
Cash flow yield	13.74%	13.79%	13.91%
Difference between remaining term and average life	17.9	14.3	10.9

Assumptions: (1) 12% GNMA. (2) Purchase price of 91. (3) Prepayment rate of 0.50 percent per month. (4) Mortgages underlying the GNMA were all 12.5%, 30-year mortgages.

Source: Lehman Brothers Fixed Income Research.

faster than 750 PSA from early 1986 through midsummer 1987, whereas GNMA 12s and 13s prepaid above 600 PSA for that entire period. The sharp decline in prepayment rates for these high-coupon securities after summer 1987 was attributable to the burn-out effect as well as to higher mortgage rates. Even after rates rose 150 basis points by October 1987, the prepayment option on these securities remained in the money by at least 200 basis points.

Among discount and current-coupon securities (9.5 percent and lower) prepayments slowed as rates rose, primarily because homeowners had less incentive to refinance. Prepayments related to housing turnover, however, remained firm, because although higher interest rates ended the surge of refinancings, they did not end the strong housing market. Existing home sales in the higher-rate environment of 1988 were slightly above those for 1986 and 1987, and new home sales equaled 1987 levels. Even mortgage rates—near 11 percent in early 1989—did not significantly slow housing turnover: Existing home sales remained above a 3.3 million annual rate until fall 1990 when the recession reduced them to an annual rate of 3.1 million units. The availability of ARMs at initial rates of 6.5 to 8 percent for most of 1988 blunted the effect of higher fixed rates; the ARM share of conventional mortgage originations stayed above 50 percent for the last four months of 1987 and all of 1988.

Examples of Burnout

A pool that has passed through a sufficient number of interest rate cycles that virtually all homeowners who are able to and are interested in refinancing have done so is considered to be fully seasoned and burned out. The pool factor has typically declined to 0.5 or lower, and the WAM is generally 240 months or less. Such pools gravitate to a stable prepayment speed and become relatively insensitive to refinancing opportunities. Table 4.11 illustrates the remaining unpaid balance of premium-coupon MBSs that remained outstanding in April 1993 in spite of many years of refinancing opportunity. It is interesting to note, for example, that 38 percent of GNMA 10.5 and 21 percent of GNMA 11 coupons were still outstanding even after the extraordinary 1991–1993 refinancing cycle.

Cyclical Burnout[16]. The burnout concept is also frequently applied to the later stages of a refinancing cycle, referring to the tendency of most homeowners to act within six to nine months of the opening of a refinancing window of opportunity to reduce mortgage interest expense. Based on the 1986–1987 experience, borrowers who failed to act within the six- to nine-month time frame became increasingly unlikely to do so. The pool would then be referred to as burned out for that cycle. *Be cautioned that the application of burnout is all too frequently hastily applied; for example, traders of IO strips start talking about burnout with the first monthly drop in PSA speed.* Figure 4.19 illustrates cyclical burnout. As the spread of available market mortgage rates fell below the mortgage rate on pools of GNMA 11s originated in 1985, prepayments "overshot"— that is, became far above normal. Even as the market spread remained below that of the pool mortgage rate, the prepayment speed of GNMA 11s slowed in 1987 and continued to do so into 1990.

Interest Rate-Path Dependency

Because of the heterogeneity in refinancing costs, not all mortgages are prepaid when the interest rate declines for the first time in the life cycle of the mortgage pool. The effect of subsequent declines in the interest rate is reduced to the extent that mortgages in the pool are represented by homeowners who will have higher refinancing

---

[16]This discussion of burnout is based largely on research by Nicole Vianna.

TABLE 4.11
MBS Coupons 10.5–15 Currently Outstanding and Percentage of Total Amount Issued (March 31, 1993)

Coupon	GNMA Current Outstanding ($ Millions)	GNMA Percentage of Total Issued	FHLMC[a] Current Outstanding	FHLMC[a] Percentage of Total Issued	FNMA Current Outstanding	FNMA Percentage of Total Issued
10.5	6,527	38	2,577	26	3,590	32
11.0	6,910	21	1,102	15	1,249	18
11.5	3,871	13	483	10	526	11
12.0	2,588	11	390	6	546	8
12.5	1,537	9	202	6	296	6
13	844	8	—	—	—	—
13.5	402	7	—	—	—	—
15	354	5	—	—	—	—

[a] Guarantor only.

FIGURE 4.19
Refinancing and Burnout of GNMA 11s

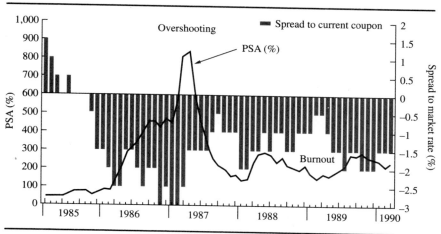

Source: Lehman Brothers Fixed Income Research.

costs compared to homeowners who prepaid in a prior interest rate cycle. The future rate of prepayments in a given pool is therefore highly dependent upon the interest rate cycles the pool has already passed through.

The pool over time will pass through cycles of higher and lower interest rates. The first opportunity to refinance will have the greatest impact on prepayments. If the pool is new (less than three years seasoned), the first down interest rate cycle it passes through will have only a moderate impact. But once the pool has seasoned, most homeowners with the inclination and financial ability to refinance will have done so. Of course, some homeowners who wish to refinance may be unable to do so—perhaps because of the lock-in effect or other reasons, such as lack of home equity or a poor credit history. Others may simply be unaware of or unconcerned about the financial benefits associated with refinancing. The second refinancing cycle will therefore see many homeowners who would have refinanced already gone from the pool, leaving a lesser number who were unable to refinance at the first opportunity and who will now do so. As each interest rate cycle and refinancing opportunity is passed fewer refinancing candidates are left in the pool.

A long period of historically low mortgage rates would remove homeowners who refinanced in prior time periods, thereby elimi-

TABLE 4.12
Historic Prepayment Data, FNMA 8.5 Percent Coupon by Issue Year
(in CPR, October 1992)

FNMA 8.5	Amount Outstanding ($ millions)	Wam (months)	WAC	CPR (%)
Total	50,993	320	9.10	21.2
1992	16,216	353	8.94	9.8
1991	17,826	342	9.11	20.1
1990	2,512	327	9.25	34.8
1989	1,601	315	9.39	43.7
1988	479	303	9.34	33.3
1987	5,032	285	9.13	30.5
1986	2,746	277	9.31	34.0
1985	534	267	9.28	36.1
1978	509	184	9.50	23.1
1977	883	174	9.29	21.6
1976	888	164	9.15	19.0
1975	387	155	9.16	17.0

Source: Lehman Brothers Fixed Income Research.

nating them as refinancing candidates in current or future periods. Historical prepayment data are often used in a misleading way. Note, for example, the historic data for FNMA 8.5s given in Table 4.12.

Question: What is the CPR of Fannie Mae 8.5s?
Answer: The CPR is 21.2 percent.
Problem: If the investor is buying FNMA 8.5s because the 21.2 CPR is an attractive prepayment speed for some investment objective, it is important to understand that 21.2 is just the average CPR for the generic universe of all FNMA 8.5s. Under PSA guidelines, the seller may deliver 1991-issue FNMA 8.5s, which have a reported CPR of only 9.8. Examine Table 4.12, and note that the CPR for various years of issue of FNMA 8.5s varies from 9.10 to 43.7. (Note also that there are large differences in the amount outstanding, which for specific pool investors can become a liquidity issue. This, of course, is not a problem for TBA trades.) For example, in the 1990-issue year only $2.5 billion was outstanding as of this report (October 1992). By contrast, $17.8 billion was outstand-

ing for the 1991 issues and $16.2 billion for the 1992 issues. Also note the disparities in the WAM and WAC for the various issues.

Clarification of collateral identity by specific year of issue, WAC, and WAM is critically important when buying CMOs and, of course, especially with IO and PO strips. Imagine the implications of buying an IO stripped off 353-month WAM paper (1992 issue) versus the shorter WAMs listed in Table 4.12.[17]

Triple D and the Pure Aging Effect

Family life cycle factors play a role as well. For example, as time passes the family grows, and if household income is also higher, a larger home will be sought. Years later the children move away, and the now empty nesters are likely to scale down to a smaller house. Finally, they may move to another region of the country to retire. Other events may occur within the pool life cycle, such as divorce, default, or an untimely death (the DDD effect).

Curtailments

Until recently partial prepayments, or curtailments, have not been considered a significant contribution to the prepayment equation. In the summer of 1991, however, Telerate's Mortgage Securities Division (MSD), the producers of the AFS, conducted a study suggesting curtailments have become fairly significant.

MSD observed that the percentage of prepayments not directly related to traditional prepayments had increased significantly during 1991 and identified the cause as an increase in both partial prepayments and foreclosures. That foreclosures had increased significantly through the 1990–1991 housing recession was well known. The rise in curtailments was a less visible but logical outgrowth of the change in consumer psychology stemming from the transition of the 1980s to the 1990s (see Curtailments Become a New Factor, page 164). Curtailments appear to be on the rise, in part as an effort to build home equity in the absence of the formerly dependable annual increase in home value. They have also been employed as

---

[17]Interest lives off principal—therefore, the longer the WAM, the greater will be the total amount of interest cash flow stream. See Chapter 14 for a further discussion of MBS strips.

an alternative investment to CDs, with their disappointing rates, which in 1992–1993 declined from the alluring 8 percent and above to the 3.5 to 4 percent range. Homeowners with 9 percent and above mortgage rates could realize a better return by partially paying down the mortgage than by leaving the money invested in short-term money market investments.

MSD derived a methodology to isolate curtailments from full prepayments. The data also take into account foreclosures, although these represent only a small percentage of the total. From data assembled by MSD it appears that more than 15 percent of homeowners made partial prepayments in 1991. Figure 4.20 shows curtailments as a percentage of total unpaid mortgage principal balance, according to MSD 1990 prepayment data. Two key points are:

1. Curtailments increase with the highest coupons, as shown in Figure 4.20. This tendency supports the possibility that the higher the mortgage rate, the more likely a partial prepayment may represent an investment alternative to lower-yielding money market securities.
2. Given that homeowners will borrow to the maximum possible leverage, the fact that curtailments are higher for seasoned loans appears reasonable—borrowers would presumably have little discretionary income to apply as a curtailment in the early years of the mortgage.

The Cash-Out Refi

The assumption is generally made that the homeowner is motivated primarily to refinance the remaining mortgage principal balance in order to achieve an economic advantage. Yet for many homeowners the decision to refinance primarily reflects a desire to extract accumulated home equity as a source of funds for the purchase of goods and services—for example, to meet tuition fees, repay debts, or make investments. According to a Federal Reserve Board study, 20 percent of refinancings in 1988 liquidized extra equity in the home beyond the amount of the existing mortgage balance.[18] The two most frequent uses of the cashed-out equity were home im-

---

[18]Federal Reserve Board, *Federal Reserve Bulletin*. Washington, DC, August 1990.

FIGURE 4.20
Partial Prepayment Analysis (1990 Curtailments as a Percentage of
Current Balance)

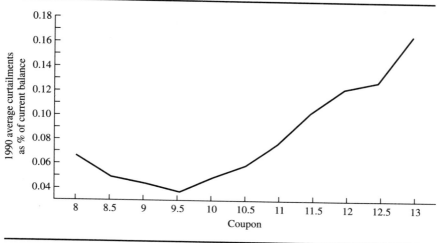

Source: Lehman Brothers Fixed Income Research.

provements and repayment of debts. The latter has likely become
more important since the passage of the 1986 Tax Reform Act,
which phased out over four years the deduction of interest paid on
nonmortgage-related consumer debt.

7. WHAT IS THE IMPACT OF PREPAYMENTS?

Whenever a mortgage in an MBS pool is paid before its stated maturity a **prepayment** has occurred. Prepayments accelerate the return
of principal cash flows to the investor and therefore have an impact
on the average life and yield of the MBS investment. Most significantly, the rate of prepayments, or **speed,** will change subject to a
number of factors with varying degrees of predictability.

The scheduled, or contractual, P&I is the monthly payment required to amortize the mortgage to its original stated maturity. The
scheduled monthly payment is referred to as **level pay** because each
monthly payment is the same, although the percentage of that payment represented by principal versus interest will change over time.
Figure 4.21 illustrates the scheduled P&I, with the cash flows con-

FIGURE 4.21
Scheduled Cash Flows, FHLMC 9 Percent Guarantor PC; 30-Year Amortization; 9.75 WAC, 30-Year WAM, Zero PSA

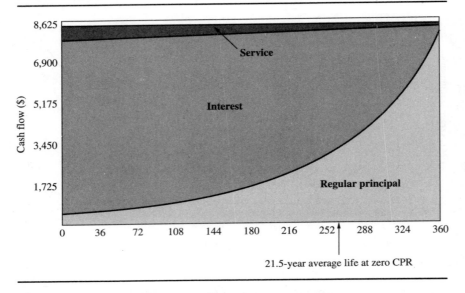

Source: Lehman Brothers Fixed Income Research.

sisting of mostly interest in the early years and then shifting to a heavier percentage of principal in the later years. Since the figure illustrates the scheduled P&I, it is at zero PSA (PSA is an index of prepayment speeds and is described on page 203).

Figure 4.22 reflects the introduction of prepayments, assuming 150 PSA. Prepayments have an impact on the pool cash flows as follows:

1. The cash flows have become *front-end* loaded.
2. The total amount of principal is *the same*—just flip-flopped.
3. The total amount of interest is *less*—interest lives off principal, and some principal has been prepaid.

Compare the pattern of principal payments and average life for an FHLMC 9 percent PC at zero PSA (Figure 4.21) with that shown in Figures 4.22 and 4.23, which show the cash flows at 150 and 75 PSA, respectively. Note that at zero PSA in Figure 4.21 the

FIGURE 4.22

Cash Flows, FHLMC 9 Percent Guarantor PC; 30-Year Amortization, 9.75 WAC, 30-Year WAM, 150 PSA

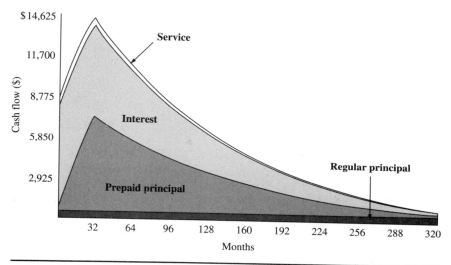

Source: Bloomberg Financial Markets.

principal payments are heavily weighted to the right side of the graph (back-end loaded). Also note that the WAL is positioned well past the midpoint (15 years) of the cash flow cycle. This is so because the average life is a time-weighted calculation. The farther away the cash flows, the more heavily they are weighted.

Now look at Figure 4.23, which illustrates the cash flows at 75 PSA. Note first that the principal payments rise slowly for about 2.5 years and then plateau. This is a reflection of the PSA curve, which defines the phenomenon that prepayments are very slow in the early years and increase gradually until the pool has achieved "normal" seasoning (30 months on the PSA curve). Next, note that even though 75 PSA is a relatively slow prepayment speed (100 PSA is the benchmark), the principal payments have shifted to the left side of the graph, giving some front-end loading to the principal-payment pattern. The WAL, because of this front-end loading, has shifted dramatically to 13.3 years, just short of the cash flow midpoint. Finally, Figure 4.24 shows how the cash flows become very front-end loaded with an acceleration in prepayments to 300 PSA.

FIGURE 4.23
**Cash Flows, $1 Million FHLMC 9 Percent Guarantor PC; 30-Year
Amortization; 9.75 WAC; 30-Year WAM; 75 PSA**

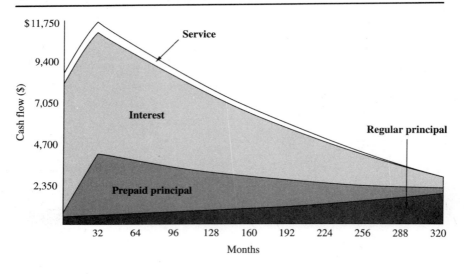

Source: Bloomberg Financial Markets.

If the MBS was purchased at a discount, accelerating prepayments enhance the realized yield because the time required to earn the unrealized discount is accelerated. When purchased at a premium price, accelerating prepayments reduce the yield because the high coupon is called away and there is less time to amortize the price premium. This effect results in price compression, causing the premium-priced MBS to underperform (for a discussion of price compression see Chapter 2).

Prepayment Volatility of Derivative Products

The impact of prepayments is magnified in derivative products such as strips or CMO residuals. The prices and yields of these securities are much more sensitive to changes in prepayment rates for the underlying collateral than are the cash flows from the collateral itself, making them potential hedging vehicles. The exceptional volatility of their returns, however, requires that investors thoroughly

FIGURE 4.24

Cash Flows, $1 Million FHLMC 9 Percent Guarantor PC; 30-Year Amortization; 9.75 WAC; 30-Year WAM; 300 PSA

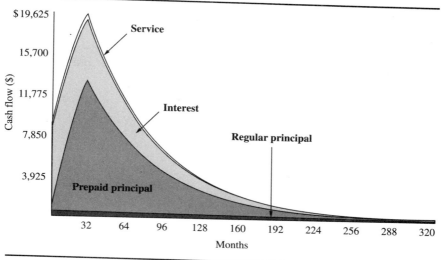

Source: Bloomberg Financial Markets.

understand the prepayment characteristics of the collateral underlying the derivative.

8. HOW DO I MEASURE PREPAYMENTS

Three standards are used to measure prepayment speed: FHA experience, CPR (single monthly mortality: SMM), and PSA (Figure 4.25).

FHA Experience

The Federal Housing Administration (FHA) has for many years tracked mortgage loan payoffs from its multibillion dollar portfolio and has found that the average FHA mortgage prepays in about 12 years. The 12-year-average-life assumption was for several years the single standard by which MBSs were priced and traded. Now it is recognized that different pools will prepay differently, some faster

FIGURE 4.25
Measuring Prepayment Speeds

FHA	Measures mortgage mortality as a percentage change from prior period unpaid principal balance.
CPR	Measures prepayments only as a percentage change from prior period unpaid principal balance.
PSA	100 PSA assumes prepayments increase 0.2% per month cumulatively for 30 months; thereafter, 6% per month.

After month 30
    75 PSA = 4.5 CPR = 14.0-year average life
   100 PSA =   6 CPR = 12.3-year average life
   150 PSA =   9 CPR = 9.8-year average life
   200 PSA = 12 CPR = 8.1-year average life
   300 PSA = 18 CPR = 6.0-year average life for 30-year
                       FNMA 9.5 MBS

Source: Lehman Brothers Fixed Income Research.

than 12 years and some slower, and the FHA prepayment standard has been replaced by more sensitive measures such as CPR and PSA.

CPR

Constant prepayment rate (CPR) was developed as an index that takes into account only principal repayments in excess of those contractually required. For this reason many people view CPR as a more sensitive index of the rate of principal repayments. This index is particularly applicable to evaluating the prepayment speed of conventionally backed Fannie Mae and Freddie Mac pools. CPR is the ratio of the difference between the amortized balance assuming scheduled amortization only and the *actual* balance *including* prepayments to the scheduled amortized balance, as shown in Equation 4.1.

$$\frac{\text{BALs} - \text{BALp}}{\text{BALs}} \qquad (4.1)$$

where

   BALs = Amortized balance assuming scheduled amortization only

   BALp = Amortized balance including prepayments

The result gives the percentage change in the unpaid principal balance reflecting *prepayments only*.

Measurements of prepayment rate may be expressed in terms of SMM and CPR. SMM reflects the percentage of outstanding principal balance prepaid each month, and CPR is simply SMM annualized. CPR reflects prepayment experience over a year, and the monthly rate may be calculated from the annual CPR rate. CPR thereby corrects for the compounding effect of SMM. When comparing rates of prepayments expressed as a percentage of FHA or as CPR, it is useful to bear in mind that for seasoned loans, 6 CPR is roughly equivalent to 100 FHA. (For a more detailed discussion of the mathematical calculations illustrating the computation of FHA, CPR, and SMM, see Calculations of Prepayment Speeds, page 204.)

PSA

In July 1985, in response to the evolving CMO market, the Public Securities Association (PSA) standardized all of the methods used to measure prepayment speed into a common standard for measuring prepayments, referred to as PSA. The PSA standard was developed to conform the very slow speed associated with newly originated loans to that of MBS pools backed by loans that have been outstanding for two and a half years (30 months) or more. Figure 4.26 illustrates the relationship between PSA and CPR. Note especially that the stated CPR differs from 100 PSA during the initial seasoning process (0 to 30 months). This differential illustrates what is referred to as the **PSA ramp.** One hundred PSA is defined as follows: zero CPR in month zero, increasing by 0.2 CPR monthly, rising to 6 CPR in month 30, and remaining at 6 CPR thereafter through maturity. Thus, 100 PSA is substantially equivalent to 100 FHA experience and to 6 CPR. Assuming a constant PSA or FHA as a predictor implies that the prepayment rate (and the CPR) will change over time according to a predefined pattern.

The PSA method may be thought of either as an idealized FHA curve or as the CPR method adjusted for fewer prepayments in the early years. Prepayments are expressed as a percentage of the PSA standard: 50 PSA, 100 PSA, and so forth. Zero PSA is equivalent to zero CPR or zero FHA—that is, no prepayments. One hundred PSA or FHA means that the pool prepays at the same rate as the PSA or FHA standard.

FIGURE 4.26
PSA Curves and CPR Equivalents

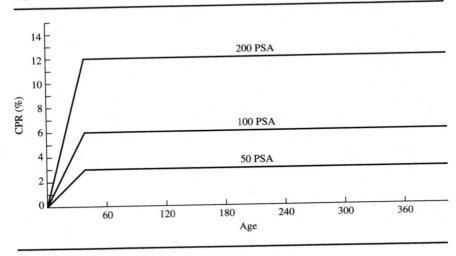

Source: Lehman Brothers Fixed Income Research.

Calculation of Prepayment Speeds

Prepayments represent principal payments made in addition to the P&I payments required under the scheduled amortization of the mortgage contract. This section examines the computation of prepayments first as SMM and then relates the SMM calculation to annualized equivalents such as CPR.

Since prepayments are simply principal payments made in addition to the scheduled principal amortization, our starting point is the **amortization factor**, which is derived from Equation 4.2 as BAL_t.

$$BAL_t = 1 - \frac{(1 + I)^t - 1}{(1 + I)^m - 1} \tag{4.2}$$

where

BAL_t = Unpaid principal balance at time t
I = Rate
m = Stated maturity

Calculation of SMM

SMM measures the monthly amount of principal payments for the pool between two periods. Since SMM measures the compound rate of reduction between the two periods, it therefore tends to smooth the pattern of prepayments over the period measured. Thus, a single large prepayment in a single month is averaged out to an SMM percentage for the period, which theoretically could be distorted if one month experienced an abnormally large one-time prepayment. For this reason some analysts prefer to examine the monthly reported factors to determine whether the monthly paydowns are steady or erratic before the calculated SMM for the period is accepted as a fair representation of the true prepayment pattern of the pool. SMM is calculated as in Equation 4.3.

$$SMM_n = 100[1 - (SF_{t+n}/SF_t)^{1/n}] \qquad (4.3)$$

where

n = The number of months between month t and month $t + n$

To calculate SMM, we must compare the actual or reported factor to what the factor based on scheduled amortization alone would have been, assuming no prepayments. If the reported factor is the same as the factor based on scheduled amortization, there were no prepayments; if the reported factor is less than the scheduled amortization factor (which, of course, is usually the case), there were prepayments.

Calculation of Prepayment Speeds

The top row in Figure 4.27 shows the actual reported factors (F_1 and F_2) for the pool at periods 1 and 2 (F_1 for period 1, F_2 for period 2). The pool factors based on the actual unpaid principal balance for this pool were 0.9878 and 0.9758 for periods 1 and 2, respectively. Compare these factors with the calculated *scheduled amortization*, BAL_1 and BAL_2, for periods 1 and 2. The actual factors (F_1 and F_2) are less than the scheduled factors, so prepayments occurred.

To derive the SMM we take a ratio of the difference between the survival factors for periods 1 and 2 (SF_1 and SF_2), which represent the number of loans that survived from period 1 to period 2, divided by SF_1 (rows 3 and 4).

FIGURE 4.27
Prepayment Rate Calculation

Month	0	1	2
Pool factors (actual)	1.000	F_1 0.9878	F_2 0.9758
Scheduled amortization unpaid balance	1.000	BAL_1 0.9984	BAL_2 0.9968
Survival factors $SF_t = F_t \div BAL$	1.000	SF_1 0.9894	SF_2 0.9789
Single monthly mortality $\left(\dfrac{SF_1 - SF_2}{SF_1} \right)$		$\left(\dfrac{0.9894 - 0.9789}{0.9894} \right) = \dfrac{0.0105}{0.9894} = 0.0106$	
Constant prepayment rate CPR $= 1 - (1 - SMM)^{12}$ $= 1 - (1 - 0.0106)12 = 12\%$			

We can determine the survival factor (SF), which is the percentage of loans that have survived (not prepaid) with Equation 4.4.

$$SF_t = F_t/BAL_t \qquad (4.4)$$

where

F_t = Reported, or actual, pool factor at time t
BAL_t = Amortization factor (from Equation 4.1)

Example. Assume we wish to calculate the SMM rate of a 10 percent mortgage at the 24th month of its amortization schedule. Assume a beginning factor of 1.0000 and a reported factor of .9455 at the 24th month.

$$BAL_{24} = 1 = \frac{(1 + .0083333)^{24} - 1}{(1 + .0083333)^{360} - 1}$$

BAL_{24} = .9883
SF_0 = 1.000/1.000 = 1.0000

where

SF_0 is at time zero, or the issue date of the pool
SF_{24} = .9455/.9883 = .9567

where

SF$_t$ is at month 24

Now having derived SF$_0$, which is 1, and SF$_{24}$, which is applied as SF$_{t+n}$ in Equation 4.3 we can calculate SMM as follows:

$$SMM_{24} = 100[1 - (.9567/1.0000)^{1/24}]$$
$$SMM_{24} = 100[1 - (.9567)^{.041666}]$$
$$SMM_{24} = .184$$

Calculation of CPR

CPRs are the annualized equivalents of SMMs. CPR is calculated from SMM as in Equation 4.5.

$$CPR = 100 \{1 - [1 - (SMM/100)]^{12}\} \qquad (4.5)$$

Following our earlier example, we see that

$$CPR = 100 \{1 - [1 - (.1842963/100)]^{12}\}$$
$$CPR = 100 [1 - (.9981570)^{12}]$$
$$CPR = 100 (1 - .9781068)$$
$$CPR = 2.189319$$

With rounding to two decimals, CPR = 2.19. Conversely, SMM may be found, given CPR, by Equation 4.6.

$$SMM = 100 \{1 - [1 - (CPR/100)]^{1/12}\} \qquad (4.6)$$

Converting between CPR and PSA

It is useful to be able quickly to convert prepayment speed data from CPR to PSA, or from PSA to CPR. When doing so, it is helpful to remember:

- 6 CPR = 100 PSA, but only with pools that are seasoned 30 months or more.
- For loans that are less than 30 months old, the exact months of age must be known or assumed.
- At 100 PSA the model assumes that speed increases 0.2 percent per month linearly, so be aware of the function of 0.2 percent related to months of age.
- Therefore, after 30 months, 100 PSA = 6 CPR.

Converting CPR and PSA of Seasoned Loans

To convert from PSA to CPR with loans seasoned 30 months or more, we divide the PSA number by 100 to convert it to a decimal and multiply by 6 (100 PSA = 6 CPR).

$$\text{Pool age} > 30 \text{ months}$$
$$CPR = \frac{\text{Percent PSA}}{100} \times 6 \tag{4.7}$$

Example: Assume PSA = 150:

$$CPR = \frac{150}{100} = 1.5 \times 6 = 9$$
$$CPR = 9$$

To convert CPR to PSA for pools seasoned 30 months or more, simply divide the CPR by 6 and multiply by 100.

$$\text{Pool age} > 30 \text{ months}$$
$$PSA = \frac{CPR}{6} \times 100 \tag{4.8}$$

Following our example, we see that

$$CPR = 9$$
$$PSA = \frac{9}{6} = 1.5 \times 100 = 150$$
$$PSA = 150$$

Converting CPR and PSA of New Production Loans

To convert CPR to PSA for pools aged less than 30 months, divide the CPR by the product of the age (m) times 0.2 (at 100 PSA the model increases the speed by 0.2 per month) and multiply by 100.

$$\text{Pool age} < 30 \text{ months}$$
$$PSA = \frac{CPR}{(0.2) \times (m)} \times 100 \tag{4.9}$$

From the example,

$$CPR = 2.4$$
$$m = 8$$
$$PSA = \frac{2.4}{0.2 \times 8} = \frac{2.4}{1.6} = 1.5 \times 100 = 150$$
$$PSA = 150$$

Be cautioned that the formula does not work for CPRs that represent time periods of more than one month—for instance, 3 months CPR—when the pool is on the PSA ramp.

This example demonstrates the reason for the creation of the PSA model. Since pools of new production loans are not as sensitive to the demographics that influence seasoned pools, the application of the CPR method will result in a misleading speed assumption (in this case, a CPR of 2.4 percent, which is "slow" compared to the norm of 6 CPR). So if the CPR method gives us a 2.4 CPR, when we convert to the PSA model we find that this pool is actually fast (150 PSA) relative to the 100 PSA norm for a new production GNMA pool (100 PSA), or at least equal to the benchmark norm for a conventional pool that is 150 PSA.

If the pool consists of new production loans, that is, with an age less than 30 months, we must take into account the number of months of age, since the PSA increases 0.2 percent per month for each month up to (but not exceeding) 30 months. Therefore, assume PSA = 150:

$$\text{Pool age} < 30 \text{ months}$$
$$\text{CPR} = (0.2 \times m) \times \frac{\text{PSA}}{100} \qquad (4.10)$$

where

m = months of age since issue

Example. Assume WAM = 352 months:

$$m = (360 - 352) = 8$$
$$\text{PSA} = 150$$

Convert PSA to a decimal:

$$\frac{150}{100} = 1.5$$
$$\text{CPR} = (0.2 \times 8)(1.5) = 2.4$$
$$\text{CPR} = 2.4$$

Drawbacks of PSA

PSA can be misleading when it is used with new production premiums that can reach ridiculously high PSAs during times of high refinancing. For example, consider FNMA 9.5s, which peaked at 1,138 PSA in October 1992. Many mortgage market observers were terrified to see such high PSAs. Look again at the conversion formula using 1,000 PSA on an MBS pool aged 6 months. Remember,

$$PSA = \frac{\text{Reported CPR} \times 100}{\text{Benchmark CPR}}$$

In the example the PSA is 1,000 and the benchmark CPR would be 1.2 (6 months × 0.2). To solve for reported CPR, what number times 100 equals 1,000 PSA? Answer: 10. What reported CPR number divided by 1.2 equals 10? Answer: 12. Therefore:

$$\frac{12}{1.2} = 10$$

$$10 \times 100 = 1,000 \text{ PSA}$$

At 12 CPR we are paying down the balance at an annual rate of 12 percent of the period's beginning unpaid principal balance. Twelve CPR is certainly a less frightening number than 1,000 PSA!

CHAPTER 5

CHANGES IN HOUSEHOLD FORMATIONS: IMPLICATIONS FOR OWNERSHIP HOUSING TURNOVER IN THE 1990S

Phillip E. Kidd

INTRODUCTION

The extended decline in long-term interest rates is approaching a bottom. When that point is reached, prepayments from refinancing of home mortgages will dwindle in the 1990s as a proportion of total prepayments. In contrast, home sales will become an even larger percentage of single-family mortgage prepayments.

In this decade, three major long-term demographic trends will have an impact on housing turnover.[1] (These demographic trends are explored in detail in Housing Turnover in the 1990s, pages 237–241.) First, the population is aging. As people age, they become less willing to change residences, thereby lowering the volume of home sales. Second, fewer households are expected to form in the 1990s as against the 1980s. As household formations fall, overall demand for new housing construction declines, cutting into a source of home sales. Third, a much smaller number of people (referred to as busters) is replacing the huge boomer cohort in the important age group of first-time home purchasers. With fewer first-time buyers, some homeowners may find it more difficult to sell their existing homes and move up to larger or more upscale homes.

The housing turnover ratio has already been inching down since the late 1980s. Given the negative implications for home sales

---

[1] In this chapter the term "housing" refers to ownership, as opposed to rental, housing unless indicated otherwise.

of these influential demographic forces, forecasting a continuation of that slide in this decade seems reasonable. The real questions, however, are: What shape will the slope of the turnover rate take in the next eight years? Will it fall at a leisurely pace? Will the decline gain momentum? Or will there be periods when the rate actually slopes upward? To answer these questions, we must first look back at what should have happened demographically in the 1980s but did not happen. With that historical background, the demographic reasons the slope of the turnover rate could change several times in the 1990s can be explored.

THE HOUSING TURNOVER RATIO: WHAT IS IT?

The housing turnover rate may be viewed as housing sales divided by the stock of housing. Housing sales include existing home sales (counting condominiums and cooperatives) plus single-family housing starts plus two or more unit starts intended for sale at the time of the start. Housing stock is defined as year-round single-family houses (attached and detached) plus year-round two to four units plus owner-occupied five or more units.

Single-family housing starts are chosen over new home sales because they offer the broadest coverage of construction that generates residential mortgage activity. New home sales cover sales only of speculative-built homes. Single-family housing starts include speculative-built homes plus owner-built homes plus contractor-built homes where a sales contract has already been signed. Homes constructed either with an existing sales contract or by the owners generally require mortgage financing. Excluding them understates the demand for mortgage credit. Year-round housing units, which include less than 10 percent vacant units, are included in housing stock because even vacant units can involve mortgage financing. Similarly, year-round two- to four-family structures are in the stock because some are condominium units, whereas in other cases an owner lives in one of the units. Mortgages on these units are generally included in single-family mortgage pools. Year-round units were not used for five or more family units because most of these are rental units, and identifying the comparatively few vacant units intended for sale is difficult. Thus, only owner-occupied five or more units were added to the housing stock.

The housing turnover rate has been slipping since the late 1980s. This is not surprising; indeed, the construction of the turn-

FIGURE 5.1
Housing Turnover Rate, 1970–1990

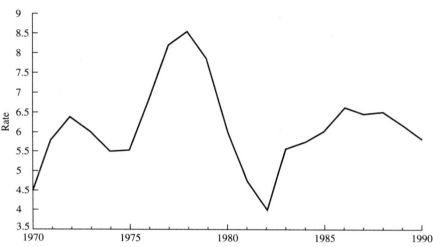

over rate implies that it will decline over time (see Figure 5.1). In most years, more new units are added to inventory than leave the stock. Thus, the denominator of the turnover rate usually expands each year. Even if housing sales (the numerator) remain at a constant high volume for several years, the rate will drop because of the growth in the denominator.

Despite this long-run downward bias, the turnover rate fluctuated considerably from 1970 to 1990. Generally, these were years of extremely favorable demographics for buying a home. Yet the sharp swings in the slope of the rate reflect abrupt changes in economic conditions that sometimes pulled with and other times pushed against the highly advantageous demographics for housing sales.

HOUSING TURNOVER IN THE 1970S AND 1980S

Boomers and Housing Sales

Boomers is the name given the group of people born between 1946 and 1964. During that 19-year period, there were actually two distinct birth waves (see Figure 5.2). In the first wave, births climbed

FIGURE 5.2
Annual Number of Births, 1935–1992

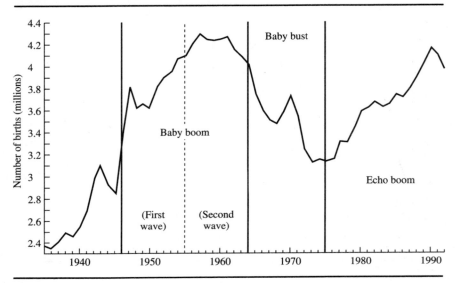

Source: U.S. Bureau of the Census.

from 2.9 million in 1945 to over 4 million in 1954. In the second wave, births leveled off, but at a rate in excess of 4 million a year from 1955 to 1964. Altogether, 76 million people were born in that time span—34 million in the first wave and 42 million in the second wave.

Since their entrance into the housing market—first in the rental apartment market in the late 1960s and then in the home ownership market in the mid-1970s—the boomers have dominated housing and mortgage market activity. Their pre-eminence will be challenged only gradually in the late 1990s, when the first of those born in the birth surge since 1976 (the echo boomers) begin entering the rental market.

When the first wave began leaving their parents' homes to set up their own residences, household formations immediately accelerated. Changes in household formations are important because they are a leading indicator of two thirds to three quarters of potential demand for residential construction in the years ahead. (The bal-

TABLE 5.1
Occupancy Status by Age of Householder

Occupancy Status	All Ages	Under 25	25–29	30–34	35–44	45–64	Over 65
			Age Group				
			1990 (%)				
Homeowner	64.1	15.3	35.9	51.5	66.4	78.1	75.5
Renter	35.9	84.7	64.1	48.5	33.6	21.9	24.5
			1980 (%)				
Homeowner	64.4	22.1	46.5	63.5	71.2	77.3	70.1
Renter	35.6	77.9	53.5	36.5	28.8	22.7	29.9

Source: Current Population Reports, U.S. Bureau of the Census, U.S. Census 1980, P-20, No. 447.

ance of the demand comes from changes in vacancies, second homes, and replacement of worn-out units.)

The age at which households are formed is equally important. Householders between 18 and 29 years of age represent the largest group of renters. Normally, young householders begin switching from apartment living to home ownership in their middle twenties, with the transition usually continuing into their forties (see Table 5.1).

In general, when first-time purchasers, especially those in the youngest age groups, enter the market, they buy existing homes. Previous owners use the proceeds from the sales to purchase either larger or more upscale existing or new homes. Thus, as younger households grow in number, their home acquisitions stimulate sales of both existing and new homes.

The 1973–1975 recession somewhat muffled the initial movement of the first wave into the home ownership market. Housing sales climbed from 2.6 million units in 1970 to 3.8 million in 1972 and then fell back to 3.3 million in 1974 when economic growth halted. As a result, the turnover rate rose early in the decade, but retreated during the recession (see Figure 5.1).

The early 1970s were only a prelude. With the economy expanding after late 1975, housing sales jumped to 5.7 million units in 1978, more than two and a quarter times the 1970 figure. Interestingly, that sales level has not been approached since. The double-dip recessions in the early 1980s slashed sales almost in half, to below 3 million units in 1982. Even the longest peacetime expansion in U.S. history only pushed sales above 5 million units, although that volume held for three years, from 1986 to 1988. More recently, the no/low growth of the early 1990s trimmed sales to 4 million units in 1991.

High Ownership Housing Demand Predicted for the 1980s

In 1978, the year of the record 5.7 million home sales, only the first wave of boomers was in the age range of first-home purchase—roughly 25 to 44 years. At that time, the expectation was that the 1980s would bring even higher sales because both waves of boomers would be rapidly forming households. For example, the Census Bureau projected that households could rise from 76 million in 1978 to 96.6 million in 1990, an increase of 20.6 million in 12 years.[2] That translated into an expected average annual increase of 1.7 million households, of which two thirds (over 1.1 million) would be between the ages of 25 and 44. Given those estimates, housing purchases were forecasted to thrive in the 1980s, but only if the economy cooperated.

The economy, of course, did not cooperate. Inflation was halted and then reversed through an extended period of restrained monetary policy. Initially, tight policy sent the economy into two recessions in the early 1980s, which hindered job growth. Once aggressive fiscal policy pushed the economy into a lengthy recovery, cautious monetary policy coupled with poor domestic savings fostered exceptionally high real interest rates throughout the rest of the decade.

Meanwhile, manufacturing, faced with intense competition from abroad, underwent a prolonged period of modernization and employee layoffs designed to regain its competitiveness. For a while, tax incentives fueled an income property construction boom. When those incentives were removed in 1985, the boom soon collapsed, causing massive job reductions and other problems that still bedevil the construction and financial industries today. More re-

---

[2]U.S. Bureau of the Census, "Projections of the Number of Households and Families: 1979 to 1995, Series B," *Current Population Reports*, P-25, No. 805, May 1979, p. 14.

FIGURE 5.3
Real Median Income of First-Time Home Buyers, 1970–1991

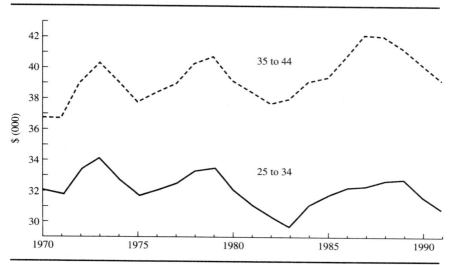

Source: U.S. Bureau of the Census, "Money Income of Households, Families, and Persons in the United States: 1991," *Current Population Reports,* P 60, No. 180

cently, weakened demand forced many service companies, which thrived throughout most of the 1980s, to cut employees and trim capacity to reduce costs and improve profits.

In retrospect, the 1980s was a time of massive restructuring of the domestic economy. Mostly that economic reshaping occurred simultaneously with the entrance of an enormous number of people (the second boomer wave combined with the continued rise in female participation) into the labor market.

Although real gross domestic product (GDP) grew for most of this period, the large expansion of job seekers plus the turmoil of reshaping much of the economy inhibited real income growth. Indeed, the real median income of households in the age range of first-time home purchase is no higher today than it was in 1980 (see Figure 5.3). In contrast, housing prices accelerated through much of the decade as the huge number of boomers moved into the ownership market, bidding up prices.

Together, minimal real gains in earnings, rising home prices, and high real interest rates created a housing affordability gap, especially among first-time buyers (see Figure 5.4). Although home sales rose in the decade, the inability of household income to match

FIGURE 5.4
Housing Affordability, 1970–1991

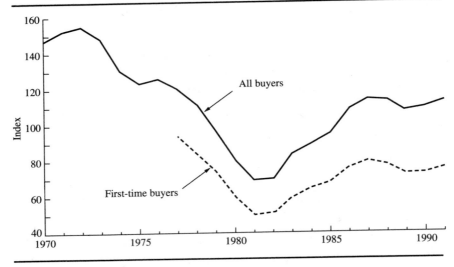

Source: National Association of Realtors.

the advances in monthly mortgage payments was an important reason sales did not reach the levels predicted for them on a strictly demographic basis in the late 1970s.

Altogether, home ownership rates for all households were just about the same in 1990 as in 1980. However, the ownership rates for households in each age group between 25 and 44 were much lower in 1990 than in 1980 (see Table 5.1). Clearly, the process of households moving from renters to homeowners was stretched out considerably in the 1980s.

Fewer Households Than Predicted

Normally, the delay in first-time home purchases would indicate larger than expected sales during the next sustainable economic expansion as boomers satisfied their pent-up demand. Even that conclusion is being questioned because of lower household formations and substantial changes in household composition in the 1980s. Actual household formations in the 1980s were far less than had been forecasted in the late 1970s (see Figure 5.5). After exceeding the projected 1.7 million annual average in 1978 and 1979, household

FIGURE 5.5

Actual and Projected Gains in Households, 1970–1990

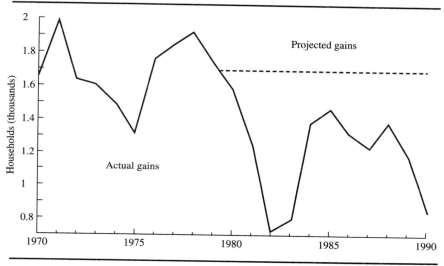

Source: U.S. Bureau of the Census, *Current Population Reports*, P-20, various issues, and P-25, No. 805.

formations plummeted to less than 0.8 million during the recessions of 1981 and 1982.

Although rising during the extended economic expansion from 1983 to 1988, the annual increase in households remained well below the 1978 projections. When the economy stumbled into a prolonged period of stagnation in 1989, household formations slumped, falling below a million per year in 1992. Overall, households actually grew at an annual rate of 1.2 million in the 1980s, about 0.5 million a year less than had been projected in 1978.

Changing Household Composition in the 1980s

Not only did the unsettled economic conditions of the 1980s hold back household formations, they also affected the composition of households being created. The change in household composition became evident in the 1970s as the first wave of boomers left home to establish their own residences (see Table 5.2)

TABLE 5.2
Household Types, 1970, 1980, 1990 (households in thousands)

Household Type	1970	1980	1990	Change		
				1970–1980	1980–1990	
All households	63,531	80,390	91,947	16,859	11,557	
Family households	51,586	59,023	64,517	7,437	5,494	
Married couples	44,755	48,725	59,798	3,970	1,983	
Other households	6,830	10,298	13,810	3,468	3,512	
Male householders	1,239	1,986	3,144	747	1,158	
Female householders	5,591	8,312	10,666	2,712	2,354	
Nonfamily households	11,945	21,367	27,429	9,422	6,062	
Male householders	4,063	8,896	N.A.	4,833	—	
Female householders	7,882	12,471	N.A.	4,589	—	
Living alone	10,851	18,262	22,580	7,411	4,318	

		Percentage of Households		*Change (%)*		
All households	100.0	100.0	100.0	26.5	14.4	
Family households	81.2	73.4	70.2	14.4	9.3	
Married couples	70.4	60.6	55.1	8.9	4.1	
Other households	10.8	12.8	15.0	50.8	34.1	
Male householders	2.0	2.5	3.4	60.3	58.3	
Female householders	8.8	10.3	11.6	48.7	28.3	
Nonfamily households	18.8	26.6	29.8	78.9	28.4	
Male householders	6.4	11.1	—	119.0	—	
Female householders	12.4	15.5	—	58.2	—	
Living alone	17.1	22.7	24.6	68.3	23.6	

Sources: U.S. Bureau of the Census, U.S. Census, 1970, 1980, and 1990, and *Current Population Reports*, P-20, Nos. 352 and 458.

In 1970, 70 percent of all households were married couples. Another 11 percent were other family households (male or female householders), and 19 percent were nonfamily households (unrelated individuals living together or persons living alone). Ten years later, married couples had declined from 70 percent to 60 percent of all households. The percentage of other family households rose slightly, from 11 to 13 percent, but the biggest gain was in nonfamily households, which climbed from 19 to nearly 27 percent.

During the 1980s, the people in the even larger second boomer wave actively formed households. They continued the trend of establishing nontraditional households begun by their older brothers and sisters of the first wave. But the pace of change was slower than in the 1970s. By 1990, the percentage of married couples had fallen from 60 percent a decade earlier to 55 percent of all households. Both other family households (13 to 15 percent) and nonfamily households (27 to 30 percent) had only modest larger shares of the total in 1990 than in 1980. In the first-home-buying age group, however, the shift from married couples to other types of households in the past two decades has been even more startling than for the entire population. In 1970, over 90 percent of all these households were family households, and married couples made up almost 90 percent of those (see Tables 5.3 and 5.4).

Twenty years later, households composed of 25- to 44-year-olds had grown by 16.7 million, from 23.5 million in 1970 to 40.2 million in 1990. Family households made up 8.8 million of that gain and nonfamily households 7.9 million. Among family households, the growth was almost evenly split between married couples and other family households. A rise in female householders accounted for almost four fifths of the advance in other family households. As a result of these changes, married couple households accounted for only 58 percent of all households in the 25-to-44 age group in 1990. That was a staggering decline from the 82 percent in 1970.

HOUSEHOLD TYPE AND HOME OWNERSHIP

While age of households is meaningful, the composition of households—married couples or some other living arrangement—within each age group is even more important in determining the type of housing (ownership or rental) that households will demand. Examining the shift in the percentage of ownership by household types

TABLE 5.3
Types of Households by Age (Households in Thousands)

Household Type	Less Than 25	25–29	30–34	35–44	45–64	65 and Over	All Ages
1990							
All households	5,049	9,018	10,831	20,393	26,683	19,973	91,947
Family households	2,630	6,002	8,151	16,300	20,634	10,801	64,518
Married couples	1,584	4,480	6,310	12,656	16,882	8,796	50,708
Other family	1,046	1,522	1,841	3,644	3,752	2,005	13,810
Nonfamily households	2,419	3,016	2,680	4,093	6,049	9,172	27,429
Living alone	1,196	1,989	2,002	3,272	5,296	8,825	22,580
1980							
All households	6,596	9,129	9,153	13,891	25,307	16,313	80,390
Family households	3,801	6,488	7,415	12,073	20,325	8,921	59,024
Married couples	2,870	5,332	6,111	9,822	17,232	7,357	48,725
Other family	931	1,156	1,304	2,251	3,092	1,564	10,298
Nonfamily households	2,795	2,641	1,738	1,818	4,983	7,392	21,367
Living alone	1,682	2,006			4,589	7,145	18,262
1970							
All households	4,431	6,098	5,604	11,812	23,060	12,526	63,531
Family households	3,559	5,417	5,210	10,988	19,190	7,222	51,586
Married couples	3,043	4,878	4,699	9,712	16,650	5,773	44,755
Other family	516	539	511	1,276	2,540	1,449	6,830
Nonfamily households	872	681	1,320	1,520	3,870	5,304	11,945
Living alone	NA	NA	NA	NA	NA	NA	NA

NA = Not available.

Sources: U.S. Bureau of the Census, U.S. Census, 1970, 1980, and 1990.

across age groups during the past two decades identifies three significant trends (see Table 5.5). First, ownership rates for each type of household—married couples, other family, and nonfamily—increase with advancing age. Second, married couples have substantially higher rates of home ownership in each group than other types of households. Altogether, slightly more than three out of four married couples owned homes in 1990, whereas slightly less than one in two other family or nonfamily households owned homes. Third, married couples achieve ownership at a much earlier age than their nonmarried peers. This discrepancy in ownership is most pronounced in the age groups under 45.

In the past, ownership rates of married couples jumped from around 30 percent when they are under 25 years of age to over 80 percent before they are 45. In contrast, other family and nonfamily households primarily remain renters until they are past 45 years of age. After that age, the sizable gains in ownership rates for both of these household types comes mainly from the growing presence of divorced persons or widows and widowers who remain in the homes they owned when they were married.

Studying the ownership rates by age and type of household in 1976, 1980, and 1990 brings out several other changes. Between 1976 and 1980 the first wave of boomers came charging into the ownership market. As they formed households, the number of nonfamily households under 35 years of age rose sharply, as did the percentage of homeowners in this group. There was also some growth in the proportion of married couples that owned homes in this age group. Only other family households, except for those under 25, did not post a gain in home ownership rates. In the above-35 age group, there were only modest changes in the ownership percentage for each household type. During the 1980s, when both waves were in the age range of first-home purchase, there was an uneven shift in ownership rates among household types. Younger (under-30) nonfamily households lost ground, but over-30 households scored impressive gains in ownership between 1980 and 1990. Meanwhile, ownership rates for other family households under 45 were far less in 1990 than in 1980.

The real surprise comes in comparing ownership rates for married couples at the beginning and end of the decade. These percentages for each age group under 45 were smaller in 1990 than in 1980, with the biggest declines registered among married couples under 35. And the number of households in the 1990 U.S. Census was 4.7 million less than had been projected in 1978 (see Table

TABLE 5.4
Distribution of Households by Types and Age Groups (%)

Household Type	Less Than 25	25–29	30–34	35–44	45–64	65 and Over	All Ages
				1990			
All households	100.0	100.0	100.0	100.0	100.0	100.0	100.0
Family	52.1	66.6	75.3	79.9	77.3	54.1	70.2
Nonfamily	47.9	33.4	24.7	20.1	22.7	45.9	29.8
Married percentage of family households	60.2	74.6	77.4	77.6	81.8	81.4	78.6
Other family percentage of households	39.8	25.4	22.6	22.4	18.2	18.6	21.4
Living alone percentage of nonfamily households	49.4	65.9	74.7	79.9	87.6	96.2	82.3
				1980			
All households	100.0	100.0	100.0	100.0	100.0	100.0	100.0
Family	57.6	71.1	81.2	86.9	80.3	54.7	73.4
Nonfamily	42.4	28.9	19.0	13.1	19.7	45.3	26.6
Married percentage of family households	75.5	82.2	82.4	81.4	84.8	82.5	82.6
Other family percentage of households	24.5	17.8	17.6	18.6	15.2	17.5	17.4
Living alone percentage of nonfamily households	60.2	76.0	75.9	83.6	92.1	96.7	85.5

TABLE 5.4 *(Concluded)*

				1970			
Household Type	Less Than 25	25–29	30–34	35–44	45–64	65 and Over	All Ages
All households	100.0	100.0	100.0	100.0	100.0	100.0	100.0
Family	80.3	88.8	93.0	93.0	83.2	57.7	81.2
Nonfamily	19.7	11.2	7.0	7.0	16.8	42.3	18.8
Married percentage of family households	85.5	90.0	90.2	88.4	86.8	79.9	86.8
Other family percentage of households	14.5	10.0	9.8	11.6	13.2	20.1	13.2
Living alone percentage of nonfamily households	NA	NA	NA	NA	NA	NA	NA

NA = Not available.

TABLE 5.5
Percentage of Home Ownership by Age Group and Household Type (%)

Household Type	Age Group						
	Less Than 25	25–29	30–34	35–44	45–64	65 and Over	All Ages
	1990						
All households	15.3	35.9	51.5	66.4	78.1	75.5	64.1
Married couples	25.7	51.1	66.4	79.2	88.4	88.5	77.9
Other family	12.7	19.1	28.6	45.2	64.1	76.7	46.2
Nonfamily	9.2	20.2	30.9	43.4	57.1	62.9	46.6
	1980						
All households	22.1	46.5	63.5	71.2	77.3	70.1	64.4
Married couples	36.5	60.6	76.7	82.5	87.1	83.0	77.8
Other family	13.2	24.6	33.6	49.8	64.4	72.9	49.5
Nonfamily	10.3	22.2	30.2	36.5	51.1	56.7	41.0
	1976						
All households	21.1	43.6	62.3	71.2	77.1	71.0	65.1
Married couples	31.3	55.3	74.2	81.1	86.0	82.8	75.9
Other family	9.0	24.6	33.3	48.2	65.3	77.7	50.9
Nonfamily	9.0	15.6	25.8	28.6	49.9	57.6	42.2

Sources: U.S. Bureau of the Census, U.S. Census 1980, and *Current Population Reports*, Nos. 311 and 447.

TABLE 5.6
Actual and Projected Households in 1990 by Type of Household
(Households in Thousands)

Household Type	Actual Households, 1990 (a)	Projection of Households, 1990 (b)	Difference (a − b) (c)
All households	91,947	96,653	(4,706)
Family households	64,518	68,487	(3,969)
Married couples	50,708	54,731	(4,023)
Other households	13,810	13,757	53
Nonfamily households	27,429	28,166	(737)

Note: The Bureau of the Census included five series of projections of household formations from 1979 to 1995 in this source. If one of the other series is used in this comparison, the results would be different. In the late 1970s, however, Series B was most often used in forecasting 1980s housing demand. Interestingly, the series with lower total households than Series B overestimated the number of married households in 1990 to a greater extent than the Series B projection.

Sources: U.S. Bureau of the Census, U.S. Census 1990, and *Projections of the Number of Households and Families: 1979 to 1995*, P-25, No. 805.

5.6). The shortfall of 4 million married couples accounts for 85 percent of this difference. Almost 70 percent of that discrepancy was in married couples in the prime first-home buying age (see Table 5.6). In retrospect, fewer than expected married couples combined with the lower ownership rates among these couples in the first-home—buying age group are the principal reasons that home sales in the 1980s were much less than had been predicted on a strictly demographic basis.

SOURCES OF DEFERRED HOME OWNERSHIP DEMAND

Pent-Up Housing Demand among Existing Households

In the 1980s, the transition from renter to homeowner for many young households never occurred. Consequently, there is still a tremendous amount of pent-up demand on the part of boomers who have not yet purchased their first home. One way to measure this potential demand is to compute the change in the number of households between ages 25 and 44 that would have owned a home if the ownership rates for each household type had been the same in 1990 as in 1980. For example, among married couples aged 25 to 29, 60.6 percent owned homes in 1980, but only 51.1 percent were homeowners in 1990 (see Table 5.5). If the 1980 rate had prevailed among the 4,480,000 married couples in this age group in 1990, then 426,000 more of them would have owned homes.

Repeating the process for each household type between ages 25 and 44 produces an eye-catching figure of 1.57 million of deferred housing purchases (see Table 5.7). Married couples with a gain of 1.47 million would account for 93 percent of the increase. Nonfamily home ownership, however, would fall in this calculation because ownership rates among that type of household actually grew between 1980 and 1990.

Will all of these households realistically become homeowners in the 1990s? Probably not all, but an exceptionally high proportion will. Most of this deferred demand is among married couples, who are most likely to have two wage earners in the household.

Next, income rises with age. Many boomers have been working for 5 to 10 years or more. They have gained experience and skills and now are being promoted into higher-level, better-paying jobs. Each of these factors boosts household income, especially in married households, making it easier to afford a home.

Finally, home ownership means more than a place to live. For most householders the home is their biggest investment. Unlike the 1980s, housing as an investment will not be based on rapid price appreciation. Instead, the economic turmoil of the early 1990s is pointing up the need for households to save against hard times. In the 1990s, homeowners will view repayment of a mortgage as one of the best ways to build equity. Therefore, even on a conservative basis, it is likely that 90 percent, or 1.4 million, of the 1.57 million households will buy that first home in the next few years.

That is not the end of it. When these households buy that first home, most of the units will be existing ones. Their acquisitions will trigger other purchases as the home sellers look for other existing or new housing. Since a third of home sales are to first-time buyers, the suggestion is that a first-time buyer's purchase generates two additional home sales. On that basis, the conversion of pent-up boomer demand for homes could add up to 4.2 million more housing sales (3 × 1.4 million households) in the next few years.

Interestingly, even if those 1.57 million households had actually owned homes in 1990, the total ownership rates for each age

TABLE 5.7
Potential Pent-Up Demand for Housing by Existing 25- to 44-Year-Old Householders

Household Types, 1990	25–29	30–34	35–44	Total
	Sales (in thousands of units)			
Married couples	426	650	392	1,468
Other family	84	92	168	344
Nonfamily	60	(19)	(262)	(241)
Total pent-up demand	570	723	278	1,571

group between 25 and 44 would still have been less in 1990 than in 1980. Behind this surprising result is the proportional decline in married couples during the 1980s (see Table 5.4).

The total ownership rate is a weighted average of the ownership rate for each type of household in the group. Married couples have much higher ownership rates at every age than other family or nonfamily households (see Table 5.5). The relative growth of these other household types with their smaller percentages of homeowners is the reason the total ownership rate for 25- to 44-year-olds would have remained below its 1980 level. If both the proportion and ownership rates of each household type for ages 25 to 44 had stayed the same in 1990 as in 1980, the potential pent-up demand for ownership housing would be double the estimated 1.57 million. This is another indication that changes in the composition of households in the 1980s continue to affect housing demands today.

Postponed Household Formations—Source of Pent-Up Demand

Comparing the actual and projected households in 1990 brings out the extent of shifts in living arrangements across the age spectrum (see Table 5.8). Specifically investigating the changes in the total and in the composition of households within three age groups—under 25, 25 to 44, and 45 and over—focuses attention on these questions: Are those missing 4.7 million households lost forever? Or has their formation been deferred? And if they are just postponed, what does this mean for housing demand in the 1990s?

TABLE 5.8

Actual and Projected 1990 Households by Age and Type of Household (Households in Thousands)

Household Type	Age					
	Under 25	25–29	30–34	35–44	Over 45	All Ages
Total households						
1990 Actual	5,049	9,018	10,831	20,393	46,655	91,947
1990 Projection	6,645	10,784	12,025	20,646	46,549	96,653
Difference	(1,596)	(1,766)	(1,194)	(253)	106	(4,706)
Married couples						
1990 Actual	1,584	4,480	6,310	12,656	25,678	50,708
1990 Projection	2,081	5,129	7,153	13,637	26,731	54,731
Difference	(497)	(649)	(843)	(981)	(1,053)	(4,023)
Other family						
1990 Actual	1,046	1,522	1,841	3,644	5,757	13,810
1990 Projection	1,223	1,587	2,161	4,065	4,715	13,757
Difference	(177)	(65)	(320)	(421)	1,042	53
Nonfamily						
1990 Actual	2,419	3,016	2,680	4,093	15,221	27,429
1990 Projection	3,341	4,068	2,711	2,944	15,103	28,166
Difference	(922)	(1,052)	(31)	1,149	118	(737)

Sources: U.S. Bureau of the Census, "Projections of the Number of Households and Families: 1979 to 1995," *Current Population Reports*, P-25, No. 805; and U.S. Census, 1990.

The prediction for total households older than 45 is close to the actual total. The mix of household types, however, is very different. Nonfamily and other family households are about 1.1 million more than expected. Married couples are 1 million less than projected. That number accounts for one quarter of the 4 million shortfall in anticipated married couples. Since there is little difference between projected and actual total households among people who were already 45 or over in 1990, household formations were not postponed in this age group. Instead, future demand for housing from this group will come as marriages, divorces, deaths, and remarriages rearrange the mixture of these households, forcing some to sell and others to buy.

In that regard, married couples are not expected to increase enough in this decade to make up the 1 million shortfall. Although people do marry and remarry in this age group, the number of marriages is not likely to offset the breakup of households due to divorces and deaths. In fact, as this group ages, other family and nonfamily households are anticipated to grow both absolutely and relatively compared to married couples.

Overall, these households will be comparatively minor contributors to housing turnover in the 1990s. First, people 45 and older have the lowest mobility of any group in the population (see Table 5.9). Second, they already have the highest rate of home ownership in the population. Third, once they acquire homes, they hold onto them, regardless of the type of household in which they live. As a result, their demand for mortgage funds is more likely to grow in the 1990s from their desire to use the equity in their homes to supplement their incomes rather than from housing turnover (see Rising Mortgage Demand among the Elderly later in this chapter).

In contrast, younger households, which were under 45 in 1990, will drive housing sales in this decade. It is in these age groups that the biggest gap exists between projected households and actual households in 1990. But a distinction must be made between households under age 25 and those between ages 25 and 44.

There were 25 percent fewer households under age 25 in 1990 than had been projected. This is a large deficit with significance for housing, but for rental demand, not ownership demand. Households under age 25 are predominantly renters (see Table 5.5). That nearly 1.6 million such households failed to form as expected, coupled with excessive overbuilding, explains much of the trouble multifamily construction experienced in the 1980s. The delay on the part of this group in forming households, however, does not

TABLE 5.9
Population Mobility

In a five-year period approximately

Two out of every three people in their 20s will move.
One out of every two people in their 30s and early 40s will move.
One out of every five people over 45 will move.

Source: U.S. Bureau of the Census, *Geographical Mobility Surveys.*

represent a carryover of delayed demand for housing from the 1980s to the 1990s. This does not mean that these missing households are unimportant for housing in the 1990s. This group will be starting the transition from rental to home ownership as its members enter the age range of first-time home purchase in the 1990s. Indeed, how many of these postponed households are formed and what types of households they will be are key factors in projecting housing sales over the next few years.

Households between ages 25 and 44 were 3.2 million fewer in 1990 than had been anticipated. Over three quarters of that decline was in married couple households. Other family households accounted for the remaining shortfall.

During the 1980s, the first wave and most of the second wave of boomers were between 25 and 44—the prime years for first-time home purchase. Thus, examining the living arrangements of this age group is crucial for learning whether deferred household formations and postponed marriages have created a delayed demand for housing that will be carried into the 1990s.

Growth in Numbers of Unrelated Adults Living Together

In the 1980s, the number of married couples between ages 25 and 44 grew 2.2 million (see Table 5.3). Meanwhile, total households increased 8.1 million. As a result, the proportion of total married couples to total households in this age group slipped from 66 percent in 1980 to 58 percent in 1990. Instead of marrying, people in this age group sought other living arrangements. One alternative life style was represented by unrelated adults living together. Overall, the Census Bureau estimates that the number of adults living together rose by about 1.7 million in the 1980s. Of that total, 1.3 million, or nearly 80 percent, were between 25 and 44 years old (see Table 5.10).

TABLE 5.10

Increase in the Number of Households with Two Unrelated Adults Living Together, 1980–1990 (Households in Thousands)

Household Type	Age Group				
	Under 25	25–34	35–44	Over 45	All Ages
All households with two unrelated adults					
1990	1,046	1,827	839	761	4,472
1980	924	1,048	297	531	2,799
Difference	122	779	542	230	1,673
Unmarried couples					
1990	596	1,188	587	485	2,856
1980	405	636	183	336	1,560
Difference	191	552	404	149	1,296

Source: U.S. Bureau of the Census, *Current Population Reports*, P-20, Nos. 365 and 450.

This alternative life style accounts for over half of the 2.5 million difference between actual and projected married couples in this age group. The significance for housing demand is that married couples have much higher ownership rates than other household types.

The Census Bureau defines two types of households containing two unrelated adults. Unmarried couples are adults of the opposite sex. Other adult households are made up of two adults of the same sex. In March 1990, the Census Bureau estimated that 2.7 million households contained two unrelated adults between ages 25 and 44. Two thirds, or 1.8 million, were unmarried couples.

Researchers at the University of Wisconsin's Center for Demographic Ecology estimate that 60 percent of unmarried couples will eventually marry each other.[3] How many of the remaining unmarried couples and other adult households will eventually separate, with the partners marrying someone else, is unknown. Based on this limited information, 1.1 million of the 1.8 million unmarried couples in 1990 could marry some time in the 1990s. Eventually, this switch from unmarried to married status could add 375,000

---

[3]Larry Bumpass and James Sweet, "Preliminary Evidence on Cohabitation," University of Wisconsin, Center for Demographic Ecology, NSFH Working Paper No. 2, 1988. Cited by Arlene F. Saluter in "Singleness in America," in U.S. Bureau of the Census, *Studies in Marriage and Family*, Series P-23, No. 162, p. 9.

units to deferred housing demand. Using the multiplier of 3, one sees that these initial purchases could stimulate as many as 1,125,000 more home sales in the 1990s.[4]

No projection was made of potential postponed sales from changes in the marital status of the remaining 1.6 million unrelated adult households (2.7 million minus the 1.1 million who are projected to marry). That decision was based on several factors.

These households could stay together; or the partners could separate and marry someone else, live with someone else, or live alone. However, the pent-up demand potential is primarily in the shift from nonmarried to married status because of the considerably higher ownership rates among married couples. In that regard, an estimate of this delayed demand has been made. Among the remaining households with partners of the same sex, the choice of lifestyle may preclude marriage.

The rise in households with two unrelated adults accounts for over half the shortfall in married couples between ages 25 and 44. Curiously, that lifestyle switch does little to explain the large difference between actual and projected total households in this age group. To examine that shortfall, we must look at individuals who are living in someone else's household.

Growth in Numbers of Children Aged 25 to 44 Living with Parents

Everyone knows families in which grown children live with their parents. What is stunning is that so many of these offspring are over 25. In March 1990, the Census found nearly 6.7 million chil-

---

[4]The estimation technique involves four steps: (1) The number of 25- to 29-, 30- to 34-, and 35- to 44-year-old unmarried couples in 1990 is multiplied by 60 percent to find the number of unmarried couples who could become married households. (2) The weighted average of ownership rates for other family and nonfamily households in 1990 for each age group is calculated. (3) The difference between the appropriate married ownership rates and the weighted average rates in each age group is found. (4) The difference in each age group's ownership rates is multiplied by the appropriate number of couples estimated to marry in order to calculate the increase in the number of households owning homes.

A weighted average of family and nonfamily household ownership rates was used because households with two unrelated adults may be classified as either other family or nonfamily household. If one of the partners has a relative living with them, the household is included in other family. The Census Bureau does not identify how many two-unrelated-adult households are in each category.

TABLE 5.11

Increase in the Number of Children 25 to 44 Years Old Living with Parents, 1980–1990 (in Thousands)

Children	Under 25	25–34	35–44	Total
		Age Group		
All 25- to 44-year-olds living with parents				
1990	3,229	1,757	1,669	6,655
1980	1,833	794	653	3,280
Difference	1,396	963	1,016	3,375
Number never married				
1990	2,725	1,278	993	4,996
1980	1,485	556	366	2,407
Difference	1,240	722	627	2,589
25- to 44-year-olds living at home as percentage of people in their age group				
1990	15.2	8.0	4.5	8.3
1980	9.9	4.7	2.6	5.6

Source: Bureau of the Census, *Current Population Reports*, P-20, Nos. 365 and 450.

dren 25 to 44 years of age living with their parents. That number was more than double the 3.3 million who were living at home in March 1980 (see Table 5.11).

If those 3.4 million people had been in two-adult households instead of in their parents' homes, 1.7 million more households would have been added to the 1990 total. If 70 percent of them had been in two-adult households and the other 30 percent living alone, there would have been 2.5 million more households. Such additional households would have reduced the 3.2 million difference between actual and projected households by 50 to 80 percent.

More older children living at home explains much about the shortfall between actual and projected total households in this age group in 1990. Not all of this growth, however, represents deferred housing demand. As people age, both the number and percentage of people living at home falls. Nevertheless, some of the people currently living with their parents will stay there.

The people most likely to leave home are persons who have never married. The Census Bureau believes that 90 percent of people who have never married will eventually marry.[5] Of the increase in 25- to 44-year-olds at home, 75 percent, or 2.6 million, have never been married. Thus, the estimate of potential ownership demand is based on that number.[6] It could take most of the decade for all of these people to leave home. When they do, many may initially establish other types of households before they marry. Moreover, a number of them may rent before they purchase a home.

To allow for the impact that all of these possibilities could have on potential housing demand, several assumptions are made. First, these people establish two-person households, which creates 1.3 million new households. Second, these new households have the same distribution as to type of household—married, other family, nonfamily—as existed in each age group 25 to 29, 30 to 34, and 35 to 44 in 1990. Third, the ownership rate for each type of household in each age group is the same as in 1990.

Based on these assumptions, the 1.3 million households have the potential to purchase nearly 620,000 homes in the 1990s. Using the multiplier of 3, one sees their deferred demand could encourage 1.85 million more home sales in this decade.

Sources of Deferred Home Sales: Synopsis

Three sources of deferred home sales among people 25 to 44 years of age in 1990 were identified:

1. Existing households	4,200,000
2. Two unrelated-adult households	1,125,000
3. Children living with parents	1,850,000
Total deferred home sales	7,175,000

The total is a sizable number. So far, however, nothing has been said about the timing with which this demand will reach the owner-

---

[5]Based upon conversations with Arlene F. Saluter of the Bureau of the Census, Population Division, Marriage and Family Statistics Branch, in November and December 1992. She indicates that the percentage of persons who are not married but who eventually will marry is now about 90 percent, down from 95 percent in earlier years.

[6]This does not mean that every never-married person in this age group will leave home. Instead, the 2.6 million is an estimate of the number of children aged 25 to 44 who will leave home and establish separate residences. The vast majority of these persons, however, will never have been married.

ship market. Yet it is both the size and the pace at which this delayed demand enters the market that will shape the ownership turnover rate in the 1990s.

HOUSING TURNOVER IN THE 1990S

Housing Starts

Before the impact of deferred demand can be determined, an assessment must be made of the housing demand that would exist in the 1990s if there was no pent-up demand carried over from the 1980s. By forecasting new ownership housing starts and existing homes sales, an estimate can be developed of total housing sales without deferred demand.

Several years ago, the average growth in total households in the 1990s was expected to be around 0.9 million a year, down from the 1.2 million average of the 1980s. This projection was made before the passage of the Immigration Act of 1990, which allows an annual additional 200,000 legal immigrants into the United States. These extra visas are meant for skilled workers who can readily be employed. They will most likely attract young persons, mostly under 35, who will quickly develop the wherewithal to purchase housing. Economists at the National Association of Home Builders (NAHB) estimate that this influx will add another 75,000 households per year.[7]

Even with these extra households, the average gain in households for the decade will still be less than 1 million a year. That annual average, however, disguises the anticipated steady decline in household formation during the 1990s. This decline is the natural result of the second boomer wave being replaced by the much smaller group of busters in the 25-to-34 age group (see Figure 5.2 and Table 5.3). Consequently, the average yearly increase in house-

---

[7]National Association of Home Builders, *The Future of Home Building 1992–1994 and Beyond.* Washington, DC: Department of Economics and Housing Policy, 1992, pp. 13–14. Also see U.S. Bureau of the Census, "Population Projections of the United States, by Age, Sex, Race, and Hispanic Origin: 1992 to 2050," *Current Population Reports,* P-25, No. 1092, by Jennifer Cheeseman Day, which incorporates new assumptions on birth rates, immigration, and longevity in the estimation of the growth of the U.S. population over the next six decades.

TABLE 5.12

New Housing Demand and Supply, 1991–1995 and 1996–2000 (Annual Average Housing Units in Thousands)

	1991–1995	*1996–2000*
Demand		
Net households formed[a]	1,055	930
Net units removed from stock[b]	200	225
Second homes, changes in net vacancies	115	145
Total	1,370	1,300
Supply		
Single-family starts	995	925
Multifamily starts	185	200
Mobile homes	190	175
Total	1,370	1,300

[a]Estimates of the annual average of household formations are based on U.S. Census Bureau, U.S. Census 1990, and *Projection of the Number of Households and Families: 1986 to 2000*, P-25, No. 986, Series C. The projections of total households for the years 1995 and 2000, used in the annual average calculation, have each been lowered by 1,350,000 households. This is the figure at which the projected number of households exceeded the actual number of households found in the 1990 U.S. Census.

[b]Net units removed from stock include demolitions, merged units, and residential units transferred to other uses *minus* conversions of existing units into additional units and transformations of nonresidential units into residential uses.

holds will fall to 930,000 a year in the second half of the decade, after averaging 1,055,000 in the first half (see Table 5.12). As household formations decrease, the other components of new housing demand—second homes, net change in vacancies, and net removals—are expected to increase moderately.

Comparing the 1980 housing stock plus housing units started in the 1980s to the housing stock in 1990 suggests that about 3.6 million units net were lost during the decade. That figure is 4 percent of the 89.3 million units in the 1980 inventory. About half of these removals are estimated to have been single-family units. Of the remaining losses, most were in the two- to four-family stock. Few such units were built in the 1980s. More important, the acceptance of condominium ownership encouraged developers to purchase existing units. These units were either renovated to add more units or knocked down to accommodate structures with more units on the same land.

The oversupply of condominiums in many, many markets has slowed the reduction in the two- to four-family inventory. Without this stimulus, net removals are expected to equal 2.5 percent of the housing stock during this decade—a percentage similar to the net loss rate posted in the 1970s. Nevertheless, the absolute number of removals will rise during the 1990s because of the continued growth of the housing stock.

Overbuilding significantly raised the vacancy rates among multifamily units in the 1980s. These vacant units will be occupied gradually in the next few years. In turn, the demand for housing starts from a net change in vacancies will shrink. After the middle of the decade, a modest pickup in second home demand combined with the earlier reduction of multifamily vacancy rates will boost these sources of housing demand.

Gains in new housing demand from these other components will blunt but not offset the drop in demand from fewer household formations. Thus, average annual housing starts will fall from 1,370,000 between 1991 and 1995 to 1,300,000 between 1996 and 2000.

Over 70 percent of the units built in the 1990s are expected to be single-family. This reflects the aging of the boomers, some of whom will be moving out of their first homes into bigger, and often new, units. Their preference for more space and amenities is a major reason mobile home placements will slide in the decade.

Interestingly, average annual multifamily starts will advance about 8 percent in the second half of the 1990s. Soon many older children currently living at home will move into their own apartments, reducing vacancy rates. Later, after 1995, the first of the echo boomers will turn 20 and start their own migration into apartment living (see Figure 5.2).

Normally, the movement of echo boomers into the apartment market would set off a strong 10-year expansion in multifamily construction. It will. But these starts will not be nearly as large as demographics would suggest. In effect, the overbuilding of rental units in the 1980s has already created a large part of the supply to satisfy that demand. That point will be obscured by the substantial shifts into and out of apartments in the 1990s of those older children now living at home. Their movements will give the impression of high demand for apartments when actually rental units will be just a brief stop on the way to home ownership.

Housing Sales

Of the units started in the 1990s, 86 percent will be intended for sale (see Table 5.13). Almost all single-family units are built for sale, and single-family starts are projected to be over four fifths of total starts. Sales of some multifamily units as condominiums will also add modestly to total ownership starts.

While some new housing is bought by households leaving apartments, the large majority of units are purchased by existing homeowners. Their actions create sales turnover in the existing inventory. Nevertheless, most existing housing transactions involve people moving among existing homes.

As new units are added, the housing stock grows each year. In turn, the opportunity for sales involving only existing homes expands. As a result, the ratio of existing home sales divided by housing starts (existing/new rate) has been increasing since the 1970s. This trend is expected to continue as the average yearly rate climbs from 2.9 in the 1980s to 3.4 in the 1990s.[8]

Based on this relationship, an estimate of existing home sales is produced, which is added to ownership starts to create a projection of total housing sales in the decade. Notice in Table 5.13 that the decline in sales between the first and second half of the 1990s is demographically related.

Household formations will decrease during the decade, lowering demand for housing starts. Next, the population is aging. That reduces people's willingness to move, lessening existing home sales, despite the projected rise in the existing/new rate during the 1990s. In this demographically driven forecast, total housing sales will fall throughout the decade. Annual sales will average 9 percent less in the first half of the 1990s than in the second half. Then yearly sales will average 7.5 percent less in the second half of the 1990s than in the first half.

---

[8]Once the forecast of ownership housing starts for the United States was complete, these starts were distributed according to changes in household formations among the regions. Next, the existing/new rate was calculated for each region and applied to the ownership housing starts for that region to estimate existing home sales in the region. This was done because the existing/new rate varies substantially among regions. Population in the South and West has been growing faster than in the East and Midwest, generating higher numbers of housing starts relative to existing home sales. Thus, the rates in the South and West are smaller than in the East and Midwest.

TABLE 5.13
Total Housing Sales, 1991–1995 and 1996–2000 (Annual Average Sales in Thousands)

	1991–1995	1996–2000
Basic demand		
Ownership housing starts[a]	1,305	960
Existing home sales	3,340	3,190
Total	4,445	4,150
Pent-up demand from		
Existing households	500	340
Two-unrelated-adult households	125	100
25- to 44-year-olds living at home	100	270
Total	725	710
All demand	5,170	4,860

[a]Almost all (98 percent) single-family starts are for sale. In the 1980s, between 20 percent and 25 percent of multifamily starts were for sale. These percentages were applied to the appropriate housing start figures in Table 5.12 to derive housing starts.

ADDING THE DEFERRED DEMAND OF THE 1980S TO THE SALES FORECAST OF THE 1990S

Much of the pent-up demand for houses from the 1980s is related to the failure of the real income of many 25- to 44-year-olds to keep pace with housing prices. Often this was the result of the restructuring of the economy, which frequently shifted people from good-paying, steady jobs to lower-paying, part-time, or even no jobs. If this deferred demand is to be satisfied in the 1990s, then growth in full-time employment must pick up from its sluggish pace of recent years. Only with solid increases in jobs will these individuals gain the wherewithal to buy homes and the confidence to commit to such purchases.

Given that economic reality, and to suggest the timing with which this delayed demand *could* hit the ownership market, a very simple assumption about the economy is made. Full-time employment will pick up in 1993 and steadily rise to above 2 million new jobs each year from 1995 to 1997 before again slumping.

Among the three types of delayed demand, the potential demand of already existing 25- to 44-year-old households will reach the market first and with the most strength (see Table 5.13).

Indeed, existing home sales and housing starts were both higher in 1991–1992 than the demographically driven forecast predicted. Even with this solid start, the sizable number of these households means that their first home purchases will add a high level of housing transactions to demographics-related sales for another five years. By about 1998 most of these households will be homeowners, and sales related to their activity will drop abruptly. Thus, the annual sales of 340,000 units for 1996 to 2000 is misleading. It is an average of very high sales in 1996–1997 and precipitously declining sales in 1998–2000.

Meanwhile, the impact of home purchases generated from unrelated adult couples getting married will take until 1994 to reach the market in force. With the economy on the mend, more of these couples will take their wedding vows. Like their already married counterparts, many of them will have two incomes for financing home purchases. As more of these couples marry in the next few years, they will aggressively pursue that first home. Almost three quarters of their stimulus of housing sales will occur between 1994 and 1997, after which their influence will dissipate rapidly.

In contrast to the first two groups, older children still at home will only slowly become a factor in housing sales. Three quarters of these people are under 35. Gains in employment will have to be on the upswing for several years before they will leave home, set up their own residences, and eventually pair off. In the next few years, advances in jobs should be sufficiently strong to bring more and more of these "children" out on their own. They will be most active in the home sales market from 1995 to the end of the decade, with 1997–1998 being their peak years of impact.

As each group goes after its home ownership dream, most of the pent-up demand will be satisfied in the years 1994 to 1997. Housing sales will rise from about 4.8 million in 1992 to just over 6 million in 1995 and 1996. In breaching the 6 million level, sales will finally surpass the previous record of 5.7 million established in 1978.[9] After 1997, however, the combination of dissipating poten-

---

[9] The housing turnover rate does not exceed the 1978 level even though more housing is expected to be sold in 1995 and 1996 than in 1978. The housing stock, which is the denominator of the rate, is estimated to be 14 million units larger in 1995–1996 than in 1978. Although the numerator—housing sales—will be 5 percent higher in 1995 and 1996, the denominator will be nearly 25 percent larger than in 1978, causing the rate in 1995–1996 to be lower than in 1978.

FIGURE 5.6
Sales Turnover Rate—United States, 1970–2000

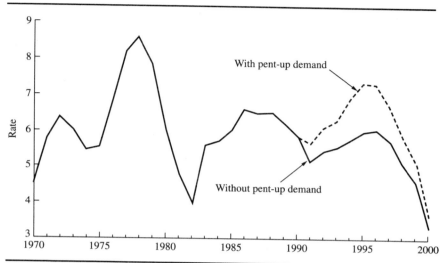

tial demand, decreasing household formations, and a slowing recovery will swiftly lower housing sales toward 3.1 million in
2000.

Comparing the housing turnover rate with and without the
pent-up demand reveals a contrast in paths through the first half of
the decade, but very similar paths in the second half (see Figure
5.6). The rate with the deferred demand jumps abruptly after 1993
and remains at a high level until 1997 as the delayed demand
surges into the housing market. The startling climb in that rate
traces a curve reminiscent of past housing cycles when the early
years of an economic recovery encouraged substantial increases in
sales. Once the rate crests in 1995–1997, its sharp plunge will be a
reminder of previous severe cyclical downturns. This time, however, the decline in the second half will likely stem as much, if not
more, from increasingly unfavorable demographics as from a falter-
ing economy. Those poor demographics will prevail into the middle
of the next decade when the echo boomers spark a resurgence in
housing sales.

If there was no delayed demand, declining household formations in the crucial 25-to-44 age group and the overall aging of the

population would be inhibiting sales. As a result, the turnover rate would wander higher from 1991 to 1996 even if the economic expansion is robust. In effect, the postponed demand only defers this slowdown until much later in the decade. By 2000, when much of this demand will have been satisfied, housing sales based on strictly demographic forces will be only slightly above the sales level in the early 1970s.

IMPACT OF PENT-UP DEMAND ON REGIONS

Like the overall pattern, each region is expected to average more housing sales in the first half of the decade than in the second half (see Table 5.14). Nevertheless, the speed and intensity with which the pent-up demand reaches a market will depend as much on the strength of the region's economic expansion as on the region's number of 25- to 44-year-olds. Thus, the turnover rate will trace different paths in each region.

The Northeast

In the Northeast, the pent-up demand rate will follow the familiar cyclical path of expansion and severe contraction of the 1970s and 1980s (see Figure 5.7). At the peak, in 1995 and 1996, sales will av-

TABLE 5.14
Total Housing Sales by Regions, 1991–1995 and 1996–2000 (Annual Average Sales in Thousands)

	1991–1995	1996–2000
Basic demand		
Northeast	675	640
Midwest	1,145	1,065
South	1,705	1,555
West	920	890
All regions	4,445	4,150
With pent-up demand		
Northeast	785	750
Midwest	1,335	1,255
South	1,980	1,820
West	1,070	1,035
All regions	5,170	4,860

FIGURE 5.7
Sales Turnover Rate—Northeast, 1970–2000

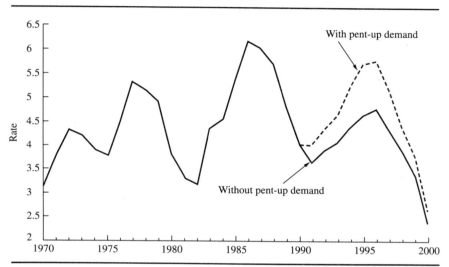

erage about 938,000, which is 1.5 percent less than the record of 975,000 set at the previous peak in 1986–1987. Several factors will mute housing sales in the Northeast.

At the beginning of the decade, the Northeast had fewer households aged 25 to 44 (under 20 percent of the U.S. total) than the other regions. Economically, the region has been struggling with recession and restructuring since 1988 and now is dealing with the downsizing of the defense industry within its borders. Despite this protracted process, there are signs that the slump bottomed in 1992. Nevertheless, recovery will take hold only grudgingly and will not gain real momentum for another year or two. Without a vigorous recovery, people, especially younger, skilled workers, will continue to leave the region for other areas with better job prospects. That will hurt the general recovery of the Northeast and weaken the impact of the deferred demand for housing.

The Midwest

The Midwest is a different story. It had the second largest total (24 percent) of households of 25- to 44-year-olds in the United States in 1990. During the early and mid-1980s, it went through a wrenching economic restructuring, particularly its manufacturing and export sectors. After years of revamping, its economic activity held up well during the nation's recent slow/no growth period. Housing bene-fited from this improvement as sales averaged around 1 million units. In turn, the turnover rate was mostly flat from 1986 to 1990 in contrast to the steep decline registered in several other areas of the country (see Figure 5.8). As employment rises in the Midwest in response to domestic and global real growth, housing sales will move from 1.1 million in 1992 to a peak of 1.6 million in 1995 and 1996. That number will surpass the previous best two-year average of 1.5 million in 1977–1978.

The South

The South is the largest region in the nation. In 1990, it had 34 per-cent of 25- to 44-year-old households. Actually, the South is com-posed of several miniregions, such as the DC/Tidewater States, the South Coastal States, the Mountain States, and the Oil States. At different times since 1980, each of these areas has suffered eco-nomic hard times, but other parts of the region always expanded fast enough to keep the economic activity of the South growing. This economic strength is demonstrated in the housing sales figures for the region. Sales between 1983 and 1990 stayed in a remarkably tight range of 1.68 million to 1.79 million. The stability of that vol-ume kept the turnover rate virtually flat during those years (see Fig-ure 5.9). With its subregions in the process of moving upward together economically, southern housing transactions will decisively break out of that range. In 1992, sales for the region were estimated at 1.8 million and will climb to over 2.3 million by 1995–1996. That figure will surpass by 13 percent the 2 million average sales posted in 1978–1979.

The West

Unlike the other regions, the West's housing turnover rate, even with the pent-up demand, is not projected to move up in the next few years, and then only weakly in the middle of the decade (see Figure 5.10). This is the result of the turmoil currently racking the California economy, specifically the southern part.

The California housing market dominates the West. In the single-family market, California historically has accounted for

FIGURE 5.8
Sales Turnover Rate—Midwest, 1970–2000

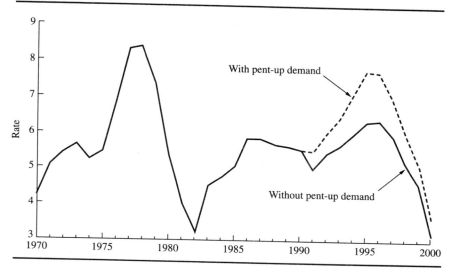

FIGURE 5.9
Sales Turnover Rate—South, 1970–2000

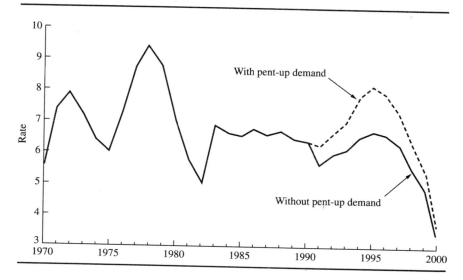

FIGURE 5.10
Sales Turnover Rate—West, 1970–2000

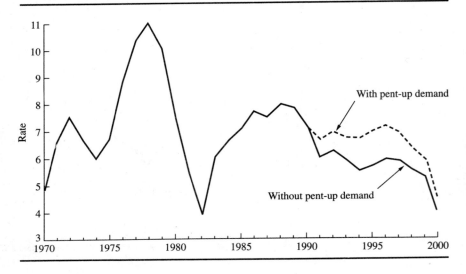

about two thirds of all originations in the region.[10] Based on the years it took the Oil Patch and more recently the Northeast to revitalize their economies, California appears only in the first stages of its restructuring. While it struggles, housing sales are expected to slip. That decline may not be as extensive as the experience of the other regions would suggest. Californians are always on the move, shifting outward to areas of less expensive housing. This pattern will continue. In the higher-cost areas, new buyers will be attracted as housing prices drop sharply. And even if immigration to the state from elsewhere in the United States and abroad slows for several years, California will still be a positive for housing sales.

Focusing only on California will overlook flourishing sales in other housing markets of the West. In some cities in the region economic expansion is already vigorously under way. In addition, many areas will benefit from California's troubles as persons or businesses originally headed for that state locate elsewhere in the region. Despite the California distraction, the West will average

---

[10]Phillip E. Kidd, "The Hottest States for Loans," *Secondary Marketing Executive*, July 1988, pp. 14–16.

about 1.05 million housing sales in the 1990s, or 7 percent more than the 0.98 million average of the 1980s.

In summary, housing sales in the Midwest and South—the regions with the currently strongest economies—will establish new record sales in 1995, hold that level in 1996, and then slide downward. In the Northeast, the top of the cycle will occur in 1995–1996 but will fall short of previous record sales. In the West, the peak, such as it is, will be in 1996–1997, but the fall from that top will be much less severe than in other regions until the very last year of the decade.

RISING MORTGAGE DEMAND AMONG THE ELDERLY

Already a demographic trend, coupled with the upheaval in the domestic business world, is creating the underpinnings of a new and powerful source of mortgage demand. By later in the decade when the demographics of first-time buyers is waning, this demand will bolster mortgage production. The demographic trend is the increase in people over 65 years of age. During the 1990s, their number will grow nearly 10 percent, from 20 million to almost 22 million. By 2000, they will account for slightly more than one in five Americans.

Most people over 65 have the income and health to enjoy a comparatively active life style. A high percentage (75 percent in 1990) own their own homes. And most of them want to live in their own home for as long as they are physically able.

In the 1990s, retirees and persons approaching retirement are increasingly being confronted with the possible reduction, or even loss, of their pension incomes. This is one of the consequences of business downsizing and restructuring and the disappearance of companies in recent years. Many of the younger elderly, those aged 65 to 75, are beginning to consider using the equity accumulated in their homes to supplement their incomes. Some will sell, invest some of the proceeds, and move to smaller, less expensive units, which they may own or rent. Such a trend will help housing turnover.

An alternative is also emerging. Organizations for older Americans are aggressively educating their members about reverse mortgages. In particular, they are using the FHA's Home Equity Conversion Mortgage Program to explain the concept. So far there have been relatively few (less than 200,000) reverse mortgages produced, but that will change. Under mounting pressure to sustain and protect their monthly income, older homeowners will steadily and noisily voice their demand for reverse mortgages.

At first, lenders may ignore this budding clamor. But that too will change. After 1996, lenders will embrace reverse mortgages as one method of countering the rapidly decreasing demand for traditional mortgages. As they do, origination volumes, which will be tumbling as the deferred demand from first-time buyers dries up, will stabilize and may even increase.

CONCLUSION

In 1978, a forecast of total households was made for 1990. It predicted a very large annual average growth in households in the 1980s. Two thirds of those new households were anticipated to form in the first-home-buying age range—25 to 44 years old. As these households bought that first home, their purchases were projected to lift housing sales to new heights.

While sales were certainly very high, they never reached their potential. The reason is that 4.7 million of those expected households have so far not been established. The questions then arise: Was the formation of these households only delayed? And if so, what would their eventual appearance in the 1990s mean for housing sales? The answers are that among persons aged 25 to 44 in 1990, there was a potential deferred demand that could trigger up to 7.2 million more housing transactions in the 1990s than a strictly demographic-based forecast would predict.

More important, several substantial changes in living arrangements have been identified among this age group that account for many households not having been formed in the 1980s. Implicit in the forecast on the size and timing of this deferred demand entering the market is an assumption that the living arrangements of many boomers will undergo further changes in the 1990s. The challenge for housing and mortgage participants is to correctly evaluate the strength and speed with which such shifts actually take place. That will involve incorporating more analysis on movements among household types to predict what the switches mean for future housing demand.

CHAPTER 6

TECHNICAL CONSIDERATIONS

KEY QUESTIONS

1. How do supply and demand factors affect MBS price performance?
2. How does the yield curve affect MBS price performance?
3. How does volatility affect MBS price performance?

1. HOW DO SUPPLY AND DEMAND FACTORS AFFECT MBS PRICE PERFORMANCE?

Change in Yield Spread

One of the most frequently encountered and vexatious aspects of MBS investing is the risk/reward of a change in the MBS to Treasury yield spread. Table 6.1 illustrates the impact on HPR of a change in MBS to Treasury spreads for 3-, 6-, and 9-month holding periods in increments of 5 basis points. The base case assumption is that spreads, interest rates, and prepayments do not change to the end of the horizon periods. Note that as spreads tighten, the price of the MBS increases—for example, from 97.02 (base price) to about 97.28 if the spreads tighten by 15 basis points. If spreads widen, the price declines to about 96 if the spread widens by 20 basis points. Note that there are marked differences in the performance measured by HPR.

    The major factors that influence the yield spread are (1) average-life drift, (2) supply/demand considerations, (3) market volatility, and (4) shape of the yield curve.

TABLE 6.1
GNMA 10, WAM 350 Months; MBS to Treasury Yield Spreads, Impact of Varying Spreads on HPR

Horizon Period (Months)	HPR			Horizon Price		
	3	*6*	*9*	*3*	*6*	*9*
MBS to Treasury spreads						
−15	13.9	12.6	11.6	97.27	97.28	97.28
−10	12.8	11.6	11.2	97.19	97.19	97.20
− 5	11.8	11.1	10.9	97.10	97.11	97.11
(0) Base	10.6	10.6	10.6	97.02	97.02	97.02
+ 5	9.5	10.1	10.2	96.26	96.26	96.27
+10	8.5	9.6	9.9	96.17	96.18	97.19
+15	7.4	9.0	9.6	96.90	96.10	96.11
+20	6.3	8.5	9.3	96.01	96.02	96.03

Average-Life Drift

If the average life of the MBS extends or contracts, the realized yield to the investor will be altered. Remember, if discount-priced MBSs shorten in average life, the realized yield will be greater; and if average life extends, it will be less. The reverse, of course, is true of premium-priced MBSs. *To the extent investor expectations are that discounts may extend or premiums contract in average life, the MBS to Treasury spread will widen.* On the other hand, of course, should investor expectations be the reverse, MBS to Treasury spreads will tighten, and the bond *will perform better than originally expected.*

Note in Figure 6.1 that the yield spread pattern closely tracks changes in interest rates. As interest rates dropped from January 1986 through March 1987 the current-coupon MBS to Treasury spread widened to more than 250 basis points. This was in anticipation of the acceleration in prepayment speeds and increase in supply of MBSs resulting from refinancing as well as higher home sales activity that took place during that time, as shown in Figure 6.2. It is particularly interesting to note from Figure 6.1 that the MBS to Treasury yield spread widened in January 1986 *before* the peak in prepayment spreads of FHLMC 12s was realized in the summer of 1986 (Figure 6.2), which demonstrates that the MBS

FIGURE 6.1

MBS to Treasury Yield Spreads, Current-Coupon GNMA versus 10-Year Treasury

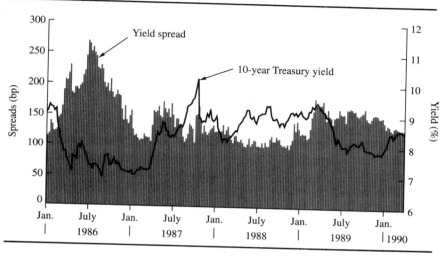

Source: Lehman Brothers Fixed Income Research.

FIGURE 6.2

FHLMC 9, 10, and 12 Percent MBS Prepayment Speeds, 1984–1987

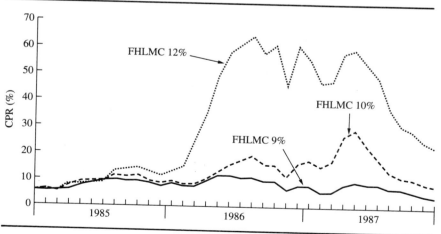

Source: Lehman Brothers Fixed Income Research.

market is highly *expectational.* This phenomenon reinforces the point that a key ingredient of the risk/reward considerations in MBS investing is to *anticipate future events that may have an impact on MBS to Treasury yield spreads.*

Supply/Demand Considerations

If the market anticipates an increase in the supply of MBSs in the near future, MBS to Treasury yield spreads will tend to widen. Also, the drops on dollar rolls will become greater. The principal supply considerations are:

- Mortgage origination level, which is a function of home sales and starts.
- Refinancings that are primarily interest rate driven, but that may also be related to consumer shifts to preferred mortgage types, for example, from ARMs to fixed, which occurred heavily in 1991 and 1992.
- Asset dispositions, as with the Resolution Trust Corporation (RTC) program.

Demand for MBS product is provided by:

- CMO/REMIC-related demand for collateral (by far the most significant demand factor following 1990).
- Investor preference for MBSs versus competitive fixed-income securities, for example, Treasuries and corporates.
- Evolution of new MBS products that fit specific investor needs, for example, PACs to match insurance company guaranteed investment contract (GIC) programs, ARMs for short-term money market funds, and hedge-related derivative products.

1989 Sales of MBSs by Thrifts

A good illustration of the impact of MBS sales on yield spreads was the 1989 debate regarding the outlook for asset dispositions by the RTC. Figure 6.3 illustrates the yield of FNMA 9s to the 10-year Treasury versus major thrift sales. As shown in the figure, a major widening of the spread accrued prior to the July and August 1989 series of thrift asset sales. Table 6.2 lists, for reference, the major

FIGURE 6.3

FNMA 9 Percent MBS Spread to Treasury versus Thrift Sales (see Table 6.2)

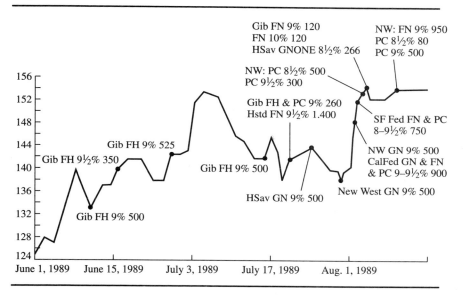

Source: Lehman Brothers Fixed Income Research.

thrift asset sales that took place between June and the middle of August 1989, which are also noted in Figure 6.3.

Origination Patterns

If the market were to expect a surge in origination volume, the MBS to Treasury yield spread would widen, of course. Of equal interest, however, was the expectation of a continuation in moderate origination activity throughout 1990 and early 1991 that prevented MBS spreads from widening when interest rates were expected to decline through the second half of 1990. Mortgage rates did, in fact, dip below 9.5 percent for the first time since 1986, hitting 9.25 percent in February 1991, and prepayment speeds accelerated considerably through spring 1991. The yield spread of Fannie Mae and Freddie Mac current coupons, however, remained close to 100 basis points throughout the bull rally of 1990 and the prepayment acceleration of 1991, in large part because investors were comfortable

TABLE 6.2
Major Asset Sales, June 1989 through August 1989

Date	Seller	MBS	Coupon (%)	Amount ($)
8-Jun-89	Gibraltar	FH	9.00	500
14-Jun-89	Gibraltar	FH	9.50	350
22-Jun-89	Gibraltar	FH	9.00	525
11-Jul-89	Gibraltar	FH	9.00	500
18-Jul-89	Gibraltar	PC and FN	9.00	260
18-Jul-89	Homestead	FN	9.50	1,400
19-Jul-89	Home Savings	GN	9.00	500
26-Jul-89	New West	GN	9.00	500
31-Jul-89	Cal Fed	PC, FN, and GN	9–9.5	900
31-Jul-89	New West	GN	9.00	500
1-Aug-89	SF Federal	PC and FN	8–9.5	750
2-Aug-89	New West	PC	8.50	500
2-Aug-89	New West	ARMS		500
2-Aug-89	New West	PC	9.50	300
3-Aug-89	Gibraltar	FN	9.00	120
3-Aug-89	Home Savings	GNOME	8.50	266
3-Aug-89	Gibraltar	FH	10.00	120
8-Aug-89	New West	FN	9.00	950
8-Aug-89	New West	PC	9.00	500
8-Aug-89	New West	PC	8.50	80

Key: GN = GNMA; FH = FHLMC; FN = FNMA.

Source: Lehman Brothers Fixed Income Research.

that origination volume would remain low as a consequence of the 1990 housing recession.

1992 MBS to Treasury Spread Patterns[1]

In January 1992, mortgage rates fell to 8.25 percent, the lowest level since the mid-1970s. Later that month, however, mortgage rates rose to nearly 8.75 percent, and as homeowners rushed to lock in rates mortgage bankers sold MBSs for forward delivery in large volume, causing the MBS to Treasury yield spread to widen in

---

[1] John Tierney and Beth Starr, *MBS Outlook.* New York: Lehman Brothers, January 1993.

January from about 75 basis points to the 10-year to about 100 basis points. As prepayment concerns subsided in April, the MBS current-coupon spread to the Treasury tightened again to about 75 basis points. By the end of July, however, the second refinancing wave of 1992 produced renewed selling pressure from mortgage bankers, which caused the current-coupon spread to widen to a 90 to 105 basis points range into the fall. A further disquieting factor was the loss of the REMIC bid in the fourth quarter, which removed what had been a stabilizing factor earlier in the year.

Some key patterns of the 1992 MBS yield spread roller coaster emerged. First, most of the 1992 spread widening appeared to be related to liquidity and supply/demand imbalances rather than to investor concern with call risk, the traditional reason attributed to refinancing-related spread widening. Second, the high cash flow generated by the refinancing activity created reinvestable funds (demand), which many institutions put back into mortgage product. The pattern then was initial spread widening caused by mortgage banker selling, which is executed for two to three months forward settlement. As the refinancing cash flows are realized by investors and the refinancing wave abates, the resulting demand tends to tighten spreads.

In the first quarter of 1993, mortgage rates again plunged, this time to below 7.5 percent. On this, the third refinancing wave of the 1991–1993 refinancing cycle, many institutions decided to step aside from mortgage paper and fled to Treasuries, where durations could be more reliably extended to participate in the powerful bull bond market rally. Another major consideration, however, was the demand for MBS collateral generated by the high level of CMO activity in recent years. (For a further discussion of the impact of issuance patterns on MBS yield spreads, see Historical Perspective: 1991–1992 versus 1986–1987 in Chapter 4.)

The CMO Bid

When CMO issuance is at a high level, a strong demand is created for the underlying collateral. Table 6.3 provides the issuance volume of agency REMICs and REMICs as a percentage of passthrough issuance for 1991 and 1992. The demand for MBSs as collateral for the burgeoning CMO/REMIC activity became so strong, in fact, that there were many months in 1991 in which the dollar amount of CMOs issued exceeded the monthly issuance

TABLE 6.3
Agency REMICs, Issuance Summary, 1991 and 1992

	REMIC Issuance ($ millions)		REMICs as a Percentage of Pass-Through Issuance	
	1991	1992	1991	1992
GNMA	33,450	32,264	59.4	39.2
FNMA	80,804	111,780	83.2	61.6
FHLMC	73,175	130,129	84.8	76.6
Total	187,429	274,173	78.2	65.2

Source: Lehman Brothers Fixed Income Research.

TABLE 6.4
Agency REMIC by Collateral Type ($ Millions)

	1991	1992
GNMA		
30-year	33,450	32,014
15-year	0	250
Total	33,450	32,264
FNMA		
30-year	67,233	77,928
15-year	13,571	31,011
Balloon	0	2,841
Total	80,804	111,780
FHLMC		
30-year	61,894	72,893
15-year	11,281	47,369
Balloon	0	9,867
Total	73,175	130,129

Source: Lehman Brothers Fixed Income Research.

volume of matching MBS collateral. Table 6.4 gives a profile of the amounts and types of collateral that backed CMOs and REMICs in 1991 and 1992.

Tables 6.3 and 6.4 do not tell the whole story, however. *Some collateral types were in far greater demand than the tables make clear. For example, 30-year collateralized FHLMC REMIC issuance in 1991 represented 107 percent of total 30-year FHLMC PCs issued that year and 106 percent for the first nine months of 1992.* (REMIC issuance slowed dramatically in the fourth quarter of 1992 as supply and prepayment-risk issues took away the CMO bid during that period.) FNMA REMIC issuance collateralized by 30-year MBSs represented 94 percent of all 1991 30-year FNMA MBS issuance and 89 percent of issuance for the first nine months of 1992.

The demand for REMICs on the part of commercial banks was a significant consideration feeding the high issuance levels of REMIC products in 1990–1991. In 1992 the full impact of the regulatory changes affecting depository institutions and insurance companies led to a strong demand for MBSs structured as REMICs, primarily by insurance companies. Table 6.5 shows the holdings of MBSs by investor category for 1988, 1991, and 1992.

The high level of prepayment volatility in 1992 caused MBS to Treasury yield spreads to widen somewhat, but nowhere near the levels reached during the 1986–1987 refinancing experience. The muting of widening yield spreads during the 1992 refinancing experience may be largely attributed to the presence of the REMIC forms. These forms redistributed the prepayment risk into less prepayment-sensitive bonds on the one hand while on the other hand concentrating the risk into other securities (strips, inverse floaters, and support bonds) that could be marketed to institutions willing to take prepayment risk for compensating yield. Generally speaking, however, the evolution of demand for MBSs does not cause MBS spreads to narrow in expectation of such demand. It is human nature to worry about possible future negative factors but to ignore probable favorable ones.

Impact of Agency Purchase Programs

The federal agencies themselves through MBS purchase programs can be an important source of demand when supply pressure widens the MBS to Treasury yield spread. According to Lehman Brothers research[2] in 1992, Fannie Mae net purchases of MBSs totaled $67.1 billion. The purchases were funded primarily by reinvesting prepayment-based cash flows or by issuing debentures. Large purchases were made in April and in October when MBS spreads widened as prepayments accelerated rapidly during the spring and fall

---

[2]William J. Curtin, *Relative Value Report.* Lehman Brothers, March 29, 1993.

TABLE 6.5
MBS Holdings by Investor Category, 1988, 1991, and 1992 ($ Billions)

1. MBSs Outstanding

	MBS ($)			REMICs ($)		
	1988	1991	1992	1991	1992	
Agency	747.7	1,156.0	1,275.6	460.0	570.0	
Nonagency	34.9	84.0	132.0	41.2	72.9	
Total	782.6	1,240.0	1,407.6	501.2	642.9	

2. MBS Holdings by Industry

	1988			1991			1992		
	Volume ($)	% of Total	% of Assets	Volume ($)	% of Total	% of Assets	Volume ($)	% of Total	% of Assets
Thrifts	308.9	39.5	21.7	186.4	15.0	18.4	178.2	12.7	18.5
Commercial banks	90.1	11.5	3.3	274.9	22.2	8.9	309.8	22.0	10.0
Life insurance companies	92.8	11.9	8.0	176.3	14.2	11.2	225.0	16.0	13.7
Mutual funds	68.2	8.7	8.4	78.7	6.3	5.8	100.6	7.1	6.3
Pension funds	70.3	9.0	9.7	157.2	12.7	16.3	185.1	13.2	18.6
Foreign investors	25.0	3.2	n.a.	85.0	6.0	n.a.	116.0	8.2	n.a.
Other	127.3	16.3	n.a.	281.5	22.7	n.a.	292.9	20.8	n.a.
Total	782.6	100.0		1,240.0	100.0		1,407.6	100.0	

3. MBS Holdings and CMOs/REMICs as a Percentage of MBS Holdings

	1991		1992	
	MBS ($)	CMOs/ REMICs (%)	MBS ($)	CMOs/ REMICs (%)
Thrifts	186.4	17.5	178.2	20.5
Commercial banks	274.9	43.1	309.8	42.1
Life insurance companies	176.3	28.4	225.0	27.3
Mutual funds	78.7	n.a.	100.6	n.a.
Pension funds	157.2	16.1	185.1	13.7
Foreign investors	85.0	58.8	116.0	56.9
Other	281.5	n.a.	292.9	n.a.
Total	1,240.0	41.7	1,407.6	44.7

Source: Lehman Brothers Fixed Income Research.

refi cycles. Lehman estimated Fannie Mae purchases approximated $6 billion in the first quarter of 1993 when MBS spreads widened again in response to supply pressures.

2. HOW DOES THE YIELD CURVE AFFECT MBS PRICE PERFORMANCE?

The shape of the yield curve has an impact on the required MBS to Treasury yield spread. For example, assume we price FHLMC 9s to yield 100 basis points over the 10-year Treasury yield. If the 10-year Treasury yield at the time is 8 percent, the FHLMC will be priced to a yield to maturity of 9 percent. To price the MBS to true value, however, we need to take into account the relative value of *each monthly cash flow*. Since we are dealing with a monthly cash flow annuity, it is not technically correct to use a single point on the Treasury curve (for example, the 10-year Treasury) to price *all* the monthly cash flows. Rather, we should price each monthly cash flow to the appropriate spread off its term point on the Treasury-maturity curve. (Nevertheless, the predominant practice is to price MBSs to a specific Treasury maturity on the yield curve.) The problem is demonstrated in Figure 6.4. The figure illustrates the principal cash flows of a FHLMC 9 percent PC at 150 PSA, which gives an 8.5-year average life. The cash flows are small the first two years or so (the PSA curve), peak at $15,000 as prepayments become significant, and trail off over a plateau as the increasing scheduled principal amortization plus prepayments reduces the corpus of the pool.

The conventional approach to pricing to cash flow yield determines the mortgage to Treasury yield spread by finding the one discount rate that, when applied to all future cash flows (P&I), produces a present value that is equal to the current market price of the security. If the Treasury curve is relatively flat, there is little difference between short- and long-term rates, and therefore the MBS will be priced fairly evenly at 100 basis points over the entire yield curve. However, if short-term rates are lower than long-term rates (a positively sloped yield curve), then the effective yield spread of the early MBS cash flows will be more than 100 basis points over the short (early-maturity) end of the yield curve. If short-term rates are higher than long-term rates (a negatively sloped, or inverted, yield curve), then the effective yield spread of the FHLMC 9 over

FIGURE 6.4

FHLMC 9 Percent Guarantor PC, 30-Year Amortization, 150 PSA, 8.5-Year Average Life

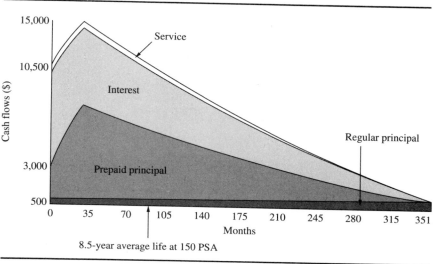

Source: Bloomberg Financial Markets.

the short-maturity Treasuries will be less, and astute investors will recognize they have a valuation problem. Figure 6.5 illustrates the three yield curve shapes at specified terms for each of the yield curves.

A more appropriate way to value the MBS cash flow annuity was proposed by Eric Smith, Mortgage Product Analyst, Merrill Lynch Mortgage Research.[3] It involves taking into account the *timing* of the cash flows, recognizing that the heaviest return of principal is realized at the short (2- to 5-year) end of the Treasury curve, with the most heavily discounted cash flows thrust out on the tail at the long (25- to 30-year) end of the curve.

Smith assumed that the mortgage to Treasury spread be determined by defining a constant spread over the entire Treasury

---

[3]Eric Smith, *The Slope of the Yield Curve and MBS Value.* New York: Merrill Lynch Capital Markets, March 1989.

FIGURE 6.5
Parallel, Steepening, and Flattening Yield Curves

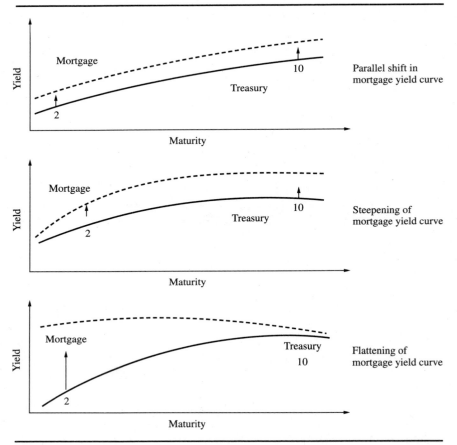

curve—a *series* of discount rates, one rate for each monthly cash flow, with each discount rate at the same spread over its equivalent-maturity Treasury yield. This approach is reminiscent of OAS technology. The method entails pricing each monthly cash flow to its appropriate-maturity Treasury rather than comparing all the cash flows to one particular point on the Treasury curve (in this case, the 10-year maturity point). Figure 6.6 points up the difference between the two approaches.

Figure 6.6 shows the spread to the 10-year Treasury held as a constant (dotted line) and then as a spread to the Treasury curve

FIGURE 6.6

FNMA 10 Percent Yield Spread to the Treasury Curve versus Yield Spread to the 10-Year Treasury Shown with FNMA Principal Cash Flows by Maturity

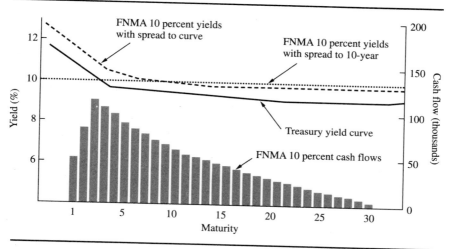

in its entirety (dashed line). In the first instance every cash flow has the same yield because all cash flows are priced at 100 basis points over one yield, that of the 10-year Treasury. In the second instance, the MBS cash flows are independently priced to monthly intervals on the Treasury yield curve. Since the Treasury curve is negatively sloped, the shorter-term MBS cash flows are priced to a higher discount factor. The composite price of the MBS will therefore be lower. Stated another way, the required MBS to Treasury yield spread will be wider. The net effect is to say *MBS to Treasury yield spreads tend to tighten when the Treasury yield curve is positive and to widen when the Treasury curve is flat to negative.*

To demonstrate the point more fully, Figure 6.7 illustrates three yield curve scenarios—a positively sloped curve, a flat curve, and an inverted (negatively sloped) curve. In all three yield curve scenarios the yield of the 10-year Treasury is held constant at 9 percent. Table 6.6 provides Treasury yields for various-maturity intervals on the Treasury yield curve ranging from 1 year to 30 years. The FHLMC 10 percent PC in the base case (positive yield curve) scenario is priced at 101–02, to yield 9.84 percent, or 84 basis points over the 10-year Treasury.

FIGURE 6.7
Positive, Flat, and Inverted Yield Curves

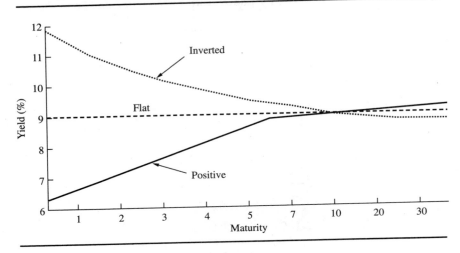

Source: Merrill Lynch Capital Markets Research.

TABLE 6.6
Treasury Yields from 1 to 3 Years (Three Yield Curve Scenarios)

Maturity Years	Positive Curve	Flat Curve	Inverted Curve
1	6.50	9.0	11.5
2	7.00	9.0	11.0
3	7.50	9.0	10.5
4	8.00	9.0	10.0
5	8.50	9.0	9.5
7	8.75	9.0	9.25
10	9.00	9.0	9.0
20	9.13	9.0	8.88
30	9.25	9.0	8.75

Source: Merrill Lynch Capital Markets Research.

Table 6.7 shows the impact on the price of shifts in the yield curve to flat and inverted slopes. The base assumes the 10-year Treasury yield is 9 percent. As the yield curve flattens and then inverts, the PC cash flows at the short end of the curve are more heavily discounted, reflecting the increase in yield of the shorter-

TABLE 6.7

Change in Price of FHLMC 10 Percent PC (Treasury Curve Positive, Flat, Inverted)

	Positive	Flat	Inverted
Price	101-02	100-00	98-31
Bp spread to 10-year Treasury	84	106	129
BEY	9.84	10.06	10.29
Spread to Treasury curve	106	106	106
Change in price	+1-02		−1-01
Change in spread (bp)	−22		+23

maturity Treasuries. This effect has the dual impact of reducing the price of the FHLMC and widening the required basis points yield spread to the 10-year Treasury. Note that the spread to the total Treasury curve remains constant. A risk of MBS investing, then, is that shifts in the shape of the yield curve may widen the stated spread to the benchmark Treasury, thereby reducing the price and performance of the MBS.

Impact on Financing Cost

The cost of financing MBS inventory is increased when the yield curve inverts. This inversion has a negative impact on market liquidity because dealers have less (or even negative) incentive to carry MBSs in inventory. This effect is reflected in the pricing of the dollar roll market: When the curve is inverted, dollar roll spreads become very tight. (The month-to-month drop reflects the cost of financing. When the curve is inverted, dollar roll drops are very narrow, but when the curve is positive, the drops widen.)

Impact of Price Volatility[4]

The MBS, as discussed previously, is a composite security consisting of two elements: a long position in a noncallable coupon bond and an implied short options position (for a description of the

---

[4]This discussion of volatility is based on William J. Curtin, Nicholas Letica, and Andrew Lawrence, *Mortgage-Backed Securities Volatility Risk.* New York: Drexel Burnham Lambert, September 1988.

series of prepayment options embedded in the MBS pool, see Valuing the Call Option in Chapter 3).

Interest rate volatility has a strong impact on the value of the option component of the MBS. The valuation process is therefore strongly related to options pricing theory. The two essential parameters of pricing-embedded options are:

1. As volatility increases, the value of a given option rises. Option buyers are therefore long volatility and hope volatility will increase; option sellers are short volatility and hope volatility will decrease.

   a. *MBS buyers are short the prepayment call option and therefore short volatility.*

   b. *An increase in volatility causes the MBS to Treasury yield spread to widen.*

2. As the time to expiration of the option shortens, the value of the option declines (time-value decay). The longer the time to expiration (the longer the MBS duration or average life), the greater the probability the option will go into the money. *As the time to expiration of the call lengthens, the impact of volatility on the option value increases exponentially* (see Figure 6.8). So rising volatility acts to increase the option value, whereas time decay deteriorates the option value.

3. HOW DOES VOLATILITY AFFECT MBS PRICE PERFORMANCE?

Volatility may be defined in statistical terms as a measure of the standard deviation from a mean set of price observations. For fixed-income securities, volatility is expressed in terms of yield or price units, generally as a percentage. For example, an annual volatility of 17 percent means that if the current interest rate is 10 percent, there is a two-thirds chance that rates one year hence will be between 8.3 and 11.7 percent (that is, 17 percent lower or higher).

Calculating Volatility

Volatility is calculated as the standard deviation of a time series of daily price or yield changes, assuming a normal distribution, as shown in Figure 6.9. The volatility is expressed as a percentage,

FIGURE 6.8
Call Option Value versus Security Price

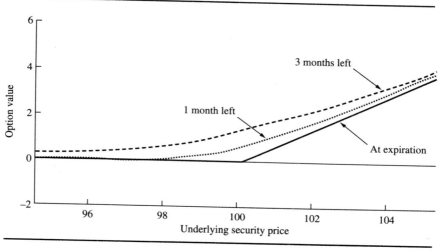

Source: Drexel Burnham Lambert.

FIGURE 6.9
Thirty-Year Constant-Maturity Treasury, Distributions of 1-Day Absolute Yield Changes

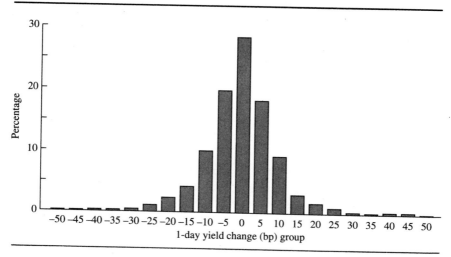

Source: Drexel Burnham Lambert.

which is the annualized deviation of the daily changes in the log of prices or yields.

Percentage Volatilities and the Log-Normal Distribution

One could compute a percentage price volatility by finding the standard deviation of daily price returns, assuming a normal distribution, and then annualizing. Daily returns would be computed as follows:

$$R - P2/P1 - 1$$

where

P = Price on the first day
$P2$ = Price on the next consecutive business day

A better way to compute the percentage volatility is to assume a log-normal distribution of prices and find the standard deviation of the logs of the daily price quotients—that is, $In(P_2/P_1)$. For the log-normal assumption to be accurate, the log of the daily price quotient and the daily return should be equal. This condition holds true if the price quotient is near 1, or:

$$In(P_2/P_1) = P_2/P_1 - 1$$

where

P_2/P_1 is congruent to 1

For 1-day price movements, this assumption is valid even on the most volatile days. For example, if a bond starts at par (P_1 = 100) and moves 5 points in one day (P_2 = 95), the price quotient P_2/P_1 = 95/100 = 0.95. The log of the price quotient $In(0.95)$ is −0.051, whereas the return $R = 0.95 - 1$ is −0.05. The log-normal method is computationally much quicker because it takes advantage of the properties of logs [$In(P_2/P_1) = InP_2 - InP_1$] and makes the price quotients equivalent to a continuously compounded return.

Linking Modified Duration to Volatility

Investors are generally familiar with the application of Macaulay's duration in measuring the percentage change in the price of a bond to a change in yield. Modified duration is the percentage change in price divided by the absolute change in yield (sometimes referred to as *dp/dy*). The modified duration of a security provides the link between price and yield volatilities.

Implied Volatility

Implied volatility is simply the market expectation of future volatility for a specified time horizon. *Calculating implied volatility is, however, far from simple since it must represent a series of prices (or yields) based on market expectations, and expectations cannot be observed directly. However, as previously pointed out, MBSs trade to a current stated yield spread to Treasuries, which reflects the market's expectations of future prepayment speeds, as well as supply and other technical considerations.* This is far truer for MBSs than for any other fixed-income security. The derivation of a series of volatility expectations is therefore critical to the MBS valuation process.

Fortunately, there is a large and liquid futures market for Treasury securities on the Chicago Board of Trade (CBOT) that can serve as a proxy for future price and yield expectations of the market. The implied volatility on the 20-year bond futures contract, for example, serves as a proxy for the market's expectations of long-term Treasury yields. With application of an OAS model (see What Is OAS? in Chapter 3 for a description of OAS models), a series of implied yields of MBSs may be derived.

Volatility Impact on MBS Performance

When volatility increases, the embedded short options in the MBSs appreciate in value, *causing the price of the MBS to underperform that of a comparable Treasury and the MBS to Treasury spread to widen.* For example, price volatility was the highest in recent memory during the powerful bull market rally in the spring of 1986. In February 1986, the implied price volatility on the CBOT was 10.7 percent. The basis points yield spread between the then-current coupon GNMA and the 10-year Treasury was about 90 basis points. *By June 1986, volatility had soared to 19 percent, and the MBS to Treasury spread had widened to 240 basis points, the widest spread of the past decade.* As the market topped out (in price) in September and trended down through the fourth quarter of 1986 and into 1987, volatility fell to a low 8 percent by March 1987. The MBS to Treasury spread narrowed back to about 100 basis points.

Volatility-Scenario Price Performance

Before discussing portfolio suggestions, it is helpful to illustrate how different securities respond to changes in volatility and interest rates. Terminal prices, terminal spreads, and rates of return for GNMA 10s under three volatility and interest rate scenarios for a 3-month horizon are shown in Table 6.8. The rates of return are for the 3-month period, not annualized. The most significant impact on returns is the interest rate movement.

The difference in the rates of return from a down 100 basis points environment to an up 100 basis points environment is approximately 800 basis points. Increasing volatility also affects return. If volatility rises from 10 to 18 percent, for example, the rates of return fall by an average of 330 basis points over the three interest rate scenarios. Notice the yield spread of the MBS to the 10-year Treasury widens as interest rates fall and also as volatility increases. Spreads widen by as much as 73 basis points when volatility moves from 10 to 18 percent (in the falling interest rate case).

TABLE 6.8
GNMA 10s, 3-Month Returns

WAM, 343 months
OAS, 56 bp with initial volatility of 12%
Starting price, 100:06
Horizon, 3 months

		CBT Implied Price Volatility (%)				
		10	12	14	16	18
−100 bp	Return (%)	7.22	6.37	5.59	4.79	4.02
	Price	105:05	104:09	103:15	102:20	101:27
	Spread[a] (bp)	130	149	166	185	203
Flat	Return (%)	3.36	2.45	1.61	0.74	−0.08
	Price	101:05	100:06	99:10	98:14	97:18
	Spread[a] (bp)	117	134	151	169	186
+100 bp	Return (%)	−1.21	−2.05	−2.85	−3.67	−4.47
	Price	96:13	95:17	94:22	93:27	93:00
	Spread[a] (bp)	105	122	139	156	173

[a]Yield of the security to the 10-year Treasury.

Source: Drexel Burnham Lambert Mortgage Research.

The price of the GNMA 8s (see Table 6.9) is not as sensitive to varying levels of volatility. As explained previously, the embedded options of the 8s are out of the money. Whereas the difference in the rate of return for the 10s is an average of 330 basis points (over the three interest rate scenarios), when the volatility assumption changes from 10 to 18 percent, it is only 270 basis points for the 8s. The larger negative returns for the 10s is a result of a greater price drop as volatility increases. For a 2 percent change in volatility, the price movement of the GNMA 8s is about 10/32 less than that of the GNMA 10s. Similarly, for equivalent volatility movements, spreads widen by about 6 basis points less for the 8s than for the 10s. This effect illustrates how sensitive the current coupon (the 10s) is to volatility changes.

Remember, the current-coupon and slight-premium MBSs will experience the greatest correlation to implied volatility. The embedded options in these securities are near or somewhat in the money (on or just over the cusp). When an option is trading near its strike price, its premium is maximized by the probability that it can move

TABLE 6.9
GNMA 8s, 3-Month Returns

WAM, 344 months
OAS, 84 bp with initial volatility of 12%
Starting price, 88:16
Horizon, 3 months

		CBT Implied Price Volatility (%)				
		10	12	14	16	18
−100 bp	Return (%)	9.28	8.52	7.77	6.98	6.19
	Price	94:28	94:06	93:16	92:24	92:01
	Spread[a] (bp)	118	130	143	157	170
Flat	Return (%)	3.11	2.45	1.79	1.09	0.39
	Price	89:07	88:20	88:00	87:12	86:23
	Spread[a] (bp)	114	126	138	150	164
+100 bp	Return (%)	−2.92	−3.47	−4.02	−4.62	−5.23
	Price	83:22	83:06	82:22	82:04	81:18
	Spread[a] (bp)	110	120	131	143	155

[a]Yield of the security to the 10-year Treasury.

Source: Drexel Burnham Lambert Mortgage Research.

into or out of the market. High-premium MBSs are the least volatile—their options are already well in the money (well above the
cusp), and discounts are in between, becoming the most volatile
when prices are upwardly biased, thereby enhancing the value of
the discount. The embedded options of discount-priced MBSs are
generally out of the money, however (well below the cusp).

In a study of the option features of mortgage securities by
Michael Waldman and Mark Gordon of Salomon Brothers,[5] the
fundamental question is, How much would mortgage securities gain
or lose in value if volatility levels changed? Figure 6.10 displays the
convexity costs and OASs of GNMAs for 1-year Treasury volatility
levels of 15, 20, and 25 percent. The corresponding mortgage rate
volatilities are 11.1, 14.7, and 18.3 percent—that is, the assumed 5
percent change in 1-year Treasury volatility results in an implied
change of about 3.5 percent in mortgage rate volatility. The convexity costs are also depicted in Figure 6.10.

FIGURE 6.10
GNMA Convexity Costs for Various 1-Year Treasury Volatility Levels

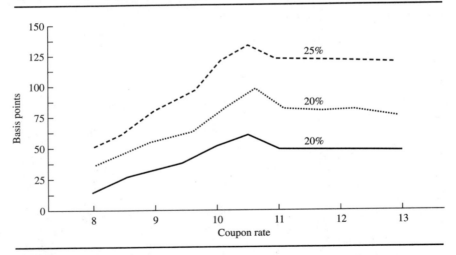

Source: Salomon Brothers Mortgage Research.

---

[5]Michael Waldman and Mark Gordon, CFA, *Evaluating the Option Features of Mortgage Securities.* New York: Salomon Brothers, 1987.

As expected, volatility changes have the greatest impact on the 10–11 percent coupon sector, where a shift in volatility in either direction causes OASs to move by 34–39 basis points. Table 6.10 gives the associated price impact of the volatility shift, that is, the price move needed to maintain the OAS provided under the base case assumption. In the case of the 10–11 percent sector, the required price move is about 1½ points.

For discount and high-coupon issues, of course, the effects are smaller. For GNMA 8s, for example, the impact of a 5 percent 1-year Treasury volatility change is about 15 basis points in OAS and about ⅝ point in price.[6]

Coupon-Sector Profile of MBS Market

The impact of prepayments on MBS to Treasury yield spreads is a function not only of higher versus lower interest rates (prepayment risk is higher with lower interest rates) but also of the coupon structure of the MBS market as a whole. When the distribution of MBS coupons is relatively high (10.5 percent and greater) the market can be said to be premium-coupon dominated. Such a structure was characteristic of the MBS market throughout the 1980s into the early 1990s. Following the 1992 refinancing cycle, however, the MBS market was substantially restructured. Table 6.11 compares the coupon structure of the MBS market of 1986 with that of the 1991–1992 market. Note that in 1986, 65 percent of all MBS coupons were 11 percent and higher! By 1992, 54 percent were below 9 percent.

The mere fact that the coupon structure of the MBS market has been restructured much lower mitigates for tighter MBS to Treasury yield spreads in two regards:

1. The MBS coupons of 9 percent and lower, which now make up over half of the MBS market, will have relatively fewer opportunities to refinance in the years ahead. Compare this to the potential prepayment sensitivity of the 1991 MBS market, with half of all MBS coupons 9.5 percent and higher.

2. Discount-priced MBSs have historically traded at significantly tighter spreads to Treasuries than premium-priced

---

[6]Ibid.

TABLE 6.10
Impact of Changes in Volatility Levels on GNMA Securities

		Volatility Level						Impact of 5% Volatility shift	
		Low		Base Case		High		1-Year Treasury	
1-Year Treasury (%) Mortgage		15 11.1		20 14.7		25 18.3			
GNMA (%)	Projected Spread at WAL (bp)	Convexity Cost (bp)	OAS (bp)	Convexity Cost (bp)	OAS (bp)	Convexity Cost (bp)	OAS (bp)	OAS (bp)	Equivalent Price Move
8	175	18	157	33	142	49	126	15	0.69
9	217	30	187	55	162	81	136	25	1.11
10	215	52	163	86	129	120	95	34	1.48
10½	202	58	144	97	105	136	66	39	1.60
11	216	48	168	85	131	123	93	37	1.35
12	263	47	216	81	182	118	145	35	1.03
13	326	45	281	76	250	109	217	32	0.82

Source: Salomon Brothers Mortgage Research.

MBSs. With such a larger percentage of the MBS market at 9 percent and below, over time these coupons will have an opportunity to trade at prices below 100, leading to a spread-tightening trend for the MBS market as a whole.

TABLE 6.11
Coupon Composition of 30-Year Conventional Agency MBSs Outstanding

As of	<9%	9%–10%	10.5%
1/86	20	16	65
12/91	18	77	5
12/92	54	46	3

Source: Lehman Brothers Fixed Income Research.

CHAPTER 7

COLLATERALIZED MORTGAGE OBLIGATION STRUCTURES

OVERVIEW

A **collateralized mortgage obligation,** or **CMO,** is a multiclass bond issue collateralized by a pool of federal agency-guaranteed mortgage pass-through securities, whole mortgage loans, or other MBS forms such as stripped MBSs. The cash flows of the underlying mortgages are used to make the P&I payments on the CMO bonds. When the collateral pool consists of federal agency-issued MBSs (Ginnie Mae and Fannie Mae MBSs and Freddie Mac PCs), the P&I cash flows are guaranteed by the issuing agency. CMOs backed by whole loans carry investment-grade ratings, generally AAA, based on credit enhancements mandated by the agencies. The amount of credit enhancement is determined by the agencies based on an examination of the underlying collateral. (For a discussion of rating agency criteria, see The Rating Agency Approach in Chapter 11.)

The key difference between a standard mortgage pass-through security, such as a Ginnie Mae pass-through, and a CMO is in the distribution of principal payments. With a standard pass-through, the P&I payments received each month from mortgage holders are passed through to all security holders on a pro rata basis. Because of prepayments, the pass-through cash flows tend to be irregular and widely dispersed over time. Furthermore, the MBS security remains outstanding as long as any of the mortgages in the underlying mortgage pool are outstanding, resulting in a long "tail" (up to 30 years).

The CMO structure substitutes a sequential retirement of a series of bond classes for the pro rata return of principal found in the pass-through. The MBS cash flows and associated prepayment options are thereby redistributed more efficiently into a series of bonds with short, intermediate, and long maturities. Of interest to long-term investors such as pension funds is the fact that the long-maturity classes of the CMO offer a measure of call protection greater than that of the generic pass-through. The reason is that the earlier classes absorb the prepayment risk when the collateral is most prepayment sensitive. By the time the later classes are paying principal the collateral has become seasoned. The CMO with certain specialized structures, such as planned amortization class PAC bonds, redistributes the prepayment option embedded in the MBS by substantially reducing the prepayment sensitivity of the PAC bonds. The prepayment risk, or optionality, is transferred to the CMO **support classes** that accompany the PACs in the CMO structure (see Anatomy of PAC Bonds, page 303).

Typically, the first class of CMO bonds receives all principal generated by the collateral pool until it is completely retired; then the second class begins to receive principal until it is retired, and so on. Interest is paid concurrently on all outstanding bonds unless they are **accrual** or **Z-bonds**. The typical CMO has four or more classes (or tranches), with the last class often being a Z-bond.[1] Figure 7.1 illustrates the cash flow distributions of a prototype four-class CMO assuming a normal prepayment pattern for the underlying collateral. The first class has a cash flow window[2] of less than 5 years and an average life of 2.3 years. The second and third classes receive level interest payments in accordance with their stated coupon rates while the first class pays down. Then the third class continues to receive level interest payments until the second class is paid down, and so on. The fourth class, a Z-bond, accrues its stated interest rate as an addition to its initial face value until all of the previous classes have been retired. Then, based on the accrued principal amount, interest is paid to the holders until the Z-bond is completely paid down, at which point the CMO is closed.

CMOs have opened the mortgage markets to many investors who might otherwise be excluded by the long maturities of standard pass-through securities or the reinvestment risk associated with monthly cash flows. However, the typical **sequential-pay** CMO structure does not eliminate the prepayment uncertainty that has long been associated with mortgage collateral. Rather, it offers a de-

---

[1]Some CMOs have been issued with only one class (plus a residual) and others with more than 20 classes.

[2]The cash flow window is the time from the first principal payment to the last, based on a prepayment projection. The end of the cash flow window represents the projected maturity date.

FIGURE 7.1
CMO Cash Flow Structure

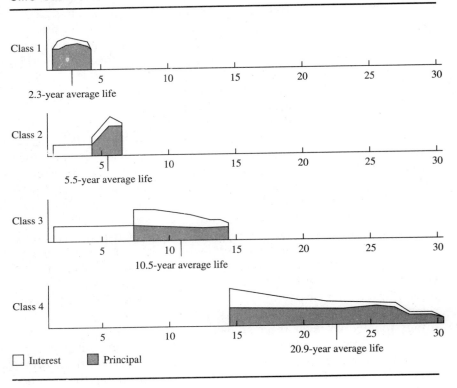

gree of prepayment protection in the sense that no principal payments may be received by a given class until all earlier classes have been retired. However, sequential payment of principal means that an acceleration of principal payments will result in early retirement not only of the first class but of all other classes as well.

Like other mortgage securities, CMOs are priced to yield a spread over Treasury securities of comparable maturity—that is, a Treasury security with a maturity that approximates the average life of the CMO bond.

Figures 7.2 through 7.4 illustrate the cash flow to the first class of a CMO at the pricing-prepayment assumption and then at slower and faster prepayment speeds.

FIGURE 7.2

Expected Cash Flows of First Class; Average Life 2.3 Years, Projected Maturity 4.75 Years

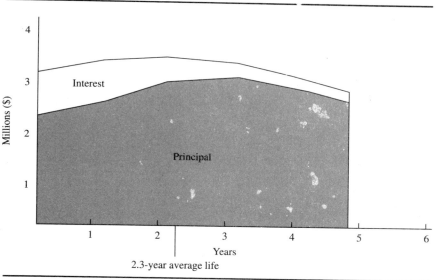

STRUCTURAL CHARACTERISTICS OF CMOS[3]

The CMO is structured so that even in the most adverse circumstances there will be adequate cash flows to satisfy all of the P&I due on the bonds. This protection is provided by structuring the CMO to a worst-case scenario—that is, to a zero-prepayment assumption. The cash flows generated by the collateral pool must be sufficient to meet the requirements of all the bonds issued under the CMO structure regardless of their coupons.

When the collateral consists of federal agency-guaranteed MBSs, the P&I due from the collateral pool is guaranteed by the agency. With whole-loan collateral, additional credit enhancements are required.

---

[3]This discussion of the structural characteristics of CMOs is based on *Collateralized Mortgage Obligations: Market View and Evaluation* by Leon Baudoin, Vice President, Lehman Brothers. New York: February 1987.

FIGURE 7.3
**Expected Cash Flows of First Class Assuming Slower Prepayment;
Average Life 3.7 Years, Projected Maturity 6.25 Years**

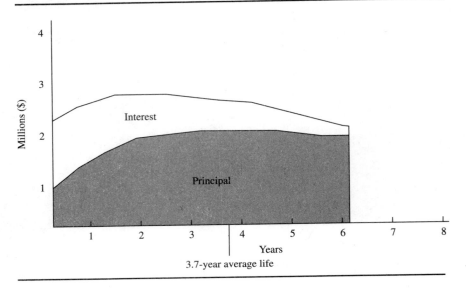

The rating agencies ensure that the CMOs will be self-supporting by requiring that the aggregate principal value, or "bond" value, of the mortgage collateral backing the bonds be greater or equal to the amount of the bonds outstanding. This requirement is applied throughout the entire CMO payment schedule: At any given payment period, the amount of bonds outstanding cannot be greater than the unpaid principal value of the collateral. Therefore, the present value of the collateral is always at least equal to the unpaid principal amount of bonds at a zero-prepay assumption. *It is because of this zero-prepay assumption that the stated maturity of the CMO bonds is so much longer than the assumed maturity used for deal pricing. CMO structuring is premised on two rules:*

1. The total principal of the collateral must always equal the sum of all principal payments scheduled for the bonds.

2. The total yield spread provided by the CMO bonds must equal not more than the purchase yield spread of the collateral, plus issuance expenses and any profit and/or residual interest to the issuer.

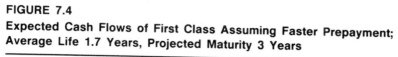

FIGURE 7.4

Expected Cash Flows of First Class Assuming Faster Prepayment; Average Life 1.7 Years, Projected Maturity 3 Years

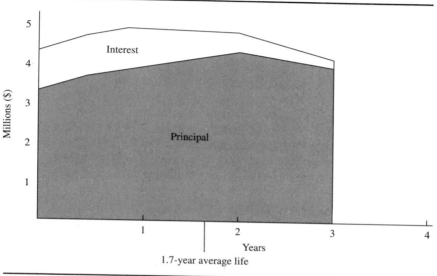

Various methods are used to calculate the bond value of a mortgage pool. The most efficient method for issuers, which still assures the safety of CMO investors, is the present value method. In one variation of this method, the bond value is the lesser of (1) the maximum collateral value of the pool—essentially its face value; and (2) the present value of the scheduled amortization—assuming no prepayment—plus the reinvestment income, using the highest CMO coupons as the discount rate (see Box 7.1). Mortgage cash flow received between CMO payment periods may be reinvested, but rating agencies assume conservative reinvestment rates: currently 4.5 percent the first year, 4 percent the second year, and 3 percent thereafter. Alternatively, a GIC may be purchased.

The present value method as well as the other types of bond value computations fully protect the investor regardless of the coupon on the collateral and its prepayment rate. If the pool consists of collateral purchased at a premium price, the bond value is parcapped—that is, the bond value is assumed at parity and is approximately equal to its face value. Therefore, even if the collateral prepays much faster than expected, the CMO structure will be

---

BOX 7.1
Maximum Collateral Value of a CMO Pool

Originally, the maximum collateral value of a pool was set simply at its face value, thus covering the case in which a premium pool prepays completely. (In this context, a premium pool is defined as a pool whose coupon is greater than the highest bond coupon.) However, rating agencies realized that if the CMO bonds were redeemed within a payment period, then it would be legitimate to have a maximum collateral value that is slightly greater than the face value of a given pool. Under a worst-case scenario—complete prepayment—the smallest possible cash flow available to service the bonds is equal to the pool's outstanding principal plus its coupon income for a month plus the reinvestment income. Discounting this sum at the highest bond coupon provides the maximum collateral value, as in the following equation:

$$MCV = \frac{FACE \cdot (1 + CC/12) \cdot [1 + (N/360) \cdot R]}{(1 + CB/12)}$$

where

MCV = Maximum collateral value
$FACE$ = Face value of the collateral
CC = Collateral coupon, in decimals
N = Number of days of reinvestment between the collateral payment and a special redemption of the CMOs
R = Minimum reinvestment rate, in decimals
CB = Highest bond coupon, in decimals

---

self-supporting since there is no unamortized price premium to be considered.

In the case of pools consisting of discount-priced collateral, the present value method involves calculating a bond value by assuming that the pools will never prepay and that all bond coupons are equal to the gross WAC of the collateral in the pool.

The bond value calculation is performed separately for each pool, and the total bond value is simply the sum of the individual values. In other words, even if the premium pools prepay very rapidly while the discount pools remain outstanding, there will still be enough cash flow to service the CMO debt.

Finally, the difference between the debt service requirement of the bonds issued and the actual cash flows generated by the collateral pool (at some prepayment experience) may be retained or sold by the CMO issuer as the *residual.*

Because of their unique structural characteristics, virtually all CMOs enjoy the highest available credit ratings by Standard & Poor's (S&P), Moody's, and Fitch rating agencies. It is important to understand why. There is a crucial difference between pay-through, or cash flow-matched, bonds such as CMOs and general corporate obligations. With a CMO, the collateral cash flow directly supports the payments on the bonds; the issuer may be thought of as a passive entity. However, with a general corporate issue the credit quality rests ultimately on the issuer's own rating.

CMOs and other cash flow-matched bonds offer investors another safety feature that they cannot obtain from other types of debt—even an AAA-rated debt. A corporate AAA can be downgraded, whereas no internally credit-enhanced CMO issue has suffered a rating downgrade.[4]

Bankruptcy Considerations

The CMO collateral pool must be held by a trustee independent of the issuer under a bankruptcy-proof trust agreement. The pool may not be invaded by a trustee in bankruptcy in any event, including bankruptcy of the issuer of the bonds or any other party to the transaction (servicer, trustee, and so on). In the event that a single-purpose CMO issuer is a subsidiary of another entity or parent, S&P generally recognizes that "the issuer would not be consolidated with the parent in case of the latter's bankruptcy." Likewise, if the parent is a savings institution and if both the issuer and its parent follow the Federal Savings and Loan Insurance Corporation (FSLIC) guidelines, the FSLIC "would not attempt to consolidate the subsidiary with the parent if appointed receiver for the latter."

Single-purpose issuers must not engage in activities that could

---

[4]A few CMOs whose credit enhancement was *external* have been downgraded only because the third party guarantor was downgraded.

directly or indirectly threaten the safety of the bonds. More precisely, when rating a CMO, S&P imposes two conditions:

1. "The issuer must engage only in activities related to the issuance of the related mortgage securities [CMOs] and must not become involved in other activities that could lead to potential insolvency."

2. "The issuer must not incur any indebtedness beyond the rated debt which, if not repaid, could result in bankruptcy proceedings against the issuer."

Optional Redemption Features

With most CMOs, the issuer has the right to redeem all outstanding bonds when their unpaid principal balance reaches a minimum threshold specified in the trust indenture (usually 10 percent of the original face amount of the bonds issued). This right is referred to as a **clean-up call** and is likely to have an impact only on the holders of the last class. However, a few CMOs permit redemption after a relatively short time, such as 10 years. CMO investors should ascertain the exact call provisions of any CMO they purchase.

The CMO Arbitrage

The economics of a CMO are generally driven by the ability to originate or purchase loans or MBSs (the CMO purchase collateral) at a relatively wide yield spread off the intermediate sector of the curve and finance it at narrower spreads off the shorter sectors of the curve, as shown in Figure 7.5.

EARLY APPLICATIONS OF CMOS

The CMO arbitrage was the key to the appeal of the CMO to builders because it enabled them to sell mortgages at a low financing cost because of the arbitrage inherent in the sequential-bond-class structure. The first few bond classes typically carried shorter average lives—2, 3, or 5 years—which were sold at a yield spread off the short end of the Treasury curve. In other words, the builder created an arbitrage, in effect, by originating, or buying, mortgages at a yield off the long-maturing end of the yield curve, whereas much of

FIGURE 7.5
CMO Arbitrage (CMO Coupon and Yield Curve Differential)

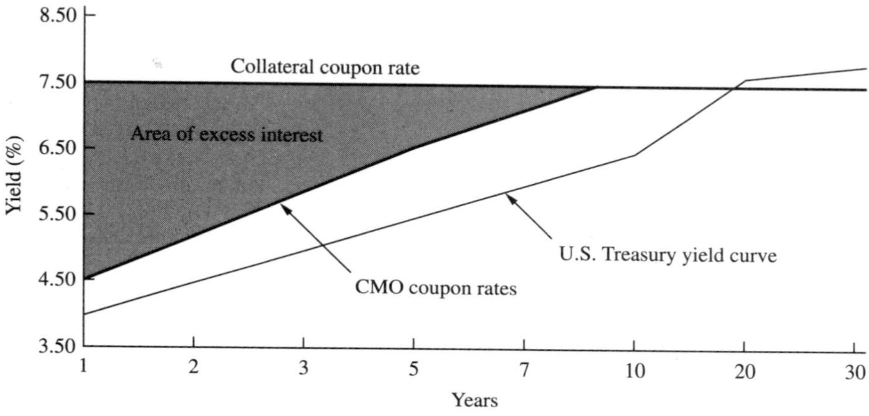

Source: Harry Forsyth.

the financing was obtained at rates pegged off the short (2 to 7 years) spectrum of the yield curve.. This arbitrage would soon be recognized as a commodity of value and traded by Wall Street dealers under the label **residual**. Dealers created special-purpose corporations that served as issuers of CMOs, utilizing as collateral MBSs they purchased in the secondary market. The dealers thus retained the arbitrage profit.

Historical Evolution of the CMO

The precursor of the CMO was the **mortgage-backed bond (MBB),** which evolved in the 1970s as the first form of mortgage security to issue bonds whose maturity was substantially shorter than that of the underlying mortgage collateral.[5] The security for the bonds was the market value of the mortgage collateral. The bonds had to be substantially overcollateralized (1.6 to 1 or more)—first, because the bondholders had to be protected against a decline in the market value of the collateral and, second, because the maturity of the bonds was substantially shorter than that of the mortgages behind

---

[5]The first MBB was issued in 1975 by California Federal Savings and Loan.

them. (Part of the objective of issuing the MBB was to structure mortgage securities that looked more like corporate bonds with short to intermediate maturities and with P&I payments that were quarterly, semiannual, or annual instead of monthly.) With more than 75 MBB issues placed by 1987, MBBs continued to be issued into the mid-1980s until they were displaced by the more popular CMO form. Most MBBs were issued by large banking and thrift institutions that had ample inventories of mortgage collateral on their books. Overcollateralizing an MBB was perhaps inefficient, but at least it was a better use of the mortgages than letting them collect dust in the bank vaults. The MBB had to be issued as a debt, not as a pass-through structure, because the original legislation approved by the Treasury in 1968 permitting the creation of mortgage pass-throughs specified the collateral had to be held in a **grantor trust** (a completely passive trust permitting no management of cash flows at the pool level). And the MBB could be issued only as a single class (i.e., 30 or 15 years, matching the maturity of the underlying mortgage collateral).

The position of the IRS had been that a trust or other entity which issues mortgage or asset-backed securities of more than one class is not exempt from taxes. In order to qualify as a tax-free pass-through entity like an REIT, all the securities must be of one class. The IRS took this position because, according to an article in *Bankers Research*,[6] it was concerned that if it allowed multiple classes, it would encourage allocations of income among entities so as to minimize taxes all around, resulting in a net loss in revenue to the government.

There have been two exceptions to this one-class rule. The major one was made by Congress, which took loans on one- to four-family housing out of the rule by providing for REMICs.[7] The minor one was made by the IRS, which ruled there could be senior and subordinate structures in the non-REMIC trust, but *the originator could not sell its interest in the subordinated class;* it had to retain it. The IRS reasoned that with the originator holding the subordinated interest, the whole transaction could be deemed a loan, sale, or partial sale. The subordinated interest was not, in that case, really a second class of securities. The prohibition against sell-

---

[6]*Secondary Market Supplement*, June 1992. Westport, CT: Bankers Research Publications.

[7]The REMIC provision was part of the 1986 Tax Reform Act.

ing the subordinated piece was never part of the IRS's written regulations, but spokespersons for the agency consistently took the position that selling was not permitted.

Eventually it turned out that S&Ls were among the largest holders of subordinated pieces and that the largest holder of S&Ls was the Resolution Trust Corporation (RTC).[8] The government wanted these subordinated pieces—many of which could be excellent investments—sold, but the IRS's position was an obstacle. Because the U.S. Government has more clout with the IRS than originators or prospective investors, the position of the IRS ceased to be an obstacle. *In April 1992 the IRS issued Revenue Ruling 92–32, which confirmed that a subordinated interest can be transferred without changing the pass-through status of the trust.*

It has always been possible to sell subordinated interest by setting up the two or more classes as different partnership interests, as a few originators such as Chrysler Credit have done. Partnerships are not taxable; rather, whatever a partnership earns or loses is treated for tax purposes as passed on to the partners. But investors tend to dislike partnership interests because of the prospect that they might be liable for debts the partnership might contract or for tort liabilities it might incur. So the IRS's change of position will help the asset-backed market to grow.

Since the MBB form could not be issued as a pass-through, it was of little use as a means of financing mortgage originations. Even the largest mortgage banking institution or bank would soon run out of capital to support the issuance of debt required to finance a major mortgage origination entity that would typically originate several million dollars of mortgages in a single week.

Pay-Through Bonds

Pay-through, or **cash flow,** bonds were introduced to the secondary market in 1981. The pay-through bond differed from the MBB in that the security for the bonds is the cash flows generated by the underlying collateral. Unlike the generic MBB, which has a fixed maturity, the pay-through's maturity and principal-repayment characteristics are dependent upon the payments realized on the mortgage collateral. First issued privately in 1976, the pay-through came

---

[8]A federal instrumentality established under FIRREA to liquidate assets of failed banks and thrifts.

into being because it satisfied two concerns. The pay-through structure enabled an issuer to realize in cash the present value of its below-market mortgage assets without selling the assets or significantly overcollateralizing the bonds. Stated another way, issuers could obtain nearly 100 percent financing on mortgage assets and avoid the tax and accounting consequences of a sale of assets.

Pay-through bonds also, of course, had to be issued as debt, not pass-throughs, under the Treasury ruling that restricted the pass-through to a single class with its maturity the same as that of the underlying collateral.

The resolution of numerous legal, tax, rating, and accounting issues delayed introduction of pay-throughs to the public bond market until April 1981 when PHM Credit Corporation brought a $39 million issue to market.

The First CMO: 1983

In mid-1983, Freddie Mac made a radical contribution to mortgage-related securities structuring. Its issue of CMOs was, strictly speaking, a pay-through bond issue except that three classes of bonds were issued instead of one. Multiclass pay-through bonds thereafter became known as CMOs. The advantage to financial intermediaries was a boon. For S&Ls, the ability to dispose of seasoned, deep-discount mortgages that could be effectively "sold" to a bankruptcy-proof entity without recognizing a loss if that entity is part of the consolidated group was compelling. In addition, the structure provided there was no material mismatch between the aggregate cash flows on the mortgage collateral and the debt service on the CMOs, which helped mitigate interest rate risk for the issuer.

These features combined to trigger a wave of CMO financings by S&L's[9] and home builders in the wake of the first Freddie Mac issue, described in Table 7.1. The impact of the offering was potent. The issue was priced approximately 85 basis points lower than the bond-equivalent yield on Freddie Mac PCs at the time of the pricing. The composite yield spread over Treasuries for the total issue was only about 75 basis points, a very attractive level to issuers.

In the year and a half following the Freddie Mac issue, 37 is-

---

[9]But not by mortgage bankers—the requirement that pre-REMIC CMOs be accounted for as debt made them inefficient as a means of financing new loan originations.

TABLE 7.1
Offering Terms of the First CMO

Class	Yield (%)	Average Life (years)	Spread over Treasuries (bp)
A-1	10.70	3.2	+40
A-2	11.37	8.6	+54
A-3	11.98	20.4	+85

Source: Freddie Mac.

TABLE 7.2
Percentage Distribution of Freddie Mac CMO Issues Purchased (by Investor Category, June 1983)

	Thrifts	Banks	Insurance Companies	Pension Funds	Others
A-1	13	23	17	4	43
A-2	7	22	21	30	19
A-3	28	8	6	38	22

Source: Freddie Mac.

sues aggregating over \$12 billion were marketed. The appeal of the CMO was broad. The distribution pattern reported by Freddie Mac for its first issue is shown in Table 7.2.

The First Private CMO Issue

In July 1983 Pulte Homes issued the first private CMO through its subsidiary, Guaranteed Mortgage Corporation. The collateral for its CMO was Ginnie Mae MBSs, a mix of level-pay and graduated-payment mortgages (GPMs). Most of the early CMO issues were by builders; Pulte was followed by American Southwest Financial Corporation, Ryland Mortgage Securities Corporation, and RYMAC (Ryland Mortgage Acceptance Corporation), to name a few.

The First Modern Conduits

The first conduit to directly access the Wall Street capital markets was Residential Funding Corporation (RFC), formed in 1982. RFC specialized in "jumbo" mortgages—those that exceed the statutory limit for loan size eligible for purchase by Fannie Mae or Freddie Mac. Mortgage Guaranty Insurance Corporation (MGIC) underwrote and insured the individual loans and provided the pool policy, and Salomon Brothers issued mortgage securities backed by the pooled loans. Still very active today, RFC is one of the largest as well as the oldest operating conduit, purchasing loans from some several hundred correspondents nationwide. RFC is notable as one of the first to utilize the CMO on a regular basis to finance mortgage originations. As early as 1987 RFC was issuing CMOs at a rate of $100 million per month.

Pre-REMIC Multiclass Pass-Through Efforts

In 1983, Sears Mortgage Securities Corporation attempted to make secondary market history with a $500 million offering of CMOs structured as pass-throughs. Such a structure had long been sought by the conduits in order to achieve sale-of-asset status rather than adding an ever-growing mountain of debt, as was required under the CMO builder-bond structure.

The Sears structure, in the eyes of the Treasury Department, represented a **multiclass pass-through,** which was not allowed under the tax law of the time. The existing legislation stipulated that a grantor trust would be exempt from taxation at the mortgage pool level only if there was only one class of securities issued against the trust. The dispute lent stimulus to a series of legislative initiatives, including the Trusts for Investment in Mortgages (TIMS) proposal. TIMS would have amended the tax law and the Securities and Exchange Acts of 1933 and 1934 specifically to permit the issuance of multiclass pass-throughs. TIMS failed to come to fruition, primarily because it prohibited the housing-related federal agencies to share in the exemption. The need for such an instrument became increasingly compelling, however, and ultimately led to inclusion of the REMIC legislation in the Tax Reform Act of 1986.

Evolution of Builder Bonds

The builder-based conduits grew rapidly with the evolution of the CMO as a financing mechanism, often referred to at the time as **builder bonds.** Builders were attracted to the CMO because of the available arbitrage. An added incentive was the builder's ability to elect installment-sale treatment for tax purposes if the mortgages the builder originated were financed and not sold. By using the mortgages as the proceeds from the sale of the homes built, the builder could amortize the profit on the sale of a house over the life of the mortgage—in essence recognizing the sale proceeds in installments represented by the mortgage payments. The trick was that by using the mortgages as collateral for the CMO they were deemed to have been financed and not sold, thereby entitling the builder to the installment-sale, or tax deferral-of-income, treatment. The Tax Reform Act of 1986 drastically reduced the ability of the builder to take this attractive tax credit, and by mid-1987 builder-bond CMOs began to taper off.

Introduction of REMICs

By the mid-1980s S&Ls were in demise, and alternative sources of mortgage capital were being looked for to sustain the housing boom. Congress became convinced of the need for a multiclass pass-through to enable originators to reach a broader range of investors with the CMO structure but with sale-of-asset treatment to enable mortgage originators to employ it in large volume.

The **REMIC**[10] provision of the Tax Act is therefore predominately tax law, that is, permitting the issuance of a multiclass pass-through without risk of taxation at the pool level. There is no structural difference between a REMIC and a CMO today; in fact, virtually all CMOs *are* REMICs. *A CMO that is not a REMIC is by definition an issuance of debt—not a sale of assets.*

The REMIC provision was a boon for some conduit builder-bond issuers—notably Ryland Mortgage Securities Corporation, the financing subsidiary of the Ryland Group, one of the biggest of the builders. Ryland found it could pass on to smaller S&Ls the advantages of REMIC's election of take-sale treatment for tax-loss purposes while retaining financing treatment for GAAP. Under this election, S&Ls with underwater loans in portfolio may create a REMIC subsidiary to which the loans are transferred with tax-loss-on-sale treatment. However, the loans are then used as collateral for funding securities, which could be issued either to a Fannie Mae REMIC or to a Ryland REMIC to become part of a larger CMO-type REMIC financing. The program became so popular that only 5 percent of the collateral backing Ryland's REMIC bond issues in

---

[10]REMIC (Real Estate Mortgage Investment Conduit), established as an amendment to the Tax Reform Act of 1986 to allow multiclass MBS forms—that is, the pay-through bond, or CMO—to enjoy pass-through status.

late 1987 and 1988 was from Ryland's own builder activities. In addition to RFC and Sears, other major conduit operations include Gemico (a General Electric Mortgage Capital subsidiary), GMAC Mortgage Corp, Citibank, Shearson Lehman Mortgage Corporation, Travelers, and Prudential.

Early Structural Innovations in CMOs

One of the earliest structural innovations was creation of the Z-bond, which enabled application of the accruals to pay down earlier bond classes in times of slow prepayments. The Z-bond was actually created to eliminate the need of a debt service reserve fund, which was required of the early Pulte Homes CMO issues because of the presence of GPM-collateralized Ginnie Maes. The GPM permits negative amortization of the mortgage (the mortgage balance increases to accrue the below-market interest payments in the early years) during a payment step-up phase. Since the Z-bond, which is an accrual bond, has negative amortization (the interest that is accrued but not paid is added to the bond principal amount), its introduction to the CMO bond structure eliminated the need for a debt service reserve fund to secure the negative amortization of the GPM. (The structural application of the Z-bond is discussed in more detail in Z-Bond Forms in Chapter 9.)

Freddie Mac, always eager for its CMOs to appeal to thrift institutions, introduced the idea of a guaranteed minimum repayment schedule, which made the first class of a Freddie Mac-issued CMO liquidity qualifying if this provision was included. With the introduction of stated maturity bonds (SMBs) in the early 1990s, this feature is no longer needed; however, it made Freddie Mac-issued CMOs attractive to financial institutions, especially S&Ls.

Other early structural innovations included a calamity clause for Pulte Homes, which enabled the issuer to accelerate its semiannual P&I payments[11] to monthly if prepayments accelerated rapidly or if interest rates fell so low that the reinvestment of cash flows became insufficient to meet the interest requirement of the bonds. Another quirk of semiannual-pay deals was to require the issuer to guarantee a minimum reinvestment rate through a sinking fund derived from the collateral cash flows.

---

[11]Pre-REMIC CMOs often paid quarterly or semiannually instead of monthly to ensure they could not be construed as pass-throughs.

TABLE 7.3
CMO/REMIC Issuance, 1983–1992

Year	Issued ($ billions)
1983	4.681
1984	10.767
1985	16.015
1986	48.317
1987	59.930
1988	78.754
1989	97.771
1990	97.5
1991	168.4
1992	274.2

Source: Lehman Brothers Fixed Income Research.

More recent innovations that are still important are PAC bonds and floating-rate CMOs (1986); stripped MBSs (1987); and an alphabet soup of innovations that came in the late 1980s, including TACs, jump Zs, super POs, and inverse floaters. Most of these forms are described and evaluated in the sections that follow.

The CMO Market in the Mid-1980s

The CMO market grew moderately after its introduction in 1983 until the REMIC legislation in 1987 gave the REMIC authority to Fannie Mae and Freddie Mac. Table 7.3 indicates the growth of the REMIC market from 1983 through 1992.

Until the federal agencies took over the REMIC market in 1987, the majority of CMO issuers were special-purpose corporations created by Wall Street firms to exploit the CMO arbitrage, which accounted for about half of all CMO issuance through the end of 1986. Home builders were second, with about 20 percent. Mortgage bankers and S&Ls made up most of the balance, which also included the first few Freddie Mac issues and some by insurance companies. Most of the S&L issuers used the CMO to dispose of seasoned mortgage loan portfolios without having to recognize the loss that would have resulted from a sale (remember, CMOs still represented issuance of debt, not asset sales).

Tax considerations made CMOs popular among home builders because prior to the Tax Reform Act of 1986 builders were able to use CMOs to raise immediate cash while benefiting from installment-sale treatment. More precisely, home builders were able to defer taxes on the profits from sales of homes by issuing mortgages to homeowners and then converting them into CMOs. However, under the Tax Reform Act of 1986, the deferral of gains from installment sales was seriously limited whenever the receivables are pledged, as they are in a CMO offering. Some builders have continued to issue CMOs for their economic benefits but not for their tax advantages.

Since 1987 when the REMIC authority was granted to Fannie Mae and Freddie Mac, these agencies have dominated the agency-guaranteed REMIC market as REMIC issuers. It is much cheaper for a prospective CMO issuer to rent the agency shelf registration and benefit from the overwhelming marketability advantage of a federal agency-issued REMIC; it is also relatively impractical for private issuers of an agency-collateralized REMIC to market REMICs on their own.

Investor Profile

Thrift institutions, primarily S&Ls, were the predominant MBS investors from the inception of these securities into the mid-1980s. With the exception of pension funds, most nonthrift institutional investors did not find the traditional pass-through an attractive investment. Prior to REMIC, S&Ls were not drawn to CMOs either because, since the pre-REMIC CMO represented purchase of corporate debt, S&Ls were restricted from CMO investing for two reasons: First, the CMO, as debt, came under a regulatory limitation that restricted S&Ls from lending more than a specified percentage of capital to one borrower (purchase of corporate debt is viewed as equivalent to a loan for purposes of the capital calculation). And, second, the CMO did not qualify under the *qualifying thrift lender* (*QTL*) test, which required S&Ls to maintain at least 80 percent of assets in qualifying assets. When Freddie Mac introduced a guaranteed minimum repayment schedule on the first class of its CMOs, the class qualified for thrift liquidity, which encouraged S&L investing in that class. Table 7.4 gives a profile of CMO investors in 1986.

By 1988 the investor profile had changed dramatically. Thrifts, particularly S&Ls, had become net sellers of assets, although they continued to buy seasoned, short-WAM MBSs and short-average-life REMICs. Commercial banks, which became highly restricted in their ability to buy municipal bonds under the Tax Reform Act of

TABLE 7.4
1986 CMO Investor Profile

Investor Type	Market Share (%)
Thrift institutions	6
Commercial banks	12
Insurance companies	7
Pension funds	11
Investment managers	14
Dealers	30

Source: Lehman Brothers Fixed Income Research.

1986,[12] sought agency-guaranteed REMICs as secure, short-term, high-yielding investments that were eligible collateral for deposits held on behalf of public bodies. The introduction of the PAC bond made REMICs attractive to insurance companies as a match for the 7- to 10-year GICs they issued. Foreign investors, particularly the Japanese, were attracted to the LIBOR-based CMO floaters. Pension funds preferred the long-dated classes, particularly the Z-bonds, which insulated them from reinvestment risk.

FIRREA Impact

With the passage of **FIRREA** in the summer of 1989 and the ensuing risk-weighted capital guidelines for depository institutions, FFIEC investment-suitability tests for banks introduced in 1992, and National Association of Insurance Commissioners (NAIC) reserve guidelines proposed for insurance company investments in 1993, commercial banks and insurance companies by the 1990s had become the principal investors in MBSs, particularly REMICs. In fact, after 1991 the REMIC deals *were* the buyer of most agency-issued MBSs to be used as collateral for the deals. Table 7.5 gives comparative investor profiles for 1991 and 1992 for all MBSs and for CMOs and REMICs. Table 7.6 underlines the significance of the demand for MBSs as deal collateral when REMIC issuance is high. As shown by the table, in 1991 the volume of REMIC issuance exceeded the 30-year Freddie Mac originations and was 94

---

[12]The Tax Reform Act of 1986 largely eliminated the classic commercial bank arbitrage of purchasing tax-exempt bonds while issuing CDs, on which the banks took as a tax deduction the interest paid to depositors.

TABLE 7.5
MBS Holdings and CMOs/REMICs as a Percentage of MBS Holdings

	1991		1992	
	MBS ($ Billions)	CMOs/ REMICs (%)	MBS ($ Billions)	CMOs/ REMICs (%)
Thrifts	186.4	17.5	178.2	20.5
Commercial banks	274.9	43.1	309.8	42.1
Life insurance companies	176.3	28.4	225.0	27.3
Mutual funds	78.7	n.a.	100.6	n.a.
Pension funds	157.2	16.1	185.1	13.7
Foreign investors	85.0	58.8	116.0	56.9
Other	281.5	n.a.	292.9	n.a.
Total	$1,240.0	41.7	$1,407.6	44.7

Sources: Inside Mortgage Securities, Lehman Brothers Fixed Income Research.

percent of 30-year Fannie Mae originations. In 1992 total REMIC issuance was only slightly less than originations. This phenomenon is referred to as the REMIC *collateral bid* and largely explains why MBS to Treasury yield spreads have remained so tight in the last few years.

PAC BONDS

A **planned amortization class (PAC)** is one type of CMO bond developed to help reduce the effects of prepayment risk. This structure was introduced in August 1986. A PAC bond provides a stable average life through creation of a sinking fund. What distinguishes the PAC bond from other CMO bond classes is the PAC pays to a pre-established schedule from cash flows that are segregated as the **PAC sinking fund.** The amount of cash flows available to the sinking fund are stable within a specified range of prepayment speeds. The PAC sinking fund takes priority over all other bond classes for the available pool cash flows. The average life of the PAC is, therefore, stabilized within the specified range of prepayment speeds, which is referred to as the **PAC bands,** or **collar.** A typical pre-

TABLE 7.6
Agency REMIC Issuance Summary

	REMIC Issuance ($ Billions)		REMIC as Percentage of Pass-Through Issuance	
	1991	*1992*	*1991*	*1992*
GNMA				
30-year	33.5	32.0	61.6	50.6
15-year	0.0	0.3	0.0	4.4
FNMA				
30-year	67.2	78.0	94.0	69.3
15-year	13.6	31.0	75.0	54.3
FHLMC				
30-year	61.9	72.9	106.9	89.8
15-year	11.3	47.4	72.3	79.2

Source: Lehman Brothers Fixed Income Research.

payment-protection range for recently issued PAC bonds might be 85 to 285 PSA (for an explanation of prepayments and PSA, see Measuring Prepayments in Chapter 4).

Identifying the Prepayment-Protection Band Range

The principal cash flows that would be available for the creation of the PAC sinking fund may best be understood by principal cash flow diagrams.

First, note the pattern of cash flows of the **scheduled amortization** of a mortgage (which is zero PSA), shown in Figure 7.6. Note that the principal cash flows are very *back-end* loaded (i.e., bundled in the later years of the principal amortization). Of course, structuring a CMO from such a distribution of principal cash flows would be extremely difficult; there is scant principal from which to retire bonds until years 17 and beyond. The average life of the scheduled amortization is about 24 years! Note that the pattern of cash flows at a relatively slow 85 PSA is also quite back-end loaded, as shown in Figure 7.7. Finally, note the *front-end*-loaded pattern of principal cash flow available at a fast 285 PSA (Figure 7.8). Thus, at a higher PSA there is ample principal cash flow for short-term bonds.

At 85 PSA, the slow-speed scenarios, the principal received from the collateral pool is relatively stable for many years and re-

FIGURE 7.6
Principal Cash Flows of $1 Million Pool, Zero PSA

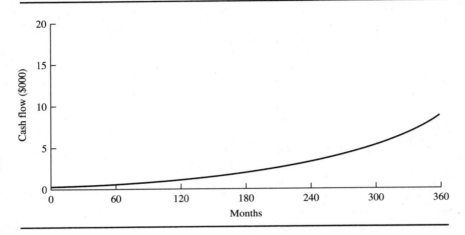

Source: Bloomberg Financial Markets.

FIGURE 7.7
Principal Cash Flows of $1 Million Pool, 85 PSA

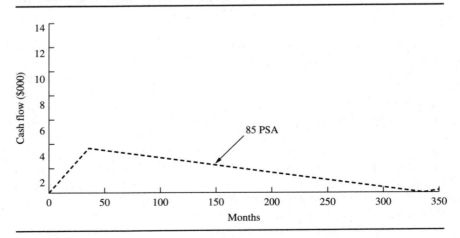

Source: Lehman Brothers Fixed Income Research.

FIGURE 7.8
Principal Cash Flows of $1 Million Pool, 285 PSA

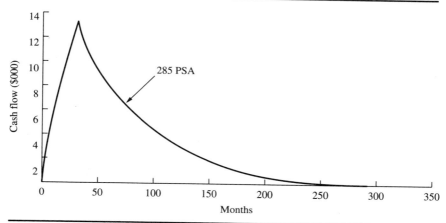

Source: Lehman Brothers Fixed Income Research.

sults in the back-end-loaded pattern previously described. These are the cash flows available to the long-dated PAC and support class bonds as long as prepayment speeds remain at moderate levels. Note that the decrease in the prepayment pattern of cash flows as the unpaid principal balance outstanding declines is offset by the increase in the scheduled principal amortization as the mortgages age.

In contrast, at the 285 PSA scenario the very front-end-loaded cash flows cause the principal payments to be greatest in the first few years, with the result that the unpaid principal balance outstanding declines very rapidly. The intersection of the 85 and 285 PSA scenarios defines the PAC sinking fund, as illustrated by the shaded area in Figure 7.9. Clearly, in the early years the principal received is greater at 285 PSA, whereas in the later years it is greater at 85 PSA. With the PAC schedule so defined, it follows that at any constant prepayment speed between 85 and 285 PSA the amount of principal available will always be in excess of the PAC schedule requirement. In fact, the earlier PAC classes in the CMO structure have **effective bands** well above the band defined by the PAC sinking fund. The vertical lines in the shaded area of Figure 7.10 show that the sinking fund may be divided into **tranches,** or classes, representing PAC bonds of varying average lives.

FIGURE 7.9
PAC Sinking Fund

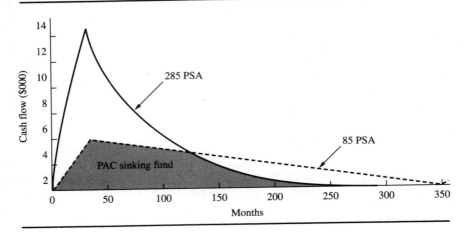

Source: Lehman Brothers Fixed Income Research.

FIGURE 7.10
CMO Principal Structure with Sinking Fund

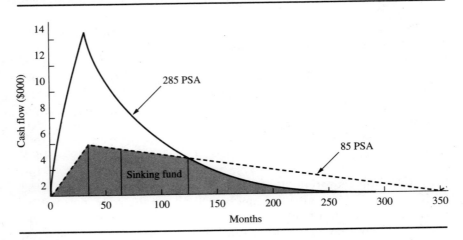

Source: Lehman Brothers Fixed Income Research.

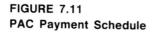

FIGURE 7.11
PAC Payment Schedule

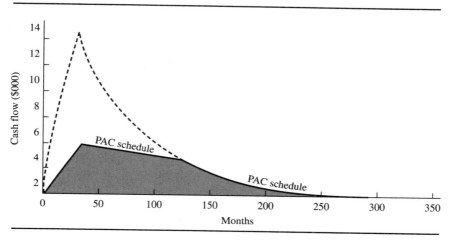

Anatomy of PAC Bonds[13]

PAC bonds achieve their stability from having a priority principal-payment schedule stipulated in the PAC bond trust indenture. According to the schedule of priorities, the PAC bonds receive a specified payment from each monthly distribution of principal from the collateral pool. The CMO bond payment requirements that can be met by the least amount of cash flows present at the fast or slow prepayment-speed scenarios define the **PAC payment schedule** (Figure 7.11). The cash flows in excess of the PAC payment schedule requirement are paid to the non-PAC bonds, referred to as **support class** or **companion bonds.** Figure 7.12 illustrates the total cash flows available from the collateral pool at 160 PSA, which is the PSA assumption used to structure the CMO in this example (referred to as the *pricing PSA assumption*). The figure also shows the amount available for the support classes at the 160 PSA assumption.

Should prepayments be so slow that the scheduled payment to the PACs cannot be paid in full that month, the PAC is to receive

---

[13]This discussion of PAC bond structure is based on *Anatomy of PAC Bonds* by Michael Bykhovsky and Lakhbir Hayre, Prudential Securities. New York: January 1992.

FIGURE 7.12
CMO Structure (Total Cash Flows Available at 160 PSA)

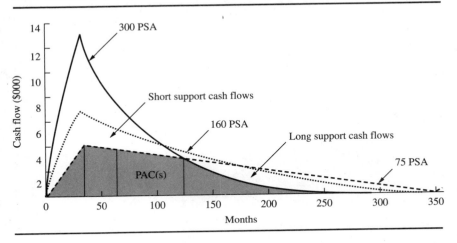

all the principal available, and the shortfall is carried forward and paid in arrears from any future cash flow containing an excess. The support classes, of course, extend in average life as they wait for principal cash flows to be available at some future date, but only after the PAC schedule has been brought fully up to date. In the event very fast prepayments generate an excess of cash flows, the PAC receives no more than its scheduled amount, with the excess paying off additional support bonds. The support bonds will now contract. Only after all the support bonds have been paid in full are excess principal cash flows applied to the PACs. Because of these features of the principal schedule, the PAC bonds can maintain a stable average life for considerable periods of fast or slow prepayments even when the PSA is outside the prepayment-protection bands.

Evaluating the PAC Band

It is very important that the lower and upper bands carry PSA limits which provide reasonable protection given the prepayment history of the specific collateral behind the PAC bond in question.

Measuring Lower-Band Adequacy

The first consideration is whether the prepayment history of the collateral lends confidence that the lower band will provide adequate extension protection during periods of slow prepayment activity. This is particularly difficult during periods of high prepayment activity, such as occurred in the early 1990s. In the spring and summer of 1992, for example, GNMA 8s were prepaying to a PSA range of 255 to 325. At such times a lower band of 90 PSA appears more than generous, but it may be well to remember that there were times in the early 1980s when GNMA 8s prepaid at 30 to 60 PSA. So don't say GNMA 8s will never prepay below 75 PSA! There may well be times ahead in the mid-1990s when history will repeat itself. What about FNMA 7 percent MBSs? In the fall of 1992 REMICs collateralized by FNMA and FHLMC 7s were structured with lower bands of 85 to 100 PSA. The PSA pricing assumption typically ranged from 85 to 285 PSA. Figure 7.13 illustrates the prepayment history of FNMA 7.5s. In the 1980s PSA speeds of 7.5s ranged from 25 to 55. Investors are cautioned, therefore, to examine closely the adequacy of lower bands as we move into what may be a slow prepayment period in the middle of this decade. In their study, Bykhovsky and Hayre presented some useful guidelines:

1. *In most cases, short-term PACs (average lives of less than two to three years) typically have little prepayment risk.* Even if there is a drastic interest-rate change over the short term (and hence a corresponding change in prepayment speeds), the non-PAC classes are still available to absorb prepayment changes.

2. *The upper collar of the PAC band is more likely to be breached than the lower collar* in times of high prepayment rates such as were experienced from the mid-1980s well into 1993. The lower collar is usually in the 70 percent to 100 percent PSA range, and prepayments on conventional mortgages are unlikely to fall below this level for an extended period of time unless an extremely severe housing recession occurs. The upper collar typically is in the 250 percent to 400 percent PSA range. Coupons exposed to significant refinancing opportunities for the first time are very likely to exceed these speeds.[14]

---

[14]Ibid.

FIGURE 7.13
FNMA 7.5 Percent MBSs, Prepayment History 1983–1992

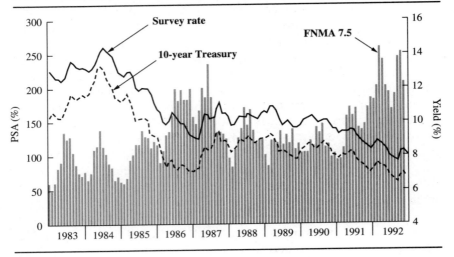

Source: Lehman Brothers Fixed Income Research.

As we move into the slower prepayment speeds likely to pre-vail in the mid-1990s, however, PACs with low-coupon collateral may experience prepayment speeds close to the lower bands for extended periods, particularly in the typically slower-speed winter months.

3. *The collateral type is a critical factor regardless of the CMO's structure.* Generally, pass-throughs with the highest prepayment volatility are relatively new current or low-premium coupons (especially FNMAs and FHLMCs), which tend to experience massive refinancings when mortgage rates drop substantially. Discount coupons provide more call protection, while seasoned premiums already have experienced a refinancing phase, making their prepayments less "elastic" in response to interest-rate changes. The discount coupons will, of course, be more prone to extension risk during periods of slower prepayment speeds.[15]

---

[15]Ibid.

Effect of Prepayments outside the Protection Range[16]

If prepayment speeds consistently fall outside the protection bands, the average life of the PAC will eventually shift, but at a slower pace than a normal CMO or MBS. The PAC sinking fund schedule always has the highest priority for payment of all the bonds in the structure. Perhaps of more practical application, the PAC bonds have a greater tolerance for prepayments that come in and out of the bands than might be expected. Stress tests demonstrate that prepayments can be below the lower band for several months a year. And if the prepayment speed falls back into the band range for the better part of the year, minimal extension will actually be realized. As discussed in 1992 Prepayment Impact on CMO Structure in Chapter 8, the 1992 refinancing experience, with prepayment speeds on some collateral coupons remaining above 500 PSA for extended periods, provided real-life testing of the call protection of PACs. In fact, some PACs actually lost most or all of their support bonds, and the PAC bands were broken. With the exception of PACs collateralized by conventional 9.5s, most survived remarkably well. The major impact of that high prepayment era was not an actual contraction in average life but rather severe erosion of the lower protection bands. If prepayments do remain below the lower band for extended periods, the PAC still has priority to all principal cash flow until the PAC bonds are fully retired. Although the average life of the PAC will extend, the degree of extension will largely depend on the proportion of support bonds to PACs in the deal structure. Generally speaking, the lower the percentage of PAC bonds in the deal, the more support bonds there are available to support the PACs. The greater the percentage of support class bonds, the more likely the PAC bond is to maintain its original average life.

If prepayments are consistently faster than the upper band of the protection range, the PAC bond will receive no more principal than its sinking fund schedule prescribes until the support bonds are fully retired. Then the degree of shortening of average life will depend upon the proportion of PAC and support bonds in the deal. The lower the percentage of PAC bonds in the deal, the more call

---

[16]This discussion of the effect of prepayments outside the protection range is based on Drexel Burnham Lambert, *CMO PAC and TAC Bonds: Call Protected Mortgage Securities.* New York: February 1989.

> **BOX 7.2**
> **Factors Contributing to Stability of PACs**
>
> 1. Most important, the PACs pay to a *predefined schedule, not to reduce given balances to zero in sequence.*
> 2. The claim of the PAC schedule on collateral principal cash flows is senior to all non-PAC classes that precede or follow it.
> 3. Most (but not all) PACs contain a provision that the PAC schedule is cumulative in claims to cash flow shortfalls.
> 4. The lower (slower prepayment) band tends actually to decline if prepayment speeds dip below the lower band.

protection the PACs will have. Box 7.2 highlights factors contributing to PAC bond stability.

In Box 7.2 the distinction drawn in (1) between paying to a schedule versus a balance is highly significant. With a standard sequential-pay structure all the collateral principal available as of a distribution date is applied to each bond class in sequential order until the balance is reduced to zero. The point in time when the balance is actually paid in full may be sooner or later depending on the timing of the cash flows—that is, in greater or lesser amounts depending on faster or slower prepayment speeds.

The PAC schedule, by contrast, specifies a specific balance, or factor, to which the bond must be paid on each distribution date. If prepayment speeds cause the principal distribution to be greater on a given distribution, the PAC cannot be reduced below its scheduled balance. If the principal amount is insufficient, in most PAC structures the scheduled balance becomes a cumulative claim on future collateral-principal distributions until the schedule is caught up.

Figure 7.14 indicates how below-band prepayment speeds might impact the collar. The figure illustrates a PAC sinking fund with a band of 125–400 PSA. Should the collateral prepay at 100 PSA for several years, which is below the low-prepayment-speed band, the realized cash flows would be represented by the solid line. After month 70 the realized cash flows exceed those needed to fulfill the requirements of the sinking fund. Note, however, two key

FIGURE 7.14

Continually Breaking the Lower PAC Band; PAC Principal Cash Flows at Constant 100 PSA

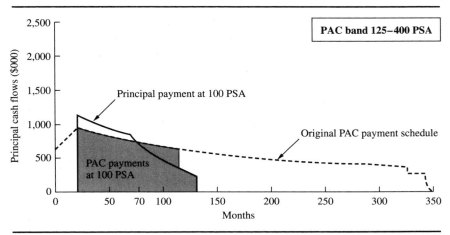

Source: Drexel Burnham Lambert.

points: First, the PAC would recoup the cash flows only if it contains the provision for shortfalls; and second, the average life would extend somewhat because of the delay in recouping the shortfall. In this case the sinking fund schedule is violated in about month 75, after which point there is a slight shortfall in the sinking fund. Note that here acceleration in prepayments above the PAC band extends the average life of the PAC.

Should the prepayment speed significantly exceed the band, for example, at 600 PSA, the average life of the PAC will shorten, as illustrated in Figure 7.15. This is so because in the instance illustrated in Figure 7.14, at 475 PSA, the non-PAC bonds were called upon to make up the shortfall to the PAC sinking fund. However, at the much higher 600 PSA the non-PACs are paid off much sooner and are, therefore, unable to cushion the PAC sinking fund. Consequently, every available dollar of cash flow is paid to the PAC, resulting in the early payments to the PAC, illustrated by the sail-shaped triangle above the PAC sinking fund in Figure 7.15.

PAC-Band Drift

Over time the effective bands will change even if the prepayment speed remains within the original band range. The band range actu-

FIGURE 7.15
Continually Breaking the Upper PAC Band; PAC Principal Cash Flows at Constant 600 PSA

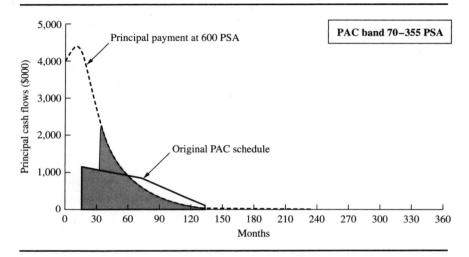

Source: Drexel Burnham Lambert.

ally tends to widen because there is *more* cash flow available than the upper band originally allowed for and less cash flow than was projected by the lower band. Furthermore, if prepayment speeds of the collateral underlying the PAC remain substantially above or below the pricing-speed assumption for a prolonged period of time, the bond will drift, or change. *This drift will, in general, occur even if the prepayment speed remains within the limits of the bands!*

The CMO bond payment requirements that can be met by the least amount of cash flows present at the fast or slow prepayment-speed scenarios make up the PAC schedule—that is, the sinking fund.

Prepayments below the Lower Band. If prepayment speeds pay consistently slower than the lower band, the deal structure will be left with more support bonds to provide call protection than was originally anticipated. There are, therefore, extra support bonds to protect the upper band, so that the upper band drifts up. However, the lower band drifts down because there is now a relatively greater percentage of collateral outstanding than was anticipated by the original pricing speed. This larger than anticipated amount of collateral generates a longer cash flow, thereby allowing a lower band to still meet the PAC schedule.

Prepayments above the Upper Band. If prepayments are faster than specified by the upper band, much of the support class has been paid off sooner than anticipated, and there will be less collateral outstanding than was originally anticipated.

Therefore, there is a lower percentage of collateral than was anticipated at the pricing speed, so the lower band drifts up because we now need a faster prepayment speed to maintain the same amount of cash flow that the larger amount of collateral originally anticipated would have generated. However, with fewer support bonds there is less call protection available to the PACs, so the upper band drifts down. If the prepayment speeds of this PAC were at 475 PSA, which is above the upper band, the impact would not be realized until the latter months of the PAC sinking fund schedule. This scenario is illustrated in Figure 7.16.

In a variable scenario, which is likely closer to reality than that of the extremes of very high or very low prepayments, as described above, the companion (non-PAC) bonds are able to do the job they were designed for. With the extra cash flows available from avoiding the extremes of the band range, the companion bonds have cash flow left over when prepayments accelerate above the prepayment-speed assumption used at pricing but not above the upper band. The upper collar of the band may therefore increase, allowing for future prepayment speeds to increase beyond the original upper limit of the band.

Prepayment Speeds within the Bands. If prepayment speeds are, in fact, higher than the minimum allowed for by the lower original band limit, the tolerance for future very slow speeds is now raised to a somewhat higher minimum because more cash flows have been disbursed than the old minimum cash flow boundary would have allowed for. Figure 7.17 illustrates how the band range would drift if the prepayment speed of this PAC collateral prepaid at 100 PSA (original band range 70–355 PSA). The new band range after three years would be 71–390 PSA.

If, in Figure 7.17, on the other hand, the actual prepayments remained within the original band but at the upper end of the allowable speed range, for example, 325 PSA, the lower band would drift much higher as a greater amount of cash flows is dissipated,

FIGURE 7.16
Continually Breaking the Upper PAC Band; PAC Principal Cash Flows at Constant 475 PSA

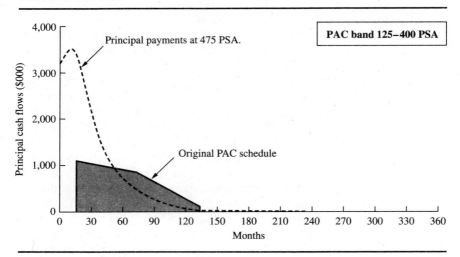

Source: Drexel Burnham Lambert.

FIGURE 7.17
PAC Bands Responding to Actual Prepayments; Prepayments within the Band Range and Near the Lower Band

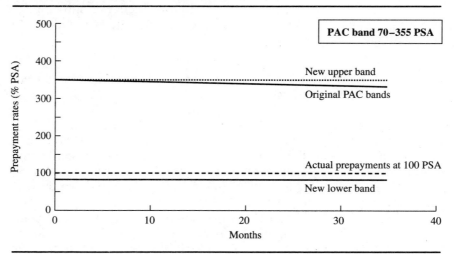

Source: Drexel Burnham Lambert.

FIGURE 7.18

PAC Bands Responding to Actual Prepayments; Prepayments within the Band Range and Near the Upper Band

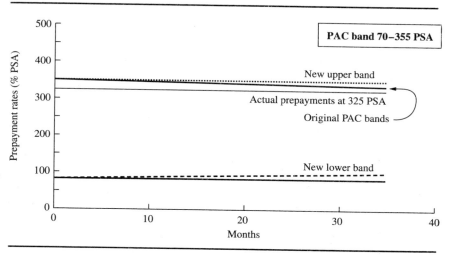

Source: Drexel Burnham Lambert.

leaving a smaller cushion to meet slower prepayment speeds should they occur. Similarly, the upper band would be able to be somewhat higher than the original 355 PSA limit, but not as high as the slower 100 PSA allowed for because more cash flows would have been disbursed. The new band range after three years for a PAC that paid at 325 PSA would therefore be 100–370 PSA. The band drift of this scenario is illustrated in Figure 7.18.

Band-Drift Synopsis

Collateral PSA below the Bands

In this scenario the structure has more supports to provide call protection; the upper band drifts up, and the lower band drifts down because there is a greater percentage of collateral remaining to support the PACs. And the greater amount of collateral provides sufficient cash flow to meet the PAC schedule at a lower and higher effective PSA.

Collateral PSA above the Bands

Now there are *fewer* supports to provide call protection; the upper band drifts down. The lower band drifts up because we have less collateral to generate principal, so the minimum PAC schedule can be met only at a faster prepayment speed.

Collateral PSA within the Bands

The upper band drifts up because payments are at a PSA below the upper band, so there are proportionately more supports left than projected in the worst-case (upper band) PSA at pricing. The lower band drifts up because collateral is being paid down faster than the minimum (lower band) PSA, so a faster speed is needed to maintain the minimum PAC schedule payments. Box 7.3 summarizes band-drift axioms.

Cash Flow Windows

The **cash flow window** within the CMO structure is the time from the receipt of the first principal payment to be paid on a tranche to the last. In general, PAC bond classes typically have relatively narrow windows (1 to 2 years for the short-average-life PACs; 2 to 5 years for intermediate PACs). Sequential-pay CMOs typically have somewhat longer windows, and support class windows may be as

---

BOX 7.3
Synopsis of Band Drift

- *If PSA is below the lower band,* the lower band drifts down (more collateral requires less speed to generate the minimum cash flow to meet the PAC schedule).
- *If PSA is above the lower band,* the lower band drifts up (less collateral needs faster speed to maintain the minimum PAC schedule).
- *If PSA is below the upper band,* the upper band drifts up (there are more supports to provide call protection).
- *If PSA is above the upper band,* the upper band drifts down (there are fewer supports to provide call protection).

FIGURE 7.19
Narrow-Window PAC, Principal Cash Flows; FNMA 1990 31-B

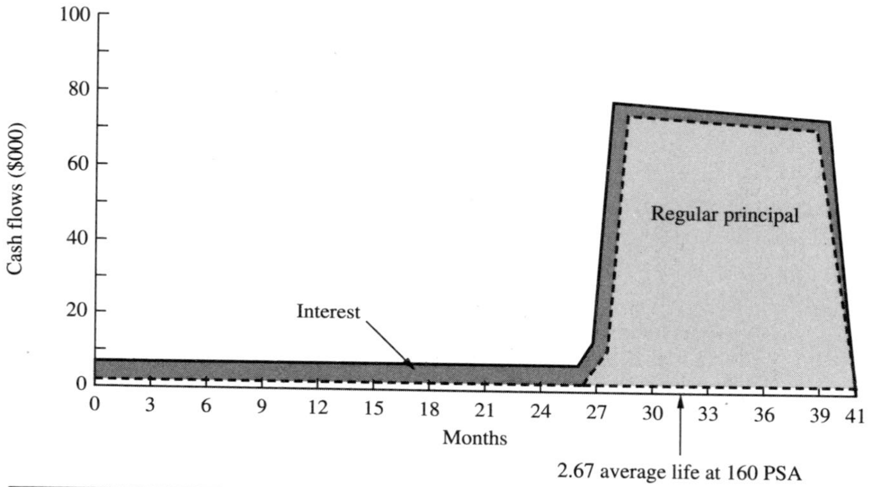

Source: Bloomberg Financial Markets.

long as 30 years. Figure 7.19 illustrates a **narrow-window PAC**. Note that the window period of a PAC bond class will not change as long as the PAC bands are not seriously violated. If they are, there is drift in the window period as the average life of the PAC extends or contracts.

Wide versus Narrow Windows[17]

Driven by investor preference for bullet-like maturities in the CMO market of the early 1990s, investor demand caused PAC bond structures to evolve from wide- to narrow-window PACs. Consequently, PACs structured with wide paydown windows typically yield 5 to 10 basis points more than narrow-window PACs with a comparable average life. In addition, in a positively sloped yield curve environment investors in wide-window PACs, in effect, purchase 3- to 5-year-average-life cash flows at the higher 7-year yields and PAC spreads. Figure 7.20 illustrates the comparative cash flow

[17]This discussion of windows is based on *Wide versus Narrow Window PACs* by Kathy Jardine, Analyst, Mortgage Strategies, Lehman Brothers, April 1991.

FIGURE 7.20
Wide- versus Narrow-Window PACs, Principal Cash Flows

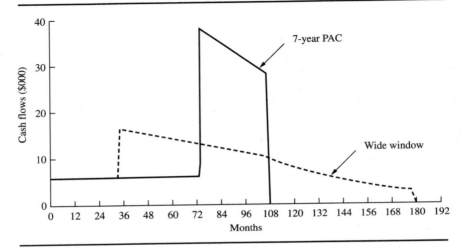

Source: Lehman Brothers Fixed Income Research.

structures of wide- versus narrow-window PACs. Table 7.7 illustrates the yield advantage of a hypothetical wide-window PAC over a comparable portfolio of 3- to 15-year-average-life PACs. The wide-window PAC in this example offers a yield advantage of 14 basis points over the narrow-window PAC. GIC managers can view their liabilities in a portfolio context and use wide-window PACs to fund their core liabilities. Spikes in the liability cash flows can then be funded using narrow-window PACs.

When the yield curve is steep, short-average-life, narrow-window PACs often offer a very low OAS, as illustrated in Figure 7.21. Note that the OAS calculates the yield spread of all the window cash flows to the entire curve—not just to a single point on the curve. The figure illustrates some key points regarding the positioning of the window on the yield curve:

1. The PAC has a 2.49-year average life but is priced off the 2-year Treasury.
2. The window cash flows start at the pricing point and continue up the curve to the 3-year point on the curve.
3. The value of the curve from the start of the cash flow window to the 2.49-year-average-life point is 31 basis points

TABLE 7.7

Yields of Wide-Window versus Narrow-Window PACs (Collateral FNMA 9.5 Percent MBSs, 4/18/91 Pricing Date)

PAC Security	Coupon (%)	Average Life (years)	Percentage of Portfolio	Yield (%)	Principle Duration (years)	Window (years)
3-year	7.50	3.45	15	7.94	2.92	3.07–4.07
4-year	7.50	4.48	09	8.20	3.66	4.07–4.91
5-year	7.50	5.48	14	8.53	4.30	4.91–6.07
7-year	7.50	7.48	28	8.77	5.42	6.07–8.91
10-year	7.50	10.97	30	9.91	7.00	8.91–13.74
Long	7.50	14.97	04	9.06	8.11	13.74–14.91
	7.50	7.64	100	8.71	5.30	3.07–14.91
Wide-window	7.50	7.64	100	8.85	5.30	3.07–14.91

FIGURE 7.21
Narrow-Window PACs Priced to Positive Yield Curve

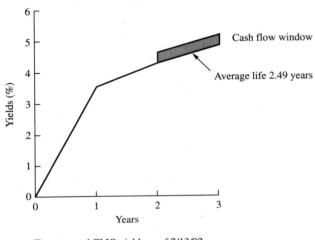

Treasury and CMO yields as of 7/13/92
 2-year Treasury yield = 5.32%
 3-year Treasury yield = 5.96%
 PAC priced at 2-year Treasury + 65 basis points = 5.97%
 2–3 year spread = 64 basis points

and must be subtracted from the stated spread, which is calculated to the 2-year point on the curve.

The fact that the investor in the 2-year Treasury is giving up 6 months of curve value (2-year pricing point versus 2.5-year average life) hurts a lot with this short-average-life PAC, but has less impact with the longer PACs, where the half-year differential between the pricing point on the curve and the longer average-life point are less meaningful.

In spite of these disadvantages, investors typically prefer the narrow window. In part, the preference appears to be related to the matching of assets to liabilities, which is important to depository institutions. The match between an asset and the liabilities supporting it is easier to conceptualize when the window period is short. In addition, the foreshortened window period lessens other risks, such as reinvestment risk, and reduces accounting problems. Another positive impact is that a narrow window will roll down the curve more quickly, enhancing its price performance over time.

TABLE 7.8
FNMA 1988 13-B Amounts

Distribution Dates	1988 13-B Amounts ($)	Distribution Dates	1988 13-B Amounts ($)
June 1988	0	July 1990	1,205,000
July 1988	0	August 1990	1,205,000
August 1988	0	September 1990	1,200,000
September 1988	0	October 1990	1,195,000
October 1988	0	November 1990	1,190,000
November 1988	0	December 1990	1,190,000
December 1988	0	January 1991	1,185,000
January 1989	930,000	February 1991	1,180,000
February 1989	965,000	March 1991	1,175,000
March 1989	1,000,000	April 1991	1,175,000
April 1989	1,035,000	May 1991	1,170,000
May 1989	1,070,000	June 1991	1,165,000
June 1989	1,105,000	July 1991	1,160,000
July 1989	1,140,000	August 1991	1,160,000
August 1989	1,175,000	September 1991	1,155,000
September 1989	1,210,000	October 1991	1,150,000
October 1989	1,245,000	November 1991	1,145,000
November 1989	1,240,000	December 1991	1,145,000
December 1989	1,235,000	January 1992	1,140,000
January 1990	1,230,000	February 1992	1,135,000
February 1990	1,225,000	March 1992	1,135,000
March 1990	1,225,000	April 1992	1,130,000
April 1990	1,220,000	May 1992	1,125,000
May 1990	1,215,000	June 1992	1,120,000
June 1990	1,210,000	July 1992	1,120,000
		Schedule concludes July 1994	0

Source: Fannie Mae.

Lockout Impact on CMO Bonds
A **lock-out** in the CMO deal structure means that the first PAC class will not receive any principal payments for two to three years (the lockout period). Table 7.8 illustrates the lockout for the first PAC (B class) in the FNMA 1988–13 REMIC. The lockout period lasted until January 1989, when the window opened and the PAC received its first principal payment.

The lockout is more properly an attribute of the support class than of the PAC. The purpose of the lockout is to stabilize the support classes by allowing the first support bond to pay as a standard sequential-pay bond during the lockout period. The short-average-life support class, therefore, has an opportunity to amortize a reasonable portion of its amortization requirement before the PAC schedule takes priority call on the cash flows. The lockout substantially stabilizes the support class if prepayment speeds are very slow. Without the lockout, the support class would, of course, extend significantly in a slow-prepayment environment because the PAC schedule would garner all the available cash flow.

The PAC bond, contrary to intuitive assumptions, is not jeopardized by the lockout. The lockout actually benefits the PAC bonds by reducing both call and extension risk, with earlier bonds benefiting somewhat more than longer-dated bonds. There are two considerations. First, the lockout reduces the total amount of the PAC payment schedule by eliminating the payment requirements to the PAC during the lockout period. There is, therefore, a smaller proportion of PAC bonds relative to support bonds. In turn, there is a relatively greater proportion of support bonds to protect the remaining PAC schedule. Second, since the supports are paid by cash flows out of the collateral with the lowest sensitivity to prepayment risk (i.e., early in the life of the pool), these supports are much less vulnerable to call risk. Even at very high prepayment speeds a larger proportion of support bonds remains outstanding to shelter the PAC bonds than would be the case with no lockout. Furthermore, these principal cash flows are not bound to a schedule, so later scheduled principal payments are more likely to be paid on time should prepayment speeds fall below the lower band.

Impact of the Yield Curve[18]

In periods of a steep yield curve a long lockout period is preferable (to avoid the reinvestment risk of the low short-term interest rates). In a flat yield curve, however, a shorter lockout may be preferred to take advantage of the relatively high short-term rates.

Forward Settlement versus Corporate Settlement
Investors who prefer to invest in new-issue CMO deals must take into consideration the yield give-up for deferring receipt of the

---

[18]This discussion of the impact on the yield curve was provided by Kenneth Scott, Vice President, Clayton Brown & Associates, Chicago.

CMO coupon until the issue settles, generally one to two months forward. For example, assume the following for a 2-year PAC:

CMO average life	2.49 years
CMO modified duration	2.00 years
Offered yield	2-year Treasury + 67 basis points
2-year Treasury yield	6 percent
LIBOR yield	4 percent
Settlement	2 months forward

Based on the above, the stated yield of this 2-year PAC would be 6.67 percent (6.00 Treasury yield plus 67 basis points spread equals 6.67 percent). However, while we wait for the issue to settle, assume we can earn only LIBOR (4 percent). We are giving up the difference, which is 2.67 percent for the two months (6.67 percent yield less 4 percent LIBOR equals 2.67 percent).

If there were a similar CMO available for current corporate delivery available at par, this CMO to be delivered two months forward is worth less, reflecting the 2.67 percent yield give-up for two months. How much less? The discount factor for two months is 2/12 of a year times 0.0267, or 0.00445. Thus the forward-settled CMO is worth 100.000/(1 − 0.00445), or 99.557. This is a decrease in price of approximately 14/32. Alternatively, if the price of the forward-settled CMO is not reduced, because the modified duration is two years, the decrease in yield is 0.00445/modified duration (which equals 0.002225), or about 22 basis points. In other words, for a forward-settled CMO offered at the same price as a corporate-settled CMO, the investor is giving up 22 basis points in yield. An investor ought to be cautious, but normally the investor is compensated for the cost of the carry. Assuming the proper lowering of cost, the nominal yield spread is 67 basis points.

The reality is somewhat worse than this would indicate. Refer back to Figure 7.21. The value of the yield curve from the 2-year to the 3-year point is 62 basis points. However, the actual average life of the PAC is 2.49 years, whereas the PAC is priced to a spread off the 2-year, a give-up of 1/2 year, which is 31 basis points. So now the yield spread adjusted for the *yield curve effect* is 67 basis points less the 31 basis points, or 36 basis points. Finally, the CMO is stated to have an average life of 2.49 years. That is true as of delivery, but delivery is two months away. An investor making the purchase today is committed to an investment of 2.49 years plus two additional months. If the 2-year to 3-year spread is 62 basis points, the investor ought to receive an additional 10 basis points. This would further reduce the purported spread from 36 basis points down to 26 basis points.

However, another adjustment needs to be made. We are comparing a PAC with a 1-year cash flow window to a 2-year Treasury, which is a *bullet maturity*. The adjustment for the window versus bullet is worth about 10 basis points, so the real comparable yield to the Treasury is only 16 basis points. The last adjustment would be for the option cost of the prepayment risk, which for a 2-year PAC is only about 2 basis points, for a net spread of 14 basis points.

It should be noted that the example given here is for a CMO priced in June 1992, a time when the yield curve was unusually steep. Therefore, the value of the curve from 2 to 3 years was more than normal. Furthermore, as one moves farther out on the curve the present value of the yield curve becomes less, and the duration of a longer-average-life CMO would, of course, be greater. Therefore, for a longer-average-life PAC, such as a 7- or 10-year, the curve effect would be a very small consideration. Also, the curve even in 1992 was not as steep past the 5-year point.

Super PAC Structure[19]

In the first quarter of 1993, in response to investor concerns with the fourth wave of prepayment acceleration of the 1991–1993 cycle, a strengthened PAC structure was developed to insulate investors from the 1992 broken PAC experience.

Super PACs are PACs with twice as many support class bonds as the usual PAC structure. In a typical PAC structure, supports represent about 32 percent of the deal. With super PACs the supports represent about 65 percent of the deal. This is reflected in the wider structuring bands of the super PACs. As shown in Table 7.9, a super PAC structure backed by conventional, 30-year 7s has a lower structuring band of 65 PSA and an upper structuring band of 450 PSA. This compares to a regular PAC, which has a lower band of 95 PSA and an upper band of 220 PSA. These wider bands sig-

---

[19]This discussion of super PACs is from *Super PACs: An Attractive Alternative to Corporates and Agencies* by Alan Jay Brazil and Jennifer Lakefield. New York: Lehman Brothers, February 1993.

TABLE 7.9
Effective PAC Bands (PSA)

Maturity	Super PAC		Regular PAC	
	Lower Band	Upper Band	Lower Band	Upper Band
1-year	65 PSA	1,500	95 PSA	700
2-year	65	793	95	380
3-year	65	639	95	315
4-year	65	536	95	265
5-year	65	477	95	235
7-year	65	452	95	225
10-year	65	450	95	225

nificantly increase the prepayment protection. The lower band of the super PAC is virtually unbreakable because it would take more than a 1,000 basis points rise in rates and a recession to push prepayments below 65 PSA. In addition, mortgage rates would need to fall almost 200 basis points before prepayments on conventional 7s act like those on conventional 9s and break the worst-case upper bands. As with all PACs, the structuring upper bands of super PACs understate the actual effective prepayment protection. These effective upper bands of the super PACs are twice those of a regular PAC.

The structure may also be created by dividing the cash flows allocated to the sinking fund of a normal PAC structure into super PACs and sub PACs. In this structure the ratio of PAC (scheduled) cash flows to support bonds is the same as that of a normal PAC. However, the super PACs have superior call protection to that of a typical PAC, and the sub PACs less. These structures may be regarded as nothing more than carving the collateral cash flows of a CMO structure in different proportions.

PAC IIs

First introduced in 1989, type II (also called tier two) PACs became popular because they offer a wide yield spread with some degree of prepayment-risk protection. However, PAC IIs are like many CMOs in that bonds with the same average life often have very different convexity, realized average life, and return expectations.

The risk/reward considerations with PAC IIs revolve around the fact that although the PAC II has a prepayment-protection band, giving it PAC-like stability in a low-volatility interest rate environment, the PAC II schedule is subordinated to the **tier one PACs,** which causes the PAC IIs to take on support class characteristics when prepayments move outside the bands. All requirements of the tier one (PAC I) schedule must be met before any principal cash flows may be dispersed to the PAC II schedule. *Remember that in the event all the support bonds are paid off, standard PAC bonds become sequential-pay, or clean, bonds, but PAC IIs become support bonds.*

CHAPTER 8

CMO VALUATION ISSUES

KEY QUESTIONS

1. What type of CMO structure do I seek?
2. What is the collateral?
3. What are the price/yield considerations?
4. How do I measure risk/reward?

1. WHAT TYPE OF CMO STRUCTURE DO I SEEK?

Maturity (Average-Life) Range

The first question most CMO investors will ask themselves is, "What maturity bracket do I seek in my investment?" Usually the question will be defined in terms of average life or of duration. The selection of a maturity, or average-life, bracket might be dictated by internal or external investment guidelines (such as no investments with an average life or stated maturity beyond five years); by a duration bogey; or by a preferred sector on the yield curve that may be expected to perform the best.

CMO Class Type

Having identified an average-life objective, the next question becomes, "How well does the proposed CMO investment fit my risk/reward parameters?" Or, "What is my tolerance for duration drift to maximize yield?" Be cautious in rationalizing the yield versus stability issue. The insatiable quest for yield tempts many investors to overrate the real value of high stated yield, which will often not be realized when prepayment volatility increases. The third question then becomes, "Do I want a sequential pay, a PAC, a support class, or perhaps a derivative (IO, inverse floater, and so on)?"

Many investors assume that the sequential-pay (often referred to as "clean") deals are best because they are relatively simple in structure and are not complicated by the "bells and whistles" of a PAC/support structure. The PAC bonds offer the least stated yield, but because of their protection bands and substantial insulation from prepayment risk, they are often the best way for investors to ensure good performance and realization of the anticipated yield. Of course, a relatively narrow yield spread with assurance it will be realized is often superior to a high stated yield that may result in disappointment. This is especially true for investors new to MBS investing. Generally speaking, the PAC class bonds represent excellent value and are even more stable in times of high prepayment volatility than is generally believed (see Impact of 1992–1993 Prepayments on CMO Structure, page 372). The support class bonds, which may offer tantalizing stated yield spreads, are often less stable than is generally believed, and the stated yield may be illusory.[1] Sequential-pay bond classes generally offer fair value for relatively modest call and/or extension risk.

Sequentials reflect the same prepayment and convexity sensitivities as the underlying collateral, although by the very fact that the cash flows have been tranched out into maturity buckets, the average-life drift for any specific class is, of course, less than that of the collateral. *The intermediate (7- to 10-year) class may be regarded as a proxy for the collateral and will have characteristics that are similar to those of the collateral, although they are more stable.*

Tables 8.1A, 8.1B, and 8.1C compare the prepayment volatility of short-, intermediate-, and long-average-life CMO bonds, respectively; Table 8.2 offers a relative value comparison of varying average-life CMO classes to comparable average-life MBSs.

Convexity Properties of CMOs

Typically, the CMO outperforms the collateral because of its structured cash flow window period. This characteristic is especially true of narrow-window PAC structures. An intermediate- or long-average-life, sequential-pay CMO will generally have greater average-life drift than the collateral—that is, will extend or shorten to a greater

---

[1]Support class bonds are usually priced to a discount because they are generally highly sensitive to prepayments. When prepayments are trending higher, a discount purchase price can provide considerable yield compensation as the average life of the bond shortens.

TABLE 8.1A
Prepayment Sensitivity Analysis, Short CMOs

		−200 bp	−100 bp	Base	+100 bp	+200 bp
AD bond FHLMC 104-C 8.45/9.0[a]	Price: 98-30+ Spread: +48					
	Yield (%)	8.41	8.41	8.41	8.41	8.41
	Average life (years)	2.32	2.32	2.32	2.32	2.32
		Structure stabilized by a series of Z-bonds				
PAC FHLMC 130-A 8.6/9.0[a]	Price: 99-06+ Spread: +51					
	Yield (%)	8.44	8.44	8.44	8.44	8.44
	Average life (years)	1.83	1.83	1.83	1.83	1.83
		No change in average life				
Sequential-pay FNMA 89-91A 8.5/9.5[a]	Price: 98-18+ Spread: +77					
	Yield (%)	8.74	8.71	8.70	8.70	8.69
	Average life (years)	1.16	1.83	1.89	2.10	2.25
		Average-life drift only 1.48 years				
Type II PAC FNMA 90-79K 8.5/9.0[a]	Price: 97-28 Spread: +98					
	Yield (%)	8.44	9.09	9.10	9.10	9.11
	Average life (years)	1.39	3.41	3.50	3.50	3.57
		Extension protection superior to sequential pay				
Stabilized support FHLMC 182-L 9.4/10.0[a]	Price: 99-30+ Spread: +89					
	Yield (%)	8.56	8.76	8.82	8.96	9.02
	Average life (years)	1.76	2.25	2.45	3.13	3.64
	Duration	1.62	2.02	2.18	2.65	2.97
		Call/extension risk similar to sequential pay				
Less stabilized support FNMA 88-21 H 7.0/9.5[a]	Price: 94-15+ Spread: +175					
	Yield (%)	15.03	10.20	9.68	8.50	8.15
	Average life (years)	0.56	1.48	1.80	3.69	5.32
	Duration	0.54	1.36	1.64	3.00	4.02
		Substantial average-life drift				

[a]Denotes CMO bond coupon/collateral pass-through coupon.

Source: Mark Rudnitsky, Vice President, CMO Trading Desk, Lehman Brothers.

TABLE 8.1B
Intermediate CMOs

		−200 bp	−100 bp	Base	+100 bp	+200 bp
PAC						
FHLMC 139-E	Price: 100-21					
9.50/9.50[a]	Spread: +95					
	Yield (%)	9.29	9.37	9.37	9.37	9.37
	Average life					
	(years)	6.77	9.14	9.14	9.14	9.14
	Some call risk; extension minimal					
TAC						
PaineWebber	Price: 90-23					
N-3 8.0/9.0[a]	Spread: +115					
	Yield (%)	9.59	9.51	9.51	9.38	9.32
	Average life					
	(years)	8.58	8.91	8.90	10.31	11.24
	Good call protection; exhibits extension risk					
Sequential pay						
FHLMC 167-C	Price: 99-05					
9.5/9.5[a]	Spread: +120					
	Yield (%)	9.56	9.61	9.62	9.62	9.62
	Average life					
	(years)	5.19	9.56	11.28	13.08	14.33
	Displays some prepayment volatility					
Support						
FHLMC 182-N	Price: 97-08+					
9.40/10.20[a]	Spread: +145					
	Yield (%)	10.14	9.91	9.81	9.79	9.78
	Average life					
	(years)	3.12	6.05	10.62	12.97	13.90
	Duration	2.72	4.58	6.65	7.46	7.73
	High call risk					
Support Z						
FNMA 90-76X	Price: 92-23+					
9.25/9.50[a]	Spread: +160					
	Yield (%)	11.41	10.30	10.08	9.98	9.94
	Average life					
	(years)	3.86	9.33	12.51	14.43	15.50
	Duration	3.84	8.71	11.72	13.75	14.84
	High call risk; protects PACs					

[a]Denotes CMO bond coupon/collateral pass-through coupon.

Source: Mark Rudnitsky, Vice President, CMO Trading Desk, Lehman Brothers.

TABLE 8.1C
Long CMOs (Deep-Discount Price)

		−200 bp	−100 bp	Base	+100 bp	+200 bp
PAC						
FNMA 90-12G	Price: 59-24+					
4.5/9.0[a]	Spread: +88					
	Yield (%)	9.70	9.28	9.28	9.28	9.28
	Average life					
	(years)	15.38	17.53	17.53	17.53	17.53
		Very stable; effective bands 0–400 PSA				
PAC						
FNMA 90-76G	Price: 79-23					
7.0/9.5[a]	Spread: +98					
	Yield (%)	9.71	9.38	9.38	9.38	9.32
	Average life					
	(years)	14.34	18.68	18.68	18.68	18.68
		Offers yield compensation for call risk				
Sequential Z						
FNMA 90-21Z	Price: 87-12					
9.0/9.0[a]	Spread: +155					
	Yield (%)	10.34	9.99	9.96	9.91	9.89
	Average life					
	(years)	12.80	18.69	19.26	20.37	21.04
		Offers yield compensation for call risk				
Whole-loan Z						
SLH 89-01 Z	Price: 90-05+					
9.5/10.92[a]	Spread: +215					
	Yield (%)	11.22	10.73	10.46	10.36	10.34
	Average life					
	(years)	9.46	14.15	19.34	21.88	22.57
	Duration	9.00	13.17	17.90	20.48	21.24
		High yield for nonagency collateral				
Support Z						
FNMA 90-76X	Price: 82-24+					
9.25/9.50[a]	Spread: +200					
	Yield (%)	16.38	10.54	10.40	10.37	10.32
	Average life					
	(years)	2.80	19.46	21.59	22.09	22.99
	Duration	2.80	17.17	19.74	20.34	21.42
		Substantial yield compensation for call risk				

[a]Denotes CMO bond coupon/collateral pass-through coupon.

Source: Mark Rudnitsky, Vice President, CMO Trading Desk, Lehman Brothers.

TABLE 8.2
Relative Value Comparison

	FHLMC 1066 PAC	Compare to
	Class B 2-Year	*Typical Clean 2-Year*
Average life (years)	2.49	2.5
Window (years)	1	5
Extension		
@ 100 PSA (years)	2.7	3.5
Comment	Compare windows, extension risk	
	Class C 3-Year	*Typical Clean 3-Year*
Average life (years)	3.49	3.5
Window (years)	1	7
Extension		
@ 100 PSA (years)	4.4	5.1
Comment	Compare windows, extension risk	
	Class E 5-Year	*7-Year Balloon*
Average life (years)	5.51	5.35
Window (years)	1	7.0
Projected final (years)	6	7
Extension		
@ 100 PSA (years)	7.8	5.78
Comment	Compare window; projected final of CMO shorter than balloon	
	Class G 7-Year	*15-Year FNMA 8.5*
Average life (years)	6.71	5.8
Window (years)	1	15
Projected final (years)	7.38	15
Extension		
@ 100 PSA (years)	9.46	6.4
Comment	CMO average life 1 year longer; also offers excellent call protection; narrow window	
	Class H 7-Year	*210 WAM FNMA 9*
Average life (years)	7.79	6.3
Window (ye3rs)	0.83	17.5
Projected final (years)	8.21	17.5
Extension		
@ 100 PSA (years)	10.97	7.71
Comment	CMO projected maturity much shorter; compare cash flow window	

Source: Mark Rudnitsky, Vice President, CMO Trading Desk, Lehman Brothers.

extent—but will outperform the collateral with intermediate price volatility. A PAC structure will generally outperform the collateral in most scenarios, and a support structure will generally underperform the collateral. There are, however, no consistent measures of how the CMO structure will perform against its comparable collateral. The performance of the CMO versus that of its collateral is a function of the price and yield at which the CMO was purchased and the relative average life of a given CMO class in comparison to the underlying collateral. Even the support class of a CMO will outperform the comparable collateral or a comparable average-life CMO class if purchased at sufficient yield spread and price volatility is moderate. As shown in Figures 8.1A and 8.1B, the yield spreads of 30- and 15-year collateral have tightened dramatically to comparable average-life PACs and to Treasuries over the past two years. This tightening may be largely attributable to the REMIC demand for collateral.

Riding the Yield Curve

When evaluating the CMO be aware of how its yield and spread to the curve change as its average life shortens and extends in the up-and-down interest rate shifts. Table 8.3 illustrates the stated yield and yield spread changes of a typical sequential-pay structure as it rides up and down the yield curve with interest rate shifts up and down 300 basis points.

As interest rates increase (+100, +300), the price and stated yield spread of the CMO decrease. In other words, as the average life of the CMO extends, not only is there a loss in its price as the CMO bond is pushed farther out on the term structure of the Treasury curve but there is a loss in the yield spread the CMO offers to the comparable-maturity Treasuries. Now farther out on the term structure of the yield curve, the Treasuries are, therefore, trading to a commensurately higher yield.

On the other hand, when interest rates decline the *stated* yield spread of the CMO widens dramatically as its average life shortens and it becomes priced to shorter-average-life Treasuries. (Of course, the required yield spread is likely to increase because of the higher prepayment speed of the underlying collateral.) A note of caution must be interjected here: the spread will widen only if the yield curve maintains its structure over time. If the Treasury curve flattens, then Treasuries of comparable average life will be at a higher

FIGURE 8.1A
Thirty-Year, Fixed-Rate MBS; Yield Spread to Treasuries, 1990–1992

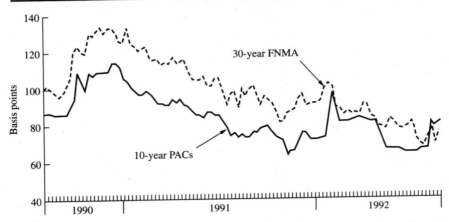

Note: Spreads are adjusted for the variance between the actual CMO average life and the reference Treasury—that is, a "2-year" PAC priced off the 2-year Treasury actually has a 2.49-year average life.

Source: Lehman Brothers Fixed Income Research.

FIGURE 8.1B
Fifteen-Year, Fixed-Rate MBS; Yield Spread to Treasuries, 1990–992

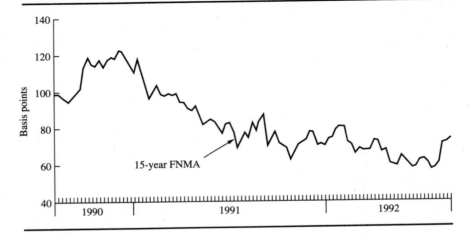

Source: Lehman Brothers Fixed Income Research.

TABLE 8.3

Riding the Yield Curve (FHLMC 1383C Sequential-Pay; Collateral, FHLMC 7.5 Percent, 30-Year PC)

Interest Rate Shift	Average Life (Years)	Yield Spread	CMO Price	CMO Price Change
−300	2.35	167	108-10	+11
−100	4.11	140	104-05	+7
0	7.13	111	97-15	0
+100	9.06	103	89-30	−8
+300	11.55	97	75-30	−22

Source: Bloomberg Financial Markets.

relative yield than at the time of the initial purchase, and the relative yield spread of the CMO will be less. Figure 8.2 illustrates the CMO yield curve as it appeared at year-end 1992.

2. WHAT IS THE COLLATERAL?

Agency-Guaranteed versus Whole-Loan Collateral

Agency-guaranteed and collateralized REMICs are the most liquid and most broadly sought category of CMO. They also trade at the tightest spread to the Treasury curve. Within the category of agency-guaranteed REMICs, other considerations are:

1. Ginnie Mae collateral is guaranteed by the full faith and credit of the U.S. Treasury and is a zero capital risk weight if purchased as a direct issue of Ginnie Mae, but 20 percent capital risk weight if the Ginnie Mae is collateral for a REMIC issued by another agency such as Fannie Mae. Ginnie Mae MBSs are all backed by FHA/VA loans, which are assumable. This feature, combined with demographic considerations, causes Ginnie Mae MBSs to be slower prepaying than conventional (Freddie Mac, Fannie Mae) MBSs. This characteristic is a plus if low prepayment volatility is an investment consideration; it is negative if faster prepays are an objective.

2. Fannie Mae and Freddie Mac collateral enjoys federal agency status with an implied federal guaranty and is 20

FIGURE 8.2
CMO to Treasury Yield Curve, December 21, 1992

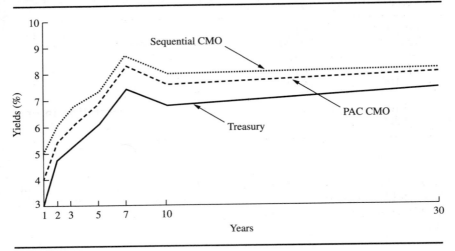

Source: Lehman Brothers Fixed Income Research.

percent capital risk weight. Fannie Mae and Freddie Mac MBSs are all due on sale and generally prepay faster than Ginnie Mae MBSs. Some investors will assume that it is best to stick with Ginnie Mae-collateralized CMOs. *However, since the Ginnie Maes are slower paying in periods of relatively low prepayments, the Ginnie Mae-backed CMOs bear greater extension risk than the faster-paying Fannie and Freddie deals.* In addition, there are relatively fewer Ginnie Mae than conventional-backed CMO deals. The longer duration of the Ginnie Maes makes it harder to structure a CMO with Ginnies.

3. Private label CMOs and REMICS are those issued by a private party but collateralized by federal agency-guaranteed MBSs. Popular in the late 1980s, few private label (by this definition) deals have been issued in recent years.

Whole-Loan Collateral

Whole-loan-backed CMOs and REMICs (often incorrectly referred to as private label issues) are generally collateralized by jumbo loans.[2] In brief, key considerations with whole-loan collateral are:

- What is the credit enhancement—letter of credit, third-party corporate guaranty, cash reserve fund, senior subordinated, and so on?
- Underwriting should conform to Fannie Mae requirements (except for loan size). Preferably loan size should not exceed $500,000.
- Geographic diversification is preferred. Concentration in one state or region increases exposure to economic risk.
- LTV ratio under 80 percent is preferred: All loans in excess of 80 percent LTV are insured to 75 percent LTV equivalent.
- Reputation and experience of the originator-servicer of the loans is very important—some do a good job, many do not. Also, note whether the issuer-servicer of the CMO was also the originator of the loans. Loans purchased wholesale from loan brokers are often poorly underwritten.

Watch Your WACs!

The WAC of the underlying collateral is the key to the prepayment sensitivity of the CMO deal structure, not the coupon on the CMO bond. You can have 8 or 9 percent coupons on CMO classes backed by 9.5 percent MBS collateral. The prepayment sensitivity of all the bond classes will be affected by the WAC of the collateral (higher WAC, greater prepayment volatility). The coupon of the bond class determines whether the bond is priced to a discount or premium. Box 8.1 provides some CMO axioms relating WAC to the prepayment sensitivity of discount- and premium-priced CMOs.

Watch Your WAMs!

The performance of all the bond classes in the CMO will also be affected by the WAM of the underlying collateral. The WAM is a good indication of the age (new production or seasoned) of the col-

---

[2]Jumbo loans are those that exceed the statutory limit of maximum loan size that may be purchased by a federal agency or included in a pool of federal agency-guaranteed MBSs.

BOX 8.1
CMO Axioms

1. Discount-priced CMO bond coupons with high-WAC collateral benefit from faster prepayments.

2. Premium-priced CMO bond coupons with low-WAC collateral benefit from slower prepayments.

3. Discount-priced CMO bond coupons with low-WAC collateral are the most stable structure—they are tantamount to *buying convexity*—and will be priced to a relatively narrow yield spread.

4. Premium-priced CMO bond coupons with high-WAC collateral are the most volatile structure—they are tantamount to *selling convexity*—and will be priced to a relatively wide yield spread. Investors who buy premium-priced classes and thereby sell convexity (i.e., assume potential prepayment volatility) in a slow prepayment environment will likely reap the benefit of the wider yield spread—the higher stated yield would then be realized.

---

lateral. *Since virtually all new CMO issues are sold before all the collateral has been secured, check the prospectus (which is supposed to be delivered before you pay for the bonds) to see that the WAM of the collateral in the deal is the same as, or very close to, what was represented when you bought the deal.* A change in WAM may affect the price of your bond. For example, purchasers of a bond IO will be alarmed if the actual WAM of the deal collateral is shorter than that represented at the time of sale (the value of the IO is a direct function of the duration of the IO cash flow stream). *If the WAM delivered is several months different from what you bought, you may be entitled to repricing.*

Collateral Features of 15-Year MBSs

CMOs collateralized by 15-year maturity MBSs are more stable than those collateralized by 30-year maturity MBSs. This is due mostly to the shorter maturity of the 15-year collateral but is also

FIGURE 8.3
Principal Payment Schedules, 15- and 30-year Collateral

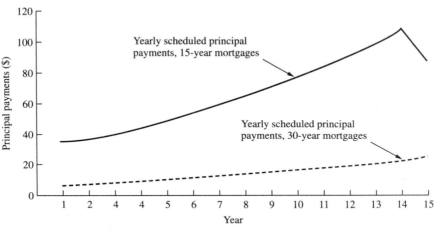

Source: Alan Jay Brazil.

because of the higher base prepayment rate of 15-year collateral. Remember, it is the early and intermediate bonds (particularly the supports) that are most prone to extension risk. It is the late-dated bonds that have the greatest call risk and therefore the highest demand on the upper band in the PAC structure with the resulting protection from extension risk and the elimination of the tail cash flows. The tail cash flows beyond 15 years in 30-year collateral are significant, and in a 30-year CMO the long-dated bonds are the more volatile bonds priced over the higher-yielding portion of the yield curve.

The 15-year collateral also provides a more favorable cash flow structure with much more principal front loaded to the early years, so there can be more PACs in the early maturities of the CMO deal structure in a 15-year CMO structure than in a 30-year structure (see Figure 8.3).

The greater stability of the 15-year collateral also allows a lower support class requirement for 15-year structures, generally 25 to 20 percent. This is in contrast to 30-year structures, which generally require 30 to 35 percent supports to PACs.

TABLE 8.4
Comparative CMO Structural Features

Feature (All CMO Structures)	Base Case	Spread to Treasury
Collateral type	FHLMC, FNMA	Base
GNMA (better call protection, zero capital risk weight)		Tighter
Whole-loan		Wider
Collateral coupon	Slight discount	Base
Low coupon (maximizes call protection)		Tighter
High coupon (Spends too much time priced over par)		Wider
Feature (PAC structures)	Base Case	Spread to Treasury
Prepayment-protection bands	85–285	Base
Wide effective bands		Tighter
Cash flow window	2 years	Base
Narrow window		Tighter

Source: Mark Rudnitsky, Vice President, CMO Trading Desk, Lehman Brothers.

3. WHAT ARE THE PRICE/YIELD CONSIDERATIONS?

The comparative structural features that affect value are outlined in Table 8.4. Yield spreads to Treasuries are indicated as tighter or wider against a base case.

Other Technical Factors[3]

Like other mortgage securities, CMOs trade at a wider yield spread to Treasuries when prepayment risk is high. Other factors are:

- *Yield Curve.* A positively sloped yield curve favors REMIC issuance by enhancing the opportunity for the CMO arbitrage. All else equal, a more positively sloped curve also allows new-issuance CMOs to be priced at wider spreads.

---

[3]This discussion of other technical factors is based on material provided by Mark Rudnitsky, Vice President, CMO Trading Desk, Lehman Brothers.

- *Collateral.* To the extent that relative collateral prices and yield spreads change, relative CMO pricing will change to reflect the performance of the collateral. For example, if the yield spread of the collateral widens versus Treasuries, REMIC spreads will also tend to widen, but less so. Notably, PAC yield spreads will widen less than sequential-pay and far less than support class bonds.
- *Absolute Interest Rate Level.* The coupon relationships outlined in the matrix will change as a function of the absolute level or rates. All else equal, a falling interest rate environment would be expected to cause a widening of MBS spreads, including PAC bonds.
- *Price of Substitute Bonds.* Relative prices of corporate bonds, asset-backed securities, short-average-life MBSs (such as balloons), agency securities, and other substitute assets will affect the pricing of PAC CMOs.
- *Technical Considerations.* Changing short-term supply/demand relationships in certain bond market sectors can explain small variations in relative MBS pricing.

Figures 8.4A, 8.4B, and 8.4C give a two-year history of 2-, 5-, and 7-year PACs (assuming current coupon, corporate delivery) versus AA-rated corporate. Note the spikes in PAC yield spreads during periods of anticipated prepayment volatility (fourth quarter 1991, first quarter 1992, and again in the summer of 1992). It is particularly interesting that the PAC to corporate spreads narrowed fairly quickly following each spread-widening episode as investors recovered from the initial realization that the prepayments were accelerating to an appreciation of the value of the PAC bond. This recovery in PAC-to-corporate yield spread persisted even as investors became concerned with the *broken* PAC[4] phenomenon that developed in the spring and summer of 1992 as the PAC prepayment-protection bands came under intense stress. The yield spread recovery of the PACs may be attributed to investors' appreciation that even in the worst-case scenario—that is, the PAC band is eliminated, resulting in a busted PAC—the PAC with little or no pro-

---

[4]A broken PAC is one in which all the support class bonds have been paid in full and there is no prepayment-protection band remaining.

FIGURE 8.4A
Yield Spreads, 2-Year PACs versus 2-Year Corporates

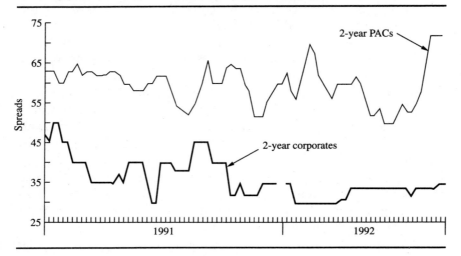

Source: Lehman Brothers Fixed Income Research.

FIGURE 8.4B
Yield Spread, 5-Year PACs versus 5-Year Corporates

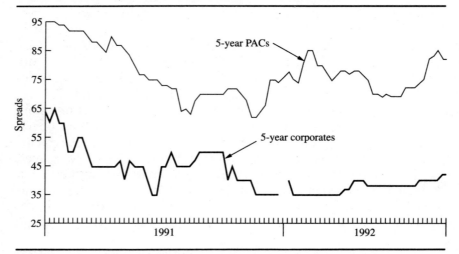

Source: Lehman Brothers Fixed Income Research.

FIGURE 8.4C
Yield Spreads, 7-Year PACs versus 7-Year Corporates

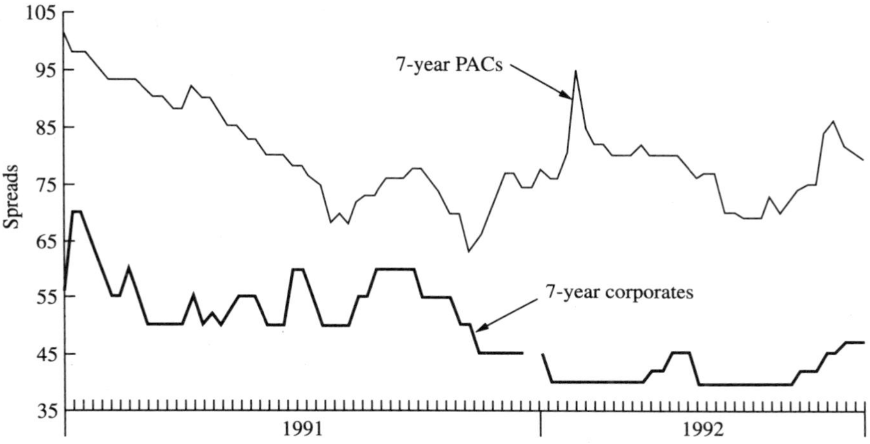

Source: Lehman Brothers Fixed Income Research.

tection band remaining would still retain greater stability than a standard, sequential-pay CMO bond or the comparable collateral.

Evaluating Your PAC Investment

The preceding discussion makes two key points: First and foremost, PAC bonds offer far greater protection from prepayment risk than a standard CMO, or for that matter an investment in the generic MBSs that underlie it; and, second, the PAC bands do not, however, provide an *absolute* guarantee against prepayment risk in any prepayment scenario.

The astute investor will examine the prepayment history of the collateral underlying the CMO. If there have been extensive periods in the past when the MBS collateral prepaid at speeds significantly faster or slower than those at the extremes of the band, the investor could be in for unpleasant surprises. On the other hand, do not be put off if the historical analysis suggests this pattern may occur for only brief periods (two or three months) during a year. Such aberrations would have minimal, if any, impact on the performance of the PAC sinking fund, as will be demonstrated more explicitly by the prepayment-stress-analysis tests explained in the next section. (See

---

BOX 8.2
Key PAC Valuation Issues

1. PAC bands respond dynamically to collateral performance.
   a. Actual PAC protection bands shift over the life of the bond.
   b. Initial PAC band ranges have different consequences with different kinds of collateral.
   c. Position, priority, and size of PAC tranches must be related to the whole CMO structure in addition to the support class bonds.
   d. PAC windows can shift dramatically.
2. Prepayment volatility affects PAC bond structure.
   a. Low-volatility projections make narrower PAC band ranges appear more attractive.
   b. Low volatility makes PAC IIs and supports appear relatively more attractive.
   c. High volatility makes PACs and accretion-directed (AD) bonds the best performers in spite of lower stated yield spreads.
   d. High volatility reduces the probability that the higher stated spread of PAC IIs and supports will be realized.
   e. High volatility causes some structures, including Z-bonds, to perform better.

Box 8.2 for a review of the PAC valuation issues discussed in this section.)

4. HOW DO I MEASURE RISK/REWARD?

Scenario Analysis of PAC Bonds

At this stage yield considerations must be addressed. Yield is often—mistakenly—the *first* and *only* question asked. The question now becomes, "How do I measure risk/reward with the CMO investment?" Most investors use **scenario analysis**, stressing the bond to varying prepayment assumptions assuming a series of interest rate scenarios, generally from up 300 basis points to down 300 basis points. Because this form of sensitivity analysis stresses the bond to instantaneous, constant interest rate shifts, it is referred to as *static scenario analysis*.

Tables 8.1A, 8.1B, and 8.1C at the beginning of this chapter are examples of static scenario analysis. Table 8.5 provides static prepayment sensitivities for the 3-, 5-, and 7-year-average-life classes of a PAC structure, the FHLMC REMIC Series 1434. The effective prepayment-protection bands vary by class, as shown in the table. The earlier classes, of course, have the widest effective bands (see Chapter 7).

The analysis in Table 8.5 shows that the principal paydown schedule is sustained unless prepayment speeds shift permanently to a prepayment rate above or below the protection bands.[5] The table also indicates that in addition to the average-life drift, the cash flow window also shifts when prepayment speeds move permanently outside the bands and the PAC becomes "broken." When a PAC becomes "broken" it becomes, in effect, a "clean," or sequential-pay, bond and typically still outperforms the collateral (it still has a cash flow window). (The performance of broken PACs is examined in Impact of 1992–1993 Prepayments on CMO Structure, page 372.)

Advantages and Disadvantages of Static Scenario Analysis[6]

The static scenario analysis just demonstrated is widely used and easy to understand. Significantly, it is the format for stress analysis required by many regulators, specifically the OCC and OTS, and was also utilized in the definition of unsuitable, high-risk investments by the FFIEC in February 1992.

Static scenario analysis is misleading because it assumes that interest rates make a single, instantaneous shift to a higher or lower rate and remain at that level for the remaining cash flow life of the

---

[5]Over time the bands will drift slightly even if prepayment speeds remain within the bands. Band shift is discussed at greater length in Planned Amortization Class Bonds in Chapter 7.

[6]This discussion of static scenario analysis is based largely on *Anatomy of PAC Bonds* by Michael Bykhovsky and Lakhbir S. Hayre. New York: Prudential Securities, January 1992.

TABLE 8.5
FHLMC 1434 7.50 Percent PAC Structure; 30-Year Summary Prepayment-Sensitivity Analysis

3-Year PAC, $24.674 Million, 5.750% at an Offering Price of 99.68875%

PSA	75	125	150	Base[a]175	225	300	400	Effective bands 95–385
Yield	5.845	5.848	5.848	5.848	5.848	5.848	5.848	
Average life	3.96	3.45	3.45	3.45	3.45	3.45	3.44	
First amortization	3.46	3.04	3.04	3.04	3.04	3.04	3.04	
Maturity	4.46	3.88	3.88	3.88	3.88	3.88	3.79	
Duration	3.54	3.13	3.13	3.13	3.13	3.13	3.12	

5-Year PAC, $47.443 Million, 6.500% at an Offering Price of 98.30321%

PSA	75	125	150	Base 175	225	300	400	Effective bands 95–285
Yield	6.857	6.893	6.893	6.893	6.893	6.896	6.958	
Average life	6.95	5.95	5.95	5.95	5.95	5.89	4.72	
First amortization	5.88	5.04	5.04	5.04	5.04	5.04	4.29	
Maturity	8.04	6.88	6.88	6.88	6.88	6.63	5.21	
Duration	5.58	4.92	4.92	4.92	4.92	4.88	4.06	

7-Year PAC, $49.586 Million, 6.750% at an Offering Price of 96.61991%

PSA	75	125	150	Base 175	225	300	400	Effective bands 95–275
Yield	7.321	7.379	7.379	7.379	7.379	7.405	7.527	
Average life	9.30	7.95	7.95	7.95	7.95	7.46	5.82	
First amortization	8.04	6.88	6.88	6.88	6.88	6.63	5.21	
Maturity	10.54	9.04	9.04	9.04	9.04	8.38	6.54	
Duration	6.85	6.11	6.11	6.11	6.11	5.83	4.79	

[a]The PSA assumption used at the time the deal was priced—the "pricing PSA assumption."

Source: Lehman Brothers Fixed Income Research.

bond. In reality, interest rates do not behave in this fashion. Interest rates are very unlikely to shift instantaneously up or down 100 or more basis points and then remain constant at that level for the life of the bond. For example, the 1991–1993 prepayment experience demonstrated that the "whipsaw" effect may be more important to test to than sudden, one-time shifts. In 1992 and again in 1993 prepayment speeds accelerated dramatically (to over 1,000 PSA for 9½ percent collateral) but were expected to be slow in the winter of 1994, creating a whipsaw. In the high-prepayment phase the support classes of some PAC bonds were significantly diminished, leaving the PAC vulnerable to extension risk should prepayments remain slow for an extended time. The static analysis, therefore, did not provide real-life economic probabilities about the performance of various CMO structures in a volatile prepayment environment. (This topic is explored more explicitly later in this chapter.)

Static analysis is also faulty because even in a zero interest rate-volatility environment prepayment speeds shift significantly, just from the seasonal effect. The static prepayment speed used for the zero-volatility (base case) assumption is an *average* PSA of the low (winter) and high (summer) PSAs. However, the impact on the PAC payment schedule, swinging from slow to fast prepayments and again to slow, is very different from the impact of a constant average. Furthermore, the damage done to the PAC schedule of variable interest rates, shifting 300 basis points for a period of time and then swinging back in the opposite direction for a time, is very different from the static scenario, which assumes one shift in interest rates is held at a steady rate for the life of the bond. This effect of the PAC band changing over time is referred to as **PAC band drift**. A dynamic, or **vector, analysis**, in which prepayment speeds are varied for periods of time, may be more instructive.

Vector Analysis of Schedules and Priorities[7]

The case studies in this section highlight the comparative average-life drift of sequential-pay, PAC, tier two PAC (PAC II), and support class structures. The vector analysis that follows illuminates

---

[7]This discussion of vector analysis was provided by Mark Rudnitsky.

the impact of prepayments on the PAC schedule when tested to a vector rather than to a static scenario. Because the variation in average life among the types of bonds examined is greatest at the short end of the CMO curve, the focus here is on the 2-year sector. In this sector the assumed yield spread ranges for these types of bonds are as follows:

PAC	2-year + 60–70 basis points
Sequential-pay	2-year + 90–100 basis points
PAC II support	2-year + 90–290 basis points

This yield spread summary shows that, within the short end of the CMO curve, the PAC II support class sector contains the widest range of spreads. While average-life-profile differences exist between bonds in the PAC and sequential-pay sectors, it is the PAC II support sector that offers investors the greatest range of yield spreads and average-life drift. There are examples of bonds, including PAC IIs and stabilized and TAC companions, that trade across a yield spread range of approximately 200 basis points. Table 8.6 describes the REMIC deals and CMO class types used as the basis for the vector analysis case studies that follow.

Case Studies 8.1 through 8.5 illustrate the varying degree of prepayment sensitivity of the different CMO bond class types shown in Table 8.6. The case studies stress the various CMO types to a vector scenario analysis. The vector format uses alternate prepayment speeds within each scenario rather than the single-prepayment assumption used in static scenario analysis. The vector pattern applied in Case Studies 8.1 through 8.5 applies an initial prepayment speed for the first six months—for example, 160 PSA, which is illustrative of the PSA assumption used for the initial pricing of the CMO deal. Then the prepayment speed is rotated to a slow prepayment speed selected to be just below the lower PAC band and then to a moderate prepayment speed selected to be just above the lower PAC band. For example, with the tier one PAC (Case Study 8.3), bands 90–450, the initial vector is 160 PSA; the slow PSA is 75, and the moderate PSA is 115. To fairly compare the prepayment sensitivities of the various CMO class types, the same initial, slow, and moderate vectors are applied to all of the bond forms examined. The rotation period for each vector is six months—that is, January to July to January, and so on.

TABLE 8.6
CMO Bond and Collateral Summary[a]

2-year PAC II	FNMA 1991-077 A, 8.25% coupon Collateral: FNMA 9% PSA bands: 110–200 Average life: 2.2 years Yield spread: 2-year + 12.5 bp
2-year AD	FHLMC 1013 D, 9% coupon Collateral: FHLMC 9% PSA bands: 0–600 Average life: 2.08 years Yield spread: 2-year + 65 bp
2-year PAC	FNMA 1991-077 PA, 7.5% coupon Collateral: FNMA 9% PSA bands: 90–450 Average life: 2.45 years Yield spread: 2-year + 60 bp
2-year sequential-pay	FHLMC 1103 A, 7.75% coupon Collateral: FHLMC 9% Average life: 2.48 years Yield spread: 2-year + 90 bp
2-year support	FNMA 1991-077 G, 9% coupon Collateral: FNMA 9% Average life: 2.28 years Yield spread: 2-year + 270 bp

[a]All examples use FNMA/FHLMC 9 percent, 30-year MBSs to eliminate variation due to collateral.

Paying to a Schedule versus to a Balance

The thrust of the case studies is twofold: first, to demonstrate the significance of paying to a *schedule* (the PACs) versus to a *balance* (the sequentials). (The structure of the PAC schedule is described in Planned Amortization Class Bonds in Chapter 7.) With the sequential-pay structure, whatever principal is received from the collateral pool in a given month is applied to the payment of the CMO bond(s), whether it is greater or less than the amount projected at the time of pricing the CMO deal. With the PAC, the schedule is defined as a specific unpaid principal balance, defined in a dollar amount, month by month, to which the PAC is to be paid. The surplus, if any, is applied to the support class bonds. Significantly, if there is a shortfall, that amount will be carried cumulatively as a debit balance. When the principal payments available from the collateral pool are sufficient to pay the full, current PAC schedule requirement plus any excess, the excess is first applied to "catch up" the PAC schedule before any principal distribution may be applied to the support class bonds.

Second, comparing the static versus vector scenarios highlights how stable the PAC forms really are, given variable prepayments that come just within the bond, albeit at a relatively slow prepayment rate. The PACs benefit from vector prepayment analysis more than do the sequentials. The static scenarios, by imposing unrealistically slow prepayment rates in perpetuity, do not reflect the strength of the PAC structure. The vector analysis shows up how unstable the support class can really be.

CASE STUDY 8.1

Tier Two PAC Structure, Bands 110–200 PSA
FNR 91-077, 77-A, 8 Percent, Due 6/25/20

Base Case 160 PSA		Static Scenario Analysis (PSA)					Variable Scenarios	
		75	100	110	200	250	V1	V2
99–07	CMO price						8.23	8.23
8.27	CBE yield	8.19	8.22	8.27	8.27	8.27	3.14	3.22
2.20	Average life	7.88	3.76	2.20	2.20	2.04		
0.1/6.9	Window	0.1/17.3	0.1/12.2	0.1/6.9	0.1/6.9	0.1/4.7	0.1/9.1	0.1/9.3

Variable Prepayment Scenario V1

Month	Speed (PSA)
07–1991	160
01–1992	75
07–1992	115
01–1993	75
07–1993	115
01–1994	75
07–1994	115
01–1995	75
07–1995	115

Analysis

A tier two (PAC II) bond was selected as Case Study 8.1 because it highlights how even this PAC form, which is subordinated to the tier one PACs incorporated in the structure, can be reasonably stable given moderate prepayment cyclicality above and below the lower band. The static scenario analysis shows the average life of the bond extends from 2.2 years to 3.76 years at 100 PSA, which is just below the lower band. The vector analysis, by contrast, illustrates the catch-up effect of its schedule in spite of multiple periods with speeds at 75 PSA, well below the 110 PSA of the lower band. The 75 to 115 PSA range used in this vector scenario replicates moderate seasonality without a slow prepayment environment such as might occur with relatively high mortgage rates. Note the extension risk in the vector stress analysis is moderate, to 3.14 years (see variable scenario V1).

Variable Prepayment Scenario V2	
Month	*Speed (PSA)*
07–1991	160
01–1992	50
05–1992	115
01–1993	50
05–1993	115
01–1994	50
05–1994	115
01–1995	50
05–1995	115

Scenario V2 stresses the PAC II to a slower 50 PSA, but for less time (4 months, from January to May) with roughly the same outcome, to a 3.22-year average life, as shown in variable scenario V2. Variable scenarios V1 and V2 both implicitly capture the stability provided by the support bonds to the PAC II class.

CASE STUDY 8.2

FHLMG 1103, 1103A, 7.75 Percent, Due 8/15/14
Sequential-Pay Structure

Base Case 160 PSA		*Static Scenario Analysis (PSA)*					*Variable Scenarios*	
		75	*100*	*125*	*140*	*200*	*V1*	*V2*
99–19+	CMO price						7.90	7.90
7.92	CBE yield	7.90	7.90	7.91	7.91	7.92	3.66	3.70
2.48	Average life	4.75	3.78	3.11	2.81	2.01	0.1/7.3	0.1/7.3
0.1/5.2	Window	0.1/9.6	0.1/7.8	0.1/6.4	0.1/5.8	0.1/4.2		

Variable Prepayment Scenario V1

Month	Speed (PSA)
07–1991	160
01–1992	75
07–1992	115
01–1993	75
07–1993	115
01–1994	75
07–1994	115
01–1995	75
07–1995	115

Variable Prepayment Scenario V2

Month	Speed (PSA)
07–1991	160
01–1992	50
05–1992	115
01–1993	50
05–1993	115
01–1994	50
05–1994	115
01–1995	50
05–1995	115

Analysis

Case Study 8.2 illustrates the prepayment sensitivity of a sequential-pay class CMO bond when stressed to a static scenario analysis
and to two vector scenarios. Although in the static scenario stress

test the sequential extends less at 75 PSA than the PAC II (to 4.75 years for the sequential versus 7.88 for the PAC II), in the variable-scenario results the sequential actually extends more than the PAC II! (Compare V1 and V2 in this analysis with the V1 and V2 results for the PAC II.)

CASE STUDY 8.3

FNR 91-077, 77-PA, 7.5 Percent, Due 12/25/07
Tier One PAC Structure Bands 90–450 PSA

Base Case 160 PSA		Static Scenario Analysis (PSA)					Variable Scenarios		
		75	90	110	450	500	V1	V2	V3
99-16	CMO price								
7.62	CBE yield	7.62	7.62	7.62	7.62	7.62	7.62	7.62	7.62
2.45	Average life	2.71	2.45	2.45	2.45	2.44	2.48	2.45	2.53
2.0/3.0	Window	2.2/3.3	2.0/3.0	2.0/3.0	2.0/3.0	2.0/2.8	2.0/3.0	2.0/3.0	2.0/3.1

Variable Prepayment Scenario V1

Month	Speed (PSA)
07–1991	160
01–1992	75
07–1992	115
01–1993	75
07–1993	115
01–1994	75
07–1994	115
01–1995	75
07–1995	115

Analysis

Scenario V1 highlights there is only moderate extension due to support of both PAC II and support tranches. Interestingly, even when the PAC is subjected to zero PSA for one full year (July 1991 to July 1992) before allowing the prepayment speed to come back to 115 PSA (just above the lower band) there is minimal extension to 2.48 years. This result is reflected in variable scenario V2. Variable scenario V3 stresses the PAC to 400 PSA for 10½ years before slowing the PSA to 90, which is the lower-band boundary.

Under this scenario sufficient support class bonds were paid down to cause the lower band to drift a bit higher. As a result, the PAC extended slightly to 2.53 years (see V3; 90 PSA is no longer the effective lower band).

The new lower band may be discovered by iterating the prepayment stress to slightly higher lower-band boundaries until the new effective lower boundary is discovered. In this case the break comes at 97 PSA, where the last extension occurs (to 2.46 years). The new lower band is therefore 98 PSA, the slowest PSA level at which the PAC does not extend beyond 2.45 years when stressed to variable scenario V1.

CASE STUDY 8.4

FHLMG 1013, 1013D, 9 Percent, Due 10/15/20
AD Bond Structure, Bands 0–600 PSA

Base Case 160 PSA		Static Scenario Analysis (PSA)					Variable Scenarios
		0	*75*	*100*	*300*	*600*	*V1*
102-12	CMO price						
7.67	CBE yield	7.67	7.67	7.67	7.67	7.67	7.67
2.08	Average life	2.08	2.08	2.08	2.08	2.08	2.08
0.1/3.8	Window	0.1/3.8	0.1/3.8	0.1/3.8	0.1/3.8	0.1/3.8	0.1/3.8

Variable Prepayment Scenario V1

Month	Speed (PSA)
07–1991	160
01–1992	75
07–1992	115
01–1993	75
07–1993	115
01–1994	75
07–1994	115
01–1995	75
07–1995	115

Analysis

The solid stability of the AD bond, which is funded from the accruals of the Z-bond, is illustrated by Case Study 8.4. Since the accrual for the Z exists at zero PSA (the Z-bond accrual is unrelated to prepayments), there is no extension risk. The call risk is very low as well, since the Z-bond is the last class in the deal structure; there will be no early call on the accrual of the Z-bond unless prepayments are so high that the entire CMO deal is paid off by its 2-year average life.

Note: The AD bond is so stable that there is no difference between the results of the static and the variable scenarios.

CASE STUDY 8.5

FNR 91-077, 77-G, 9 Percent, Due 5/25/20
Support Class Structure

Base Case 160 PSA		Static Scenario Analysis (PSA)					Variable Scenarios
		75	100	125	140	200	V1
98–11	CMO price						
9.7162	CBE yield	9.29	9.30	9.38	9.54	9.95	9.31
2.25	Average life	22.44	18.26	8.32	3.64	1.54	15.27
0.1/4.1	Window	20.6/24.2	15.2/21.0	0.1/15.9	0.1/8.2	0.1/2.5	0.1/19.0

Variable Prepayment Scenario V1

Month	Speed (PSA)
07–1991	160
01–1992	75
07–1992	115
01–1993	75
07–1993	115
01–1994	75
07–1994	115
01–1995	75
07–1995	115

Analysis

Case Study 8.5 illustrates the relatively high prepayment sensitivity of the support class bond, which has the widest stated yield spread but the lowest priority in the distribution of physical cash flow. The results of the variable scenario analysis are similar to those of the sequential-pay bond (Case Study 8.3), but with more extension. The prepayment volatility of this bond is, of course, due to its use in stabilizing all other bonds with higher priority. The support is the

TABLE 8.7
FHLMC 1320, Class I (PAC II), Static Scenario Analysis

Collateral: FHLMC Gold 7 percent, 15-year
WAC, 7.778; WAM, 14 years, 6 months
Price 101-26, base PSA 140
Bands 100–160 PSA

	Static PSA Assumptions					
	50	100	140	200	350	500
Average life	10.88	3.35	3.35	2.74	1.67	1.29
First principal payment	2/03	10/92	10/92	10/92	10/92	10/92
Last principal payment	1/04	6/00	6/00	10/96	8/94	2/94
Yield (%)	6.82	6.37	6.37	6.24	5.75	5.37

first bond to be paid from excess cash flows and the last to be paid when cash flows are diminished by a low level of prepayments.

Vector Analysis à la Bloomberg[8]

A form of variable-prepayment rate, or vector, analysis available to users of the Bloomberg analytic system is illustrated in Figure 8.5. The Bloomberg vector analysis offers a variety of high/low and whipsaw variables, as shown in Table 8.7. The vectors in the table use 140 PSA as the base prepayment speed. The base PSA is the assumed pricing prepayment speed of a given collateral pool or MBS-structured transaction. The high and low PSA vectors are, respectively, double the base PSA and half the base PSA, that is, 240 and 70. In Table 8.7, 140 is the base PSA assumption for the FHLMC Series 1320 REMIC, Class I (PAC II). Figure 8.5 illustrates the Bloomberg vector paths.

The static scenario analysis for a PAC II, described in Table 8.7, shows that the average life ranges from the base 3.35-year average life to more than 10 years (slow PSA) and to just over 1 year (fast PSA). The yield increases as it extends and declines as it contracts because the security was priced to a premium.

---

[8]Bloomberg Financial Markets provides market data, information, and analytics for fixed-income securities, commodities, and equities.

FIGURE 8.5
Bloomberg Vector Paths

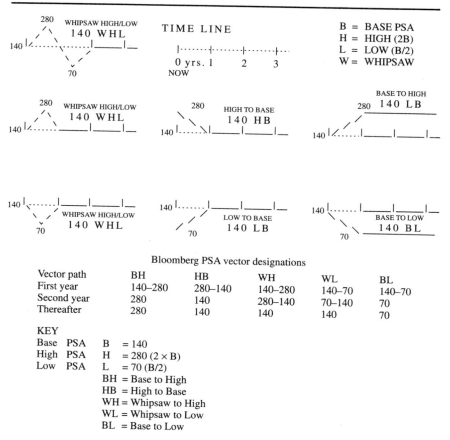

Bloomberg PSA vector designations

Vector path	BH	HB	WH	WL	BL
First year	140–280	280–140	140–280	140–70	140–70
Second year	280	140	280–140	70–140	70
Thereafter	280	140	140	140	70

KEY
Base PSA B = 140
High PSA H = 280 (2 × B)
Low PSA L = 70 (B/2)
BH = Base to High
HB = High to Base
WH = Whipsaw to High
WL = Whipsaw to Low
BL = Base to Low

Note: The key designates the variable-prepayment scenario (vector) selected: for example, Base to High (BH) means start with the base pricing PSA assumption and stress to a faster PSA, which will be twice the base PSA; the Whipsaw to High (WH) means the PSA shifts from the base PSA (140) to the high (280—twice the base) and returns to the base.

Source: Bloomberg Financial Markets.

Table 8.8 shows that the average-life volatility is substantially less than that of the static analysis within a variety of variable scenarios. Except for the base-to-low (BL) the average life does not ex-

TABLE 8.8
FHLMC 1320, Class I (PAC II), Vector Scenario Analysis

Vector	BH	HB	WH	WL	LB	BL
Average life	2.05	3.35	3.35	3.35	3.35	9.16
First principal payment	10/92	10/92	10/92	10/92	10/92	10/92
Last principal payment	3/95	6/00	6/00	6/00	6/00	1/03
Yield	5.99	6.37	6.37	6.37	6.37	6.78

Source: Bloomberg Financial Markets.

tend beyond 3.35 years or shorten below 2 years under variable prepayment assumptions.

OAS Methodology

Static and perhaps even dynamic scenario analysis, although useful, nevertheless tells relatively little about the impact of passing through cycles of rising and falling interest rates and prepayments. OAS analysis encompasses more scenarios and is able to cover the dynamics of changing interest rates. OAS incorporates the analyst's best estimate of the empirical relationships between prepayments and mortgage interest rates.[9] It is also a relative value measure; for example, a *CMO class may have significant average-life volatility but still be undervalued because it is priced at a spread wide enough to compensate for the risk.* Remember, the OAS methodology is not an absolute—it is, rather, a measure of the relative risk/reward.

Essentially, the OAS methodology measures the option cost of the collateral behind the CMO.

The option cost is measured by the differences in the **zero volatility** OASs (when interest rates stay at their current levels and the PAC schedule is met) and at a specified volatility (e.g., 15 percent). The OAS at a specified volatility factors in the effect of interest-rate and prepayment variations on the PAC. The difference between these two OAS figures indicates the

---

[9]OAS does interpret the implied forward rates of a positive yield curve as an indication of increasing interest rates, and the prepayment model linked to the OAS model will project declining prepayments as part of the investment horizon. In times of a steep yield curve with accelerating prepayment speeds, this interpretation can lead to a misreading of the OAS value of prepayment-sensitive securities—for example, IOs, such as occurred in the spring and summer of 1992.

net effect of interest-rate contingency on the PAC's cash flows (with a zero option cost indicating that the PAC has essentially no cash-flow uncertainty).[10]

The option cost, then, is the difference between the OAS at zero volatility and the OAS at some volatility assumption (i.e., 15 percent).

Bykhovsky and Hayre point out other factors contributing to the option cost—for example, "As might be expected, option cost generally increases with the weighted average life (WAL) of the PAC. However, other factors such as the size and type of the supporting classes and whether there is a lockout period can have an important effect." Thus, the CMO structure itself is a determining factor in the option cost of its component bonds. The OAS analysis, which is a "stochastic-valuation methodology," as Bykhovsky and Hayre point out, is extremely valuable in deriving a better sense of relative value among a population of bonds that may be apparently comparable in coupon, collateral, and average life but that have structural differences.

Distributional Analysis—or a Look inside the Black Box
Bykhovsky and Hayre continue:

> The option cost indicates the net cost to an investor of the interest-rate uncertainty of a bond's cash-flows. As mentioned earlier, it is obtained using an averaging process over a large number of randomly generated interest-rate paths. It is useful to examine the security's behavior over the individual paths for several reasons. First, in statistical analysis, the individual observations often provide information and insight that is lost in an average. To quote Mark Twain, "If I stick my head in an oven and my feet in an ice-box, then on average my body is at a perfect temperature."

OAS Interest Rate-Volatility Case Studies[11]

This section, utilizing an OAS model, examines the average-life drift of several CMO structures based on a distribution of average lives derived by the model. For each simulated interest rate path the OAS model measures the probabilities of the different paths

---

[10]Bykhovsky and Hayre, *Anatomy of PAC Bonds.*

[11]This discussion of OAS interest rate volatility is based on studies prepared by Chuck Webster, Senior Vice President, Manager, Lehman Brothers Mortgage Analytics Department.

and calculates the cash flows by applying the prepayment model to the distribution of interest rate paths. The OAS model can even identify the starting and ending points of the principal-paydown cash flow windows. One product of this process is a distribution of average lives.

To illustrate the process, Chuck Webster examined several CMO bond classes from the FNMA 1991–82 PAC bond structure. The deal structure, average life, pricing, OAS, and distribution data are shown in Table 8.9. The data for the bonds used in the case studies are in boldface type. The table served as a point of reference for the case studies on CMO average life and price-volatility analysis prepared by Webster.

The yield spread information together with the standard deviation of average-life and price-volatility data present a telling methodology for measuring risk/reward. Case Studies 8.6 through 8.13 look at some classes more closely.

Short-Average-Life PAC Classes
The 2- and 3-year PACs (PA, PB, PC, etc.) show a very small standard deviation in average life, meaning that even with considerable prepayment volatility their average-life drift would not exceed a few months. Case Study 8.6 examines a very stable bond, the 2-year average-life PB class PAC.

CASE STUDY 8.6

OAS Analysis, FNMA 1991-82 PB
PAC Class Bond: 2-Year Average Life

Base Data		Average-Life Distribution	
Observations	200	99%	2.63
Mean average life	2.43	95	2.47
Standard deviation	0.1498	90	2.47
		10	2.47
		5	1.56

The standard deviation of average life is only 0.15—about 1 month. The average-life distribution indicates that 95 percent of the time this bond maintains an average life within 2.5 years—so it is very stable. Figure 8.6 illustrates the average life of this PAC.

TABLE 8.9

FNMA 1991-82 PAC I Bond and Pricing Summary; Collateral, FNMA 9 Percent MBS; WAC 9.70; Pricing PSA, 160, WAM, 357 Months

Class Name	Bond Type	Spread (bp)	WAL (Years)	OAS	CC[a]	SD[b] Avg. Life	SD Price	Stated Yield (%)
PACs								
PA	PAC	1-yr. + 48	1.23	16	1	0.02	0.63	5.96
PB	**PAC**	**2-yr.** + **66**	**2.47**	**41**	**3**	**0.15**	**1.70**	**6.81**
PC	PAC	3-yr. + 77	3.44	46	8	0.37	2.79	7.33
PD	PAC	4-yr. + 105	4.44	51	13	0.64	4.02	7.76
PE	**PAC**	**5-yr.** + **82**	**5.84**	**47**	**15**	**1.03**	**5.74**	**8.04**
PG	PAC	7-yr. + 77	7.90	38	30	2.02	9.57	8.37
PH	PAC	10-yr. + 83	9.63	54	28	2.48	10.01	8.63
PJ	PAC	10-yr. + 83	10.61	52	20	2.72	10.01	8.63
PK	PAC	10-yr. + 88	11.38	55	16	2.89	11.29	8.68
PL	PAC	10-yr. + 108	12.85	71	8	3.25	11.63	8.88
PM	**PAC**	**10-yr.** + **108**	**14.33**	**67**	**24**	**3.87**	**11.47**	**8.88**
PX	PACZ	5-yr. + 157	5.84	83	40	1.42	10.05	8.79
PZ	PACZ	15-yr. + 164	15.47	102	28	4.49	23.05	9.58
ADs								
A	AD	2-yr. + 104	2.68	88	5	0.20	1.94	7.68
B	AD	2-yr. + 104	2.54	98	1	0.01	1.92	7.68
C	AD	7-yr. + 103	7.86	92	6	0.79	7.09	8.64
D	**AD**	**10-yr.** + **107**	**12.86**	**86**	**10**	**11.49**	**9.86**	**8.88**
E	AD	15-yr. + 137	14.85	107	12	3.76	11.03	9.18

(continued)

TABLE 8.9
(Concluded)

Class Name	Bond Type	Spread (bp)	WAL (years)	OAS	CC[a]	SD[b] Avg. Life	SD Price	Stated Yield (%)
Supports								
G	PACII	2-yr. + 136	2.16	40	76	1.86	4.90	7.61
J	**PACII**	**7-yr. + 88**	**6.45**	**26**	**67**	**3.65**	**8.19**	**8.49**
K	PACII	7-yr. + 112	6.63	35	56	5.04	8.84	8.73
L	**Support**	**2-yr. + 286**	**2.25**	**10**	**114**	**4.67**	**6.70**	**9.11**
M	Support	2-yr. + 149	2.25	-50	120	4.67	5.55	7.74
O	Support	4-yr. + 199	4.76	64	69	6.56	9.32	9.24
P	Support	7-yr. +	7.					
Q		10-yr. +	13.					

[a]CC = Convexity cost.
[b]SD = Standard deviation.
Note: IO, residual, and floater and inverse floater classes are not shown.

Source: Chuck Webster, Senior Vice President, Manager, Lehman Brothers Mortgage Analytics Department.

FIGURE 8.6

OAS Distribution of Average Life: FNMA 1991-082 PB, 2-Year PAC (200 Observations)

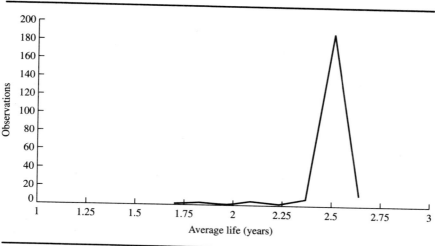

The greater the weighted average life, the greater the deviation in WAL. Take, for example, the PE class, a 5-year-average-life PAC bond. Although still a fairly stable bond, it does have a standard deviation of 1 year. The detailed data from the OAS model are given in Case Study 8.7.

CASE STUDY 8.7

OAS Analysis, FNMA 1991-082 PB
PAC Class Bond: 5-Year Average Life

Base Data		Average-Life Distribution	
Observations	200	99%	7.13
Mean average life	5.40	95	5.85
Standard deviation	1.0292	90	5.85
		10	5.45
		5	2.17

The data tell us that out of 200 observations 99 percent will be within 7 years, 95 percent within 5.8 years, and only 5 percent within less than 5 years. Case Study 8.8 looks at the same data for a 15-year-average-life PAC, the PM class.

CASE STUDY 8.8

OAS Analysis, FNMA 1991-82 PM
PAC Class Bond: 15-Year Average Life

Base Data		Average-Life Distribution	
Observations	200	99%	21.47
Mean average life	15.42	95	17.97
Standard deviation	3.8687	90	17.64
		10	13.09
		5	5.24

The mean average life is 15.4 years, a tad beyond its advertised 14.33 years, and the standard deviation in average life is almost 4 years! Ten percent of the time the average life can be 13 years or shorter; it can be as long as 21.47 years. This is not to say this is a bad bond, but the analysis does point out how average-life drift can increase over the years.

The price volatility data are also interesting:

Base Data		Average-Life Distribution	
Observations	200	99%	118.17
Mean average life	101.69	95	111.03
Standard deviation	11.4653	90	103.11
		10	94.50
		5	66.70

So the price can range from up to $118 to down to $67.

It is interesting to compare the 15-year-average-life PAC to a 12-year-average-life AD, the D Class (Case Study 8.9).

CASE STUDY 8.9

OAS Analysis, FNMA 1991-82 D
AD Bond

Base Data		Average-Life Distribution	
Observations	200	99%	12.87
Mean average life	11.49	95	12.87
Standard deviation	2.4060	90	12.87
		10	10.87
		5	3.82

The OAS analysis confirms there is no extension risk in the AD, but it can really shorten up if prepayment speeds get high enough to pay off the bond issue down to the Z-bond accruals. However, 90 percent of the observations are longer than a 10-year, which indicates a very stable bond.

PAC II Class

The PAC IIs have been popular because they offer relatively high yield with a modicum of prepayment-risk protection with moderate scheduled cash flows. Case Study 8.10 looks at the 7-year-average-life PAC II, the J class.

CASE STUDY 8.10

OAS Analysis, FNMA 1991-82 J
PAC II Bond

Base Data		Average-Life Distribution	
Observations	200	99%	12.24
Mean average life	7.0	95	8.44
Standard deviation	3.6519	90	7.29
		10	4.03
		5	1.24

The data show the J class does indeed have a mean average life of 7 years, with a standard deviation of 3.65 (versus 2.02 for the PG 7-year PAC). The average-life distribution shows that 15 percent of the observations are less than 7 years, and 90 percent of the time average life will be close to 7 years. The maximum extension is 12.24 years.

The risk/reward question remains: How much convexity are you willing to give up for how much yield? This 7-year PAC II offers 11 basis points more spread to the 7-year Treasury than the G class PAC I with a give-up of 12 OAS.

Short-Average-Life Support Class

Now let's go for the yield and examine a short-average-life support class bond, the 82-L (Case Study 8.11). This bond is actually two 2.25-year-average-life support class bonds, the 82-L and 82-M. Since the 82-L has the higher stated yield, 9.11 percent (2-year plus 286), we shall examine it first.

CASE STUDY 8.11

OAS Analysis, FNMA 1991-82-L Class
Support Class Bond

Base Data		Average-Life Distribution	
Observations	200	99%	19.30
Mean average life	5.22	95	7.48
Standard deviation	4.6660	90	3.23
		10	1.54
		5	0.66

This is a 2-year average-life bond? It has a mean average life of over 5 years, but 10 percent of the time average life will be less than 3 years and 10 percent of the time over 7 years. The maximum extension of the bond is 19 years—quite an achievement for a bond advertised as a 2-year! So at a zero-volatility assumption this bond would produce a great yield. But with any prepayment volatility it has no truly definable average-life expectations—it is a 7-year as often as it is a 1-year. Figure 8.7 illustrates graphically the wide distribution of average lives for this bond.

As for price volatility, the bond has a standard deviation in price of 6.70 percent (compared to 1.7 percent for the 2-year PAC and 4.9 percent for the 2-year PAC II). The 82-M support class, priced at the 2-year Treasury plus 149 basis points, also has a WAL standard deviation of 4.67, and the OAS model confirms its tighter spread is no bargain, giving it an OAS of −50 with a convexity cost of 120.

FIGURE 8.7

OAS Distribution of Average Life: FNMA 1991-082 L, 2-Year Support (200 Observations)

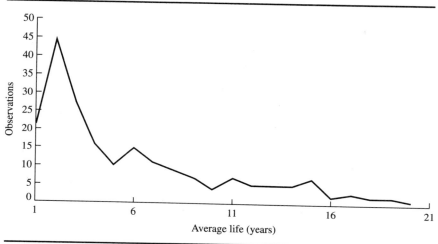

As this text has pointed out, the OAS technology is still far from perfect, but when such low OAS numbers with such high convexity cost are assigned to a bond, the investor should see a red flag: A lot of analysis should be employed before that high "stated" yield is pursued.

The deal summary table (Table 8.9) also shows the OAS does not always go lock-step with the yields. Note the PAC Z at the bottom of the PAC class of bonds, the 82-PZ with an OAS of 102. Case Study 8.12 examines it. Remember, the Z-bond is an accrual bond with a coupon that accrues until the prior coupon-paying classes are refined. The PZ becomes coupon paying in 15 years at the pricing prepayment-speed assumption of 160 PSA.

CASE STUDY 8.12

OAS Analysis, FNMA 1991-82 PZ
PAC Z-Bond

Base Data		Quantiles, Average-Life Distribution		
Observations	200	100% max.	21.67	99%
Mean average life	14.81	75% Q3	18.25	95
Standard deviation	4.4898	50% med.	15.71	90
		25% Q1	11.30	10
		0% min.	3.92	5

The price analysis is particularly interesting. Because the Z-bond does not pay a coupon for a long time, investors want to be compensated for waiting, so the PAC Z is priced at a spread of 164 to the 20-year Treasury. Compare this to the other long-average-life bond, the E class AD at 137 to the 20-year Treasury. Also, the price of the Z is more volatile than a coupon-paying bond. If yields decline, investors are very happy to have their cash flow locked in, reinvesting at the accrual rate of the Z—so in bull markets the Z-bond moves up in price very nicely. However, when yields are rising, the Z-bond holder is disappointed not to have the cash flows returned so they could be reinvested at the higher yields. Note the OAS price-volatility analysis in Case Study 8.13.

CASE STUDY 8.13

OAS Analysis, FNMA 1991-82 P2
AD Bond

Base Data		Quantiles, Average-Life Distribution		
Observations	200	100% max.	111.24	99%
Mean average life	80.30	75% Q3	99.60	95
Standard deviation	23.0456	50% med.	83.99	90
		25% Q1	63.63	10

FFIEC Suitability Test

Depository institutions subject to FFIEC suitability guidelines and other investing constraints imposed by their regulators must determine the suitability of the investment (see "Regulatory Considerations" in Chapter 1). Examples of three CMO structures subjected to the test are provided in Tables 8.10A, 8.10B, and 8.10C. The difficulty with the analysis is that it shows the PAC bond breaks at 84 and 286 PSA (Table 8.10A); the sequential bond extends to 8.9 years average life at 150 PSA (Table 8.10B); and the support class bond shortens to 1.72 years at 300 PSA. These experiences will occur *only* if instantaneously upon purchase the PSA of the collateral underlying these bonds rises or falls to the levels shown—*all for the life of the bond!* Note the support class fails the FFIEC test because its average life extends more than 4 years at 75 PSA and its price changes 25.3 percent in the interest rates up 300 basis points environment.

Although this static scenario analysis gives some indication of the relative prepayment sensitivity of the PAC versus the sequential, for example, the scenarios have little bearing on real-life risk/reward investing considerations assuming PSA spreads will rise up and fall down in cyclical waves over time, as do interest rates. Variable-prepayment assumptions, or vector analysis, provide a somewhat better measure of the average-life volatility of these bonds. However, since many regulatory bodies incorporate the up/down 300 basis points static scenario test as part of their definition of investment suitability, the exercise is required for depository institutions. For financial intermediaries not directly affected by these investment guidelines, the ability of the bond to pass these suitability tests is a liquidity issue not to be ignored.

Total-Return Analysis—Advantages and Limitations

Advantages

Total-return analysis, also referred to as horizon analysis, is instructive because it demonstrates the projected *performance* of the CMO to changing interest rate and prepayment assumptions. The performance is measured by calculating the price at the end of a predetermined horizon holding period, generally six months to a year, based on a series of up-and-down static interest rate and prepayment-rate scenarios. The principal benefit of horizon analysis is that it is a straightforward, easy to understand analytical technique which projects performance with a minimum of "black box" esoterica. An example of a horizon analysis is given in Table 8.11, which compares the performance of the FHLMC Series 101 REMIC, class F to its underlying collateral, FNMA 9 percent recent MBSs.

This comparison of total returns shows that the bullish investor seeking good risk/reward would find the class F of this REMIC an attractive alternative to the collateral that is more stable across the

TABLE 8.10A
FFIEC High-Risk Security Test: FHLMC 1320 C PAC Bond; Protection-Band Range: 85–285 PSA

| Tsy. (bp) | Test 1 | | | Security | | Test 2 | | Test 3 | |
| | Security | | Max. | | | WAL | Change | Price | Change |
Shift	PSA	WAL	WAL	Yield	Price	Actual	Max.	Actual	Max.
−300	575	1.82		2.90	107-1	−1.28	−6.0	6.1%	17%
−200	525	1.93		3.99	105-11	−1.17	−6.0	4.4	17
−100	300	2.75		5.48	103-24	−0.35	−6.0	2.8	17
0 bp	200	3.10	10	6.66	100-29	n/a		0.0	
+100	150	3.10[a]		7.66	98-07	0.00[a]	+4.0	−2.7	17
+200	115	3.10[a]		8.66	95-20	0.00[a]	+4.0	−5.2	17
+300	75	3.19		9.70	92-27	0.09	+4.0	−8.0	17

[a]Note the average life (WAL) does not change at these scenarios—it is still within its band range.

Source: Bloomberg Financial Markets.

TABLE 8.10B

FFIEC High-Risk Security Test: FHLMC 1316 B Sequential-Pay Bond

Tsy. (bp)	Test 1 Security		Max.	Security		Test 2		Test 3	
Shift	PSA	WAL	WAL	Yield	Price	WAL Actual	Change Max.	Price Actual	Change Max.
−300	800	1.00		3.27	108-04	−1.77	−6.0	2.2%	17%
−200	650	1.16		4.42	108-04	−1.61	−6.0	2.2	17
−100	400	1.64		5.84	109-04	−1.14	−6.0	1.3	17
0 bp	195	2.77	10	7.61	110-17	n/a		0.0	
+100	150	3.38		8.90	108-23	1.60	+4.0	−1.6	17
+200	125	3.87		10.11	105-30	1.10	+4.0	−4.1	17
+300	110	4.25		11.27	102-21	1.48	+4.0	−7.1	17

Source: Bloomberg Financial Markets.

TABLE 8.10C
FFIEC High-Risk Security Test: FHLMC 1320 I Support Class Bond

Tsy. (bp)	Test 1			Security		Test 2		Test 3	
	Security		Max.			WAL	Change	Price	Change
Shift	PSA	WAL	WAL	Yield	Price	Actual	Max.	Actual	Max.
−300	575	1.02		2.73	104–01	−1.55	−6.0	4.0%	17%
−200	525	1.10		3.81	103–06	−1.48	−6.0	3.2	17
−100	300	1.72		5.40	102–14	−0.86	−6.0	2.5	17
0 bp	200	2.58	10	6.70	99–31	n/a		0.0	
+100	150	3.19		8.31	96–19	0.61	+4.0	−3.4	17
+200	115	3.19		9.31	94–03	0.61	+4.0	−5.9	17
+300	75	8.98		11.77	74–23	6.40	+4.0	−25.3	17

Source: Bloomberg Financial Markets.

TABLE 8.11
Holding-Period Comparison: FHLMC R101 F versus FNMA 9 Percent MBSs

	Yield Curve Shifts						
	300	*200*	*100*	*0*	*−100*	*−200*	*−300*
			Holding-Period Returns				
FNMA 9%	−3.21	0.77	4.71	7.67	8.26	8.19	8.64
FHLMC R101 F	−4.17	0.52	5.45	8.02	11.92	14.20	14.52
Differences	−0.94	−0.25	0.74	0.35	3.66	6.01	5.88
			Holding-Period-Return Assumptions				
FNMA 9%							
PSA	136	149	182	279	465	448	601
Average life	8.42	7.97	6.99	4.77	3.02	2.48	2.28
Spreads	118	118	118	138	148	148	148
FHLMC R101 F							
PSA	140	154	210	349	503	568	612
Average life	7.67	7.67	7.67	6.82	4.36	3.67	3.28
Spreads	75	75	75	125	145	165	185

Source: Lehman Brothers Fixed Income Research.

range of interest rate scenarios but lacks the higher performance of the class F in the down interest rate scenario. Of course, there are other bond classes in this REMIC that would be even more stable than the collateral, but at a tighter yield spread to the Treasury curve.

Limitations

An important question is how the repricing of the asset at the end of the horizon period is calculated. For example, assume the total return is to be calculated for a one-year horizon. Most horizon analyses assume the base case spread to the Treasury curve is unchanged. If the MBS is priced at a yield spread to the 10-year Treasury of 100 basis points, with the 10-year Treasury at 8 percent, the MBS will be priced at a discount factor of 9 percent (8 percent Treasury yield plus 1 percent spread). The base case (zero prepayment-volatility assumption) price one year from now will then be the same 9 percent plus reinvestment (with one year less remaining to maturity).

In the down 200 basis points (−200) scenario, the discount factor used will be 7 percent (assuming the Treasury is −200 to 6 percent plus the 1 percent spread). But this is not realistic—if yields are down 2 percent, the prepayment risk is much higher, and the yield spread to the Treasury should be wider. For example, assume that with the decline in interest rates to 6 percent the prepayment speed of the collateral has accelerated significantly and investors now require a yield spread to the Treasury curve of 150 basis points. The discount factor is now 7.5 percent (6 percent Treasury yield plus 1.5 percent for the spread).

The investor should also ask what reinvestment assumption is used. One shortcoming of the internal rate of return (IRR) or yield to maturity (YTM) calculations used in total-return analysis is that the electronic price calculator assumes the coupon is reinvested at the coupon rate—not a very good assumption if we are testing an MBS with a wide spread to intermediate Treasuries! The reinvestment assumption should be closer to the federal funds rate or to LIBOR—and increased or decreased by the amount of change in the interest rate scenario (i.e., up or down 300 basis points).

Finally, what about changes in the shape of the yield curve? If the yield curve steepens, three things are likely to happen: (1) the reinvestment assumption drops (short rates have decreased more than long rates); (2) the MBS to Treasury yield spread is likely to narrow because the REMIC arbitrage is improved; and (3) the required yield spread could actually widen if the collateral is on the cusp and prepayments are expected to accelerate. (For a further discussion of the impact of the yield curve on MBS value, see How Do I Apply Relative Value Analysis? in Chapter 3.)

Market Comparables

Investors should compare a proposed MBS investment to both intrasector (i.e., similar average-life MBSs) and intersector comparables (MBS vs. asset-backed securities and corporate bonds). Tables 8.12 and 8.13 suggest some intra- and intersector comparables.

Impact of 1992–1993 Prepayments on CMO Structure

The 1992–1993 prepayment experience had a profound impact on CMO structures and on how MBS investors and analysts viewed prepayment and OAS analysis and the effect of prepayments on

TABLE 8.12
Intrasector Comparables

Proposed MBS	MBS Comparables
30-year TBA	10-year sequential CMO
30-year seasoned	7-year sequential CMO
	7-year PAC
15-year seasoned	7-year balloon
	7-year AD
7-year balloon	5-year PAC
	5-year AD

MBS structures. Following the 1992 refinancing experience, the bands of PACs backed by 9.5 collateral were, in fact, mostly destroyed. As a consequence, PACs became similar to sequential tranches. This resulted in the phenomenon referred to at the time as "busted" PACs, meaning PACs backed by 9.5 and 10 percent collateral were left with no effective bands. By mid-year 1992 the actual bands for 5-year-average-life PAC classes collateralized by FNMA 9.5 percent collateral had drifted, as shown in Table 8.14. The table shows that by June 1992 the effective bands had drifted, with significant increases in the lower band to the 125–133 PSA range.

By the third quarter of 1992 most PAC structures backed by 9.5 percent MBS collateral had no prepayment-protection bands remaining, and by year-end 1992 PACs backed by 9 percent MBSs

TABLE 8.13
Intersector Comparables

Proposed MBS	MBS Comparables
30-year TBA	10-year Treasury
	10-year callable Telephone
15-year	7-year Treasury
5–7 year balloon	5-year ABS
PAC	Comparable average-life
	ABS

TABLE 8.14
PAC Band Shift for 5-Year PACs; Collateral, FNMA 9.5 Percent MBS

Deals Issued	Case Study Equivalent	WAM 11/91	Actual 6-Month PSA	PAC Bands (PSA)	
				11/91	6/92
9	265	28.2	756	94–284	125–265
8	MS	25.2	743	88–322	133–289

had lost most of their bands, as illustrated in Table 8.15. As of December 1992, support bond balances were 14 percent of their original balances.

The change in effective bands from 1991 to 1992 for several representative PAC structures is shown in Table 8.16. The collateral type backing the PAC structure is given in the table.

Performance of Broken PACs

Even with their prepayment-protection bands gone, the broken PACs offered potential good relative value to the comparable MBS collateral in the fall of 1992. Remember, broken PACs become sequential-pay-type bonds, but with the tighter cash flow window typical of the PAC structure. This tight window enables the broken PAC to roll down the curve effectively and thereby outperform the generic MBS in price responsiveness. Table 8.17 compares the OAS of selected PACs to the collateral backing them.

TABLE 8.15
PAC/Support CMO Backed by FNMA 9s, January 1991 Issue

Original pricing speed: 150 PSA
Structuring bands: 90–275

PAC Bond	Average Life (Years)	Effective PAC Bands	
		At Issuance	After 24 Months
3-year	3.5	90–373	155–225
5-year	5.9	90–289	None
7-year	7.9	90–274	None
10-year	10.9	90–273	None

TABLE 8.16
PAC Band Drift

Bond	WAL (Years)	Collateral Type	WAM	Effective PAC Bands	
				12/91	10/92
FNR 91–138K	4.6	15-yr. FN 8.5	166	85–239	105–221
FHLMG 11371	7.2	30-yr. FH Gold 8.5	337	93–233	87–228
FNR 90–057G	4.2	30-yr. FN 9.0	321	93–289	135–276
FNR 90–053G	7.2	30-yr. FN 9.0	318	95–285	127–276
FNR 90–106G	2.7	30-yr. FN 9.5	329	90–272	183–230
FHLMC R101F	4.0	30-yr. FH, 75-day 9.5	302	68–315	None

Why the OAS Models Were Misread in 1992

Table 8.17 shows the fair value of the broken PACs was high. However, for several months during the late summer and early fall of 1992 the yield spreads of the broken PACs widened to the extent that sellers of these bonds, or those marking to market, did experience a loss in price. The panic selling of broken PACs by nervous investors created a severe lack of liquidity for these broken PACs. However, investors who were able to hold the broken PACs through the end of the 1991–1993 prepayment cycles or who bought them at the wide yield spreads in the late summer of 1992 and through the winter of 1993 realized good performance with them.

The broken PACs became attractive in the winter of 1993 as a function of the burnout pattern of prepayments that made

TABLE 8.17
Broken PACs Compared to Collateral, January 21, 1992

Security	Collateral	Coupon %	Price	PSA	Projected Avg. Life (Years)	OAS (bp)
FNR 90–112P	FN 8.5s	8.5	104.00	280	5.2	151
FNR 91–39G	FN 9.0s	8.5	104.59	300	5.2	132
FNMA 8.5s	—	8.5	105.06	345	5.3	105
FHLMG-1288H	FH 9.0s	9.0	109.11	353	8.3	121
FHLMC 68-F	FH 9.0s	9.0	106.50	300	4.5	134
FNMA 9.0s	—	9.0	106.12	373	4.1	111

certain premium-priced MBS coupons appealing at that time. The 1992 experience with the impact of three unprecedented prepayment cycles on the structure and value of PACs highlighted some key points:

1. Know the collateral behind the PAC deal and understand its structure. PACs collateralized by seasoned current-coupon (7 to 8 percent) collateral fared significantly better than those with 9½ and 10 percent collateral.

2. Appreciate that OAS and prepayment models are powerful analytic tools but may not be able to predict extremes such as the 1991–1993 triple prepayment spikes, or for that matter other variables related to real-life economics such as yield curve shape and homeowner psychology.

CHAPTER 9

CMO BOND FORMS: PAC II, SUPPORT, TAC, Z-, AND AD BONDS

TIER TWO PACS

First introduced in 1989, **tier two (PAC II)** PACs became popular because they offer a wide yield spread with some degree of prepayment-risk protection. However, PAC IIs are like many CMOs in that bonds with the same average life often have very different convexity and realized average life and return expectations.

The risk/reward considerations with PAC IIs revolve around the fact that although the PAC II does have a prepayment-protection band, giving it PAC-like stability in a low-volatility interest rate environment, the PAC II schedule is subordinated to the tier one PACs, which causes the PAC IIs to take on support class characteristics when prepayments move outside the bands. All requirements of the tier one (PAC I) schedule must be met before any principal cash flows may be dispersed to the PAC II schedule. *Remember that in the event all the support bonds are paid off, standard PAC bonds become sequential-pay, or clean, bonds, but PAC IIs become support bonds.*

Relative Value Analysis of Tier Two PACs

In the short-average-life sector, tier two PACs can offer an attractive risk/reward relative to PACs or sequential-pay bond classes. Although the PAC IIs are generally priced at a lower yield than sequential-pay bonds, they may perform well relative to both sequential pay and short-term PAC structures in a low-volatility environment. Tables 9.1A through 9.1C compare a PAC, a PAC II, and a sequential-pay bond on a total rate of return, option-adjusted spread, and average-life frequency analysis basis.

TABLE 9.1A
CMO Structure Characteristics

	PAC FNMA 1990 54-B	PAC II FNMA 1990 59-G	Sequential-Pay FNMA 1990 43-A
Price	98-20	99-15	98-15
Spread	3-year + 66 bp	3-year + 83 bp	3-year + 93 bp
Yield	9.74%	9.91%	10.01%
Window	13 months	23 months	76 months
Coupon	9.30%	9.75%	9.50%
Collateral	FNMA 9.5%, 15-year	FNMA 10s	FNMA 10s
WAC	10.12%	10.70%	10.68%
WAM	14.33 years	29.83 years	29.17 years
Prepayment bands (PSA)	90–275	125–250	NA

Source: Lehman Brothers Fixed Income Research.

The PAC II illustrated in Table 9.1C provides about 17 basis points of incremental yield relative to a PAC bond in the base case (zero scenario). Furthermore, the PAC outperforms the PAC II only if interest rates decline by over 125 basis points or rise by over 200 basis points. The FNMA 1990 54-B is a 3-year PAC; the FNMA 1990 59-G is a 3-year PAC II; and the FNMA 1990 43-A is a 3-year sequential structure. The OAS on the PAC, the PAC II, and the sequential-pay bond are 54, 52, and 43 basis points, respectively. The OAS reveals that the sequential-pay tranche does not compensate the investor for the duration drift, whereas both the PAC II and the PAC provide compensation. It should be noted that the slightly higher OAS on the PAC is due to its superior performance when interest rates fall by more than 150 basis points.

PAC II Structures[1]

There are significant differences in performance among the population of PAC II bond forms depending on how the payment schedule is structured. Three types of principal-paydown schedules are described here: (1) level-payment schedule, (2) lockout-payment schedule, and (3) barbell-payment schedule.

Level-Payment Schedule
When structuring short-average-life PACs, the amount of principal that is available for the PAC schedule is dictated by the lower band. If prepayments are faster than the lower band, principal is available for other short-average-life tranches.

As a result, the amount of principal that makes up the PAC II paydown schedule is simply the difference in principal payments between the lower-band PSA of the first tier PAC and the lower-band PSA of the second tier PAC. The simultaneous paydown of the first tier PACs and PAC IIs causes the PAC IIs to have a relatively level paydown schedule. An example of this type of PAC II is FHLMC 1087-J (see Figure 9.1). The PAC II payment schedule is relatively large at first and then declines because the principal-paydown difference between the lower bands of the first and second

---

[1]This discussion of PAC II structures is based largely on DLJ Mortgage Research, *What the Street Does Not Tell You About Pac IIs* by Thomas Silvia, Vice President. New York: DLJ, July 1991.

TABLE 9.1B
Twelve-Month HPR Analysis

Scenario[a]	12-month HPR (%)	YTM (%)	Duration	WAL	Terminal[b] NAV as Percentage of Face	Terminal Spread (bp)	PSA Speed
			PAC				
−150	23.67	9.74	2.90	3.41	102-23	0.73	220
−100	11.68	9.74	2.90	3.41	101-21	0.66	190
−50	10.70	9.74	2.90	3.41	100-19	0.66	180
0	9.73	9.74	2.90	3.41	99-18	0.66	175
+50	8.78	9.74	2.90	3.41	98-18	0.66	145
+100	7.82	9.74	2.90	3.41	97-17	0.66	120
+150	6.78	9.74	2.90	3.49	96-15	0.66	80
			PAC II				
−150	12.34	9.00	2.73	3.20	102-27	1.15	320
−100	11.85	9.91	2.92	3.46	102-10	0.95	225
−50	10.87	9.91	2.92	3.46	101-08	0.83	210
0	9.89	9.91	2.92	3.46	100-06	0.83	185
+50	8.93	9.91	2.92	3.46	99-05	0.83	160
+100	7.97	9.91	2.92	3.46	98-04	0.83	150
+150	7.02	9.91	2.95	3.46	97-04	0.83	140

TABLE 9.1B
(Continued)

Scenario[a]	12-month HPR (%)	YTM (%)	Duration	WAL	Terminal[b] NAV as Percentage of Face	Terminal Spread (bp)	PSA Speed
			Sequential				
−150	12.05	10.16	1.89	2.15	102-07	1.10	320
−100	11.40	10.90	2.23	2.61	101-06	1.05	255
−50	10.77	10.04	2.56	3.08	100-11	0.98	210
0	9.98	10.01	2.79	3.42	99-13	0.93	185
+50	8.87	9.98	3.08	3.87	98-05	0.92	160
+100	7.71	9.97	3.21	4.09	96-27	0.90	150
+150	6.41	9.95	3.35	4.33	95-14	0.89	140

[a]Interest rate scenarios are for up/down changes of ±50, 100, and 150 basis points with a 1-month phase-in for each 50 bp step up/down.

[b]NAV = Net asset value at end of horizon period for investment (one year).

Source: Lehman Brothers Fixed Income Research.

TABLE 9.1C
Relative Value Comparison

Scenario	HPR (%)	YTM (%)	Duration	WAL	Terminal NAV as Percentage of Face
		Buy Advantage PAC II to PAC			
−150	−0.33	0.16	−0.17	−0.22	−0-04
−100	0.17	0.17	0.01	0.05	0-21
−50	0.17	0.17	0.01	0.05	0-20
0	0.16	0.17	0.01	0.05	0-20
+50	0.15	0.17	0.01	0.05	0-19
+100	0.14	0.17	0.01	0.05	0-19
+150	0.24	0.17	−0.04	−0.03	0-21
		Buy Advantage PAC II to Sequential			
−150	0.29	−0.26	0.84	1.04	1-20
−100	0.45	−0.18	0.69	0.85	1-04
−50	0.10	−0.13	0.36	0.39	0-28
−0	−0.09	−0.10	0.13	0.04	0-25
+50	0.06	−0.07	−0.16	−0.41	1-00
+100	0.25	−0.06	−0.29	−0.62	1-09
+150	0.61	−0.05	−0.43	−0.87	1-22
		OAS Performance			
Spread		+66		+83	+93
OAS		+54		+52	+43
Convexity cost		12		31	50

Source: Lehman Brothers Fixed Income Research.

tier PACs declines with time (see Figure 9.2). This tendency limits the amount of principal that can be scheduled to the PAC II, which extends its paydown window. It is characteristic of all PAC IIs.

Lockout-Payment Schedule

When the first tier PACs do not begin to pay down for several years, the PAC II may have large principal paydowns during the early part of its paydown schedule while the first tier PACs are "locked out." Once the first tier PACs begin to pay, the amount of principal available to the PAC II is only the differential of principal cash flow between the lower bands of the first and second tier

FIGURE 9.1
Principal Paydown, FHLMC 1087-J

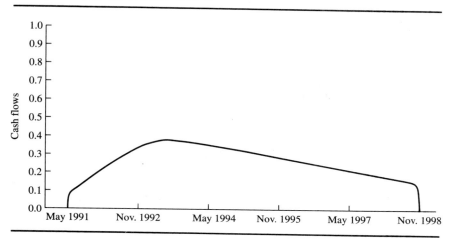

Source: DLJ Mortgage Research.

FIGURE 9.2
Collateral Principal Cash Flows, FHLMC 1087-J

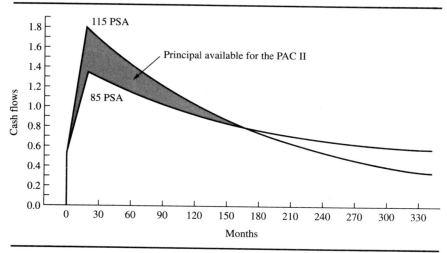

Source: DLJ Mortgage Research.

FIGURE 9.3
Principal Paydown, FNMA 1991 35-L

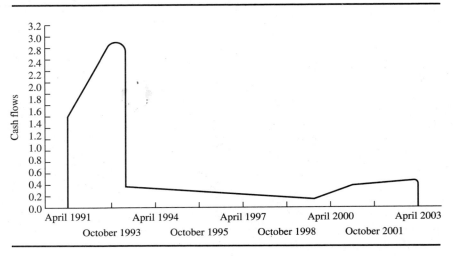

Source: DLJ Mortgage Research.

PACs. This effect produces a tail of principal that extends the average life of the PAC II. This type of PAC II partially replaced the short-average-life companion bonds that received the locked-out cash flow in earlier structures. Roughly 40 percent of the short-average-life PAC IIs are structured with first tier PACs that are locked out. An example of this type of PAC II is FNMA 1991 35-L (see Figure 9.3).

Barbell Payment Schedule. PAC IIs may also have an uneven principal payment schedule because the principal return is barbelled. The barbell is created when the principal schedule is concentrated at two separate points over the life of the security. An example of this type of PAC II is the FNMA 1991 22-K (see Figure 9.4).

A quick review of the average-life profiles of the three bonds just examined shows that the FHLMC 1087-J, the level-payment bond, is the most volatile outside its band. One should not hastily conclude, however, that the level-pay issue offers the least value. Investors can gain a tremendous amount of insight into a bond by running future cash flows to see how the security changes over time, which will determine how the marketplace will evaluate the

FIGURE 9.4
Principal Paydown, FNMA 1991 22-K

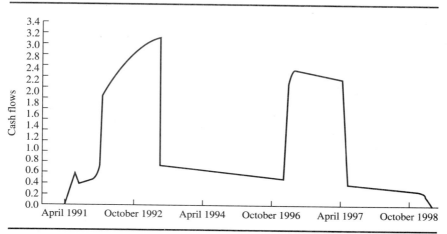

Source: DLJ Mortgage Research.

security. Table 9.2 shows the average-life sensitivity of the three PAC IIs two years from now. The average-life change for the FHLMC 1087-J is by far the most beneficial of the three PAC IIs. The average life shortens on the FHLMC 1087-J at every PSA, whereas it extends at every PSA for the FNMA 1991 35-L and hardly shortens for the FNMA 1991 22-K. The level-pay bond has the advantage of being priced in the future off a shorter part of the curve, which, in a positively sloped environment, will enhance its return versus the other PAC IIs.

Investment Implications of PAC II Structures

The structure of each PAC II has a dramatic effect on the investment characteristics of the bond. If the first tier PACs are locked out, the PAC IIs receive a large portion of their principal during the lockout period and the remainder over an extended period of time. This amplifies three separate risks: reinvestment risk, duration risk, and price risk. A PAC II with a long principal tail and a PAC II with a level payment of principal that have the same initial duration will exhibit significantly different performances because of these risks.

Reinvestment risk occurs because a PAC II with a large early paydown schedule may return as much as 70 percent of the princi-

TABLE 9.2
Average-Life Analysis, Selected PAC II Bonds

	Average Life					
Bond/PSA	75	100	115	150	200	250
06/26/91						
FHLMC 1087-J	16.63	7.17	3.44	3.44	3.44	3.10
FNMA 1991 35-L	5.33	3.37	3.37	3.37	3.37	3.66
FNMA 1991 22-K	8.86	5.27	3.56	3.22	3.22	3.22
08/26/93						
FHLMC 1087-J	13.83	6.10	2.28	2.26	2.26	1.80
FNMA 1991 35-L	10.80	5.55	5.56	6.56	6.66	6.21
FNMA 1991 22-K	9.65	5.60	3.30	2.83	2.83	2.83
	Change in Average Life from 6/91 to 6/93					
FHLMC 1087-J	−2.00	−1.07	−1.18	−1.18	−1.18	−1.30
FNMA 1991 35-L	5.49	2.19	2.19	2.19	2.19	2.55
FNMA 1991 22-K	0.79	0.33	−0.25	−0.39	−0.39	−0.39

Source: DLJ Mortgage Research.

pal in the first two to three years. These principal cash flows are then subject to reinvestment risk, which the level-pay bonds do not face. With a steep yield curve, the reinvestment of the early cash flows will cause this type of PAC II to underperform.

The remaining portion of principal on the PAC II extends in average life because of the long tail of principal cash flow. The price risk of the bond is increased because it now has a longer duration. A steep yield curve forces the remaining principal to be priced at the higher yields generally prevalent farther out on the term structure of the Treasury curve. The result is the bond underperforms a level-pay PAC II.

PAC II Window Structure
Tier two PACs often have wide windows in contrast to the typically narrow windows of tier one PACs. Table 9.3 gives examples of some PAC II windows. Note that all the PAC II windows shown display significant volatility in how much they contract or extend. For example, the 1-year window of the FHLMG 1217-N at pricing is quite narrow but extends far more than would a tier one PAC window at 100 PSA. The FHLMG 1212-M, with a 26-year window

TABLE 9.3
PAC II Window Structures

REMIC and Class	Average Life (Years)	PSA			Window at (Years)			
		Pricing	High	Low	Pricing	High	Low	Band
FHLMG 1217-N Collateral: PC 8s	5.6	160	520	100	1.1	0.2	4.0	125–215
FHLMG 1184-NC Collateral: PC 8s	7.5	160	500	100	9.0	0.5	2.9	130–190
FHLMG 1212-M Collateral: PC 8s	5.4	190	500	100	25.8	0.4	25.5	130–190

at pricing, is not typical of even a tier two PAC but illustrates that the unwary investor may be surprised to see such a long tail if it was not discovered (or disclosed) prior to purchase. Note also how much the window shrinks at 500 PSA (to 0.4 years).

Total-Return Analysis

A total rate of return analysis demonstrates that a long principal tail will have a significant negative impact on the performances of PAC IIs. The FHLMC 1087-J is a 3-year PAC II with a level principal-return schedule. The FNMA 1991 35-L is a PAC II with a tail of principal paydown. A one- and two-year rate of return for each issue is summarized in Table 9.4. The rate of return analysis demonstrates that PACs with a level-principal schedule are superior investments to PAC IIs with a tail of principal. The one- and two-year expected rates of return are higher for the FHLMC 1087-J than for the FNMA 1991 35-L by 37 and 94 basis points, respectively.

Liability Matching

The principal tail and barbell effect complicates asset/liability management. On the other hand, the level-pay issues can be effectively applied to match liabilities without the fear of duration risk and average-life volatility.

Volatility

Over the past several years investors who have purchased PAC IIs have done well when interest rates remained stable and market prepayment rates remained in a narrow range; PAC II investors did not fare so well in the high prepayment environment of 1992–1993 when many PAC IIs became support class bonds. Typically, investors who purchase PAC IIs have expectations that volatility will remain low and, therefore, will benefit the most from well-structured, level-pay PAC IIs.

Not All PAC IIs Are Equal: PAC II Windows

Some PAC IIs do have relatively tight windows and reasonable tolerance for volatility; for example, the FHLMG 1062-O, a 2-year PAC II, has a 1.75-year window. With 5-year-average-life PAC IIs,

TABLE 9.4

Selected PAC II CMO Structures (Average Life and Rate of Return Comparison)

Bond	Price ($)	Average Life		Expected Rate of Return				
		Begin	End	−200	−100	0	+100	+200
1-Year								
FHLMC 1087-J	98.53	3.44	2.75	11.78	10.20	8.53	6.79	5.04
FNMA 1991 35-L	98.58	3.37	3.62	10.75	9.62	8.09	6.71	5.36
Differential	0.95	0.07	−0.87	1.03	0.58	0.44	0.08	−0.32
2-Year								
FHLMC 1087-J	99.63	3.44	2.27	9.19	8.99	8.56	8.19	7.78
FNMA 1991 35-L	95.68	3.67	5.67	8.17	7.87	7.59	7.40	7.22
Differential	0.95	0.07	−3.30	1.02	1.12	0.97	0.79	0.56

Source: Lehman Brothers Fixed Income Research.

TABLE 9.5
Dynamic Sensitivity Analysis, FHLMG 1062-L 1.25-Year PAC II, Bands 115–270

	Scenarios				
PSA Speed for	*(1)*	*(2)*	*(3)*	*(4)*	*(5)*
Months 1–24	150	150	150	115	350
Months 25–36	150	75	200	115	350
Months 37–48	150	75	200	115	350
Months 49–maturity	150	150	150	115	350
Yield	7.50	7.50	7.50	2.49	7.50
Average life	1.25	1.25	1.25	1.25	1.25
First amortization	0.04	0.04	0.04	0.04	0.04
Maturity	1.79	1.79	1.79	13.21	1.79
Duration	1.19	1.19	1.19	2.0	1.19

the window may more typically be 12 to 15 years, but there are also 5-year-average-life PAC IIs with a window of 30 years!

The 1062-L 1.25-year PAC is also quite stable. Note the dynamic sensitivity analysis illustrated in Table 9.5. The pricing speed assumption was 150 PSA, given in the first column as a static scenario, priced at a slight premium of 100.30. Scenario 1 was the pricing assumption, which shows this PAC II to have an average life of 1.25 years and a yield of 7.5 percent and to be priced at a slight premium of 100.30. The cash flow window is 1.75 years (from 0.04 to 1.79). Scenario 2 stresses the PAC II to 75 PSA from months 25 to 48, and there are no changes. Scenario 3 stresses the PAC II to 200 PSA for the same period, and again there is no impact. Scenarios 4 and 5 are static slow- and fast-prepayment stresses. In scenario 4 the PSA speed is held constant at 115 PSA for its life. Scenario 5 is the high-PSA stress, with the bond held constant at 350 PSA for its life, and again we see no impact.

The static sensitivity analysis of a barbell PAC II presents some surprises for the unwary investor, which are illustrated in Figure 9.5. The FHLMG 1261-O was priced at 101.26 at the time of stress testing at a base case PSA of 165 to yield 7.38 percent, a spread of 155 basis points to the 3-year Treasury. The collateral is FHLMC 8s, 358-month WAM.

The base case PSA in Figure 9.5 (solid line) shows a barbell payment schedule with a very long tail, providing a cash flow window of about 9 years—long for a PAC trying to be a 3-year-aver-

FIGURE 9.5

Static Sensitivity Analysis, FHLMG 1261-O, 3-Year PAC II, Bands 120–200 PSA

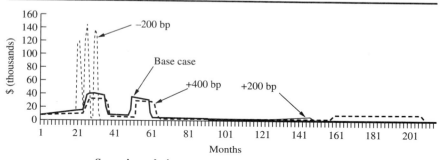

Scenario analysis

	−200	Base	+200	+400
Yield	6.96	7.38	7.48	7.70
Average life	2.05	3.42	4.15	7.60
Duration	1.89	2.93	3.38	5.08
PSA	712	150	112	88

Source: Matthew Josoff, Lehman Brothers Fixed Income Research.

age-life bond. The unsuspecting investor, on passing the first hump of the barbell, might assume that the cash flow schedule has been satisfied. However, the investor would not only be surprised by the second hump in about year 5 but would be downright discouraged on realizing the length of the cash flow tail.

The barbell is a function of the CMO structuring process in which 2-year cash flows (first hump) were combined with 5-year cash flows (second hump) to create a 3-year-average-life bond. In the fast-prepayment-speed scenario in Figure 9.5 (dashed line; rates down 200 basis points, PSA 712) there are three successive spikes as the two humps and the tail are scrunched together in quick succession. In the slow-prepayment-speed scenario (dotted line; rates up 400 basis points, PSA 88) there is a low-elevation plateau of cash flows reserved for the now long-suffering investor that stretches over the last five years of the very long cash flow window.

Figure 9.6 illustrates the amortization pattern of the monthly unpaid principal balance for the 1261-O under the various scenarios.

FIGURE 9.6
Monthly Principal Balance, FHLMG 1261-O, 3-Year PAC II

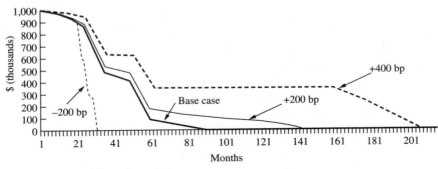

Scenario analysis

	–200	Base	+200	+400
Yield	6.96	7.38	7.48	7.70
Average life	2.05	3.42	4.15	7.60
Duration	1.89	2.93	3.38	5.08
PSA	712	150	112	88

Source: Matthew Josoff, Lehman Brothers Fixed Income Research.

PAC Capital Appreciation Bond CMOs: An Investment Alternative for Retirement Planning[2]

Individual investors seeking to combine the attractive yield and average-life stability of PAC CMOs along with Z-bond attributes may consider an investment in **PAC capital appreciation bond (CAB) CMOs.**

Comparison with Z-Bonds

PAC CAB CMOs are often compared to Treasury strip Z-bonds because they are purchased at a deep discount and are designed to accrue to par, assuming the underlying collateral prepays within the PAC bands of a particular tranche. Since the investor receives no

---

[2]This discussion of PAC capital appreciation bond CMOs was provided by Julia M. Rosado, Vice President, Mortgage Securities Product Manager, Lehman Brothers Fixed Income Division.

income until the principal-payment window begins, there is minimal reinvestment risk.

Treasury Z-bonds return principal in one single payment at maturity, whereas PAC CABs pay an amount representing P&I over a period of time, generally one to two years. As with all CMOs, the period when principal is returned is referred to as the principal-payment window. Principal-payment windows vary among structures at issuance. Once in the secondary market, the window drifts because prepayments may affect the structure. Principal-payment windows, and therefore average lives, change in different prepayment environments.

The Mechanics

If interest rates rise, causing prepayments to fall below the lower PAC band, the principal-payment window extends slightly, causing the average life to extend. In this scenario the PAC CAB continues to accrue at its coupon rate to a total greater than par.

In the opposite scenario, if interest rates drop significantly and the collateral prepays faster than the upper band, the PAC CAB has a shorter principal-payment window, causing a shorter average life, thereby accruing to a total less than par.

In either case, once principal payment commences accrual ceases, and monthly payment reflecting P&I begins. The PAC CAB at this point becomes an interest-bearing security based on the remaining principal balance and the original accrual rate until its final maturity. P&I is not differentiated but is made in one payment. Table 9.6 illustrates the prepayment sensitivity of a PAC CAB.

TABLE 9.6
FNMA G92–31 PAC CAB CMO; Accrual Rate, 8 Percent; PAC Bands, 85–240 PSA

	Base Case				
Mortgage rate	10.50	9.50	8.50	7.50	6.50
Change in rates	+200	+100	0	−100	−200
Prepayment assumption PSA	75	100	160	240	375
Average life (years)	14.6	13.9	13.9	13.9	9.5
Yield to average life at $31.78 (%)	8.39	8.40	8.40	8.40	8.53

Interest Rate Scenario

The PAC CAB described in Table 9.6 is collateralized by 30-year Ginnie Mae pass-throughs. By combining the stability of Ginnie Mae prepayments along with current and future interest rate projections, the base case prepayment assumption is 160 PSA. There are seven PAC CAB tranches in this structure.

TARGETED AMORTIZATION CLASS BONDS

First introduced in 1986, **targeted amortization class (TAC)** bonds pay to a schedule established by casting out the collateral cash flow to a single prepayment assumption that generally is the deal-pricing prepayment speed. The schedule for a TAC that has been added to a sequential-pay PAC structure is defined by the projected cash flows at the pricing speed assumption. In the case of a support class TAC, the schedule consists of the projected principal remaining after the PAC schedule requirements are met. Therefore, TACs do not enjoy a prepayment-protection range set by bands; there is just one PSA speed at which the TAC schedule is satisfied, usually the PSA assumption used to price the deal. Therefore, TAC bonds provide reasonable call protection but no extension protection. If prepayments exceed the pricing speed, the excess is paid to the support classes first. Therefore, the TAC has a modicum of call protection, although less than a PAC (prepayments in excess of the PAC schedule are paid to the support classes until they are exhausted, and then to the TACs). Obviously, the larger the short support classes are in relation to the TAC, the more stable will be the TAC. If prepayments fall below the pricing speed, however, the TAC will extend.

Table 9.7 compares the average lives of the 10-year tranche for three hypothetical CMOs under various prepayment-rate scenarios. Each CMO has three classes: At the pricing speed of 135 PSA, each first tranche has an average life of 3.4 years; the second tranche has an average life of 10.9 years; and the third tranche is a long-maturity, coupon-bearing sequential class. If prepayments rise above the pricing speed, the average lives of the PAC and TAC tranches remain relatively stable, whereas the sequential class shortens dramatically.

TACs and PACs react very differently when prepayment rates decline, however. The average life of the PAC is constant until pre-

TABLE 9.7
CMO Sensitivity Analysis, Average Life under Selected PSA Speeds

PSA	Sequential	PAC	TAC
50	19.0	10.9	19.0
100	13.6	10.9	13.6
135	10.9	10.9	10.9
200	7.9	10.9	11.3
275	5.9	10.9	11.1
450	3.7	7.8	6.9

Source: Drexel Burnham Lambert.

payment rates fall below 50 PSA, the lower boundary of the protection band. The TAC, however, lengthens exactly as the comparable sequential tranche at speeds under 135 PSA. The yields at which PACs and TACs trade reflect this difference in average-life stability. Sequential-pay, 10-year bond classes typically offer higher yield than comparable PACs. TACs provide a compromise for investors who do not expect prepayment rates to fall below 100 PSA. In that case, a TAC provides much of the average-life stability of a PAC, with a yield moderately above the spread of the comparable average-life PAC.

TAC Cash Flows at Prepayments above the TAC PSA Rate[3]

The average life of the TAC sometimes lengthens when actual prepayments fall within a range of rates above the TAC PSA rate. In some structures, the TAC schedule may not be broken initially. The support bonds that had been absorbing the excess are retired before the TAC is paid down. Therefore, the TAC receives all of the principal cash flow from the remaining collateral. This cash flow is not enough to cover the principal payment schedule of the TAC, and, cash flows are received beyond the original maturity date. If the collateral consistently prepays at 200 PSA, for example, the average

---

[3]This discussion of TAC cash flow prepayments is based largely on *CMO PAC and TAC Bonds* by William J. Curtin and Paul Van Valken. New York: Drexel Burnham Lambert, February 1989.

FIGURE 9.7
FNMA 1992-50 TAC; WAL Graph

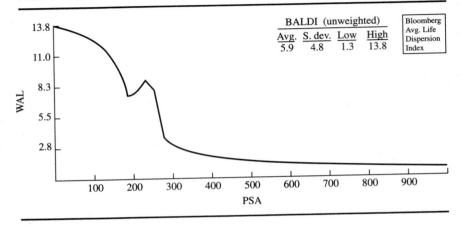

BALDI (unweighted)				Bloomberg Avg. Life Dispersion Index
Avg.	S. dev.	Low	High	
5.9	4.8	1.3	13.8	

Source: Bloomberg Financial Markets.

life of the TAC lengthens. Figure 9.7 illustrates the hump as the TAC lengthens when the collateral pays in a range of 200–250 PSA.

TAC Cash Flows at Very Fast Prepayments

If prepayment rates are very fast over a long period of time, all of the other non-TAC classes are retired and the TAC is the only outstanding bond. The TAC bond then receives all of the remaining principal payments, which results in higher payments in the early months than originally scheduled. If the increase in payments is early and significant enough, the average life of the TAC bond shortens at PSA speeds of 300 and higher (see Figure 9.7). The TACs, for example, shorten to 6.9 years if the collateral consistently prepays at 450 PSA. The PSA rate at which the TAC's average life begins to shorten depends upon the collateral and the TAC structure. To compare call protection of a TAC to other TACs and other callable securities, the investor should find the first constant PSA rate that causes the average life of the TAC bond to shorten (all prepayment rates above this rate also cause the TAC to shorten) and then estimate the interest rate movement necessary to cause prepayment rates to increase to this level. The magnitude of this interest rate movement indicates the amount of call protection of the specific TAC bond.

The TAC PSA rate, like the PAC band, changes each month that prepayments are not equal to the current TAC PSA rate. In fact, the TAC may actually develop a narrow band. When prepayment rates are below the TAC PSA rate, more dollars are outstanding than were expected. At this point, a constant PSA rate that is slightly slower or faster than the original TAC PSA rate now generates sufficient principal to meet the scheduled principal payments of the TAC. The TAC does not suffer any additional principal shortfall and develops a weak prepayment band.

Support TACs

The cash flows of a support TAC are generally derived from the cash flows available to the short-average-life support class. The TAC schedule would then be defined as the principal cash flows attributable to the support at the pricing speed assumption. The support TAC has less call protection than a sequential-pay or standard TAC because it must absorb the principal payments in excess of the PAC schedule once the PAC support classes have been paid off.

Reverse TACs

The payment rules may simply be altered to create a TAC with extension-risk protection and little or no call protection. These bonds will typically be structured from the long-average-life support classes and priced at deep discounts to compensate the investor for the call risk, since they are typically long-average-life securities; the extension risk is limited in any event to 6 or 10 years. These bonds are referred to as **reverse TACs,** or sometimes **anti-TACs.**

Z-BOND FORMS

The **Z-bond,** or **accrual bond,** has a coupon attributed to it, but the coupon is not paid out until all prior classes have been satisfied; at that point the Z-bond commences paying P&I monthly, just as a standard CMO bond. The Z designation is a reflection of the zero-coupon nature of the Z-bond during its accrual phase. Here the similarity to a Treasury strip, or zero, ends. In the case of a Treasury zero coupon bond, there is no economic benefit to the bondholder until maturity. With the Z-bond, the accrual itself represents an economic benefit to the investor from day 1 because of the accrual addition to the principal balance of the Z-bond—which, by the way, is reinvested, representing another benefit to the investor. The traditional position of the Z-bond within the CMO deal structure is that it is the last to pay. Note, however, that a Z-bond need not necessarily always be the last bond class—the Z-bond may be positioned anywhere in the deal structure, but it is always an accrual bond for some portion of its existence. Therefore, typically the Z-bond has a relatively long duration and, because of its accrual feature, offers reinvestment-risk protection. Z-bonds are purchased at a discount and accrue to par. Those that are near the end of their accrual phase can trade to a premium if the anticipated paying coupon warrants a premium price. There are many variations of the Z-bond structure, and they are explored in this chapter, including PAC, TAC, and **support Zs,** as well as **jump Zs, sticky jump Zs, cumulative** and **noncumulative,** and **toggle jump Zs.**

The Accrual Structure

As mentioned earlier, the Z-bond coupon is not paid out for some time but accrues, cumulatively, to the Z-bond itself. The accrual is added to the unpaid principal amount of the bonds, so that the original face amount of the bonds issued under the Z-structure accrues to considerably more than the original face amount in 8 to 10 years. Figure 9.8 illustrates the accrual pattern of the FHLMG 1090-Z, which has an 8.5 percent accrual rate and an original average life of about 15 years.

Table 9.8, which, is simply a factor table, illustrates how the unpaid principal balance of the 83-Z bond grows over time as a function of the accrual. Note that the factor grows instead of amortizing to a smaller number. This pattern reflects the accrual characteristic of a 83-Z bond. At the pricing assumption of 175 PSA the factor reaches its maximum of 351 in year 15. Since we started with a factor of 100, this means in 15 years $1 million face amount of Z-bonds will accrue to $3.5 million face.

Note in Table 9.8 that at a slower payment speed, for example, 100 PSA, the factor does not peak until year 19 at 464. At first this may appear to be a favorable outcome. However, implicit to a slower PSA is the implication that interest rates have risen, meaning the investor is locked into the 9 percent accrual when market interest rates rise to higher levels; the investor would have preferred having the cash flow returned sooner to be reinvested at the higher interest rates. Also, remember the axiom that when MBSs pur-

FIGURE 9.8
Z-Bond Cash Flows, FHLMG 1090-Z, 8.5 Percent Accrual

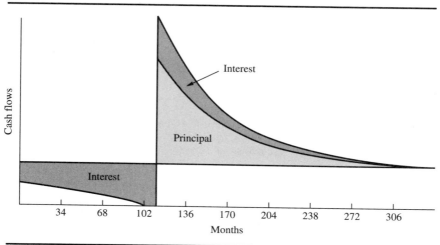

Source: Bloomberg Financial Markets.

chased at a discount (in this case at about 84¾) extend duration the investor loses yield.

On the other hand, if prepayment speeds accelerate to 300 PSA, the bond converts to a peak accrual of 157 in year 6 (Table 9.8). Again, higher prepayment speeds assume lower interest rates, so one would assume the investor would prefer not to receive the cash sooner. However, since the faster prepay implies lower interest rates, the investor is happy to have the accrual reinvestment locked into higher rates. And, again, the Z-bond would be purchased at a discount, and receiving the rate for cash flows purchased at a discount always enhances the yield.

Table 9.9 is a static sensitivity analysis of the FHLMG 83-Z. The table shows that if the prepayment speed declines to 100 PSA, the average life extends to 23.23 years, and the realized yield declines from over 10 percent to 9.93 percent, reducing the effective spread to Treasuries (as it extends) from 190 basis points to 175 basis points. If the prepayment speed accelerates to 300 PSA, the average life shortens to less than 15 years, the yield is 10.39 percent, and the effective spread widens to 221 basis points over a shorter point on the term structure of the Treasury curve. Because of these characteristics, Z-bonds may be highly volatile in price per-

TABLE 9.8
83-Z Bond Cash Flow Factor Table, FHLMG 9 Percent, 2019,
Pricing Assumption 175 PSA

	PSA				
Year	0	100	175	300	500
1	100	100	100	100	100
2	109	109	109	109	109
3	120	120	120	120	120
4	131	131	131	131	131
5	143	143	143	143	143
6	157	157	157	157	157
7	171	171	171	171	171
8	187	187	187	187	187
9	205	205	205	205	135
10	224	224	224	224	93
11	245	245	245	245	64
12	268	268	268	219	44
13	293	293	293	176	30
14	321	321	321	141	21
15	351	351	351	113	14
16	384	384	312	90	10
17	420	420	270	72	7
18	459	459	233	57	4
19	502	464	200	44	3
20	549	416	170	35	2
21	601	369	144	27	1
22	657	324	120	21	1
23	719	281	99	16	1
24	786	239	80	12	0
25	860	199	64	8	0
26	860	160	49	6	0
27	726	123	36	4	0
28	576	87	24	2	0
29	406	51	14	1	0
30	215	17	4	0	0

formance—a consideration that makes them unsuitable investments for most banks and thrifts, which need to keep their invested assets in relatively stable, short-term investments. However, Z-bonds can be very attractive for buy and hold accounts such as pension funds and other managed funds seeking long-duration investments and for whom high potential price volatility is not a concern.

TABLE 9.9
FHLMG 83-Z Bond Sensitivity Analysis

	Low	Base	High
PSA	100	175	300
BEY	9.93	10.08	10.39
Spread to Treasury (bp)	175	190	221
First P&I (year)	17.72	14.22	10.47
Average life (years)	23.23	19.73	14.73
Projected maturity (year)	29.55	29.55	29.55
Price 84 25/32			

Applications of Accrual

The accrual is generally directed to the payment of prior sequential-pay bonds, to support the PAC bonds or to fund ADs. This diversion of the Z-bond accrual to the support or payment of other bonds is often misconstrued as robbing Peter to pay Paul. This is not so. Remember, the accrual is not interest in the sense that an IO strip is an existing cash flow stream of interest. The accrual simply represents future cash flows that are borrowed for earlier use. Since the accrual is applied within the deal structure to retire bonds now that would have to be paid eventually, it may be viewed simply as synthetically created collateral that may be applied to pay bonds today and then reappear later in the form of additional face amount Z-bonds. Another way to view the accrual is to realize that when we use the accrual to pay down bonds, the debt liability has been reduced, but we retain the same amount of unpaid principal amount of collateral. There is a mathematical balance retained within the CMO deal structure such that the sum of the unpaid principal balance of bonds always equals the sum of the collateral principal.

A good way to think of the Z-bond is that it is getting positive interest payments but negative principal payments, so that the total cash flow to the Z-bond is zero while it is accreting. These negative cash flows may be "sold" as another bond class, such as AD bonds. Table 9.10 demonstrates the process of converting a 30-year, interest-bearing bond into a Z-bond plus AD bond. The table shows the unpaid principal balance, interest, principal payments, and total cash flow of a 9 percent interest-bearing bond in the four left-hand columns. The Z-bond cash flows are shown in the middle columns and the AD cash flows in the four right-hand columns. The sum of

TABLE 9.10

Carving Interest-Bearing Bond into Z-Bond plus AD ($; Window, 16–30 Years; 9 Percent Coupon)

Year	Interest-Bearing Bond (Average Life 23 Years) Beginning Balance	Interest Payment	Principal Payment	Total Payment	Z-Bond (Average Life 23 Years) Beginning Balance	Interest Payment	Principal[B] Payment	Total Payment	AD Bond Class (Average Life 9.6 Years) Beginning Balance	Interest Payment	Principal[B] Payment	Total Payment
1	300.00	27.00	0.00	27.00	82.36	7.41	(7.41)	0.00	217.64	19.59	7.41	27.00
2	300.00	27.00	0.00	27.00	89.77	8.08	(8.08)	0.00	210.23	18.92	8.08	27.00
3	300.00	27.00	0.00	27.00	97.85	8.81	(8.81)	0.00	202.15	18.19	8.81	27.00
4	300.00	27.00	0.00	27.00	106.66	9.60	(9.60)	0.00	193.34	17.40	9.60	27.00
5	300.00	27.00	0.00	27.00	116.26	10.46	(10.46)	0.00	183.74	16.54	10.46	27.00
6	300.00	27.00	0.00	27.00	126.72	11.41	(11.41)	0.00	173.28	15.59	11.41	27.00
7	300.00	27.00	0.00	27.00	138.13	12.43	(12.43)	0.00	161.87	14.57	12.43	27.00
8	300.00	27.00	0.00	27.00	150.56	13.55	(13.55)	0.00	149.44	13.45	13.55	27.00
9	300.00	27.00	0.00	27.00	164.11	14.77	(14.77)	0.00	135.89	12.23	14.77	27.00
10	300.00	27.00	0.00	27.00	178.88	16.10	(16.10)	0.00	121.12	10.90	16.10	27.00
11	300.00	27.00	0.00	27.00	194.98	17.55	(17.55)	0.00	105.02	9.45	17.55	27.00
12	300.00	27.00	0.00	27.00	212.53	19.13	(19.13)	0.00	87.47	7.87	19.13	27.00
13	300.00	27.00	0.00	27.00	231.66	20.85	(20.85)	0.00	68.34	6.15	20.85	27.00
14	300.00	27.00	0.00	27.00	252.50	22.73	(22.73)	0.00	47.50	4.27	22.73	27.00
15	300.00	27.00	0.00	27.00	275.23	24.77	(24.77)	0.00	24.77[d]	2.23[d]	24.77[d]	27.00[d]
16[b]	300.00	27.00[b]	20.00	47.00	300.00[c]	27.00	20.00	47.00[d]	0.00	0.00	0.00	0.00
17	280.00	25.20	20.00	45.20	280.00	25.20	20.00	45.20	0.00	0.00	0.00	0.00
18	260.00	23.40	20.00	43.40	260.00	23.40	20.00	43.40	0.00	0.00	0.00	0.00
19	240.00	21.60	20.00	41.60	240.00	21.60	20.00	41.60	0.00	0.00	0.00	0.00
20	220.00	19.80	20.00	39.80	220.00	19.80	20.00	39.80	0.00	0.00	0.00	0.00
21	200.00	18.00	20.00	38.00	200.00	18.00	20.00	38.00	0.00	0.00	0.00	0.00
22	180.00	16.20	20.00	36.20	180.00	16.20	20.00	36.20	0.00	0.00	0.00	0.00
23	160.00	14.40	20.00	34.40	160.00	14.40	20.00	34.40	0.00	0.00	0.00	0.00
24	140.00	12.60	20.00	32.60	140.00	12.60	20.00	32.60	0.00	0.00	0.00	0.00

TABLE 9.10
(Concluded)

Year	Interest-Bearing Bond (Average Life 23 Years)				Z-Bond (Average Life 23 Years)				AD Bond Class (Average Life 9.6 Years)			
	Beginning Balance	Interest Payment	Principal Payment	Total Payment	Beginning Balance	Interest Payment	Principal[a] Payment	Total Payment	Beginning Balance	Interest Payment	Principal[a] Payment	Total Payment
25	120.00	10.80	20.00	30.80	120.00	10.80	20.00	30.80	0.00	0.00	0.00	0.00
26	100.00	9.00	20.00	29.00	100.00	9.00	20.00	29.00	0.00	0.00	0.00	0.00
27	80.00	7.20	20.00	27.20	80.00	7.20	20.00	27.20	0.00	0.00	0.00	0.00
28	60.00	5.40	20.00	25.40	60.00	5.40	20.00	25.40	0.00	0.00	0.00	0.00
29	40.00	3.60	20.00	23.60	40.00	3.60	20.00	23.60	0.00	0.00	0.00	0.00
30	20.00	1.80	20.00	21.80	20.00	1.80	20.00	21.80	0.00	0.00	0.00	0.00
31	0.00	0.00	0.00	0.00	0.00	0.00	(0.00)	0.00	0.00	0.00	0.00	0.00
Total		621.00	300.00	921.00[e]		433.64	82.36	516.00[e]		187.36	217.64	405.00

[a]The negative principal of the Z-bond accrues to the Z as it pays the AD bond.
[b]The interest-bearing bond pays interest only to year 16; thereafter, it pays to reduction of principal as well.
[c]The Z-bond accrual compounds at 9 percent for 15 years, so it grows to $300 million interest-bearing bond principal at year 16.
[d]At end of year 15 the AD bond matures, and the Z-bond starts paying P&I in year 16: $27 interest + $20 principal = $47.
[e]The total cash flow interest-bearing bond = $921. The Z-bond total cash flow, $516, plus AD total, $405, = $921.

the Z-bond plus AD bond cash flows at all times are equal to the total cash flows of the original coupon bond. Note these key points with reference to Table 9.10:

1. The negative principal of the Z-bond equals the interest payment of the Z-bond (canceling out to zero) and becomes the principal payment of the AD bond until the AD bond is paid in full at the end of year 15.

2. Since the coupon bond pays interest only until year 16 ($27) that interest is available as an accrual to the Z-bond, and, in turn, as synthetic principal paid by the AD bond ($7.41 the first year, then compounding at the 9 percent accrual rate). The remainder of the $27 ($27.00 − $7.41 = $19.59) secures the AD bond interest. Therefore, the $27 of the original coupon bond interest becomes a synthetic P&I cash flow for the AD bond.

3. The discounted face amount of the Z-bond ($82.36) accrues, compounded at 9 percent, to $300 by year 16. Thus, an investor would pay $82.36 in year 1, which accrues to $300 by the end of year 15.

4. At the end of year 15, the Z-bond becomes a "payer"; that is, it begins paying P&I. The AD bond has been retired, ending its claim on the accrual.

5. The sum of the interest and principal payments of the interest-bearing bond ($921.00) equals the sum of the Z-bond cash flow ($433.64 + $82.36 = $516.00) plus the AD cash flow ($187.36 + $217.64 = $405.00): $516.00 + $405.00 = $921.00.

Z-Bond Impact on CMO Structure

Because of the ability to apply the accruals to pay earlier bond classes, the inclusion of a Z-bond enables more bonds to be created in the early portions of the CMO structure. Table 9.11 compares the number of short-average-life bonds that can be included in a CMO that contains a Z-bond versus one that does not. Of course, if these accruals are sold as an AD bond they would also not be available for other bonds. The table illustrates a more generic application of the accruals.

Note in Table 9.11 that there can be $19 million bonds in the class A of the CMO that has a Z-bond, whereas there can only be about $14.4 million class A bonds in the structure without a

TABLE 9.11

Comparison of Two CMO Structures: One with a Z-Bond, One without a Z-Bond

Quarterly pay, 30-day delay
Collateral: GNMA 9%, 30 years to maturity, $100 million (face amount)

If the Last Tranche Is a Z-Bond

CMO Class	Comparable Treasury (%)	Bond Amount ($ Millions)	Bond Coupon (%)	Average Life 100 PSA (Years)	Spread over Treasury (bp)	Price (%)
A	6.37 (2-year)	19.076	7.400	2.20	80	99.968
B	6.95 (5-year)	23.740	8.300	5.30	130	99.874
C	7.55 (10-year)	46.284	8.875	10.60	190	96.181
D	8.18 (20-year)	10.900	8.875	21.27	240	74.386
Total		100.000				

If the Last Tranche Is a Coupon Bond

CMO Class	Comparable Treasury (%)	Bond Amount ($ Millions)	Bond Coupon (%)	Average Life 100 PSA (Years)	Spread over Treasury (bp)	Price (%)
A	6.37 (2-year)	14.443	7.400	2.20	80	99.969
B	6.95 (5-year)	20.300	8.300	5.30	130	99.873
C	7.55 (10-year)	20.300	8.300	5.30	130	99.873
D	8.18 (20-year)	36.606	8.875	21.40	170	91.446
Total		100.000				

Source: Lehman Brothers Fixed Income Research.

Z-bond. The class A bonds have the lowest coupon (7.4 percent) and the tightest spread (80 basis points to the 2-year Treasury) of all the bond classes. Also note that there is a give-up. The 20-year-average-life coupon bond in the second structure requires only 170 basis points yield to the 20-year Treasury versus 240 basis points for the Z-bond. Even though the yield spread requirement is higher (most investors prefer a coupon), the Z-bond amount is only $10.9 million, whereas the long-coupon bond principal amount is $36.6 million—so the Z-bond is a good trade-off.

Utilizing the same concept, we see that the ratio of PAC to support bond classes can be greater when the structure includes a Z-bond because there is additional support provided for the PACs by the Z accruals. Investors should be wary, however, of PAC structures relying for support on Z accruals when the Z has been restructured in some of the ways described in the following sections, especially if the Z is a jump Z.

Multiple Z-Bond Structures

Since 1989 many CMO and particularly PAC structures have included several Z-bonds with average lives ranging from 5 to 20 years. Often there is a series of sequential Zs with average lives of 5, 7, 10, and 20 years. Another variation is to structure a pair of short and long Zs with one or more coupon-paying bonds in between. The long-dated Z usually donates its accrual to early, short-average-life bonds, whereas intermediate Zs typically direct their accrual to pay earlier-maturing Zs as they convert to coupon-paying bonds. The Z accruals, because of their synthetic nature, offer almost total flexibility in where they are added to the deal structure and may be used to permit the issuance of more earlier-class bonds, whether sequential-pay, PAC, or Z-bond classes. Similarly, the accrual may be used to stabilize a volatile intermediate support that might otherwise be difficult to sell.

PAC Z-Bonds

Remember, there are no clean, or standard, sequential-pay bonds within a PAC CMO structure. All bonds within the structure are either PAC or support class bonds, as is the Z-bond when it is part of a PAC support structure.

When the Z accruals are derived from the PAC cash flows, they retain the stability provided by the PAC bonds. This characteristic means not only greater average-life stability but also more reliable insulation to reinvestment risk, since the **PAC Z** is far less likely to extend during high interest rate periods or to pay off sooner in falling interest rate environments. PAC Zs are, therefore, particularly attractive to investors seeking to lock in a reinvestment rate, match fund a GIC, or lock in a spread to the maturity of a liability. And portfolio managers looking for an MBS with which to extend portfolio duration in a bullish interest rate environment would be well served by PAC Zs.

Support Zs

Support Z accruals are derived from the cash flows outside the PAC bands and therefore are quite unstable. Support Zs typically possess relatively little call protection and so are priced to deep discounts. Investors with cash flows not supported by liabilities at all, or by liabilities with no targeted maturity (for example, core pass-book savings accounts), may be able to accept the extension risk of intermediate support Zs and benefit from the relatively high yield spread offered on them. Pension funds purchasing long-dated support Zs should be wary of the utter lack of call protection of these bonds.

Jump Zs

One form of support Z introduced in 1989 was the jump Z. A jump Z is one in which the maturity sequence shifts in priority upon striking a specific event. The event could be a specific PSA speed (for example, 250) or an interest rate level (for example, a 10-year Treasury yield of 8 percent or below). Achieving the event activates a trigger that causes a shift in the payment priority of the Z, generally from some intermediate to long position within the maturity sequence to the first in the sequence. In other words, if the trigger of a 15-year-average-life jump Z is activated, that bond shifts ahead of what was formerly the first (A) bond in the bond-maturity sequence. Clearly, then, a jump Z is the ultimate in a bond with no call protection. Investors who bought these bonds were sometimes looking to make a high-profit bet on interest rates (rates drop to the trigger level, and the jump Z, always sold at a deep discount, "jumps" and pays off in a few months, providing the investor with a windfall profit—and, of course, lots of reinvestment risk). The worst aspect of the jump Z is that once it jumps, its accruals are obviously no longer available to support whatever they were to pay off or stabilize. Thus, support bonds stabilized by the jump Z accruals extended severely, and PAC structures with the lower-prepayment bands dependent on jump Z accruals were seriously impaired during the high-prepayment period of 1991–1992. Some jump Zs had prepayment-speed-designated triggers so sensitive that the Z jumped on the seasonal impact alone. Table 9.12, which compares the average life of a standard Z-bond (FHLMC 137–12) to that of a jump Z (FHLMC 1010–20), points up the impact the jump feature has on the yield.

The jump Z trigger in Table 9.12 is 150 PSA. Note that at 151 PSA the jump Z average life shortens to less than 1 year. At the 151 PSA "strike" the jump Z moves to first priority in the distribution of principal and therefore pays off very fast. The benefit to the jump Z holder is a sudden, large pickup in yield to 17.48 percent. The detriment to the CMO deal structure is that any bonds created from the accruals will also pay off very fast but without an incremental benefit in yield: An AD bond created from these accruals probably would have been priced at or close to par. Worse, if the jump Z accruals had been used to stabilize other bonds or to support the PAC bonds, that support is swiftly lost, thereby weakening the entire structure of the CMO issue.

Cumulative and Sticky Jump Zs

There have been a number of variations on the trigger structure. Many provided that cumulative events were required to trigger a jump, for example, a 3-month cumulative prepayment speed of 225 PSA. By contrast, a noncumulative trigger required only that a single PSA number be observed once. A sticky jump Z is one that having once activated its trigger makes a permanent shift in payment priority regardless of future events. A nonsticky jump Z reverts back to its former priority should the event or conditions that activated the trigger cease to exist.

By late 1991 criticism of and concern about the jump Z, particularly the sticky variety, had become so intense that the form ceased to be included in the deal structure. The jump Z experience was an unfortunate example of Wall Street innovation producing confusion and concern in the market beyond any benefit that might have been provided to some deal structures.

TABLE 9.12
Average-Life Sensitivity, Z-bond versus Jump Z

	PSA	Average Life (Years)	Yield (%)
Z-bond	100	26.4	10.46
FHLMC 137-12	150	24.1	10.77
Price 72	151	24.1	10.79
Jump Z	100	26.2	9.39
FHLMC 1010-20	150	24.1	9.41
Price 94-16	151	0.7	17.48

AD BONDS

AD bonds represent a stable structure with short, final stated maturities whereby a separate class of bonds is funded by the Z-bond accruals. The characteristics of ADs, also called **VADMs (Very Accurately Defined Maturity)** or **stated maturity bonds (SMBs)** are as follows:

1. The AD bond cannot extend because the Z-bond accruals exist in their scheduled amount at zero PSA.

2. There is minimal call risk because there is no principal downstreaming to the accrual cash flows. The accruals are derived solely from interest due but not paid out on the Z-bond at zero PSA.

3. A 5-year AD has a 5-year final stated maturity and is a liquidity-qualifying bond. The most common form of AD bond structure is a sequential series of ADs structured from all the Z-bond accrual and paid concurrent with the PAC classes. The accrual, which is precisely known based solely on the coupon attributed to a specific face amount of Z-bonds at zero PSA, may be carried into absolute maturities by simply specifying in the prospectus that the accrual "shall be paid first to the AD-1 until it is paid in full, then next to the AD-2," and so on. Thus, a series of ADs with absolute final stated maturities of 5, 7, 10, and 50 or more years may be structured out of the accruals.

4. The short-maturity (5-year or less) ADs are liquidity qualifying for thrift institutions and any other institutions with a statutory restriction on investing beyond a certain maturity, for example, 5 years.

5. Short-maturity ADs enjoy considerable call protection because the accrual cash flow of a 5-year AD is not shortened unless prepayment speeds become so high that the entire CMO bond issue is paid off in less than 5 years. In that event there would, of course, be no accrual beyond the 5 years, and the bond would prepay early. ADs are therefore extremely stable, with zero extension risk at any prepayment speed and moderate call risk only at prolonged PSAs above 400 to 600.

Figure 9.9 gives the cash flows of a 5-year-maturity AD. Note that the accrual has been structured into a synthetic P&I cash flow so the investor is not buying an IO. Remember, the accrual is not an IO—it is a synthetic cash flow created from an accrual owed to the bond issuer at a later date.

Table 9.13 illustrates the principal payment schedule of 5-, 10-, and 13-year AD bonds together with the Z-bond accruals.

FIGURE 9.9
FNMA 1992-122A AD: Cash Flow Window at 300 PSA

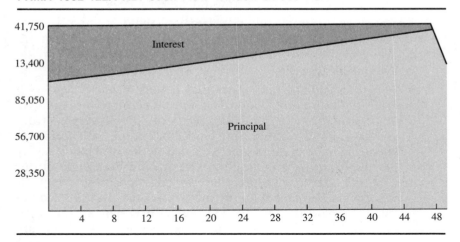

Source: Bloomberg Financial Markets.

TABLE 9.13
Schedule of AD Bond Principal Payments ($)

| | Principal Paid | | | |
| | 5-Year | 10-Year | 13-Year | Interest Accrued/ |
Year	Final	Final	Final	Accrual Bond
1	2,251,366			2,251,366
2	2,462,559			2,462,559
3	2,693,564			2,693,564
4	2,946,239			2,946,239
5	3,146,272	76,345		3,222,617
6	0	3,524,920		3,524,920
7	0	3,855,582		3,855,582
8	0	4,217,262		4,217,262
9	0	4,612,871		4,612,871
10	0	5,013,020	32,570	5,045,590
11	0	0	5,518,901	5,518,901
12	0	0	6,036,612	6,036,612
13	0	0	6,411,917	6,411,917

Alternate SMBs

The alternate SMBs described here, such as the ADs, have short final stated maturities, but their source of cash flow is not from the Z-bond accrual. Although they have absolute final maturities with no call risk, SMBs may have considerable call risk. The cash flow source of the SMB is the scheduled amortization of the MBSs that make up the collateral for the CMO bond issue.

If prepayment speeds rise to fairly high levels (400 PSA or above) for prolonged periods of time, the reduced amount of collateral remaining will not have sufficient scheduled amortization to pay off the SMB by its final stated maturity. To protect the SMB from such an eventuality, increasing amounts of prepayments are applied to pay down the balance of the SMBs according to a formula provided in the prospectus (see Stated Maturity Bond Schedule in Chapter 10). Figure 9.10 illustrates the propensity of the average life of the SMB to shorten, sometimes dramatically, at high prepayment speeds.

FIGURE 9.10
FNMA 1992-68A SMB: Cash Flow Window at 600 PSA

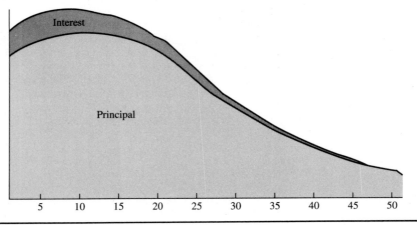

| | | | | | | | | | |
|5|10|15|20|25|30|35|40|45|50|

Source: Bloomberg Financial Markets.

SUPPORT CLASS BONDS[4]

The PAC structure does not reduce or eliminate prepayment risk for the entire CMO issue; rather, it redistributes that risk. Thus, the stability of the PAC bonds is created by transferring the uncertainty of prepayments to the support bonds. Due to volatile and uncertain prepayment rates on most mortgage collateral, the support classes must absorb the prepayment risk so that the PAC bonds can meet their objective. This section examines the dynamic interaction of the PAC and support classes when prepayment rates vary from the pricing speed assumption.

In the CMO structure, the support bonds are created from excess principal after the PAC sinking fund schedule is met, based upon the pricing prepayment assumption. For purposes of analysis, support bonds may be divided into three classes: those intended to support relatively short-term PACs, those supporting intermediate-

---

[4]This discussion of support class bonds was provided by Kevin McDermott, Vice President, CMO Trading Desk, Lehman Brothers. Mr. McDermott is now with Nomura Securities, New York.

TABLE 9.14
Factors Influencing Support Volatility

Factor	Comment
1. Percentage of PACs in deal structure	Positive correlation with volatility; with more PACs, greater volatility of supports
2. Size of support versus total remaining supports	Generally, volatility decreases if remaining supports are large
3. Average-life base case	Short supports—extension risk Intermediate—both call and extension risk Long supports—call risk
4. Stablizing deal structure features: Lockouts Z	Special structuring features can reduce volatility
5. Collateral	Discount collateral generally lowers average-life volatility

Source: Lisa A. Brown, Vice President, First Union Securities, Charlotte, NC. Presented at Infoline Mortgage-Backed Securities Seminar, New York, April 1991.

term PACs, and those supporting long-term PACs. Support class bonds are all volatile, but *under conditions of little rate fluctuation (low volatility) or when purchased at deep discounts, they can outperform the PACs.*

Table 9.14 provides key points relating the performance of support class bonds to prepayment volatility. The primary risk on the short-term support bonds is *extension risk*—that is, that the pay-out will stretch out and the investor will not get the principal back as soon as expected. Extension risk of the support class may be limited if the related PAC has lockout provisions. Also, adding a Z-bond can reduce the extension risk on the PAC supports.

With the intermediate-term support bonds, there is both extension risk and call risk; prepayments might cause the bonds to be paid off before the investor expects, as well as after. Discount collateral may help prevent early prepayment; and, where prepayment takes place, the investor gets the discount back early, thus increasing the realized return.

For long-term support bonds, extension risk is not a problem. Rather, it is call risk that the investor must take into account. Here, buying bonds based on the discount collateral may help, just as it may for intermediate support bonds.

TABLE 9.15
Structure of PAC CMO: FNMA REMIC 1988-13; Pricing Date, 4-27-88; Pricing Speed, 165 PSA; Collateral, FNMA 9.5; 10.25 Percent WAC, 28.9-Year WAM

Bond Class	Tranche Size ($ millions)	Bond Type	Stated Maturity	Average Life (Years)	Projected Maturity
13-A	93.00		11/25/11	3.3	7/96
13-B	75.50	PAC	8/25/12	3.4	7/94
13-C	80.25	PAC	5/25/18	10.8	5/90
13-D	36.25		1/25/35	10.8	6/01
13-Z	15.00	Z	5/25/18	19.9	4/17
Total	300.00				

Source: Lehman Brothers Fixed Income Research.

Table 9.15 gives the structure of an actual PAC CMO—FNMA REMIC 1988–13. This CMO is collateralized by FNMA 9.5s and contains two PAC bonds with protection ranges from 75 to 300 PSA (classes 13-B and 13-C). To support these PAC bonds the issue contains three support classes: 13-A, 13-D, and 13-Z. At the new-issue pricing speed of 165 PSA, the PAC bonds pay off concurrently with the support bonds.

Class 13-A in Table 9.15 has a short average life (3.3 years) with a final projected maturity in year 9. Class 13-D has an intermediate average life (10.8 years) with a first projected payment in year 9 and a projected maturity in year 14. Class 13-Z has a long average life (19.9 years) with the first payment projected for year 14.

Figure 9.11 illustrates the principal distribution of the FNMA 1988–13. At 75 PSA, the pattern of the principal return for the support bonds shifts, as shown in Figure 9.12. As expected, the scheduled sinking fund for the PAC bonds is unchanged, but the support bonds absorb the effect of slow prepayments by extending. The average life of class 13-A more than triples, from 3.3 years to 11 years, and its final projected principal payment occurs in year 17 instead of year 9. Class 13-D lengthens from an intermediate average life to 16.8 years with a final projected maturity of 19 years. Class 13-Z remains a long-average-life security, lengthening by more than 3 years to a 23.3-year average life with the first projected payment in year 19.

FIGURE 9.11
Principal Cash Flows: FNMA 1988-13, 165 PSA

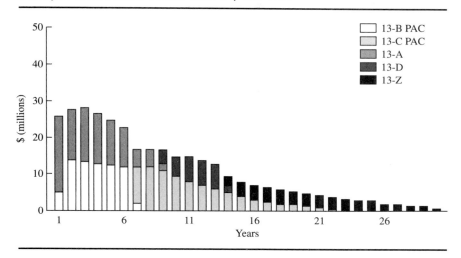

Source: Lehman Brothers Fixed Income Research.

FIGURE 9.12
Principal Cash Flows: FNMA 1988-13, 75 PSA

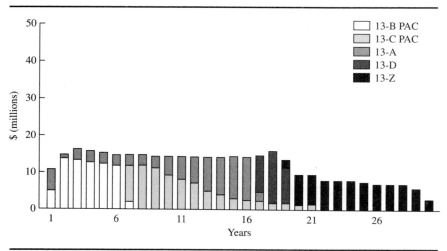

Source: Lehman Brothers Fixed Income Research.

FIGURE 9.13
Principal Cash Flows: FNMA 1988-13, 300 PSA

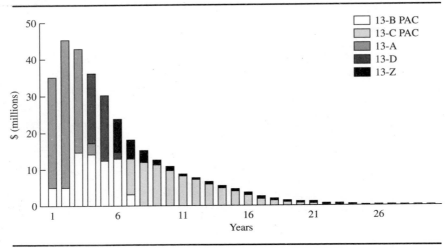

Source: Lehman Brothers Fixed Income Research.

On the other hand, in a high-prepayment-rate environment of 300 PSA, the brunt of the prepayment risk is absorbed by the long and intermediate support classes (Figure 9.13, classes 13-D and 13-Z). The PAC sinking fund schedule remains intact at 300 PSA, but this call protection is achieved at the expense of the severely shortened average lives of the support classes. Class 13-A shortens from 3.3 years to 1.4 years. Class 13-D shortens from a 10.8-year average life to 3.6 years with a projected maturity of 4.6 years. Class 13-Z shortens from 19.9 years to 8.8 years with the first projected payment in 4.6 years.

The severe call risk associated with the intermediate and long support bond classes casts a dark cloud over these bonds, but investors may find a silver lining in this extreme shortening effect: They are purchasing bonds priced to a discount, which results in a higher realized yield when prepayments accelerate. Investors who believe prepayment rates are increasing are more likely to buy the bonds at a deep discount; then, if the principal is returned much earlier than projected, they realize a significant yield gain. The deeper the discount, the greater the possible reward to the investor.

A number of structural modifications may be utilized to mitigate the prepayment volatility of support class bonds:

1. The interjection of a 2- to 3-year lockout on the first PAC class directs all collateral principal payments made during the lockout period to the support class. (For a further description of the lockout and its impact on the PAC structure, see Chapter 7.)

2. The band range may be narrowed. Raising the lower band to a higher PSA level increases the collateral principal available for the early support class. Lowering the upper band increases the principal cash flow available for intermediate to longer-dated support classes.

3. The back-end cash flows (tail) of the PAC schedule may be paid to the longer-dated support classes. In addition, some of the stable cash flows from a PAC can be redirected to specific support classes. When PAC cash flows are so directed they are referred to as a **component**.

4. Z-bond accruals may be directed to stabilize specific support bonds. Furthermore, if prepayments slow down, the Z-bond extends, thus generating more accrual to stabilize the support class for which the Z is the beneficiary. The addition of the Z accruals also helps to stabilize the window drift of the support bonds.

5. The spread risk to the support class holder may be reduced by lowering the coupon of supports exhibiting call risk, thus pricing the bond to a discount; the investor is thereby compensated with an increase in realized yield if prepayments accelerate. Conversely, if the coupon is increased for a support bond bearing extension risk, the support will be priced to a premium, and the support bond investor will realize a higher yield if the support extends.

Table 9.16A outlines the deal structure of the FNMA 1990 28 REMIC offering. It includes six PAC bonds, two support classes, a residual, and—note in particular—five Z-bond classes. The presence of such a generous allocation of Z-bonds lends substantial backing to the support classes. With such a structure there is creation of what is often described as a stabilized support class.

The average-life sensitivity of the 1990 28-G support class is shown in Table 9.16B for static prepayment scenarios ranging from 75 to 225 PSA. Note the average-life drift is fairly moderate for a support class, ranging from 5.8 years in the base case to 13 years at the slow PSA and 1.5 at the fast PSA. The analysis of the variable-

TABLE 9.16A

CMO Bond Summary, FNMA 1990 28 REMIC; Collateral, FNMA 9 Percent MBS; PSA, 160

Bond Class	Bond Type	Original Size ($ Thousands)	Coupon	Stated Maturity	Average Life (Years)	Variable Scenario Interval	PSA
28-A	PAC	50,623	9	7-25-97	0.91	July 92	160
28-B	PAC	30,784	9	2-25-14	2.11	Nov. 92	90
28-C	PAC	46,338	9	4-25-16	3.11	March 93	160
28-D	PAC	68,762	9	9-25-18	4.61	Nov. 93	90
28-E	PAC	53,631	9	3-25-20	6.20	March 94	160
28-T	PAC	10,000	9	3-25-00	7.22	Nov. 94	90
28-U	Z	29,077	9	8-25-07	8.91	March 95	160
28-V	Z	11,395	9	8-25-12	11.61	Nov. 95	90
28-W	Z	9,467	9	1-25-19	15.61	March 96	160
28-X	Z	1,385	9	3-25-20	22.56	Nov. 96	90
28-G	Support	121,372	9	3-25-20	5.88	March 97	160
28-H	Support	24,776	9	9-25-16	13.17	(to life)	
28-Y	Z	16,500	9	3-25-20	0.36		
28-Z	Z	15,500	9	3-25-20	20.23		
28-R	REMIC	10,390	9	3-25-20	0.00		

TABLE 9.16B

Bond Class Price-Sensitivity Analysis FNMA 1990 28-G

Prepay	75 PSA	125 PSA	140 PSA	185 PSA	225 PSA	Variable
Price	99-8	99-8	99-8	99-8	99-8	99-9
Yield	9.21	9.24	9.25	9.27	9.39	9.15
Average life	13.22	6.56	4.97	3.68	1.51	7.13
Window	10.3/15.6	0.1/11.7	0.1/10.4	0.5/9.6	0.2/2.8	0.2/12.3
Yield spread	71	107	131	164	250	101

BOX 9.1
Support Class Axioms

1. The greater the proportion of supports to PACs, the more stable the PACs and the less stable the supports.
2. Short-average-life supports can lengthen (from 2 to 14 years), but have little room to shorten in average life.
3. Long-average-life supports have substantial call risk (a 14-year may shorten to less than 2 years), but have limited extension risk—they are already a long average life.
4. The last support class in a balloon or 15-year structure has virtually no extension risk.

---

prepayment scenario, starting with July 1992 and continuing thereafter, stresses the G support class to 90 PSA in the November–March interval and allows it to return to the 160 PSA pricing speed assumption for the March–November interval. The average life extends only to 7 years, demonstrating that it has quite reasonable extension-risk protection because of the support from the Z-bond accruals. Box 9.1 contains a summary of axioms pertinent to support class bonds.

Support Class Case Studies

The prepayment volatility of CMO support classes may differ dramatically depending on the overall deal structure. Compare the four support classes in Table 9.17—all with short average lives but with dramatically differing sensitivities to prepayments.

Case Study 1
Class 1990 59-H Support Class

The bond summary in Table 9.18 shows there are five PAC classes totaling $131.25 million, a PAC II of about $30 million, two support classes totaling $124.7 million, and a $7.5 million Z class. The points to note in this structure are:

TABLE 9.17
Comparative Support Class Structures

Case Study	Deal	Class	Coupon (%)	Collateral	Pricing	Curve Point	Spread (bp)
1	FNMA 1990-59	H	10.00	FNMA 10	185	3-year	+135
2	FHLMC 57	A	9.50	FHLMC 9.5	165	3-year	+110
3	FHMA 1989-59	H	9.25	FNMA 9.5-59	165	4-year	+127
4	FHLMC 191	I	9.50	FHLMC 10	185	3-year	+105

1. The 1990 59-H support is a quite large class ($92 million), almost one third of the total deal.
2. The Z class, which can add stability to the support classes, is quite small.
3. The 59-H support has no lockout (as shown by the CMO bond sensitivity analysis in Table 9.19, where the window opens at period 0.1).

TABLE 9.18
$300 Million FNMA 1990 59-H Deal Structure;[a] Collateral, FNMA 10 Percent MBS

Bonds Issued ($ Millions)		Coupon (%)	Type	Average Life (Years)	Spread	Bands
A	15.65	9.6	PAC	4.50	4-year + 80	100–300
B	30.80	9.6	PAC	5.98	5-year + 95	100–300
C	26.40	8.0	PAC	7.98	7-year + 95	100–300
D	37.70	7.0	PAC	10.99	10-year + 100	100–300
E	20.70	7.0	PAC	17.79	30-year + 112	100–300
G	29.99	9.75	PAC II	3.46	3-year + 83	125–225
H	92.00	10.0	Support	3.46	3-year + 138	
J	32.70	10.0	Support	12.26	10-year + 150	
Z	7.54	10.0	Z	20.92	30-year + 203	

[a]Residual classes totaling $6.52 million.

The sensitivities of the 1990 59-H (Table 9.19) show:

1. The total average-life drift is 11.75 years from 12.27 (slow prepay) to 1.52 (fast prepay), so the bond displays substantial extension and call risk. From the base case 3.14-year average life to the 75 PSA scenario it extends 9.13 years to 12.27 years; at the 350 PSA scenario it shortens 1.62 years, from 3.14 to 1.52 years. On balance, then, this bond has considerable extension risk but limited call risk.
2. The realized yield spread declines in both the slow- and fast-prepay scenarios, so it displays severe negative convexity.
3. The enticement of a relatively wide-stated yield spread (135 basis points to the 3-year Treasury) will not be realized in the event of any significant interest rate volatility. Therefore, this bond is not a good candidate for total-return investors.

TABLE 9.19

Prepayment-Sensitivity Analysis, FNMA 1990 59-H, 10 Percent 7/25/20; Support Class Priced at 100 14/32

Yield curve shift	+300	+200	+100	Base	−100	−200	−300
PSA	75	125	160	185	200	275	350
Average life	12.27	7.00	4.33	3.14	2.70	1.80	1.52
Window	0.1/19.1	0.1/14.9	0.1/11.6	0.1/8.6	0.1/6.8	0.1/3.4	0.1/2.5
Bp spread	110	112	131	135	130	126	115

Case Study 2
FHLMC 57-A Support Class

The bond structure in Table 9.20 shows there are four PAC classes totaling $117.53 million (29.38 percent). The class A support class also enjoys support from the large class B Z-bond, which pays concurrent with it. Thus, this support has structural characteristics surrounding it that compare favorably to the FNMA 1990 59-H. The principal negative consideration is that the 57-A support is a very large class, representing 43 percent of the total deal—so if prepayments are slow in the early years, the bond will take a long time to pay off.

TABLE 9.20

$400,000 FHLMC R57 Deal Structure;[a] Collateral, FHLMC 9.5 Percent PC

Bonds Issued ($ Millions)		Coupon (%)	Type	Average Life (Years)	Spread	Bands
A	171.395	9.5	Support	3.33	3-year + 110	
B	56.07	9.5	Z/support	3.54	3-year + 122	
C	46.80	9.5	PAC	4.94	5-year + 88	85–340
D	38.95	9.5	PAC	7.95	7-year + 99	80–300
E	26.82	9.5	PAC	10.95	10-year + 110	75–300
F	4.96	9.5	Z/PAC	15.50	15-year + 125	50–300
G	45.00	9.5	Support	20.71	20-year + 100	

[a]Residual class totaling $100 million.

The sensitivities of the FHLMC 57-A (Table 9.21) show:

1. The total average-life drift is 7.76 years from 9.93 (slow prepay) to 1.52 (fast prepay), which is less than the FNMA 1990 59-H.

2. The yield spread declines in the slow-prepayment scenario as it extends on the curve, but widens in the fast-prepay scenario (because it is priced at a discount).

3. This bond could be rewarding for an investor willing to make the risk/reward bet that prepayment speeds are not likely to slow down in the foreseeable future.

TABLE 9.21
Prepayment-Sensitivity Analysis, FHLMC 57-A, 9.5 Percent, 7/15/20; Support Class Priced at 99 20/32

Yield curve shift	+300	+200	+100	Base	−100	−200	−300
PSA	75	103	150	165	185	225	350
Average life	9.93	7.87	3.85	3.17	2.49	1.77	1.52
Window	0.1/17.4	0.1/13.4	0.1/11.4	0.1/10.0	0.1/8.0	0.1/4.7	0.1/2.9
Bp spread	68	92	99	110	123	126	132

Case Study 3
FNMA 1989 52-H Support Class

The bond structure in Table 9.22 shows there are six PAC class bonds totaling $165.14 million for 55 percent of the deal supported by the 52-H, which makes up 29 percent of the total structure.

TABLE 9.22
FNMA 1989 52-H Deal Structure;[a] Collateral, FNMA 9.5 Percent MBSs

	Bonds Issued ($ Millions)	Coupon (%)	Type	Average Life (Years)	Spread
A	26.97	8.70	PAC	1.2	1-year + 75
B	33.88	8.60	PAC	3.4	3-year + 80
C	24.97	8.75	PAC	5.0	5-year + 105
D	29.24	8.95	PAC	7.8	7-year + 115
E	30.59	9.15	PAC	10.9	10-year + 125
G	19.49	6.00	PAC	17.4	20-year + 90
H	86.90	9.25	Support	3.5	3-year + 150
J	40.00				
K					

[a]Residual class totaling $11 million.

The sensitivities for the FNMA 1989 52-H (Table 9.23) show:

1. The total average-life drift is 11.52 years from 12.64 (slow prepay) to 1.12 (fast prepay).
2. The yield spread declines in the slow-prepay scenario (average life extending up the curve), but the spread increases significantly in the fast-prepay scenario (shortens on the curve) because it is priced to a discount.
3. A comparison of the stated yield of the 52-H support (3-year plus 150) and that of the PAC (4-year plus 80) suggests that the support appears to be the cheaper bond. However, at 300 PSA the PAC still realizes a spread of 75 to the 3-year, whereas the support spread has shrunk to 126. Of course, if the investor wants to make a prepayment bet, the support can be a winner—but investing for performance (total return) and making a prepayment bet are not the same thing.

TABLE 9.23

Prepayment-Sensitivity Analysis, FNMA 1989 52-H, 9.25 Percent, 2/25/15; Support Class Priced at 98 9/32

Yield curve shift	+300	+200	+100	Base	−100	−200	−300
PSA	75	125	150	165	185	225	350
Average life	12.64	6.50	4.61	3.76	2.95	2.08	1.12
Window	2.2/17.1	0.1/12.9	0.1/10.6	0.1/9.1	0.1/7.0	0.1/4.6	0.1/2.2
Bp spread	85	111	127	150	181	256	277

Case Study 4
FHLMC 191-I Support Class

The bond structure in Table 9.24 shows there are five PAC classes (counting E1–E8 as one) totaling $137.55 million, or 69 percent of the total. There are two PAC II classes totaling $46 million, which are subordinated to the PAC bond classes. The 191-I is a large ($150.4 million) support class, which, however, is assisted by the two far less stable (J and K class) supports that follow it, as well as by the accruals from the Z.

TABLE 9.24
$400 Million FHLMC 191-I Deal Structure;[a] Collateral, FHLMC 10 Percent PCs

Bonds Issued ($ Millions)	Coupon (%)	Type	Average Life (Years)	Spread	Bands[c]
A	39.795	8.80	PAC	4.50	4-year + 72	90–350
B	19.380	9.20	Z			
C	53.630	8.00	PAC	7.96	7-year + 85	90–310
D	14.580	9.00	PAC	9.65	10-year + 95	90–300
E1–E8[b]	19.550	9.50	PAC	15.00	15-year + 95	90–300
F	10.000	7.00	PAC	21.46	30-year + 100	45–300
G	27.000	9.00	PAC II	11.50	10-year + 125	110–225
H	19.000	9.50	PAC II	21.39	30-year + 150	110–225
I	150.440	9.50	Support	3.09	3-year + 105	
J	10.000	9.00	Support	3.09	3-year + 210	
K	10.000	10.00	Support	3.09		
L	10.000	9.50	Support	10.07	10-year + 150	
Z	8.000	9.50	Z	19.93	30-year + 215	

[a]Residual classes totaling $8.815 million.
[b]The E1 through E8 classes are referred to as PAC CABs.
[c]Note the effective bands decline as the bond maturities increase.

Base Case PSA 185

Note from the information in Table 9.25 that the total average-life drift is 8.05 years, and the structure enjoys reasonable stability in the fast-prepay scenario, but carries 7 years of extension risk from the base case 3.07 years to 10.18 years at the 75 PSA prepayment speed.

TABLE 9.25
Prepayment-Sensitivity Analysis, FHLMC 191-I 9.5 Percent; 9/15/21; Support Class Priced at 99 25/32

Yield curve shift	+300	+200	+100	Base	−100	−200	−300
PSA	75	125	160	185	200	275	350
Average life	10.18	5.20	3.15	3.07	3.06	2.43	2.13
Window	0.1/20.9	0.1/15.6	0.1/9.9	0.1/9.0	0.1/8.6	0.1/4.0	0.1/3.3
Bp spread	65	88	105	105	105	117	114

Scenario-Sensitivity Analysis

Because support bonds are very prepayment sensitive, the standard static scenario analysis portrays them in a worst-case—and certainly unrealistic—risk/reward profile. For investors able and will-

TABLE 9.26
Sensitivity Analysis, 10-Year Support Class

FNMA 1989 52-J	*FNMA 1989 37-J*
FNMA 9.5s	FNMA 9.5s
WAC 10.15 percent	WAC 10.23 percent
WAM 11/17	WAM 4/18
Six PACs in deal	Six PACs in deal
No TAC in deal	TAC bond in deal
	(more of the deal principal is scheduled)
Support Z in deal	Clean Z in deal
	10-year support is primary support piece

Source: Lisa A. Brown, Vice President, First Union Securities, Charlotte, NC. Based on a presentation on CMOs, New York, March 1991.

ing to take a fair amount of prepayment risk, *it is worthwhile to look at several different interest rate scenarios before investing,* with the specific characteristics of all the securities in the pool in mind.

There are *dangers in considering only static sensitivity analysis,* particularly when evaluating support classes. Two different PAC support bonds may look quite similar on the assumption that prepayment speeds will immediately move to an interest rate level and remain there for the life of the bond. A dynamic sensitivity analysis is considerably more enlightening.

Lisa Brown, vice president of First Union Securities, constructed an instructive dynamic sensitivity analysis (also referred to as vector analysis) consisting of two tables, with each table covering the same two securities. Table 9.27, which follows the collateral description in Table 9.26, describes what happens to the two 10-year PAC support bonds assuming the PSA immediately rises or drops to a given level and stays there. Table 9.28 describes what happens if the prepayment rises to 490 PSA for one year and then drops to levels between zero and 275 PSA.

Table 9.26 summarizes the key structural differences between the FNMA 1989 52-J and FNMA 1989 37-J REMICs, both deals containing a 10-year-average-life support class bond.

Note that whereas the bonds look fairly similar when prepayment rates immediately go to a static PSA speed and remain there, they look quite different in Table 9.28, where they soar for a year and then drop. A prospective investor who looks only at the "static analysis" contained in Table 9.27 will miss the impact of prepayment volatility.

TABLE 9.27
Static Yield/WAL Analysis

	PSA	0	50	75	100	135	165	275	475
				FNMA 1989 52-J 10-Year Support					
	Yield	9.643	9.653	9.660	9.670	9.689	9.714	9.993	10.707
+ 170 vs. 10-year	WAL	22.757	19.808	18.139	16.417	13.956	11.755	4.410	1.718
at 135 PSA (97-15	Duration	9.027	8.640	8.366	8.034	7.453	6.799	3.430	1.510
price)									
LOWER PRICE	Beg. pay	12/25/12	7/25/09	7/25/07	6/25/05	7/25/02	10/25/99	12/25/93	4/25/92
	End. pay	7/25/14	2/25/12	9/25/10	4/25/09	4/25/07	7/25/05	8/25/97	4/25/93
			EXTENDS MORE						
				FNMA 1989 37-J 10-Year Support					
	Yield	9.689	9.689	9.689	9.689	9.689	9.698	9.687	9.672
+ 170 vs. 10-year	WAL	20.811	17.439	15.763	14.125	11.858	9.844	3.028	0.483
at 135 PSA (99-12	Duration	8.725	8.193	7.858	7.475	6.836	6.139	2.523	0.452
price)									
CLOSER TO 10-year	Beg. pay	7/25/11	12/25/07	3/25/06	6/25/04	1/25/02	10/25/99	7/25/93	4/25/91
IN BASE CASE	End. pay	2/25/12	12/25/08	5/25/07	10/25/05	9/25/03	11/25/01	8/25/94	10/25/91
							SHORTENS MORE		

WHICH ONE DO I BUY? The static scenario analysis assumes prepayments remain static for the life of the bond. The analysis therefore is muddy, and the risk/reward choice unclear.

Source: Lisa Brown, Vice President, First Union Securities, Charlotte, NC.

TABLE 9.28
Dynamic Analysis (Scenario Analysis)

	PSA	0	50	75	100	135	165	275
		FNMA 1989 52-J 10-Year Support						
490 PSA for 12 months								
Then:	WAL	23.03	19.74	17.92	16.02	13.12	9.88	3.55
	Duration	9.62	9.15	8.82	8.41	7.61	6.36	3.02
	Beg. pay	1/25/12	1/25/08	10/25/05	6/25/03	1/25/99	9/25/94	4/25/92
	End. pay	11/25/13	3/25/11	10/25/09	4/25/08	2/25/06	3/25/04	2/25/95
		FNMA 1989 37-J 10-Year Support						
490 PSA for 12 months								
Then:	WAL	0.3	0.3	0.3	0.3	0.3	0.3	0.3
	Duration	0.29	0.29	0.29	0.29	0.29	0.29	0.29
	Beg. pay	1/25/90	1/25/90	1/25/90	1/25/90	1/25/90	1/25/90	1/25/90
	End. pay	6/25/90	6/25/90	6/25/90	6/25/90	6/25/90	6/25/90	6/25/90

Note: The dynamic sensitivity analysis demonstrates dramatic differences between the bonds when stressed to the shock of a very high 490 PSA for one year, returning thereafter to a lower-volatility interest rate environment. Note the 89 37-J now displays a shorter average life in *all* static scenarios. The key distinction is that, in the 1989 37-J deal structure, the 10-year support class *is* the support, including the TACs, which adds to the total of scheduled principal in the deal structure. In the 1989 52-J deal, the support Z is providing the call protection and does not have the additional burden of providing call protection to the TACs.

Source: Lisa Brown, Vice President, First Union Securities, Charlotte, NC.

The following appendix includes definitions of REMIC and CMO bond forms provided by Freddie Mac. Also included for the benefit of readers who have the Bloomberg analytics with passport is the CMO passport acronym.

APPENDIX

Standard Definitions for REMIC and CMO Bonds

FHLMC Acronym	Unless Otherwise Denoted, the Interest Pay Method is Fixed Coupon	CMO Passport® Acronym[a]
	Principal Pay Types	
AD	Accretion Directed—bonds that pay principal from specified accretions of accrual bonds. ADs may, in addition, receive principal from the collateral paydowns.	AD
COM	Component—bonds comprised of non-detachable components. The principal pay type and/or sequence of principal pay of each component may vary.	C
NSJ	Non-Sticky Jump—bonds whose principal paydown is changed by the occurrence of one or more "triggering" event(s). The first time and each time the trigger condition is met the bond changes to its new priority for receiving principal and reverts to its old priority for each payment date that the trigger condition is not met.	NJ
PAC	Planned Amortization Class—bonds that pay principal based on a predetermined schedule established for a group of PAC bonds. The principal redemption schedule of the PAC group is derived by amortizing the collateral based upon two collateral prepayment speeds. These two speeds are the endpoints for the "structuring PAC range." A PAC group is therefore defined as PAC bonds having the same structuring PAC range. A "group" can be a single bond class. CMO Passport further defines PAC bonds as indicated below:	PAC

FHLMC Acronym	Unless Otherwise Denoted, the Interest Pay Method is Fixed Coupon	CMO Passport® Acronym[a]

Principal Pay Types

PAC	**Sub-types: Pxy** The first number of the sub-type (shown above as 'x') will indicate the relative position in which the bond's PAC group will receive principal up to its PAC schedule(s). The second number (shown above as 'y') will indicate the relative position, starting from the last bond group and moving in reverse order, in which the bond's PAC group will receive principal in excess of the amount stipulated by the PAC schedule. Both numbers will be relative to other PAC and TAC groups in the deal. If no other groups exist then both numbers will be '1'.	PAC
PAC Z RTL	Capital Appreciation Bonds—accrual bonds similar to Z bonds issued with initial principal balances per "unit" of $1,000 or less. Most CAB accretion schedules are derived by discounting $1,000 back over the expected life of the CAB bond at its stated coupon.	CAB
SCH	Scheduled—bonds that pay principal to a set redemption schedule(s), but do not fit the definition of a PAC or TAC.	SCH
SEQ	Sequential Pay—bonds that start to pay principal when classes with an earlier priority have paid to a zero balance. SEQ bonds enjoy uninterrupted payment of principal until paid to a zero balance. SEQ bonds may share principal paydown on a pro rata basis with another class.	SEQ
SJ	Sticky Jump—bonds whose principal paydown is changed by the occurrence of one or more "triggering" events. The first time the trigger condition is met the bond changes to its new priority for receiving principal and remains in its new priority for the life of the bond.	KJ
STP	Pro rata Principal Strip—bonds that pay principal in some fixed proportion to the aggregate collateral paydowns.	G

FHLMC Acronym	Unless Otherwise Denoted, the Interest Pay Method is Fixed Coupon	CMO Passport® Acronym[a]
SUP	Support—bonds that receive principal payments after scheduled payments have been paid to some or all PAC, TAC and/or SCH bonds for each payment date.	SUP

TAC	Target Amortization Class—bonds that pay principal based upon a predetermined schedule which is derived by amortizing the collateral based on a single prepayment speed.
	
	CMO Passport further defines TAC bonds as indicated below:
	
	Sub-types: Txy
	Each TAC group will be defined uniquely within a deal. The TAC bonds within each TAC group will all carry the same bond type. A group is defined as TAC bonds having the same structuring speed. A "group" can be a single bond class.
	    The first number of the sub-type (shown above as 'x') will indicate the relative position in which the bond's TAC group will receive principal up to its TAC schedule(s).
	    The second number (shown above as 'y') will indicate the relative position, starting from the last bond group and moving in reverse order, in which the bond's TAC group will receive principal in a greater amount than stipulated by the TAC schedule.
	    Both numbers will be relative to other PAC and TAC groups in the deal. If no other groups exist then both numbers will be '1'.
		TAC

XAC	Index Allocation—bonds whose principal paydown is allocated based upon the value of some index.	XAC

Interest Pay Types

ARB	Ascending Rate Bonds—bonds that have predetermined coupon rates which take effect one or more times on dates set forth at issuance.	ARB
EXE	Excess—bonds which are entitled to collateral principal and interest paid which exceeds the amount of principal and interest obligated to all bonds in the deal.	E

FHLMC Acronym	Unless Otherwise Denoted, the Interest Pay Method is Fixed Coupon	CMO Passport® Acronym[a]
FIX	Fixed—bonds whose coupons are fixed throughout the life of the bond.	FIX
FLT	Floater—bonds whose coupons reset periodically based on an index and may have a cap and/or floor. The coupon varies directly with changes in the index.	F
INV	Inverse Floater—bonds whose coupons reset periodically (like Floaters) based on an index and may have a cap and/or floor. The coupon varies inversely with changes in the index.	I
IO	Interest Only—bonds that receive some or all of the interest portion of the underlying collateral and little or no principal. IO bonds have either a notional or nominal amount of principal. A notional amount is the amount of principal used as a reference to calculate the amount of interest due. A nominal amount is actual principal that will be paid to the bond. It is referred to as nominal since it is extremely small compared to other classes.	IO
PO	Principal Only—bonds that do not receive any interest.	PO
PZ	Partial Accrual—bonds that accrete interest (which is added to the outstanding principal balance) and receive interest distributions in the same period. These bonds have a stated coupon which is equal to the sum of the accretion coupon and interest distribution coupon.	AZ
W	WAC coupon—bonds whose coupons represent a blended interest rate which may change in any period. Bonds may be comprised of non-detachable components some of which have different coupons.	W
Z	Accrual—bonds that accrete interest which is added to the outstanding principal balance. This accretion may continue until the bond begins paying principal or until some other event has occurred.	Z

FHLMC Acronym	*Unless Otherwise Denoted, the Interest Pay Method is Fixed Coupon*	*CMO Passport® Acronym[a]*
	Other Types	
L	Retail—a separate and unique field on each system indicates that a bond is a retail bond. Retail bonds are bonds designated to be sold To retail investors.	*
LIQ	Liquidity—bonds intended to qualify as a "liquid asset" for savings institutions. LQ bonds are any agency issued bonds that have a stated maturity of 5 years (or less), or any non-agency issued bonds that have a stated maturity of 3 years (or less), in each case from issue date.	LQ
R,RS, RL	Residual—bond that is designated for tax purposes as the residual interest in a REMIC.	R
TBD	To Be Defined—bonds that do not fit under any of the current definitions.	TBD

[a]CMO Passport is a registered trademark of Merrill Lynch Mortgage Capital Inc.

Source: Freddie Mac.

CHAPTER 10

CMO STRUCTURING
CONSIDERATIONS

BASIC CMO STRUCTURES

A REMIC structure[1] is keyed to the levels of PAC bonds included in the deal:

1. Zero levels of PACs are a sequential deal (Figure 10.1).
2. One level of PAC is a simple PAC deal with stable support bonds (Figure 10.2).
3. Two levels of PACs are a PAC/PAC II/support structure (Figure 10.3), and so on.

Each level[2] in the structure may be thought of as a miniature CMO, ready to be tranched into sequential-pay and parallel-pay bonds. Structures with several classes are not necessarily more difficult to understand if they are conceptualized in terms of cash flow levels and tranching within levels.

Stability and Volatility of Classes

The benchmark of stability is the sequential-pay bond structure, which has roughly the same prepayment stability as the MBS collateral itself.

---

[1] This discussion of REMIC structures is based on a series of seminars on REMIC deal structuring presented by Laurence Penn, Senior Vice President, Manager, MBS Derivatives Desk, Lehman Brothers.

[2] The levels are segregated by their position in the priority of principal cash flow distribution—for example, scheduled cash flows (PACs) versus support cash flows.

FIGURE 10.1
Basic Sequential Structure

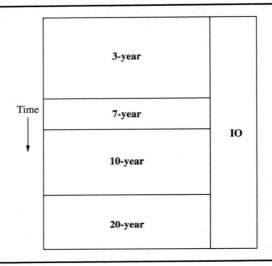

Source: Lehman Brothers Fixed Income Research.

FIGURE 10.2
Basic PAC/Support Structure

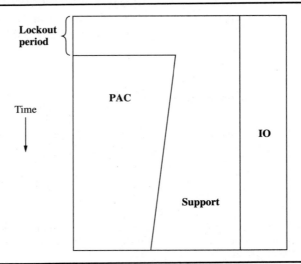

Source: Lehman Brothers Fixed Income Research.

FIGURE 10.3
PAC/PAC II/Support

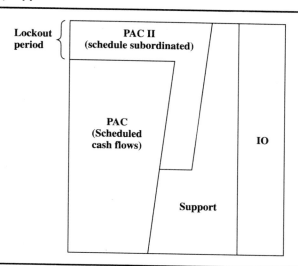

Source: Lehman Brothers Fixed Income Research.

Hierarchy of Cash Flow Priorities

- With a PAC structure stability is provided by the PAC pre-payment-protection bands (wider is more stable).
- With a PAC II structure stability is provided by PAC II bands (wider is more stable) and by the percentage of PACs in the deal relative to the percentage of support bonds. The lower the percentage of level-one PACs, the more stable the PAC IIs, since fewer bonds with scheduled cash flows have priority over the PAC IIs. Finally, stability is provided by a lockout on the PACs because during the lockout period PAC IIs are not competing for cash flow with the level-one PACs.
- With support class bonds prepayment volatility is influenced by the percentage of higher-priority bond classes that have scheduled cash flows (for example, PACs and PAC IIs). The greater the percentage of support class bonds, the more stable will be the PACs.

Typical percentages of PAC (I and II) scheduled cash flows to support classes are 60 to 70 percent PACs to 30 to 40 percent supports with 30-year collateral and 70 to 80 percent PACs to 20 to 30 percent supports with 15-year collateral (since 15-year collateral has less extension risk, support requirements are less; see Collateral Features of 15-Year MBSs in Chapter 8). Z-bonds also provide stability. This stability may be directed to any desired classes in the deal, but it is usually directed to ADs, PAC IIs, and supports (since sequential classes and PACs are already stable enough). However, if less stable forms of the Z-bonds (such as support Zs or jump Zs) are employed, the stability of the deal structure may be jeopardized (see Z-Bond Impact on CMO Structure in Chapter 9).

THE CMO DEAL STRUCTURE

The basic CMO arbitrage structuring process consists of the following four steps:

1. Start with a block of potential MBSs or mortgage collateral, which it is to be hoped may be accumulated in size. Estimate as accurately as possible the WAM of what will ultimately be delivered.

2. Model a few basic structures with the collateral, creating generic classes that are widely distributable:

   a. Simple sequential-pay (3-, 7-, 10-, and 20-year-average-life) interest-bearing bonds (Figure 10.4).

   b. A simple PAC structure (3-, 4-, 5-, 7-, 10-, and 20-year-average-life PACs with salable PAC bonds and 3-, 7-, 10-, and 20-year support bonds; Figure 10.5). The PAC structure is created in two steps: First, separate the cash flows into two levels of principal-distribution priority—for example, PAC and support bond classes. Second, carve each level of cash flows sequentially. Each of these structures may also have some IO if it is necessary to strip the collateral coupon to create lower coupons for the CMO bond classes.

3. Estimate market-required yield spreads on these generic classes, and, using current Treasury and collateral prices, determine the economics of the simple deal structure. *At this point, the arbitrage will almost always be negative* (even if the arbitrage is slightly positive, it may be smaller than a reasonable bid/offer spread). If the arbitrage is positive, it is

FIGURE 10.4
Sequential-Pay Structure

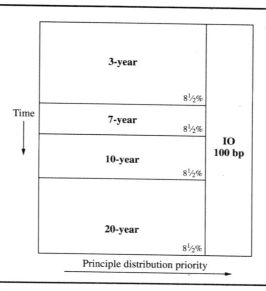

Source: Lehman Brothers Fixed Income Research.

easy to print an arb CMO and sell these simple, liquid bonds. Therefore, the target collateral is typically bid up to a level at which the arb disappears *in this structure*. Nevertheless, if the arb is positive from time to time and one moves quickly, a deal may be created with this simple structure at market levels.

4. Choose one of the basic structures. If the generic arbitrage is negative, which is usually the case, there are basically only two ways of creating arbitrage:

   a. If possible, sell some of these generic classes at rich, through-the-market levels.

   b. Start the process of carving. Carving involves splitting a bond class into two pieces and selling the pieces for more than the market value of the original underlying class. *The pieces are not necessarily sold at rich levels; in fact, they may even be sold at cheap levels. The point is that the market is more receptive to the way individual pieces may*

FIGURE 10.5
Simple PAC Structure Fully Tranched

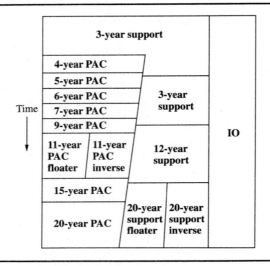

Source: Lehman Brothers Fixed Income Research.

> *have redistributed the risk of the prepayment option as it exists in the original structure.*

As orders are garnered either on generic classes at through-the-market levels or on efficiently carved subpieces, the arbitrage in the deal should start to improve. If the basic arbitrage on the generic structure is very negative, increasing it to positive levels will probably be impossible, even with rich orders or carving. However, if the basic structure is only slightly out of the money, such orders may bring the structure into the money.

DEAL CARVING

Examples

1. *Premium discount structure.* A 9 percent, 20-year PAC with good bands backed by FNMA 9s sells at a spread of 30-year + 117. However, one can split this class into a 7 percent

FIGURE 10.6
Carving Discount PAC plus IO from Full-Coupon PAC Bond

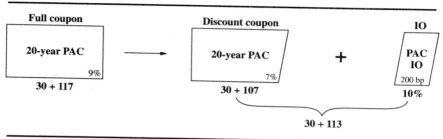

Source: Lehman Brothers Fixed Income Research.

PAC together with a Z PAC IO.[3] Figure 10.6 illustrates this type of deal carving. The 7 percent PAC sells at a spread of 30-year + 113, for a price pickup of over a quarter point on the total class. It is hard to argue that any one of these three securities is relatively rich or cheap, since each is part of a well-developed market (PACs and PAC IOs), but the subpiece execution is definitely more efficient.

2. *Alternative premium/discount structure.* Strip 50 basis points off 9 percent collateral providing 8.5 percent bonds. The premium/discount structure is created by reallocating the distribution of principal and interest as shown in Figure 10.7, D-1 and D-2.

The IOette is generally used to strip the collateral coupon to lower coupon bonds, as shown in Figure 10.8. As shown in the figure, 50 basis points is stripped from 9.5 percent collateral, leaving 9 percent for the bond coupons.

The coupon-stripping process may be carried further to strip a small IO off a particular bond class or several bond classes. Such a strip is called a *bond IO*. If the bond being stripped is a PAC bond class, it will be called a PAC IO. In the latter case the IO carries the PAC prepayment-protection band with it, creating an IO with call

---

[3]IOettes, bond IOs, and PAC IOs are discussed in more detail in Chapter 14. In summary, an IOette is a strip off the entire block of collateral; a bond IO is a strip off one or more specific bond classes; and a PAC IO is a strip off a PAC bond class.

FIGURE 10.7
Premium/Discount Structure

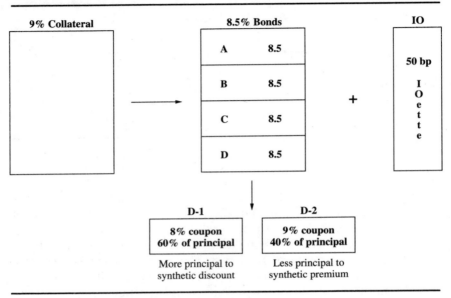

Source: Lehman Brothers Fixed Income Research.

protection! Figure 10.9 illustrates the creation of 7 percent and 7.25 percent coupon PAC bonds by stripping 100 basis points off two PACs among a series of 8 percent coupon PACs. The 8 percent PAC coupons were created by stripping a 100 basis points IOette from a block of 9 percent FNMA MBSs.

The cost (or pickup) of yield spread in a bond class resulting from coupon-stripping is a function of the yield required to market the IO being stripped: If the IO requires a much higher marketing yield (i.e., is much cheaper) than the underlying bond, then the stripped bond must be created much richer than the original full coupon in order to preserve economics. PAC IOs and IOettes are the two most common forms of CMO derivative IOs.[4] Since IOettes are typically marketed at a higher yield than PAC IOs,[5] it costs

---

[4]The bulk of the IO strip market is the Fannie Mae Trusts (see Chapter 14).

[5]The PAC IO may be sold richer than the IOette because the PAC IO carries with it the PAC prepayment-protection band.

FIGURE 10.8
PAC Bond Structure with IOette Stripped from 9.5% Collateral

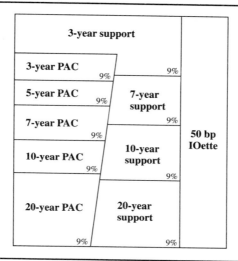

Source: Lehman Brothers Fixed Income Research.

more to strip coupons on clean sequential bonds than on PAC bonds. Thus, for 10-year PACs, a coupon stripped down 50 basis points may be produced 3 basis points richer, but a 10-year (clean) sequential bond stripped down 50 basis points may be produced 5 basis points richer.

3. *Z/AD bond structure.* An 8.5 percent, 20-year, interest-bearing, sequential-pay class sells at a yield of the 30-year Treasury plus 130 basis points. However, one can split this class into a 20-year Z-bond and a series of ADs (Figure 10.10; see AD Bonds in Chapter 9 for a description of AD and SMB bond classes). The 20-year Z-bond starts with a smaller balance (it will accrete up to the size of the 20-year interest-bearing bond). A good way to think of the Z is that it is getting positive interest payments but *negative principal payments;* therefore, the total cash flow to the bond is zero while it is accreting (see Z-Bond Forms in Chapter 9).

FIGURE 10.9
Creation of Bond IO from 8 Percent PAC Bond

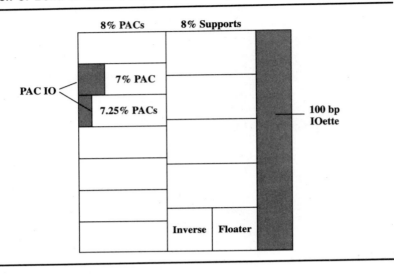

Source: Lehman Brothers Fixed Income Research.

FIGURE 10.10
Carving Z-Bond plus AD Bond from Interest-Bearing Bond

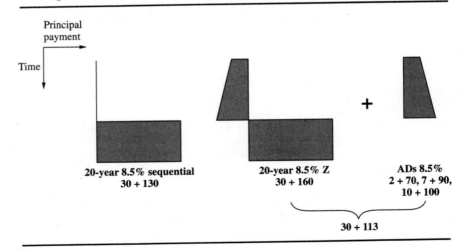

Source: Lehman Brothers Fixed Income Research.

Selling the 20-year Z-bond at the 30-year Treasury plus 160 basis points and selling the 9-year ADs at the 10-year plus 84 basis points provides an execution equivalent to the 30-year plus 117 basis points on the interest-bearing 20-year bond, for a savings of 13 basis points (which equates to well over a point in higher price!). Actually, the 9-year AD at the 10-year plus 84 basis points is further carved sequentially into a 2-year, 7-year, and 12-year AD at yield spreads of 2-year plus 70, 7-year plus 90, and 10-year plus 100, respectively.

4. *Floater/inverse structure.* Assume that a $40 million, 20-year, interest-bearing, support class bond with a 9 percent coupon trades at a 9.76 percent yield for a dollar price of $95. One can split this class into $30 million of a floating-rate class at 1-month LIBOR plus 80 basis points with a 12 percent cap, together with $10 million of an inverse floater (Figure 10.11; for a discussion of floating and inverse-floating CMO bond classes, see Chapter 12).

The formula for the inverse floater is 33.6 − 3 × 1-month LIBOR (with a zero percent floor). If one can sell the floater at par and the inverse at $84 for a yield of 15.65 percent (assuming 1-month LIBOR at 7 percent), then the 20-year, 9 percent support bond will have been sold at an effective price of $96, for a 1-point arbitrage (about 12 basis points of yield on the total bond class).

5. *Reallocation of cash flows.* We can carve out more and less volatile cash flows into other bond classes. For example, we can split a moderately volatile support class bond into a

FIGURE 10.11

Carving a Floater/Inverse Floater from a 20-Year Interest-Bearing Support Bond

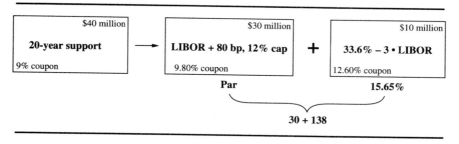

Source: Lehman Brothers Fixed Income Research.

more stable bond together with a more volatile support bond. A typical example is PAC II bonds, which are carved out of the support class bonds of a deal, leaving the more volatile support class bonds alongside the PAC IIs.

6. *Component bond structure.* The more stable cash flows of the PAC I, or the accretion from the Z-bond, may be combined with support class cash flows to stabilize the support bond, thus reducing the market yield required to market the supports. Such combining of cash flows from one category (scheduled cash flows) to the other (support cash flows) results in the creation of a **component bond** (see Figures 10.12A and 10.12B).

Figure 10.12A provides a diagram of the deal structure of the FHLMC 1164 REMIC deal. The K class is a component bond consisting of a portion of the PAC class cash flows (K-1), which have also been apportioned to the F class as K-5 and to the TAC cash flows as K-3. Figure 10.12B shows how the component cash flows form a barbell pattern as they are redistributed across the deal structure.

Yield Curve Impact on Deal Structure

A common misperception is that the main provider of CMO arbitrage is the steepness of the yield curve and that whenever the yield curve is steep it is advantageous to carve up collateral sequentially. Historically, the volume of CMO issuance has had very little correlation with the shape of the yield curve; in fact, even as the yield curve was flat to inverted through 1989 and the first half of 1990, CMO issuance remained at a relatively high level. Whereas a steepening of the yield curve may lead to a temporary spurt of deals, collateral spreads will quickly readjust as the first few arb CMOs are printed, after which arbitrage will have to be extracted the hard way again—through carving.

Nevertheless, the slope of the yield curve does have an impact on the yield spreads at which CMO bonds with various principal-payment windows may be produced on an arbitrage basis. For example, a $100 million, 3-year, 8 percent coupon paying over a 7-year period may be priced at the 3-year plus 100. If we carve this bond sequentially into $43 million of a 1-year bond with a 3-year window, $14 million of a 3-year bond with a 1-year window, and

FIGURE 10.12A
FHLMC 1164 Deal Structure

FRIO									
Floater N									
IOette O									
A	B	C	D	E	K–5	G	H	J–2	L
J–I									
K–L					F			K–3	M
PAC IO I								R	
								RS	
PACs								TAC	Supports

Source: Lehman Brothers Fixed Income Research.

$43 million of a 5-year bond with a 3-year window and price the
pieces at 2-year plus 75, 3-year plus 105, and 5-year plus 120, then
the resulting execution is equivalent to a 3-year plus 123, or a
give-up of 13 basis points in yield spread, which equates to a loss of

FIGURE 10.12B
Component Bond Cash Flows

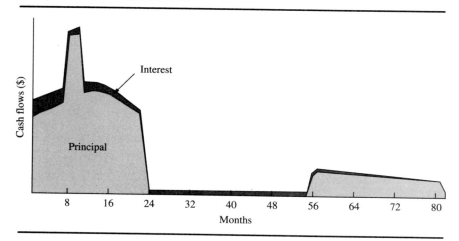

Source: Lehman Brothers Fixed Income Research.

about 3/8 of a point in price. Thus, it often *costs* to carve sequentially and tighten windows. In a steep yield curve environment, and for a given average life, narrow-window bonds must generally be created at much tighter spreads than their wide-window counterparts in order to preserve deal-making economics.

THE STEPS IN STRUCTURING THE FHLMC 182: A CASE STUDY[6]

This case study examines the structuring process of a specific REMIC transaction, the FHLMC REMIC 182 deal. Table 10.1 summarizes the deal structure.

Figure 10.13 illustrates the relative positioning of the bonds at the pricing speed assumption of 185 PSA. Note there is a 3-year lockout on the PACs to stabilize the support class bonds. The normal diagram positioning of PAC cash flows to the left and supports to the right is reversed to reflect the relationship between the PAC IO and the PACs. Note the PAC IO in this case is a strip off all the PAC bonds.

The following steps are involved in the structuring process:

1. We know that we will have trouble marketing intermediate-maturity support class bonds if they are created with dollar prices too close to par. Accordingly, we first strip 60 basis points of interest off the 10 percent coupon of the Freddie Mac PC collateral, leaving 9.40 percent coupons available to the CMO bonds. The 60 basis points stripped create an IO class (in this case the IO is an IOette). This IO class is critically important to the deal, since without it we would have unsalable 10 percent coupon, intermediate support bonds; it becomes our "hurdle" class, which we must be able to place in order to execute the deal.

At this point, we have carved out only class Q, the IO class (see the deal summary). As we market this IO, we find that we can sell this class to a particular buyer in a *combination trade* with 10-year Z-bonds structured within the same deal. Since we are doing a PAC

---

[6]The FHLMC 182 case study was prepared by Laurence Penn.

TABLE 10.1

FHLMC REMIC 182, $400,250,000 PAC Bond Structure; Collateral, FHLMC 10 Percent PCs; WAC 10.70, WAM 350 Months; PAC Bands 100–300 at 185 PSA

Bond Class	Description	Amount ($)	Coupon (%)	Average Life (Years)	Treasury (Tsy. bp)	Price	Effective Bands (PSA)
182-A	PAC	15,000	9.00	1.59	2 + 50	99.856	0–490
182-B	PAC	21,520	9.00	3.48	3 + 68	99.52	100–360
182-C	PAC Z	15,430	9.40	4.24	4 + 85	100.33	100–310
182-D	PAC Z	25,666	9.40	5.49	5 + 97	100.187	100–320
182-E	PAC	55,450	8.00	7.68	7 + 93	92.45	100–300
182-F[a]	PAC Z	4,646	9.40[b]	9.35	10 + 125	98.04	100–300
182-G	PAC CAB	11,776	9.40[b]	10.06	10 + 114	38.875	NA
182-H	PAC	24,300	7.00	11.52	10 + 99	83.34	100–300
182-I	PAC CAB	5,163	9.40[b]	13.06	10 + 115	29.31	NA
182-J	PAC CAB	5,662	9.40[b]	13.81	10 + 115	27.31	NA
182-K	PAC	25,100	7.00	18.24	30 + 100	79.12	75–300
182-L	TAC	118,500	9.40	2.48	2 + 97	99.77	195
182-M	Support	29,300	9.40	5.84	5 + 138	98.25	NA
182-N	TAC	18,700	9.40	10.65	10 + 149	96.875	250
182-O	TAC Z	19,000	9.40[b]	11.68	10 + 170	93.52	250
182-P	Support Z	11,000	9.40[b]	20.95	30 + 205	84.87	NA
182-Q	IO	250	970.00[c]	8.50	10 + 368	4401.65[d]	NA
182-S	PAC IO	200	1063.39[c]	11.42	30 + 205	6640.42[d]	100–300
182-R	Residual	8,400	9.40	0.42	2 + 815	96.56	NA

[a]Structured as a "total-return" bond.
[b]Accrual rate until interest paying.
[c]Since the IO has a nominal principal balance it carries a super premium "coupon."
[d]Since the "coupon" is high on a de-minimus (minimal) balance, the price is expressed as a 4-digit number.

Source: Freddie Mac.

FIGURE 10.13
FHLMC REMIC 182, Cash Flow Structure at 185 PSA

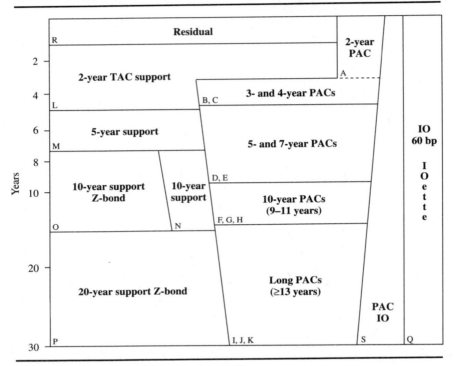

Source: Lehman Brothers Fixed Income Research.

structure, the only Z-bonds we can create are support Z-bonds or PAC Z-bonds. It turns out the 10-year support Z-bonds have too much duration drift for the combination, whereas PAC Z-bonds do not offer enough yield to meet market requirements. However, a *combination* of 10-year PAC Z-bonds and 10-year support class Z-bonds, together with the IO class, produces a yield/duration profile that attracts a specific buyer to produce an order to buy the combination. Therefore, we proceed to structure the deal around this order, which ultimately is filled in the form of class F (PAC Z), half of class O (support Z), and class Q (IO).

2. The next step is to create PAC and support bonds from our new "raw material" of 9.40 percent bonds. We choose 100 PSA and 300 PSA as appropriate lower and upper bands for

PACs backed by FHLMC 10s. We also structure the PACs to begin paying after three years (the lockout), since this structure helps to stabilize the support classes, which may have first priority on the cash flow for the first three years. (Don't be confused that we also have a 2-year PAC in the deal, class A, which pays for the first three years; how this is created will become apparent later.) These bands and lockouts produce $195 million of PAC bonds (which start paying principal after three years) and $205 million of support bonds.

3. We now begin tranching the PAC bonds and companion bonds separately. On the PAC side, we know that we have orders for 4- and 5-year PAC Z-bonds from one particular customer; we have demand from retail for PAC Z-bonds (PAC CABs) as zero coupon bond substitutes in the 10- to 13-year area; we have demand for long-discount PACs; and, finally, we have to structure a 10-year PAC Z for the combination trade. We thus carve out, in succession, class B (3-year PAC), class C (4-year PAC Z), class D (5-year PAC Z), class E (7-year PAC), class F (10-year PAC Z), class G (PAC CAB), class H (10-year PAC), class I (PAC CAB), class J (PAC CAB), and class K (20-year PAC).

4. As we carve out the PACs, we must also select the PAC coupons. Since we are "carving" PACs out of a "block" of a $195 million, 9.40 percent PAC bond, any PAC coupons below 9.40 percent must be accompanied by a piece of PAC IO, which represents the excess interest spread between the reduced PAC coupon and the 9.40 percent bond coupons created by the IOette. This PAC IO sells at comparatively higher yields than PAC bonds (spreads of plus 150 to plus 200 to the curve), so we want to create only discount-priced coupons on a PAC if we can get *significant* yield spread savings on the PAC by doing so. It turns out in this situation that we *can* get significant savings on interest-bearing classes by stripping down coupons, but not on PAC A bonds. Therefore, we create full 9.40 percent coupons on all of our PAC Z bonds, 9 percent coupons on our short interest-bearing PACs, an 8 percent coupon on our 7-year PAC, and 7 percent coupons on our 10- and 20-year interest-bearing PACs.

Remember, Z-bonds create "accretions" (negative principal payments) that may be used to amortize earlier classes. Moreover, the accretions on *PAC* Z-bonds (e.g., classes C, D, F, G, I, and J in our deal) are *fixed within the PAC bands, so they can be used to create additional PACs*. This is the source of the payments for class A, the 9 percent coupon, 2-year PAC with a 3-year stated maturity.

We have finished carving the PACs, so based on the PAC coupons we have also created a PAC IO (class S). There is one further twist: The buyer of the IO/PAC Z/support Z combination, the crucial sale in the deal, wants the PAC Z (class F) to have call protection even greater than that for ordinary PACs. We therefore make the F class a total-return PAC, which will be call protected not only by support bonds but also by other PACs! If prepayments are high (above the upper PAC band of 300 PSA), classes G, H, I, and J get called out before class F, even though they are longer PACs and therefore would normally get called out after class F. Meanwhile, the other PAC classes are unaffected. *This is an example of shifting cash flow priorities.* Table 10.2 shows the average-life performance of the F class. Note that at the high 350 and 400 PSA speeds the average life actually extends, from 9.35 years (within the 100–300 PSA bands) to 11.54 years at 350 PSA. At 400 PSA it shortens again slightly to 10.24 years.

5. Finally, we must carve our $205 million, 9.40 percent support bonds. We are looking to create a 6-month-average-life residual (class R) for thrifts with net operating losses (at the time this was the most efficient way to lay off the tax effects of a residual); a stable 2-year (class L) for commercial banks; a 5-year (class M) for both retail and institutional clients; a 10-year Z (class O) for the IO/PAC Z/support Z combination; a 10-year interest-bearing support (class N) for retail; and a long 20-year Z (class P). The two Z-bonds help protect the other classes from extension. We use the 5-year to call

TABLE 10.2

Prepayment-Sensitivity Analysis (FHLMC Series 182, Class F PAC Z, Bands 100–300)

PSA speed	75	115	185	225	350	400	
Yield	9.71	9.72	9.72	9.72	9.70	9.70	
Average life	10.47	9.35	9.35	9.35	*11.54*	*10.24*	extends
First amortization	10.13	9.05	9.05	9.05	10.80	9.63	
Maturity	10.80	9.63	9.63	9.63	12.38	10.88	

FIGURE 10.14
Cash Flow Structure at 75 PSA

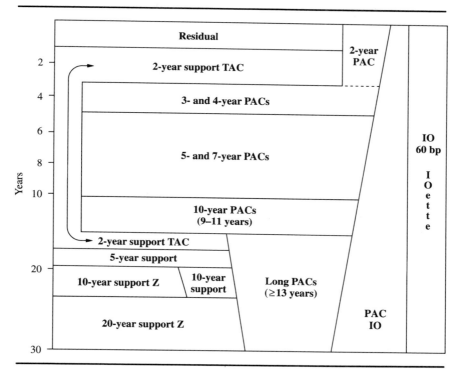

Source: Lehman Brothers Fixed Income Research.

protect the 2-year at prepayment speeds above 195 PSA, and we use the 20-year Z and the 10-year interest-bearing support to call protect the 10-year Z at speeds above 250 PSA (to improve the profile of the combination trade). Our structure is now complete.

The sensitivity of the structure to changes in prepayments is illustrated in Figures 10.14 and 10.15. Figure 10.14 gives the changes in cash flows that take place at 75 PSA. Note that, in general, at the slow 75 PSA speed the support classes extend significantly in time, whereas the PACs extend only moderately (remember, this is a static scenario—the assumption is that prepayments drop to 75 PSA and remain there for life, thereby breaking the lower band). Also note that the 2-year support TAC curls around the PACs it

FIGURE 10.15
Cash Flow Structure at 350 PSA

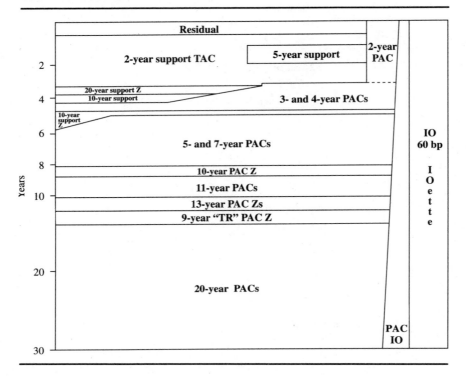

Source: Lehman Brothers Fixed Income Research.

supports and extends out to about 15 years. The 5-year support extends to almost 20 years, as does the 10-year support. Note also that the PAC IO increases its portion of cash flow significantly. The IOette would also increase in cash flow value, although the figure does not clearly reflect this pattern.

Figure 10.15 illustrates the cash flow dynamics at a static acceleration to 350 PSA. The 5-year support, which supports the 2-year PAC, is squeezed almost to oblivion. The 20-year support Z jumps in front of the 10-year support and almost disappears, and the 10-year support Z vanishes. Of particular interest is the K class 9-year total-return PAC Z, which actually extends when prepayments accelerate—now *that* is call protection! In addition, the 20-year PAC extends its cash flows. The PAC IO, as we would expect, shrivels significantly, as would the IOette.

CHAPTER 11

WHOLE-LOAN
MORTGAGE-BACKED
SECURITIES

EVOLUTION OF THE WHOLE-LOAN MARKET

The securitization of whole loans was initiated in 1977 by Bank of America with the first issuance of a private pass-through. (For more information on the early development of nonagency pass-throughs and builder bonds, see Pre-REMIC Multiclass Pass-through Efforts in Chapter 7.) The whole-loan MBS market consists primarily of nonconforming loans that do not meet federal agency purchase or pooling criteria because of their size (jumbo loans) or underwriting standards.[1]

Market Development

The nonagency-guaranteed MBS market started growing in earnest following the introduction of CMOs by Freddie Mac in 1983. From the $1.6 billion issuance level in 1983, nonagency MBS issuance grew moderately to about $5 billion in 1986, doubled to over $10 billion in 1987, crested in 1988 at $16 billion, and grew steadily to $24.4 billion in 1990 (see Figure 11.1). In 1991, with the advent of the Resolution Trust Corporation (RTC)[2] and the S&L asset-disposition program, nonagency-issuance levels soared to nearly $50 billion. In 1992, $89.5 billion was issued. In 1993 whole-loan MBS issuance is estimated to total about $92.5 billion.

---

[1]The vast majority of nonconforming loans that do meet Fannie Mae/Freddie Mac underwriting standards are jumbo. However, some jumbos may not meet these standards.

[2]The RTC was established by FIRREA to execute the liquidation of failed thrift and banking institutions.

FIGURE 11.1
Whole-Loan Issuance, 1983 through 1992

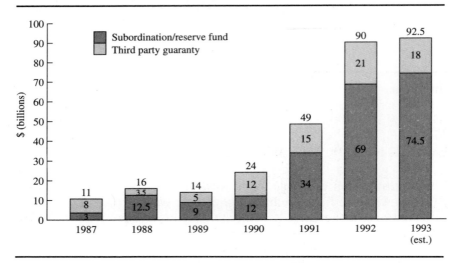

Source: Lehman Brothers Fixed Income Research.

The 1988 issuance increase was in large part related to the broadening utilization of the senior/subordinated structure of credit enhancement for the MBS structure. Under this structure a portion of the collateral pool is segregated as a subordinated, or B, class to absorb any losses, thereby protecting the senior class bonds, which are typically rated AAA or AA. The principal rating agencies are Moody's Investor Service, Standard & Poor's, and Fitch Investors Service as well as Duff & Phelps.

Before the introduction of the senior/subordinated structure, credit enhancement had been provided by private mortgage insurers or bank letters of credit (LOCs). However, with the start of the real estate-related woes in 1987 that eventually plagued the real estate market for years after, many private insurers and banks faced deteriorating balance sheets, calling into question the viability of third party corporate or banking guarantees. By 1988 it was generally recognized that the best credit enhancement in a subordinated structure is the whole-loan collateral itself. The event that, in fact, made the senior/subordinated structure possible was the REMIC legislation, which permitted the issuance of a multiclass pass-through. Before REMIC, a senior/subordinated structure would not have been possible as a pass-through issue.

1989 Issuance Declines

In 1989 the volume of nonagency pass-through issuance fell to $12.2 billion, primarily because of a decline in ARM origination that year. The drop was also a consequence of the uncertainty generated by the new capital requirements mandated by FIRREA, which were widely anticipated during 1988 and ultimately implemented in January 1989. Responding to these new capital requirements, the Federal Reserve Board established guidelines requiring banks that held the subordinated B class to reserve capital against the entire amount of the bond issue; the OTS required thrift institutions to reserve capital against the amount of the subordinated portion only. These guidelines temporarily discouraged banks and thrifts from continuing with the issuance of senior/subordinated structures.

1990—A Recovery Year

The primary reason for the reacceleration of MBS issuance beginning in 1990 was the entry of the RTC, which in the second half of 1991 issued over $10 billion in single- and multifamily MBSs. According to a Bear Stearns report,[3] the growth in private mortgage conduits was also a contributing factor. "Issuers such as Residential Funding Corp (RFC) and Chase Mortgage Finance issued more than three times as many whole loan securities in 1990 ($10.8 billion) as they did in all preceding years ($3.1 billion)," the report pointed out, and "the conduits need less capital than the banks and thrifts," it was noted. In addition, the conduits do not have the regulatory constraints on holding the subordinated classes that are imposed on banks and thrifts. Furthermore, by 1991 a secondary market had begun to develop for the subordinated B class bonds (usually rated A to BBB but sometimes not rated), enabling the subordinated classes to be sold by issuers constrained to hold them. The landmark issue on that score was the $260 million RMC 111 series 1992-A issued by Ryland Mortgage Securities and underwritten by Lehman Brothers. It consisted of four classes rated A to B,

---

[3]*An Introduction to Whole Loan Securities* by Brian P. Lancaster. New York: Bear Stearns, September 30, 1991.

three of which were offered publicly and one privately. The transaction aggregated the subordinated classes of a number of fixed- and adjustable-rate mortgage pass-through securities that had been previously issued. The success of this offering significantly expanded the secondary market for the subordinated classes.

The market for the nonagency MBSs expanded even more in 1992, in large part stimulated by demand from insurance companies, who were encouraged by newly imposed risk capital regulations (see Chapter 1) to seek high-yielding alternatives to their traditional concentration on commercial real estate and below-investment-grade corporate bonds. Money managers also bought the nonagency deals in larger volume as market liquidity increased, largely as a result of the RTC program.

Issuer Profile[4]

The primary issuers of mortgage pass-throughs have been mortgage conduits and the mortgage banking subsidiaries of thrifts, commercial banks, and insurance companies. During the 1986–1989 period, five issuers accounted for 42 percent of the pass-through market, with Citicorp commanding a 22 percent share. At present, the principal issuers of private MBSs include the names shown in Table 11.1A. Whereas many of the leading issuers are large residential mortgage originators, small institutions have also been able to participate in this market by channeling their mortgage loans into conduit programs. Table 11.1B lists the lead underwriters of private-issue MBSs in 1992.

Market Composition

During the 1980s, thrift institutions were the predominant buyers of the nonagency MBSs, and they strongly preferred the adjustable-rate pass-throughs. In the late 1980s, changing regulations encouraged insurance companies to shift away from commercial loans and low-grade corporates (see Chapter 1) into nonagency MBSs, with a strong preference for the CMO structure. The entry in 1991 of the RTC as an issuer caught the attention of money managers, who also

---

[4]This discussion of issuer profile is based on *Understanding the Private Label Pass-through Market.* New York: Lehman Brothers Fixed Income Research, May 1990.

TABLE 11.1A
Issuers of Whole-Loan Fixed-Rate MBS Issues, 1992

1992 Rank	Issuer	Fixed-Rate Issuance through 6/2/92 ($ in millions)	Share of 1992 YTD Issuance (%)
1	Pru Home Mortgage	4,511	17.6
2	RTC[a]	4,273	16.6
3	RFC[b]	3,961	15.4
4	Chase Mortgage	2,620	10.2
5	Capstead Mortgage	2,549	9.9
6	SMART[c]	2,411	9.4
7	Citicorp Mortgage	1,203	4.7
8	SEARS Mortgage	861	3.3
9	GE Morgage Corp.	778	3.0
10	Marine Midland	650	2.5
	Total issuance	25,713	92.6

[a]The RTC is not a jumbo conduit.
[b]Residential Funding Corporation.
[c]Shelf issue name for Lehman Brothers.

Sources: Inside Mortgage Capital Markets, Lehman Brothers Fixed Income Research.

strongly favored the CMO. The predominant form of the nonagency MBS structure therefore shifted from the pass-through to the CMO form. About $26 billion of nonagency MBSs issued in 1992 was backed by ARMs. Since the late 1980s the bulk of fixed-rate whole-loan MBSs have been issued as CMOs in REMIC form or as ARM pass-through forms (see Table 11.2).

STRUCTURAL FORMS[5]

The Pass-Through Structure

The pass-through structure consists of a single class of securities with scheduled interest and principal payments from the underlying mortgages passed on to the certificate holder, usually on the 25th of

---

[5]This discussion of structural forms is based on *Understanding the Private Label Pass-through Market.*

TABLE 11.1B
Whole-Loan MBS Underwriters in 1992

Rank	Underwriter[a]	1992 Underwriting ($ in millions)	Number of Deals
1	Lehman Brothers	14,218.11	45
2	Kidder Peabody	11,642.17	43
3	First Boston	10,366.15	39
4	Merrill Lynch	10,185.93	34
5	Bear Stearns	8,650.88	26
6	Goldman Sachs	7,767.99	24
7	Salomon Brothers	6,890.29	22
8	Prudential-Bache Securities	4,738.99	18
9	Citicorp/Citibank	2,434.43	12
10	PaineWebber	2,277.63	9
11	Morgan Stanley	1,522.65	8
12	Greenwich Capital Markets	1,325.43	6
13	Donaldson Lufkin Jenrette	1,071.92	8
14	Dean Witter	989.00	1
15	Residential Funding Corporation	974.57	9
16	Smith Barney	956.99	4
17	Nomura	185.00	1
18	NationsBank Capital Markets	105.79	1
19	Daiwa Securities	74.70	1
	Private placements	$3,087.72	20
	Totals	$89,466.32	331

[a]For purposes of this ranking, full underwriting credit was given to the lead manager of the deal.

Source: Inside Mortgage Securities.

each month. The pass-through rate is set at least 25 basis points below the lowest mortgage coupon rate in the collateral pool. For example, a pool of 30-year mortgages with coupons ranging from 8.25 to 9 percent and a WAC of 8.45 percent would normally be structured as an 8 percent pass-through security. In this way, the servicer can collect on each loan an average servicing fee of 45 basis points but not less than 25 basis points. The rating agencies require minimum servicing fees of 25 basis points for fixed-rate loans and 37.5 basis points for adjustable-rate loans. Adequate servicing fees ensure good performance on the part of the servicer and enable another servicer to take over if the original servicer defaults.

TABLE 11.2
Nonagency MBS Issuance, Pass-Through and CMO Forms, 1986–1992 ($ millions)

Year	Total	Fixed Rate[a]	ARM[b]
1986	6,994	NA	NA
1987	11,101	9,044	2,057
1988	15,421	3,303	12,118
1989	14,238	7,812	6,426
1990	24,430	16,812	7,619
1991	49,350	30,599	18,750
1992	89,466	63,448	26,018

[a]From 1988 forward the bulk of fixed-rate nonagency MBSs have been issued as REMICs structured as CMOs.
[b]Nonagency ARMs for the most part have been issued as pass-throughs.

Sources: Inside Mortgage Securities, Financial World Publications, and Lehman Brothers Fixed Income Research.

The CMO Structure

Whole-loan-backed MBSs have since 1988 been structured predominately as CMOs, usually as REMICs. The CMO tranching for whole-loan-structured transactions is similar to that of the agency-issued REMICs, although typically with somewhat fewer tranches and with less frequent use of the more esoteric CMO derivatives.

Super Senior Structure

An innovation with whole-loan CMOs is the super senior structure, wherein a mezzanine class is carved out of the AAA senior bonds. The mezzanine class is generally rated AAA, but it is subordinate to the super senior bonds. This structure provides the super senior class generally with 15 percent or more of varying levels of subordination. Two super senior structures are depicted in Figures 11.2A and 11.2B, which illustrate Lehman Brothers' super senior structures issued out of its SMART[6] shelf. Compare the mezzanine structures illustrated in the two figures. Note that in Figure 11.2A

---

[6]SMART is Lehman Brothers' acronym for its private MBS shelf—Structured Mortgage Asset REMIC Trust.

FIGURE 11.2A
SMART 1991-1 Deal Structure

Smart 91-1

Senior bond second loss Parallel pay Mezzanine (AAA rating)	Super senior cash flow (Tranched into clean sequential-pay bonds)
First loss GE pool policy	7%

Source: Lehman Brothers Fixed Income Trading.

the subordinated mezzanine class pays concurrent with all the classes in the bond issue. Although this is certainly acceptable since the senior class bonds are being retired in greater principal amount than is the case with the subordinated class bonds, the structure in Figure 11.2B is clearly stronger since there are no payments of principal from the collateral until the senior class bonds are fully retired. Note that from a potential investor's point of view, although

FIGURE 11.2B
SMART 1991-2-8 Deal Structure

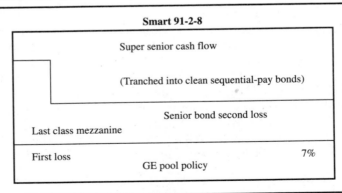

Source: Lehman Brothers Fixed Income Research.

committing to a long maturity on a subordinated bond may be less attractive, there is substantial call protection from prepayments in this structure. From mid-1993 forward the senior/subordinated structure largely displaced dependence on the GEMICO pool policy, in large part because of the evolving secondary market for the subordinated bond classes.

The Parties to the Transaction

The servicer function is primarily to collect the monthly mortgage payments from the homeowner and forward them to the custodial account held by the trustee. Often there is a master servicer who receives the payments from subservicers who perform the actual collection of P&I due from the homeowners. The master servicer then remits these payments to the trustee. The latter collection and remittance structure is more typical when large conduit operations are performing the servicing function. The conduits are generally formed for the primary purpose of channeling the proceeds of mortgage capital raised regularly from the capital markets through residential mortgage bond issues underwritten and sold to institutional investors by primary investment banking firms. The subservicers are mortgage bankers and/or mortgage brokers operating in regional markets. The mortgage loans originated in the primary mortgage market are often sold **servicing released** to the master servicer, in which case the servicing function is transferred to the master servicer.

The custodial account held by the trustee is segregated in a bankruptcy-proof account, meaning that in the case of insolvency by the trustee or the master servicer these deposited funds may not be claimed by a trustee of the bankrupt estate.

The servicer for the bond trustee is required to remit on a timely basis the monthly cash flow required of the unpaid principal amount of mortgages originated and held as collateral for the bond issue regardless of whether or not collected from the homeowners. As such, any delinquent payments past due 30 days or in foreclosure must be advanced as though paid on a timely basis until the delinquency is cured or the foreclosure process is completed. The ultimate proceeds from a foreclosure therefore appear to the trustee and to the bondholder as current, and when passed through as proceeds from foreclosure they appear as a regular prepayment. Thus, mortgage originations with a high delinquency and/or foreclosure rate appear to the bond investor as fast prepay. For this reason the servicer (or master servicer) to the bond trustee must have a rating no lower than at least one rating category below that of the mortgage-backed bonds issued—that is, to service for an AAA bond issue the servicer must be rated at least AA. With most structured transactions the issuer of the bonds is also the servicer, or more typically the master servicer.

CREDIT-ENHANCEMENT STRUCTURES[7]

The form of credit enhancement determines the method for protecting the bond investor against loss from foreclosures on defaulted loans. The prevalent form of credit enhancement is the senior/subordinated structure. Other forms include pool insurance, LOCs, and bond insurance. Limited corporate guarantees were used in the mid-1980s but are not in favor at present.

Senior/Subordinated Structures

With the senior/subordinated structure the bonds are divided into a senior class, referred to as the A portion (usually rated AAA or sometimes AA), and a subordinated class, the B portion (which may be rated from AA to BBB or nonrated). The A portion is, in turn, generally tranched into CMO bond classes. Increasingly the subordinated B portion is being tranched as well. The A class bonds are generally tranched by average life, as with a typical CMO. The B class, if tranched, is tranched by credit exposure into a first, second, . . . and last loss.

Subordinated Class Structures

The amount of the total bond issue to be subordinated is determined by the rating agencies utilizing an econometric model. The model stresses the mortgage collateral to economic scenarios; the more severe the scenario that the bond structure survives, the higher the rating. As a general rule, if the credit enhancement sur-

---

[7]This discussion of credit-enhancement structures is based on *Understanding the Private Label Pass-through Market*.

vives a Houston, Texas, scenario, the bonds would typically be rated AA; if the structure survives the 1930s Depression the bond issue is rated AAA. *Do not be misled into believing the amount of subordination alone is an indication of the credit soundness of the bond structure. Prime-quality collateral may require only 6 to 7 percent subordination to be awarded AAA; on the other hand, with lesser-quality collateral, a 10 percent subordination might be awarded only AA!*

There are two ways to maximize the credit-enhancement function of the subordinated class: establishment of a reserve fund and implementation of a shifting-interest structure.

1. Reserve Fund

The reserve fund structure is common with RTC-issued transactions. The RTC has favored establishing the reserve fund with a deposit of cash, or a cashable bank-issued LOC. The reserve fund may also be established by diverting principal cash flows due the subordinated class to a reserve fund until a pre-established level is realized.

2. Shifting-Interest Structure[8]

In a shifting-interest structure mortgage prepayments are "shifted" from the subordinated class to the senior class during the first 5 to 10 years of the transaction. As a result, the senior class is paid down faster, and the balance of the subordinated class declines much more slowly through scheduled principal payments. The early retirement of the senior class in a shifting-interest structure causes its average life to shorten.

Examine the layers of loss priorities within the B class structure, as illustrated in Figure 11.3. The D class takes the first loss in the event of mortgage defaults and represents 1 percent of the $100 million total collateral. In other words, with a 1 percent loss experience, the D certificates are wiped out. This is not a 1 percent default experience—the loss experience represents the amount lost (not recovered) on the defaults. For example, a 40 percent loss experience with a 2.5 percent default rate would produce a loss percentage of 4 percent ($0.40 \times 10 = 4.0$). This first-loss piece is

---

[8]This discussion of shifting-interest structures was provided by John Tierney and Chris Ames, Lehman Brothers Fixed Income Research, July 1992.

FIGURE 11.3
Senior/Subordinated Shifting-Interest Structure

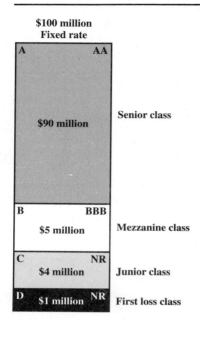

$100 million
Fixed rate

A   AA

$90 million   **Senior class**

B   BBB
$5 million   **Mezzanine class**

C   NR
$4 million   **Junior class**

D $1 million   NR   **First loss class**

Senior/subordinate structure
In the senior/subordinate structure, the A class is protected from credit losses by the D, C, and B classes in that order.

Shift-interest mechanism
The shifting-interest nature of this structure causes all prepayments that the B, C, and D classes would be entitled to receive be paid to the A class for the first 5 years for fixed-rate loans and 10 years for adjustable-rate loans. Thereafter, on a predetermined sliding scale the B class will start receiving a portion of prepayments.

Hypothetical loss scenario
$4 million of loans default on which we have a 50 percent recovery ($2 million) and resultant loss of $2 million. The $2 million recovery will be treated as a prepayment, causing the A class to be reduced to $88 million. The $2 million loss reduces the class D balance to zero and class C to $3 million.

(To simplify the above analysis we have ignored amortization.)

Source: Lehman Brothers Fixed Income Trading.

generally not rated and is not sold by the bond issuer. (For a further discussion of calculating the loss experience and the tolerance of the credit-enhanced structure to withstand foreclosure loss, see The Rating Agency Approach, page 480.)

The B and C certificates make up the core of the subordinated B class credit enhancement. The C certificates in this structure were rated BBB by S&P; the C was nonrated. However, the second-loss certificate often was rated, most probably BB. The B, C, and D bonds make up the total B class of bonds, which provide 9 percent loss coverage for the AAA senior bonds, the A class.

Figure 11.4 illustrates the cash flow support of shifting interest for a simple A/B structure. The senior (A) class is initially 85 percent of the transaction, with the subordinate (B) piece accounting for the remaining 15 percent. Assuming a prepayment speed of 200 PSA and zero default experience, the B class increases to 31 percent

FIGURE 11.4

A and B Classes as a Percentage of Total Unpaid Principal Balance at 200 PSA

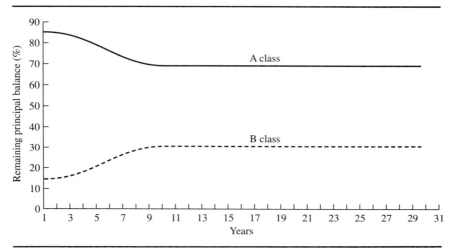

of the remaining balance over the first 10 years and then remains constant for the balance of the term as prepayments are allocated on a full pro rata basis. (If there were no shifting-interest feature and no losses, the A and B percentages would remain at their initial levels over the life of the structure.) Shifting-interest securities are structured so that the subordinated class will actually increase during the early years under even fairly extreme prepayment and loss scenarios. Shifting-interest structures provide additional credit enhancement for the senior class in several ways:

1. Defaults and losses typically are low on pools of new mortgages, then gradually rise to a peak around year 4 or 5 (see Figure 11.5). The growth in the subordinated class roughly mirrors the increasing exposure to defaults and losses.

2. As the subordinated class grows, it provides a larger buffer against potential losses.

3. Paying down the senior class relatively quickly further reduces its exposure to losses. In addition, the senior class has a shorter and more stable average life across a range of interest rates and prepayment rates, which is a desirable investment characteristic for many investors.

FIGURE 11.5
Mortgage Loan Default Distribution

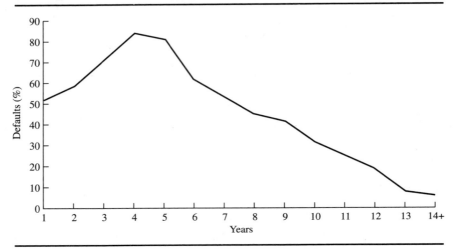

Source: Standard & Poor's.

Typical Shifting-Interest Structures.   S&P has developed basic criteria for structuring shifting-interest securities that depend to a large degree on whether the collateral is fixed-rate or adjustable-rate mortgages. Typically, if the collateral is fixed-rate mortgages, the lockout period during which the subordinated classes receive no prepayments is 5 years. During the next 4 years prepayments are still allocated disproportionately to the senior class, but the subordinated classes receive an increasing share each year. Thus, in year 6 the subordinated classes receive only 30 percent of their full pro rata share of prepayments. The share rises to 40, 60, 80, and 100 percent during years 7 to 10 and remains at 100 percent in subsequent years. Alternatively, in year 6 the senior class receives 100 percent of its pro rata allocation plus 70 percent of the share of the subordinated class. In years 7 to 10 the senior class receives 60, 40, 20, and zero percent of the subordinated class share of prepayments. Additionally, if in any month the senior class share of the total collateral outstanding rises above the original senior share, prepayments are directed to the senior class until the original share is restored. The parameters for ARMs are similar except that the lockout period is 10 years instead of 5.

These basic parameters may vary from transaction to transaction depending on the quality of the collateral, or trade-offs, among certain givens, such as initial size of the subordinated class, length of the lockout, length/timing of the phase-in schedule, and delinquency triggers.

Pool Insurance

A pool insurance policy insures defaults on the underlying mortgages up to the amount required for AA or AAA rating. The insurance company providing the pool policy must have a rating equal to or higher than the desired rating on the pass-through. Currently the largest issuer of mortgage pool insurance is GEMICO (General Electric Mortgage Insurance Company). Others that provide pool insurance include MGIC (Mortgage Guaranty Insurance Company), PMI (Private Mortgate Insurance Company), and UGI (United Guaranty Insurance Company).

A pool policy does not cover all types of losses. Additional insurance protection must be obtained for bankruptcy, fraud, and special hazards. A bankruptcy bond protects against court orders that may modify the mortgage debt. Fraud insurance protects investors from misrepresentations of the borrower or lender during the application process that could render a mortgage invalid or unenforceable against the borrower. Special-hazard insurance protects investors from physical damages, such as earthquakes and vandalism, that are not covered by the borrower's standard homeowner's policy.

Bank Letters of Credit

The bank issuing the LOC must be rated at least as high as the related bond issue. Since there are no limitations on the scope of coverage under these guarantees, no additional insurance for special hazards, bankruptcy, and fraud is required.

LOCs have become less prevalent than the senior/subordinated and pool policy form because they are expensive, and only a few mortgage originators can obtain them on an unsecured basis. Also, the risk-based capital regulations have made it unattractive for banks to impair their capital by guaranteeing the loss on large mortgage bond issues.

Bond Insurance

Bond issuers are also employed to guaranty structured MBS financings. These insurers include Financial Surety Association (FSA), which is the most commonly used; Financial Guaranty Insurance Company (FGIC); Municipal Bond Insurance Association (MBIA); and AMBAC Indemnity. The bond insurer's guaranty covers the entire senior class, thus affording the pass-through an Aaa/AAA rating by virtue of the bond issuer's corporate debt rating.

COLLATERAL EVALUATION ISSUES[9]

We have discussed how investors of privately issued pass-through and CMO bonds are protected from loss by delinquencies (payments late beyond 30 days) and foreclosure. The principal credit risk associated with private-issue MBSs is default by the homeowner. *Most significant to the issue of default is its infrequency in association with the American homeowner.* According to data provided by the Mortgage Bankers Association, the national delinquency rate runs between 4.5 and 6 percent of total residential debt, *with the percentage actually going into foreclosure less than 0.5 percent!*
  The principal determinants of default, according to research by Lehman Brothers, appears to be related to home price appreciation, or more specifically the lack of it; the LTV ratio (the lower the better); and change in employment status.

Home Price Appreciation

According to Lehman Brothers, the most important variable by far in explaining default is home price appreciation. Lehman analysis shows that default activity is very negatively correlated with the robustness of the local housing market. Defaults are low during periods of strong housing markets and rise sharply when home price appreciation is sluggish (or negative). Figure 11.6 illustrates the sensitivity of default probability to home price appreciation.

---

[9]This discussion of collateral evaluation is based on *Understanding the Private Label Pass-through Market.*

FIGURE 11.6

Default Probability as a Function of Home Price Appreciation

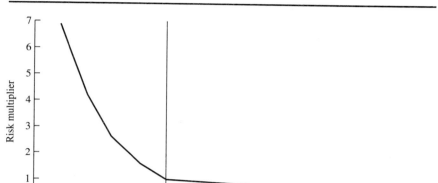

Source: Lehman Brothers Fixed Income Research.

An examination of the interaction between home price appreciation and default activity in five different metropolitan statistical areas (MSAs) by Lehman provides insight into the strength of this relationship over time. The MSAs that encompass New Orleans, Houston, Boston, Minneapolis, and San Francisco have experienced widely differing rates of price appreciation on residential real estate since the mid-1970s (see Table 11.3). NAR median home price data by MSA indicate that a house acquired in San Francisco in 1977 appreciated in value by about 310 percent (10.60 percent annualized rate) over the 14-year period ending June 1990. Except during the recession years of the early 1980s, this increase occurred steadily over the period. In New Orleans, on the other hand, cumulative price appreciation for houses acquired in 1977 was a much more modest 35 percent (2.20 percent annualized rate); and homes purchased during the 1980s have on average declined in value. Other regions have experienced more uneven home price appreciation over time: Homes bought in Houston during the first half of the 1980s when the regional housing market was booming have generally declined in value, whereas those purchased before 1980 or after 1986 have achieved modest gains.

TABLE 11.3

Cumulative Home Price Appreciation (%) for Selected MSAs (Origination to Second Quarter 1990)

| MSA | Origination Year | | | |
	All	1987–1989	1983–1986	1977–1982
New Orleans	1.2 (5)[a]	−12.3 (5)[a]	−16.4 (5)[a]	14.8 (5)[a]
Houston	26.2 (4)	10.2 (2)	−5.9 (4)	39.4 (4)
Boston	30.2 (3)	−1.6 (4)	22.0 (2)	202.8 (2)
Minneapolis	32.8 (2)	9.0 (3)	19.5 (3)	73.2 (3)
San Francisco	128.4 (1)	26.9 (1)	71.6 (1)	259.7 (1)

[a]The number in parentheses denotes rank for the period indicated in the column heading.

Source: Lehman Brothers Fixed Income Research.

The foreclosure rates as of September 1990 for mortgages originated in the cities listed in Table 11.3 over the 1977–1989 period bear a striking relationship to home price appreciation. Table 11.4 summarizes foreclosure rates, cumulative home price appreciation, and relative rankings for several groupings of origination years. For each group the rank correlation between foreclosure rate and home price appreciation is either −0.90 or −1.0. For loans originated during 1977–1982, New Orleans had the highest foreclosure rate (0.735 percent) and the lowest price appreciation (14.8 percent), whereas San Francisco had the lowest foreclosure rate (0.113 percent) and the highest price appreciation (259.7 percent). Foreclosure rates and relative ranking for an MSA may also vary with origination year. Loans originated in Boston during 1987–1989 experienced the highest foreclosure rate of all five cities (and the second lowest price appreciation rate), but loans originated during 1977–1982 had the second lowest foreclosure rate (and the second highest price appreciation rate), behind San Francisco.

LTV Ratio

LTV ratios have historically been good predictors of foreclosure rates. LTV is the ratio of mortgage debt to the lower of the home's purchase price or appraised value. If a mortgagor's equity in the home is greater than the interest past due, there is an economic incentive to continue paying the mortgage. The rating agencies as-

TABLE 11.4

Ranked Foreclosure for Selected MSAs as of September 1990

	Origination Year			
	1977–1982	*1983–1986*	*1987–1989*	*1977–89*
Foreclosure rate (%)				
New Orleans	0.735 (1)	1.746 (1)	0.530 (2)	0.784 (1)
Houston	0.483 (2)	1.061 (2)	0.317 (4)	0.441 (2)
Boston	0.270 (4)	0.445 (3)	0.591 (1)	0.419 (3)
Minneapolis	0.461 (3)	0.339 (4)	0.403 (3)	0.337 (4)
San Francisco	0.113 (5)	0.129 (5)	0.086 (5)	0.085 (5)
National	0.283	0.364	0.254	0.285

Source: Lehman Brothers Fixed Income Research.

sume increasing foreclosure risk for mortgages with LTVs above 80 percent based on empirical data from the mortgage insurance industry. Statistically, loans with LTV ratios of 90 percent are 1.5 times as likely and those with 95 percent LTVs are 3 times as likely to default as loans with LTVs of 80 percent.

Even though higher LTV loans have greater foreclosure risk, their loss severity is usually no greater than lower LTV loans. The reason is that individual loans with LTVs above 80 percent usually have private mortgage insurance that covers the excess of the loan balance over the 75 percent LTV ratio. This coverage greatly reduces the degree of loss suffered in the event of foreclosure. Under the Lehman credit-adjusted spread (CAS) framework, loans with an initial LTV of 80 percent carry a risk multiplier of 1; the multiplier falls to 0.4 for 50 percent LTV loans and rises to 1.7 for 95 percent LTV loans.

Employment Status

Clearly the loss of employment by the wage earner in a one-income family will greatly increase the probability of default by that homeowner. However, if there has been adequate home price appreciation and the LTV at closing was conservative and based on a realistic appraisal, the actual loss to the MBS bond investor will be none or very small.

On the other hand, the homeowner who remains well employed is highly likely to continue with the regular mortgage payments even if there has been depreciation in the home equity and/or if the

LTV was (or still is) relatively high. Homeowners who can easily afford to make the mortgage payment are highly unlikely to invite default unnecessarily.

Other Mortgage Credit Issues[10]

There are other mortgage credit issues, which may be summarized as follows:

Loan Purpose

A mortgage undertaken to purchase the primary home is best for obvious reasons: The homeowner is making an investment in shelter for the household and will be highly motivated to protect it. This is referred to as a **purchase mortgage**. The equity takeout mortgage, also called a **cash-out refi,** is a less desirable mortgage because the homeowner is reducing the home equity. Almost all lenders impose a much lower LTV requirement to qualify for a cash-out refi, and some investors of whole-loan-backed bonds restrict the percentage of these loans they will accept as collateral for the bond issue. Also, most lenders will commit to an equity take-out refi only on the primary residence of an owner-occupied home. Loans for second homes, recreation homes, and investor properties are seldom allowed as collateral for prime mortgage pools backing bond issues designed for AAA taxing.

Property Type

The single-family, detached, owner-occupied home is the preferred property type. Townhouses, low-rise condominiums, and two- to four-family homes are somewhat less desirable. The rating agencies assume the default rate on these property types is about 1.2 times that of a single-family, detached unit. High-rise condominiums are the least desirable and are considered twice as likely to default as single-family homes.

Loan Type

The common 30-year, level-payment mortgage carries by far the lowest credit risk of any mortgage loan. Risk elements in mortgage

---

[10]This discussion of other credit issues is based on *Understanding the Private Label Pass-through Market.*

loans that have been identified include short-term buydowns and GPM structures because when the buydown or reduced-payment structure of the GPM ends, the homeowner may face payment shock.

ARMs also bear higher default risk than level-pay mortgages. Variations in the ARM loan structure can also bear on the credit risk. Examples include the volatility of the index (LIBOR and CMT are more volatile than COFI) and negative amortization. (See Chapter 13 for a discussion of negative amortization with respect to ARMs.)

Geographic Dispersion

Historically, pools with the lowest default risk are made up of mortgages distributed over a wide geographic area. Pools that are geographically concentrated are expected to experience 1.5 times as many foreclosures as pools that are geographically diverse. The rating agencies prefer pools with no greater concentration than 5 percent in any one zip code. In areas with higher economic risk, such as southern California in the early 1990s and Massachusetts and Texas in the late 1980s, the rating agencies may require additional credit enhancement to compensate for loss of home price appreciation, poor employment prospects, and other negative demographic and economic considerations.

Seasoning of Loans

As loans age, or become more seasoned, the mortgage pool risk is deemed to decrease. Based on data from private mortgage insurance companies, S&P found that 95 percent of losses occur by year 7 of a pool's life. Seasoned loans have stable credit quality for several reasons:

1. Homeowners have shown an ability to pay the monthly payments year after year.

2. House price appreciation since the inflationary period of the early 1970s has lowered the effective LTV of most loans with the possible exception of some loans originated in 1988 and 1989 at the peak of the 1980s surge in home prices and those in areas that have suffered economically, such as the Northeast and Southwest.

3. The paydown of principal has lowered the current LTV even if housing prices have not appreciated in certain areas.

FIGURE 11.7
Default Probability as a Function of Pool Age

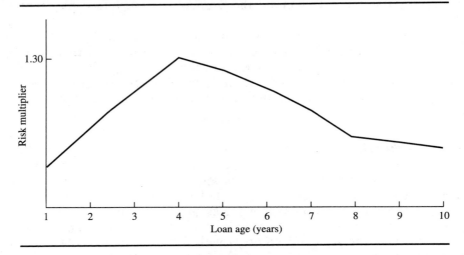

Figure 11.7 illustrates the pattern of defaults with pool age. Note defaults rise fairly quickly to a peak at year 4 and level off after year 7.

Loan Size

The size of the loan is another credit-quality factor. Very large loans (over $600,000) may suffer a greater decline in value in an economic downturn because of a limited market for the underlying properties. The larger the market value decline, the more likely the mortgagor will default due to a loss of equity in the property.

Loan Servicing

Loan servicing is another important aspect of pool risk. Servicing is the administration of fees and payments associated with the mortgage loans. The servicer's responsibilities are outlined in a participation and servicing agreement executed with the sale of a whole-loan mortgage pool or in a pool servicing agreement for a securitized pool. The servicer's duties include:

• Collecting and remitting P&I payments.

- Administering mortgage escrow funds for paying taxes and insurance.
- Contacting delinquent mortgagors and administering foreclosure proceedings.
- Handling aggregate reporting and distribution to investors.
- Segregating funds for the payment of pool expenses.
- Advancing funds on delinquent loans to meet payments to certificate holders.

The servicer is entitled to an annual fee that is deducted from interest payments on the mortgage loans before they are passed through to the certificate holders. In most pools, the servicer is required to make regular P&I payments, whether or not they have been collected from the borrower, up to the time of or through foreclosure. This requirement is called **MBS servicing** because it mirrors Fannie Mae's requirements for servicing MBSs.

For MBS servicing, the servicer is entitled to reimbursement from the foreclosure sale proceeds of any advances made or other costs incurred. When a pool contains both senior and subordinated classes, the servicer is obligated to advance an aggregate amount sufficient to assure payment at least to the senior certificate holders.

Underwriting

The issuer's loan underwriting procedures also affect collateral quality. Underwriting guidelines have changed greatly in the recent past, with more loans underwritten to standards that differ from Fannie Mae and Freddie Mac requirements. Recently, Fannie Mae and Freddie Mac have added programs that allow alternative documentation: The borrower may submit other or alternative credit information, such as bank statements instead of verification of deposit and W-2 payment stubs rather than verification of employment. Low-documentation programs are acceptable when the loans exhibit offsetting criteria, such as low LTV ratios or good payment histories on seasoned loans.

Loan Documentation
Loan documentation is critical to the underwriting process. In addition to the obviously necessary note and mortgage, title policy, and

appraisal, the documentation demanded from the borrower is also critical. Documented verification of employment, income, and ability and willingness to pay are critical to good loan underwriting.

Reduced-Documentation Loans.[11]   In the face of competitive pressure streamlined underwriting is often resorted to as a means of increasing loan-origination volume. Unfortunately, it is also a means of significantly reducing credit quality.

Reduced-documentation loans were spawned in the 1986–1987 refinancing boom when the volume of loan applications soared, straining the processing capability of loan originators. Lenders found they could provide faster turnaround by eliminating time-consuming verifications of employment and deposit. They reasoned that borrowers with equity in their houses would be unlikely to default. As a result, low-documentation loans typically required substantial down payments of 25 percent or more. Thus, even if the lender had to foreclose, the house could be sold and the loan balance recovered as long as the appraisal was accurate.

Low-documentation programs seemed an ideal way to meet lenders' needs to stay competitive as well as to increase efficiency in a paper-intensive industry. By 1987, a significant part of the nonconforming market used low documentation, and secondary market agencies introduced programs of their own. Freddie Mac announced both low and alternative documentation on May 15, 1987. The new guidelines were designed to reduce the time and cost of loan origination without sacrificing quality.

Alternative Documentation. For loans on owner-occupied properties with total LTV ratios (including second mortgages) up to 90 percent, alternate forms of documentation could be used to verify employment and income, source of funds, and payment history for the previous mortgage or rent. The allowable LTV for this program was subsequently increased to 95 percent.

For a borrower who was not self-employed, the most recent month's pay stubs, two years of W-2 forms, and telephone confirmation from the employer could replace the verification of employment (VOE) form. The verification of deposit (VOD) form could be

---

[11]This discussion of reduced-documentation loans is based on "Low Documentation Loans" by Claude Seaman, Vice President, Underwriting, PMI Mortgage Insurance Company. In *Secondary Market Reports*. Washington, DC: Freddie Mac, Summer 1991.

replaced by the account statements of the three most recent months or by evidence of a sale of assets.

Low Documentation. For loans with total LTVs no higher than 70 percent on owner-occupied properties that are the borrowers' principal residences, Freddie Mac accepted the borrowers' signatures in place of VOEs. This program was available to self-employed borrowers as long as they had operated their businesses for two years.

On a negotiated basis Freddie Mac also purchased low-documentation loans with LTVs above 70 percent and loans with documents waived in addition to the VOEs. However, Freddie Mac often required mortgage insurance for these loans. In this way, Freddie Mac had the assurance that another loan underwriter would screen the loans and would share in any losses.

Freddie Mac called its rules "reduced" documentation; PMI Mortgage Insurance Company's program was called "limited" documentation; and similar plans went by the name "streamlined." Fannie Mae had an alternative-documentation program known as TimeSaver and a low-documentation program called TimeSaver Plus. Full documentation had become the exception rather than the rule.

What Went Wrong. By not verifying certain credit aspects of the borrower and relying instead on the collateral, low-documentation loans represented a much greater underwriting challenge for mortgage lenders and insurers than full or alternative-documentation loans. Without adequate verifications of employment and source of down payment, low-documentation programs became invitations for abuse.

In 1988 and 1989 competition led lenders to relax their underwriting standards, compounding what turned out to be serious problems with these loans. Low-documentation loans were increasingly aimed at marginal borrowers making smaller down payments. Eventually, the typical down payment dropped to 20 percent. To make matters worse, undisclosed borrowed-down payments turned loans that were meant to have 75 to 80 percent LTVs into 90 percent LTV loans.

As the real estate market softened, the degree of risk associated with these loans increased considerably. Lenders, particularly in the Northeast, discovered that low-documentation loans had a relatively high incidence of delinquency, even with LTVs as low as 70 percent.

THE RATING AGENCY APPROACH[12]

The rating agencies have designed models to determine the amount of insurance protection required to cover losses on whole-loan-backed pools. S&P bases its assumptions on a worst-case scenario patterned after the Great Depression. From 1925 to 1929, 11.8 percent of fully amortizing, single-family loans is estimated to have entered foreclosure, and between 1930 and 1934 the rate is estimated to have been 15.9 percent. Over the 10-year period, property values decreased an estimated 25 to 30 percent.

S&P requires sufficient insurance on the pool to protect investors in the event of a severe economic downturn. Specifically, insurance must cover a 32 percent decline in market value for AA rating and a 37 percent decline for AAA rating. The rating agency has determined, based on Depression era statistics, that the highest national foreclosure frequency for fixed-rate, fully amortizing loans with LTVs of 80 percent or less would be 10 percent for AA rating and 15 percent for AAA rating. S&P's loss-severity assumptions include property value losses and foreclosure costs equal to 25 percent of the mortgage balance.

To receive at least S&P's AA rating, the loan collateral must first meet the criteria that define a **prime pool**. *A prime pool is one consisting of level-pay, fixed-rate loans on owner-occupied, single-family, detached properties with a weighted average LTV of 80 percent or lower.* The pool must have insurance to cover a minimum potential loss of 4 percent of the pool's balance. The loss percentage is calculated as follows:

Loss Calculation

Initial property value	$100		
Investor's interest = 80% LTV		80	
Less: Assume 32% loss in			
property value in foreclosure:	32	32	
Adjusted property value		68	
Investor's loss in property value			12
Less: Assume foreclosure costs equal 25%			
of adjusted property value:	20		
Net foreclosure loss			20
Total investor loss			32

---

[12]This discussion of the rating agency approach is based on *Understanding the Private Label Pass-through Market.*

Loss severity = Investor loss/Investor investment
= 80/32
= 40% loss severity
Assume 10 percent default rate
Required credit enhancement = Loss severity × Default rate
= 0.4 × 10.0
= 4 percent pool policy of subordination

Fixed-rate pools that are not prime generally require credit enhancement equal to 5 to 10 percent of the pool for an AA rating. ARMs with 2 percent annual caps and 6 percent lifetime caps usually require 150 percent of the credit enhancements for a similar fixed-rate pool. To evaluate whole-loan pools it is useful to look at the rating agency standards compared to recent historic loss experience. S&P assumes, based on foreclosure experience during the 1930s, that 10 percent of an AA-rated pool will go into foreclosure over the pool's life. However, foreclosure data made available by the MBA show that annual conventional mortgage loan foreclosure rates, as a percentage of outstanding mortgage balances originated by mortgage bankers from 1986 to 1989, ranged from 0.18 to 0.59 percent. Because the data represent all types of conventional mortgage loans nationwide, they may not accurately reflect expected foreclosure experience for any one pool. Regional delinquency statistics are important because jumbo mortgages tend to be concentrated in a few geographic areas. Table 11.5 compares national average delinquency and foreclosure rates for conventional residential loans with delinquency and foreclosure rates of states typically

TABLE 11.5

Delinquency and Foreclosure Rates, Nationwide and in Selected States

	Delinquency Rate (%)	Foreclosure Rate (%)
National average, 1989	3.42	0.59
Connecticut	3.44	0.25
Massachusetts	3.27	0.36
New Jersey	3.26	0.47
New York	3.80	0.30
Illinois	3.13	0.33
California	1.98	0.18

Source: Mortgage Bankers Association Newsletter, *National Delinquency Survey,* February 22, 1990 (data as of December 31, 1989).

included in whole-loan pools. The use of 1990 data enables reflection of the July 1990 to March 1991 economic recession as well as the post-1988 slump in home prices.

A whole loan with prime characteristics originated by an institution with low foreclosure rates should experience minimal losses, and a whole-loan pool backed by credit enhancement sufficient to provide AA or AAA rating should experience no losses. Table 11.6 illustrates the degree of losses necessary to deplete a pool's credit enhancement *based on a 10 percent pass-through with a 7 percent pool policy. The table assumes that one third of the losses occurs at the beginning of years 2, 3, and 4. The pool policy provides insurance protection against foreclosures totaling 15 percent of the pool and recovery rates as low as 60 percent.* These foreclosure and loss rates are more severe than those of the Depression era and far more severe than actual recent foreclosure history.

THE STANDARD DEFAULT ASSUMPTION[13]

Understanding default rates is critical for analyzing the investment characteristics of nonagency mortgage securities, especially subordinated classes. To facilitate the standardization of stress tests and market disclosure of pool-specific default activity, Lehman Brothers developed a standard default assumption (SDA) curve. The SDA curve is similar in concept to the PSA prepayment curve currently used to analyze prepayment risk in mortgage securities. Investors may use multiples of the SDA curve to stress whole-loan-backed mortgage securities, depending upon the nature of the underlying collateral and the economic outlook of individual investors. The PSA adopted the SDA curve as the industry standard on May 25, 1993.

The standard (100 percent SDA) gives the annualized default rate on a pool of mortgages as a function of the loan age, as illustrated in Figure 11.8. The default rate over any month is expressed as a percentage of the loan balance at the beginning of the month. The SDA standard assumes that the conditional default rate (CDR) starts at an annualized rate of 0.02 percent during month 1. There-

---

[13]This discussion of the standard default assumption is from a May 25, 1993 announcement from the Public Securities Association.

TABLE 11.6
Remaining Pool Policy

Recovery Rates (%)	Default Rates (1/3 defaults at the beginning of years 2, 3, and 4)								
	0%	2%	4%	6%	8%	10%	12%	14%	15%
100	7.0	7.0	7.0	7.0	7.0	7.0	7.0	7.0	7.0
90	7.0	6.8	6.7	6.5	6.3	6.2	6.0	5.8	5.0
80	7.0	6.7	6.3	6.0	5.6	5.3	5.0	4.7	4.0
70	7.0	6.5	6.0	5.5	5.0	4.5	4.0	3.5	3.0
60	7.0	6.3	5.6	5.0	4.3	3.6	3.0	2.3	2.0
50	7.0	6.1	5.3	4.4	3.6	2.8	2.0	1.2	0
40	7.0	6.0	4.9	3.9	2.9	1.9	1.0	0	0
30	7.0	5.8	4.6	3.4	2.3	1.1	0	0	0
20	7.0	5.6	4.3	2.9	1.6	0.3	0	0	0

Assumptions: 7 percent pool policy, 10 percent pass-through rate; 210 PSA, 360 WAM at origination; servicer advances scheduled P&I; recoveries occur 12 months after foreclosure.

Source: Lehman Brothers Fixed Income Research.

after, the CDR grows at an annualized rate of 0.02 percent every month until it reaches an annualized rate of 0.6 percent at month 30. After month 30, the default rate is assumed to hold constant from

FIGURE 11.8
Standard Default Assumption

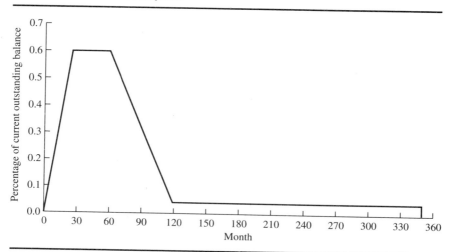

month 30 to month 60. The default rate then declines at a rate of 0.02 percent per month from month 60 to month 120 and to an annualized rate of 0.03 percent for the remaining life of the pool (less 12 months, the time assumed to be required to liquidate the last default). The decline in the CDR from month 60 to month 120 reflects the decline in default rates with pool seasoning. An SDA of 200 implies default rates that are twice the rate implied by the SDA; an SDA of 50 translates to half the level of the SDA standard.

Interaction of SDA and Prepayment Rates

Cumulative defaults represent the total of all mortgages from the original pool that have either defaulted or are delinquent and certain to default. Since the SDA specifies the default rate to be applied to the previous month's performing balance and not on the original balance, cumulative defaults will depend on the prepayment assumption. For a given SDA, higher prepayment rates result in lower cumulative default rates. For instance, 100 SDA for a 30-year, 8 percent pool of mortgages implies a cumulative default rate of 2.78 percent at 150 PSA and only 2.08 percent at 300 PSA. Table 11.7 illustrates this effect.

TABLE 11.7
Cumulative Defaults over Life: Sensitivity to Prepayment Rates and Default Rates (30-Year, 8 Percent Mortgage Pool)

Prepayment Rate (PSA)	Default Rate (SDA)			
	50	100	200	300
100	1.56	3.09	6.08	8.97
150	1.40	2.78	5.47	8.08
200	1.26	2.51	4.95	7.32

Source: Public Securities Association.

CHAPTER 12

FLOATING-RATE CMO STRUCTURES

One of the most important CMO innovations of the mid-1980s was the floating-rate class, or **CMO floater**.[1] It was developed for investors who need or prefer short-duration, adjustable-rate assets. In times of a positively sloped yield curve the floater, which is priced to the short-term, lower-yielding portion of the Treasury curve, provides much of the economics that drive a CMO transaction. As of year-end 1992 floater outstandings amounted to $11 billion.

CMO FLOATER CHARACTERISTICS

The CMO floater coupon has an adjustable interest rate that is reset periodically at a constant spread over an index, usually LIBOR. The maximum interest rate to which the coupon can reset is restricted by a single life cap, but there are generally no periodic caps. The cap is almost always a single interest rate, but in some early deals there was a series of interest rates, called step-up caps, allowing a gradual upward adjustment in the floating rate.

The early floater deals were structured to be the first tranche of a CMO and usually carried a short average life, typically not beyond 7 years. The margin over the index was about 50 basis points over LIBOR, and the highest caps normally ranged between 500 and 600 basis points over prevailing LIBOR. As the floater gained wide acceptance among investors, more tranches, and in some cases all tranches, became floaters. In the early 1990s it became more common to structure floaters out of a long-average-life support class using a floater/inverse floater structure. Under such structures the

---

[1]The first floating-rate CMO was introduced in September 1986 by Lehman Brothers.

floater would more often have an average life of 19 years with a margin over LIBOR of close to 100 points.

CMO Floater Structure

The five structural considerations with CMO floaters are the (1) index, (2) margin, (3) coupon cap, (4) collateral, and (5) class deal position.

Index
The **index** is the benchmark for the floater coupon. The most common indexes are **LIBOR,** Treasury-based indexes such as the **CMT,** and the **COFI.**

LIBOR. In general, a LIBOR-based CMO floater is indexed to the LIBOR corresponding to its payment frequency, which is usually monthly but may be reset to three- or six-month intervals. The interest rate on the floater is usually reset two business days prior to the CMO payment date. On each reset day, at 11 A.M. London time, the CMO bond trustee determines the appropriate LIBOR by surveying interest rates quoted by the London offices of four reference banks. The four quotations are averaged and rounded to the nearest 16th to arrive at the index rate. The interest payment on the floater is then determined, assuming a 30/360-day basis.

CMT. Floaters indexed to the CMT reset monthly to any of the published CMT indexes, typically the 1-, 7-, or 10-year CMT. The 1-year CMT is the most common. The reset date is generally the last day of the month.

COFI. Floaters indexed to COFI almost universally use the 11th District COFI, which is derived from the monthly cost of funds of thrift institutions in the 11th District of the FHLB system (California, Arizona, and New Mexico).

Index Frequency. The **index frequency** determines the length of time between resets—monthly, quarterly, annually, and so on. It is important to note that except for LIBOR-based floaters the reset frequency often differs from the interval of the index itself; for example, 1-, 7-, and 10-year CMT-indexed floaters ordinarily reset monthly.

Investors sensitive to the shape of the yield curve will wish to tailor their CMO floater investments accordingly. In times of rising interest rates, a monthly reset would presumably be preferred. When interest rates are declining, a three- or six-month reset may be preferred.

Margin

The **margin** determines the floater coupon:

$$\text{Floater coupon} = \text{Index value} + \text{Margin}$$

The margin spread is narrow for short-average-life CMO floater classes backed by stable collateral and may range to over 100 basis points for a 20-year-average-life support class. The margin spread is also a function of how much the interest rate cap is out of the money and of the relative volatility of interest rates. In general, the margin spread is a function of the factors shown in Table 12.1.

Margin Spread. In general:

- The shorter the average life, the narrower may be the spread to the index.
- The lower the cap rate, the greater the required spread to the index.
- The greater the average-life extension risk, or the higher the cap rate, the greater the required spread to the index.

Coupon Cap

The coupon cap sets the maximum interest rate the CMO floater may achieve. The cap is an implicit interest rate option embedded into the security. The purchase of a floating-rate CMO bond, therefore, may be viewed as consisting of two transactions: purchase of a short-, intermediate-, or long-term floating-rate bond and sale of a series of interest rate caps, one for each reset interval over the life of the bond. Investors in CMO floaters are, therefore, short the interest rate cap option (where there is an associated inverse floater the inverse floater investor is long this cap, as discussed in Understanding Inverse Floaters on page 500).

TABLE 12.1
Determinants of Margin Spread

Factor	Margin Spread Wider	Margin Spread Narrower
Bond class average life	Long	Short
Cap premium priced	Low	High
Collateral	Premium priced	Discount priced
Market volatility	High	Low

Since there is a margin spread, the floater coupon will be capped at a level above that of the floater coupon by the amount of the margin. That level is referred to as the **strike level**. Figure 12.1 illustrates the relationship among the floater coupon, margin, cap, and strike.

Example:

> Coupon cap = 10 percent
> Margin   = 75 basis points
> Strike   = 9.25 percent

If LIBOR = 9%   Investor receives 9.75% (Index + Margin)
If LIBOR = 9.25%   Investor receives 10%   (Index + Margin)
If LIBOR = 10%   Investor receives 10%   (Index flat)
If LIBOR = 10.75% Investor receives 10%   (Index − 75 bp)

As the example and Figure 12.1 illustrate, with a 10 percent cap and a 75 basis points margin the coupon paid to the floater investor reaches its maximum value when LIBOR is at 9.25 percent, which is the strike level.

$$\text{Strike level} = \text{Cap} - \text{Margin}$$

In the example, when LIBOR is at 9 percent, the floater cap is said to be out of the money; at 9.25 percent it is at the money; and at any level above 9.75 percent it is in the money.

Valuation Considerations

Volatility Impact

Interest rate volatility has an impact on the performance of the CMO floater. If volatility is high, the floater will be in and out of the money at frequent intervals. If volatility is low in a low interest

FIGURE 12.1
CMO Floater Coupon Set at LIBOR plus 75 Basis Points, 10 Percent Cap

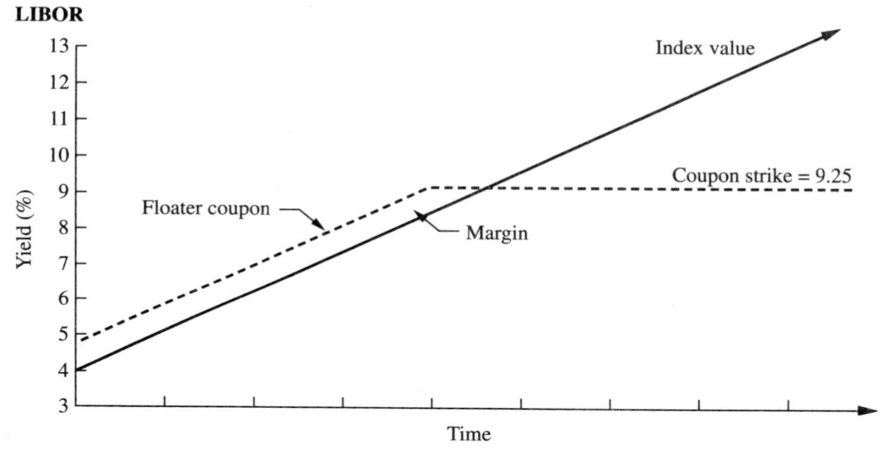

rate environment, the floater investor will receive the index and margin coupon indefinitely; if volatility is low in a high interest rate environment, the floater investor will own, in effect, a fixed-rate bond. Only in the late 1980s did some floaters actually hit their caps, and that was only for a few months. At the time interest rate volatility was high, and total-return investors, such as money managers, found the capped floaters attractive because they were able to buy capped floaters discounted to attractive yields.

Price to Discount Margin

CMO floaters are generally priced to a **discount margin (DM).** The floater is priced at or close to par as a new issue, but in secondary market trading the floater is priced to a premium or discount, depending on three variables: (1) the relation of the index plus margin to current short-term interest rates, (2) the present value assigned to the interest rate cap, and (3) the relative level of market volatility.

As long as the cap is reasonably above the strike level, the floater will trade close to par. However, as the floater coupon approaches the strike the market will assign greater value to the cap, which will cause the price of the floater to decline below par. As market volatility rises, the value of the cap increases. Therefore, if market volatility increases when the floater coupon is near (but not at) the strike level, the floater will trade to a discount price before the coupon hits the strike level.

Prepayment Risk

Prepayment activity also affects the pricing of a floater, especially when interest rates are rising. In a rising interest rate environment, prepayment speeds will likely decline, and the weighted average life of the floater will extend. As the average life extends, the time that the investor is exposed to the interest rate cap is extended, thereby increasing the investor's risk. Stated another way, the time value of the cap is increased. Since both volatility and time extension increase, the value of the interest rate cap increases and the price of the floater declines. Remember, since the floater investor is short the cap, the value of the cap becomes a minus in the pricing equation.

CMO Principal Structures

When floating-rate CMOs were first developed, the principal outstanding on a floater was gradually paid down, as with other fixed-rate tranches. This type is called a sequential-pay floater. The counterparty to the floater was a floating-rate residual. Recently, an inverse floater has been developed that shares the principal paydown of the collateral with the floater. The fixed-rate classes of the early deals were structured to carry deep-discount coupons, so that even with the floater at its maximum (capped) coupon, the total coupon interest owed the CMO bondholders would not exceed the total coupon income of the collateral pool. Figures 12.2 and 12.3 illustrate the bond structure of the early deals, which contain floater classes that pay concurrent with other fixed-rate, deep-discount coupon tranches. The structure illustrated in Figure 12.2 is the most conservative, with the floating class paying concurrently with the first fixed-rate bond class. The floater depicted in this type of structure would be priced to the narrowest spread to LIBOR of any floater structure shown in Figures 12.2 through 12.5.

The structure in Figure 12.3 is similar to that in Figure 12.2 except the floater class generally represents a greater percentage of the total offering and pays parallel to the first two fixed-rate classes. However, it is also a relatively conservative structure, and given collateral priced to conservative prepayment-speed assumptions, it offers moderate protection against average-life extension. This

FIGURE 12.2
CMO Floater Structured as Concurrent Pay with First Fixed-Rate Class

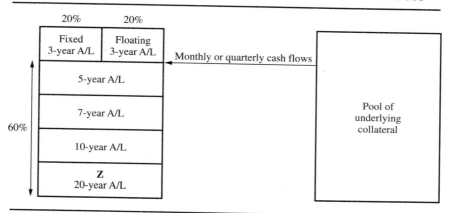

Source: Lehman Brothers Fixed Income Research.

FIGURE 12.3
CMO Floater Structured as Concurrent Pay with First Two Fixed-Rate Classes

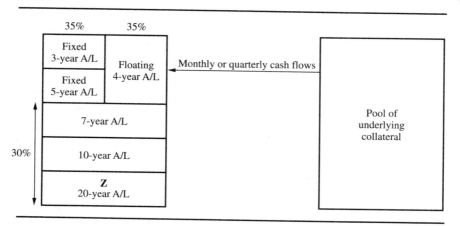

Source: Lehman Brothers Fixed Income Research.

structure would likely be priced to a somewhat wider spread to LIBOR than the first structure and offers good risk/reward if priced to a conservative prepayment assumption. The typical average-life range for this structure is 3 to 5 years.

Figure 12.4 illustrates a floater class created as a **collateral strip**. In this structure the floater class pays parallel with all the fixed sequential-pay bonds; its average life is, therefore, the average life of the underlying collateral. This structure would be priced to a wider spread to LIBOR than either of the first two, but the typical average-life range of this structure is 7 to 10 years.

Figure 12.5 illustrates a single-class, all-floater issue. The floater, since it *is* the bond issue, has the average life of the underlying collateral. This uncommon structure was issued using premium-priced collateral to minimize the average life. However, with premium collateral there is potential the prepayment speed can slow, resulting in extension of the average life. The typical average life range of this structure at pricing was 2 to 7 years.

Super Floaters

Super floating-rate CMOs leverage the floating-rate coupon by a multiplier less a spread to LIBOR. For example, the coupon might be determined as:

$$\text{Coupon} = 2 \times \text{LIBOR} - 75 \text{ basis points}$$

The super floater structure has been infrequently created, although it has been in demand to hedge portfolios against interest rate risk should rates rise suddenly and unexpectedly. The super floater can be combined with interest rate swaps or IO strips to hedge against a decline in interest rates.

Fixed-rate swaps provide attractive off-balance sheet leverage. In order to replicate the spread results of the matched swap structure with on-balance sheet securities, one would need to find fixed-rate assets with spreads to LIBOR that are double those of fixed-rate swaps. For example, if the super floater can be financed with zero carry and combined with a fixed-rate swap that has a 200 basis points initial spread to LIBOR, then the combination will have a 200 basis points ROA. If in place of a swap one were to use a fixed-rate asset with a 300 basis points spread to LIBOR, then the average ROA would be only 150 basis points. Although the fixed-rate asset may have a larger spread to LIBOR, it is an on-balance

FIGURE 12.4

**CMO Floater Structured as Collateral Strip Concurrent Pay with All
Sequential Fixed-Rate Classes**

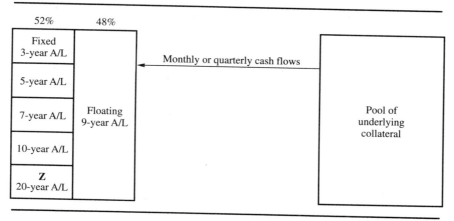

Source: Lehman Brothers Fixed Income Research.

FIGURE 12.5

CMO Structured as a Single-Class All Floater

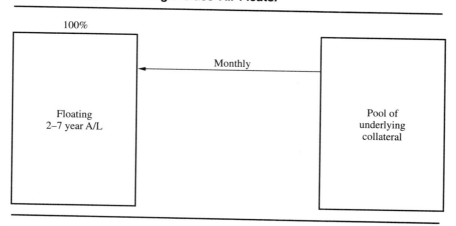

Source: Lehman Brothers Fixed Income Research.

sheet asset and therefore increases the denominator in the ROA calculation.

The prepayment option may actually be a benefit in these structures. As interest rates rise and prepayments slow, the balance of super floaters might be higher than expected or even exceed the swap balance. This is an excellent outcome because the super floater security performs very well in higher interest rate environments whereas the fixed-rate swaps perform poorly. In high interest rate environments one would prefer more super floaters than swaps.

Conversely, when rates decline and prepayments accelerate, the balance of the super floater may be much lower than expected. This is also fortuitous. When rates are low the super floater performs poorly and the fixed swaps perform very well. In low interest rate environments one would prefer more swaps than super floaters.

By combining super floaters and bullet-maturity swaps rather than 30-year, fixed-rate mortgages to create ARMs synthetically, one avoids the tail risk of the fixed-rate mortgages at the end of the holding period. The expected price risk of the super floater alone should be lower than that of ARMs or fixed-rate mortgages. These structures do expose investors to Treasury/LIBOR basis risk; however, the risk is similar to that of Treasury ARM positions, which are funded with LIBOR deposits or repos.

UNDERSTANDING INVERSE FLOATERS[2]

This section introduces inverse floaters through description of their structure and investment characteristics.

Background

An **inverse floater** is a floating-rate security whose coupon adjusts to an index in the opposite direction as the index—that is, it adjusts inversely with the index at specified adjustment intervals. The most

---

[2]This discussion of inverse floaters is based on research and writing by Laurence Penn, Senior Vice President, Manager, Derivatives Trading Desk; Alan Jay Brazil, Senior Vice President, Mortgage Strategies; and Andrew Davilman, Vice President, Mortgage Derivatives Trading Desk, Lehman Brothers.

common indexes are the 1- and 3-month LIBOR and COFI and the 1-year CMT. The 7- and 10-year CMT are also used.

Inverse floaters represented one of the fastest growing sectors of the MBS market in the early 1990s, with issuance exceeding 35 billion through 1993. Inverse floaters are created in the process of structuring floating-rate CMO classes from fixed-rate collateral (see Chapter 7). The recent strong demand for CMO floaters and a steep, positive yield curve led to an increased supply of inverse floaters starting in 1991. Because of their superior credit quality and high yield, inverse floaters have become popular with nontraditional mortgage investors, principally money managers, pension funds, and overseas investors.

Federal agency-guaranteed inverse floaters typically offer among the highest yields within the MBS market, although they do not necessarily contain the highest risk; whole-loan backed, AAA-rated inverse floaters offer somewhat higher yields. The increased yield is offered as compensation for a combination of potential price volatility and a relatively illiquid secondary market. Portfolio managers can choose inverse floaters with structural characteristics that control both average-life variability and responsiveness to interest rate changes (with floors).

Structure

An inverse floater is a security whose coupon moves in a direction opposite to the movement of interest rates. Each inverse floater is accompanied by a parallel floating-rate security with a coupon that moves in the same direction as interest rates. These two securities are backed by fixed-rate collateral and are structured so that the impact of a higher coupon on one class is exactly offset by a correspondingly lower coupon on the other class.

The inverse floater coupon resets to a formula, such as coupon = 40.00 − 4 × 1-month LIBOR:

$$\text{Coupon} = \text{Cap} - M \times \text{LIBOR}$$

where

Inverse cap = 40 percent
Multiplier = 4.0
Index   = 1-month LIBOR

In this formula, 40 percent is the cap on the inverse floater because it is the coupon that results from a LIBOR value of zero percent. The multiplier of 4.0 determines the impact of index movements on the inverse floater coupon—in this case, the coupon changes inversely by four times the change in the index. For example, if the index (LIBOR) were to *decrease* by 1 percent (100 basis points), the inverse floater coupon would *increase* by 400 basis points. By contrast, the associated floater coupon would *decrease* by 100 basis points.

With a floater/inverse floater structure the multiplier on the inverse is generally equal to the proportion of floaters to inverse floaters. Thus, a structure with $20 million principal amount of inverse floaters and $80 million of floaters will have a multiplier of 4.0.

Leverage Relationships

The value of the multiplier determines whether the inverse is a low-, medium-, or high-leverage floater. In general:

Low leverage	Multiplier 1 to 2 times
Medium leverage	Multiplier 2 to 4.5 times
High leverage	Multiplier 4.5 times or greater

Lower-multiplier inverse floaters have an additional feature, the coupon floor, which is the minimum guaranteed coupon on the security regardless of the index level. Inverse floaters with higher multipliers (4.0 in the example just given) have an implied floor of zero. In a floating-rate structure, lower caps increase the upside potential of the inverse floater, whereas higher floors limit the downside risk.

Creating an Inverse Floater

Inverse floaters, and their accompanying floating-rate tranches, may be created from any class of a CMO structure. Inverse floaters are created by splitting a fixed-rate bond into two floating-rate components—a floating-rate bond and an inverse structured such that the floater and inverse floater coupons always equal the original fixed-rate coupon. The creation of an inverse floater is a two-step process (see Figures 12.6A and 12.6B).

FIGURE 12.6A

FNMA 1991-42 REMIC PAC Support Bond Class Structure

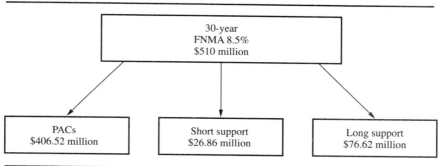

Source: Lehman Brothers Fixed Income Research.

Step 1: Select the Maturity and Call Protection

Figure 12.6A shows that $510 million of 30-year FNMA 8.5s was divided into PAC and support class bonds to create the basic structure of FNMA 91–42. Any of the resulting CMO classes was a candidate to be structured as an inverse floater and a floating-rate tranche. In most cases, the investor chooses the characteristics of

FIGURE 12.6B

FNMA 1991-42 REMIC Long Support Class Carved into Floater/Inverse Floater

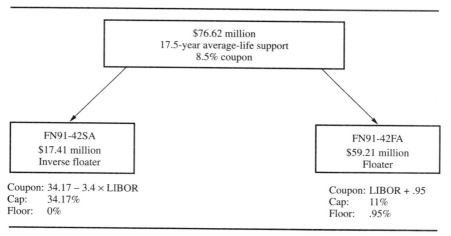

Source: Lehman Brothers Fixed Income Research.

the inverse: the maturity (in this example, 5- or 25-year average life) and the degree of call protection (either the stable PAC tranches or the higher-yielding support classes). In this structure the long support class was split into a floater (FNMA 91–42FA) and an inverse floater (FNMA 91–42SA).

Step 2: Select the Inverse Floater Parameters

In this example, the long support class was stripped into two parallel classes—an inverse floater and a floating-rate security. As shown in Figure 12.6B, the $76.62 million 8.5 percent support class (17.5-year average life) was split into $17.41 million inverse floaters (with a coupon of 34.17 − 3.4 × LIBOR) and $59.21 million floaters (with a coupon of LIBOR + 0.95). The coupon on both securities is reset monthly based on the level of 1-month LIBOR. The coupon on the inverse floater has a cap of 34.17 percent and a floor of zero. The floor and cap on the floating-rate class coupon are 11 percent and 0.95 percent, respectively. These caps and floors ensure that the WAC on the two classes never exceeds 8.5 percent, the coupon on the underlying CMO support class.

The coupon on the inverse floater moves inversely with the level of interest rates, giving the inverse unique investment characteristics. For example, a 10 basis points decline in the 1-month LIBOR leads to a 34 basis points increase in the coupon of the FNMA 91–42SA inverse floater (the 3.4 multiplier times the 10 basis points) and a 10 basis points reduction in the floater coupon. Since there are 3.4 times as many floaters as inverse floaters, a 10 basis points decline in the floater coupon exactly offsets the 34 basis points increase in the inverse coupon. A range of potential fluctuations in the coupons on the two securities in response to the level of the 1-month LIBOR is shown in Table 12.2.

Investment Characteristics

- The performance of inverse floaters is determined by the characteristics of the underlying CMO class and the parameters defining the coupon on the inverse floater.
- As with the yields on fixed-rate CMOs, inverse floaters backed by support classes yield more than those backed by sequential-pay or PAC classes. Premium inverse floaters usually offer higher yields than discount inverse floaters.

TABLE 12.2
Coupons on FNMA 91-42SA (Inverse) and FNMA 91-42FA (Floater) for Different Levels of LIBOR

LIBOR (%)	Coupon (%)		WAC (%)
	Inverse Floater	Floater	
0.00	34.17	0.95	8.50%
2.00	27.37	2.95	8.50
4.00	20.57	4.95	8.50
6.00	13.77	6.95	8.50
8.00	6.97	8.95	8.50
10.00	0.17	10.95	8.50
10.05	0.00	11.00	8.50
12.00	0.00	11.00	8.50

- Inverse floaters with high floors offer less downside risk and are priced at lower yields.

Three sets of variables determine the performance characteristics of the inverse floater: the parameters that describe the inverse floater coupon (multiplier, cap, floor, and floating-rate index); the attributes of the underlying CMO class and collateral (the coupon of the collateral and the type of CMO class, e.g., PAC or support); and the shape of the yield curve.

The economics of an inverse floater are similar to those of a leveraged repurchase transaction. The inverse floater buyer has purchased, in effect, a leveraged position in the "mother" fixed-rate bond from which it was derived. The inverse buyer has, in effect, borrowed the economics of the fixed-rate bond, funding in the short-term market at a rate equivalent to the value of the floater bond. The inverse buyer receives the spread between the values at any given time of the inverse coupon and the coupon of the original fixed-rate bond.

This transaction is similar to receiving the spread between a fixed-rate bond and the carrying cost of a repurchase agreement, a transaction familiar to all depository institutions. There are two essential differences, however: First, the inverse buyer has usually leveraged the economics by the multiplier applied to the index value; second—and very important—the inverse buyer cannot receive a value below zero. There can all too easily be a negative carry on the repurchase agreement. The floor of the inverse would be zero if the maximum leverage has been applied, but it could be above zero if less than the maximum leverage has been applied.

The investor needs to understand that the value of the inverse floater is affected by economic factors other than just the multiplier of the index. For example, if the inverse is a support class that was purchased at a discount, accelerating prepayments would increase its value; if it was purchased at a premium, declining prepayments would increase its value (and vice versa). The inverse investor will be affected by the value of the underlying fixed-rate coupon bond. If interest rates rise, the value of the fixed-rate bond underlying the floater inverse will decline. Therefore, one may derive the value of the inverse floater by deducting the market value of the floater from the value of the "mother" fixed-rate coupon bond. Since the floater generally remains priced close to par, most of the change in the value of the inverse will be attributable to the change in the value of the original fixed-rate bond; and that change in value will be leveraged as a function of the multiplier on the inverse.[3]

Valuing the Inverse Floater Cap

From the preceding discussion it should be clear that the value of the inverse floater is closely related to the economics of the floater bond. Whereas the investor in the floater is short the cap on the floater coupon, the buyer of the inverse is *long* the floater cap. The cap on the floater prevents the inverse coupon from going below zero—or, depending on the leverage, can provide an above-zero floor for the inverse. (Logically, the cap on the floater provides the floor for the inverse, since the inverse is the mirror of the floater, and the sum of the floater and inverse components must always equal the economics of the "mother" fixed-rate coupon bond.) The value of this cap may be determined in one of two ways: (1) from the value implied by the forward-rate curve together with a volatility assumption and (2) through pricing a series of over the counter caps. The mathematical derivation of the cap value is given in "Inverse Floater Math," which follows.

---

[3]See *Understanding the Pricing of Inverse Floaters* by Michael Winchell and Michael Levine, Risk Management, Bear Stearns & Company. New York: Bear Stearns, October 1991.

Inverse Floater Parameters

The **multiplier** determines the impact of index movements on the inverse floater coupon. For an inverse with a multiplier of 3, the coupon changes inversely by three times the movement of the index. In a floater and inverse floater structure, the multiplier on the inverse is generally equal to the proportion of floaters to inverse floaters. A higher multiplier leads to a higher base case yield in a positively sloped yield curve environment. (The higher multiplier implies a large proportion of low-yielding floaters and, consequently, a small proportion of high-yielding inverse floaters.) Inverse floaters with low multipliers attempt to balance investor desires for both higher yield and more stable yield profiles. Multipliers as low as 0.4 have been created that offer a judicious mix of incremental yield and relatively stable yield profile.

The **cap** sets the ceiling, whereas the **floor** indicates the minimum for the coupon on the inverse floater. The impact of caps and floors on the inverse floater is straightforward: A higher cap increases the upside potential of the inverse floater, and a higher floor limits the downside risk of the inverse. The caps and floors on the inverse floater ensure that the structure is self-supporting.

Although most inverse floaters have used 1-month LIBOR as their index, many have also been tied to movements of the COFI or the 7- and 10-year CMT yield.

Inverse Floater Math

The creation of an inverse floater is a zero sum game; the combination of the floater and inverse floater coupons and principal amounts must at all times equal the coupon and principal amount of the fixed-coupon CMO class from which the floater/inverse structure was derived. Mathematically, the relationships defined in Equation 12.1 must be maintained:

$$(Fc \times Fp) + (INVc \times INVp) = (Bc \times Bp) \tag{12.1}$$

where

Fc	=	Floater coupon
Fp	=	Floater principal
$INVc$	=	Inverse coupon
$INVp$	=	Inverse principal
Bc	=	Coupon of original fixed-bond class
Bp	=	Total principal of original fixed-bond class

If we assume an original fixed-coupon class of $10 million with a 9 percent coupon, there will be a total of $900,000 (0.9 × 10 million) of coupon to divide between the floater and the inverse. Further, assume LIBOR is at 5.5 percent.

Example 1: Using the Maximum Coupon Leverage[4]

Total principal of floater and inverse floater	$10 million
Underlying collateral coupon	9.0%
Current LIBOR	5.5%
Floater cap	11.0%
Floater margin (spread over LIBOR)	80 bp
Coupon leverage	Maximum

Floater Coupon

Floater coupon = Current LIBOR + Floater margin

Floater coupon = 5.5 + 0.80 = 6.30%

Maximum Coupon Leverage

$$\text{Maximum coupon leverage} = \frac{\text{Collateral coupon}}{\text{Floater cap} - \text{Collateral coupon}}$$

$$\text{Maximum coupon leverage} = \frac{9}{11.0 - 9.0} = 4.5$$

Floater Principal

$$\text{Floater principal} = \frac{\text{Coupon leverage} \times \text{Total principal}}{(1 + \text{Coupon leverage})}$$

$$\text{Floater principal} = \frac{4.5 \times 10,000,000}{(1 + 4.5)} = \$8,181,818.18$$

Inverse Principal

Inverse principal = Total principal − Floater principal

$$\begin{aligned}\text{Inverse principal} &= \$10,000,000 - \$8,181,818.18 \\ &= \$1,818,182.82\end{aligned}$$

---

[4]This example is from *Inverse Floating Rate CMOs: Concepts and Strategies* by Bella Bora, Brian Lancaster, and Jane Tang, Financial Analysis and Structured Transactions Group, Bear Stearns & Company. New York: Bear Stearns, October 4, 1991.

Inverse Coupon

The total amount of interest paid to the floater and inverse floater in any time period must be less than or equal to the total interest available from the underlying collateral coupon. Equation 12.2 may be written as:

$$
\begin{pmatrix} \text{Floater} \\ \text{coupon} \end{pmatrix} \times \begin{pmatrix} \text{Floater} \\ \text{principal} \end{pmatrix} + \begin{pmatrix} \text{Inverse} \\ \text{coupon} \end{pmatrix} \times \begin{pmatrix} \text{Inverse} \\ \text{principal} \end{pmatrix}
$$

$$
\leq \begin{pmatrix} \text{Collateral} \\ \text{coupon} \end{pmatrix} \times \begin{pmatrix} \text{Total} \\ \text{principal} \end{pmatrix} \tag{12.2}
$$

In this example, a total of \$900,000 of interest will be split between the two tranches (9.0/100 × \$10,000,000).

If the floater coupon is 6.3 percent and \$515,454.54 of interest is allocated to the floater tranche (6.3/100 × 8,181,818.18), then the remaining \$384,545.46 of interest (\$900,000 − \$515,454.54) is allocated to the inverse floater. The initial inverse floater coupon is calculated by dividing this amount by the inverse principal expressed as a percentage (\$384,545.46/1,818,181.82) × 100, which is 21.15.

From Equation 12.2 we obtain:

$$
\text{Initial inverse coupon} \leq \frac{\begin{pmatrix} \text{Collateral} \\ \text{coupon} \end{pmatrix} \times \begin{pmatrix} \text{Total} \\ \text{principal} \end{pmatrix} - \begin{pmatrix} \text{Floater} \\ \text{coupon} \end{pmatrix} \times \begin{pmatrix} \text{Floater} \\ \text{principal} \end{pmatrix}}{\text{Inverse principal}}
$$

$$
\text{Initial inverse coupon} = \frac{9.0 \times 10,000,000) - (6.3 \times 8,181,818.18)}{1,818,181.82} = 21.15\%
$$

The inverse coupon is always expressed as a function of the inverse cap and leverage (see Inverse Cap, which follows):

Inverse coupon = Inverse cap − (Coupon leverage × Current **LIBOR**)

Inverse Floor

The floor refers to the minimum coupon that the inverse floater can reset to. It is computed by assuming that the floater coupon has reached its life cap:

$$
\begin{pmatrix} \text{Collateral} \\ \text{coupon} \end{pmatrix} \times \begin{pmatrix} \text{Total} \\ \text{principal} \end{pmatrix} - \begin{pmatrix} \text{Floater} \\ \text{cap} \end{pmatrix} \times \begin{pmatrix} \text{Floater} \\ \text{principal} \end{pmatrix}
$$

$$
\geq \begin{pmatrix} \text{Inverse} \\ \text{floor} \end{pmatrix} \times \begin{pmatrix} \text{Inverse} \\ \text{principal} \end{pmatrix} \tag{12.3}
$$

In this example, if the floater coupon is equal to its life cap of 11 percent, then all of the $900,000 interest available (11/100 × 8,181,818.18) is allocated to the floater, and no interest is allocated to the inverse floater. The floor is calculated by dividing this amount by the inverse principal (0/1,818,181.82), which is zero.

From Equation 12.3 we may derive Equation 12.4:

$$\text{Inverse floor} \leq \frac{\left(\begin{array}{c}\text{Collateral} \\ \text{coupon}\end{array} \times \begin{array}{c}\text{Total} \\ \text{principal}\end{array}\right) - \left(\begin{array}{c}\text{Floater} \\ \text{coupon}\end{array} \times \begin{array}{c}\text{Floater} \\ \text{principal}\end{array}\right)}{\text{Inverse floater principal}} \quad (12.4)$$

$$\text{Inverse floor} = \frac{9.0 \times 10,000,000) - (11.0 \times 8,181,818.18)}{1,818,181.82} = 0\%$$

Note that if the coupon leverage is at its maximum, the floor will always equal zero.

Inverse Cap

The inverse cap is the maximum coupon that the inverse floater can reset to. It is computed by assuming that LIBOR is equal to zero. When LIBOR is zero, the floater coupon is equal to its margin.

$$\left(\begin{array}{c}\text{Collateral} \\ \text{coupon}\end{array} \times \begin{array}{c}\text{Total} \\ \text{principal}\end{array}\right) - \left(\begin{array}{c}\text{Floater} \\ \text{coupon}\end{array} \times \begin{array}{c}\text{Floater} \\ \text{principal}\end{array}\right)$$

$$\geq \left(\begin{array}{c}\text{Inverse} \\ \text{cap}\end{array} \times \begin{array}{c}\text{Inverse} \\ \text{principal}\end{array}\right) \quad (12.5)$$

In this example, the floater coupon is equal to 0.80 percent when LIBOR is zero. The interest allocated to the floater is $65,454.55 (0.80/100 × 8,181,818.18), and the remaining $834,545.45 of interest ($900,000 − $65,454.55) is allocated to the inverse floater. The inverse cap is calculated by dividing this amount by the inverse principal expressed as a percentage, $834,545.45/$1,818,181.82 × 100, which is 45.90 percent.

In Example 1 (p. 502) the cap and margin characteristics of the floater are a given, which is typically the case; since the volume of floaters is usually substantially greater than that of the inverse, the floater characteristics are market driven. The *leverage*, or multiple, is generally a function of what orders can be generated for what type of inverse. Typically, the greater the leverage, the greater the CMO economics, since the floater is the lower-yielding bond, thereby maximizing the CMO arbitrage. However, it is not always possible or desirable to structure the maximum-leveraged inverse. With lower leverage, a floor can be added to the inverse floater that will enhance the marketability of the floater and reduce the yield at which it must be sold. Example 2 illustrates creating specific coupon leverage, which permits adding a floor (in this case 3 percent) to the inverse.

Example 2: Using a Specific Coupon Leverage[5]

Total principal of floater and inverse floater	$10 million
Underlying collateral coupon	9.0%
Current LIBOR	5.5%
Floater cap	11.0%
Floater margin	80 bp
Coupon leverage	3.0

Floater Coupon

$$\text{Floater coupon} = (5.5 + 0.80) = 6.30\%$$

Floater Principal

$$\text{Floater principal} = \frac{3 \times \$10,000,000}{(1 + 3)} = \$7,500,000$$

$$\text{Floater principal} = \$10,000,000 - \$7,500,000 = \$2,500,000$$

Inverse Coupon

$$\text{Inverse coupon} = 33.60 - (3 \times 5.5) = 17.10\%$$

Inverse Floor

$$\text{Inverse floor} = \frac{(9 \times 10,000,000) - (11 \times 7,500,000)}{2,500,000} = 3.00\%$$

---

[5]*Inverse Floating Rate CMOs.*

Inverse Cap

$$\text{Inverse cap} = \frac{(9 \times 10,000,000) - (0.8 \times 7,500,000)}{2,500,000} = 33.60\%$$

Coupon and Type of Underlying CMO Collateral

Structuring inverse floaters with low-coupon collateral allows them to be priced at a lower yield because the inverse shares the characteristics of its collateral. Lowering the coupon on the underlying CMO class by stripping or by using discount collateral improves its convexity characteristics. A synthetic discount coupon (for example, an 8 percent coupon created from 9 percent collateral) allows for a lower dollar price on the underlying CMO class and inverse floater. Using discount collateral provides average-life stability, since interest rates would have to decline significantly before the underlying mortgages would face major refinancings. Therefore, inverse floaters backed by low-coupon CMO classes should trade at lower yields than those backed by current-coupon and premium CMO classes.

Inverse floaters structured from PAC CMO classes offer greater average-life stability and lower yield than those backed by regular CMO classes. In the same way, inverse floaters backed by support classes offer investors higher yields than those backed by comparable average-life sequential-pay CMO classes to compensate for their greater average-life volatility. Yield differences between PACs and support classes are amplified in inverse floaters because the convexity characteristics of the CMO class being restructured are passed along to the smaller inverse floater class.

Impact of the Yield Curve

A steep yield curve makes a large percentage of the coupon income from the underlying CMO class available to the inverse floater. For example, if LIBOR falls and the yield curve steepens, the yield on the inverse floater increases.

Behavior of Inverse Floater Coupons. Table 12.3 lists some of the wide range of inverse floaters available to the investor. The five sample inverse floaters have a wide span. Their multipliers range from a low 0.4 (security 1) to a high of 109 on the superpremium inverse floater (security 5). These securities also exhibit a variety of

TABLE 12.3
Selected Characteristics of Five Inverse Floaters

Security	Name	Type	Collateral WAC	WAM	Tranche Type	Average Life (years)	Inverse Coupon (%)	Floater Coupon	Floor (%)
1	FNMA 91-82s	FNMA 9.0	9.7	357	PAC II	5.4	9.0	$12.07 - .4 \times \text{LIBOR}$	8.5
2	FNMA G-13s	GNMA 9.5	10.0	342	Clean	18.82	8.5	$16.10 - 1 \times \text{LIBOR}$	0
3	FNMA 91-57s	FNMA 9.5	10.05	345	PAC	10.99	7.0	$17.67 - 1.75 \times \text{LIBOR}$	0
4	FNMA 91-42s	FNMA 8.5	9.24	339	Support	19.53	8.5	$37.4 - 3.4 \times \text{LIBOR}$	7.85
5	FNMA 91-90	FNMA 10	10.62	324	Clean	7.39	10.0	$1149.95 - 109 \times \text{LIBOR}$	0

FIGURE 12.7
Inverse Floater Structures (Comparative Performance of Inverse Coupon
to Changes in Index Value)

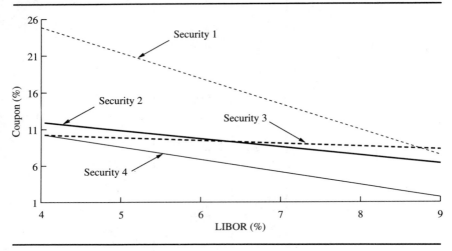

Source: Lehman Brothers Fixed Income Research.

structure types, including PACs (securities 1 and 3), supports (security 4), and clean or sequential pay (securities 2 and 6). Figure 12.7 shows the coupon pattern of four of the inverses described in Table 12.3 for their response to changes to the index value.

Impact of Deal Structure

Inverse floater buyers are affected not only by the leverage of the multiplier and prepayments but also by the stability versus volatility of the bond structure. In this section, examples compare the performance of high- versus low-leveraged and stable versus unstable deal structures.

Table 12.4 illustrates the price and yield parameters of a range of inverse floater structures, including low and moderate leverage as well as PAC, sequential, and support structures. Note that some of the structures include floors. The table illustrates the relationships between maximum leverage (zero floor) and the floor, price, and basis points yield spread to the curve. In general, the greater the leverage and the lower the floor, the lower the price and the wider the spread. Note the very stable PACs have reasonably high

TABLE 12.4
Inverse Floater Structures

Source	WAL (Years)	Multiplier	Cap (%)	Floor (%)	Price ($)	Treasury Yield (%)	Spread (bp)
PAC							
Low leverage							
5-year PAC	5.85	0.40	11.25	7.01	99-09	7.68	154
10-year PAC	10.98	0.40	11.83	7.71	99-15	8.06	166
15-year PAC	14.98	0.40	11.91	7.85	97-24	8.06	196
10-year PAC II	10.98	0.70	14.22	7.01	99-12	8.06	231
PAC II							
Low leverage 3-year	3.45	0.40	11.16	6.94	99-13	0.05	212
Moderate leverage 3-year	3.45	3.38	33.75	0.00	98-02	7.05	785
Support							
Low leverage 2-year	2.28	0.40	11.93	7.85	98-28	6.63	371
Moderate leverage 2-year	2.28	3.89	39.67	0.00	96-01	6.63	1,293
Low leverage 8-year	8.67	0.40	11.89	7.85	95-14	8.06	254
Moderate leverage 8-year	8.47	3.89	39.28	0.00	86-25	8.06	1,234

floors and very little discount and offer a moderate yield spread to the curve.

The 3-year-average-life PAC II, low-leverage inverse with a floor near 7 percent, offers a spread of 212 basis points (Table 12.4); the 3-year PAC II with a zero floor offers more discount and a much higher—785 basis points—spread to the curve (7.85 percent, which when added to the 7.05 percent Treasury yield, gives an initial yield of 14.90 percent). The relationships are the same with the supports, with the prices discounted even more and the spread pickup even greater. Note how dramatically the spread picks up with the zero floor! Those floors are expensive, but if the yield curve flattens sooner than expected the investor is at least stopped out at somewhere near the Treasury yield prevalent at the time of initial pricing. Investors who bought these inverses when they were offered in the summer of 1991 realized yields of 30 to 40 percent by late 1992 as the yield curve steepened and LIBOR fell to just over 3 percent.

Inverse Case Studies

The case studies that follow illustrate many of the different inverse floater structure types.

Case Study 1
Low-Leverage Inverse

> FNMA 1991–90 sequential-pay class
> Collateral, FNMA 10s
> Floor, 8.2%; cap, 12.34%; average life, 10.35 years at 150 PSA
> Coupon = 12.34 − 0.4 × 1-month LIBOR

In Case Study 1 the 10-year-average-life tranche of the FNMA 1991–90 REMIC was restructured as a floater/low-leverage inverse floater with a 0.40 multiplier, a high (8.2 percent) floor, and a 12.34 percent cap. Note the coupon on this inverse will move in the opposite direction as LIBOR, with a 10 basis points decline in LIBOR resulting in a 4 basis points increase in the coupon of the inverse. Table 12.5A illustrates the coupon differentiation of the inverse (structured as the LL class) and the coupon of the sequential-class bond from which it was structured. Table 12.5B compares the sensi-

TABLE 12.5A
Coupon Differentials for LL Inverse and Fixed-Coupon CMO

Security	Changes in LIBOR (bp)						
	−300	−200	−100	0	100	200	300
LL inverse	11.09	10.69	10.29	9.89	9.49	9.09	8.69
Fixed-rate	9.00	9.00	9.00	9.00	9.00	9.00	9.00
Advantage	2.09	1.69	1.29	0.89	0.49	0.09	−0.31

tivity of the LL class versus the fixed-rate CMO to interest rate shifts.

Case Study 2
Low-Leverage Inverse with Floor

FHLMC Gold 1993-02 support class

Collateral, GNMA 8s

Coupon = $14.25 - 1 \times$ 1-month LIBOR

Floor, 5.5%; cap, 14.25%; average life, 22.36 years at 150 PSA

In Case Study 2 the low-leverage inverse with a 5.5 percent floor has been structured from the 20-year support tranche of the FHLMC 1993–02 REMIC deal. Since the inverse is from a support class, it will have a high degree of sensitivity to prepayment volatility, ranging in average life from 22 years at the slow 90 PSA to 0.8 years at the fast 400 PSA. The yield table in Table 12.6 is generally referred to as a **seven-by-seven** because it shows seven LIBOR sce-

TABLE 12.5B
Yields and Yield Differentials for LL Inverse and Fixed-Rate CMO

Security	Shifts in Interest Rates (bp)						
	−300	−200	−100	0	100	200	300
LL inverse	11.69	12.24	10.77	10.35	9.89	9.47	9.05
Fixed-rate	9.75	9.66	9.58	9.51	9.48	9.46	9.45
Advantage	1.94	1.58	1.19	0.84	0.41	0.01	−0.40
Average life of both	4.77	5.92	7.74	10.11	11.82	13.24	14.46

narios across the top horizontal axis and seven prepayment speeds on the vertical axis. Each square of information under a LIBOR yield and opposite a PSA provides a yield and duration number. For example, at the base case, LIBOR is 3.25 percent, the PSA is 150, and the inverse yield is 11.45 percent with a 7.66-year duration. Since prepayment speeds are linked to interest rate shifts, the seven-by-seven is generally read diagonally, as shown by the numbers in boldface type. This approach reflects the relationship between rising and falling LIBOR rates and slowing and accelerating prepayment speeds, assuming *parallel* shifts in the yield curve (i.e., that LIBOR moves up or down by the same amount as the 7- or 10-year Treasury: It is, of course, the 7- and 10-year sector of the Treasury curve that drives prepayment rates). If a flat yield curve is to be assumed (LIBOR shifts but the 7- to 10-year maturity sector does not), then the table would be read on a horizontal axis at the desired PSA level (for example, in Table 12.6 at 150 PSA from 11.45 percent left to 8.31 percent).

Eliminating the Extremes

Some of the scenarios in Table 12.6 seem highly unlikely, especially those in the lower-left and upper-right quadrants. For example, it does not seem probable that the prepayment speed would accelerate from 150 to 400 PSA in an environment in which LIBOR increases by 400 basis points (lower-left quadrant) or that prepayments would decline to 90 PSA if LIBOR dropped to 0.25 percent. And it seems equally unlikely that LIBOR would even drop to 0.25 percent (upper-right quadrant). Most investors accept the premise that the nine scenarios adjacent to the base case (boxed areas) contain the most likely outcomes. Here the base case is a yield of 11.45 percent at 150 PSA with LIBOR at 3.25 percent. Due diligence calls for a check on the risk/reward of the extremes of the diagonal line (boldface numbers) and the flat-curve scenario (the numbers on the horizontal axis to the left of the base case).

Balloon Inverse Floaters

Inverses structured from 5- or 7-year balloon MBSs benefit from the short, stable average life of the balloon collateral. The short stated final maturity of the balloon protects the inverse holder from extension risk and indefinite exposure to the possibility of a contin-

TABLE 12.6
LIBOR to Prepayment-Sensitivity Analysis: FNMA 1993-02 20-Year Support Inverse, $19,727,697; Price, $98-16, Purchase Yield, 11.45

| | LIBOR Rates (%) | | | | | | | Average |
	6.25	5.25	4.25	3.25	2.25	1.25	0.25	Life (years)
	LIBOR Rises			Base	LIBOR Declines			
90 PSA	**8.30**	9.34	10.39	11.44	12.49	13.55	14.61	
	8.26	8.15	8.06	7.98	7.92	7.86	7.82	27.15
100 PSA	8.30	**9.34**	10.39	11.44	12.49	13.55	14.61	
	8.24	**8.13**	8.03	7.96	7.89	7.83	7.79	26.65
125 PSA	8.30	9.35	**10.39**	11.44	12.50	13.55	14.61	
	8.18	8.05	**7.95**	7.86	7.79	7.73	7.67	24.98
150 PSA	8.31	9.35	10.40	**11.45**	12.50·	13.56	14.62	
	8.02	7.87	7.76	**7.66**	7.57	7.50	7.44	22.36 ·
250 PSA	9.37	10.37	11.37	12.37	**13.38**	14.40	15.41	
	1.37	1.36	1.36	1.35	**1.34**	1.34	1.33	1.57
350 PSA	10.01	10.98	11.96	12.94	13.92	**14.91**	15.90	
	0.90	0.90	0.90	0.90	0.90	**0.89**	0.89	1.01
400 PSA	10.29	11.25	12.22	13.19	14.16	15.14	**16.12**	
	0.79	0.79	0.79	0.78	0.78	0.78	**0.78**	0.87

uously rising LIBOR. Case Study 3 illustrates the economics of a balloon inverse.

Case Study 3
Low-Leverage Balloon Inverse Collateral

FHLMC 5-year balloon PC, 6.5s

Coupon = 18.00 − 2.25 × 1-month LIBOR

Floor, 0.00 percent; cap, 18.00; average life, 3.34 years at 300 PSA

In Case Study 3 the inverse has a purchase yield of 11.12 percent and an average life of 3.34 years at 300 PSA (Table 12.7). Again, the table should be read diagonally, following the boldface numbers. Note that the average-life drift is within a tight range of 1.64 years, which demonstrates its stability. The yield ranges from

TABLE 12.7
LIBOR to Prepayment-Sensitivity Analysis: FHLMC 5-Year Balloon
Inverse; 6.5 Percent, $8,921,250.00; Price, $99-04, Purchase Yield, 11.12

PSA	LIBOR (%)						
	6.25	5.25	4.25	3.25	2.25	1.25	0.25
100	**4.20**	6.48	8.78	11.10	13.44	15.80	18.17
	4.35	4.09	3.85	3.62	3.42	3.23	3.05
200	4.20	**6.48**	8.78	11.10	13.44	15.80	18.17
	4.33	**4.08**	3.84	3.62	3.41	3.22	3.05
225	4.20	6.48	**8.78**	11.10	13.44	15.80	18.17
	4.30	4.05	**3.81**	3.59	3.39	3.21	3.03
300	4.22	6.50	8.80	**11.12**	13.45	15.81	18.18
	3.97	3.74	3.53	**3.34**	3.16	2.99	2.83
500	4.28	6.55	8.85	11.16	**13.49**	15.83	18.20
	3.20	3.03	2.88	2.73	**2.60**	2.47	2.36
750	4.37	6.64	8.92	11.22	13.54	**15.88**	18.23
	2.44	2.33	2.23	2.13	2.04	**1.96**	1.88
900	4.44	6.70	8.97	11.27	13.58	15.91	**18.25**
	2.08	2.00	1.92	1.84	1.77	1.71	**1.64**

18.25 percent at the low LIBOR (it appears unlikely LIBOR would fall to 0.25 percent) to 4.20 percent with LIBOR at 6.25 percent.

PAC Inverse

The PAC structure allows the inverse investor to take advantage of the high yield offered by an inverse while the PAC structure stabilizes the yield such that at PSA speeds within the band range the yield is fairly stable. The PAC structure is also attractive to inverse buyers because of the prepayment stability provided, especially the protection against extension risk. (Most inverse floater buyers don't mind being called out early, since it reduces the LIBOR exposure. This is especially true of inverses purchased at a discount, which, in most cases, is preferable to paying a premium.)

Case Study 4
FNMA 1992 G-93 Short-Average-Life PAC Inverse

Collateral, GNMA 8s

Coupon = 17.31 − 1.92 × 1-month LIBOR

Floor, 0.00%; cap, 17.31; PAC bands, 95–225 PSA

Table 12.8 illustrates the stable average life of this inverse, which in most scenarios offered a yield in a range from upper single digits to mid-teens, a very attractive offering at the time, when long-maturity Treasuries were yielding in the low 7s and LIBOR was at 3.19 percent.

Other Indexes
Other indexes may be used to take advantage of specific market conditions. Two such indexes are the COFI, for its lag, and the 7- and 10-year CMT, for its close correlation to prepayment rates.

COFI Inverses.   If short-term rates are anticipated to decline for some time, a COFI inverse will leverage the benefit to the investor of the steepening yield curve because of the lag inherent in the COFI index. The COFI lags several months behind the current level of short-term rates. (For a description of the lag in the COFI index, see The COFI Rate Lag in Chapter 13.) COFI also offers the advantage that it is a low-volatility index and historically has not risen above 9 percent, probably because thrift institutions in periods of rising interest rates become highly efficient at hedging out further rising interest rate exposure. For these reasons, low-leverage COFI inverses generally outperform the COFI floater, even for a considerable time after short-term interest rates have started to move up.

CMT Indexes.   The 7- and 10-year CMT indexes were created to make an inverse floater that would be a better hedge for an IO strip than the LIBOR inverse. In 1991, concern about the potential for an acceleration in prepayments made it increasingly difficult to sell IO strips without a hedge.

Declining interest rates are the obvious risk to IO investors. The inverse floater, which thrives on a decline in the index rate of the inverse, presented itself as an ideal hedge for the IO. However, IO investors were leery of the hedge benefit of the LIBOR-based inverse because it is mortgage rates that drive prepayment speeds, not

TABLE 12.8
LIBOR to Prepayment-Sensitivity Analysis: FNMA PAC Inverse,
$50,629,926.28; Price, 99-0; Purchase Yield, 11.69

| | LIBOR (%) | | | | | | | Average |
PSA	6.188	5.188	4.188	3.188	2.188	1.188	0.188	Life (Years)
75	**5.73**	7.70	9.68	11.66	13.67	15.68	17.70	7.02
	5.58	5.18	4.83	4.51	4.22	3.96	3.72	
100	5.77	**7.73**	9.70	11.70	13.69	15.70	17.72	5.98
	4.89	**4.58**	4.31	4.05	3.82	3.61	3.41	
125	5.77	7.73	**9.70**	11.70	13.69	15.70	17.72	5.98
	4.89	4.58	**4.31**	4.05	3.82	3.61	3.41	
155	5.77	7.73	9.70	**11.70**	13.69	15.70	17.72	5.98
	4.89	4.58	4.31	**4.05**	3.82	3.61	3.41	
200	5.77	7.73	9.70	11.70	**13.69**	15.70	17.72	5.98
	4.89	4.58	4.31	4.05	**3.82**	3.61	3.41	
250	5.78	7.74	9.71	11.70	13.69	**15.70**	17.72	5.76
	4.75	4.46	4.20	3.97	3.75	**3.54**	3.36	
350	5.85	7.80	9.77	11.74	13.73	15.73	**17.74**	3.37
	3.88	3.69	3.51	3.35	3.20	3.05	**2.92**	

LIBOR, and mortgage rates are more keyed to the 7- and 10-year-maturity sector of the Treasury curve. Wall Street therefore created the 7- and 10-year CMT index as one that would respond to interest rate changes and that would be more in tandem with prepayments than the LIBOR inverse, which is indexed off the very short end of the maturity spectrum. The difficulty is that the floater of the 7- and 10-year CMT is a difficult sale because floater buyers prefer an index more sensitive to the short end of the yield curve. There is, therefore, a limited supply available of the 7- and 10-year inverses.

IO INVERSE FLOATERS

An **inverse IO** is structured either by combining the IOette of a CMO bond class into an inverse floater, creating a **floating-rate IO (FRIO),** or by stripping an inverse floater into IO and PO components (an IOette is a portion of the CMO bond coupon stripped off to reduce the bond coupon; see "PAC IOs and IOettes" in Chapter 14).

The inverse IO is a self-contained hedge because it is an IO strip that is at the same time an inverse floater. If interest rates decline, the acceleration in prepayments reduces the unpaid principal balance of collateral, thereby reducing the total amount of coupon generated (interest lives off principal). The coupon value is increasing, however, since the IO *is* an inverse floater and its index is rising, resulting in a higher coupon, even as the **notional amount** of IO is declining because the underlying collateral is paying down with prepayments. The inverse IO, in a declining-yield environment, therefore, has a coupon rising in value but declining in amount.

When interest rates increase, the inverse IO coupon is declining, but since interest rates are rising, prepayment speeds slow and the collateral life is extended, thereby producing a greater amount of the lesser coupon. This hedge concept will only work, of course, if the index is responsive to the same dynamics that drive prepayment rates—which might not be the case if the index is LIBOR, unless LIBOR rises and falls parallel with mortgage rates.

Case Study 5
FNMA 1992–83 Inverse IO[6]

Coupon, FNMA 8s
Coupon 18.7 − 2.1 × 1-month LIBOR

The FNMA 92–83 class S security is a deep-discount inverse floater carved out of a 20-year CMO support class. A combination of a deep-discount dollar price ($62) and cash flows that are extremely sensitive to fast prepayments results in investment characteristics comparable to a super PO. Investors can employ these inverse floaters to hedge portfolios and to take advantage of interest rate and prepayment views. Specifically, the FNMA 92-83S inverse floaters can be used to hedge the prepayment/call risk on mortgage portfolios or to protect a servicing portfolio from fast prepayments. Furthermore, unlike other prepayment hedges such as super POs and prepayment swaps and caps, investors can earn high returns on deep-discount inverse floaters under most of the probable scenarios. The deep-discount inverse floater structure results in the creation of a minimal

---

[6]This inverse IO case study was provided by David Quint, Vice President, Mortgage Strategies, Lehman Brothers.

amount of cheap IOs. In contrast, POs and super POs can be created only by stripping off the entire collateral coupon.

In addition to benefiting from fast prepayments in a declining-rate environment, investors in the FNMA 92-83S inverse floaters can benefit from a short-term acceleration in prepayments caused by a housing recovery, should it occur. Combinations of high-coupon IOs and FNMA 92-83S inverse floaters may be used to synthetically create securities that benefit from both an increase in housing turnover and an eventual slowdown in refinancing activity.

Structure and Characteristics of FNMA 92-83S

The FNMA 92-83 class S inverse floater was structured out of a 7 percent, 20-year support class CMO backed by 30-year FNMA 8s (see Figure 12.8). This discount, 7 percent coupon support CMO is stripped into two classes—a two-thirds floater class (R) and a one-third inverse floater class S.

Since the floater is priced close to par, the benefits of the dollar discount on the 7 percent support CMO are magnified in the inverse floater. Figure 12.8 and Table 12.9 describe the structure and performance characteristics of this bond.

FIGURE 12.8

FNMA 1992-83S REMIC Support Class Carved into Floater/Inverse Floater Structure

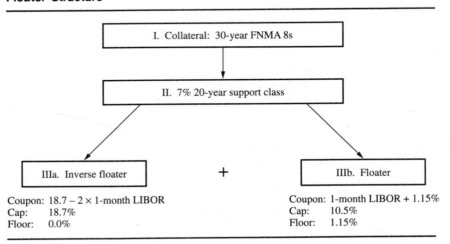

Source: Lehman Brothers Fixed Income Research.

TABLE 12.9
FNMA 92-83 Class S: Pricing and Yield

Price	Initial Coupon	Initial LIBOR	Coupon	PSA	Projected	
					Average Life	Yield
62-00	18.7 − 2 × LIBOR	4.0625	10.575%	165	20 years	18.18%

Security Characteristics

A discount of 38 points from par gives the FNMA 92-83S a price comparable to that of POs backed by FNMA 8s. Table 12.10 compares the characteristics of these two securities. The FNMA 92-83 class S offers a yield advantage of approximately 10 percent over FNMA Trust 85 POs.

Average-Life Variability

Since the underlying CMO class backing FNMA 92-83S is a support class bond, the security benefits from the leverage of a super PO with modest increases in prepayments lead to very sharp reductions in average life. A decline in rates of under 100 basis points could cause prepayments on FNMA 8s to rise to 350 PSA, resulting in a decline in the average life of FNMA 92-83 class S of 20 years to under 3 years (Table 12.11). In contrast, the average life of the FNMA Trust 85 PO is projected to decline from 7.5 years to 2.3 years.

The support class of the FNMA 92-83S security receives priority over the PAC classes if prepayments exceed the structuring speed of 165 PSA. Thus, the FNMA 92-83S may be viewed as a

TABLE 12.10
FNMA 92-83S versus FNMA 8 POs

Security	Coupon (%)	Price	PSA	Yield (%)	Effective Duration
FNMA 92-83S (inverse floater)	10.75	62-00	165	18.18	26
FNMA TR 85 PO	0.0	61-00	165	8.26	9.3

TABLE 12.11
Average-Life Variability: FNMA 92-83S versus FNMA 8 POs

		PSA					
		125	150	165	250	350	450
FNMA 92-83S	Yield (%)	11.49	14.79	18.18	27.12	38.38	46.72
Inverse floater	Average life (years)	23.6	21.6	20.0	7.5	3.0	2.3
FNMA Trust 85	Yield (%)	6.79	7.6	8.26	11.81	16.56	21.86
PO	Average life (years)	8.7	7.8	7.3	5.4	3.9	3.0

long position in a prepayment option struck at 165 PSA.. In addition, over 70 percent of the 92-83S is PAC classes, further leveraging the value of the prepayment option inherent in the companion.

Cap of 10.5 Percent on Floater
Since the 7 percent CMO support class has been stripped into an inverse floater and a floater class with a cap of 10.5 percent, we can view the inverse floater as a leveraged purchase of the underlying CMO class partially (two thirds) funded by issuing a LIBOR floater with a cap of 10.5 percent. Thus, an investment of $1 million in FNMA 92-83S represents the purchase of $2 million of 20-year caps at a LIBOR of 10.5 percent. In a steep yield curve environment with high levels of volatility this cap becomes extremely valuable.

Prepayment Sensitivity
The FNMA 92-83S benefits from prepayment rates above 165 PSA. Over the three months prior to pricing the bond, FNMA 8s prepaid on average 200 PSA. The deal structure was made in the spring of 1992—a time when prepayment expectations were high. A prepayment rate of 250 PSA would boost the yield from 18.20 to 24 percent. In fact, even a 300 basis points increase in LIBOR accompanied by prepayment rates of 250 PSA would lead to yields of approximately 14.8 percent (see Table 12.12).

TABLE 12.12
Price Sensitivity of FNMA 92-83S to LIBOR and Prepayment Rate

PSA	LIBOR (%)				
	7.06	6.06	5.06	4.06	3.06
125	8.47	11.50	14.66	17.92	21.27
150	8.67	11.67	14.80	18.04	21.36
165	8.88	11.88	14.99	18.20	21.15
250	14.82	17.86	20.93	24.03	27.15
350	23.85	26.69	29.56	32.48	35.44
450	29.12	31.97	34.86	37.79	40.75

Applications

Combinations of high-coupon IOs and current-coupon POs can provide investors with superior prospective returns, as shown in Table 12.13. Support inverse floaters with low dollar prices often offer investors a cheap alternative to current-coupon POs. A portfolio of 55 percent FNMA Trust 111 IO (FNMA 9.5s) and 45 percent FNMA 92-83S inverse floaters (portfolio 1) have provided a yield of 14.4 percent in the base case. If rates decline by 300 basis points, the combination would yield 15.4 percent, whereas a 300 basis points increase in rates would result in a yield of 12.4 percent (see Figure 12.9). A comparable-duration combination constructed using FNMA 8 percent POs as a substitute for FNMA 92-83S (portfolio 2) would have a 35 percent weighting in IOs and a 65 percent weighting in POs. The inverse floater portfolio outperforms the PO

TABLE 12.13
Inverse/IO versus IO/PO Combination (Prices as of 4/23/92)

Security	Market Weight (%)	Price	PSA	Yield (%)
Portfolio 1				
FNMA 92-83S inverse	45	62-00	165	18.18
FNMA TR 111 IO	55	33-24	360	7.36
Total	100			14.98
Portfolio 2				
FNMA TR 85 PO	65	61-00	150	8.18
FNMA TR 111 IO	35	33-24	360	7.36
Total	100			7.96

FIGURE 12.9
Portfolio 1 versus Portfolio 2 (Relative Performance Comparison)

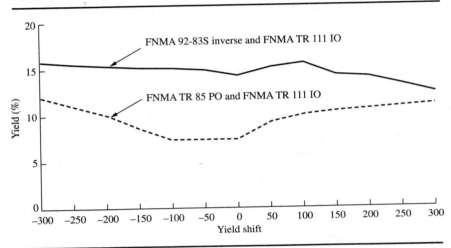

combination by 645 basis points in the base case, by 345 basis points if rates decline 300 basis points and by 175 basis points if rates rise by 300 basis points.

Because servicing portfolios have IO-like characteristics, investors can use FNMA 92-83S to hedge servicing portfolios. By changing the proportion of the inverse portfolio hedge, investors can achieve a yield profile that is bullish or bearish relative to the yield profile, shown in Figure 12.9.

CHAPTER 13

ADJUSTABLE-RATE MORTGAGE SECURITIES

INTRODUCTION

Traditional investors in ARM securities have generally purchased these securites as a means of obtaining an interest rate-sensitive asset representing a good match against interest rate-sensitive liabilities. For such a purpose, ARMs have not represented a perfect asset because of their caps. More recently, nontraditional investors, such as money managers and ARM funds, have purchased ARMs as a short-duration, relatively high-yielding investment. Either way, for many investors the biggest hurdle to becoming involved in the ARM securities market is evaluating the effect of the embedded prepayment and interest rate cap options on the investment performance of the ARMs. This chapter describes the basic forms of ARM securities, their investment characteristics, and the key analytical frameworks used to identify relative value among ARM securities.

BACKGROUND

With $11.5 billion of agency and $55 billion of privately securitized ARM pools outstanding at year-end 1992, ARMs now represent a significant portion of the MBS market (Table 13.1). Note that about one third of ARMs outstanding was privately issued. ARMs were introduced in 1981 when the Federal Home Loan Bank (FHLB) first permitted federal S&Ls to originate and invest in ARMs. In 1982 Fannie Mae encouraged ARM originations by announcing its ARM purchase program. The early ARMs were pure floaters with no caps and no limitations on how low an initial rate (often referred to as the teaser rate) might be on the ARM. With the high interest rate environment of 1983–1984, however, regulators

TABLE 13.1
ARM Security Issuance 1986–1992 ($ Millions)

	GNMA	FHLMC	FNMA	Privately Issued	Total
1992	11,211	15,288	12,138	26,018	64,655
1991	2,379	6,952	11,366	17,516	38,213
1990	717	16,194	12,251	7,619	36,781
1989	522	16,700	15,783	6,426	39,431
1988	1,802	7,287	18,328	12,118	39,536
1987	2,040	4,500	8,500	2,057	17,097
1986	961	1,500	6,000	0	8,461

Source: Lehman Brothers Fixed Income Research.

and legislators became concerned about the prospect of accelerating defaults if there were no controls on how high the rate might adjust to. There was also concern about the potential consumer payment shock related to very low teaser rates that could adjust several hundred basis points at the first adjustment date. The major turn came in 1983 when Fannie Mae announced a standardization of ARM structures that would be eligible for adjustable-rate MBSs issued by it. The Ginnie Mae and Fannie Mae ARM MBS programs were actually initiated in 1984. Freddie Mac followed in 1986 with modifications to the cap, index, and teaser-rate structure that Freddie Mac would consider for purchase. In 1987 Fannie Mae announced the cost of funds-indexed (COFI-) ARM structure it would purchase. Also in 1987, Fannie Mae introduced ARM Megapools, which permitted giant pools to be created by aggregating smaller pools, permitting stratification of reset dates. Freddie Mac introduced a similar program, the WAC pool concept, in 1989. Figure 13.1 shows the distribution of ARM securities by index type in 1992.

ARM Market Share

When mortgage rates rose to above 12 percent in the early 1980s, consumers were attracted to the low teaser rate offered on ARMs because the lower rates allowed more people to qualify for loans. Figure 13.2 shows the relationship between fixed mortgage rates and the share of mortgage originations represented by ARMs: The initial surge in the ARM share closely matched rising fixed mortgage rates in 1981–1982, with the ARM share falling off somewhat

FIGURE 13.1

ARM Securities Outstanding by Index Type, December 31, 1992

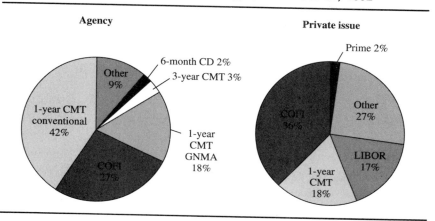

Source: Lehman Brothers Fixed Income Research.

FIGURE 13.2

ARM Share of Originations and the Fixed to ARM Mortgage Rate Spread

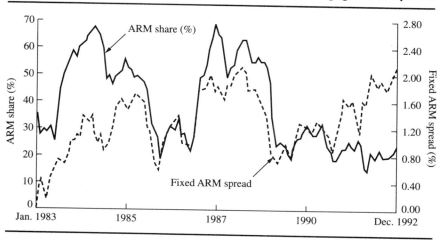

Source: Jeff Biby, Lehman Brothers.

when rates declined in 1983. Since 1986, with fixed mortgage rates in the 9 to 11 percent range, consumers have viewed ARMs not as the choice of last resort but in light of the comparative savings available with the lower ARM rate. By the end of 1988, about half of all residential mortgage originations was represented by ARMs. The annual market share of ARMs as a percentage of total mortgage originations has fluctuated widely, from about 20 percent to nearly 70 percent, depending primarily on the interest rate spread between the initial teaser rates on ARMs and the fixed mortgage rates (Figure 13.2).

STRUCTURAL CHARACTERISTICS OF ARM SECURITIES

All ARM securities have an **index,** which is the base reference value for the ARM coupon, a **margin,** or **spread,** which specifies the amount (expressed in basis points) by which the coupon exceeds the index (ARM coupon = Index + Margin) and **caps** (periodic and lifetime). **Periodic caps** restrict the amount by which the ARM coupon may increase at each **reset interval,** or adjustment date. The **life cap** is the maximum rate the coupon can achieve under any circumstance. It is important to note the ARM coupon will be effectively capped at an index value below the cap rate equal to the cap minus the margin.

Index

The index is the base reference value for the ARM coupon. There are two major categories of indexes: those that are based on a capital markets interest rate (CMT, Treasury bill, LIBOR) and others that are based on an accounting measure (COFI, which is based on the monthly cost of funds of S&Ls). Table 13.2 lists the most commonly used indexes.

CMT
The 1-year **CMT** is the most common CMT index. It is based on the weekly average yields of all current actively traded Treasury securities with one year remaining to maturity. It is updated every Monday by the Federal Reserve Board and is published in Schedule

TABLE 13.2
Common ARM Indexes

1-year CMT
3-year CMT
5-year CMT
6-month T-bill
11th District cost of funds index (COFI): Cost of funds for member thrifts in the FHLB's 11th District (San Francisco)
National median cost of funds index (NMCOFI): National median cost of funds for all FHLB system thrifts
LIBOR

H15 of the *Federal Reserve Bulletin*. It is also published on Telerate, page 7052.

COFI

The 11th District **COFI** is based on the monthly weighted average cost of funds of federally insured S&Ls in the 11th District of the FHLB of San Francisco, which encompasses Arizona, California, and Nevada. The index is calculated by dividing the total monthly interest expense of the institutions by the *average* principal amount of liabilities outstanding during the month. The result is then annualized and adjusted for the number of days in the month. The index value is published on the last business day of the month by the FHLB of San Francisco. It is also published on Telerate page 7058.

The national median cost of funds index (**NMCOFI**) represents the median cost of funds for all thrifts regulated by the FHLBB, where the cost of funds is calculated for each thrift as monthly interest expense divided by average liabilities. This index generally moves with COFI, though it is slightly less volatile and tends to lag COFI. ARM securities based on NMCOFI are similar in structure to COFI-ARM securities.

COFI Rate Lag. The COFI is calculated with some delay and therefore contains a two- or three-month lag, or **lookback** (usually three months). It is announced one month after the month to which it refers, but the ARM coupon is not adjusted for one month or more (usually two months) afterward, resulting in a three-month lookback in most cases. For example, the COFI for December is announced as the COFI value at the end of January. The new COFI-ARM accrues at this rate (plus the security margin) during February and pays at this rate in March. As a result of this process, investors in COFI-ARMs can experience a lag of four months or so behind the actual trend of interest rates. In times of declining interest rates this lag is beneficial to the ARM investor, who continues to earn the past higher interest rate as current yields are declining. However, when interest rates are rising, the COFI-ARM investor may experience a *negative carry* if the cost of liabilities rises faster than the return on the COFI-ARM coupon. Figure 13.3 illustrates the lag of the COFI versus the CMT ARM. Note that the COFI is also less volatile.

Reset Frequency

The coupon and payment **reset frequency,** or **reset interval,** determines how often the coupon and payment reset. Both coupon and payment resets are important determinants of value. In general, the reset period matches the maturity of the index. For 1-year Treasury-indexed ARMs, the coupon resets once a year, and the monthly payment adjusts accordingly on the reset date. On many

FIGURE 13.3
COFI versus 1-Year CMT Lag of Indexed Interest Rate

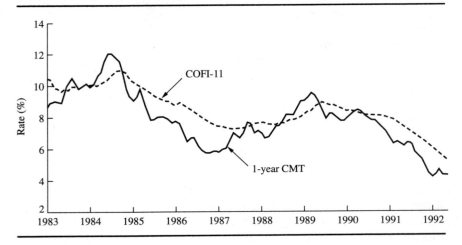

Source: Lehman Brothers Fixed Income Research.

TABLE 13.3
One-Year CMT-Indexed ARM

Assume on January 1, 1993 these values:	
CMT index	6.00%
Margin	1.75%
Coupon	7.75 (Index + Margin)
Caps	2.00% periodic, 11.00% life
ARM coupon rate	7.75%
1/1/93–12/31/93	(6 + 1.75 = 7.75)
Assume 1-year CMT increases to 8.25 percent on January 1, 1994:	
Index value	8.25 (1/1/94)
Margin	1.75
Calculated coupon	10.00
Cap	2.00
Cap reference rate	7.75
Maximum coupon 1/1/94	9.75

COFI-ARMs, however, the coupon resets monthly, whereas the borrower's monthly payments adjust annually.

Margin

The margin, or spread, is the amount by which the ARM coupon exceeds the index value *subject to the interest rate cap*. The margin for Fannie Mae and Freddie Mac CMT ARMs ranges from 175 to 225 basis points. For Ginnie Mae CMT ARMs the margin may be 100 or 150 basis points. The margin for COFI-ARMs is typically 125 basis points.

Caps

With ARMs, there are usually both **periodic caps** and **lifetime caps**. The periodic cap controls the maximum amount by which the ARM can adjust at each reset date or interval. There are two types of caps—**interest rate caps** and **payment caps**. Table 13.3 illustrates the effect of the periodic interest rate cap on a CMT ARM. The table illustrates a 1-year CMT ARM with a coupon rate of 7.75 percent from January 1993 to year-end 1993 (1 year). On January 1, 1994 the ARM should adjust to the index value (now 8.25 percent)

TABLE 13.4
COFI-ARM

Assume on January 1, 1993 these values:
    Index   6.25
    Margin   1.25
    Coupon   7.50
    Caps   7.5% payment cap, 12.0% life cap

Assume COFI increases to 8.5 percent on January 1, 1994:
    Index   8.50
    Margin   1.25
    Calculated coupon 9.75

---

plus the margin (1.75 percent) to 10.00 percent (8.25 + 1.75 = 10.00, the calculated rate). However, there is a 2 percent periodic cap, so the ARM cannot increase above 9.75 percent (7.75 + 2.00 = 9.75). The ARM investor is therefore denied the economics of any coupon income above 9.75 percent.

The second type of per interval cap is a *payments* cap. The payments cap restricts the amount by which the home mortgage payment of P&I may increase. Table 13.4 illustrates a COFI-ARM with a 7.5 percent payments cap. The coupon from January 1992 to year-end is 7.5 percent. On January 1, 1993 the COFI has risen to 8.5 percent. The coupon would adjust to 9.75 percent (8.50 + 1.25, the index plus margin) except for the payments cap, which restricts the borrower's payment from increasing more than 7.5 percent, or $52 per month. Therefore, the maximum payment of P&I is $751 per month (699 + 52). The interest portion of the payment at 9.75 percent would be $800 per month. The difference, $49 (800 − 751 = 49), is added to the unpaid principal balance of the mortgage. This is referred to as **negative amortization.** We must now apply the payments cap calculation to determine the maximum allowable monthly payment:

Total P&I at 7.5% $699 per month

Total P&I at 9.75%   857 per month

Interest payment at 9.75%   800 per month

7.5% payment cap:
  7.5 x 699 = 52

The maximum monthly payment increase is $52.00. Therefore, the maximum monthly payment is $751, leaving $49 as negative amortization ($800 − $751 = $49).

When negative amortization reaches a certain level, typically 125 percent of the original loan balance, the borrower's payment is adjusted to a level sufficient to fully amortize the loan balance over the remaining term regardless of the payment caps. Another way of limiting negative amortization is to recalculate the mortgage P&I schedule at specific intervals (i.e., every five years) to fully amortize the unpaid principal balance. This practice is sometimes referred to as **rebenching** the loan.

Lifetime Coupon Rate Cap

The **life cap** defines the maximum coupon rate an ARM can have during its lifetime. ARMs typically have a lifetime cap of 5 to 6 percent above the initial coupon rate. Don't forget the coupon is capped at the cap rate less the margin!

Teaser Coupon Rate

The **teaser rate** is the relatively low initial rate offered on most ARMs. This rate is used by mortgage lenders to entice homeowners into ARMs and is typically 50 to 200 basis points below the fully indexed rate (current index plus security margin) and is the rate until the first adjustment date.

Stratified Reset

A security backed by loans all having the same reset date is commonly referred to as a single reset pool. However, some pools diversify reset risk by combining loans with different reset dates into the same pool. This diversification of coupon reset dates is commonly referred to as stratification, or the security is said to have a *stratified reset*. A stratified reset makes the security more responsive to changes in the current index because the coupon resets more frequently.

FEDERAL AGENCY ARM PROGRAMS

All of the federal agencies issue and guarantee pools of ARM securities. Figure 13.4 is a quick reference guide to the agency ARM programs. Whereas both Fannie Mae and Freddie Mac sponsor programs based on all of the major indexes, Fannie Mae is the dominant originator of COFI-ARMs. Freddie Mac had securitized the greater share of CMT ARMs until the early 1990s when the Ginnie Mae CMT ARM program picked up momentum. Ginnie Mae securitizes only FHA-insured mortgages indexed to the 1-year CMT.

Ginnie Mae ARM Program Summary

- Ginnie Mae securitizes only ARMs that are issued by FHA and issues its ARMs under its GNMA-II program as multiple-issuer pools.
- The only index used is the 1-year CMT.
- The margin is usually 150 basis points. Margins of 100 or 200 basis points are allowed but seldom used.
- All of the mortgages in a given ARM pool reset in the same month, and there is no negative amortization since the coupon and payment reset at the same time.
- The ARM coupon resets annually on the first of the month in one of the following months: January, April, July, or October.
- The coupons of GNMA ARMs are restricted by a 1 percent periodic interest rate cap, unlike most other 1-year CMT ARMs, which have a 2 percent periodic cap.

Freddie Mac ARM Program Summary

- Freddie Mac issues ARM PCs based on the 1-year CMT through both its Cash and Guarantor swap programs. Freddie Mac issues COFI-ARMs only through its Guarantor swap program.
- The majority of Freddie Mac ARM PCs outstanding are backed by 1-year CMT loans with a 2 percent periodic coupon rate cap, and Freddie Mac is the predominant issuer of conventional 1-year CMT ARM pools.

FIGURE 13.4
Summary of Agency ARM Programs

	GNMA II	FHLMC		FNMA		
	1-Year CMT	1-Year CMT	COFI	1-Year CMT	COFI	NMCOFI
Net margin (bp)	150	150–225	125	150–225	125	175
Coupon-adjustment frequency	Annual in either Feb., May, Aug., or Nov	Annual, semiannual	Monthly	Annual, semiannual	Monthly	Monthly
Payment-adjustment frequency	Annual, same as coupon	Annual, resets 1 month later than coupon	Annual	Annual, same as coupon	Annual	Annual
Periodic coupon rate (±)	1%	1 or 2%	Varies	1 or 2%	None	None
Lifetime coupon cap (±)	5%	5–6%	Varies	5–6%	Varies	Varies
Periodic payment cap (±)	None	None	7.5%	None	7.5%	7.5%
Negative amortization	None	None	Permitted. Limited to 125% of original loan balance. Payment recast every 5 years.	None	Permitted. Limited to 125% of original loan balance. Payment recast every 5 years.	Permitted. Limited to 125% of original loan balance. Payment recast every 5 years.
Underlying collateral	FHA/VA ARM loans	Conventional, first-lien, 1–4-family ARMs	Conventional, first-lien, 1–4-family ARMs	Conventional, first-lien, 1–4-family ARMs	Conventional, first-lien, 1–4-family ARMs	Conventional, first-lien, 1–4-family ARMs

Source: Walter Booker, Paine Webber.

TABLE 13.5
Freddie Mac ARM PC Series

Pool Prefix	PC Characteristics
35	2% annual capped, Treasury ARM Cash
39	COFI, ARM Guarantor
40	2% annual capped, convertible, Treasury ARM Guarantor
42	COFI, scheduled payment of principal ARM Guarantor
60	2% annual capped, Treasury ARM Guarantor
63	1% annual capped, convertible Treasury ARM Guarantor
64	1% annual capped, Treasury ARM Guarantor
71	2% annual capped, convertible, Treasury ARM Cash
72	1% annual capped, convertible, Treasury ARM Cash
74	Annual or semiannual, rate-capped, NMCOFI, ARM Guarantor
75	Annual or semiannual, rate-capped, Treasury ARM Guarantor
76	5-year rate-capped, Treasury ARM Guarantor
77	Annual or semiannual, rate-capped, COFI, ARM Guarantor
78	2% annual capped, 3/1 and 5/1, Treasury ARM Guarantor
79	COFI, multifamily Guarantor
84	Weighted average, ARM Giant Guarantor
86	3-year rate-capped, Treasury ARM Guarantor
87	Miscellaneous ARM Guarantor
94	Payment-capped, Treasury ARM Guarantor

Source: Freddie Mac.

- Common types of Freddie Mac ARM PCs (see also Table 13.5) are as follows: Standard ARM PCs adjust their coupons and payments on the same date. Pools of ARM mortgages with a variety of adjustment dates, coupons, and margins are issued under Freddie Mac's Giant ARM program.
- Freddie Mac issues stratified reset ARM pools under its WAC ARM PC program.

Fannie Mae ARM Program Summary

- Fannie Mae's largest ARM program is based on the 11th District COFI index.
- The **coupon** adjusts monthly, subject to a 5 to 6 percent lifetime interest rate cap above the initial coupon rate.
- The **lookback** is generally two or three months prior to the coupon reset date.

- Scheduled mortgage payments adjust annually, subject to a 7.5 percent payment cap.
- Negative or accelerated amortization may result since the coupon rate adjusts more frequently than the scheduled payment.

Negative amortization is limited to 125 percent of the original balance. If negative amortization reaches this level, the payment is adjusted to fully amortize the principal balance over the remaining life of the mortgage at the current coupon rate, regardless of the payment caps. In addition, the monthly payment is recast every five years to adjust to a level that fully amortizes the principal balance.

- Fannie Mae also has a CMT-indexed ARM program whose characteristics are very similar to those of Freddie Mac.
- Fannie Mae issues stratified reset pools under its FLEX ARM program.

FASB 91: ACCOUNTING FOR ARM SECURITY INVESTMENTS[1]

FASB 91, "Accounting for Nonrefundable Fees and Costs Associated with Originating or Acquiring Loans and Initial Direct Costs of Leases," requires that any origination fees and purchase discount or premium be amortized over the life of the investment using a level-yield methodology. The level yield is the internal rate of return that discounts the projected cash flows to the purchase price. In the case of mortgage investments, FASB 91 allows the investor to incorporate a reasonable prepayment assumption into the level-yield calculation. With ARM securities that carry teaser rates, projected cash flows should also reflect the escalation of the coupon rate to the fully indexed level, assuming that interest rates remain stable. In principle, amortization procedures are the same for both fixed and adjustable-rate securities. For ARMs, however, FASB 91 effectively allows most, if not all, purchase discount to be taken

---

[1] This discussion of FASB 91 accounting was provided by John Tierney.

into income during the first one to three years the investment is owned.

Amortizing the Purchase Discount on ARM Securities under FASB 91

FASB 91 allows most purchase discounts for ARMs to be taken into income during the first one to three years the investment is owned. Table 13.6 gives the amortization schedule for a hypothetical ARM with a current coupon of 8.14 percent, 10 years to maturity, and a price of 96-08. The purchase discount on this annual-pay ARM is almost completely amortized in two years.

The level yield is calculated in column N, where cash flows (annual payment and prepayment cash flows) are discounted to the initial market value of $96,250, giving an internal rate of return or level yield of 11.41 percent. The level yield is used to calculate the effective interest income of the ARM (column J). The purchase discount is then amortized (column K) or taken into income. A small amount of purchase discount remains after two years because the level yield is slightly higher than the fully indexed ARM rate in this example (11.41 percent versus 11.38 percent).

This front loading of purchase discount is justified because ARMs are priced with the expectation that teaser rates will hold the coupon rate below the fully indexed level for about two years. However, if the purchase discount reflects an interest shortfall projected to continue over the life of the ARM (as it does in this example), FASB 91 accounting will cause the purchase discount to be taken into income over the life of the security. In practice this happens on ARMs with smaller than normal adjustment margins. In addition, origination fees capitalized and amortized under FASB 91 are treated as principal balance, not as teaser rates.

FASB 91 also requires that the level yield of mortgage securities be restated if actual or projected cash flows differ materially from original projections. This requirement can have a substantial impact on reported income for securities purchased at a significant discount (below 90) or premium (above 105). For securities priced near par, however, even major changes in prepayment activity have relatively little impact on the level yield. For ARM securities, prices rarely stray more than a few points from par because the ARM coupon adjusts toward market rates at regular intervals.

TABLE 13.6
Amortizing Purchase Discount of ARM Securities under FASB 91

Principal	$100,000	Lifetime cap	12.75%
Initial coupon	8.14%	Maturity	10 years
Fully indexed coupon	11.38%	Prepayment	18 CPR
Adjustment margin	2.13%	Price (32s)	96.25 (96–08)
Adjustment cap	2.00%		
Level yield	11.41%		

	Amortization Schedule								Purchase Discount Amortization				
	A	B	C	D	E	F	G	H	I	J	K	L	M	N
Year	Beginning Balance	Coupon %	Payment	Stated Interest	Amortization	Ending Balance	Prepayment	Ending Balance	Book Value	Effective Interest	Purch. Amort.	Discount Balance	Book Value	Cash Flow
				$C-(A\times B)$	$C-D$	$A-E$		$F-G$		$I(11.41\%)$	$J-D$	$I-K$	$H-L$	$C+G$
0	100,000							100,000	96,250			3,750	96,250	(96,250)
1	100,000	8.14	14,997	8,140	6,857	93,143	16,766	76,377	75,467	10,979	2,839	911	75,467	31,763
2	76,377	10.14	13,336	7,745	5,591	70,786	12,741	58,044	57,998	8,609	864	46	57,998	26,077
3	58,044	11.38	11,430	6,603	4,828	53,216	9,579	43,637	43,604	6,616	13	33	43,604	21,009
4	43,637	11.38	9,373	4,964	4,409	39,228	7,061	32,167	32,144	4,974	10	23	32,144	16,434
5	32,167	11.38	7,686	3,659	4,027	28,140	5,065	23,075	23,060	3,667	8	15	23,060	12,751
6	23,075	11.38	6,302	2,625	3,678	19,397	3,492	15,906	15,897	2,631	6	9	15,897	9,794
7	15,906	11.38	5,168	1,809	3,359	12,547	2,258	10,289	10,284	1,813	4	5	10,284	7,426
8	10,289	11.38	4,238	1,170	3,067	7,221	1,300	5,921	5,919	1,173	3	2	5,919	5,538
9	5,921	11.38	3,475	674	2,801	3,120	562	2,558	2,558	675	2	1	2,558	4,037
10	2,558	11.38	2,849	291	2,558	0	0	0		292	1	(0)	0	2,849

Source: John Tierney.

537

Procedures for applying FASB 91 to ARM securities vary. For example, a level yield may be calculated initially and used throughout the life of the security, with the assumption that revising the level yield would not have a material impact on reported income. Or the level yield may be revised prospectively as prepayment or interest rate expectations change based on the most recent cost basis and projected future cash flows. However, differences between prior expectations and actual experience are assumed not to be material and are not incorporated into the revised level-yield calculation. The most conservative approach is to recalculate the level yield to reflect both differences between projected and actual experience and changes in the prepayment or interest rate outlook. (See Chapter 15 for further information on procedures for applying FASB to ARM securities.)

PREPAYMENT CONSIDERATIONS[2]

ARM securities, like fixed-rate MBSs, are exposed to prepayment risk. Homeowners who take out ARMs generally have the right to prepay their mortgage at par at any time. The prepayment option is, in effect, a long call option position for the homeowner because the owner can call the mortgage away from the security holder. At the same time, the security holder is short a bundle of call options, one for each mortgage in the collateral pool. Consequently, the security holder receives a premium for writing these call options in the form of a higher yield or, alternatively, a wider spread to the Treasury curve.

Compared to fixed-rate MBSs, the historical data for analyzing ARM prepayments are limited; however, available evidence indicates that prepayments on ARM securities tend to be both faster and less predictable. Economically, the cost of ARM prepayment activity to the investor may be fairly small. Since the coupon rate on ARM securities adjusts toward the market level periodically, the reinvestment risk associated with prepayments is reduced. In addition, the prices of ARM securities rarely stray more than a few points from par because of the adjustable-rate feature, minimizing

---

[2]This discussion of ARM prepayments is based on *Evaluating ARM Securities* by John Tierney. New York: Lehman Brothers, June 1989.

the capital gain/loss effect of prepayment activity. Because less is known about the relationship between ARM prepayments and demographic and interest rate factors, however, there is more uncertainty about the timing of cash flows and the average life of ARMs in different interest rate scenarios. Figure 13.5 provides prepayment data for selected ARM securities for 1992 and January 1993.

ARM securities tend to prepay faster than fixed-rate MBS pools largely for demographic reasons. The ARM is a less conservative loan than the fixed-rate mortgage, and most homeowners would prefer a fixed-rate loan given feasible economics to do so. The ARM, therefore, is utilized largely as an affordable mortgage when the home buyer cannot qualify for the desired mortgage amount at the higher, fixed rate. In time, as the economics of the homeowner improves, a refinancing into a fixed-rate mortgage will generally be undertaken at the first opportune time. ARMs are also favored by highly mobile home buyers who expect to be in the home only a short time (five years or less) and who are inclined, therefore, to take the lower rate of the adjustable under the assumption they will move before the rate reaches a level above that of the alternative fixed rate.

Yield Curve Effect

The shape of the yield curve has a profound impact on ARM prepayments. When the yield curve is steep and the volatility of long-term interest rates is low there will not be many opportunities to refinance into a fixed-rate mortgage. However, in a flattening yield curve environment if the ARM rate loses its advantage over the fixed rate, ARM borrowers are likely to make the switch and lock in the fixed rate when the opportunity to do so arises.

Convertible versus Nonconvertible ARMs

In the late 1980s ARMs were increasingly originated with a conversion feature. In general, the conversion feature provides that the ARM may be converted to a fixed-rate mortgage at a rate determined as a spread over the agency commitment rate for fixed-rate mortgages in effect at the time, usually 0.625 percent for Fannie Mae and 0.375 percent for Freddie Mac. In addition, the borrower may be required to pay a processing fee. The option to convert may not be exercised before the end of the first year but

FIGURE 13.5

Aggregate ARM Prepayment Rates, October–December 1992 and January 1993

	January 1993				Past 3-Mo.	Past 1-Yr.	1992			12-Mo. High
	Amount Outstanding ($ millions)	CPR	Chng.	Pct. Chng.			Dec.	Nov.	Oct.	
GNMA 1-year CMT	19,412	3.8	−2.2	−37	5.5	8.7	5.9	5.9	6.6	8.3
Conventional 1-year CMT										
Nonconvertible										
FNMA	7,944	12.9	−4.6	−26	16.2	17.5	17.5	17.2	16.7	20.0
FHLMC series 60	11,705	13.2	−2.3	−15	15.0	17.3	15.4	14.9	15.1	21.9
Convertible										
FNMA	8,905	13.1	−6.7	−34	19.3	27.0	19.8	21.9	22.5	31.5
FHLMC series 40	9,994	17.1	−2.3	−12	20.3	31.3	19.4	21.7	24.3	36.8
COFI Monthly										
FNMA 30-year	4,180	20.9	−6.9	−25	24.4	25.6	27.8	24.3	24.6	32.0
FNMA 40-year	8,380	19.3	−1.4	−7	21.0	20.8	20.7	23.9	19.3	24.0
FHLMC 30-year	4,567	21.7	−1.4	−6	21.8	22.4	23.1	20.5	30.3	27.5

Source: Jeff Biby, Lehman Brothers.

FIGURE 13.6
Prepayments for Convertible and Nonconvertible ARMs

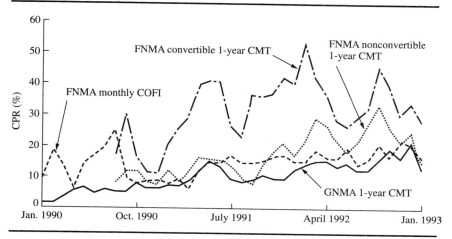

Source: Jeff Biby, Lehman Brothers.

must be exercised by the end of the fifth year. In general, the conversion option has not been exercised with much frequency because the homeowner can usually refinance into a new fixed-rate mortgage at a better rate than the rate offered under the conversion option. However, in the 1991–1992 experience convertible ARMs prepaid considerably faster than nonconvertibles, as shown in Figure 13.6. The figure shows that convertible ARMs prepaid significantly faster than nonconvertibles during the 1991–1992 refinancing cycle. The reason appears linked to the historic low levels reached by fixed-rate mortgages in this period. Apparently, many holders of the conversion option felt they should take advantage of the opportunity to convert to a fixed-rate mortgage. A major advantage of the convertible ARMs in 1992 was the feature of virtually instantaneous conversion; during the peak of the refinancing crush, processing time for a regular refinancing extended out for three or four months. Many holders of the ARM convertibility option elected to convert rather than gamble on losing out on what many of them viewed as a once in a lifetime opportunity. Those with nonconvertible ARMs apparently preferred to sit with the lower rate on the ARM and were more willing to bide their time regarding refinancing.

Note in Figure 13.6 that the COFI-ARMs prepaid faster than the CMTs. The reason is probably related to the lag of the COFI, which caused COFI-ARM borrowers to become disenchanted with the relatively high rate on the COFI-ARM as fixed rates were rapidly declining.

EVALUATING ARM SECURITIES

The ARM contains a number of embedded options that complicate the evaluation process. The ARM option basket includes prepayment options, a series of periodic caps (at each reset), and a lifetime cap.

Investors in capped ARMs are really "long" an uncapped floater and "short" a series of put options. The cap may best be viewed as a put option with the level of the next periodic cap equal to the strike price. If the next adjustment is scheduled to exceed the cap, then the mortgagor will exercise the option to put a security with a yield at the cap level to the investor.

The relationship of an ARM's fully indexed value to the passthrough coupon will greatly affect its value. Note the following example:

Option Strike Price		*Current at the Money Level*	
Current ARM coupon	7%	Current index level	7.75%
Annual rate cap	±2%	Reset margin	2.00%
Next cap and coupon level (put option strike price)	9%	Fully indexed rate	9.75%

In this example, if the ARM were an uncapped floater, the scheduled reset would be 9.75 percent (7.75 percent index + 2 percent margin). However, because of the 2 percent periodic rate cap, the mortgagor will limit the investor's coupon to an artificially low level of 9 percent. This is clearly a valuable option that the investor is effectively short, since the investor is unable to collect the additional 75 basis points in coupon that would otherwise be remitted if the ARM were uncapped. Consequently, this rate cap has a tangible negative impact on the pricing of the ARM.

ARM Pricing Methodologies[3]

A number of methodologies are employed to value ARMs. For the most part they may be segregated into static yield measures and dynamic yield measures. Static yield measures include discount margin and net effective margin.

Discount Margin

The **discount margin (DM)** uses traditional yield to maturity measures to calculate the margin adjusted for a discount or premium price. For example, the DM of a CMT + 175 ARM priced at 100 that has no payment delay is 175 basis points. If the ARM is priced to a discount, the DM is greater than 175; if priced to a premium, the DM is less. The DM does not take into account the impact of changes in prepayments or interest rates on the implied prepayment option and caps embedded in the pool.

Net Effective Margin[4]

The **net effective margin (NEM)** measures the average yield spread over the base index that the ARM security provides in a stable interest rate environment. The NEM resembles the cash flow yield calculation used to price MBSs. As in that calculation, the NEM assumes a single prepayment speed/interest rate scenario (and a reinvestment assumption) and discounts the cash flows to an average-life and interest rate scenario, but does not account for changing prepayment speeds or the impact of interest rate volatility on the caps. The NEM may be thought of as the margin, or spread, over the index the investor would receive if there were no caps, or if interest rates did not change more than the per interval cap would allow.

The major drawback of the NEM measure is that it is highly dependent upon the interest rate assumption used. For a fully indexed par security under a constant-rate assumption, the NEM is the security margin adjusted for bond-equivalent yield conversion. If a changing interest rate scenario is used, the NEM deviates from the security margin. A rising-rate assumption lowers the NEM because of the adjustment limitations imposed by the caps. A falling-

---

[3]Ibid.

[4]For Bloomberg users NEM is called BEEM (bond-equivalent effective margin).

TABLE 13.7
Net Effective Margins, Different Scenarios

Scenario	Net Effective Margin[a] (bp)
Stable	191
Rising	173
Falling	206

[a]Bond-equivalent yield basis.
Assumptions: Price = 100
Coupon = 8.75%
Security margin = 1.75%
Annual cap = 2.00%.

rate scenario increases the NEM. Table 13.7 compares the effective margins under different interest rate scenarios. Changes in the price and delay days also affect the NEM, just as they would affect the yield on fixed-rate securities. Because of the importance of the interest rate assumptions in the NEM calculation, a common practice is to perform the analysis for several interest rate paths. Whereas this approach provides better insight into the performance of the ARM under various scenarios, it will not fully capture the values of the caps and floors.

OAS Analysis
The OAS methodology derives the expected spread, or margin, that will be realized over the index, taking into account interest rate and prepayment rate volatility. The OAS model derives the value of the caps and of the prepayment option (see "Understanding Option Adjusted Spread" in Chapter 3). Since the ARM investor is short the caps, the value of the caps is a cost, or minus, and must be subtracted from the stated margin to the index to derive the **option-adjusted margin (OAM)**.

Table 13.8 is a quick reference guide to the application of OAS to the valuation of ARM MBSs (Table 13.9). The row labeled *Base* in Table 13.9 provides margin, time to the next reset, and cap characteristics for a benchmark 1-year CMT ARM. The vertical columns show how the OAS changes as each of the characteristics is changed. By holding the price constant at 98-17 the OAS is forced to change in response to alterations in the base case state of the

TABLE 13.8
Guide to the OAS Analysis of ARMs in Table 13.9

Row	Comment
Base	Benchmark ARM
Teaser	A higher teaser (initial) rate allows higher OAS.
Reset	A sooner reset has more OAS value (time always has an option value).
Life cap	Lower life cap reduces OAS.
Periodic cap	Imposition of a periodic cap introduces option cost, reduces OAS.
Volatility	Lower volatility (15 percent versus 18 percent in the base case) reduces option cost, and OAS is higher. Higher volatility (20 percent) lowers OAS.
Change in the yield curve	Holding the OAS constant, declining interest rates result in price increase, and vice versa.

benchmark ARM. In real markets, the price would adjust up where OAS is higher than that of the benchmark and down where the OAS is lower. Changes in characteristics are shown in boldface type in the rows contained in the body of Table 13.9.

OAM[5]

The OAM represents the margin, or spread, over the index that the ARM investor would earn if the investor purchased caps and sold floors to create an uncapped, freely floating ARM. OAM is a measure of intrinsic value in ARMs and is derived by adjusting the price of the ARM to account for the values of the various caps and floors built into the ARM. The NEM based on the adjusted price is the OAM.

The simplest example of this method is an ARM floater with a life cap and no periodic adjustment caps. The life cap is analogous to the caps traded in the swap market. These caps have varying strike rates and maturities. For example, if an investor sells a 10 percent cap, the investor has to make a payment if the index rate rises above 10 percent (the cap holder receives the difference between the index rate and the cap rate on settlement date). These

---

[5]Tierney, *Evaluating ARM Securities.*

TABLE 13.9
OAS Valuation of ARM Securities

Case	Price	OAS	Effective Margin	Teaser Rate	Time to Reset	Life Cap	Periodic Cap	CMT 1-Year	Volatility
Base*	98–17	126	132	7.50	12	14.00	NA	8.28	18
Cash Flow									
Teaser rate	98–17	152	159	8.50	12	14.00	NA	8.28	18
Time to reset	98–17	153	160	7.50	6	14.00	NA	8.28	18
Option Value									
Life cap	98–17	110	132	7.50	12	12.00	NA	8.28	18
Periodic cap	98–17	107	128	7.50	12	14.00	2.0	8.28	18
Volatility	98–17	135	132	7.50	12	12.00	NA	8.28	15
Volatility	98–17	119	132	7.50	12	12.00	NA	8.28	20
Change in Yield Curve									
Down 200	100–16	126	124	7.50	12	14.00	NA	6.28	18
Up 200	96–05	126	158	7.50	12	14.00	NA	10.28	18

*Values for base case ARM.
Margin = 150, Reset period = 12 months, CPR = 18, Volatility = 18%, Fully indexed rate = 9.78.

Source: Chuck Webster, Lehman Brothers.

caps may also be viewed as a series of put options. The price of the cap is equal to the sum of the values of the put options. An ARM with a life cap, therefore, may be viewed as a long position in a pure floater and a short position in a cap or series of put options. The purchaser of the floater is, in effect, buying a pure floater and selling a cap. In order to remove the risk of the coupon capping out, the security holder would have to buy a cap with the same maturity and strike rate as the life cap.

The pricing of an ARM with a life cap can, therefore, be broken down into the price of a pure floater and the price of a cap.

Price of pure floater = Price of ARM + Price of life cap

Consider a hypothetical ARM with an 8.5 percent coupon, a 13 percent life cap, a security margin of 150 basis points, and a market price of $100.5. If the life cap is worth 3.5 points, the adjusted price, or the price of a comparable floater, is the sum of the market price of the ARM and the price of the cap. Assuming the index is currently at 7 percent, the NEM in a stable-rate scenario is calculated for the pure floater and the original ARM as follows:

	Price	NEM (bp)
Pure floater	104.0	110
ARM	100.5	175

The NEM of the pure floater is the OAM for the ARM security. The OAM of 110 basis points is significantly lower than the NEM of 175 basis points for the ARM because the NEM does not capture the burden of the life cap, which is valued at 3.5 points.

The basic approach just described is used to value the major caps and floors in ARMs. Periodic and life caps are the main components of the option valuation. The market price of the ARM is then adjusted to derive the price of a hypothetical pure floater and the OAM.

Adjustment Caps
The valuation of the periodic adjustment caps is not as straightforward as the valuation of the life cap. Although the periodic caps may be treated as call and put options, the difficulty in valuation lies in trying to determine the level at which the coupon will reset every year. Making this determination is important because the adjustment limits are based on the coupon rate of the prior period.

For the first year, the reset level can easily be determined because the initial coupon rate is known. An FHLMC 7 percent ARM with a 200 basis points adjustment limit and one year remaining to the next reset has a cap of 9 percent and a floor at 5 percent. These limits may be treated as put and call options. However, the second year's adjustment cap and floor are not known with certainty because they depend on the actual reset level of the coupon. Determining the adjustment limits for later years becomes increasingly difficult because the limits depend on the interest rate path.

Currently, the valuation of the adjustment limits may be simplified because of the low initial rate (teaser) on most ARMs. Under these circumstances, the first year's cap is much more restrictive than the first year's floor. Consequently, the security holder must be compensated for the extra cost of the cap relative to the benefit of the floor. As one goes out farther in time, the effect of the teaser rate diminishes. At this point, the price of the floor approximately offsets the price of the cap. The options approach values only the first two years' adjustment limits as an approximation of the value of all the adjustment limits.

In order to value the adjustment limit of the second year, the cap and floor levels must be determined. The simplest approach would use a constant interest rate assumption. This assumption, however, overlooks the shape of the current yield curve and the forward rates implied by the yield curve. Implied forward rates are used for pricing caps in the swap market, and the same approach is adopted here.

Interaction between Adjustment Limits and Life Cap

The periodic adjustment limits and the life cap are not independent. The adjustment caps may limit the coupon in certain interest rate environments, whereas in other environments the life cap may supersede the adjustment cap. The effects of the caps overlap and may have to be considered in tandem. For most securities, however, the adjustment cap limits the coupon adjustment to a level well below the life cap during the first two years. Thus, only the adjustment limits have a significant impact on the value of the security for the first two years. For the remaining period, only the effect of the life cap is taken into account. The interaction between the adjustment limits of the later years and the life cap is considered insignificant and is not taken into account. Despite these simplifications, this method values the most important caps and floors and provides a reasonably good measure of OAMs.

Duration

The traditional modified duration measure estimates the impact of a change in interest rates on a security's price, assuming stable cash flows. Modified duration, however, is not an effective measure for securities with embedded options, such as ARM securities, because the cash flows are interest rate sensitive. As interest rates change, caps may be triggered, causing the cash flow profile to change. The OAS model estimates the duration of the ARM security, taking into account the impact of a change in interest rates on both the projected cash flows and the price. The estimate is done by shifting the current Treasury yield curve up and down by a small amount, generating new interest rate scenarios and ARM security cash flows based on the modified yield curves and then recalculating the security price based on the initial OAS estimate. The duration is then calculated as the percentage change in price divided by the change in the Treasury yield curve.

CHAPTER 14

STRIPPED MORTGAGE-BACKED SECURITIES

INTRODUCTION

Stripped mortgage-backed securities (SMBSs) were the first major MBS derivative innovation since the creation of CMOs in 1983. SMBSs were introduced in 1986 as synthetic-premium and discount securities, in large part in response to the frustration related to the negative convexity displayed by MBSs during the 1986–1987 refinancing experience. In 1987, Fannie Mae introduced fully stripped MBSs. As of April 1993, SMBSs outstandings totaled $87 billion, according to data provided by Bear Stearns.

The SMBSs, in essence, split the hybrid MBS into its basic interest and principal components, thereby capturing the divergent prepayment effects to maximum leverage. Figure 14.1 compares the present value of the interest and principal portions of MBS cash flows across PSA rates ranging from zero to 400. The figure illustrates SMBS cash flows with PSA speeds declining at the left of the graph and rising at the right. Implicitly interest rates are rising from right to left and declining from left to right. Note that the **principal only (PO)** portion displays positive convexity as its cash flows move to the left (down interest rate) portion of the graph. The **interest only (IO)** portion, meanwhile, shows itself to be the first fixed-rate security to actually *increase in price as interest rates are rising* (moving to the right side of the graph). This unique characteristic of the interest portion would, of course, come to be known as **negative duration.**

CHARACTERISTICS OF SMBSS

An important element relating to SMBSs is that the IO and PO strips are one-dimensional securities whose *value bears a direct relation to movements in prepayment rates, but not necessarily to inter-*

FIGURE 14.1

Present Value of MBS Interest and Principal Cash Flows across PSA Speeds

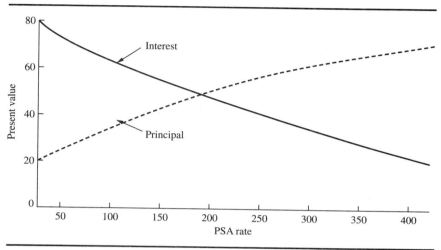

Source: Harry Forsyth.

est rates. PO strips tend to outperform the market when interest rates are going down. However, during these same periods, the downward movement in the prices of IOs tends to be disproportionately large. The converse is true during periods of rising rates, although the PO tends not to lose price either as readily or as much when prepayment rates *decline* as does the IO when prepayments *increase.* This tendency will be referred to as the **asymmetric price performance** of SMBSs. It is important to recall here that investors tend to have the *perception* of a link between a change in interest rates and prepayment rates. It is indeed a fact that SMBS prices have a marked tendency to lead other sectors of the market in anticipation of interest rate changes and that in general interest rate changes do have a direct bearing on prepayment rates. In a steep yield curve environment this may not always be so, however. Short-term rates might increase, whereas intermediate-term rates remain unchanged; or in an inverted yield curve environment the reverse might occur if short-term rates declined. In both of these curve-flattening scenarios short-term interest rates could change with little or no impact on prepayment rates.

All SMBSs have distinct properties that make them attractive to investors and hedgers alike. First, SMBSs grant holders the ability to capture the asymmetric performance characteristics of the interest and/or principal portions of the underlying strip collateral. Second, the inherent leveraging of the prepayment-option value enables SMBS holders to obtain much greater returns on invested dollars *when the timing of the SMBS acquisition is correct.* Finally, this leveraging of option value also makes SMBSs potentially valuable hedging instruments. The investment characteristics of PO and IO SMBSs are summarized in Box 14.1.

HISTORICAL PERSPECTIVE

During the spring and summer of 1986, the realization that the value of pass-through MBSs can actually decline during a bull market rally was reinforced, as was the discovery of the option component of the MBS. Part of this process of a rapidly evolving insight into MBS cash flow dynamics was the further realization that in a bear market the value of an IO would increase! Holders of high-coupon MBSs found that the prices of their securities were eroding as interest rates were coming down. The growing need to cope with the negative convexity characteristic of pass-through MBSs provided the incentive for the creation of SMBSs.[1] This innovation took the reallocation of collateral interest and principal payments to its essential ingredients.

Wall Street and Fannie Mae MBS analysts found that they were able to divide the interest and principal cash flow from a single FNMA pass-through pool, reallocate it to different classes of securities, and by so doing create synthetically high and low pass-through coupons. FNMA designed one class of SMBSs that received most of the principal cash flow (synthetic discount) and one that received most of the interest cash flow (synthetic premium). The collateral for the first SMBS was an 11 percent FNMA MBS, which was converted into 5 percent synthetic-discount and 605 per-

---

[1]Richard Roll, then at Goldman Sachs, is credited with introducing the stripping concept to Fannie Mae in September 1986 to enhance the structure of a substantial collateral bid requested by Fannie Mae.

BOX 14.1
Investment Characteristics of SMBSs

PO Characteristics

- Long (positive) duration.

- Strong positive convexity.

- All PO cash flow is returned at par.
  IRR increases when PSA accelerates.
  IRR decreases when PSA slows.

- Investor uses:
  As a bull market prepayment hedge.
  To lengthen portfolio duration.
  As a proxy for zero-coupon Treasuries.

- Key attributes of PO cash flows:
  The PO consists of a stream of principal cash flows. These cash flows, which are purchased at a discount, are always returned at par—and the investor ultimately receives back all the cash flows. The value issue is one of timing: The sooner the cash flows are returned, the greater will be the present value of the future cash flows.

IO Characteristics

- High current yield.

- Negative duration.

- Interest lives off principal; therefore,
  IRR increases when PSA slows.
  IRR decreases when PSA accelerates.

- Investor uses:
  To hedge interest rate-sensitive investments.
  To shorten portfolio duration and add yield.
  As a bear market-biased investment.

(continued)

BOX 14.1 (*concluded*)

- Key attributes of IO cash flows:
  The IO consists of a cash flow stream of interest. The foremost consideration when investing or trading in IOs is that interest lives off principal: Without principal no interest is generated. Therefore, unlike with POs, no definitive amount of interest cash flow is returned with IOs. Simply stated, the longer the collateral life is extended, the greater will be the total of interest cash flows generated. Conversely, if prepayment speeds accelerate, the interest cash flow stream will be less than expected; *if prepayments accelerate dramatically, the interest cash flows returned could be less than the original dollars invested, resulting in a negative IRR.*

---

cent synthetic–premium-stripped securities.[2] Simply stated, the synthetic-discount SMBS was allocated a lesser proportion of the underlying 11 percent coupon against 99 percent of the principal, whereas the synthetic premium was allocated a little more than half the available coupon but only 1 percent of the principal.

Because of the perceived link between interest rate movements and prepayment rates, one "strip" would be a bullish investment and the other bearish. The strip receiving the mortgage principal offered substantial potential for gain should prepayments accelerate, and the interest strip offered protection against price erosion during periods of rising rates and falling prices (slowdown in prepayment rates).

This first SMBS was issued in July 1986 and was identified as FNMA SMBS Trust 1986-A1 (synthetic discount) and A2 (synthetic premium). Subsequent SMBS issues were given the next letter in the alphabet and therefore became known as **alphabet strips.**

---

[2]In the first FNMA SMBS, holders of the 5 percent coupon SMBS received 4.95/11 of the interest payments and 99/100 of all principal payments. Holders of the 605 percent net SMBS received 6.05/11 of the interest payments and 1/100 of all principal. To create the synthetic coupon rates for class A1, simply divide the 4.95 percent interest allotment by the 99 percent principal allotment. To calculate the coupon rate for the A2 class, use the same math; that is, 6.05 percent of the interest, divided by 1 percent, equals 605 percent.

FNMA issued a total of 12 alphabet strips, and then the market evolved away from the interest portion/principal portion synthetic coupon of these first transactions to the creation of all-interest and all-principal strips, which were much more like other stripped securities. Like Treasury or agency strips, the next generation of SMBSs allotted all of the interest to one class of bonds and all of the principal to another class, creating the now familiar IO and PO SMBSs. As discussed in Chapter 10, the stripping process can be extended to the creation of bond IOs, IOettes, PAC IOs, and synthetic combinations, which are examined at the end of this chapter.

At the time Fannie Mae developed this innovation, there was a great deal of premium-price resistance to premium-priced MBSs trading at prices above 102. At one point, an inverted price curve for higher-coupon MBSs actually came about. From late 1985 through early 1987, single-family mortgage rates decreased from over 12.5 percent to 8 percent. Before 1985, rates had been as high as 18 percent. When homeowners began to realize that they could refinance their mortgages and decrease monthly payments by as much as 30 to 40 percent, the mortgage banking community was deluged with requests to refinance. The resultant pickup in MBS prepayment rates was unprecedented (see 1986–1987 Revisited in Chapter 4). A price inversion in the high-coupon sector resulted as more investors began to price their holdings based upon cash flow yield calculations (see Table 14.1).

The boxed prices in Table 14.1 show the severity of the price compression when FNMA 11s and 12s traded at or close to the same price much of the time from February through April. In April and June 1986, the price relationship between 11s and 12s actually inverted! (For a further discussion of price compression of premium-priced MBSs, see Premium MBSs in Chapter 2.)

SMBS Recombinability

In an effort to enhance the liquidity of the secondary market for SMBS issues, FNMA provided that its SMBS certificates include a convertibility feature enabling IOs and POs stripped from the same FNMA SMBS Trust to be exchanged for Fannie Mae megapool pass-through MBS certificates (minimum $200 million). Once recombined the reformed megapool cannot again be stripped. Freddie Mac has also granted holders of its Giant SMBSs the same

TABLE 14.1

Price Compression of FNMA 10, 11, 12, and 13 Coupons, Month-End Prices January–July 1986 (in 32nds)

FNMA MBS Coupons	Jan.	Feb.	March	April	May	June	July
10	99^{06}	101^{26}	102^{24}	103^{22}	100^{04}	100^{22}	101^{20}
11	102^{28}	104^{18}	105^{08}	105^{2}	103^{30}	103^{20}	104^{30}
12	104^{26}	104^{20}	105^{08}	104^{24}	104^{04}	103^{06}	104^{14}
13	105^{28}	105^{16}	105^{14}	105^{06}	105^{00}	104^{04}	104^{30}

Source: Bloomberg Financial Markets.

recombining option, as have some private issuers. In January 1993, Freddie Mac introduced the Gold MAC program with FHLMC Series 146, which allows repeat recombining and restripping of a REMIC issued as a Gold MAC. Combinations of synthetic premiums and discounts, IOs and POs, all backed by the contributing PC collateral, may be offered by the participating underwriters. For example, a combination of (1) a 6 percent synthetic-discount PC and a 1.5 percent IO, (2) a PO and a synthetic-premium 15 percent PC, and (3) a PO and a 7.5 percent IO could all be issued initially. Each of these Series 146 strips, in turn, can be restripped into different coupon combinations, recombined with other Series 146 strips, or exchanged for a corresponding portion of the underlying contributing PC collateral.

The benefit the convertibility option provides to the SMBS market is sometimes referred to as **arbitrage pricing**. Here is how it works: We know from the 1992 refinancing experience that when interest rates are declining IO strip prices tend to decline with more momentum than PO strip prices accelerate. However, at a point the IO price declines so rapidly that the sum of the IO and PO prices is less than the price of the underlying collateral. When this becomes the case, arbitrageurs will enter the market, buy the undervalued IOs, and recombine them with POs to create the standard MBS at a cost that will provide a profit.

RISK/REWARD CONSIDERATIONS[3]

It is prudent to consider that SMBS investing should not be regarded as a passive or buy and hold investment strategy. Examine the pass-through rate, WAM, and the prepayment sensitivity of the MBS collateral underlying the strip. Finally, to be realistic, expect the worst-case scenario associated with the prepayment-sensitivity analysis of any strip, and do not expect consistent liquidity. Then ask if your portfolio can absorb the worst-case yield and still perform to its expectations. If it can, the risk/reward may be acceptable. Always remain prepared to liquidate the SMBS holdings as soon as adverse prepayment changes become apparent. Remember, the market loss and or hedge cost of a highly prepayment-sensitive derivative in a high-volatility environment can be very painful. In the 1992 prepayment experience some investors in IOs backed by cusp coupon collateral (conventional 9.5, in particular) did, in fact, lose some or most of their initial invested capital, or what would be referred to in accounting terms as the basis. (Remember, it is not technically correct to refer to loss of principal with respect to IO investing, since what is purchased is interest cash flow only, on a "notional" amount of principal in which the IO investor has no direct participation.)

With this cautionary note in mind, it appears likely that the post-1991–1993 economic and demographic environment suggests less prepayment volatility, which may well provide favorable investing for SMBSs. Nevertheless, SMBS investors must remain alert to unexpected spikes in volatility.

Price Patterns[4]

The S-Curve Pattern of SMBSs
Since prepayments are the predominant factor that drives SMBS price performance, the pattern of prepayments largely dictates the price pattern of an SMBS. The S curve illustrated in Figure 14.2 re-

---

[3]This discussion of risk/reward was provided by Harry Forsyth, Vice President, Yamaichi International (America) Inc.

[4]This discussion of the S curve is based on concepts described in Lackbhir Hayre, *Overview of the Stripped Mortgage-Backed Securities Market.* New York: Prudential-Bache Capital Funding, May 1990.

FIGURE 14.2
Typical Prepayment Pattern for FNMA 9.5s

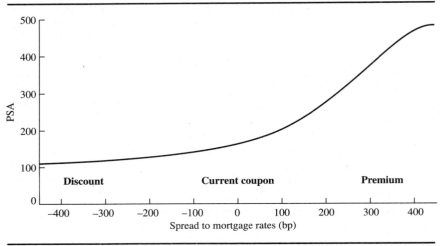

Source: Prudential Bache Financial Strategies Group.

flects the typical prepayment pattern of a generic pass-through MBS. The lower-left portion of the figure shows that when the MBS pass-through coupon (or more properly the WAC) is below current mortgage rates, prepayments are slow. This is because housing turnover represents the only contributor to any prepayment activity, which would be sluggish if the pass-through rate of 9.5 percent were 400 basis points below the mortgage rate, implied at about 13.5 percent (9.50 + 400 = 13.50), a rate unaffordable for most homeowners. As the mortgage rate declines to 1 to 2 percent below the pass-through rate (implied mortgage rate 7.5 to 8 percent), the incentive to refinance stimulates prepayments dramatically. Finally, if mortgage rates persist at low or even lower levels, burnout takes effect, and prepayments begin to plateau (see Chapter 4 for a discussion of the economic incentive to refinance and of burnout).

Price Impact of S Curve and Risk/Reward
The price curve of an IO SMBS tends to trace an S pattern inverse to that of the prepayment pattern for intuitively apparent reasons. When prepayments are slow, the IO cash flow is maximized, and therefore its price will be at a relatively high level. However, as the S curve implies, as market mortgage rates rise above the WAC of

the MBS underlying the IO, the risk/reward of investing in the IO becomes less favorable (the S curve implies prepayments will plateau at between 50 and 100 PSA). The risk/reward of "paying up" for the IO becomes more negative because any volatility will imply there is more risk that prepayments will increase rather than decrease further. The yield spread the IO must offer versus Treasuries begins to widen, thereby further depressing the price. Thus, the price of the IO tends to plateau at a maximum level and to not increase even if prepayments continue to slow (at this point, probably gradually).

By the same token, when prepayments accelerate, the price of the IO drops rapidly, but after time, as the S curve implies, prepayment burnout causes the prepayment speed to plateau. The IO price likewise levels out as the risk/reward of this IO, now at relatively cheap levels, improves, with greater probability that prepayment speeds will at worst stabilize and perhaps even decline rather than rise further. The investor-required IO to Treasury yield spread begins to narrow as the risk/reward becomes more favorable, thereby further supporting the price of the IO. The implied price curve of an IO might then appear as in Figure 14.3.[5]

These prepayment characteristics impart a strong optionlike element to the return profile of IOs. For IOs backed by high-premium collateral, there is little downside risk if rates fall further but much upside opportunity if rates rise. As rates continue to rise, IO prices level off as prepayments fall to the base turnover rate. At low mortgage rates, the high-coupon-backed IO is long an at-the-money put that is similar to a long put on Treasury or mortgage securities.[6] In addition, this IO is short an out-of-the-money put with a strike at the point where the prepayment slowdown levels off. For IOs backed by discount- or current-coupon collateral, there is little upside potential if rates rise further but significant downside risk if rates fall. This return profile is similar to a short at-the-

---

[5]Figure 14.3 and the commentary that follows were provided by Alan Jay Brazil, *Using OTC Options to Enhance IO Performance*. Lehman Brothers, April 1993.

[6]A put gives the holder the right to sell or "put" the underlying security to the seller or writer of the put at a predetermined strike price. If the price of the underlying security rises above the strike price and remains there, the put expires out of the money, and the investor's loss is limited to the option premium paid. If the price falls below the strike price, the investor's return equals the difference between the strike price and the market price, less the option premium paid.

FIGURE 14.3

Projected Price Pattern, FNMA 9.5 IO, Interest Rate Shift from +200 to −200 Basis Points

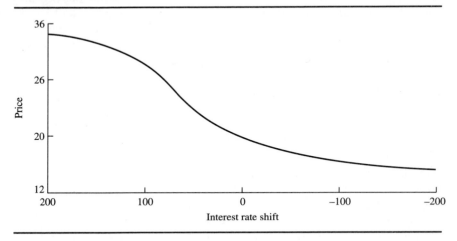

Source: Alan Jay Brazil.

money call and a long out-of-the-money call.[7] The out-of-the-money call option is struck at the level where prepayments peak and then slow due to burnout. Box 14.2 provides a synopsis of risk/reward in strips investing.

Duration Patterns of SMBSs

To better comprehend the contracyclical properties of IOs and POs, see Table 14.2.[8] The table illustrates a theoretical price-yield rela-

---

[7]A call option gives the holder the right to purchase or "call" a security from the writer of the call option at a predetermined strike price. If the price of the underlying security falls below the strike price and remains there, the option expires out of the money, and the investor's loss is limited to the option premium paid. If the security price rises above the strike price, the call option holder's return is equal to the difference between the market price and strike price of the underlying security less the option premium paid.

The option writer's return profile is the mirror image of the option buyer's. If the call option expires out of the money, the option writer's return is limited to the option premium received from the option purchaser. The option writer has significant downside risk if the option expires in the money, because the loss is the difference between the market value and the strike price of the underlying security less the option premium received.

[8]Table 14.2 and the commentary that follows were provided by Harry Forsyth.

BOX 14.2
Risk/Reward Considerations in Strip Investing

MBS Price Structure	Risk/Reward	
	IO	PO
Discount	High downside, minimal upside	High upside, minimal downside
Current coupon	High downside, some upside	Good upside, minimal downside
Low premium	High downside, fair upside	Fair upside, some downside
High premium	Minimal downside, high upside	Minimal upside, high downside

Source: Adapted from Lackbhir Hayre, *Overview of the Stripped Mortgage-Backed Securities Market.* New York: Prudential-Bache Capital Funding, May 1990.

tionship of POs to IOs using a discount to present value pricing model (this model does not take into account the expectational value of the prepayment option).

Table 14.2 shows that the prices and yields of the IO and PO move in the opposite direction to the changes in prepayment rates.

TABLE 14.2

Price and Yield Changes across Changing Prepayment Rates (FNMA 9 Percent MBS; WAC, 9.75 Percent; WAM, 29 Years, 4 Months)

PSA Rate	Price Changes		Yield Changes		Duration Changes	
	PO	IO	PO	IO	PO	IO
0	19.656	79.844	3.493	16.396	18.834	5.377
50	33.531	65.875	5.162	13.733	12.783	4.752
100	43.688	55.719	7.200	11.004	9.633	4.230
150	51.344	48.063	9.453	8.207	7.713	3.792
200	57.250	42.156	11.785	5.338	6.425	3.423
250	61.875	37.500	14.114	2.392	5.505	3.112
300	65.625	33.781	16.409	−0.634	4.817	2.846
400	71.250	28.156	20.858	−6.946	3.858	2.421

Source: Harry Forsyth.

FIGURE 14.4A
Principal Cash Flow, FNMA 9 MBS, Prepayment-Speed Range Zero to 300 PSA

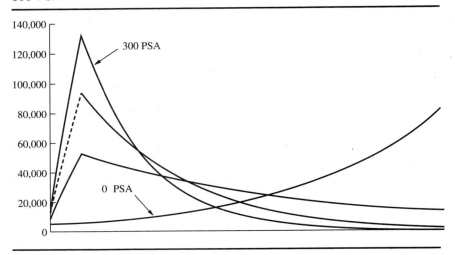

Source: Harry Forsyth.

The key to why this is so may be found in the duration column. The duration listed for the PO is approximately the same as its average life for the PSA rates. Remember that average life (as it applies to a nonbullet security such as a pass-through MBS) may be loosely defined as the average period of time that the principal balance of a security is outstanding. (See Chapter 2 for a specific definition of average life.) Figure 14.4A illustrates the principal cash flows of a FNMA 9 percent MBS at PSA speeds ranging from zero to 300. Note at zero PSA the principal cash flows are back-end loaded. This is the familiar pattern for the scheduled amortization of a mortgage where the amortization of principal is small in the early years and builds into a meaningful amount from about 17 years onward. At 300 PSA the principal is front-end loaded. A longer average life (duration) implies that the principal will be returned over a longer period of time.

In the case of the IO, longer duration results in a greater capacity of the collateral to generate more coupon interest for a longer time, which will be passed through to the IO investors. Conversely, a shorter average life and duration mean that principal will be re-

FIGURE 14.4B

Interest Cash Flow, FNMA 9 MBS, Prepayment-Speed Range Zero to 300 PSA

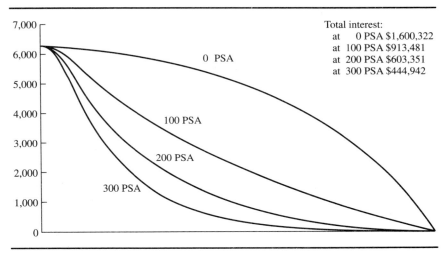

Source: Harry Forsyth.

turned faster, and a smaller amount of interest will be paid. Figure 14.4B illustrates the interest cash flows for the FNMA 9. Note that the total dollars of interest cash flows decline as the PSA speed increases. This illustrates the central characteristic of the IO: *Interest lives off principal, and as the principal is called away with rising prepayments the interest cash flows are dissipated.*

The actual cash flows of GNMA 11 percent SMBSs are illustrated in Tables 14.3A and 14.3B. Table 14.3A shows the principal cash flows of a GNMA 11 percent PO at 15, 35, and 40 CPR. The return of principal at 40 CPR is substantially faster than at a slower 15 CPR. Nevertheless, the full $1 million of original principal is ultimately returned, so the risk/reward of PO investing is basically a timing issue. Note that at 40 CPR almost 80 percent of the principal is returned by the third year; at 15 CPR only about 40 percent is returned by year 3.

Table 14.3B illustrates that the total return of interest cash flows can be substantially less with an IO at the high CPR speed. Indeed, the $217,665 received at 40 CPR could be less than the original amount invested!

TABLE 14.3A

GNMA 11 Percent PO Strip, Principal Cash Flows

Years	15 CPR		35 CPR		4 CPR	
1	$153,795	15.4%	$352,900	35.3%	$402,678	40.3%
2	130,549	13.1	228,599	22.9	240,729	24.1
3	110,796	11.1	148,014	14.8	143,851	14.4
4	94,015	9.4	95,794	10.0	85,912	8.6
5	79,759	8.0	61,961	6.2	51,278	5.1
6	67,647	6.8	40,053	4.0	30,591	3.1
7	57,359	5.7	25,873	2.6	18,236	1.8
8	48,623	4.9	16,702	1.7	10,858	1.1
9	41,201	4.1	10,768	1.1	6,460	1.1
10	34,902	3.5	6,936	0.7	3,839	0.6
11	29,552	3.0	4,464	0.4	2,278	0.4
12	25,006	2.5	2,867	0.3	1,349	0.2
13	21,151	2.1	1,842	0.2	800	0.1
14	17,881	1.8	1,179	0.1	472	0.1
15	15,102	1.5	750	0.1	275	0.0
16	12,745	1.3	480	0.0	166	0.0
17	10,748	1.1	308	0.0	97	0.0
18	9,052	0.9	192	0.0	51	0.0
19	7,616	0.8	122	0.0	30	0.0
20	6,399	0.6	79	0.0	16	0.0
21	5,368	0.5	50	0.0	12	0.0
22	4,495	0.4	25	0.0	3	0.0
23	3,755	0.4	13	0.0	—	0.0
24	3,132	0.3	12	0.0	—	0.0
25	2,599	0.3	—	0.0	—	0.0
26	2,155	0.2	—	0.0	—	0.0
27	1,777	0.1	—	0.0	—	0.0
28	1,460	0.0	—	0.0	—	0.0
29	1,192	0.0	—	0.0	—	
30	176	0.0				
	$1,000,000		$1,000,000		$1,000,000	

WAC, WAM, and Age Considerations

The WAC of the collateral from which the IO is stripped has an impact on the sensitivity of the IO. A high-WAC IO would be expected to be more prepayment sensitive than a low-WAC IO. The WAM also will have an impact. Obviously, a long-WAM IO will have more time to generate more interest cash flow than a short-WAM IO (see Watch Your WACs and Watch Your WAMs in Chapter 2).

Be especially watchful of the WAC on the IO delivered on a newly issued CMO. Sometimes the WAC of the collateral actually

TABLE 14.3B

GNMA 11 Percent IO Strip, Interest Cash Flows

Years	15 CPR		35 CPR		40 CPR	
1	$102,016	16.0%	$90,818	35.4%	$87,823	40.3%
2	86,307	13.6	58,753	22.9	52,445	24.1
3	72,971	11.5	37,987	14.8	31,302	14.4
4	61,654	9.7	24,544	9.6	18,667	8.6
5	52,052	8.2	15,847	6.2	11,125	5.1
6	43,909	6.9	10,223	4.0	6,624	3.0
7	37,000	5.8	6,587	2.6	3,941	1.8
8	31,145	4.9	4,240	1.7	2,343	1.1
9	26,181	4.1	2,725	1.1	1,388	0.6
10	21,976	3.5	1,750	0.7	823	0.4
11	18,413	2.9	1,122	0.4	488	0.2
12	15,401	2.4	717	0.3	286	0.1
13	12,850	2.0	458	0.2	169	0.1
14	10,693	1.7	292	0.1	99	0.1
15	8,872	1.4	184	0.1	58	0.0
16	7,331	1.2	116	0.1	34	0.0
17	6,033	0.9	74	0.0	20	0.0
18	4,940	0.8	46	0.0	12	0.0
19	4,017	0.6	29	0.0	8	0.0
20	3,243	0.5	17	0.0	0	0.0
21	2,595	0.4	12	0.0	0	0.0
22	2,048	0.3	8	0.0	0	0.0
23	1,593	0.3	0	0.0	0	0.0
24	1,212	0.2	0	0.0	0	0.0
25	894	0.1	0	0.0	0	0.0
26	631	0.1	0	0.0	0	0.0
27	413	0.1	0	0.0	0	0.0
28	237	0.0	0	0.0	0	0.0
29	90	0.0	0	0.0	0	0.0
30	3	0.0	0	0.0	0	0.0
Total	$636,717		$256,560		$217,665	

delivered to the trustee upon issuance of the CMO is different from the WAC estimated when the deal was marketed, generally four to six weeks prior to issuance. *If the actual WAC is higher than what was described when you committed to purchase the IO, you may well be entitled to a repricing.*

Seasoning, or age, considerations are also very important. An IO stripped off seasoned collateral will likely be less prepayment sensitive than a pool that is 2 to 3 years of age (see Triple D and the Pure Aging Effect in Chapter 4).

OAS Pricing of SMBSs[9]

Because of the high sensitivity of SMBSs to changes in prepayments and their high optionality, traditional pricing methods, such as the discount to present value application illustrated in Table 14.2, are of limited value. The OAS methodology described in Chapter 3 should provide better results. A note of caution is due, however. It is important to bear in mind when applying OAS to prepayment-sensitive securities that because of limitations and some bias still inherent in models that are dependent on reference to pre-1992 prepayment and home sales patterns, OAS tends to favor bear market-directed MBSs such as IOs. In particular, during the steep yield curve environment in the first quarter of 1992, some models indicated OAS values of 800 and above when in retrospect the option cost was evidently much higher than the models indicated. As new information from the 1992–1993 refinancing cycles is implanted in the models, OAS will likely prove to be a more reliable measure of risk/reward in highly prepayment-sensitive MBSs.

Figure 14.5 compares the OAS-derived projected price profile of the IO to the actual prices for the period December 7, 1992 through July 1, 1993. Note that the deviation between the projected and actual prices is widest during the February–March 1993 period, just before the April surge in refinancings. This OAS-derived projected price was influenced by the positively sloped yield curve in effect at the time, resulting in high OASs for the IOs. The pricing of IOs was, in fact, strongly negatively affected by the rapid decline in interest rates and the acceleration in refinancing applications that occurred during the period (see the following sections on the asymmetric pricing of SMBSs).

Asymmetric Pricing of SMBSs[10]

The asymmetric pricing of the IO versus the PO may be illustrated from the price history of the two, which is illustrated in Figure 14.5 for the FNMA Trust 33 SMBSs in the first half of 1993. The high

---

[9]Figure 14.5 and the discussion of OAS pricing that follows are based on research developed by Vernon H. Budinger, Consultant, Financial Strategies, Global Advanced Technology Corporation, New York.

[10]The figures relating to and the discussion of asymmetric pricing of SMBSs that follow are based on research provided by Vernon H. Budinger.

FIGURE 14.5

OAS Projected Price, FNMA 9 IO versus Actual Price, December 7, 1992 through July 1, 1993

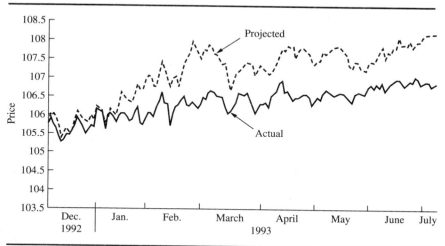

Source: Vernon Budinger, Global Advanced Technology.

price of the period for the Trust 33 IO was 26–08 on December 16, 1992, which was also the date of the low price for the PO at 79–15. The figure shows that the IO price dropped precipitously from mid-January 1993 to March 4, 1993, whereas the PO price rose over the same period. The significant point is that the IO price decline from December 17, 1992 to March 4, 1993 was 9–24, or 37.14 percent, whereas the PO appreciated only 13.93 percent over the same period. Again, duration tells the story. The *negative* duration[11] of the IO on December 17 was −12.87, about twice the 7.19 (positive) duration of the PO. By March 4, 1993 the duration of the IO had declined to −9.29 versus 13.27 for the PO. Table 14.4 provides selected pricing data for the period.

Figure 14.6 compares the December 7, 1992 through June 24, 1993 prices of the FNMA SMBS Trust 33 IO and PO combined to the prices of FNMA 9s, the Trust 33 collateral, and the Trust 33 IO. The figure shows that most of the time the price of the IO and

---

[11]This is option-adjusted duration, or OAD (see Option Adjusted Duration in Chapter 3).

TABLE 14.4
FNMA Trust 33 IO and PO, December 17, 1992 through June 24, 1993

| Date | Selected Prices ($) | |
	IO	PO
12/07/92	26	80-03
12/16/92	26.08	79-15
3/04/93	16.16	90-16
3/26/93	18.12	87-31
4/14/93	18.20	88-06
6/18/93	20.20	86-12

Source: Global Advanced Technology Corporation.

FIGURE 14.6
FNMA 9 Percent Collateral versus FNMA Trust 33 IO/PO Combination

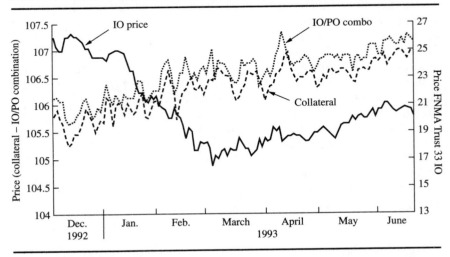

Source: Vernon Budinger, Global Advanced Technology.

FIGURE 14.7
Ten-year Treasury Yield versus FNMA Trust 33 IO Prices

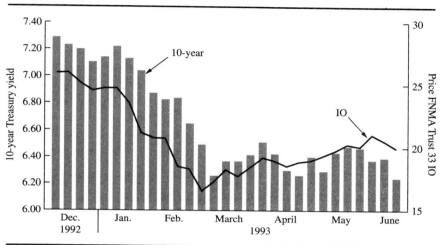

Source: Vernon Budinger, Global Advanced Technology.

PO combined is greater than the price of the underlying FNMA 9 percent collateral by a spread of ⅛ to ½ a point.

Interest Rate Impact on SMBS Prices[12]

Figure 14.7 plots the yield of the 10-year Treasury against prices of the FNMA Trust 33 IO from December 11, 1992 through June 24, 1993. The figure shows there is a strong correlation between price changes of the SMBSs to the 10-year Treasury yield. Note that the IO price reached its bottom just before the 10-year reached its low yield of the cycle on March 4. The figure also shows signs of burn-out on the underlying FNMA 9 percent collateral. The 10-year yield on April 29 and on June 24 is at about the same yield as on March 4, but the price of the IO has drifted higher at each of these two yield points following the March 4 low.

---

[12]The figures relating to and the discussion of interest rate and refinancing impact on SMBS prices that follow are based on research by Vernon H. Budinger.

FIGURE 14.8
**MBA Refinancing Index versus FNMA Trust 33 IO, December 11, 1992
through June 24, 1993**

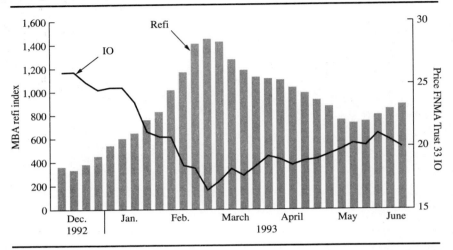

Source: Vernon Budinger, Global Advanced Technology.

Refinancing Impact on SMBS Prices

Figure 14.8, which tracks the Trust 33 IO price against the MBA
refinancing index, may hold an explanation for the upward ramping
of the IO price in the face of the repeated dips in the 10-year Treasury yield in the May–June 1992 period. Note that the refi index
reached its highest level on March 4, coincident with the low price
of the IO. However, the refi index was much lower on April 29 and
June 24. The 10-year Treasury yield appears to be a good coincident indicator of the *direction* of the IO price; the refi index appears to better indicate the *amount* of price change that may occur.
The 1992 price history of the FNMA SMBS Trust 2 IO is illustrated in Figure 14.9.

Note in Figure 14.9 the decline in price of the Trust 2 IO from
about $34 in early March 1992 to just under $21 in late July (a
decline of about 38 percent in four months). This price drop occurred as the second wave of 1992 prepayments struck in April,
with the realization that prepayment speeds would not ramp down
in the spring as had been anticipated. This wave was followed by
the third wave of the 1992–1993 cycle, which occurred during the

FIGURE 14.9

Price History, FNMA Trust 2 IOs, January 30, 1992 through March 29, 1993

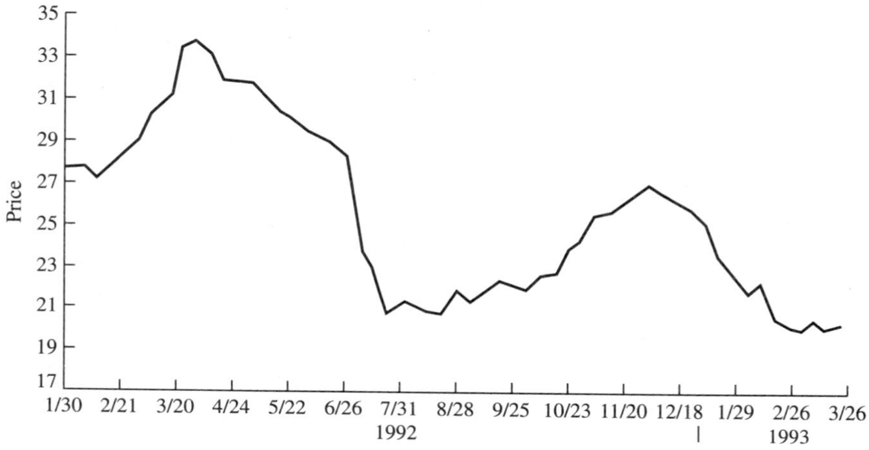

Source: Bear Stearns & Co.

first half of 1993. (See Tracking the 1992–1993 Prepayment Experience in Chapter 4.)

Price Volatility[13]

Because of the inherent leveraging of SMBSs, there is generally a greater price volatility associated with this sector of MBSs. (For a discussion of the impact of volatility on the value of the prepayment option, see Volatility Price Impact in Chapter 2.) Nowhere, however, are the implications of volatility more important than in its application to the SMBS market. Understanding what contributes to volatility in SMBS price patterns provides the next, and perhaps most important, clue as to why SMBS prices and yields move so dramatically in opposite directions.

During periods when the bond market undergoes a secular move to higher or lower interest rates,[14] investors and speculators

---

[13]This discussion of price volatility was provided by Harry Forsyth.

[14]A secular move in interest rates is generally associated with a major shift in economic activity. Typically, when the economy slows down there is less demand for

alike endeavor to restructure their portfolios so that they can take advantage of future trends in the direction of rate movements. Typically, this means an order imbalance will develop between IOs and POs as investors' holdings change according to the dictates of an emerging market trend. *The result is more demand for one type of SMBS and more supply of the other, which will have a depressing effect on the prices of the security being purchased.* Because of the leveraged optionality of SMBSs, these price movements have a tendency to be more pronounced than those of nonstripped securities, resulting in greater price and yield volatility associated with SMBSs.

Comprehending volatility in the SMBS sector is really a function of understanding how prepayment rate changes affect changes in the value of one's SMBS holdings. Ownership of collateral[15] grants holders the advantage of the receipt of both the interest and principal components of mortgage cash flow. Therefore, as prepayments speed up or slow down, there is a natural offset to the positive and/or negative changes in option value resulting from the changes in prepayment patterns. *Naturally, as compared to ownership of an IO or PO, the receipt of both interest and principal at the same time has a tendency to smooth out return, or reduce volatility. Conversely, if either of the cash flow components is removed, what is left, either the interest or principal, will reflect a greater sensitivity to changes in prepayment rates.*

Timing Considerations

It is apparent from the preceding discussion that SMBSs are highly sensitive to shifts in prepayment speeds and that their pricing is highly directional. For example, when investors anticipate that prepayment speeds will accelerate, the prices of deep-discount POs may move up sharply, well ahead of the actual realization of faster

---

money—that is, less borrowing by individuals and corporations. At the same time, savings rates have a tendency to go up. This phenomenon results in marked decreases in interest rates. Conversely, when economic activity increases, rates usually rise. A good example can be garnered from the period starting in late 1990 and continuing through 1993 when mortgage rates decreased by over 250 basis points.

[15]Agency pass-through MBSs are referred to as collateral by Wall Street. During recent years 70 to 90 percent of all new-issue FNMA and FHLMC pass-through securities have been used to secure varying kinds of REMIC issues. The figure for GNMA MBSs is somewhat lower (see Supply/Demand Considerations in Chapter 6).

prepayments. Conversely, with the appearance of any concern that prepayment speeds will accelerate, IO prices will generally drop dramatically, again in anticipation of possible rising prepayments and well before an accelerating prepayment trend has become apparent. SMBS investors are loath to pursue PO and IO prices once prepayment trends become obvious. The risk/reward of SMBS investing is so leveraged that substantial upward price moves are made only when the SMBS is extremely cheap and the risk/reward equation is highly favorable. Once the SMBS has become fairly priced to an established trend, price gains become sluggish, whereas price declines occur with increasing frequency with any adverse prepayment volatility. The same applies to hedging applications. IOs can become so expensive to hedge in a high-prepayment environment that it is seldom worthwhile.

Liquidity

SMBSs have achieved a reasonable amount of liquidity in the Fannie Mae Trust SMBSs, which are large issues and are modeled on Bloomberg. However, in times of rapidly declining interest rates, such as occurred in 1992 and 1993, the demand for IOs becomes sporadic. And when the loss of coupon from prepayments leads to negative carry, the dealer community becomes reluctant to bid IOs for position at almost any price. Ultimately, of course, the arbitrage pricing eventually assures a bid at some level, but in times of high price volatility it will likely be below fair value.

The liquidity for CMO-issued SMBSs is not as good as that for the FNMA trusts. Bond IOs and IOettes represent fairly small issues in and of themselves, with each one custom created to meet the needs of one particular deal structure (see CMO Bond SMBSs at the end of this chapter). The CMO SMBS issues can represent excellent value, however, especially the IOs stripped from the PAC bonds because of the protection afforded by the PAC bands.

Current Yield, or Carry Cost[16]

A significant consideration for SMBS investors is the cost of carry. When investing and trading in strips it is essential to track changes in the book yield, particularly in the case of IOs.

---

[16]This discussion of current yield and carry cost was provided by Harry Forsyth.

Changes in the **monthly book yield** or IRR, as it relates to POs, is a straightforward function of the changes in prepayment rates. The process simply requires calculating the additions to, or subtractions from, discount appreciation that the original prepayment rate indicated. To calculate the monthly book yield of an IO SMBS, however, additional considerations must be employed as follows:

Monthly book yield = [(Collateral coupon/12) − (Book price × CPR/12)]/Book price

The **cost of carry,** or book yield, calculation is shown in examples 1 and 2.

Example 1: Fast Prepayment Speed
Assume:

> Purchase price: $30 (30%)
> Collateral: FNMA 10 percent MBS
> Collateral prepayment rate: 60 CPR

Then:

> Book price × CPR/12 = (.30) × (60/12) = .30 × 5 = 1.5

> Book yield = [(10/12) − 1.5]/.30 = −2.22 percent

Note that when the write-down of original invested dollars (the **basis**) from prepayments (reduction of the basis) exceeds coupon income, the IO investment is said to be at a **negative carry**. If prepayments accelerate for a prolonged period of time, the write-down of prepaid principal becomes greater, whereas the coupon income becomes progressively smaller (less principal, less coupon). The negative carry (book yield) therefore grows exponentially to the *negative.*

Example 2: Moderate Prepayment Speed
If the CPR rate slows to 12 percent the following month, the calculation would change to:

> Book price × CPR/12 = (.30) × 12/12 = .30 × 1 = .3
> [(10/12) − .3]/30 percent = 1.78 percent

In example 2 we derive a positive carry number as opposed to the negative number experienced by the IO holder when a higher prepayment rate assumption is applied.

INVESTMENT PROPERTIES OF THE POS[17]

During times of significant price appreciation in the PO market, the performance characteristics of POs in portfolios should be carefully evaluated. Although the PO price should appreciate when interest rates decline and prepayments are expected to accelerate, POs backed by high-premium collateral may not provide much actual upside in a rally. In the analysis that follows, two PO issues are evaluated versus comparable-duration Treasuries. The returns under both a long-term shift in prepayment expectations and changes in actual prepayments are assessed. It is demonstrated that some POs may underperform Treasuries under some scenarios. *Unless the PO can be purchased at a substantial discount, portfolio managers are cautioned to temper expectations of high price appreciation in POs and employ them primarily for hedging high-premium MBSs or IOs.*

POs are often used by portfolio managers to extend the duration of portfolios. Furthermore, the positive convexity that POs offer has enabled them to trade at narrow or negative yield spreads over Treasuries. These characteristics of POs will generally be fulfilled when they are trading at low dollar prices in the 50s and 60s. At higher price levels, however, POs may not offer the performance characteristics expected of them.

Case Study: POs in a High-Prepayment Environment

Two PO issues are used as the basis for the case study: FNMA S-210 and FNMA S-6 backed by FNMA 7.5 and FNMA 9.0 collateral, respectively. Their characteristics are given in Table 14.5. Table 14.6 summarizes the yield and total returns of FNMA S-6 under various prepayment assumptions.

FNMA S-6 PO in April 1993 was priced to yield only 4.67 percent to the street median PSA speed of 463.[18] Based on the January–March 3-month historical PSA of 633, this PO yielded

---

[17]This discussion of investment properties of POs is based on Andrew Davidson and Thomas Ho, "Assessing Value in POs," *CMO Commentary*, April 6, 1993.

[18]The street median PSA is a composite of 1-year projected PSAs from a representation of Wall Street PSA assumptions as reported to Telerate Information Systems.

TABLE 14.5
Characteristics of Two POs

Issue	Collateral	WAC	WAM	Price	Duration
FNMA S-210	FNMA 7.5	8.07	356	69-01+	14.5
FNMA S-6	FNMA 9.0	9.69	268	87-25	7.7

6.65 percent. However, it appeared unlikely that this high PSA could be maintained for an extended period. In comparison, a similar-duration Treasury (approximately 10-year maturity) yielded 6.30 percent. Therefore, unless prepayments were to continue to be very fast, the PO would yield less than comparable Treasuries, as shown in Table 14.5

Table 14.6 shows the total returns of the PO under a one-year holding period. If the PSA assumption remains unchanged at 500 PSA, the total return is 4.86 percent. A comparable Treasury returns 6.10 percent over one year. In order to roughly match this Treasury total return, the long-term PSA expectation has to rise to 550 PSA. Alternatively, given the same 500 long-term PSA expectation, the Treasury return can be matched if the 12-month actual PSA is 660.

The return analysis considers only the unchanged interest rate scenario. Does the PO offer any additional positive convexity over the Treasury? Without performing analysis over various interest rate shifts, the magnitude of the upside on the PO can be estimated. Assume that the PO prepays completely at the end of one year, giving it a terminal price of 100. Under this scenario, the total return is 14.42 percent. This is slightly higher than what the comparable Treasury would return in a down 100 basis points scenario. Even if the PO pays off completely in one month, the cash has to be reinvested, and this limits its maximum upside. It is thus very unlikely that the PO would outperform Treasuries if rates drop significantly.

Under rising rates, the PO may also have difficulty outperforming the Treasury. Due to the then high prepayment expectation on FNMA 9 collateral, there was a substantial downside risk in prepayments. A significant drop in prepayments under rising rates would extend the duration of the PO and cause it to underperform Treasuries. If rates shift up by 100 basis points, the total return is projected to be −3.4 percent for the PO in comparison to −1.2 per-

TABLE 14.6
Yield and Total Return (TR) of FNMA S-6 PO

	500 PSA	463 PSA (Street Median)	633 PSA (3-Mo. Hist.)		500 PSA	550 PSA	660 PSA/12 Mos.; Long Term at 500 PSA
Yield	5.08	4.67	6.65	TR	4.86	6.13	6.14

cent for the Treasury. In summary, unless prepayment rates are sustained at higher than expected long-term forecasts under different interest rate scenarios, POs may not provide good performance.

Now consider the performance of the FNMA S-210 backed by 7.5 percent collateral. The yield and total-return profile are outlined in Table 14.7. This bond has a longer effective duration of 14.5 years, which is longer than a 30-year Treasury. Compared to the 30-year Treasury that yields 7.06 percent, this bond would outperform the Treasury at 300 PSA. However, if the long-term PSA expectation and the actual PSA drop to 250, the one-year return diminishes greatly, to 2.40 percent. If the actual PSA drops to 200 for 12 months and prepays at 300 long term thereafter, the return drops to 6.92 percent, which is approximately equal to the 30-year Treasury return. Finally, if the PSA is 400 for 12 months and then 300 long term thereafter, the return is 8.41.

With respect to convexity, the FNMA S-210 PO offers significantly more upside than the FNMA 9 PO, due to its lower dollar price and prepayment expectation. Assuming the PO is at 100 at the end of one year, the total return is 45.0 percent. Nevertheless, its performance versus comparable Treasuries is highly dependent on the actual prepayment experience and changes in long-term prepayment expectations.

INVESTMENT PROPERTIES OF THE IOS[19]

As pointed out in the introduction to this chapter, IOs are vulnerable to significant loss in return during periods of high prepayment volatility. The reduced return or negative return due to a prepayment spike can lead to a situation in which a large yield spread narrowing or a significant drop in the long-term prepayment expectation is necessary to recover the lost income. Given the level of prepayment risk in IOs, investors are advised to stress proposed IO investments to a whipsaw scenario analysis (see Vector Scenario Analysis in Chapter 8) before adding IOs to enhance current yield or shorten duration.

---

[19]This discussion of investment properties of IOs is from Andrew Davidson and Thomas Ho, "IOs: Risk of Prepayment Spike," *CMO Commentary,* March 23, 1993.

TABLE 14.7
Yield and Total Return (TR) of FNMA S-210 PO

	300 PSA	197 PSA (street median)	90 PSA (3-mo. hist.)		300 PSA	350 PSA	250 PSA	200 PSA/12 Mos.; Long term at 300 PSA	400/12 Mos.; Long term at 300 PSA
Yield	7.69	5.52	3.36	TR	7.67	11.95	2.40	6.92	8.41

In an environment of high prepayment volatility, an IO investor may wait for prepayments to stabilize at lower levels or for yield spreads to narrow to recoup what was lost while prepayments were significantly faster than the expected long-term average. This may be possible as long as the prepayments spikes are not at extremely high levels for an extended period of time. However, the risk always exists of losing so much principal balance that it is difficult or impossible to regain the lost income or market value. Such was, in fact, the case in 1992 when many investors of 9.5 percent coupon-backed IOs lost a large portion of their original investment dollars. This risk varies depending on the coupon level and the extent of the prepayment whipsaw.

Case Study: Effect of Prepayment Spike on IO Value

Two IO strips backed by FNMA 8s and FNMA 9s are the basis for this case study. The price levels of two issues as of mid-March 1993 are given in Table 14.8. The total-return numbers are the annualized returns over a six-month holding period assuming a reinvestment rate of 3.25 percent. Suppose actual prepayments spike up over the investment period due to a whipsaw in rates after the IOs are purchased. Also, assume that at the end of six months rates and prepayment expectations come back to the initial levels. The impact on total returns is summarized in Tables 14.9 and 14.10. As expected, the less-seasoned FNMA 8 IO is less affected by a six-month prepayment spike. If actual prepayments come in at 450 PSA, the total return goes down to 8.07 percent if yield spreads remain unchanged. In order to realize the anticipated return of 10.01 percent of the stable PSA scenario, the horizon yield spread has to narrow by 37 basis points. With 550 PSA, the required spread tightening is 74 basis points to earn the 10.01 percent return.

TABLE 14.8
FNMA 8 and FNMA 9 IO Levels

Issue	Collat.	WAC	WAM	Price	PSA	Yield	Total Return
FNMA 196	FNMA 8	8.49	354	26-25+	350	10.18	10.01
FNMA 6	FNMA 9	9.69	268	18-24	500	10.00	9.61

TABLE 14.9
Impact of Prepayment Spike on FNMA 8 IO

Init. PSA	6-Mo. Act. PSA	Horizon PSA	Horizon Yield	Horizon Price	Total Return	Required Spread Narrowing (bp)
350	450	350	10.18	25-02+	8.07	
			9.81	25-11	10.01	37
350	550	350	10.81	25-02+	6.13	
			9.44	25-20	10.01	74

The seasoned FNMA 9 IO exhibits a significantly greater vulnerability to prepayment spikes. Given a six-month PSA of 600, the return drops dramatically to 1.35 percent. For 700 PSA and higher, the total return is highly negative unless the yield spread narrows by hundreds of basis points. With 900 PSA, the horizon yield has to decline to 0.05 percent to earn a return of 9.62 percent. This exhibits the dramatic decline in yields required to offset the loss of principal balance in whipsaw scenarios.

The loss due to the prepayment surge can also be recouped if the long-term prepayment expectation falls. For the FNMA 9 IO after the 900 PSA spike, a return of 9.62 percent can be attained without a narrowing of the horizon spread if the long-term PSA

TABLE 14.10
Impact of Prepayment Spike on FNMA 9 IO

Init. PSA	6-Mo. Act. PSA	Horizon PSA	Horizon Yield	Horizon Price	Total Return	Required Spread Narrowing (bp)
500	600	500	10.00	18-23	1.35	
			7.64	19-22	9.61	236
500	700	500	10.00	18-23	-6.97	
			5.21	20-26	9.59	479
500	800	500	10.00	18-23	-15.36	
			2.68	22-04+	9.62	732
500	900	500	10.00	18-23	-23.84	
			0.05	23-23	9.62	995

falls by approximately 125 to 375 PSA. This is a significant drop in the long-term PSA given an unchanged yield curve. For the 700 PSA shock, however, the long-term PSA would only have to decline by 60 PSA. For portfolio applications, lower-coupon IOs represent a relatively conservative approach for yield-enhancement and duration-shortening strategies. Lower-coupon IOs should provide more stability than higher coupons and are less vulnerable to severe prepayment shocks.

CMO Structuring Case Study[20]

This case study is based on a CMO structure utilizing 7.5 percent MBS collateral to create a pro forma CMO deal. Assume the collateral is purchased at a price of 99.5 and the yield curve at the time of deal pricing is positively sloped with a 200 basis points yield differential between the 1-year bill and the 10-year Treasury note. To maximize the CMO arbitrage, the CMO will be structured with as many short-term PAC classes as possible (to leverage off the steep yield curve). Therefore, if we can create 1-, 2-, 3-, and 5-year-average-life PACs, we should be able to achieve the best possible execution on the proceeds from the sale of the CMO. Because the deal receives its cash flow from mortgages with a 30-year maturity, the CMO structure obviously must also include longer-term classes. For simplicity, assume that the spread relationship between the CMO classes and the yield curve, as shown in Figure 14.10, exist at the time of pricing the CMO issue.

We can now structure a $100 million new-issue CMO, as illustrated in Table 14.11. Using the structure in the table, we can create a $100 million preliminary deal that would result in $98 million in sale proceeds. Remember that the cost of the collateral was equal to $99.5 million. The key to the deal structure here is to derive another $2.5 million so that we can create a profitable arbitrage. Refer again to Figure 14.10, which shows the CMO coupons and the yield curve. Note the area on the figure that is defined by the yield axis, the collateral coupon rate line, and the CMO coupon rate line and you may discern a triangle. This triangle area represents excess coupon, or collateral coupon income (interest income), over and above

---

[20]This CMO structuring case study was provided by Harry Forsyth.

FIGURE 14.10
CMO Coupon, Yield Differential

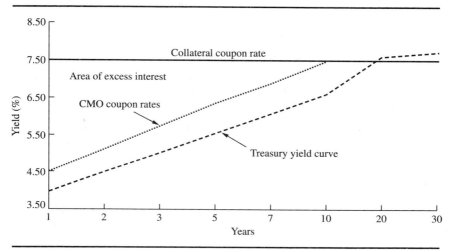

Source: Harry Forsyth.

the amount that will be necessary to pay interest on the CMO classes (interest expense). As of the issue date, $543,750 will be necessary to pay the first month's interest expense. However, the collateral will generate $625,000 in interest income, resulting in an $81,250 excess interest or cash flow surplus. When the preliminary analysis of an arbitrage CMO results in the potential creation of extreme amounts of excess interest, it can be capitalized upon by the

TABLE 14.11
$100 Million CMO Deal Structure

Coupon Rate (%)	Amount ($ millions)	Average Life (years)	Sale ($ millions)
4.50	10,000	1	10,000
5.00	10,000	2	10,000
5.25	10,000	3	10,000
6.50	20,000	5	19,500
7.50	25,000	10	24,500
7.50	25,000	20	24,000
Total	100,000		98,000

inclusion of an IO class as the **residual interest**[21] in the deal structure.

The next step in the structuring process is modeling the deal at varying prepayment rates to estimate the amount of excess interest there will be over the life of the deal. This step will determine whether the present value of all of the excess interest payments can be sold as an *IO strip*. On the surface, the deal should be doable. The spread between collateral interest income and CMO interest expense is approximately 13 percent in the first month and, given the historical prepayment experience attributable to 7.5 percent collateral, that percentage should not depreciate to any meaningful extent over time. We will now total the excess interest using the prepayment speed at which the deal will be sold and discount it to a present value dictated by current market yield requirements. If the present value of the excess interest cash flow exceeds the $2.5 million necessary to create our arbitrage, we can create an IO class and structure a CMO deal.

In summary, we sold this CMO assuming a prepayment rate equal to 170 PSA, and that assumption resulted in total excess interest income of approximately $10 million over the life of the deal. We discounted the $10 million back to a present value, using an 8 percent discounting factor, which resulted in net proceeds equal to approximately $3,974,800.

HEDGING WITH SMBSS[22]

SMBSs were created (ostensibly) so that holders of generic MBSs would have additional options with which to hedge their holdings. To the extent that a holder of pass-through MBSs hedges the portfolio with other mortgage securities, basis risk should be eliminated. The original intent for the utilization of SMBSs was to augment one's portfolio and not to provide speculators with the possibility of creating big portfolio gains. However, because of the extreme potential for gain embedded in most SMBSs (when the acquisition is made at the correct point in the cycle), sometimes investors find

---

[21]A residual interest in a CMO is the cash flows remaining after meeting all debt service, deal structure, and trustee expenses.

[22]This discussion of hedging with SMBSs was provided by Harry Forsyth.

themselves in the position of speculating on the direction of prepayments and not using the SMBSs as hedges. A true hedge, in fact, requires the investor to acquiesce to the reality that to hedge against risks requires a willingness to sacrifice some portion of the potential profit of a favorable market event in exchange for protection against unfavorable events.

The objective of any hedging strategy is to add to a portfolio securities that possess cash flow and/or performance characteristics that are contrary to those of the original securities held. A correctly executed hedge will provide the hedged portfolio with gains that will directly offset losses anticipated by interest rate and prepayment rate shifts. Additionally, investors are reluctant to execute cross-sector hedges, that is, purchase a Treasury security to hedge an MBS.[23] To the extent that investors are able to add discount-priced hedges to their portfolios, an element of leverage is introduced which may result in greater return on invested dollars and greater downside protection.

Ideally, the hedging medium selected should possess both the *contrary cash flow and pricing attributes that the hedged securities do not.* A hedging strategy employing SMBSs must utilize strips of the same WAC and WAM as those of the MBSs to be hedged. For example, if a portfolio of high-coupon pass-through MBSs is hedged against prepayment risk with POs, for the hedge to be effective the cost of negative convexity associated with the pass-through MBSs should be offset by the positive convexity of the PO. The assumption that must be made is that the acceleration in the prepayment rate of the PO will be equal to or greater than the option cost of the pass-through. To the extent that the positive cash flow pickup in the PO position is not sufficient to offset the pass-through's negative convexity, the hedge relies on a liquidation of the PO to create an offsetting appreciation in price. The lack of liquidity associated with SMBSs may, however, cause disparities between model-generated projections and actual value at the time a hedge is to be unwound.

---

[23]Cross-sector hedges introduce an additional element of risk into the equation, referred to as basis risk. Basis risk refers to risk arising out of a one-dimensional price movement in one sector of the bond market and not another. Typically, basis risk becomes a factor during periods when supply/demand influences affect one sector and not another. An example might be a widening spread relationship between pass-through MBSs and the Treasury 10-year note just prior to a quarterly refinancing.

Leveraging the Hedge Ratio with SMBSs

Another important ingredient of a correctly executed hedge is the *ratio* of the position held to the hedge that is added. Owing to the far greater price sensitivities of IOs and POs to changes in prepayment rates than those of the generic MBS, it is not necessary to add an equal amount of SMBSs to arrive at the appropriate hedge ratio. Stated another way, because of the disparity in duration characteristics of SMBSs (POs have very long durations, whereas IOs have *negative* durations), the greater price volatility of the SMBSs for a given change in price enables the hedge ratio to be leveraged. To determine the principal balance of securities that are to be added to protect a position against loss, one must estimate how changes in interest rates and/or prepayments affect the value of the MBS holdings. As an example, assume that one holds a 9 percent, 30-year FNMA pass-through purchased at a price of 103. Further assume that interest rates are projected to decline, which will expose the FNMA position to call risk. To offset the negative convexity, the portfolio manager decides to purchase a PO, also collateralized by FNMA 9s. All things being equal, the only decision that must be made is how large a PO position should be added to create a gain equal to the expected loss in the position held. If the value of a pickup in prepayment rate exerts a 10 percent increase in the market value of a PO and a 5 percent decrease in the value of the FNMA pass-through, POs would be added on a 1:2 ratio. For every $1 million of FNMA MBSs held, $0.5 million in principal balance of POs would be added.

Interaction of Interest Rate and Prepayment Rate Risks

Interest rate risk may be defined as the risk associated with the degree to which changes in the levels of interest rates affect the present value, or price, of future cash flows over a given holding period. The timing and reinvestment rates associated with monthly mortgage payments are also affected by interest rate shifts. *Prepayment rate risk* may be defined as the risk associated with the changes in the timing and rate at which future payments of unscheduled principal are received. To perceive a direct correlation between prepayment rate risk and interest rate risk is correct. However, *the two risk factors must be evaluated separately if one is to construct an effective hedging strategy.*

Why Hedge?

With respect to MBS portfolio management, the price at which a position is sold is a function of *both* the market interest rate *and* the MBS to Treasury spread requirement at the time of sale. For example, assume the sale of $1 million 8 percent FNMA pass-through MBSs, which were purchased at 8 percent (99.468 percent of its face amount) and then sold discounted to a market yield of 9 percent, to realize a price of 94.066 percent, which results in a $54,020 loss. On the other hand, the same pass-through sold at 7 percent would result in a $54,430 gain. In this example, we used a 150 PSA prepayment rate to calculate both prices. However, when we factor in a higher prepayment rate, the pricing changes rather dramatically. To yield 7 percent at 200 PSA, the price will drop to $104.67; at 250 PSA to $104.08; and at 300 PSA to $103.60. *The price drop reflects the loss in yield resulting in the shorter duration as prepayments accelerate.* Because of the yield loss, or call risk, the price must be reduced to maintain the original yield basis since there is less time to write down the premium. There is also a reduced coupon annuity because of the loss in principal. This is a further illustration of negative convexity (see Chapters 3 and 6). To offset the potential for lack of performance that may be experienced by a negatively convex MBS, investors may add securities to their portfolios that possess cash flow and/or performance characteristics which are contrary to those of the MBSs held. This is called hedging, and the prudent portfolio manager will likely wish to hedge high-volatility MBSs.

Common MBS Hedging Strategies

Portfolio Hedging

Portfolio hedging is largely a question of properly matching durations to neutralize interest rate risk. This is difficult to do with SMBSs because of the difficulty of devising a good option-adjusted duration for the SMBSs. For example, when SMBSs were introduced, IOs were hailed as the preferred means of hedging a Treasury or agency portfolio from interest rate risk. After all, since the IO value goes up when interest rates rise, IOs were thought to be a perfect hedge against interest rate risk. A typical portfolio strategy is to shorten the duration of the portfolio with the addition of IOs; since the IOs have negative duration, they can enable the bullish portfolio manager to gain price performance with the addition of long-duration Treasuries without extending the duration of the portfolio overall. Suppose a portfolio has a duration of 5. If the portfolio manager wishes to benefit from the price appreciation potential of longer-duration Treasuries, the addition of IOs with a negative duration of -12 would permit the addition of considerable long-duration Treasuries without causing an extension of the portfolio overall beyond its target duration of 5. *The risk, of course, is that the bull market will persist longer than anticipated, and the IO will prepay sooner than anticipated, thereby being eliminated as a duration hedge.* However, because of the asymmetric response of IOs to changes in interest rates, a dependable ratio with which to hedge noncallable securities with SMBSs has so far proved elusive.

MBS durations can often be better matched to SMBSs than the noncallable securities. For example, a position of long-duration MBSs, such as discount-priced GNMAs, could be shortened in duration with the addition of IOs, so this strategy centers on coupon rate and duration matching. To the extent that any shift in rates portends possible discrepancies in duration-matched assets and liabilities, SMBSs can be added to a portfolio to protect against possible losses. Emphasis should be placed upon the management aspects of this hedging strategy, with regular monitoring to assess the potential need to rebalance the ratios of the hedge as changes in prepayment rates are anticipated.

Hedging Mortgage Servicing

Purchase of PO or SPO Strips to Offset Paydown Losses in Servicing Portfolios. From an analytical point of view, a mortgage-servicing portfolio has basically the same duration attributes as an IO. Mortgage servicers can therefore purchase POs that have the same WAC and WAM and as similar as possible geographic mix as the mortgages to be hedged. Generally, the mortgage bankers who employ this strategy introduce as much leverage into the hedge as possible by either purchasing a **super PO (SPO)**[24] at a substantial discount or by using borrowed funds to leverage the PO purchase if it can be carried profitably. It is important to bear in mind the risks

---

[24]A super PO is a support class with no coupon. Since it is a support bond, it receives all the prepayments in excess of the PAC schedules, and when prepayments are high it will prepay much faster than a standard PO.

of hedging servicing with POs stripped from collateral of a different WAC from that of the loans underlying the servicing portfolio to be hedged. For example, the hedger may be tempted to buy POs from a higher WAC pool. The risk of doing so is that the higher WAC MBSs may be burned out (see the discussions of burnout in Chapters 3 and 4) and therefore will not respond as quickly as the loans in the servicing portfolio if they are on the cusp.

This strategy is again one of duration matching. Here the servicing, which is simply the basis points spread income withheld from the gross WAC (mortgage rate), has a negative duration that is the same as that of similar WAC and WAM IOs. Therefore, the long positive duration of the properly matched PO will provide a hedge. However, since the gain in prepayment cash flow of the PO must click in at the same time the servicing income is being lost, the PO or SPO must be carefully matched to have the same prepayment sensitivity as the mortgages providing the servicing income.

Hedging IOs[25]

Hedging IOs with OTC Options. The quantitative analysis of SMBSs must take place within a context that correctly weighs the option value of the securities. Because SMBSs are much more sensitive to changes in prepayment rates than pass-through collateral, coming to grips with their option value is essential. The results of any quantitative analysis will therefore be more accurate if the analysis is done recognizing the optionality of the SMBS. As with options, when an investor incorrectly anticipates interest rate and, therefore, prepayment rate movements, returns will be asymmetrical. Option positions often expire out of the money. When a bet is made with an incorrectly timed acquisition of an IO or PO, like an option, the needed cash flow and/or price performance will be lacking. Needless to say, incorrectly anticipated performance can exert a negative influence on a "risk-controlled" trade.

Simply stated, the owner of an IO is short the call options embedded in the underlying MBS collateral. The owner of a PO, conversely, is long the call. Given the standard measurements of volatility, both actual and implied, one should be able to price the long or short position into potential ownership of an IO or PO. The

---

[25]This discussion of hedging IOs was provided by Alan Jay Brazil.

calculation should simply value the call and then add or subtract its value into the SMBS pricing. If the SMBS price does not accurately reflect the option's value, as is often the case, the acquisition should be avoided. Remember that convexity is a measurement of the duration drift of a given security. Convexity, as an analytical valuation tool, can also be viewed as the value of the volatility of an SMBS and, when converted to basis points, should approximate the option cost in an OAS measurement. Therefore, the OAS of a given SMBS should vary from the static spread in an amount equal to its option cost. In this context, there will be an inverse relationship between positive convexity and negative option cost, and vice versa.

Long-dated Treasury strips can be used both to hedge IO MBSs and to increase holding-period returns in their MBS portfolio.[26] In particular, these trades give the following results:

- On a duration and dollar-matched basis, the strip and IO combination provides generally higher total returns and yields than comparable-coupon pass-throughs.
- The Treasury strip is an ideal hedge for an IO, even in bullish environments, with the high positive convexity of the strip offsetting the large negative convexity of the IO.

Hedging an IO is difficult because its duration, even option-adjusted duration, changes dramatically as yields move, reflecting its large negative convexity. Thus, in a rally its duration shortens; as rates rise its duration lengthens. The long-dated Treasury strips are ideal hedging securities for IOs because they have large positive convexity relative to Treasury coupons. This convexity can then be used to offset the negative convexity of the IO.

INVERSE IO[27]

An IO stripped from an inverse floater (see Chapter 12) produces an IO where the underlying coupon (an inverse floater) is declining in value when interest rates are rising (so the amount of coupon to contribute to the IO becomes smaller). At the same time, the dura-

---

[26]This discussion of hedging IOs with Treasury strips was provided by Alan Jay Brazil.

[27]This discussion of the inverse floater IO is by Andrew Davidson and Thomas Ho, *CMO Commentary*, April 27, 1993.

tion of the IO cash flows are extending (interest rates rise, prepayment spreads slow). Conversely, when interest rates decline, the inverse floater coupon underlying the IO is increasing (generating more coupon for the IO), whereas the duration of the inverse IO is shrinking (prepayment speeds accelerate). The inverse IO is therefore viewed as a self-hedge, which will be so *only if LIBOR is rising and falling parallel with the longer-term rates that drive prepayment speeds.*

Funding Cost Risk versus Prepayment Protection

Inverse floater IOs can be viewed as a leveraged investment in which a CMO bond is funded to a spread off LIBOR. When the underlying CMO bond is a well-protected TAC, the inverse floater IO may have negligible prepayment risk. For investors who believe the yield curve will remain steep, these bonds offer an inexpensive method of financing with short-maturity LIBOR rates. Further, the WAL of these bonds can be short, and they can be used as short-term investments offering substantial yields. However, investors should be aware of the possible high price volatility due to the long effective duration.

If the market uses "guilty by association" as a rule, then an inverse floater IO may be an opportunity for some astute investors. Why? Simply put, bonds labeled as inverse floater IOs are not mere combinations of two evils. These bonds may have characteristics that fit certain portfolio applications.

When prepayment speeds are high, as was the case in the 1992–1993 period, the fear of prepayment spikes sent IO prices plummeting. The anticipation of rising short interest rates, as 1-month LIBOR reached the historic low of 3.14 percent in the spring of 1993, made inverse floaters risky investments. But some inverse floater IOs can be well protected from severe prepayment risk. This feature significantly dampens the overall risk exposure of these bonds. The key to analyzing inverse IOs is to understand the deal structure.

Case Study
Structuring an Inverse Floater IO under a Steep Yield Curve

Consider FNMA 93-48 as an inverse floater case study. The deal was priced on March 11, 1993 at 380 PSA and is backed by 15-year

TABLE 14.12
FNMA 93–48 Deal Structure

Tranche	Principal Type	Coupon Type	Size ($mm)	Coupon (%)	WAL (years)
F	TAC	Floater	37.5	3.33	1.2
S	Notional	IO	37.5	4.68	1.2
B	Support	PO	9.9	0.00	4.7
C	Support	Fixed	52.6	9.50	4.7

FNMA 8s (gross WAC 8.65 percent). The other deal has only four tranches. Table 14.12 provides the deal summary.

The market data are based on April 21, 1993. The 1-year and 10-year Treasury yields were 3.14 percent and 5.86 percent, respectively, with a 272 basis points yield spread. The FNMA 93-48 deal summarized in Table 14.12 has two components: the short-term, composed of tranches F and S, and the long-term, composed of tranches B and C.

Tranche F floats off monthly LIBOR with a 20 basis points spread. The floater has a lifetime cap of 8 percent and a floor of 0.20 percent. The difference between the collateral coupon rate and the floating rate pays the inverse floater tranche S.

Tranche F is a TAC bond with a TAC schedule at 380 PSA. The principal payments are made to pay down the TAC up to the scheduled amount. Any excess is absorbed by the support tranches. Therefore, tranche F is protected from call risk but is exposed to extension risk. The amount of support bonds is very significant, consisting of 62.5 percent of the deal (many PAC bonds are supported by only 30 percent of the deal).

On the long-term portion of the deal, the support tranche has a high coupon rate of 9.5 percent. In order for the 8 percent collateral to support the tranche C coupon, POs are created. Therefore, the POs are also support tranches with a high exposure to call risk.

Figure 14.11 depicts the cash flow (principal and interest) of the collateral and its allocation to the four tranches at 800 PSA. At prepayment speeds below 380 PSA, a significant portion of the principal payments of the support bonds (tranches B and C) follow those of tranches F and S. However, at the high PSA speeds, these support bonds are paid down to offer the TAC bonds protection.

FIGURE 14.11
Monthly Cash Flows of FNMA 93-48

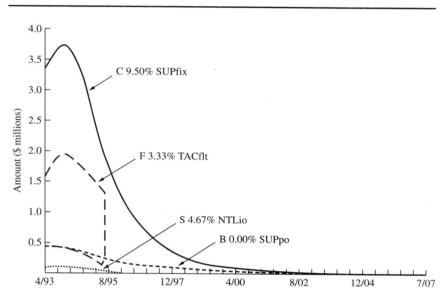

Source: CMO Commentary.

Inverse Floater and IO Features: Risks That Are Publicized

Tranche S is an inverse floater with only the IO component. In general, inverse floaters can be viewed as a leveraged investment in a CMO bond, with a significant percentage of the bond financed at a spread to LIBOR with a cap on the funding cost. In this case, the purchase of $1 million notional value of tranche S is equivalent to the purchase of $1 million par 8 percent coupon TAC bond (the underlying bond) with its principal schedule defined as tranche F. The investment is funded by $1 million LIBOR plus 20 basis points financing, capped at 8 percent. Since the WAL of the bond is only slightly more than a year, the 8 percent cap is inconsequential.

   In contrast to a typical inverse floater, the inverse floater IO does not receive any principal. Nevertheless, inverse floater IOs are clearly very sensitive to the changes in the funding cost. In particular, the size of the coupon is driven by the LIBOR rate, and the pre-

FIGURE 14.12
Monthly Cash Flows, FNMA 93-48S

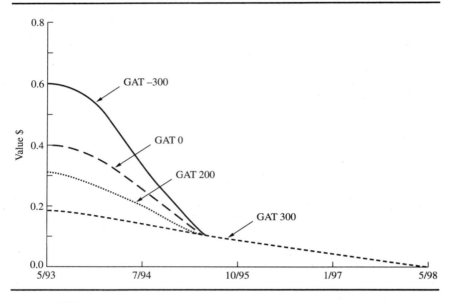

Source: CMO Commentary.

payment rate is affected by a combination of the long rate and the shape of the yield curve.

If LIBOR falls, tranche S will receive more coupon income. If the underlying bond extends when prepayments slow down, tranche S will generate cash flows for a longer period. This behavior is depicted in Figure 14.12, which compares the cash flows of tranche S under seven scenarios. The scenarios represent instantaneous parallel shifts in interest rates. The figure shows that the cash flows are higher for lower interest rate levels and longer for higher interest rate levels when prepayments are lower.

The TAC Feature: The Protection That Is Built into the Deal Structure

According to the preceding analysis, the value of the inverse floater IO lies in the ability to fund a bond at a relatively low rate. Since tranche S is linked to the TAC bond (tranche F), this inverse floater IO also has protection from the call risk. Considering the deal has

62.5 percent support bonds, the protection from the prepayment risk is substantial.

To analyze the impact of prepayment risk on tranche S, consider the bond cash flows under different PSA speeds. But this time, let us keep the interest rates fixed. The effective PAC collar is defined as the minimum and maximum of all the speeds that ensure the scheduled paydown of the TAC bond. The effective PAC collar is calculated to be 266 to 1,546 PSA for tranche S. Within this very wide collar the bond has a WAL of 1.32 years.

This analysis shows that the call risk of the bond is quite limited. For the inverse floater IO cash flow to be affected by the prepayment speed would require a sustained speed in excess of 1,546 PSA. Meanwhile, the bond would benefit from a slow prepayment speed, leading to an extension of WAL. The bond extends to a WAL of 2 years at 160 PSA. Figure 14.12 confirms these observations. The cash flows of scenarios 100–300 have extended payments. But as the interest rates fall, the cash flows do not shorten because of the protection from the support bonds.

Valuing the Inverse Floater IO

The value of tranche S depends on the combined effect of the extension of the bond and the level of the LIBOR rate. For simplicity, we shall analyze the bond assuming the short and the long rate move in tandem. Let us use the indicative price of 5-17. This is the price of the IO on 100 notional par. The summary of analytics is given in Table 14.13.

At the price of 5-17, the bond offers a spread of 230 basis points over the 1-year Treasury. The bond has a high effective duration since it is a leveraged investment. Since the bond is an IO, it is somewhat surprising to see that it has a negative option cost and a high positive convexity. To understand this behavior, let us evalu-

TABLE 14.13
Tranche S Analytics

Price	Yield at 380 PSA	Spread (bp)	Option Cost	Effective Duration	Effective Convexity
5-17	5.44	230/1-Year	−38	12.18	19.97

TABLE 14.14
Price Sensitivity of Tranche S

Rates	−200	−134	−67	0	67	134	200
Price	7.76	6.99	6.24	5.53	5.33	4.98	3.92

ate the performance profile. Consider interest rates rising and falling 200 basis points and calculating the price assuming constant OAS (Table 14.14).

When interest rates fall, tranche S is protected from call risk. Therefore, the price rises as the funding cost decreases. However, a rise in interest rates does not lead to a significant drop in prices. This is because the rise in the funding cost is partially offset by the extension of the WAL of the bond, leading to the bond's positive convexity around the base case scenario. Note that if interest rates rise more than 100 basis points, the cost of funding dominates the bond value again.

Summary of Inverse IO Investment Properties

The value of an inverse floater IO depends crucially on the combination of LIBOR rates and prepayment expectations. In the case of bonds like tranche S, where there is significant protection against call risk, we should still consider the effect of extension.

The inverse floater IO performs best when prepayments slow down, leading to an extension in the bond while short rates fall. The worst scenario is when the yield curve flattens, with higher funding rates accompanied by lower long-term rates, resulting in higher prepayments. In portfolio applications, the inverse floater IO should also be evaluated versus comparable effective duration alternatives.

Since the value of the inverse floater IO is very sensitive to the funding cost, investors are advised to consider first the value of the underlying TAC bond. The next step is to determine the value of the floater. The fair value of the inverse floater IO is the value of the underlying TAC bond net of the floater value.

Derivative Applications

Combining an Inverse Floating-Rate MBS with an IO

The inverse floater's coupon value increases (usually with leverage) as interest rates decline. Inverse floaters are therefore bull market biased (inverse floaters typically have long-duration properties). As with any MBS, however, there will always be premium-price resistance because of the potential for increases in prepayments. Inverse floaters are, therefore, possessed of a certain amount of call risk; for example, if an inverse floater with a duration of $d + 1$ is matched against liabilities with a duration of d, the negative duration properties of an IO of similar, or greater, coupon rate collateral will offset the duration mismatch. Furthermore, the idea is if rates are rising (inverse coupon declines), the increase in interest (and mortgage) rates would reduce prepayments, thereby extending the duration of the IO and enhancing its value.

There can be considerable basis risk with this hedge, however, because the inverse floater coupon responds to changes in LIBOR, whereas the IO prepayments would be responsive to changes in the 7- or 10-year Treasury. The risk would be a curve flattening on the 5-year and less sector of the Treasury curve, whereby the inverse floater coupon would go down; and there would be no impact on prepayments to enhance the value of the IO. Or a rally at the long end of the curve might accelerate prepayments, causing the IO to pay off and leave the inverse floater unhedged.

The Creation of a Position of Synthetic Securities

This strategy involves the purchase of opposing IOs and POs, or adding IOs or POs of differing coupon rate collateral, to blend rates and create a custom-built security in anticipation of prepayment rate shifts. This strategy utilizes the acquisition of an IO or PO whose coupon is either way in or way out of the money and combining it with an IO or PO with the opposing price and/or yield. *For example, one would ideally combine an IO stripped from high-coupon collateral exhibiting burnout with a PO stripped from CUSP or current-coupon collateral to achieve optimal results.* (For an example of combining IOs and POs, see Applications at the end of Chapter 12.)

Table 14.15A provides the components of a synthetic portfolio consisting of an IO and an inverse floater. Table 14.15B illustrates the return profile of combining the IO and inverse floater of the FHLMC REMIC. The up-down changes in LIBOR are shown on the horizontal row at the top of the table; changes in the PSA speeds are shown on the vertical column to the left of the table. The base price assumptions are that LIBOR is 5.25 percent with the col-

TABLE 14.15A
Components of IO Inverse Synthetic Combination Portfolio

Amount ($ thousands)	Component	Price ($)	Yield (%)
19,167	FHLMC 1191-G inverse floater	77-00	14.51
66,176	FHLMC 1191-I IO	41-00	11.22
42,416	Synthetic combination		12.73

lateral prepaying at 125 PSA. (See the bold box at the center of the table with a 12.26 percent yield.) Assuming parallel shifts in LIBOR and the yield of 7- and 10-year Treasuries,[28] as LIBOR increases to 8.25 percent, the PSA speed slows to 80 and the return of the IO inverse combination declines to 9.75 percent (upper-left quadrant of the table). The return of the combination declines because the inverse coupon goes down as the index value (LIBOR) goes up. The return decline would have been far more severe, however, had the collateral underlying the inverse floater not extended in average life as the prepayment speed slows from 125 to 80 PSA. With the extension in collateral average life the IO has more time to pay out the now smaller coupon.

In the other direction, as LIBOR declines from 5.25 percent to 2.25 percent, the coupon value is obviously going up. However, the average life of the underlying collateral is shrinking, so even though the inverse coupon value is becoming greater, it has far less time to pay it, so the value of the IO cash flows are diminished. However, there is one other very important benefit contributed by the collateral. Recall the collateral principal was purchased at a deep discount and with prepayment speeds high (375 PSA under this scenario). The rapid return of principal at par mitigates the negative impact of the high PSA speed on the IO. The result is the yield on the combination overall in the low interest rate, high-prepayment speed scenario holds at 6.64 percent (lower-right quadrant of the table).

To view the returns in a flat yield curve scenario, simply read the yields horizontally across the 125 PSA row. For example, if LIBOR rises to 8.25 percent and the PSA speed does not change,

---

[28]Most MBS analysts view the yield of the 7- and 10-year sectors of the Treasury curve to be a lead indicator of the future direction of prepayment speeds.

TABLE 14.15B

7 × 7 Matrix of a Deep-Discount Inverse Floater and IO Combination

	8.25% LIBOR	7.25% LIBOR	6.25% LIBOR	5.25% LIBOR	4.25% LIBOR	3.25% LIBOR	2.25% LIBOR
80 PSA	9.75%	11.08%	12.37%	13.62%	14.83%	16.03%	17.20%
95 PSA	9.19%	10.55%	11.86%	13.14%	14.38%	15.59%	16.79%
110 PSA	8.67%	10.05%	11.39%	12.68%	13.94%	15.18%	16.39%
125 PSA	8.20%	9.60%	10.95%	12.26%	13.53%	14.78%	16.00%
165 PSA	7.75%	9.04%	10.29%	11.52%	12.73%	13.92%	15.09%
275 PSA	7.84%	8.36%	8.89%	9.43%	9.98%	10.54%	11.12%
375 PSA	3.87%	4.31%	4.76%	5.22%	5.68%	6.15%	6.64%

Source: Lehman Brothers Fixed Income Research.

the yield of the combination is 8.20 percent. The poorest results would come about if the prepayment speed were to accelerate as LIBOR is increasing (combination yield 3.87 percent, lower left quadrant), a seemingly unlikely event.

SMBSS IN CMO DEAL STRUCTURING

CMO Bond SMBSs

In recent years the emphasis on strip origination has shifted to strip forms created from the CMO structure. Chapter 10 illustrated the application of coupon stripping to reduce the coupon of the CMO bonds below that of the collateral pass-through rate. For example, in a period of declining interest rates and on a steeply positive yield curve, the coupon that is the current coupon may be too high to enable sale of the short-maturity bond classes of the CMO without a substantial premium price. If the current coupon is 7.5 percent and the yield spread from the 2-year Treasury to the 10-year Treasury is 250 basis points, the coupon of the 2- through 5-year-average-life CMO classes will have to be well below 7.5 percent.

Figure 14.13 illustrates the creation of an **IOette** and PAC IO from the deal structure. The IOette illustrated in the figure represents 100 basis points stripped off the 9 percent coupon of the CMO deal collateral and various amounts stripped off the first three PAC bond classes (see the discussion that follows on PAC IOs).

Even though an IOette is a strip of only interest, in pre-1993 REMIC deals there was required to be a small amount of principal attached to the tranche to satisfy REMIC requirements. What this translates into is that paying 4–07 for a 100 basis points strip off $500 million of 9.5 percent collateral is the same as paying 4220–00 for $500,000 original face with a 1009.5 percent coupon. The point is that when a small amount of principal is attached to a bond that is interest only, it creates an extremely high coupon and dollar price in order for the cash flows to match out.

IOette Math

The math involved in figuring proceeds and accrued interest on IOettes is the same as for any other bond; just watch the decimals.

FIGURE 14.13

Creation of IOette and PAC IO from FNMA Collateral in CMO Deal Structure

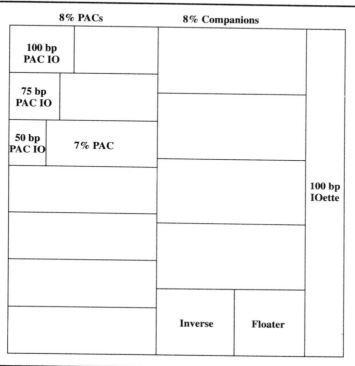

Source: Lehman Brothers Fixed Income Research.

For the IOette, with $500,000 original face, a 1009.5 percent coupon, and a dollar price of 4220–00:

Proceeds = Face × Dollar price/100
= 500,000 × 4220/100 = $21,100,000

Accrued = Face × Coupon/360 × Days of accrued
(assume 20 days of accrued)
= 500,000 × 10.095/360 × 20 = $280,416.67

The only other thing to remember when considering an IOette is that it is similar to a super premium coupon bond. One might pay par for an 8 percent coupon bond and 102–00 for a bond with an 8.5 percent coupon. How much would be paid for a bond with a 1,000 percent coupon? The same way a premium bond loses yield the faster it pays down (because 2–00 is lost every time a dollar of principal is repaid at par), an IOette's price amortizes down to par over time, and prepayments of principal are returned at par (so the loss is, in this case, 4120–00 for every dollar returned at par). Remember, the longer the principal is outstanding, the longer the holder gets that enormous coupon and forestalls the loss due to repayment (at par) of principal that was purchased at a premium.

PAC IOs

A **PAC IO** is a form of bond IO. A bond IO is simply some amount of basis points stripped off the coupon of a particular CMO bond class. For example, the IOette in the deal structure illustrated in Figure 14.13 consists of 100 basis points off the 9 percent collateral pass-through coupon, leaving 8 percent as the coupon available for the CMO bonds. However, in a steep yield curve environment that is too high a coupon for the short-average-life CMO bonds to be sold without a high premium price; therefore, additional coupon interest must be stripped from those classes. The most prevalent form of bond IO is one stripped from the PAC bond classes, which creates a PAC IO. The PAC IO may be created from stripping various amounts of coupon interest from several PAC bond classes, as illustrated in Figure 14.13. However, a PAC IO is often created from just one PAC bond.

Structural Characteristics of PAC IOs

The most significant structural characteristic of the PAC IO is that, since it has been stripped from a PAC bond, the PAC IO *carries with it the prepayment-protection band of the underlying PAC bond.* So we have an IO with call protection! A second significant structural feature of the PAC IO is that it has substantial call protection during the period of the principal lockout on the underlying bond. Finally, remember the call- and extension-risk properties of CMO bonds:

- Short-average-life PACs have wide effective bands and maximum call protection.
- PAC bonds offer relatively little extension potential.
- Intermediate PACs have narrower effective bands, but provide additional call protection with lockouts.

- Short- and intermediate-average-life sequentials lack call protection but offer extension potential.
- Long-average-life sequentials enjoy call protection by being the last bonds to be paid off.
- Busted PACs still have some call protection from the lockout and have good extension protection.

An interesting opportunity with PAC IOs can potentially be found at the end of a prepayment cycle with PAC II IOs or busted PAC IOs that have just enough call protection to survive some amount of remaining prepayment activity but then can extend as the prepayment cycle winds down. However, beware: This strategy is for the brave at heart who can afford to withstand the risk of longer than anticipated prepayment activity. The most *conservative* strategy would be purchase of an IO stripped from a super PAC that typically has effective upper bands in excess of 400 PSA (see Chapter 7 for a description of super PAC structures).

Tables 14.16A and 14.16B illustrate vector scenarios stressing the FNMA 1991 182S PAC IO backed by FNMA 9s. With Table 14.16a all speeds are static; that is, the yields are generated from running the collateral at the specified speeds for their entire lives. The difference between Table 14.16A and Table 14.16B is that in Table 14.16B we run the initial speeds for two years instead of one year. The *worst* thing that can happen to a PAC IO is for the collateral to run faster than the upper band for the entire life of the bond. The *two best* things that can happen to PAC IOs are to run slower than the lower band for the life of the bond or to run faster than the upper band for a couple of years and then slow down inside the

TABLE 14.16A
Vector Scenario Analysis, FNMA 1991 182S

	Year 1	Year 2	Year 3–Maturity	Base Yield (%)
Scenario 1	195 PSA	195 PSA	195 PSA	9.75
Scenario 2	325	325	195	9.75
Scenario 3	325	195	195	9.75
Scenario 4	350	350	195	9.75
Scenario 5	350	195	195	9.75
Scenario 6	400	400	195	9.82
Scenario 7	400	195	195	9.75

TABLE 14.16B
Vector Scenario Analysis, FNMA 1991 182S

	Year 1–2	Year 3	Year 4–Maturity	Base Yield (%)
Scenario 1	195 PSA	195 PSA	195 PSA	9.75
Scenario 2	325	325	195	9.82
Scenario 3	325	195	195	9.75
Scenario 4	350	350	195	9.96
Scenario 5	350	195	195	9.75
Scenario 6	400	400	195	10.65
Scenario 7	400	195	195	9.82

bands for the remainder of its life. Scenario 6 in Table 14.16B shows a yield of 10.65 percent if the bond runs for three years at 400 PSA and then slow to within the bands for the rest of its life.

CHAPTER 15

ACCOUNTING FOR INVESTMENTS IN MORTGAGE-BACKED SECURITIES

Raymond J. Beier[1]

INTRODUCTION

This chapter examines how an MBS investor should apply **generally accepted accounting principles (GAAP)** to determine (1) the amount of reported income or loss generated by a security during a financial reporting period and (2) the amortized cost basis of that security.

Income or loss reported each period will generally depend on the type of security purchased, the purchase price paid, the unamortized balance of the purchase premium or purchase discount, the coupon rate, the remaining term to maturity, actual and anticipated prepayments, the current level of interest rates, and whether the investment is reported on the investor's balance sheet at amortized cost or market value. The GAAP discussed in this chapter apply to all MBS investments, including government-guaranteed agency securities, REMICs, CMOs, and all of their derivatives.

At first glance, investors who report investments in their financial statements solely at current market value (as contrasted to historic cost) may conclude that the accounting principles defining the interest method are not relevant to them. Even so, these investors still must distinguish between realized and unrealized gains and losses in their periodic financial statements. And making that determination requires the investor to compare the investment's current market value to its amortized cost basis at each financial reporting

---

[1]Partner, Coopers and Lybrand, New York.

date. Accordingly, these investors must use the interest method described in this chapter or a similar method to determine the amortized cost basis.

Issues concerning whether investors should use market value or amortized cost to account for their investment securities, regulatory accounting,[2] accounting by issuers of CMOs and REMICs, and federal income tax consequences[3] are beyond the scope of this chapter. Additionally, the intent of this chapter is to summarize the basic concepts of applying GAAP to MBSs rather than to address the many intricacies that can arise with certain MBSs. These complexities are dependent on the many individual characteristics of the security purchased, including, among others, terms of interest payments, the general level of prevailing interest rates, and anticipated prepayments.

FINANCIAL ACCOUNTING GUIDANCE

The authoritative accounting literature, **Statement of Financial Accounting Standards (SFAS),** "Accounting for Nonrefundable Fees and Costs Associated with Originating or Acquiring Loans and Initial Direct Costs of Leases" **(FASB 91),** generally requires that investors account for their investments in MBSs using the interest method (also known as the effective-yield or the level-yield method). The standard also provides specific guidance and techniques illustrating how the **Financial Accounting Standards Board (FASB)** believes investors should apply the interest method.

Nevertheless, FASB 91 does not answer all the questions that may arise about investments in certain types of MBSs. For example, the interest method clearly applies to debt securities, but certain MBSs are issued in equity form (e.g., residual interests). Nor does FASB 91 address how an investor should apply the interest method to MBSs that have a risk or loss, such as high-premium securities, for example, interest-only MBSs. (See FASB 91 Accounting for ARM Security Investments in Chapter 13.)

---

[2]See Chapter 1 for accounting and regulatory guidelines regarding market value accounting, risk-weighted capital, and FFEC investment guidelines.

[3]See the appendix to this chapter for some general tax-accounting considerations.

Legal Form of the Security

Because accountants usually account for investment securities substantially based upon their legal form,[4] certain MBSs have created a special problem from an accounting standpoint. Many MBSs are legally equity securities (e.g., PCs and certain residuals), but behave exactly like other MBSs that are legally debt instruments.

The accounting profession addressed and solved this problem by means of the FASB's **Emerging Issue Task Force (EITF)** Consensus 89–4, "Accounting for a Purchased Investment in a Collateralized Mortgage Obligation Instrument or in a Mortgage-Backed Interest Only Certificate" (EITF 89–4). Basically, the consensus requires investors of MBSs issued in legal form as equity but that possess "debt-like" cash flow streams to account for those investments as debt using the interest method. The task force developed the following criteria to assist "equity-form" MBS investors in making this "form over substance" determination:

- The investor did not contribute assets to the MBS entity.
- The collateral backing the MBSs is either government-agency securities or mortgage loans that offer only a remote possibility of credit loss.
- The MBS entity will self-liquidate when assets are fully collected and obligations fully paid.
- The collateral may not be managed as a portfolio, and the investor may not substitute collateral.
- It is highly unlikely that the investor would have to contribute funds to the MBS entity to cover administrative expenses or other costs.
- No other investor in the MBS entity has recourse to the investor.

Obviously, in today's market almost all forms of MBSs that are issued in equity form would qualify as "debt-like" investments using these criteria. The consensus refers to MBSs that meet these

---

[4]Debt investments generally represent cash flow streams that are collectible under preset terms and conditions. Excluding certain types of preferred stock, most equity investments represent an interest in the residual cash flows of an entity. Accordingly, the accounting rules applied to debt investments differ from those applied to equity investments.

criteria and to those that are issued in legal form as debt as "non-equity CMO instruments" (e.g., most REMIC classes categorized as regular interests).

High-Risk CMO Investments

EITF 89–4 also distinguishes MBSs that have little or no principal component as an element of its expected future cash flow stream (e.g., IOs or certain residuals) from all other MBSs. EITF 89–4 refers to these MBSs as "high-risk CMO instruments" and specifies an application of the interest method, which differs from that applied to other MBS investments, referred to as the "prospective" method. Investors are to apply the "retrospective" method to investments in all other MBSs. Both methods are discussed in the next section.

This reference for accounting purposes as "high risk" does not refer to potential market risk (although these securities typically are considered risky in terms of prepayment and/or price volatility by market participants), but simply the risk that an investor may not recover a significant portion of the original investment because there is little or no principal designated for that class of security. For example, although changes in prepayment speeds will have a significant impact on the return on investment of a PO certificate, the investor can still expect to recover the investment. The same is not true for IOs if prepayment speeds increase dramatically. Market participants will sometimes refer to "high-risk" securities as high-premium securities.

EITF 89–4 provides that "high-risk CMO instruments" are those that have a *potential for loss of a significant portion of the original investment* due to changes in (1) interest rates, (2) the prepayment rate of the assets of the CMO structure, and (3) earnings from the temporary reinvestment of cash collected by the CMO structure but not yet distributed to the holders of its obligations (e.g., reinvestment earnings). In applying this guidance, some accountants have concluded that an MBS has the potential for a significant loss of a portion of its original investment when the purchase price paid exceeds 125 (assuming par is 100; therefore, the premium is 25). Other accountants use a lower benchmark. As a practical matter in today's MBS market, controversies are rare in making this assessment because premiums on MBSs are either nominal or far in excess of 25 percent.

APPLICATION OF THE INTEREST METHOD

Interest Method Defined

From an accounting perspective, the **interest method** represents an effective yield calculation, which at the acquisition date discounts the MBS's future series of annual cash flows to the purchase price paid to future value. The investor's yield calculations should consider all components of the purchase price, including purchase premium or discount, accrued interest existing at the purchase date, and any other fees or costs. In addition, other factors may have impact on the yield calculation, for example, anticipated prepayments and the MBS's payment delays.

As described in FASB 91, the objective of the interest method is to determine the amount of interest income recognized for each accounting period using a constant effective yield applied to the MBS's net carrying value.[5] The interest income recognized each period includes the amortization or accretion of any purchase premium or purchase discount. In addition, whereas FASB 91 allows MBS investors to anticipate prepayments in their calculation of effective yield, the retrospective and prospective methods differ on the accounting for prepayment experience that deviates from original estimates.[6] MBS investors also should note that at each balance sheet date, whether either the retrospective or prospective method is used, an MBS's net carrying value *generally represents the present value of the defined future cash flows discounted at a calculated effective yield.* And finally, when estimating prepayments many investors rely primarily on reports forecasting prepayments that are published by the major security firms. Other investors sometimes

---

[5]For financial reporting purposes, the net carrying value (also referred to as book value) represents the following components: purchase price paid, remaining balance of discount or premium, purchased accrued interest, and any other unamortized fees or costs.

[6]While market participants might automatically assume that accounting rules require that prepayments be estimated, FASB 91 was not written with only MBS investments in mind. It permits but does not require investors to anticipate prepayments when estimating future cash flows for calculating the effective yield, but only when the investor owns a large number of similar loans, or pools when prepayments are probable; and when the investor has the option, timing and amount can be reasonably estimated. As a practical matter, most MBS investors anticipate prepayments when calculating effective yields.

use historical prepayment speeds (e.g., the preceding 3 months or 12 months) in projecting prepayments.

Retrospective Method

As discussed earlier, *an investor should apply the* **retrospective method** *to all MBSs other than those designated as "high risk."* Therefore, most MBSs, including agency securities, PACs, TACs, CMO floaters, inverse floaters, POs, and Z-bonds, are accounted for using the retrospective method.

Under this method, in each accounting period when actual prepayment experience differs from the original projections, FASB 91 requires that an investor perform a new effective yield calculation. *The investor should perform the recalculation as of the original purchase date using actual prepayment experience to date and a revised projection of future cash flows based on the revised prepayment projection.* The investor should adjust the MBS's carrying amount to the corresponding amount that would have occurred had this updated effective yield calculation been applied at the time of purchase. The accounting adjustment can be either a write-up or a write-down to the MBS's net carrying value and would increase or decrease reported interest income for that period. (A write-up should not exceed the original basis of the MBS as of the trade settlement date.) Therefore, interest income for that period will consist of the income resulting from the effective yield calculation adjusted by the write-up or write-down to the MBS's carrying value.

FASB 91 provides cases illustrating how an investor should apply the interest method. Although the cases are quite general, they are helpful in understanding the FASB's approach to the interest method. Table 15.1 is a useful guide that cross-references FASB 91, its cases, and EITF 89–4 to the retrospective and prospective methods.

Example
To better illustrate the application of the retrospective method and the required accounting adjustments, assume an investor who does not use market value accounting purchases the A bonds of a hypothetical (and simplified) CMO. Assume the hypothetical CMO is collateralized with $100 million principal amount of 5-year balloon mortgages (with a remaining term to maturity of 55 months) that have an 8.125 percent fixed annual interest rate. The CMO has four

TABLE 15.1
Cross Reference to Accounting Literature That Applies to Accounting for Investments in MBSs

Types of Investments	Applicable Accounting Pronouncement	Prepayment Assumptions	Accounting Method Required for Changes in Prepayments	Cross Reference to Illustrative Cases in FASB 91	
MBSs other than those designated "high risk." This category includes agency securities, PACs, TACs, POs, floaters, Z-bonds, etc.	FASB 91	Not required by FASB 91 but usually done in practice.	Retrospective method. Under this method, effective yield is based on actual cash flows to date and future estimates of prepayments; at end of each accounting period carrying value of investment is adjusted.	MBSs whose interest rate is fixed.	See FASB 91, paragraph 18 and Cases 3 and 4.
				MBSs that have scheduled interest rate increases and decreases (e.g., ARMs).	See FASB 91, paragraphs 18(a), 18(b), and Cases 5, 6, and 7.
				MBSs whose interest rate floats.	See FASB 91, paragraph 18(c) and Cases 8 and 9.
"High-risk" MBSs. The most common security of this type is the IO.	Emerging Issues Task Force, issue number 89–4	Required by EITF 89–4	Prospective method. Effective yield is based on carrying value of investment and future estimates of cash flows. No adjustments to carrying value except in limited circumstance.	None. FASB 91 does not apply to "high-risk" MBSs.	

classes of sequential-pay bonds (A, B, C, and D) and an E bond that is primarily an IO. The B, C, and D bonds pay coupon interest of 7.5 percent, whereas the A bond pays a 6 percent coupon and has a principal amount of $35 million. The example assumes that there are no payment delays between the collateral payment date and the bond payment date. The investor purchases the A bond at $34,475,000 plus one day of accrued interest amounting to $5,833 and has a corporate bond-equivalent yield of 8 percent. At settlement date, the PSA on the collateral is expected to be 175. The difference between the 8 percent yield and the 6 percent coupon rate occurs primarily because the $519,167 discount is amortized over the life of the A bond, which has an expected life of less than 2 years. The projected cash flows of the A bond at settlement date are shown in Exhibit A in the appendix to this chapter.

The investor decides to update accounting records at the end of month 2. Actual cash flows for months 1 and 2 and revised estimates for the remaining months are shown in Exhibit B in the appendix. Using the retrospective method, a new effective yield calculation is performed as of the settlement date. Exhibit B shows that at the end of month 2, using the revised cash flows, the book value of the A bond should be $31,324,119 instead of $31,183,803, as shown in the original effective yield calculation in Exhibit A. The investor must increase the investment balance to $31,324,119 while reducing income recognized for the two-month period by $5,900 and reducing cash by $146,216.[7]

Prospective Method

EITF 89–4 provides that MBS investors of "high-risk" instruments (primarily IOs) use the **prospective method** of accounting for changes in prepayments. At the end of each accounting period (as-

---

[7]Under the retrospective method, total income recognized for the two-month period should be $428,664 based upon the cash flows and effective yield calculation in Exhibit B ($216,943 + $211,721 = $428,664). The original effective yield calculation shown in Exhibit A generated income for the two-month period of $434,564 ($218,863 + $215,701 = $434,564). If the investor had made preliminary accounting entries for month 2 using the results of the cash flow estimates in Exhibit A, the investor would have to make an adjustment, reducing income by $5,900 ($434,564 + $428,664 = $5,900). Actual cash received for the two-month period per Exhibit B was $3,585,378, whereas estimated cash flows per Exhibit A were $3,731,593, necessitating the $146,216 adjustment ($3,731,593 − $3,585,378 = $146,216).

suming actual prepayments and revised estimates differ from estimates used at the purchase date), the investor should recalculate the effective yield by equating the MBS's net carrying amount at the recalculation date to the present value of the revised estimate of future cash flows. Interest income for that period will be the amount determined by the revised effective yield calculation; there is no adjustment to the MBS's net carrying amount (except for one exception, which is described below). Rather, the difference between actual and anticipated cash flows during the holding period is rolled forward into future periods by means of the revised calculation.

For example, if prepayments on an IO are faster than what was anticipated at the purchase date, the yield that equates the present value of the revised estimated future cash flows to the IO's carrying value declines. Although no loss is recognized at the recalculation date, the investor would recognize a reduced amount of income for future periods as compared to the original calculation. If in another subsequent period the prepayment speed declines, the yield that equates the present value of the newly revised estimated cash flows to the IO's carrying value would increase as compared to the first recalculation date. Accordingly, interest income for that subsequent period and future periods would be higher than that determined in the first recalculation.

In contrast, under the retrospective method, when the prepayment speed first changed, the investor would recognize a write-down for accounting purposes to reduce the IO's net carrying value. In the second instance of prepayment-speed change, the investor would then recognize a write-up to increase the IO's net carrying value.

The only time an investor adjusts a "high-risk" MBS's carrying value is when the "realization test" is performed. If the MBS's net carrying value ever exceeds the undiscounted estimated future cash flows, the investor should record a write-down equal to that difference. The new carrying value becomes the cost basis of the MBS and is used in all future calculations of effective yield. The investor is prohibited from postponing loss recognition into future periods by means of a negative effective yield.

Example

Assume a different investor purchases the E bond of the hypothetical CMO just described for $464,344, comprised of $50,000 principal amount and $412,875 premium plus accrued interest of $1,469.

In the CMO structure, the E bond pays 7.5 percent interest on the principal amount in addition to the interest from the 150 basis points that were not allocated to the A bonds. See Exhibit C for the projected cash flows of the E bond at settlement date.

At the end of month 1, the investor updates the accounting records by determining the yield that equates actual month 1 cash flows and future projections of cash flows to the purchase price, which is the carrying value of the E bond at the beginning of month 1. That yield annualized is 12.5 percent. The investor records income of $4,673 in period 1. See Exhibit D for those cash flows.

At the end of month 2, the investor solves for the yield that equates month 2 actual cash flows and future estimated cash flows (note that the PSA slowed to 125) to the carrying value at the end of period 1. That carrying value is $422,101, and the resulting yield annualized is 15.9 percent. Month 2 interest income is $5,601, and remaining unamortized premium is $339,007. These cash flows are shown in Exhibit E.

It is important to note that no accounting adjustments are made for financial reporting purposes to the carrying value of the E bond. The differences between actual cash flows and subsequent estimates (in this case, prepayments have slowed down) are "accounted for" by adjusting the yield. For example, month 1 income is based on an annualized rate of 12.5 percent, whereas month 2 income is based on an annualized rate of 15.9 percent.

Retrospective Method and Prospective Method Summarized

To better understand these accounting methods, it might be useful for an investor to focus on the differences between the retrospective and prospective methods.

The retrospective method requires that an investor solve for a new carrying value using the yield that equates actual cash flows to date and revised estimates of the MBS's future cash flows (as of the recalculation date) to the purchase price paid for the MBS. The MBS's "old" carrying value is adjusted up or down to the "new" carrying value. In essence, the effects of prepayments are recognized in the period of change, which introduces an element of earnings volatility not present with the prospective method.

The prospective method requires the investor to solve for the yield that will equate future estimated cash flows to the current carrying value. The investor makes no adjustment to the MBS's carrying value (except in the limited circumstance described earlier). The effects of prepayments essentially are deferred and recognized in future periods.

And finally, with respect to the retrospective method, while effective yield calculations are performed for each individual MBS, the net accounting adjustment recorded in an accounting period represents the aggregate of each adjustment determined for all MBSs in the investor's portfolio.

Floating-Rate Securities

FASB 91 allows an investor two choices to account for changes in cash flows of a floating-rate MBS that occur because of changes in the interest rate index of the security. The investor may determine the amortization pattern of premium or discount and the resulting effective yield using the index in effect at settlement date. The resulting pattern of discount or premium reduction remains fixed throughout the term to maturity, regardless of future changes in the index. Alternatively, the investor may recalculate the pattern of premium or discount amortization and resulting effective yield each time the index changes. However, FASB 91 does not provide clear guidance on how to account for cash flow changes resulting from both changes in interest rates and prepayments.

The FASB addressed this issue in a September 1991 exposure draft dealing with investments and prepayment risks.[8] Although the exposure draft was never issued as a final statment, the FASB concluded that cash flow changes resulting from changes in the MBS's index should be accounted for in the period of change. Changes in cash flows resulting from prepayment differences should be accounted for using the retrospective method. The FASB did not stipulate a specific technique for implementing this conclusion. One approach discussed in the exposure draft was to apply the retrospective method using hypothetical cash flows resulting from freezing the index at the settlement date and actual and projected cash flows from principal repayments.

---

[8]The exposure draft, "Accounting for Investments with Prepayment Risk," is dated September 16, 1991. An exposure draft is used by the FASB to publish its preliminary conclusions on topics for which it plans to issue a final statement on accounting standards.

Since the exposure draft was not issued, this method is not required. Historically, investors have dealt with the lack of guidance by using a variety of methods that are generally based on interest-method concepts. Until the FASB issues further guidance (and none currently is planned), MBS investors continue to have latitude in how they apply the interest method to floating-rate MBSs.

MBS investors must, nevertheless, comply with certain limitations prescribed by FASB 91, particularly as they relate to floating-rate MBSs. FASB 91 addresses the accounting for MBSs whose terms contain scheduled interest rate increases (e.g., teaser rates on ARMs). Paragraph 18(a) generally prohibits the recognition of interest income at the effective yield if it would cause the net carrying value of the MBS to exceed the amount at which the debtor could settle the obligation. This situation might occur when coupon interest is less than interest income as determined by the interest method.

For MBSs with scheduled rate decreases, the coupon interest received early in the life of the MBS will exceed the interest income determined under the interest method. Paragraph 18(b) requires the investor to defer the excess amount into future periods when the effective yield exceeds the coupon interest.

Payment Delays

As described in Chapter 2, payment delays slightly reduce the yield to an investor. FASB 91 is silent on payment delays and their effect on the interest method. It is not surprising, then, that some investors include the impact of payment delays in their effective yield calculation while others do not. Because payment delays usually do not have a dramatic impact on the reported income of an MBS for financial accounting purposes, investors have flexibility in how they treat payment delays.

Accrued Interest

Unless an investor takes delivery and settles an MBS immediately after the end of an interest-accrual period (e.g., the end of a month), the purchase price includes an amount representing interest earned by the seller for the period from the record date to the settlement date. From the investor's perspective, this accrued interest becomes part of the purchased MBS's basis to be returned at the next interest payment date and will affect the investor's yield. As with payment delays, FASB 91 is silent on this issue. So while some investors consider accrued interest in their effective yield calculation, others do not.[9] Most accountants are not troubled by this inconsistency because the financial accounting effects usually are not significant. In the example provided regarding the A and E class bonds, accrued interest was included in determining the effective yield calculations.

Concluding Comment

The accounting adjustment required in any period when actual and future anticipated prepayments are deemed to differ from original estimates represents the fundamental difference between the retrospective and prospective methods. Under existing accounting rules as described above, "high-risk" MBSs are accounted for using the prospective method. Accordingly, "high-risk" MBS investors generally avoid current-period accounting adjustments to the investment account balance when the prepayment speed changes.

Notwithstanding the current acceptance of the prospective method, there remains a divergence of opinion within the accounting profession as to its appropriateness. While no changes in the accounting rules are anticipated, MBS investors should be aware that the FASB preferred, in the September 1991 exposure draft, that all MBS investments (including "high-risk" MBSs) be accounted for using the retrospective method. At least partly because of industry opposition, the exposure draft was canceled, and it is not clear what further action, if any, the FASB plans on this topic.

---

[9]Whether accrued interest is included in the calculation often depends on the type of security purchased. Investors in "bond-like" structures frequently exclude accrued interest in the calculation, whereas investors in IO-type securities frequently include accrued interest in the calculation.

APPENDIX TO CHAPTER 15

EXHIBIT A
Projected Monthly Cash Flows of A Bonds at Settlement Date

Month	PSA	Beginning A Bonds	Principal Reduction	Interest Payable	Total Cash Flow	Carrying Value	Discount	Discount Amortization	Book Income
						34,480,833			
1	175	35,000,000	1,678,329	175,000	1,853,329	32,846,367	519,167	43,863	218,863
2	175	33,321,671	1,711,656	166,608	1,878,264	31,183,803	475,304	49,092	215,701
3	175	31,610,015	1,743,578	158,050	1,901,628	29,486,958	426,212	46,733	204,783
4	175	29,866,437	1,774,057	149,332	1,923,389	27,757,208	379,479	44,307	193,640
5	175	28,092,380	1,803,057	140,462	1,943,519	25,995,970	335,171	41,819	182,280
6	175	26,289,323	1,830,544	131,447	1,961,991	24,204,694	293,353	39,268	170,714
7	175	24,458,779	1,856,485	122,294	1,978,779	22,384,866	254,085	36,657	158,951
8	175	22,602,293	1,880,852	113,011	1,993,863	20,538,003	217,428	33,989	147,001
9	175	20,721,442	1,903,615	103,607	2,007,222	18,665,654	183,439	31,265	134,872
10	175	18,817,827	1,924,749	94,089	2,018,838	16,769,393	152,174	28,487	122,577
11	175	16,893,079	1,944,231	84,465	2,028,696	14,850,821	123,686	25,659	110,124
12	175	14,948,848	1,962,039	74,744	2,036,784	12,911,562	98,028	22,781	97,525
13	175	12,986,809	1,978,156	64,934	2,043,091	10,953,261	75,247	19,856	84,790
14	175	11,008,652	1,992,566	55,043	2,047,609	8,977,582	55,391	16,886	71,930
15	175	9,016,087	2,005,253	45,080	2,050,333	6,986,204	38,505	13,875	58,955
16	175	7,010,834	2,016,207	35,054	2,051,262	4,980,820	24,630	10,824	45,878
17	175	4,994,626	2,025,420	24,973	2,050,393	2,963,136	13,806	7,736	32,709
18	175	2,969,206	2,032,885	14,846	2,047,731	934,863	6,070	4,613	19,459
19	175	936,321	936,321	4,682	941,002	0	1,458	1,458	6,139

Notes: (1) The A bonds have a 6 percent coupon rate and are purchased at 98.5 percent of par plus $5,833, representing one day of accrued interest. (2) The A bonds will pay off in 19 months at a projected PSA of 175 percent. (3) The A bonds generate an annual yield of 7.88035 percent and a corporate bond-equivalent yield of 8.01087 percent. The annual yield of 7.88035 percent converted to a monthly rate is used for the effective yield calculation.

EXHIBIT B
Actual and Projected Monthly Cash Flows of A Bonds at End of Month 2

Month	PSA	Beginning A Bonds	Principal Reduction	Interest Payable	Total Cash Flow	Carrying Value	Discount	Discount Amortization	Book Income
1	175	35,000,000	1,997,147	175,000	2,172,147	34,480,833	519,167	41,943	216,943
2	130	33,002,853	1,248,217	165,014	1,413,231	32,525,629	477,224	46,707	211,721
3	125	31,754,636	1,681,370	158,773	1,840,144	31,324,119	430,517	45,127	203,900
4	125	30,073,266	1,706,099	150,366	1,856,466	29,687,876	385,390	42,883	193,249
5	125	28,367,167	1,729,817	141,836	1,871,653	28,024,659	342,507	40,587	182,423
6	125	26,637,350	1,752,502	133,187	1,885,689	26,335,429	301,921	38,240	171,427
7	125	24,884,848	1,774,134	124,424	1,898,559	24,621,167	263,681	35,844	160,268
8	125	23,110,713	1,794,696	115,554	1,910,249	22,882,876	227,837	33,399	148,953
9	125	21,316,018	1,814,167	106,580	1,920,747	21,121,580	194,438	30,908	137,488
10	125	19,501,851	1,832,532	97,509	1,930,041	19,338,321	163,530	28,371	125,880
11	125	17,669,319	1,849,775	88,347	1,938,122	17,534,160	135,159	25,790	114,136
12	125	15,819,543	1,865,881	79,098	1,944,979	15,710,174	109,369	23,165	102,263
13	125	13,953,662	1,880,837	69,768	1,950,605	13,867,458	86,204	20,500	90,268
14	125	12,072,826	1,894,629	60,364	1,954,993	12,007,122	65,704	17,795	78,159
15	125	10,178,196	1,907,248	50,891	1,958,139	10,130,287	47,909	15,051	65,942
16	125	8,270,949	1,918,682	41,355	1,960,037	8,238,090	32,859	12,270	53,625
17	125	6,352,267	1,928,923	31,761	1,960,685	6,331,678	20,589	9,454	41,215
18	125	4,423,343	1,937,964	22,117	1,960,081	4,412,209	11,135	6,604	28,721
19	125	2,485,379	1,945,798	12,427	1,958,225	2,480,848	4,531	3,722	16,149
20	125	539,581	539,581	2,698	542,279	538,772	809	809	3,507
						0			

Notes: (1) At the end of month 2, the investor recalculates the effective yield using the retrospective method. Months 1 and 2 represent actual cash flows, whereas months 3 through 20 represent updated projections of prepayments. Under these revised cash flows, the A bonds pay off in 20 months. (2) The revised annual effective yield is 7.81123 percent, and the corporate bond-equivalent yield is 7.93945 percent. (3) The investor must adjust the carrying value of A bonds to $31,324,119 at the end of month 2.

EXHIBIT C

Projected Monthly Cash Flows of E Bonds at Settlement Date

Month	PSA	Beginning A Bonds	Principal Reduction	Interest Payable	Total Cash Flow	Carrying Value	Discount	Discount Amortization	Book Income
						464,344			
1	175	50,000	2,398	44,063	46,460	421,622	(414,344)	(40,324)	3,739
2	175	47,602	2,445	41,950	44,395	380,739	(374,020)	(38,438)	3,512
3	175	45,157	2,491	39,795	42,286	341,625	(335,582)	(36,623)	3,172
4	175	42,666	2,534	37,600	40,134	304,337	(298,959)	(34,754)	2,846
5	175	40,132	2,576	35,366	37,942	268,930	(264,205)	(32,831)	2,535
6	175	37,556	2,615	33,096	35,711	235,459	(231,374)	(30,856)	2,240
7	175	34,941	2,652	30,792	33,444	203,976	(200,518)	(28,830)	1,961
8	175	32,289	2,687	28,455	31,142	174,534	(171,687)	(26,756)	1,699
9	175	29,602	2,719	26,087	28,806	147,181	(144,932)	(24,633)	1,454
10	175	26,883	2,750	23,690	26,440	121,967	(120,299)	(22,464)	1,226
11	175	24,133	2,777	21,267	24,045	98,939	(97,834)	(20,251)	1,016
12	175	21,355	2,803	18,820	21,622	78,140	(77,583)	(17,995)	824
13	175	18,553	2,826	16,349	19,175	59,616	(59,588)	(15,699)	651
14	175	15,727	2,847	13,859	16,706	43,407	(43,889)	(13,363)	497
15	175	12,880	2,865	11,351	14,215	29,553	(30,527)	(10,989)	362
16	175	10,015	2,880	8,826	11,706	18,093	(19,538)	(8,580)	246
17	175	7,135	2,893	6,288	9,181	9,062	(10,958)	(6,137)	151
18	175	4,242	2,904	3,738	6,642	2,496	(4,821)	(3,663)	75
19	175	1,338	1,338	1,179	2,516	0	(1,158)	(1,158)	21

Notes: (1) The E bonds are an IO with a principal amount of $50,000 and are purchased at 925.75 percent of par plus one day of accrued interest totaling $1,469. (2) The E bonds will pay off in 19 months at a projected PSA of 175. (3) The E bonds generate an annual yield of 9.99593 percent and a corporate bond-equivalent yield of 10.20642 percent.

EXHIBIT D

Actual and Projected Monthly Cash Flows of E Bonds at End of Month 1

Month	PSA	Beginning A Bonds	Principal Reduction	Interest Payable	Total Cash Flow	Carrying Value	Discount	Discount Amortization	Book Income
						464,344			
1	175	50,000	2,853	44,063	46,916	422,101	(414,344)	(39,389)	4,673
2	130	47,147	2,364	41,548	43,912	382,585	(374,954)	(37,153)	4,395
3	130	44,783	2,401	39,465	41,866	344,702	(337,801)	(35,482)	3,984
4	130	42,382	2,437	37,349	39,786	308,505	(302,320)	(33,760)	3,589
5	130	39,945	2,472	35,202	37,673	274,044	(268,560)	(31,989)	3,212
6	130	37,474	2,505	33,024	35,528	241,369	(236,570)	(30,170)	2,854
7	130	34,969	2,536	30,817	33,353	210,530	(206,400)	(28,303)	2,513
8	130	32,433	2,566	28,582	31,148	181,575	(178,097)	(26,390)	2,192
9	130	29,868	2,594	26,321	28,915	154,550	(151,707)	(24,430)	1,891
10	130	27,274	2,620	24,035	26,655	129,504	(127,277)	(22,426)	1,609
11	130	24,653	2,645	21,726	24,371	106,482	(104,851)	(20,377)	1,348
12	130	22,008	2,668	19,395	22,063	85,528	(84,474)	(18,286)	1,109
13	130	19,340	2,690	17,043	19,733	66,685	(66,188)	(16,152)	891
14	130	16,650	2,710	14,672	17,382	49,998	(50,036)	(13,978)	694
15	130	13,940	2,728	12,285	15,012	35,506	(36,058)	(11,764)	521
16	130	11,212	2,744	9,881	12,625	23,251	(24,294)	(9,511)	370
17	130	8,469	2,758	7,463	10,221	13,272	(14,782)	(7,221)	242
18	130	5,710	2,771	5,032	7,803	5,607	(7,562)	(4,894)	138
19	130	2,939	2,782	2,590	5,372	293	(2,668)	(2,532)	58
20	130	157	157	139	296	0	(136)	(136)	3

Notes: (1) At the end of month 1, using the prospective method, the investor solves for the yield that equates actual cash flows in month 1 plus projected cash flows in all future months to the carrying value of the E bonds at the beginning of month 1 (i.e., the purchase price), (2) The new annual effective yield is determined to be 12.49518 percent. The corporate bond-equivalent rate is 12.825 percent. The investor would record income in month 1 of $4,673, representing 29 days of earned interest.

EXHIBIT E
Actual and Projected Monthly Cash Flows of E Bonds at End of Month 2

Month	PSA	Beginning A Bonds	Principal Reduction	Interest Payable	Total Cash Flow	Carrying Value	Discount	Discount Amortization	Book Income
						464,344			
1	175	50,000	2,853	44,063	46,916	422,101	(414,344)	(39,389)	4,673
2	130	47,147	1,783	41,548	43,331	384,371	(374,954)	(35,947)	5,601
3	125	45,364	2,402	39,977	42,379	347,092	(339,007)	(34,877)	5,100
4	125	42,962	2,437	37,860	40,297	311,400	(304,130)	(33,255)	4,606
5	125	40,525	2,471	35,712	38,183	277,349	(270,876)	(31,580)	4,132
6	125	38,053	2,504	33,535	36,038	244,991	(239,296)	(29,854)	3,680
7	125	35,550	2,534	31,328	33,863	214,379	(209,441)	(28,077)	3,251
8	125	33,015	2,564	29,095	31,659	185,565	(181,364)	(26,250)	2,845
9	125	30,451	2,592	26,835	29,427	158,600	(155,114)	(24,373)	2,462
10	125	27,860	2,618	24,551	27,169	133,536	(130,741)	(22,447)	2,104
11	125	25,242	2,643	22,244	24,887	110,420	(108,294)	(20,473)	1,772
12	125	22,599	2,666	19,916	22,581	89,304	(87,821)	(18,451)	1,465
13	125	19,934	2,687	17,567	20,254	70,236	(69,371)	(16,382)	1,185
14	125	17,247	2,707	15,199	17,905	53,262	(52,989)	(14,267)	932
15	125	14,540	2,725	12,814	15,538	38,431	(38,722)	(12,107)	707
16	125	11,816	2,741	10,413	13,154	25,787	(26,615)	(9,903)	510
17	125	9,075	2,756	7,997	10,753	15,377	(16,713)	(7,655)	342
18	125	6,319	2,769	5,569	8,337	7,244	(9,058)	(5,365)	204
19	125	3,551	2,780	3,129	5,909	1,431	(3,693)	(3,033)	96
20	125	771	771	679	1,450	0	(660)	(660)	19

Notes: (1) At end of month 2, using the prospective method, the investor solves for the yield that equates actual cash flows in months 1 and 2 plus updated projected cash flows in all future months to the carrying value of the E bonds at the beginning of month 2. The carrying value at the beginning of month 2 is $422,101. (2) The revised annual effective yield is 15.92286 percent, and the new corporate bond-equivalent yield is 16.46050 percent. The investor would record income in month 2 of $5,601.

GLOSSARY

A

ABS   See **asset-backed security.**

Accretion directed (AD) bond   A bond derived from the Z-bond accrual. AD bonds have short final stated maturities, usually 5, 7, 10, and 13 years. AD bonds also display excellent call protection. Also referred to as a VADM (very accurately defined maturity) or stated maturity bond. The 5-year stated maturity of the AD bond is liquidity qualifying for thrift institutions. It is therefore sometimes referred to as a liquidity bond.

accrual bond   Also known as an accretion bond or a Z-bond in a CMO issue. A bond on which interest accrues, but is not paid to the investor during the time of accrual. Instead, the amount accrued is added to the amount of remaining principal of the bond and is paid at maturity.

alphabet strips   The series of synthetic discount and premium SMBSs issued by Fannie Mae, so called because their issue series were identified by letters of the alphabet.

amortization factor   The pool factor implied by the scheduled amortization assuming no prepayments.

anti-TAC   See **reverse TAC class bonds.**

arbitrage pricing   A phenomenon in which the existence of an arbitrage supports the price of one or more of the components of the arbitrage, as in the case of IO SMBSs.

ARMs (adjustable-rate mortgages)   A mortgage that features predetermined adjustments of the loan interest rate at regular intervals based on an established index. The interest rate is adjusted at each interval to a rate equivalent to the index value plus a predetermined spread, or margin, over the index, usually subject to per-interval and to life-of-loan interest-rate and/or payment-rate caps.

asset-backed security (ABS)   A security that is collateralized by loans, leases, receivables, or installment contracts on personal property (not including real estate).

asset valuation reserve (AVR)   A capital reserve account established under guidelines promulgated by the NAIC against losses due to credit loss.

asymmetric price performance   A situation in which the price of two securities which should move in opposite directions in the same proportion do not (as with IO and PO strips).

average life   Also referred to as weighted average life (WAL). The average number of years that each dollar of unpaid principal due on the mortgage remains outstanding. Average life is computed as the weighted average time to the receipt of all future cash flows, using as the weights the dollar amounts of the principal paydowns.

AVR   See **asset valuation reserve.**

B

balloon mortgage   Mortgage loans that involve regular monthly payments for interest plus either no or partial amortization of the loan principal, so that at the end of the term of the mortgage there is a lump-sum payment of the remaining unpaid principal balance.

band   See **PAC band.**

band drift   See **PAC band drift.**

basis   Refers to the original invested dollars as the reference book equity for investments not possessing a principal value (as with IO strips and residual interests).

basis risk   A risk that the price of a hedge instrument does not move as expected relative to the increase or decrease in the market price of the hedged loan or security.

BEPR   See **breakeven prepayment rate.**

BEY (bond equivalent yield)   See **corporate bond equivalent (CBE).**

bond IO   An IO consisting of some portion (in basis points) of the coupon of one or more bond classes of a CMO structure.

book profit   The cumulative book income plus any gain or loss on disposition of the assets on termination of the investment.

breakeven prepayment rate (BEPR) The prepayment rate of a MBS coupon that will produce the same CFY as that of a predetermined benchmark MBS coupon. Used to identify for coupons higher than the benchmark coupon the prepayment rate that will produce the same CFY as that of the benchmark coupon; and for coupons lower than the benchmark coupon the lowest prepayment rate that will do so.

builder bonds Pay-through (CMO) bonds issued as debt obligations by builders. In the mid- 1980s CMOs issued by builders to take advantage of the installment sales accounting treatment of booking the profit on a home sale were referred to as builder bonds.

builder buydown loan A mortgage loan on newly developed property that the builder subsidizes during the early years of the development. The builder uses cash to buy down the mortgage rate to a lower level than the prevailing market loan rate for some period of time. The typical buydown is 3 percent of the interest-rate amount for the first year, 2 percent for the second year, and 1 percent for the third year (also referred to as a 3-2-1 buydown).

burnout The decline of prepayments over time holding the refinancing incentive constant. Burnout measures the reduction in prepayment sensitivity of a pool as the refinancing potential of the home borrowers remaining in the pool is exhausted.

buydowns Mortgages in which monthly payments consist of principal and interest, with portions of these payments during the early period of the loan being provided by a third party to reduce the borrower's monthly payments.

C

call option The right to purchase a security at a predetermined price on or before a specified date.

call risk The risk that prepayments will cause the MBS pool collateral to be paid faster than anticipated with the resulting loss of anticipated coupon income.

cash flow window The time period, measured in days, from the day of the first payment of principal to the last payment or to the final (or projected final) maturity.

cash-flow yield (CFY) The monthly rate of return of the MBS derived by using the actual age, or WAM, of the mortgages underlying the pool, and projecting the monthly cash flows according to a prepayment assumption. The projected cash flows are then discounted to present value using a current market required rate of return.

cash-out refi A refinance made in an amount in excess of the original mortgage amount to liquidate home equity.

CBE (corporate bond equivalent yield) Also referred to as bond equivalent yield (BEY), CBE is an adjustment to the mortgage yield to reflect assumed semiannual payment of cash flows rather than monthly. Converting monthly MBS cash flows to semiannual equivalent allows a more meaningful comparison of MBSs values to corporate and government bonds. The conversion primarily reflects the benefit to the MBS holder of reinvesting MBS cash flows monthly rather than semiannually, as is usually the case with other fixed-income securities.

CDR See **conditional default rate.**

CFY See **cash-flow yield.**

clean CMO bond See **sequential pay CMO bond.**

clean-up call The right to pay-off the remainder of the CMO bond issue when the unpaid principal balance reaches a stated percentage of the original face value of the CMO issue (usually 10 percent).

CMO floater A CMO bond whose coupon resets periodically to an index (usually LIBOR) plus margin, subject to caps and sometimes floors. The coupon varies directly to changes in the index.

CMOs See **collateralized mortgage obligation.**

CMT See **constant maturity treasury.**

COFI (cost of funds index) See **11th District Cost of Fund Index.**

co-insurance Under FHA a program in which the private lender and HUD share the credit risk on the loan.

collar (Prepayment collar) See **PAC band.**

collateralized mortgage obligation (CMO) A multiclass bond issue collateralized by a pool of MBSs or mortgage loans, or derivative MBS forms such as POs.

collateral strip A portion of the entire collateral of a CMO structure allocated to support a floater. The collateral strip is off the entire block of collateral and therefore will have the average life of the underlying deal collateral.

companion bond   See **support class bond.**

component bond   A bond structured from cash flows allocated to two or more sectors of the CMO deal structure, generally in the form of scheduled cash flows added to support cash flows to create a more stable bond.

conditional default rate (CDR)   The observed actual default rate of loans within a specified geographic area or sector under consideration.

conduit   An organization that buys mortgages from correspondents, packages the loans into collateral pools held by a trustee, and sells mortgage securities through the capital markets.

conforming loans   Loans within the statutory size limit eligible for purchase or securitization by the federal agencies.

constant maturity treasury (CMT)   An index derived from the weighted average yield of a range of Treasury securities adjusted to a constant maturity (most commonly one year, but also 3, 5, 7, and 10 years). The index is computed as a weekly average and published in the Federal Reserve Board H-15 statistical release.

constant prepayment rate (CPR)   A measure of principal prepayments expressed as a ratio of prepayments to the prior month's outstanding principal balance.

construction loan certificate (CLC)   A primary program of Ginnie Mae for securitizing FHA- insured and co-insured multifamily, hospital, and nursing home construction advances.

convexity   A measure of the shape of the price/yield curve. Convexity explains the difference between the prices estimated by standard duration and the actual market prices of a security resulting from a change in market required yield.

convexity cost   The amount by which the value of the prepayment option reduces the convexity value of the MBS.

CDR   See **conditional default rate.**

corporate bond equivalent   See **CBE.**

coupon cap   The maximum interest rate to which the interest rate of a variable rate security may reset.

cumulative jump Z-bond   A jump Z with the trigger for the shift in payment priority specified as a sequence of cumulative events such as requiring a 3-month cumulative PSA rather than a single event.

current coupon For Ginnie Mae securities, the pass-through rate applicable to the maximum allowable VA rate in effect at the time. The current-coupon Freddie Mac PC is that currently offered in the Freddie Mac Cash program PC dealer auctions.

current loan balance Also referred to as the current face, or the outstanding loan balance. The current monthly remaining principal of a certificate computed by multiplying the original face of the pool by the current principal balance (factor).

current yield The coupon divided by the price.

curtailments Partial prepayments made in excess of the scheduled payments regularly or sporadically to reduce the principal balance of the mortgage.

cushion bond With reference to MBSs, the tendency of premium-priced MBSs to hold price when market yields are rising because of the anticipated slowing of prepayment speed.

cusp The point where the price of the MBS reflects a current market interest rate where the mortgage loans underlying the MBS pool are presumed to have crossed the threshold for refinancing.

custom pool The single-issuer approach in which an individual issuer assembles a pool of mortgages against which he issues and markets securities, as in the GNMA-I program.

D

delayed issuance pool Refers to MBSs that at the time of issuance were collateralized by seasoned loans originated prior to the MBS pool issue date.

discount margin (DM) The yield spread over the underlying index discounted to reflect pricing variances from par—i.e., the DM is reduced if a premium price is paid, and widened if a discount price is paid. DM assumes monthly equivalent yield (MEY) rather than BEY.

duration A measure of the percentage change in price for a percentage change in yield with the price to yield relationship inverse. Duration is also sometimes referred to as the weighted average time to the receipt of the present value of the sum of future cash flows.

E

effective bands The actual maximum and minimum prepayment speed that may be tolerated by a specific PAC bond class without shifting its average life. The effective bands of short average life PACs are generally wider than the stated band.

11th District Cost of Funds Index (COFI) The COFI Index is based on the average cost of funds for member institutions of the 11th district of the Federal Home Loan Bank (composed of Arizona, California and Nevada). The index is computed by dividing monthly interest expense by the average liabilities and multiplying by 12. It is released by the Federal Home Loan Bank of San Francisco at the close of business on the last business day of each month and refers to the preceding month.

F

FASB The Financial Accounting Standards Board, the governing body on establishing and reviewing accounting practices.

factor The proportion of the outstanding principal balance of a security to its original principal balance expressed as a decimal.

fail A trade is said to fail if on or after the settlement date the seller does not complete delivery of the securities to the buyer.

Federal Home Loan Mortgage Corporation See **Freddie Mac.**

FHA prepayment experience The percentage of loans in a pool of mortgages outstanding at the origination anniversary, based on annual statistical historic survival rates for FHA-insured mortgages.

first call With CMOs, the first payment of principal; the start of the cash-flow window.

floor The minimum yield level to which the coupon of a variable rate security may reset.

48-hour rule The requirement that all pool information, as specified under the PSA Uniform Practices, in a TBA transaction be communicated by the seller to the buyer before 3 P.M. EST on the business day 48 hours prior to the agreed settlement date.

forward delivery   A transaction in which the settlement will occur on a specified date in the future at a price agreed upon on the trade date.

forward sale   A method for hedging price risk which involves an agreement between a lender and an investor to sell particular kinds of loans or securities at a specified price for forward delivery.

forward trade   A transaction in which the settlement will occur on a specified date in the future at a price agreed upon on the trade date (see also **TBA**).

Freddie Mac (Federal Home Loan Mortgage Corporation)   A Congressionally chartered corporation that purchases residential mortgages in the secondary market from S&Ls, banks, and mortgage bankers and securitizes these mortgages for sale into the capital markets.

G

GAAP   Generally accepted accounting principles mandated by the Financial Accounting Standards Board (FASB).

generic   Refers to the characteristics and/or experience of the total universe of a coupon of MBS sector type; that is, in contrast to a specific pool or collateral group, as in a specific CMO issue.

gestation repo   A type of reverse repurchase agreement between mortgage firms and securities dealers. Under the agreement the firm sells federal agency-guaranteed MBSs and simultaneously agrees to repurchase them at a future date at a fixed price.

Ginnie Mae   See **Government National Mortgage Association.**

GMCs (guaranteed mortgage certificates)   First issued by Freddie Mac in 1975, GMCs (like PCs) represent undivided interest in specified conventional whole loans and participations previously purchased by Freddie Mac.

GNMA midget   A GNMA pass-through security backed by fixed-rate mortgages with a 15-year maturity. GNMA midget is a dealer term and is not used by GNMA in the formal description of its programs.

GNMA-I   MBSs on which registered holders receive separate principal and interest payments on each of their certificates, usually directly from the servicer of the MBS pool. GNMA-I MBSs are single-issuer pools.

GNMA-II MBSs on which registered holders receive an aggregate principal and interest payment from a central paying agent on all their certificates. Principal and interest payments are disbursed on the 20th day of the month. GNMA-II MBSs are backed by multiple-issuer pools or custom pools (one issuer but different interest rates that may vary within one percentage point). Multiple-issuer pools are known as "jumbos." Jumbo pools are generally larger and often contain mortgages that are more geographically diverse than single-issuer pools. Jumbo pool mortgage interest rates may vary within one percentage point.

"gnomes" A pre-1991 term referring to Freddie Mac's 15-year, fixed rate pass-through securities issued under its Cash program. Following introduction of their Gold Program in October 1990 Freddie Mac phased out the 75-day delay program together with usage of the "gnome" term. The term "gnome" is therefore no longer in common usage.

gold program Refers to the Freddie Mac PC program introduced in October 1990 that extended the timely payment guarantee by Freddie Mac to both principal and interest and reduced the interest delay to 14 days.

good delivery and settlement procedures Refers to PSA Uniform Practices such as cutoff times for delivery of securities and notification, allocation, and proper endorsement.

Government National Mortgage Association (Ginnie Mae) A wholly owned U.S. government corporation within the Department of Housing and Urban Development. Ginnie Mae guarantees the timely payment of P&I on securities issued by approved servicers and that are collateralized by FHA-insured, VA-guaranteed, or Farmers Home Administration (FmHA)-guaranteed mortgage.

GPMs See **graduated-payment mortgages.**

graduated-payment mortgages (GPMs) A type of stepped-payment loan in which the borrower's payments are initially lower than those on a comparable level-rate mortgage. The payments are gradually increased over a predetermined period (usually 3, 5, or 7 years) and then are fixed at a level-pay schedule, which will be higher than the level-pay amortization of a level-pay mortgage originated at the same time. The difference between what the borrower actually pays and the amount required to fully amortize the mortgage is added to the unpaid principal balance.

grantor trust A mechanism for issuing MBSs wherein the mortgage collateral is deposited with a trustee under a custodial or trust agreement.

guaranteed mortgage certificates See **GMCs.**

guarantor program Under the Freddie Mac program the aggregation by a single issuer (usually an S&L) for the purpose of forming a qualifying pool to be issued as PCs under the Freddie Mac guaranty.

H

haircut The margin or difference between the actual market value of a security and the value assessed by the lending side of a transaction—for example, a repo.

hedgers Those who engage in the use of a hedge, see **hedging.**

hedging A technique employed by securities traders and investors to offset price risk by taking an opposite position from that of the position held; that is, to hedge a position in a security owned by selling short a like or substitute security such as a financial futures contract.

holding period return (HPR) See **total rate of return.**

I

immediate settlement Delivery and settlement of securities within five business days.

implied call The right of the homeowner to prepay, or call, the mortgage at any time.

implied volatility The market expectation of future volatility for a specified time horizon.

IMR See **interest maintenance reserve.**

in the money A call option that may be exercised to the economic advantage of the holder at the call option price, or strike.

index The benchmark reference for the coupon of an adjustable rate mortgage or CMO floater.

interest maintenance reserve (IMR) A capital reserve account established by the NAIC against losses resulting from interest rate risk.

interest only security (IO) The interest-only portion of a stripped MBS. With IO securities, all the interest distribution from the underlying pool collateral is paid to the registered holder of the IO based on the current face amount of the underlying collateral.

interest delay See payment delay.

interest-rate swap An agreement whereby two parties agree to exchange payment terms, usually by exchanging fixed for floating, but may also be used to swap maturity terms, for example, 3-month LIBOR for 6-month LIBOR.

internal rate of return (IRR) The value, measured in terms of yield, received on an investment to its maturity, including reinvestment income at the stated coupon rate of the security. The IRR takes into account the function of the coupon to price—i.e., discount or premium.

inverse floater A CMO tranche with a variable-rate coupon that is formulated to an index such that the coupon declines when the index value increases.

inverse IO An IO strip consisting of the coupon on an inverse floater.

IOette An IO consisting of some portion (in basis points) of the coupon of the entire collateral of the CMO Structure.

IRR See **internal rate of return.**

J

jumbo loans Loans that exceed the statutory size limit eligible for purchase or securitization by the federal agencies.

jumbo pools Pools formed by Ginnie Mae, Fannie Mae, or Freddie Mac by aggregating loans from several originators into large pools generally representing one month of loan originations.

jump Z A Z-bond in which the maturity sequence shifts in priority upon striking a specific event. For example, the bond trust may specify that if the collateral PSA reaches 250 PSA, the prepayment priority of the Z-bond will shift to a specified earlier position in the CMO structure, usually to first pay.

L

lag response of prepayments   There is typically a lag of two to three months between the time the WAC of an MBS pool has crossed the threshold for refinancing and when an acceleration in prepayment speed is observed.

level pay   The characteristic of the scheduled principal and interest payments due under a mortgage such that the *total monthly* payment of P&I is the same while characteristically the principal payment component of the monthly payment becomes gradually greater while the monthly interest payment becomes less.

LIBOR   The London Interbank Offered Rate on Eurodollar deposits traded between banks. There is a different LIBOR rate for each deposit maturity. Different banks may quote slightly different LIBOR rates because they use different reference banks.

liquidity bond   A bond structured to qualify as a "liquid asset" for savings institutions. Liquidity bonds have a final stated maturity of 5 years or less (see **accretion directed bond** and **stated maturity bond**).

loan-to-value ratio (LTV)   The percent of the original purchase price represented by the mortgage.

lock-in effect   The inability of a mortgage borrower to respond to a refinance opportunity because of lack of cash to meet loan closing expenses, lack of home equity to qualify, or a poor credit rating.

lock-out   With PAC bond CMO classes, the period before the PAC sinking fund becomes effective. With multifamily loans, the period of time during which prepayment is prohibited.

LOCOM   Accounting acronym for lower cost of market.

log-normal distribution   A distribution of statistical data that follows a typical bell-shaped pattern.

look back   The date prior to the coupon reset date that sets the index value—usually the prior month, or in the case of a COFI ARM 2 or 3 months back.

LTV   See **loan-to-value ratio**.

M

management and guarantee fee A portion of the service spread in basis points paid to the entity (usually a federal agency) for guaranteeing the payment of principal and interest due from an MBS pool.

mandatory securities valuation reserve (MSVR) Capital reserves required by the National Association of Insurance commissioners against losses due to credit and/or interest rate risk.

manufactured housing securities (MHSs) Loans on manufactured homes—that is, factory-built or prefabricated housing, including mobile homes.

margin The amount, in basis points, added to the index to establish a coupon.

mark-to-market The process whereby the book value or collateral value of a security is adjusted to reflect current market value.

MBS servicing The requirement that the mortgage servicer maintain payment of the full amount of contractually due P&I payments whether or not actually collected.

MBSCC (Mortgage-Backed Securities Clearing Corporation) A wholly owned subsidiary of the Midwest Stock Exchange that operates a clearing service for the comparison, netting, and margining of agency-guaranteed MBSs transacted for forward delivery.

MHSs See **manufactured housing securities.**

Mobile home securities See **manufactured housing securities.**

Modified duration The percentage change in price of a security that results from a small change in yield.

Money market notes (MMNs) Publicly traded issues that may be collateralized by mortgages and MBSs.

Monte Carlo simulation A method of casting out randomly generated interest-rate paths through the interest-rate generator of an OAS model.

mortgage-backed bond A mortgage-backed bond is a general obligation of the issuer, secured by mortgage collateral, where the issuer retains ownership of the mortgages. The bond is secured by the market value of the underlying mortgages. Since the value of the mortgages will decrease over time as a result of principal amortization and prepayments, the market value of the collateral must exceed the value of the bonds issued. Unlike pass-through securities, the cash flow on a mortgage-backed bond is not directly related to the cash flow of the underlying mortgage collateral. Interest on the bond is paid semiannually at a predetermined rate and principal is paid at maturity.

mortgage pipeline   The period from the taking of applications from prospective mortgage borrowers to the marketing of the loans.

MSVR   See **mandatory securities valuation reserve.**

multi-class pass-through   A CMO structured as a REMIC and qualified for sale of asset accounting treatment.

multifamily loans   Loans usually represented by conventional mortgages on multifamily rental apartments.

multiple-issuer pools   Under GNMA-II program, pools formed through the aggregation of individual issuers' loan packages.

multiplier   The factor which leverages the coupon of an inverse floater.

N

narrow window PAC   A PAC bond with a very closely defined cash flow window, generally one to not more than 2 years.

negative amortization   A loan repayment schedule in which the outstanding principal balance of the loan increases, rather than amortizing, because the scheduled monthly payments do not cover the full amount required to amortize the loan. The unpaid interest is added to the outstanding principal, to be repaid later.

negative carry   A situation with IO SMBSs in which the reduction of principal, or basis, exceeds the coupon income.

negative convexity   Describes securities that produce a negatively sloped price/yield curve. With negatively convex securities, price changes of the security are in the same direction as that of a change in yield, as with premium priced MBSs and IO SMBSs.

negative duration   A situation in which the price of the MBS moves in the same direction as interest rates.

net effective margin (NEM)   A measure of the yield spread over the security's current index rate that is required to discount all future cash flows back to the original price. NEM is a static application of BEY. NEM may be viewed as the expected spread over the index value that could be realized if interest rates and prepayment rates remain unchanged.

net present value (NPV) The current worth or value of a dollar amount to be received or paid over a period of time at a future date. The current worth is the price derived by discounting the future cash flows by a current market required yield.

notification date The day the option is either exercised or expires.

notional amount The reference principal amount in a derivative transaction such as with a swap or SMBS.

NPV See **net present value.**

O

OAS See **option-adjusted spread.**

option-adjusted duration (OAD) The price sensitivity of the MBS taking into account the impact of prepayments.

option-adjusted margin (OAM) The effective margin derived by an OAS model taking into account the value of any interest rate or payment rate caps and the repayment option.

option-adjusted spread (OAS) The expected yield spread of the MBS over the entire treasury curve adjusted for the value of the prepayment options embedded in the loan collateral underlying the MBS.

original face value The principal amount of the mortgage as of its issue date.

origination The making of mortgage loans.

out of the money A call option that at the time offers no economic incentive to exercise the call.

P

PAC See **planned-amortization class.**

PAC band The highest and lowest possible prepayment rates that can be sustained until maturity of the PAC bond. Also referred to as the prepayment collar.

PAC band drift The variance from the original high and low PSA speed parameters of the PAC band resulting from prepayment speeds that have paid persistently at substantial variance from the pricing PSA speed.

PAC CAB (planned amortization capital appreciation bond)   PAC CABs are CMOs which are often compared to zero coupon bonds because they pay no income until maturity approaches, and are available at deeply discounted dollar prices. PAC CABs are designed to accrue at their nominal coupon rate to par, at which point the PAC CAB investor may begin to receive monthly payments reflecting principal and interest, assuming the underlying collateral prepays within the PAC bands.

PAC IO   A bond IO stripped from a PAC bond. The IO thus carries with it the PAC prepayment protection band.

PAC payment schedule   The amount of principal reduction specified in the trust indenture for each monthly payment.

PAC sinking fund   The principal cash flows identified as scheduled cash flows as defined by the prepayment band, or collar.

PAC II   A PAC with a payment schedule subordinated to a Tier One PAC.

PAC Z-bond   A Z-bond derived from the scheduled cash flows of a PAC CMO structure.

pairoff   A buy-back to offset and effectively liquidate a prior sale of securities.

parity price   The price at which the yield of the MBS equals its coupon. The parity price of an MBS is less than 100 because of the interest payment delay.

pass-through rate   The net interest rate passed through to investors after deducting servicing, management, and guarantee fees from the gross mortgage coupon.

path-dependent discounting   The discounting back to present value the projected cash flows using a sequence of short-term interest rates and averaging the present values over all interest- rate paths generated by the OAS model.

pay through bond   A general obligation of the issuer secured by the cash flows of MBSs pledged as security collateral to the bond trustee. This form, introduced in 1981, is more efficient than the MBB and was the precursor to the CMO.

payment cap   The maximum payment rate which the borrower on a variable rate loan may be caused to pay.

payment delay   The time lag in days from the first day of the month following the month of issuance of the pool to the date where the pass-through of principal and interest is actually remitted to the investor. The payment delay for GNMA MBSs is 14 days; for FHLMC 75- day program PCs 44 days and for Gold Program PCs 14 days; for FNMA MBSs 24 days.

permanent loan certificates (PLCs)   Upon completion of construction projects, certificates that may be exchanged for CLCs. PLCs are issued with the suffix "PL" following the pool number.

planned-amortization class (PAC)   A CMO bond class that has a planned amortization schedule similar to contributions to a sinking fund. With the PAC, principal payments are directed to the payment schedule on a priority basis in accordance with a predetermined payment schedule, with prior claim to the cash flows before other CMO classes. Similarly, cash flows received by the trust in excess of the PAC payment schedule are allocated to other bond classes. The average life of the PAC is therefore very stable over a wide range of prepayment experience.

PLCs   See **permanent loan certificates.**

PO   See **principal-only security.**

pool factor   The outstanding principal balance divided by the original principal balance with the result expressed as a decimal. Pool factors are published monthly by the bond buyer for Ginnie Mae, Fannie Mae, and Freddie Mac MBSs.

positive convexity   Describes securities that produce a positively sloped price/yield curve. With positively convex securities, price changes are inverse to the direction of changes in yield.

prepayment   A principal payment made in excess of the scheduled amortization of the mortgage. May also refer to the satisfaction of a mortgage prior to its scheduled maturity.

prepayment collar   See PAC bands.

price compression   The tendency of MBSs to lose ability to appreciate in price when the mortgage loans in the underlying pool have passed the threshold for refinancing.

price value of a basis point (PVBP)   The change in the price of a security that results from a basis-point change in yield.

prime pool   A prime pool is one consisting of level-pay, fixed-rate loans on owner-occupied, single family detached properties with a weighted average LTV of 80 percent or lower.

principal-only security (PO)   The principal-only portion of a stripped MBS. For PO securities, all of the principal distribution due from the underlying collateral pool is paid to the registered holder of the stripped MBS based on the current face of the underlying collateral pool.

project loan certificate (PLC)   A primary program of Ginnie Mae for securitizing FHA-insured and co-insured multifamily, hospital, and nursing home loans.

project loan securities   Securities backed by a variety of FHA-insured loan types–primarily multifamily apartment buildings, hospitals, and nursing homes.

project loans   Usually FHA-insured and HUD-guaranteed mortgages on multiple-family housing complexes. Includes as well nursing homes, hospitals, and other development types.

projected maturity date   With CMOs, the final payment at the end of the estimated cash flow window.

PSA   See **Public Securities Association.**

PSA   A prepayment model developed by the PSA based on an assumed rate of prepayment each month of the then-unpaid principal balance of a pool of mortgages. Used primarily to derive an implied prepayment speed of new production loans, 100 percent PSA assumes a prepayment rate of 0.2 percent a month in the first month following the date of issue, increasing 0.2 percent per month thereafter until the 30th month. Thereafter, 100 percent PSA is the same as 6 percent CPR.

PSA ramp   A line drawn from 0 CPR at time zero to 6 CPR at the 30th month of time with a slope calculated as increasing 0.2 percent per month.

PTC   Participants Trust Company was chartered in March 1989 to provide a book-entry clearing and settlement system for GNMA MBSs. PTC also disburses P&I to its members and facilitates borrowing and lending by its participants through book-entry transactions.

Public Securities Association (PSA)   The trade association for primary dealers in U.S. government securities, including MBS dealers.

purchase mortgage A loan secured by real estate made for the purpose of buying the real estate in question.

put option An option giving the holder the right to deliver a loan or security at a prearranged price within an agreed-upon period.

PVBP See **price value of a basis point.**

R

RAMs (reverse-annuity mortgages) Mortgages in which the bank makes a loan for an amount equal to a percentage of the appraisal value of the home. The loan is then paid to the homeowner in the form of an annuity.

RAP See **regulatory accounting procedures.**

rate lock An agreement between the mortgage originator and the loan applicant guaranteeing a specified interest rate for a designated period, generally about 60 days.

real estate mortgage investment conduit See **REMIC.**

rebenching A restructuring of a mortgage loan of which the payment has been capped and added to the loan balance for the maximum time. Under a rebenching the loan is restructured to pay in full to the original remaining maturity.

reclamation A claim for the right to return or the right to demand the return of a security that has been previously accepted as a result of a bad delivery or other irregularity in the delivery and settlement process.

record rate The date determines who is entitled to payment of principal and interest due to be paid on a security. The record date for most MBSs is the last calendar day of the month (however, the last day on which they may be presented for transfer is the last business day of the month). The record date for CMOs and ABSs varies with each issue.

regulatory accounting procedures (RAP) Accounting principles required by the FHLBB that allow S&Ls to elect annually to defer gains or losses on the sale of assets and amortize these deferrals over the average life of the asset sold.

remaining principal balance (RPB) The amount of principal dollars remaining to be paid under the mortgage as of a given point in time.

REMIC (real estate mortgage investment conduit) A pass-through tax entity that can hold mortgages secured by any type of real property and issue multiple classes of ownership interests to investors in the form of pass-through certificates, bonds, or other legal forms. A financing vehicle created under the Tax Reform Act of 1986.

repo (repurchase agreement) An agreement of one party to purchase securities at a specified price from a second party and a simultaneous agreement by the first party to resell the securities at a specified price to the second party on demand or at a specified price.

reported factor The pool factor as reported by the bond buyer for a given amortization period.

residuals Remainder cash flows generated by pool collateral and those needed to fund bonds supported by the collateral.

reverse repo (reverse repurchase agreement) An agreement of one party to purchase securities at a specified price from a second party and a simultaneous agreement by the first party to resell the securities at a specified price to the second party on demand or at a specified later date.

reverse TAC A TAC with extension protection but not call protection. These bonds are typically structured from the long average life support class cash flows.

risk-controlled arbitrage (RCA) A self-funding, self-hedged series of transactions that generally utilize mortgage securities as the primary assets.

S

scenario analysis See sensitivity analysis.

scheduled amortization The mortgage principal and interest payments due to be paid under the terms of the mortgage not including possible prepayments.

seasoned MBS pools Those that have been issued with specific pool numbers and that have been outstanding at least 30 months. The PSA further defines seasoned Ginnie Mae pools as 30-year, single family pools with coupons at 9 percent or less with maturities of 2008 or earlier; coupons over 9 percent but less than 10 percent with a maturity at 2009 or earlier; and coupons 10 percent or higher with a maturity of 2010 or earlier.

sensitivity analysis Stressing a bond for prepayment rate, yield, and price changes to up/down interest rate scenarios, generally to instantaneous and constant interest rate shifts up/down 100, 200, 300 basis points.

sequential pay CMO A CMO structure in which the tranches, or bond classes, pay down in sequential order with no concurrent pay components. Also referred to as a "clean" CMO structure.

service fee A portion of the servicing spread retained by the mortgage servicer to manage the mortgage payments due from the homeowner and remittance of amounts due to the MBS pool investors.

servicing spread The differential, in basis points, between the mortgage coupon rate and the pass-through coupon. The servicing spread consists of the service fee and a management and guarantee fee.

seven-by-seven A form of price to yield and prepayment sensitivity table which shows seven yield levels across the top horizontal row of the table (usually LIBOR or CMT) and seven PSA speeds on the vertical axis with yields and durations in the body of the table.

75-day program Refers to the original Freddie Mac PC program with a stated payment delay of 75 days (actual 44 days).

speed A Wall Street dealer term that refers to the rate of principal prepayments of a pool of mortgages as calculated by the FHA, CPR, PSA, or other methods of measuring prepayments.

split-fee option An option on an option. The buyer generally executes the split fee with first an initial fee, with a window period at the end of which upon payment of a second fee the original terms of the option may be extended to a later predetermined final notification date.

spot lending The origination of mortgages by processing applications taken directly from prospective borrowers.

standard default assumption (SDA) A default assumption that the CDA starts at an annualized rate of 0.02 percent during month 1. Thereafter the conditional default rate increases at an annualized rate of 0.02 every month until it reaches an annualized rate of 0.6 percent at month 30. After month 30 the default rate is assumed to hold constant from month 30 to month 60. The default rate then declines at a rate of 0.02 percent per month from month 60 to month 120 and to an annualized rate of 0.3 percent for the remaining life of the pool (less 12 months, the time assumed to be required to liquidate the last default).

stated maturity   For the CMO tranche, the date the last payment would occur at zero CPR.

stated maturity bond (SMB)   A bond structured from the z-bond accruals or the scheduled amortization of the collateral for a CMO. Both structures have absolute final stated maturities; the latter structure does display some call risk.

stated maturity date   For an MBS pool is calculated as the last payment date of the latest- maturing mortgage in the pool.

steady state   As the MBS pool ages, or four to six months after it has passed at least once through the threshold for refinancing, the prepayment speed tends to stabilize within a fairly steady range. (Also referred to as short-term burnout.)

sticky jump Z   A sticky jump Z is one that having once activated its trigger makes a permanent shift in payment priority regardless of future events.

strike level   The point, expressed as index value, or yield, or price, at which the cap on a floater is in effect.

strip mortgage participation certificate (strip PC)   Ownership interests in specified mortgages purchased by Freddie Mac from a single seller in exchange for strip PCs representing interests in the same mortgages.

strip PC   See **strip mortgage participation certificate.**

stripped mortgage-backed securities (SMBSs)   Securities that redistribute the cash flows from the underlying generic MBS collateral into the P&I components of the MBS to enhance their use in meeting special needs of investors.

super floater   A floating rate CMO wherein the coupon is leveraged by a multiplier less a spread to LIBOR: Coupon = 2 × LIBOR − 75 basis points.

super PO (SPO)   A support class bond with no coupon. Since the SPO is a support bond, it receives all prepayments in excess of the PAC schedules, and when prepayments are high it will prepay much faster than a standard PO.

support Z-bond   A Z-bond derived from the support class cash flows of a PAC CMO structure.

support class bond   A bond within the CMO structure that absorbs the prepayment volatility of specified PAC bond classes.

support TAC   A TAC derived from support class cash flows. The TAC schedule would then be defined as the principal cash flows attributable to the support class at the deal pricing speed assumption. These bonds are usually structured from the short average life support class cash flows.

swaption   In connection with hedging, a forward-swap agreement whereby the buyer pays an initial fee to enter a swap at a later date at a specified rate.

T

TAC   See **targeted amortization class bond.**

tail   The principal cash flow that extends from the average life point to the final maturity date of the pool. Sometimes the term "tail" also refers to the odd amount in an MBS pool.

tandem programs   Under Ginnie Mae, mortgage funds provided at below-market rates to residential mortgage buyers with FHA Section 203 and 235 loans and to developers of multifamily projects with Section 236 loans initially and later with Section 221(d)(4) loans.

targeted amortization class (TAC) bond   A CMO bond that has a payment schedule only at the pricing speed used to price the original CMO deal. TAC bonds generally offer a modicum of call protection but may exhibit substantial extension potential.

TBA   See **to be announced.**

teaser rate   The initial first year rate of an adjustable rate mortgage. The term "teaser" refers to the fact the initial rate is often set below the index plus margin value for the first year.

threshold for refinancing   The point when the WAC of an MBS is at a level to induce homeowners to prepay the mortgage in order to refinance to a lower-rate mortgage—generally reached when the WAC of the MBS is 75 basis points or more above currently available mortgage rates.

Tier One PAC   A PAC with the most senior scheduled cash flows.

Tier II PACs, Type II PAC   See **PAC II.**

to be announced (TBA) A contract for the purchase or sale of a MBS to be delivered at an agreed-upon future date but does not include a specified pool number and number of pools or precise amount to be delivered.

total rate of return A measure of the return earned to a pre-defined horizon including coupon and reinvestment income plus/minus market gains or losses. (Also referred to as holding period return, or HPR).

tranche Also known as class. CMOs generally have several tranches; each bond issued under the CMO is considered a separate tranche or class, each with different maturities and interest rates and/or accrual structures.

V

VADM Very accurately defined maturity. (**See accretion directed bonds**.)

variance rule Specifies the permitted minimum or maximum quantity of securities that can be delivered to satisfy a TBA trade. For Ginnie Mae, Fannie Mae, and Freddie Mac pass-through securities, the accepted variance is plus or minus 2.0 percent per million of the par value of TBA quantity.

vector sensitivity analysis stressing a bond for changes in prepayment rate, yield, and price changes to variable up/down interest-rate shifts of different amounts for varying periods of time.

volatility A measure of the standard deviation from a mean set of price observations

W

WAC See **weighted average coupon.**

WAM See **weighted average maturity.**

WARM See **weighted average remaining maturity.**

weighted average coupon (WAC) The weighted average of the gross interest rates of the mortgages underlying the pool as of the pool issue date, with the balance of each mortgage used as the weighting factor.

weighted average life (WAL) See **average life.**

weighted average loan age (WALA) The weighted average of the number of months since the date of origination.

weighted average maturity (WAM) The WAM of an MBS is the weighted average of the remaining terms to maturity of the mortgages underlying the collateral pool at the date of issue, using as the weighting factor the balance of each of the mortgages as of the issue date.

weighted average original loan term (WAOLT) The weighted average loan term as of the original date of issue of the pool.

weighted average remaining maturity (WARM) The average remaining term of the mortgages underlying an MBS.

Y

yield curve effect The impact of a positively-sloped yield curve on prepayments by the creation of shorter maturity, lower cost options for refinancing such as 15-year, balloon, and ARM loans.

yield to maturity (YTM) The rate of interest earned to the final maturity date of the bond assuming reinvestment of the bond coupon from each payment date to the maturity date at the rate of the bond coupon rate.

Z

Z-bond Also known as an accrual bond or accretion bond; a bond on which interest accretes interest but is not paid currently to the investor but rather is accrued, with the accrual added to the principal balance of the Z and becoming payable upon satisfaction of all prior bond classes.

zero prepayment assumption The assumption of payment of scheduled principal and interest with no prepayments.

zero-volatility OAS The spread, in basis points, to the entire Treasury curve of a CMO cash flow window or MBS discounted to the existing forward curve and assuming that interest rates do not change. It is the benchmark OAS assuming no prepayments.

INDEX